Practical Marketing Research

A GUIDEBOOK FOR MARKETING INSIGHTS

Chuck Chakrapani, PhD
Ken Deal, PhD
Jordan A. Levitin, MBA

Standard Research Systems

Copyright © 2020, 2023 by Standard Research Systems

All rights reserved. No part of this publication may be reproduced, distributed or transmitted in any form or by any means, including photocopying, recording, or other electronic or mechanical methods, without the prior written permission of the publisher, except in the case of brief quotations embodied in critical reviews and specific other noncommercial uses permitted by copyright law. For permission requests, write to the publisher, addressed "Attention: Permissions Coordinator," at the address below.

Practical Marketing Research/Chuck Chakrapani, Ken Deal and Jordan A. Levitin —1st ed. (minor revisions 2023)
ISBN 978-0-920219-79-9

THE AUTHORS

Chuck Chakrapani, MA, MSc, PhD, FSS, CAIP, FCRIC

Dr. Chuck Chakrapani is president of Leger Analytics and a Distinguished Visiting Professor at the Ted Rogers School of Business. He was formerly the CEO of Millward Brown Canada. Chuck has held academic appointments at the London Business School in England and at the University of Liverpool. He is a prolific writer and has written more than 30 books and 1,000 articles on various subjects - statistics, marketing research, investment strategies and other areas. He was also, for a long time, the Editor-in-Chief of *Canadian Journal of Marketing Research* and of *Marketing Research* magazine published by the American Marketing Association. Chuck, a Fellow of Royal Statistical Society and CRIC, was a past president of the Professional Marketing Research Society of Canada. He is a founding board member CIRC and CAIP and served on the board of MRII as well. His website is *http://www.ChuckChakrapani.com*

Ken Deal, MBA, PhD, CAIP, FCRIC

Dr. Ken Deal is Professor Emeritus at the DeGroote School of Business where he has taught courses in marketing analytics, marketing research and strategic marketing analysis in the MBA programme. His scholarly and professional work on designing new treatments, services and products in health, pharmaceuticals and children's mental health and new pricing products for the electricity market has appeared in many peer-reviewed journals. Ken is past president of the Professional Marketing Research Society of Canada, a Lifetime Fellow of the Canadian Research Insights Council (CRIC), a Certified Analytics and Insights Professional and has been qualified as a marketing research expert by Canadian and US courts. *https://ca.linkedin.com/in/ken-deal-ph-d-a345a*

Jordan A. Levitin, MBA, CAIP. FCRIC

Jordan Levitin has been a marketing insights practitioner for four decades, partnering with clients from virtually all sectors of endeavor - business, government, politics and not-for-profits. His work has covered all facets of practice, both qualitative and quantitative, including their transformation into today's leading edge, digital and AI applications. Jordan has served as President of Canada's Professional Marketing Research Society and was a perennial instructor in its professional development program. He is a founding Board Member of the Certified Analytics and Insights Professionals (CAIP) of Canada and has lectured at several Canadian colleges and universities. In 2023 he was named a Lifetime Fellow of the Canadian Research Insights Council (CRIC) and was recognized for Excellence in Teaching by York University. *https://ca.linkedin.com/in/jordan-levitin-mba-caip*

Dedication

To Nancy, for all that she is
Chuck

To my wife, Barbara Deal, with all my love and admiration.
Ken

To the two men who elevate and energize my life,
my husband Francisco Juarez and our son Aaron.
Jordan

Gratitude

No matter how isolating the craft of writing a book is to the authors, eventually many people contribute to its creation. Here we acknowledge with gratitude those who contributed to the book significantly.

- *Robert Wong* and *John Tabone* of CAIP were instrumental in providing the impetus we needed to finish the book, we had been working on for a long time.
- *Arundati Dandapani* of *Generation1.ca* patiently and expertly beta-read the book.
- *Nancy Kramarich* basically wrote Chapter 13.
- *Annie Pettit*, who was initially to be a coauthor and generously let us use her contributions.
- *Lisa Covens, Marjut Huotari, Ann Christelis, Luc Dumont, Ian Large, K. Edwin Sheppard* and *Allison Watson* who either read parts of the book or helped in other ways.
- *Rob Williams* designed the brilliant cover.
- The team at *LS Graphics* who designed and maintain the book's companion website.

Our thanks to all of them.

In addition,
Chuck would like to thank *Jean-Marc Leger* and *Anne-Marie Marois* and his team at *Leger Analytics* for their unfailing support to whatever he undertakes to do.

Introduction

Practical Marketing Research is the third incarnation of a book written in 1992[ii] and rewritten in 2005[iii]. There have been approximately 15 years between each of these three versions of the book, reflecting the enormous changes that have taken place in the intervening years.

Back in the early nineties, most survey interviews were carried out by landline telephones, door-to-door interviewing was still common, desktop and laptop computers were not universal, and big data would have been a sample of 1,000. By the mid-2000s, the world had changed dramatically. Everything started happening online, including most marketing research interviews, in North America in any case.

Fifteen years later, and we are in the middle of another major upheaval in marketing research. The emphasis and resources are moving away from data collection, interpretation and report writing to data analytics, integration and insight generation. We believe that marketing insights will be based on multiple sources and types of data and will be intensely facilitated by Artificial Intelligence (AI).

AI will impact everything. Secondary research will become faster and far more effective, design options will multiply, qualitative research will include minute analyses of voice and facial expressions to uncover deeper emotions, quantitative coding will be faster and identify emotions behind word patterns, 'synthetic data' will reduce the need for respondents by fabricating how they are likely to respond. AI will pull in comparative data, spot patterns and contradictions and perform our initial analysis for us. In fact, AI will democratize marketing insights by putting powerful data collection and analysis tools into the hands of those with no specific training or experience. The appropriate use of these powerful AI tools still requires a foundation of understanding, making a comprehensive guidebook to marketing research application, methodology and interpretation more important than ever.

These disruptions we are seeing in the industry have made this book challenging to write. Standing at this intersection of the past, the present and the future, we wondered what approach we should take in this version of our book. Emphasize the traditional approach? Emphasize what is being done now, knowing that it may be dated within the next few years? Emphasize the future, which will make the book less useful for current learners? The fact that different countries are at different stages of this evolution did not help either.

What we have done is to make this version relevant to current learners. We used our best judgment, and we hope those decisions have made this book a solid foundation for today's new practitioners and an important reference book for those with more experience. In any case, we have established a website, *PracticalMarketingResearch.com,* which we will use to update any changes. There is a companion volume to this book, *Analytics of Customer Insights*, which we encourage you to read as well.

Even though many things have changed, our fundamental objectives have remained the same.

They are:
- to provide the practical knowledge required to carry out marketing research, while being theoretically sound
- to emphasize practical applications as a means of understanding the theory
- to minimize the number of topics that may be of theoretical value with minimal practical applications
- to make the book universally relevant and
- to provide a considerable amount of additional material through the companion website *PracticalMarketingResearch.com.* Please remember that the website is an integral part of the book and make sure that you refer to it to get the full benefits of using this book.

If you have any comments, please share them with us through the book's website.

Chuck Chakrapani
Ken Deal
Jordan A. Levitin

[i] Chakrapani, Chuck & Ken Deal. *Marketing Research: Methods and Canadian Practice,* Prentice-Hall 1992.

[ii] Chakrapani, Chuck & Ken Deal. *Modern Marketing Research,* Pearson, 2005.

Contents

THE AUTHORS	3
Introduction	5
1. What is Marketing Research and How Does It Work	9
2. How to Prepare For a Marketing Research Project	33
3. How to Carry Out Secondary Research	73
4. How to Draw Samples	93
5. How to Conduct Qualitative Research	129
6. How to Design a Questionnaire	173
7. How to Measure Attitudes, Behaviour, and Traits	237
8. How to Manage the Mechanics of Quantitative Research	273
9. How to Analyze the Data	315
10. How to Present the Findings	367
11. How to Research Common Marketing Problems	410
12. What are the Responsibilities of Marketing Researchers?	457
13. How to Carry Out Global Marketing Research	477

UNIT 1

What is Marketing Research and How Does It Work

Introduction

We designed this book to introduce you to and improve your understanding of the field of marketing research. In this introductory unit, you will develop an overview of marketing research's role within the broader marketing function:

- appreciate the full range of contributions it can make towards decision making;
- meet the players and their functions;
- be introduced to the methodologies and activities;
- develop an overview of the marketing research industry's structure; and
- learn about education opportunities and industry associations.

Subsequent units will delve more deeply into the details.

Why does Marketing Research Exist?

At the heart of our discussion is the **commercial market system** through which we **exchange** things of value (a product or a service) for something of equal value (usually money). For example:
- A juice manufacturer sells their beverages to consumers, through a retail partner (a store) in exchange for a few dollars (or other local currency);
- A bank provides money to a family to buy a home (a mortgage) in exchange for interest payments;
- An amusement park sells an experience to visitors in exchange for an entry fee; and
- A government provides services to its citizens in return for taxes paid on purchases or income.

The two key players in this exchange are those who provide the product or service (providers) and those who buy it (customers).

Marketing is the set of activities that are used to *initiate*, *enhance*, and *support* this exchange between providers and customers. For example:
- The juice manufacturer will set up 'sampling' stands in supermarkets so shoppers can **try** their new flavour, thereby increasing awareness of its improved taste;
- The bank will **advertise** its flexible 'skip a payment' offer to attract mortgage seekers who are concerned about unexpected expenses;
- The amusement park will **offer** a 'half-price' Tuesday to attract more visitors during low traffic days; and
- The government will **improve access** to library books by offering an automated online reservation and renewal website

Marketing research exists for only one reason – to *help managers make better marketing decisions*. It does this by providing relevant insights into the marketing environment, competition, and consumers' behaviours, needs, and attitudes.
- The juice manufacturer might research to test a variety of alternative juice flavours to understand which one consumers are most likely to buy before production begins.
- The bank would research to explore consumers' motivations and barriers to applying for a mortgage before deciding that 'skip a payment' will be a driver to attract potential new homebuyers.
- The amusement park could undertake pricing research to project the profit potential of a discount day by determining how much traffic would increase at each of several alternative entry fee levels.
- The government might conduct research to understand how important improved access to library books is compared to other services that could be improved with the same budgetary funds.

Of course, many marketers make excellent decisions without marketing research. They may be able to rely on their intelligence, rich and diverse experience, good contacts, and tremendous insight. They are paid to make the right marketing decisions, whether or not they have marketing research to rely upon.

When marketing research gives the marketer access to **objective market information** that has been gathered and analyzed specifically to help with their decisions, they are more confident in the outcome and are better able to convince others of the wisdom of their decision. They are also then able to pay more attention to those other facets of the decision for which there is no objective market information.

As with any human interaction, marketing involves a series of **relationships** between:
- those who *manufacture* products or *offer* services;
- business partners who help *get them to market* (distributors and retailers); and
- the *end customer* (an individual, household, business, or some other end-user).

The links can be **direct**, for example, when a customer opens a new bank account at a bank branch, she is in direct contact with the provider of the service. When a customer buys fresh vegetables at a farmer's market, they are probably buying directly from the family that planted the seeds. Or when a tourist does a wine tour and buys a few bottles of wine, they like to purchase directly from an estate winery.

On the other hand, it can be relatively **indirect** – when a manufacturer sells its product through a distributor to a retailer who then sells it to the end-user. Even a call to a customer care line won't put the customer into direct contact with the provider because the call center has been 'outsourced' to a third party.

Tool manufacturers such as Black and Decker, Makita, and Porter-Cable don't sell directly to the public and, consequently, never actually see or talk to end-users. They rely on their business partners, such as Home Depot, to offer their tools to the public, to complete transactions and to maintain those positive relationships that motivate customers to buy other tools using their brand name.

The more indirect the relationship, the less the provider knows about their end-consumer. For example, *why would Ian (who is about to build a chicken coop) buy a Makita cordless drill from Home Depot?* Makita really should know this if their marketing information and product development are to give potential customers convincing information about their products.

Ian has probably answered in his own mind all the questions that Makita needs answered. He might have *consciously* thought through some issues when shopping for the drill, and subconsciously answered others without fully thinking them through. And he has probably not discussed this decision with anyone else but may have heard comments about Makita. Neither Home Depot nor Makita will get information about Ian's decision unless they ask him. This could be the beginning of a marketing research project. Either Makita or Home Depot could begin this marketing research project for their own reasons.

Makita might be concerned about:
- the relationship between Ian and Home Depot, which might be the only direct connection Ian has with Makita;
- they may be interested in his relationship with the call center, which may be run by a third-party management company; and
- if he was pleased or displeased with the availability, purchase, warranty registration and after-sales service,

Makita would focus on *all* possible connections between purchasers of Makita products and relevant business partners. Any glitch in these interactions could have severe negative ramifications on Makita's future sales. They will also want to know:
- if Ian takes pride in owning a high end, quality power tool;

- how he perceives the Makita brand and its products compared to other brands he might find in the store;
- whether or not he told friends, neighbours, family or acquaintances about the experience; and
- how he felt the drill performed compared to his expectations.

Home Depot, on the other hand, is interested in knowing if Makita's products are a better fit with its customers' needs than other brands of power tools. They'll want to know:

- if the products are priced right for each market;
- if specific promotions would be useful at moving more of Makita's products during particular seasons; and
- if offering Makita products enhances Home Depot's own image with its customers.

If Home Depot were enticed by Makita to cooperate in the project, both companies, as well as their customers, would benefit from the research.

Here are some other examples of business situations that would benefit from marketing research:

The manufacturer of a breakfast cereal wants to know:

- how potential buyers use cereal (breakfast versus snack);
- what they pair it with (for co-branding with their juice brand?);
- what price is going to optimize sales, market share, and profits;
- how receptive consumers will be to alternative flavours; and
- how consumers see *themselves*, what needs they are striving to meet in the morning and how they want their breakfast cereal to reflect on them (champion, athlete, healthy eater, fun and permissive parent).

A public transit agency may be examining alternative payment methods and will need to know how users would react if

- cash fares are increased;
- or bus tickets are phased out;
- or a new 'smart card' that can be loaded up with rides is launched.

A publisher of computer software may want to know the requirements of a given type of business so that packages that deliver on currently unmet needs can be written and marketed. They may want:

- to test beta versions of a new app;
- to understand how to optimize the combination of elements in the offer to maximize customers' interest; and
- might even need consumer reaction to select from several alternative names for their offer.

Marketers have a tremendous need for relevant, timely, and insightful market information to help them make crucial decisions that will impact their company's bottom line.

What is Marketing Research?

Marketing research deals with the observation, collection, processing, analysis, and communication of information on people's attitudes, feelings, intentions, personal characteristics (geo-demographics), and behaviours towards products, services, and those organizations and people involved in any aspect of marketing.

ESOMAR, the international association of marketing researchers, provides a commonly accepted definition of marketing research:

> Market research, which includes social and opinion research, is the systematic gathering and interpretation of information about individuals or organizations using the statistical and analytical methods and techniques of the applied social sciences to gain insight or support decision making. (ESOMAR, World Research Codes and Guidelines 2009)

You will note that the above definition includes a broader range of activities beyond 'marketing' to include all forms of marketing and social research such as consumer and business, qualitative and observational studies, competitor intelligence, sociological and psychological investigations.

In reality, marketing research is in the process of evolving. Digital media has vastly expanded the range of human interactions and has led to new ways to access consumers' thoughts and behaviours. In addition to asking and observing, marketing research can now track and measure communications in real-time – picking up references to client products in tweets, Facebook posts, Instagram mentions and other social media. The internet (or online) is not only a method of conducting research, but it also has become a source. And rather than discrete research projects, marketing research now thinks in terms of insight generation through multiple tracks of information curation. Marketers perform experiments online to determine which communication elements most highly influence prospective customers. But let's take a step back, and build an understanding of time-tested, foundational research methods.

There are several ways to dissect marketing research. One of these is by the source of information. **Primary research** refers to those projects that are explicitly designed to *generate new data and information* to meet the objectives of a marketing problem. Whether the study is a survey, a focus group, mystery shopping, or an online experiment, it produces data or information that did not exist before. Sometime after the primary research project is finished, someone else might retrieve and use that data for a slightly different purpose, and at that point, it becomes secondary data. **Secondary research** refers to the search, retrieval, and analysis of information not *initially* collected for the purpose at hand. The original data might have been obtained using any of the marketing research methodologies that are used for primary research (e.g., surveys, focus groups, etc.), or it may exist in a government census or customer database. The distinguishing difference between primary and secondary information is that the latter already existed before the marketing question was first asked.

Unit 3 will focus on secondary research, while the rest of this book will deal almost exclusively with primary research.

What does Marketing Research do?

In more specific terms, marketing research:
- **specifies** the information required to address the relevant marketing issues;
- **designs** the methods for collecting the pertinent information;
- **manages** and implements the data collection process;
- **analyzes** the resultant data;
- **transforms** the findings into usable marketing insights;

- **communicates** those insights and their implications to the marketing managers; and
- **recommends** a course of action on the marketing issue.

These and other similar definitions characterize marketing research from an academic perspective. However, marketing research is not a discipline that fits into neatly defined boundaries. Nor is its scope clearly defined and static. The subject matter can and usually does include diverse areas such as ethnography, social and psychological research, loyalty tracking, advertising testing, and tracking, advocacy research, geo-demographics, and political polling. It also includes competitive intelligence, data mining, web-scraping, re-analysis of historical records, and other related functions.

The bulk of marketing research is carried out to improve the marketing of goods and services through better decision making. It also contributes to the development and refinement of **public policy** through more informed decisions by public sector managers and politicians. For example, a new government program designed to promote and support job creation among small businesses might benefit at the design stage from a deeper understanding of the needs of small business owners. It also provides weight to the arguments of those who **advocate** for a specific policy direction. For example, an agricultural lobby group agitating for more favourable treatment for domestically produced foods might conduct research that shows a vast majority of citizens prefer to buy home-grown foods over imported foods.

This list of **typical problems** that might be handled by marketing researchers provides a good sense of the **scope** of the field, including how to:

- prioritize new ways for electricity customers to buy electricity
- determine the best long-range strategy for an over-the-counter drug
- discover which scent would make a perfume most desirable to a specified target audience
- decide on which features your grocery supermarket chain and its four main competitors excel and how best to compete
- map the changing tastes for wine among younger adults
- measure the experience of travelers who stay at a specific hotel
- design parenting courses to ideally suit the needs of parents of children with mental disabilities
- optimize the mix of potential features that could be offered on a new version of a popular mobile phone
- determine the best marketing strategy to expand the number of women in the 19 to 35-year-old age group who buy and read a women's magazine
- help members of a specific religious group understand how their members across the country might prioritize outreach initiatives
- identify the potential impact on the sales of jet fuel at your fixed based operators (FBOs - service stations for airplanes) across the country if a large chain from another country decides to enter the market
- determine the best price at which your new subcompact car should enter the market and which other subcompacts this car will compete against most directly
- understand if the demand for snowboards and wakeboards is growing or declining

- understand how the general public perceives the effectiveness of your not-for-profit community organization
- evaluate how much of the public's affinity for your corporation can be attributed to its environmental policies
- assess the degree to which citizens might support or oppose a proposed ban on government employees wearing religious symbols in the workplace
- analyze the role and impact of bank branch managers on customer satisfaction and loyalty
- understand residents' likes and dislikes regarding your community recreation programs
- research the public's image of your corporation and compare with perceptions of other similar corporations
- predict how a political party will fare in the upcoming election including understanding:
    - which party is viewed more favourably?
    - which parties are gaining or losing momentum?
    - what factors are influencing voter preferences?
    - who are the undecided voters and what are their triggers?
- identify who is reading your magazine?
    - what are their demographics?
    - what do they like and dislike about the magazine?
    - what motivates a person to subscribe to the magazine?
    - how can we better understand their lifestyles and priorities?
- investigate the country's citizens' current mindset with relation to
    - requiring CEOs to attest to the accuracy of their firms' financial statements
    - requiring officeholders to put their personal business interests in blind trusts
    - a new free trade deal with another country
    - federal government initiatives to combatting global warming

What are the Different Types of Marketing Research?

If *marketing* research serves the broader function of providing information that will help the organization develop and implement more effective marketing strategies, tactics, and procedures, *market* research is a sub-category that focuses on understanding the market for a particular good or service. The two terms are often used interchangeably.

Market research makes use of secondary information as well as primary marketing research to profile consumers, competitors, market conditions, pricing, behavioural patterns, etc. in a specific market category. It builds a foundational understanding of the operating environment for brands in the marketplace. A quick profile of the market might be obtainable from reports produced for members of a marketing association or from **government census agency** reports.

More detailed and focused information might necessitate a marketing research survey specifically tailored to the organization's needs. Often, marketing research surveys provide both types of information. For example, almost all studies contain descriptive demographic questions that might include residence location (6-digit postal codes or zip codes), residence type, education, age, income, occupation, household composition, and other profiling variables. Sometimes, behavioural information such as shopping locations, usage patterns, and the frequency of purchase are collected in a survey. All of this helps the organization better understand the environment in which it operates or intends to operate.

> Example. An international beverage company has had great success with a brand of carbonated, tropical fruit drinks marketed to teenagers in the southern hemisphere and would now like to introduce this brand to northern hemisphere countries. However, it doesn't know how much Europeans and North Americans know about these exotic flavours, how they are consuming existing carbonated and fruit-based beverages, how they relate to the brands that are currently in the marketplace. They would like to understand where their brand might fit into this marketplace and what needs it could optimally target.

Innovation Research is another sub-category of marketing research that is focused primarily on helping companies develop and optimize new product ideas. Work in this area focuses on identifying the types of products or services that would meet consumers' needs in a specific category and how those products should be configured to attract as many potential buyers/users as possible.

> Example. A local snack food firm is working on a line of organic, vegan protein snacks and has developed 25 different potential products that it could produce, package, and sell. However, before it makes all of the required investments, it wants to measure the potential for success (and even forecast sales) for each of the ideas. Ideally, they will want to understand the optimal range of products (some sub-group of the 25 potential products). This would allow it to invest in those products most likely to be successful launches – and reduce their risk of failure.

Optimizing products and services during the innovation process can also make use of:
- **insight** screening – what insights consumers are most likely to respond to
- **idea/concept screening** – which new product ideas have the best chances of success
- **feature** optimization – what combination of features will please the most consumers
- **volumetric forecasting** – how many units of a new product are likely to be sold in the first year after launch
- **line** optimization – how many flavours or format options will bring in the most buyers without putting unnecessary variants on the shelf
- **pricing** research – what is the price point that will maximize revenue
- **packaging** design research – which of several alternative packaging designs are most likely to catch consumers' eyes on the shelf, be linked to the brand and communicate the crucial positioning messages

Loyalty Research is another sub-category of marketing research that focuses on tracking the relationship between an organization and its customers. It is most common in sectors where the organization knows its customers and is likely to have data already collected on its customers. For example, we see two-way relationships like this between consumers and their financial institutions, universities, airlines and hotel chains. Loyalty research generally involves ongoing tracking of perceptions of the company and its competitors on measures that are considered essential to retaining their business.

> **Example**. A national airline knows that its reputation hinges on its passengers' experience at many touch-points – buying tickets, checking in, gate and boarding, and in-flight. It continually tracks how passengers feel they are treated at each point to ensure any potential problems are caught and corrected early and to ensure it maintains its ranking against key competitors.

Advertising and Communications Research is a specialized field that has two components: (a) **copy testing** the advertising before it is launched to ensure that it communicates what is intended and does so in a way that captures consumers' attention and creates the necessary linkage to the brand, and (b) **tracking** the performance of the advertising after it is launched to ensure it continues to be active and has not worn out. Most advertising research, like loyalty research, involves ongoing research programs.

> Example. A financial institution runs advertising to support its positioning as a welcoming, comfortable, and 'easy' banking solution. It has created a new series of television commercials that are intended to communicate this freshly and are concerned that the ads may undermine the positioning they have painstakingly built over many years because it takes such a different tack. The financial institution wants to test each commercial and compare it to global benchmarks to ensure each will stand out, will be linked to the company, will persuade consumers to bank there and will create the emotional perceptions that it is intended to.

Public Affairs Research is another branch of research that is not always linked with marketing research. This segment of the industry focuses on government policies, corporate reputation, and political message testing and tracking in much the same way marketing research does for commercial enterprises. Many of the same methodologies and techniques are used, and researchers can move from one segment to the other. Public affairs research can focus on understanding citizens'/voters' needs, test political communications messages, optimize the mix of public policy positions, and test innovative new messages.

> Example 1. A national association of agricultural producers wants the government to impose tariffs on produce imported from other countries, making domestic produce more competitive. They conduct research to show that the majority of citizens is in favour of these tariffs and understands that they will safeguard local jobs.

> Example 2. The Health Ministry is in charge of implementing the government's new policy to allow physician-assisted dying and needs to understand who might object and how their concerns are framed so that it can find ways to address these concerns through regulations or communications. They conduct research to measure reactions to the new policy and collect and code concerns that arise. They might also test several alternative ways to frame the communications on the new policy.

Who Uses Marketing Research?

Marketing managers use marketing research. So do product managers, media planners, advertising executives, educational managers, government bureaucrats, politicians, managers of non-profit organizations, the legal system, and, in fact, any person or organization that needs information from the public.

The use of marketing research is pervasive in most countries in the world. The expansion of the internet over the past decade and the widespread use of computers and smartphones in virtually all countries of the world means that marketing research can be conducted just about anywhere.

The bulk of commercial marketing research is conducted for **firms that market their products and services to the public**. These might range from consumer packaged goods companies (food, beverage, personal and household care products, non-prescription pharmaceuticals, etc.), durables manufacturers (automobiles, appliances, etc.), the transportation and hospitality sector (airlines, car rental, hotels, restaurants, etc.), retailers, pharmaceuticals, health care and other sectors.

Various levels of **government** are responsible for a large amount of marketing research.

Example. Census organizations account for a tremendous volume of marketing research studies, not only through the 'national census' but with on-going data collection programs.

National, provincial, or state governments typically conduct research to understand their citizens' needs and preferences, and likely reactions to upcoming policy changes. They will often research outside their jurisdictions, for example, to understand the tourism market better.

Municipal governments might conduct marketing research to assess the social and economic impact of large public development projects. At the same time, private land developers do marketing research to show municipal planning committees that the public is not opposed to the type of development that they propose.

Industry associations representing specific groups in the economy exist to protect and promote the interests of their members and to provide communal services. Examples might include a national organization of manufacturers or professional associations representing teachers, accountants, doctors or lawyers. They may represent a specific industrial sector such as steel manufacturers, dairy farmers, or home builders, etc.

These associations conduct marketing research to make market information available to all their members. These studies can be quite extensive and substantially help the association's members better understand the overall market for their product or service. Generally, these findings do not provide competitive information. Some of the association's members might conduct their own studies to identify their business's own unique competitive advantages.

Industry associations also conduct public opinion research to bolster their lobbying efforts with governments on their members' behalf.

Media planners in advertising agencies must determine how to spend their clients' advertising budgets for maximum impact. Sales representatives for newspapers, television and radio networks and other media use readership, viewing and listening studies to show prospective advertisers the profiles of those who are accessing their media content. The advertiser then has a much better basis for deciding how best to reach their target market with their advertising dollars.

Apart from these apparent uses, marketing research is also used to prove and disprove points of view for **legal** or **regulatory** purposes.

> Example. A manufacturer may commission research to isolate facts that can be used in an advertising campaign without violating government 'truth-in-advertising' regulations. They may want to claim that "two out of three consumers preferred drink A over drink B." The direct purpose of the research is not so much to collect information for decision-making to provide evidence that advertising claims are true.

Marketing research is also used to help the courts understand if **trademarks** are being infringed upon.

> Example. Labatt's Breweries owns the Oland Breweries of Nova Scotia. Oland introduced Oland Export in the 1920s and has owned a Canadian trademark registration for its Oland Export ale label since 1951. In 1996, Labatt attempted to introduce that brand into the Ontario market. Molson began proceedings in the Ontario Superior Court of Justice against Labatt and Oland, contending that Oland's marketing of its Export was likely to confuse beer drinkers with Molson Export and that Oland was attempting to pass off its beer for those of Molson. A survey was conducted for Molson by a marketing research expert to identify confusion. When Mr. Justice Kealey of the Ontario Superior Court of Justice dismissed the Plaintiff's (Molson) actions with costs payable to the Defendant (Oland), Molson proceeded to litigate this matter in the Federal Court of Canada. Another survey was conducted. In both cases, an expert hired by Labatt's reviewed the studies and submitted affidavits to help the courts understand the value of the marketing research findings.

Marketing research is sometimes used to provide evidence in other types of legal cases. There are cases on record in which the income tax arm of government had carried out studies to determine the meaning of a word to determine the tax eligibility. Although marketing research is used in different types of court cases, those relating to intellectual property are probably where it is most frequently used.

Who Carries out Marketing Research?

Marketing Research Companies:

Marketing research is usually carried out by companies that specialize exclusively in marketing research.

A *professional* marketing research firm professionally conducts its business. Of course, "professional manner" can mean different things to different people. Many countries around the world have national marketing research societies that provide well-defined codes of ethics and professional conduct that its members are obliged to uphold. Membership in such associations is often the hallmark of a "professional" marketing research company.

Consolidation over the past decade has resulted in several large **full-service global firms**: GfK, Ipsos, Kantar, and Nielson are among the largest. Each has specialized divisions that can execute almost any type of marketing research project.

> Example. One of these firms might have a highly-visible public affairs and polling division, a section that specializes in advertising research, another that does new product concept testing, another focused on market understanding, and all operate within a standard corporate structure. While they do different types of research, each division is staffed by subject-matter and methodological experts, and all use common fieldwork, data management, and corporate (HR, Finance, office management) resources.

In a tier below those large, generalist organizations are **mid-sized research companies** that are more focused. They may be a significant player in a particular country or region or may have been created with a specific sector focus (e.g., consumer packaged goods) or methodology (e.g., audience measurement).

Some companies **specialize** in very **specific types** of research, such as political polling or public policy research, automotive research, health sector research, or new product research. The principals and practitioners in these firms may have specialized training or years of experience in these sectors.

> Example. A highly specialized area of research exists to support legal cases. They may provide empirical proof of confusion in copyright infringement cases or recruit parallel juries to try out arguments before they are used in a courtroom.

These mid-sized companies and specialized firms might have their own fieldwork and data components. Still, they may just as easily contract out these functions to companies that **specialize** in some **functional aspects** of research such as recruiting or moderating group discussions, computer tabulation of the data, special statistical analysis of the data or fieldwork interviewing.

Most marketing research is contracted to companies that specialize in professional marketing research. However, many accounting, engineering, and general **management consulting** companies list marketing research as one of their services. Very often, the marketing researchers in those firms determine the needs of the client and then subcontract at least the fieldwork and often a high percentage of the project to professional marketing research firms and sometimes to several independent researchers.

Independent market researchers can often earn an excellent living with a small number of clients, offering consulting, qualitative moderating, or specialized analysis. The current era of **'virtual' companies** also makes it easy for independent professional marketing researchers to pull together a team to execute a specific research project by subcontracting components of the project to others.

Finally, it is important to recognize the **'do it yourself'** sector in marketing research. Anyone can write a questionnaire and get answers with easily accessible online tools. Survey Monkey is perhaps the most visible option for non-researchers to collect information.

Marketing Research Professionals

When we talk about marketing research, we generally think of a **professional marketing researcher** who has been educated in the field, has substantial experience in all or almost all phases of marketing research, and is actively involved in providing marketing research services for most or all of their workweek. In some countries, education, experience, and/or exams can earn a researcher a professional certification or designation.

Researchers can be **suppliers**, working for the marketing research company that undertakes the studies. Within supplier organizations, there are several essential roles. Many of the functions in the list below will be explained in later chapters.

- **Management**. Senior management in marketing research firms – the people who run the company and make strategic decisions – are often marketing researchers themselves. It is a profession and is best managed by people who understand how the elements of the business function. But just like management in any company, they are focused on strategic directions, human resources (staffing and training), financial management, product development, and relationships with important clients.
- **Client Service**. Marketing research is essentially a relationship-driven profession. Those who work in a client service function are primarily responsible for building and maintaining those relationships by seeking out potential clients, gaining their confidence, keeping them informed of the firm's capabilities, writing proposals to bid on research projects, overseeing and delivering on the projects and managing the relationships between projects. It has often been said that only a researcher can sell research; so people who are in this role must have a broad view of marketing research methodologies and deliverables. They often come up through the ranks from an analyst role.
- **Research Managers**. This function overlaps with and leads into client service. These are project managers and analysts who are responsible for the many stages of running marketing research studies. They may work through the costing for proposals, write initial proposal drafts, write early versions of a questionnaire, oversee the logistics of data collection, ensure the resulting data is error-free and undertake the initial steps of turning that data into the story that will eventually be delivered to the client as a report or presentation. Besides, they are often responsible for maintaining the company's project and financial management systems at the project level by setting up jobs, triggering invoices, tracking expenses, etc.
- **Marketing Science Personnel**. There is often a separate specialist role within marketing research firms that undertake more sophisticated statistical analyses. These may range from analysts with specialized training to experienced statisticians, and they generally have access to complex data manipulation and modelling techniques. Their role is to go beyond what the numbers say and pull out more complex relationships in the data. Often, a strong marketing science function is what separates the simple charting of numbers from telling a story. This function is now often referred to as marketing analytics or marketing data science.

Example: A firm's survey of candy usage patterns can be analyzed by looking at the whole population and breaking it down in tables by age, region, gender, etc. But the story becomes much more insightful if the firm's marketing science department runs an attitudinal segmentation analysis to find groups in the population that differ in their personal relationship with candy – e.g., indulgers, purists, connoisseurs, avoiders, etc.

- **Data Processing Personnel**. This is the role that bridges data collection and the reporting function. Raw data that comes in from the fieldwork must be cleaned and organized in a way that research managers and client service executives can pull out the story and prepare a report. Their role is generally to create the data tables and ensure they are accurate.
- **Questionnaire Scripters**. Much of today's research is conducted using web-based surveys. The questionnaires for these surveys have to be programmed so that they work smoothly on any device – from desktop computers to mobile phones. Scripting is a programming function that takes the finished questionnaire prepared by research managers and client service executives and writes the logic to ensure the data is captured correctly when a respondent selects an answer and that the flow (skip patterns, terminations, etc.) happens as intended. If this function is not properly done, the resulting data will likely have irreparable flaws, so quality control and careful testing are absolutely necessary (and time-consuming).
- **Interviewers**. When telephone and face-to-face interviews are conducted, trained interviewers are necessary. They may work in a facility where their work is supervised, such as a central telephone call center or mall intercept facility, or they may be sent out to knock on the doors of people's homes or intercept people on the street or at an event. Specialized interviewers are often employed for 'executive' interviewing, for example, when conducting pharmaceutical research with doctors. Their training ensures that they understand how to find the right respondents, read the question exactly as written, record responses accurately and without interpretation, and avoid influencing the respondent as much as possible.
- **Coders**. The responses to open-ended questions need to be organized and coded so that the story will emerge. This is a specialized role that requires a good understanding of the intent of the study and the focus to spot keywords in a large volume of text-based responses.

Example: A financial institution may want to know why older customers go to the bank branch to pay their bills rather than use online banking services. If it is the first time this question has been asked, the researchers don't know what to expect. That's why it is asked as an open-ended question. When the raw text comes back from the survey, the chief coder reads through a portion of the comments and creates groupings that capture the full range of reasons given. They then have the entire coding team read all of the responses and slot each one into one of the coded reasons. This will provide the client with an empirical read on the barriers to online banking among this age group.

- **Moderators**. In qualitative research, the moderator combines client service, interviewer, coder, and analyst into one single role. Moderators work with clients to design the research approach and conduct qualitative interviews, ethnography, or focus groups themselves, analyze what emerges, create the story and recommendations, and write the report. The integration and complexity of this role mean that it is one that is still commonly undertaken by independent researchers. It is at once close to the ground and very strategic.

- **Recruiters**. This is a specialized role that provides participants for qualitative research. Recruiters build and maintain databases of willing participants and can assemble focus groups or set up personal interviews with the types of people that the study needs to hear from.

Example: A manufacturer of vaping products is looking for direction on flavours that would be particularly appealing to younger male adults. A series of focus groups is to be set up for two consecutive evenings, and a recruiter is brought in to find participants that are males aged 19 to 29. On each evening, the first group will be with young men who are experienced vapers, and the second will be with young men who have not yet tried vaping but would be open to it. The recruiter checks her database for young men in the age range and calls them, using a carefully worded recruitment guide, to find out their experience with vaping and to invite those who qualify to the groups.

- **Panel / Community Managers**. In the web-based and online research environment, there is no ability to sample a population randomly. So, a pool of pre-recruited respondents is necessary from which to pull a representative sample for a specific survey. A later chapter will go into the sampling function in depth. This is an infrastructure role that requires significant ongoing investment in recruitment, incentives, quality management, and project management and is often handled by specialized supplier companies. As web-based surveys continue to expand, panel management is becoming increasingly collaborative with the companies working together to ensure every project gets the respondents it needs.

Example: A company called FieldCo has, over time, built up an online panel of 750,000 Britons who are willing to complete surveys in return for collecting points that can be redeemed for merchandise. While this panel is not strictly representative of the UK population, it is a pool from which representative samples can be drawn. The panel is carefully managed to weed-out and replace any participant who is not who they say they are, or who does not faithfully complete surveys sent to them. FieldCo is a supplier that uses this panel to provide samples for the surveys of other marketing research companies.

Respondents / Participants. Marketing research would not exist without those people who complete surveys and participate in online communities, interviews, or focus groups. They give us their time, describe their behaviour and attitudes, and offer their opinion, often in return for a small incentive but also because they appreciate being asked. They feel that their participation may improve products that are important to them. As an industry, we have a responsibility to ensure they are appreciated and treated with respect.

Many of these roles are described in great detail in the units that follow.

Several roles on the client-side are crucial to marketing research.

- **Research or Insight Managers.** This is the client-side counterpart to the research firm's client service role. They work within their organization to support the marketing function with consumer insights. Their responsibilities would include consulting with marketers in the company, determining their needs for marketing information, informing them of procedures that could obtain that information, writing requests for proposals, finding well-qualified marketing research firms, awarding the contracts, monitoring the project, ensuring that the project meets all requirements, performing any additional analysis that might be needed, interpreting the findings for relevance, archiving the research for on-going internal use, communicating the results to the appropriate managers and maintaining contact with those managers to determine if the study served the needs and identify if any additional research is required. This certainly sounds like a tremendous amount of responsibility, and it is.

- **Brand Managers.** The Insight Manager's internal client is often the individual who manages the brand. It is his or her responsibility to chart the best pathway to growth, be it through positioning, advertising, line extensions, sponsorships, etc. Marketing research provides consumer insights into how the brand is perceived and used and what barriers or opportunities it may face. Marketing research can also be used to test new formulations and line extensions, new packaging designs, new advertising copy etc. In smaller organizations, where there is no insight manager, the brand managers often deal directly with the marketing research firms.
- **Marketing Managers.** This is the individual who has a broader view of the company's marketing – perhaps covering multiple brands and products or services. They may be more experienced users of marketing research than the brand manager and can use their broader perspective to commission more wide-sweeping strategic research (e.g., portfolio optimization studies, master brand development, franchise extension into new categories, etc.)
- **Research and Development Staff**. If a new product is being developed, these people are involved in creating it. In a food or beverage company, this person may be able to adjust the taste, texture, or aroma to appeal more to respondents. In a household or personal care product, there may be other attributes that can be fine-tuned, such as developing products for those with sensitive skin or creating more eco-friendly packaging. These people are very interested in hearing how consumers perceive the product.

In smaller markets, client organizations may be too small to justify a fully staffed and resourced insight management group capable of overseeing every aspect of their research programs. In these cases, they may contract their marketing research to outside **consultants**. These are individuals or small firms that act as "insight departments for hire," working on an hourly basis or on a retainer to provide the client organization with all the functions that would otherwise be handled by an internal insight manager.

The benefit of this arrangement is that when there are no research projects underway, the client organization is not paying salaries. When there is a project to be done, they can bring in an experienced research practitioner who also knows the organization's business. There is also a degree of comfort, knowing that an impartial consultant can find the best marketing research supplier for each job that needs to be done.

How does Marketing Research Function?

In a "full-service" marketing research arrangement, the research firm offers all or almost all of those services that are typical components of quantitative survey projects. These include:

1. consulting with the client to fully understand the business issue, alternative decisions that could be made, and information required to choose between those alternatives
2. helping the client define the research project's purpose, objectives, and scope;
3. understanding how to provide best the necessary information needed to choose between alternative decisions;
4. designing a questionnaire to elicit the required information from respondents sampled from the relevant population in society;
5. developing the sampling process to ensure that the sample respondents are appropriately selected from the relevant universe;
6. determining the analysis or the range of analyses that will be used to provide information best suited to the client's needs;
7. designing and executing the fieldwork in the best way possible, given the study objectives, questionnaire, sampling, and budget;
8. analyzing the data to extract important marketing and market information;
9. interpreting the research findings to maximize the marketing benefit to the client;
10. presenting the results to the client in written and oral forms with clear recommendations on which alternative decision will lead to greater success; and
11. helping the client activate the findings through on-going consulting, follow-ups or workshops.

Some of these functions can be **subcontracted** to other firms.

Example. A firm wins a project that requires telephone interviewing. They may not have their own call centre or may have one that can't handle the volume of interviews needed. So, they bring in another firm that specializes in fieldwork and can partner with the winning firm to get the job done. Or a project may call for a particularly sophisticated statistical analysis. While the firm can do many types of analyses themselves, they know a statistician who works independently and specializes in this type of analysis. They bring this individual in on a contract to do the analysis and hand it back to the primary contractor to integrate into their report and presentation.

Many of these full-service professional marketing research firms offer a variety of approaches to conducting research: custom or ad hoc research, standardized studies, syndicated research, and omnibus studies.

Custom research is primary research designed and executed for one client and to satisfy one specific need for marketing information. As its name implies, it is *tailored* to the client's desires. When a marketing research firm does many similar custom projects, they will begin to have very similar components.

Example. Brand tracking studies generally have a similar structure and ask the same types of questions. They may start with a series of brand awareness, usage, and loyalty questions before getting into a battery of brand image statements.

There can be substantial differences among industry sectors, and each company within an industry might want their study to be conducted somewhat differently from studies done for competitors.

Some client companies would prefer to undertake custom studies with research firms that do _not_ work with their competitors because of the highly strategic nature of the work. However, that may mean trading off industry expertise for exclusivity. This is particularly acute in smaller markets where there are not a lot of experienced firms to choose from.

Standardized studies might have begun as customized research that served a need for one client organization but then evolved into a type of study that other client firms wanted to use. Over time, many of these studies became standardized and are currently offered to any client. Standardized studies are always conducted in the same way, regardless of the client.

> Example. Many global firms have highly standardized and pre-scripted questionnaires for new product concept testing. Using identical questionnaires across all studies permits the creation of normative databases so that clients can compare the results of their tests to industry benchmarks.

Sometimes a standardized study begun by one marketing research firm has spawned a mini-industry focusing on variations of that standardized study. Customer satisfaction research is one of the most widely used examples of standardized studies. Many firms offer their own particular twist on customer satisfaction measurement, and each of these would be considered a standardized study if the questionnaire and field methodology is fixed, and it is offered in the same form to any interested client.

Syndicated studies are entrepreneurial efforts by marketing research firms to sell continuing business and to establish an image as an expert in a field. They are designed and executed to fill a need among several client organizations at the same time. The syndicated study is often designed and completed at the expense of the research firm, and then the report is sold to any client that needs the information.

> Example. Enviro Research has identified a need within the home building sector for information on the projected extent of home renovations for the coming year: how many homeowners are planning to renovate their kitchens or bathrooms, how many are planning to change windows or doors, how many are planning to build extensions or finish basements or replace their roof shingles; and how much they are expecting to spend on the work. While door and window manufacturers, builders, and municipal governments could all benefit from this information, they would not have the budgets on their own to conduct this research. So, Enviro creates the questionnaire, collects and analyzes the data, and writes an extensive report. They own the study, but they sell the report to anyone who wants to buy it. If they can sell ten reports, they will cover the cost of the research, and every additional sale is profit.

Multiple buyers for the same report mean each client pays far less than they would have for a custom study and could mean substantial profits for the supplier if enough reports are sold.

Omnibus services are another way for clients to get access to market information with a smaller price tag. They are _shared-cost_ studies that carry questions for several clients on the same questionnaire. This means that each client can have a large sample respond to their questions (and common demographic questions) while paying only a small share of the study costs.

The total cost of a marketing research study is comprised of both fixed and variable costs.

- The **fixed costs** include designing the project, the typical components of the questionnaire, the sampling and incentives, and the costs expended to obtain and analyze the demographic questions as well as the research firm's overhead that are allocated to the study,
- The **variable costs** include the time needed to design questions for each client, interviewing time, data preparation time, and the time to analyze the data and to prepare the report for each client.

Overall, the cost to each client is less than what they would spend if each company had a custom study designed and executed for the same general purpose. However, because the prices are calculated on a cost-per-question basis, they are most cost-effective when only a few questions are needed.

Collaboration and Virtual Project Teams

Not all marketing research firms can carry out all types of research, or even all parts of every project. It is increasingly common for different firms to collaborate or to bring in individual consultants to assemble the skills, resources, and expertise needed for a project.

Example. An experienced qualitative research team may be exceptional with general public focus groups but may lack the technical understanding and vocabulary to do pharmaceutical interviews with doctors. So, the qualitative team brings in a 'subject matter expert' to do those interviews and draft the report. Or a small research firm may be comfortable conducting simple cross-tab analyses on their studies but bring in a marketing science consultant for more advanced analytics when needed. Or an independent market research practitioner might sub-contract the fieldwork on a quantitative study to another firm so that she doesn't need to undergo the expenses of building that infrastructure herself.

Firms to which project components are subcontracted make up a relatively significant part of the marketing research industry. This collaboration extends into other fields as well. There are **marketing, management, accounting, financial and engineering consulting firms** that advertise marketing research as one of their services. Some do, but most would subcontract the marketing research to a marketing research specialist if such a job were obtained.

These consulting firms would assist their clients in defining their needs for marketing research, identifying the objectives and scope of the project, and help interpret the findings at the end of the research study. Some of the large accounting firms employ several professional marketing researchers and have full marketing research departments. However, it is rare for these companies to have the study fielding capabilities.

Some **advertising agencies** also say that they conduct marketing research. Mostly, the marketing research personnel in advertising agencies act in the same manner as insight managers in other client companies: they determine what research their advertising clients want, help with the initial design of the project, subcontract the execution of most of the actual marketing research and then assist the client in understanding and interpreting the findings.

How is Marketing Research related to Decision Making?

Marketing research information is used by management to make more informed decisions; for example:

- How can our firm continue to prosper in an increasingly competitive environment?
- Is there more opportunity for our brand to grow if we position it differently?
- Should our company introduce a new product/service to complement our current offer?
- What is the optimal combination of features that will help this new product/service succeed?
- Might our new advertising message antagonize the consumer?
- What media are best suited to getting our message out to our key target audience?
- What messages would be most effective in inoculating our corporate image against social media misinformation?
- What are the pain points in our customers' path to purchase, and how might we minimize or remove them?
- Are our front-line staff following proper procedures with every customer interaction?
- How can we disrupt 'habitual' purchasing and make customers notice our new product on the shelf?

Of course, marketing research information is **only one component** in the marketing decision-making process. A brand's success could be affected by pricing, product formulation, product distribution, the competence of the sales force, the effectiveness of the advertising campaign, the activities of competitors, the relationships developed by the company with its customers, and other factors. Research may show an opportunity for a brand, but its success is ultimately determined by how brand management puts it in front of consumers and how the marketplace reacts.

Marketing research doesn't dictate management decisions. It can only advise and guide the decision-maker by providing valuable information and insight upon which to make better decisions. The value of marketing research lies in its contribution to **reducing the risk** of making bad marketing decisions.

While quantitative survey research plays a significant role in this, qualitative research, competitive intelligence, and research-based on secondary information also contribute significantly to improving the quality of management decision making.

How can Marketing Research Help Decision-making?

Ideally, research should assist firms in the **strategic** and **marketing planning process**, from goal setting, planning and implementation, through to evaluation of the efforts.

Strategic planning allocates a company's resources to achieve its objectives. It is a continuing process of assessing the organization's current resources, diagnosing its current situation, forecasting its status in the future, developing a set of alternative strategic directions, choosing a strategy, implementing that strategy, and providing for the strategic and tactical control of that plan.

The **marketing planning** process ensures that firms have the information they need to determine the potential or actual success of their marketing plans as they are being developed and implemented. It is the responsibility of the professional marketing researcher to ensure that research information is valid, reliable, up-to-date, and suitable for its intended use.

The **marketing decisions**, in turn, are components of the comprehensive strategy for the organization. Many companies and public organizations have strategic planning processes that require marketing decisions to be made at appropriate points and to be based on expert judgment and sound information. This need for data to support strategic planning is a key motivator for marketing research activity.

One of the best ways of appreciating the breadth of information that marketing research can provide to an organization is to follow the strategic planning process through its many phases. By asking, "How do you know that?" and "What information do you need to make that decision?", many marketing research tasks can be identified to enhance the strategic plan. Marketing research can play as valuable a role in measuring the needs and desires of the public for library resources and services as it can in private business in assessing the needs of new features for home carpet cleaning, or for microwavable frozen entrees.

In strategic planning, *the current planning gap* identifies the distance between where the organization thought it would be at a point in time and where that organization is at that time on key indicators. A **gap** between what the organization knows and what it thinks it needs to know to compete in the marketplace effectively motivates the need for obtaining information based on marketing research. Such a gap could be desired sales of a product in a market segment and the current sales in that segment.

Marketing research and information from the organization's operations should provide substantial input to this gap analysis. The organization's *mission* would have specified what the organization ideally intends to achieve. The objectives are more practical manifestations of what the organization strongly desires to achieve at particular points of time. The *strategic market audit* is an investigation of the capabilities and resources of the organization to plan strategically and to execute those plans.

Once the current gap is identified, the reasons for the gap's existence ("diagnosis") and the prediction of the gap's implications for the organization ("prognosis") are studied. The *future planning gap* can then be estimated. This specifies that if the organization continues with its present strategy for the next year, for example, then the gap between objectives and achievement will be a certain size. Rather than changing strategy based on the current planning gap, the organization needs to project the effects of its strategy for long enough to see whether the strategy is perhaps correct. Still, the timing was a bit too ambitious. Maybe the organization just has to wait another year, and everything will be fine. Or, of course, the reverse might be true. Marketing research can be helpful at this stage to estimate the likely response of the public to current marketing strategies during the next year or so.

If it is determined that a change of strategy is needed, then *alternatives* must be identified and assessed. The organizational and marketing strategies will foster a reformulation of the marketing actions of the company through the development of a new or modified *marketing mix*. To determine new service and product directions, changes to existing services and products, revised pricing, more effective advertising and distribution that better meets the needs of the organization's public, the needs and wants of that public must be measured through marketing research. Similarly, the development of "programs" to inform and motivate the public to make better and more effective use of the organization's services and resources should be the subject of marketing research.

After the strategic plan is *approved*, the plan for the "implementation" of the strategy is developed. Then the services and resources that the marketing research identified as needed and desired are "offered" to the public through communication and distribution. It is crucial at this stage that *tactical control* mechanisms are established to measure the effectiveness of the organization's day-to-day mechanisms in providing the resources and services. In parallel, the *public's opinions and needs* must be sensitively measured to identify their reactions to those resources and services and how the new strategies provide them.

It is nearly impossible to get any strategy working exactly right without monitoring the market and organizational activities and perhaps to refine the strategy as sensitively and as quickly as possible.

At the end of the planning cycle is the detailed evaluation of the strategic plan in terms of objective measures on internal and external performance criteria. Naturally, marketing research is again needed to identify the reactions of the several segments of the public to the many facets of the strategic plan and its implementation.

It is relatively easy to see that there are many opportunities for marketing research to contribute to the more effective allocation of a company's resources and improved marketing decisions.

Where to get Marketing Research Information from?

General information related to marketing research can come from several sources.

Industry Associations

Many countries around the world have **national marketing research associations** that provide several services to the industry, including:
- A meeting place for networking and socializing
- Professional development and education opportunities
- Published codes of ethics and good practice
- Standards and audit processes
- Certification programs
- Journals, newsletters and conferences
- Directories of members and services
- Job advertising and placement services
- Public relations campaigns
- Group insurance and/or health benefits
- Advocacy on public policy issues that might affect the marketing research industry

Industry associations may offer **professional development** opportunities ranging from the occasional guest speaker at a social gathering to a full syllabus of courses leading to certification.

Standards are essential in ensuring a common, industry-wide understanding of how ethical marketing research is conducted. They are prepared, updated, and policed by special standards committees. As technologies evolve, new standards are written, for example, covering research with children or in online environments. Respect for the client and for the respondent are critical components of any list of standards.

Some national associations have tackled the tricky question of **certification** by offering an educational curriculum and an exam leading to a designation – for example, "Certified Marketing Research Professional." In some markets or organizations, clients require that at least one certified researcher is involved in every project.

Conferences provide an informal, non-competitive environment for sharing new approaches and learning to ensure the industry as a whole keeps up with trends and fine-tunes its practices against new realities in the consumer space.

Public relations is a particularly important role for these national associations. The industry survives only if members of the public are willing to participate in studies. The public must have a positive impression of the role of marketing research in making their lives better. In an age of social media, it is also crucial that misperceptions be caught and corrected as quickly as possible.

Public policy advocacy is crucial to ensuring that marketing research is not lumped in with telemarketing and other selling ventures when regulations are created. Policymakers are often unaware of the role that marketing research plays in a market economy and need to be educated to avoid removing a resource for informed decision making.

ESOMAR is a global organization that offers networking and professional development opportunities on a worldwide scale. Their standards are often adopted by the national associations to ensure consistency around the globe – particularly when client organizations are increasingly global.

Educational Opportunities

National associations provide professional development opportunities, and many business programs offer at least one course in marketing research. However, universities and colleges are increasingly offering diploma or degree programs in marketing research. These may be stand-alone or integrated into commerce or business programs. The types of courses may include:

Quantitative Research Techniques
- Marketing Research Fundamentals
- Questionnaire Design
- Marketing Research Statistics & Data Analysis
- Measuring Brand Equity
- Measuring Customer Satisfaction, Loyalty and Retention
- Marketing Analytics/ Marketing Science

Qualitative Research techniques
- Qualitative Marketing Research
- Moderator Training

Secondary Research
- Competitive Intelligence
- Data Mining Techniques

Reporting
- Storytelling Techniques

- Market Segmentation Research

The Business of Marketing Research
- Proposal Writing
- Selling Marketing Research
- New Technologies in Marketing Research
- Ethical Issues in Marketing Research

Educational programs generally use a textbook like the one you are now reading to provide detailed 'how-to' guidance.

Concluding Comments

At this point, you will have developed an overview of the function of marketing research and the role it plays in making better marketing decisions. You now understand the various roles played by practitioners on both the supplier and client-side and are aware of the different types of marketing research and how they are conducted. We've wrapped up with a section on industry and educational resources that are available to those who are in or wish to enter the marketing research field.

In the following chapters, you will have the opportunity to develop a deeper understanding of the mechanics and practice of marketing research.

UNIT 2

How to Prepare For a Marketing Research Project

Introduction

In Unit 1, you were introduced to the field of marketing research and the various players and stakeholders. In the following pages, you will move on to learn how these stakeholders work together to:
- understand what marketers need to create, fine-tune, position and market their products and services to consumers; and
- to design research projects that will give them the direction they need to make marketing decisions.

Start with the Marketing Problem

Marketing research plays a crucial role in keeping brands **relevant**. It provides the information that marketers need to ensure their products and services grow by **filling a need** in consumers' everyday lives. Marketing research is how marketers **listen**.

But listening needs a focus. A research project can only help solve a **marketing problem** when it is **precisely and adequately articulated**.

What is the business decision that is to be made, and what information will help you make that decision?

This may seem obvious, but it is not unusual to find a research request that is a grab bag of nice-to-know questions with no focus and no apparent direction. This happens when marketers and brand managers are simply asked to send in questions they'd like answered.

The more players that are involved, the more important is the duty to define the marketing problem accurately. A research partner may not have the corporate experience or insider knowledge to see what the client organization considers obvious.

If the end-user of marketing research does not define the problem clearly from the start, the final information is unlikely to help solve the marketing problem that generated the request. You might end up asking the wrong questions, collecting information from the wrong people, using the wrong type of analysis and drawing the wrong conclusions. The **most important thing** is to understand the marketing decisions that need to be made.

> Example. Let's drop in on Stella. She's an insight manager with Big Juice Company and has been asked to create and execute a market research study that will help the company increase its share of sales of the juice category.
>
> Stella's first step is to talk to Richard, the brand manager, to understand what the findings will be used for. Richard tells her that sales have been falling and that he believes the brand's current consumers are ageing and becoming more health conscious. He wants to target younger, more active consumers who are not as concerned about sugar content.
>
> The second step is to understand what alternative actions might be taken. Stella learns from Richard that he might redirect some of his sponsorship efforts away from health sector charities and focus more on sports teams. He is also interested in launching a sports drink line extension.
>
> The third step is to determine what information is needed to select between the alternative actions. Together, Stella and Richard decide that they need to create a study that will determine what triggers lead younger consumers to choose one brand of juice over another. They also need to understand if those triggers are the same as among the current consumers of Big Juice, or if they might be a turn-off for them.
>
> The fourth step is to decide who is best able to provide this information. Would it be the principal grocery shopper, current customers, store managers or younger sports fanatics?
>
> At this point, Stella has a clear idea of the marketing problem. She drafts the following problem definition for approval by her stakeholders:
>
> > Big Juice has been a category leader for several decades, but slipping sales and the appearance of a new wave of start-up competitors has led the company to conclude that renewal is needed.

Its current buyers tend to be older and are turning away from the juice category because of health concerns.

Big Juice will need to understand how best to drive brand growth among current and potential juice buyers, mainly targeting a younger demographic.

With the marketing problem clearly defined, Stella can determine that a customer satisfaction survey, focusing only on current customers, won't provide any information to attract potential customers. Instead, a market segmentation study among the general population would collect information on the needs of different groups within the population, whether they drink Big Juice or not.

Marketing decisions should be part of a regular planning process with appropriate timelines built-in for effective research solutions. However, there are times when consumer feedback is required quickly because of an urgent need to respond to a crisis.

Secondary research may be required if you have only a few hours to come up with a solution. You could look through the results of research conducted in the past (archival research), or access data available from existing syndicated reports or from government data collection agencies (e.g., Statistics Canada or the U.S. Census Bureau).

A well-constructed marketing problem definition will make that desk research faster and more effective and, consequently, less expensive.

Why are Marketing Problems not Appropriately Defined?

A proper marketing problem definition is *so essential* to a successful research outcome that it is surprising how little discipline and focus there often is around this step. The reasons are often:
- a lack of experience,
- extreme time pressures, and
- the absence of a research perspective at the decision table.

Example. When Stella first started asking, "What decisions will be based on this research?" she might have received a broad range of answers from her stakeholders:
- "We need to understand how to make our brand 'number one.'"
- "I just need to know more about my customers."
- "Maybe none. We'll just keep doing what we're doing unless something jumps out."
- "I want to segment the market based on key drivers of customer retention."

Difficulties with problem definition can arise from three factors:
- failing to distinguish between the marketing objectives and the marketing research objectives;
- trying to identify latent, habitual or subconscious behaviour patterns by direct questioning;
- confusing the objectives with the scope of the study.

Failing to distinguish between marketing objectives and marketing research objectives

Marketing decision-makers think in terms of *marketing* opportunities to be exploited, *marketing* problems to be solved, and *marketing* objectives to be achieved. They will want to know:
- How to outsmart the competition?
- Why is the market share of our product going down?
- What can be done to increase the sales of our product?

After listening to these marketing objectives, a **researcher** may be tempted to define the marketing *research* objectives in similar terms:
- To assess the factors contributing to gaining a competitive edge
- To find out why the market share of Product X is going down
- To find out how the sales of Product X can be increased.

These objectives are not wrong but, as they are worded, it is hard to solve them by using marketing research alone.

Research objectives must be written in a way that can be answered *directly* by the research study. Problems that *cannot* be explained by the survey can then be easily identified at this stage before resources are allocated. Otherwise, the researcher might be blamed for failing to solve a problem that the research was never able to answer.

> Example. Richard, Big Juice's brand manager, is concerned about increasing sales for his product. Stella, his insight manager colleague, realizes that her research suppliers will have a challenge learning "how to increase sales" from consumers.
>
> On the other hand, she knows that research might identify whether buying dynamics are shifting, whether needs are changing in the marketplace overall or differentially among the several market segments, if there are shortcomings in Big Juice's positioning against consumer needs, particularly in the face of competitor Chic Juice's new ad campaigns. This speaks directly to solutions that marketing research can identify.
>
> Richard would then have the information he needs to begin creating an updated positioning for Big Juice's product and identifying relevant themes for his marketing communications, advertising and sponsorships and the channels that would get that message to the right consumers in segments that have greater potential for growth in juice consumption.
>
> The research objectives must be specific enough that they can be achieved solely through the research. With this in mind, Stella might write the following research objectives for her suppliers to respond to.
>
> Segment the general population across Canada on key juice purchasing attributes and identify the following for differences among segments;
>
> - the frequency with which consumers buy the category and the quantity per purchase occasion;
> - the rate with which consumers purchase specific brands and the amount per purchase occasion;

- what other products tend to be bought and used together with the brand, and whether there have been any changes in these other products;
- whether there have been any recent changes in claimed usage;
- consumer preferences for juice and related beverages for each segment;
- whether consumers feel that the brand is inferior to competing brands and has become more so in the recent past;
- whether consumer perceptions of the brand have changed in the recent past and the direction of those changes;
- whether consumers use another product as a substitute and whether the tendency to use a substitute has changed;
- what the proportion of buyers is in different demographic groups;
- whether there have been any changes in external influences, such as government regulations or inability to visit the stores carrying the product, that might have affected sales of the brand; and
- meeting these research objectives may or may not fully solve the marketing problem. they do, however, pertain directly to the consumers who are subjects of the research.

Another example. Frank is the Director of Insight for Brothers Cosmetics. His organization would like to increase the price of OatLather, one of their brands of soap, but he wants to make sure that this will result in increased profitability. That is the marketing problem in very broad terms. In discussions with the brand managers, Frank has determined the following facts:

1. An increase in the unit price would increase the unit profit. This is purely a maneuver to increase the profit margin and has nothing to do with the cost of producing OatLather.

2. If people buy fewer bars of OatLather or switch to other brands because of the new pricing, then the brand's total profitability could decrease rather than increase.

Frank will need to determine how consumers—in particular current users of OatLather —would react to a price increase. Working with his research suppliers, Frank has established that a research project could tell Brothers Cosmetics:

- whether consumers of the soap category are price-conscious, i.e., aware of the prices they pay for soap;
- whether category consumers are price sensitive—price points play a significant role in the choice of brands they buy;
- whether consumers of OatLather are price sensitive;
- the degree of loyalty to OatLather among current users;
- the extent to which OatLather users will remain loyal (continue to buy our brand) if the price is increased;
- whether current OatLather users will switch to a competitive brand, or simply buy fewer units of OatLather if they find the price increase to be unacceptable; and
- whether OatLather can be positioned to have an essential appeal among buyers of upscale bath and beauty products.

Frank will be able to sharpen, extend, reduce, or modify these initial research objectives as discussions with the brand manager and suppliers continue. For example, he may have to delete some objective if the resultant questionnaire turns out to be overly long. He may also find that there is not enough money in the budget for the length of the questionnaire required to cover all these topics. He may have to go back to the brand team and ask them to prioritize and remove those objectives that are less important.

Confusing Latent Variables with Manifest Variables

Here are two fundamental concepts when we are designing a research study: manifest and latent variables.

Manifest variables are those aspects of the consumer that can be directly observed or physically proven. These include demographics such as age, income or education, which can be verified with a birth certificate, pay stub or school diploma. It can be the number of boxes of cereal bought last month, which can be observed by looking into a shopping cart, purchase diary or photograph of their kitchen cupboard.

Latent variables are those aspects of the consumer that cannot be directly observed, such as people's attitudes and opinions. We know that they bought something but can't observe "why." One of the significant challenges in marketing research is measuring people's attitudes.

For example, if we were designing a research project to understand why people buy the latest version of an expensive mobile phone, we could simply ask them directly. This would give us a few critical insights. But they may not be willing to tell us that they buy it to improve their social status. In fact, an even more severe threat to validity is that they may not even be aware of the real reasons for their behaviour.

Example 1.
RESEARCH OBJECTIVE: To identify the reasons why upscale adults consume alcohol.
The reason offered by the respondent on a questionnaire: "To relax with friends."
Latent behaviour: Alcohol dependency or addiction.
Better research method: Use an indirect research method, for example, projective techniques (see Unit 4).

Example 2.
RESEARCH OBJECTIVE: To determine how likely medical doctors would be to prescribe a specific brand of a pharmaceutical product to treat Alzheimer's disease.
The reason offered by an MD in a personal interview: "I typically prescribe Brand X for that disease."
Latent behaviour: The likelihood of future prescribing behaviour is unknown, given that new and better drugs are continually being researched and made available.

Better research method: Present MDs with several pharmaceutical products in a conjoint experiment and ask them to choose the one they would prescribe for a specific type of patient. Repeat this with different selections of products and various types of patients.

Marketing research projects generally include questions that will measure *both* types of variables.

Manifest variables can be measured with direct, structured and undisguised questions, and consumers can be expected to provide direct, accurate answers. They will tell us their age and education level as well as the model of car they drive, the restaurants they visit or the brand of orange juice they buy.

The **latent** component is not as easy. Attitudes reside deep in our conscious and subconscious mind. By nature, attitudes can't be observed. In some cases, consumers can't or won't provide answers to attitudinal questions. For example, people may refuse to say they are sexist or racist. Indeed, some people may not believe that they are sexist or racist even though their behaviours may suggest otherwise.

Direct questioning (e.g., are you racist?) only provides partial, and sometimes misleading, information. Sophisticated statistical analysis, such as latent class analysis, can be used to identify latent variables if the right questions have been asked.

How Latent Variables are related to Latent Constructs

> The first type of latent variable that we consider is a single question where the respondent's correct answer can never be observed nor proven. This is referred to as a **hypothetical construct** (something we think exists but cannot demonstrate). Let's consider customer loyalty. There are two key components of loyalty: behaviour and attitude.

Behavioural loyalty refers to repeat purchases of a brand. For example, some consider a customer loyal to a brand if they bought it four out of the last five times. Others might say it is one out of every two purchases. Whatever the criterion, behavioural loyalty relies on the observable and measurable action of buying a brand. Purchasing is a manifest variable because it is observable.

Of course, this behavioural loyalty may happen because there is only one accessible store that carries only one brand.

Attitudinal loyalty is a mental state where a consumer feels they need just one brand to satisfy all or most of his or her needs. We could try to measure it by simply asking people how loyal they are to a brand, but this is unlikely to be sufficient. It is a hypothetical construct that we attempt to measure using several latent variables, which together can capture the essence of the construct. The attitudinal element of brand health could include a sense of 'closeness' to the brand, how it makes consumers feel about themselves, how using the brand might make others see them and how they would feel if it were out of stock.

Taken further, behavioural loyalty (how much they buy) can be combined with attitudinal loyalty (how they feel about the brand) to create a larger latent construct of **'brand health.'** It would be the role of the analysis phase to bring all these variables together into a single brand equity measure.

Other examples of hypothetical latent constructs are quality, corporate reputation and customer satisfaction.

Confusing Research Objectives with the Scope of the Study

The third problem encountered when trying to clearly define the marketing research problem is confusing the *objectives* of the study with the *scope* of the study.

Objectives outline the exact *purposes* for conducting the study. At the end of the project, the findings must have addressed each specific objective and must align with marketing-oriented solutions. The **scope** of the study relates to how the project *will be conducted*. It will describe the relevant geographical regions, the type of people to include, the breadth of analysis to perform and the period during which the study must be conducted.

The scope must, of course, relate directly to the objectives. If it doesn't, or if the objectives are poorly developed, then the scope of the study might not be relevant to solving the marketing problem.

> Example (continued). So, if we drop in on Frank of Brothers Cosmetics again, he'll remind us that they had developed a range of research objectives around the impact of a price increase on his OatLather soap brand. The scope of the study might outline the following requirements:
> - that he needs to hear from current OatLather users who are soap brand decision-makers for their household;
> - that he wants to investigate the behaviours and attitudes of upscale bath and beauty customers;
> - that the research is to be conducted in the region where OatLather is available (e.g. the Scandinavian and Baltic countries of Sweden, Norway, Denmark, Latvia, Lithuania and Estonia); and
> - that peak purchasing season for OatLather is during the winter when harsh conditions boost the sales of the brand.

How to Define the Marketing Research Problem

Marketing research objectives must describe the information needed to choose the actions that will solve the marketing problem. The following four steps can help us do this:
1. State the marketing problem
    - *The sales of our brand are not increasing.*
2. Explicitly state the factual information implied in the marketing problem
    - *The total unit sales of our brand have been flat over the past three years across all geographic regions where it is sold.*
3. State the possible causes that might have led to this problem
    - *The market for the category has expanded but not to the benefit of our brand.*
    - *The market for the category has eroded since last year but not to the detriment of our brand.*

- *The market has shrunk, to our detriment.*
- *The market is static and so are our sales and the sales of our primary competitors.*

4. List what you would like to know about the market
   - *You may want to test all four possible reasons, or you may already know which one is the real problem. Depending on your knowledge, you may list the types of information related to each reason that can be obtained through marketing research.*

In defining the marketing problem, it is essential to consider what is already known from **past studies**, and what can be sourced from **secondary sources** of information.

We should also consider the **hypotheses** to be tested. These are the decision-makers' *understanding* of the marketing environment that needs to be proven or disproven.

The scope is then fleshed out from the objectives and can be modified to fit the resources available. The scope of the study describes the breadth of all the information in the study, including the sample frame and the main lines of questioning.

For example, in terms of sampling frames, i.e., the direct source of the sample:
- a broad scope might include a sample drawn from the population of all North Americans 18 years of age or older;
- a narrow scope might consist of restricting the sample to those Canadians who own a single-detached home in the lower mainland of British Columbia.

In terms of a questionnaire,
- a narrow scope might be to ask respondents only about the last purchase of a product;
- a broad scope might be to ask about the previous purchase, the previous five purchases, their current attitudes about the product, and their intentions regarding upcoming purchases.

Answering the following questions will help to clarify the objectives and scope of the project.

1. What is the **marketing problem** for which a solution is sought? (What marketing decision will be based directly on the information collected?)
2. What is the **marketing research problem**?
3. What information is required to solve the problem?
4. What sources can provide the required information?
5. What part of the required information can be obtained from consumers directly?
6. What part of the required information can be obtained from secondary sources?
7. What resources are available for collecting this information?
8. How broad or narrow will each study component be?
9. Once research findings become available, how can they be used to solve the critical marketing problem?
10. What additional information can be collected?

The reason for collecting *additional* information can be twofold: to augment the primary information collected and to maximize the benefit derived from the project. The marginal cost of asking a few more questions on a survey will be small compared to the total cost of the project. Keep in mind, however, that a low financial cost to the researcher or client could translate into burden and fatigue for respondents.

By formalizing the information needs in this way, we can *clarify* the problem, set realistic *goals* for the research, *weed out* information that is not relevant and *define* the scope very clearly.

The *objectives* of the study are less negotiable than its *scope* because the objectives relate to the primary purpose of the study. However, we may have to cut a few of the objectives due to budget, time constraints, or limits to respondent availability or patience.

Can this Study Provide Answers to the Problem?

If the answers provided by a marketing research study are to be believed, they must be **reliable** and **valid**. These two words are often grouped together or used interchangeably, but they do have two distinct meanings.

Reliability is one key indicator of the quality of the research. It refers to the *consistency* of measurements: if a particular observation can be *replicated* using the same measurement procedure and a similar sample drawn from the same population, then the study is considered reliable. If some aspect of the design is *not* well controlled across the measurement occasions, then these measurements could be statistically different and unreliable.

Reliability is only *one* necessary component for a measurement instrument and process to be considered valid. Other requirements must be met, as well.

> Example. The fastest way to lose 5 kilograms is to adjust your bathroom scale so that it reads lighter. Even if your actual weight stays precisely the same, you will seem to weigh 5 kg less. And no matter how many times you weigh yourself on the adjusted scale, it will reliably indicate that you weigh 5 kilograms less. The consistency makes it a reliable scale. Of course, it is not a valid measurement.

Validity means that you correctly measure what you intend to measure. The bathroom scale does not generate valid measurements because it provides a reading that is 5 kilograms lower than your actual weight. If the scale *always* provided your *actual* weight, it would be *both* reliable and valid.

So, if an instrument is *not* reliable, it *cannot* be valid. But, if it is reliable, it might or might not be valid. And, if the instrument is valid, it must be reliable.

Naturally, both clients and their research suppliers want to build high quality research mechanisms that provide accurate (valid) and consistent (reliable) findings.

> Example (Contd.) Let's reconsider the problem faced by Big Juice's insight manager Stella and her brand manager colleague Richard. Big Juice company engaged in a research study to measure brand linkage – whether consumers identified their unique bottle design with their product. Intercept interviews were conducted among 'health juice' buyers in six different malls in the same region. Care was taken to set up the same sample (age, income, education, brand usage) and the same interview protocol in each mall, but the results varied greatly from one location to another. Stella felt that because the results were not consistent, they were not valid. She checked in with a senior member of her supplier's team, and he agreed that if the samples were drawn from the

same population and used the same methodology, a reliable research process would not produce measurements that are statistically different. Are these conclusions appropriate?

What are Marketing Research Projects Like?

When deciding on the design for a marketing research project, it is important to work through three essential components: The **type** of marketing research project, the **information requirements**, and the field **methodology.**

1. Types of Marketing Research Projects

Identifying the correct *type* of project is a critical step in the design process. Some common types include:

- Usage and attitudes
- Market landscaping
- Insight, idea and concept screening
- Product design optimization
- Product testing
- Pricing optimization
- Advertising copy testing
- Brand or advertising tracking
- Segmentation
- Packaging testing
- Claims testing
- Customer satisfaction
- Mystery shopping

Many problems can be translated quickly and accurately into one of these standard research types.
- If sales are dropping, we might do a *customer satisfaction* study.
- If we need to look for innovation opportunities, we might do a *market landscape* study.
- If we need to narrow a list of potential product innovations, we might do a *concept screening* study.

However, sometimes, prematurely assigning a marketing problem to a research type can lead to the incorrect design and the subsequent collection of information that does not address the project objectives.

The **primary aim** of a research design is **to answer the research questions** (and address the marketing problem) effectively while keeping the costs at a reasonable level. The marketing scope, the marketing research objectives, and the projected budget will help determine the design.

2. Information Requirements

Each of these *types* of research studies can be designed to provide **exploratory**, **descriptive**, or **causal information**. Here, in brief, are the differences between the three types.

Exploratory: When little is known about the topic, and we collect learning in a relatively open-ended manner to] (for example)
- formulate the marketing problem more precisely
- develop hypotheses
- establish priorities
- eliminate impractical ideas
- clarify concepts and language.

Descriptive: To explain the current state of the market and marketing by, for example:
- describing characteristics of certain groups
- estimating the proportion of people in a population who behave a certain way
- making specific predictions .

Causal: To attempt to explain what **triggers** or **barriers** lead to specific consumer behaviours or attitudes by using sophisticated design and analysis techniques.

We tend to focus too often on the descriptive, merely collecting information that will tell us what people do or say. However, including an exploratory phase will help us discover new insights that exist beyond our current understanding. By the same token, causal analysis might help us uncover the triggers and barriers that spur the behaviour we need to impact or change.

This usually represents a sequence of projects – we would explore first, then describe to ensure we have substantial information about the market and consumers before we undertake the more sophisticated causal studies. Let's look at each in more depth.

Marketing Problems and Research Techniques

Type of Research Study	Marketing Problem/Issue	
Usage and Attitude Studies	Who and how many use the product category/brand? What are the differences between heavy and light users? What are the main features of their behaviour and habits—frequency of purchase, brand loyalty, what do they mix it with?	What are their attitudes, beliefs, values to existing brands? What are their product requirements? What are the brand's strengths and weaknesses? Tell me everything I ever wanted to know about ___!
Concept Tests	Which of a number of alternative new product ideas has the most appeal? Is the idea easy to understand? What expectations and associations does it generate? Do you perceive distinct benefits for this product over those products currently on the market? Are the claims about this product believable? Would you buy this product?	Would you replace your current brand with this new brand? Would this product meet a real need? What improvements can you suggest in various attributes of the concept? How frequently would you use the brand? Who would use the brand? What share potential does it have? If I reposition my brand this way, will it work?
Product Testing	Which is the preferred prototype? How much is the "improved" formulation liked? Will consumers buy a "cost-reduced product? Is our product acceptable to consumers? Is our product marginally or much better/worse than the competition?	Can we get away with substituting carob for chocolate? Does the product we've developed deliver its promise? Which brand is better—ours or P&G's?
Segmentation Studies	How does the market segment (demographics, psychographics, behaviour, attitudes, lifestyles)? How large are the segments? What is the potential of the segments?	How can each segment be reached with ads? Can I improve my brand's current positioning? Are there any gaps in the market that can be exploited?
Tracking Studies	What are the levels of brand and advertising awareness over time? What are the progressing levels of trial and purchase? Is there any conversion to occasional and regular usage? Is the advertising communicating, compared to last quarter, last year, etc.?	How have attitudes toward the brand changed? How has our brand's image changed relative to that of competitive brands?
Advertising Research	How believable is our advertising? How relevant is our advertising to the target consumers? How much do the target consumers like our advertising? How much power does our advertising have over the receivers?	To what does our advertising appeal? Does our advertising provide the information that the consumers want? Has our advertising shifted consumer attitudes?
Test Marketing	How will our new brand fare in an actual market situation? How well does the new brand gain retailer interest? How does the new brand do against real competition?	Is the marketing plan strong enough to gain initial trial? Does repeat purchase build as expected after initial trial? Which is the best name out of the alternatives?
Name Testing	Which name connotes the benefits that consumers want most? Is the name easily pronounced?	Does the name have any secondary meanings? Is the name remembered? Do the target consumers like the name?
Package Research	Which package communicates best on the shelf? Which package is most visually appealing? Which package is most useful to consumers?	Which package produces the best imagery of the brand to consumers?
New Product Research	How effective is our advertising in building awareness of the new brand? Which brands will our new brand compete against? How effective is our marketing plan in encouraging initial trial?	Will the brand characteristics entice consumers to repeat purchase? How strong is the likability of the brand? How can we answer all of the above as inexpensively as possible?

Exploratory Research

Suppose that the marketing team has identified an issue and calls a meeting with their marketing research colleagues. Someone at that first meeting recognizes that the **issue** is **not understood well enough** to have a precise hypothesis that can be tested.

The company needs to **explore the basic nature** of the marketing issue before it can even begin to plan an effective fact-gathering study. At this point, there is little to rely on but the experience of the company's marketing staff and research team.

> Example (contd.) Frank, the brand manager at Brothers Cosmetics, has asked his research team to attend a meeting to help him understand price sensitivity for OatLather soap. He may never have done research on the brand in the past, and the product may be priced simply at 'par' with similar products. But he does know that the product is made with premium ingredients, has an odd, rough texture, and has a smell that he believes men in particular enjoy. But he doesn't know what impact, if any, these characteristics have on consumers' willingness to buy the product and whether or not they might be willing to pay a premium for it. Frank is in a place where he could benefit from exploratory research.

It is always tempting to get the research team to define the project and jump directly to a descriptive or causal study, but that means the company will be confining itself to its **current understanding** of the marketing issue and will not challenge itself to consider new learnings. In a rush to field an extensive data collection exercise, the team risks losing focus on the marketing problem. And if not correctly designed from the start, a project cannot be saved by manipulations in the analysis phase. Even a fast turn-around study needs to be built on thoughtfully developed hypotheses.

The **main output** from an exploratory study is a solid understanding of the nature of the marketing problem and a set of intuitive hypotheses that can be tested through descriptive or causal research.

Descriptive Research

Descriptive research begins with a good understanding of the marketing problem and the marketing research objectives. This understanding is based on **experience**, on **learnings** from past studies, and **exploratory research**.

This knowledge may lead to well-defined hypotheses about the relationship between variables and the state of the market and marketing that can be tested in a quantitative survey.

Past experience can be easy to source. The senior marketing or research staff may have conducted similar work in the past. Even the freshest brand manager has access to research consultants or experienced suppliers who can draw on experience. Astute organizations archive their past research for quick access.

> Example (contd.) Richard and Stella are both relatively new employees at Big Juice Company. Still, Richard's direct manager, Alice, has been in the business for several decades and can help steer

them towards colleagues who do similar studies several times a year and towards an experienced research supplier who has a great deal of experience in the field that they need to explore.

The end report of a descriptive study might provide an overview of category purchase and usage dynamics, brand awareness and usage, brand perceptions, portraits of the type of people who are heavy users of the client's product, of competitive products and of switchers and non-users.

Causal Research

Suppose the same company has a fairly solid understanding of all of the variables that play a role in their customers' behaviour. Still, they want to understand the hierarchy of triggers and want to answer the question, "What is the most effective trigger that pushes consumers to choose one brand over another?"

> Example (contd.) Frank, at Brothers, might know that consumer's like OatLather Soap and that its critical points of differentiation are its texture, smell and exfoliation characteristics. He may also know that the product is positioned as 'premium' primarily because of where people expect to find it on the shelf. However, to effectively execute positioning advertising in the future, he needs to know which of these characteristics are most important, which ones differentiate OatLather from other brands, and which ones are most likely to trigger purchasing at a premium price.

Causal research may be the most beneficial type of research, but it is often challenging to get approval for research because it is the most **expensive** to execute. It is costly because it is generally **very complex**, requiring broad and multi-faceted sample designs, carefully constructed and intricate questionnaire designs, advanced analytics and more insight-focused analysis. As a result, it also requires highly qualified project directors, analysts and interpreters of the findings.

The intention of causal research is to be able to conclude specific cause-and-effect relationships that can be used to direct the highest level of marketing decisions.

> Example (contd.) Frank is hoping to be able to give Brothers Cosmetics' ad agency direction that will help them design an effective and focused positioning campaign. They must identify the key trigger that will raise awareness of the brand and alter perceptions to the point that consumers will prefer OatLather over the competition and will be able to justify a higher price point.

A key element that will help make this happen is **advanced modelling** on the data once it is collected. Strict causality requires the design, execution and interpreting of formal experiments. Weak causation can be established by using a method called structural equation modelling (SEM). Analysis by **structural equation** modelling to investigate causal hypotheses depends on:
- developing a set of hypothetical relationships
- asking the appropriate survey questions that will confirm and measure these relationships
- and then applying a specific analytical technique to create a model that explains how a key marketing *result* (e.g., customer retention or brand equity) is achieved.

The modelling will not only tell us *how* it is achieved, but *how it relates* to *other* marketing activities, consumer attitudes and personal characteristics.

In practice, projects are not necessarily identified as strictly exploratory, descriptive or causal. A well-designed project brings in the right tools to explore, if necessary, to collect descriptors and to explain the causal relationships when needed.

Causal Research and the Design of Experiments:

Establishing one or more variables as the cause of some phenomenon is one of the most challenging and complex tasks in research. The focus of proper causal research is on the design, execution, analysis, and interpretation of experiments. Sometimes these experiments are conducted in laboratories and other times they are set in actual market conditions. In the marketing research world, a laboratory might be as simple as an office or boardroom, or as complicated as a fully mocked-up grocery store with real products on the shelves.

A straightforward experiment to understand the effect that price has on soft sales might be designed to be conducted in a laboratory.

- First, the range of prices and several specific prices for a product would be identified. Let's say that four prices, ranging from $1.79 to $2.49, were selected for a 1.5-litre bottle of the soft drink Schpritz.

- Second, a large sample would be randomly selected and recruited from the relevant population of interest, perhaps young adults between the ages of 18 and 34.

- Then, one-quarter of the respondents would be shown the bottle of Schpritz and asked how likely they would be to buy the drink at $1.79. The second group, also a randomized selection of one-quarter of the total sample, would be asked their purchase likelihood at $1.99, the third group at $2.29, and the fourth group at $2.49.

Other questions could also be asked to identify purchase frequency and to understand the demographic profile of each group to ensure that they were comparable. The differences in purchase likelihood and frequency among the four groups could be attributed to the price levels only because the products and the study environments would be the same, and the sample groups would be nearly identical in critical attributes.

Now, think about moving the laboratory finding into the real world. Laboratory administration has the benefit of eliminating unrelated stimuli that could influence the subjects' responses. However, the results from laboratory experiments are sometimes difficult to generalize to the real marketing environment in which consumers make their product choices.

What might compromise the findings? Of course, no soft drink is without competition. The laboratory experiment presented only Schpritz to the subjects, but what would happen if other brands of soft drinks as well as other juices, energy drinks, and bottled waters, were available? What if Schpritz was priced lower or higher than the alternatives? What if the person's best friend was exerting influence to purchase a different drink? What if another customer was blocking the fridge containing the Schpritz?

> Experiments can be very complicated to design, administer, and interpret. But they provide the best opportunity to test the effect of variation in product attributes and other variables on critical responses of consumers. In fact, well-designed experiments can take advantage of sophisticated statistical techniques called conjoint analysis, A/B testing and uplift modeling to test these variations.

3. Field Methodology

The third element is to select the most appropriate **research methodology** to get the right information from the right respondents in a context that is as close as possible to real life.

For example, if we are testing a new pizza snack that we want young teen males to buy at convenience stores, we need to find a methodology that will put the product in the hands of some of these young consumers, perhaps away from the influence of their parents. Or, if we want to gauge how parents feel about their children's experiences at an amusement park, we need to find these visitors fairly efficiently and interview them as close to the experience as possible. Or, if we are testing the effectiveness of a potential new television advertisement, it should be shown to the target audience as part of a mix of programming and other ads, on a screen that resembles what they will see in their own home.

There is a wide range of potential field methodologies that we could use, including:
- Ethnography
- Digital bulletin boards
- Pop-up online communities
- Standard focus groups
- Virtual focus groups (via a video link)
- Social listening
- Face-to-face interviews (in person or via a video link)
- Telephone interviews
- Voice recognition automated interviews
- Self-administered web-based surveys
- Self-administered paper questionnaires
- Eye-tracking
- Facial recognition
- Neurological measurement.

There are several questions a researcher needs to ask when exploring methodology options:
- Who is my intended target? Are there influencers who should be included?
- Where am I most likely to find this target efficiently, inexpensively and in a mood to participate?
- Is the information best collected by quantitative or qualitative methods?
- Does the information I need already exist from a source I can tap into, such as secondary research? Or, will I need to conduct primary research?

- Is the data going to be available from a shared, syndicated study that I can buy into, or will I need a custom study explicitly designed to my needs?
- Am I asking just a few questions that can ride on a relatively low-cost omnibus study? Do we have a proprietary panel I can tap into, or should it be a larger scale custom study?
- Will the target for the information I need require the participation of an interviewer or can the target respondent provide answers directly through a self-completion questionnaire; or does the information we need lend itself to alternative methods like passive observation, social listening, facial recognition or neuroscience (measuring brain activity)?

By asking questions like these, the researcher can arrive at a research design that would be appropriate to the problem. It may be easy to *simply choose* the method that provides the greatest *comfort for the researcher.* But experienced researchers are more likely to arrive at suitable research designs by mentally *eliminating the inappropriate* ones and evaluating the ones that are left against the set **criteria**.

Proper research designs depend on:
- How well it **suits the problem** being researched
- How well it **suits the type of respondent** being interviewed
- Whether or not the cost of the design **fits the budget**
- The **level of accuracy** required (often tied to the degree of risk in the decision being made)
- **Length of the interview**
- **How quickly** the study must be turned around
- Whether or not it fits **other project specs** that may be variable.

For example, the pizza snack test will require interviews in a central location where the snacks can be prepared as they would be in the convenience store. Ideally, the test would be conducted in a store, but that might introduce sampling bias (is the store's location representative of the full market? Is it near a particular type of school?). So, a test lab with a recruited sample of male teens from across the city may make more sense.

Parents' satisfaction with an amusement park might best be measured with a short intercept interview as respondents have completed their visit to the amusement park and are on their way to the exit. It is an on-going tracking program the cost per interview should be low, and the questions should be very simple. So, this can be a self-completion paper questionnaire handed out by park staff.

The advertising test can use a standard online methodology that inserts the potential advertisement into a series of other advertisements and asks highly standardized questions to test proven key success factors. The cost of failure, with an expensively shot ad airing through an extensive national media buy means that a large sample will be required to ensure a high degree of accuracy.

Keep in mind that research designs are not mutually exclusive. Custom designing a study for a specific marketing research problem might involve some ethnographic work to explore and prepare, followed by a quantitative web-based survey to collect hard data, augmented by social listening and followed up with in-depth qualitative deep dive with a few of the respondents from the quantitative study.

How is Data Collection Designed?

We often equate marketing research with surveys, but there are many different methods for obtaining consumer information, particularly as technology evolves.

- Sometimes it is necessary to look a consumer in the eye and probe their responses if we are to get through the superficial layers of 'easy responses.' In these cases, only ethnography or in-depth interviews would do.
- Sometimes you need to capture what consumers are seeing, hearing, tasting or feeling 'in the moment.' In this case, a mobile survey triggered by participation at a specific location will be appropriate.
- Other times, a multi-country quantitative survey with large samples of respondents is needed to track loyalty for a major corporation.
- A quick glimpse at social media participants' opinions on a topic may focus on Twitter, Facebook and Instagram over the last three days.

Moreover, because a specific project may have all three information needs – exploratory, descriptive and causal - one project could use multiple information collection techniques.

1. Qualitative Research

"Qualitative research" refers to studies that collect verbal and non-verbal information from personal interactions with a relatively small number of respondents. Qualitative research is intended to find insights, create hypotheses or understanding, but *not* to count, measure or extrapolate to larger populations.

The stereotypical 'qualitative' approach is a classic focus group with 8 to 10 respondents. But in reality, the field is far more diverse. Here are some examples:

- **Focus groups** are carefully mapped-out discussions with eight to ten people to explore a specific topic through semi-structured interactions between a moderator and the participants and between the participants. Focus groups are generally held in specially designed facilities with audio and video recording and a one-way mirror so the clients can observe. Smaller groups are sometimes required (6 to 8) if the topic is more specialized and the participants more expert, or if the intent is to break down social barriers and delve deeply into sub-conscious feelings.
- **Virtual or online focus groups** are similar in structure and approach, but rather than gathering participants in one room, they join the discussion from their home or workplace through a video link such as Zoom or Teams. Virtual groups have the benefit of including people from different regions and save on travel costs for the moderator and clients but are sometimes thought to miss the visual cues, and body language is evident in face-to-face groups.
- **In-depth personal interviews** are discussions that one moderator has with one respondent to explore a respondent's perceptions of a specific topic qualitatively. It is generally

comprehensive and often used for more sensitive matters or with respondents who might be hard to reach or sensitive to interaction with others. In-depth interviews can be conducted in person or via a video link.

- **Dyads** and **Triads** are small groups of two or three respondents, sometimes known to each other, to create a more intimate and profound discussion.
- **Ethnography**: A qualitative researcher spends time with a subject, perhaps in their own home, or on a shopping expedition, observing behaviour and interactions and collecting impressions before asking probing questions.
- **Virtual or Online Ethnography**: The qualitative researcher interacts with participants over the internet, often over several days, asking them to record and report on their routines in real-time, post photos, explore new ideas, share impressions and reflect on their motivations.
- **Bulletin Boards and Communities**: Web-based communities that share some characteristic and interact on an ongoing basis with researchers (in a bulletin board) and with each other (in a community) to respond to questions as they arise, co-create and develop new ideas.

Sometimes qualitative research is the only research conducted on a topic. More often, it is used to obtain information during the *exploratory* phase of studies to collect vocabulary, create hypotheses and initiate understanding. It can also be used **after** a quantitative study to gain a more in-depth understanding or to provide colour-commentary to explain the results better.

An interesting, but rare approach, is to present findings from a survey to a focus group and to ask them to explain the results with real-world examples and insights.

Qualitative research is explored in considerable detail in Unit 5.

When is Qualitative Research Most Useful?

A qualitative approach might be chosen when a company needs to:
- understand how real customers feel about the brand;
- discover the language and vocabulary that customers use when talking about brands in the product category;
- probe for deeper motivations that don't surface in casual conversations;
- explore the impact of social interaction on the evolution of perceptions;
- expose brand managers to frank discussions by their customers about the company's brand and its competitors;
- obtain background information;
- trace salient behaviour patterns, attitudes, and motivations;
- explore reaction to alternative concepts;
- identify potential problem areas;
- pilot or amplify quantitative studies;
- generate hypotheses for further testing by quantitative research methods.
- do a 'disaster check' before making a significant change;

Some of these situations can also be tested using *quantitative* research. These guidelines cannot be used as an absolute set of criteria for determining whether one should do a qualitative study. However, as one gains experience in research, it becomes easier to determine the appropriateness of a qualitative approach for a given problem.

2. Quantitative Research

The term **quantitative research** is used to describe any research project in which the interpretation depends on the <u>numbers</u> collected from the investigation.

In its most formal sense, quantitative research refers to studies that yield results with a **known or assumed degree of accuracy**, although as sampling moves away from strict probability sampling, the calculation of this 'accuracy' is put into question. Chapters 5 and 9 will explore this in greater depth.

Some of the common **characteristics** of quantitative research include:
- Numerical data based on many data points
- Representative samples of respondents reflecting the target group
- Results collected through formal, strictly structured and consistent questionnaires
- Findings that are presented numerically (e.g., tables, graphs, equations, infographics)
- Interpretation based on numerical relationships rather than the intuition of the researcher
- Used more for measuring and evaluating than investigating or exploring

Technological advances mean that researchers have an even broader range of methods they can use to collect numerical data than even a few years ago.
- **Eye-tracking** captures how consumers look at the packaging or at store shelves, and how the pathway that their eyes move along when the pack design changes or when the product arrangement on the shelf changes. AI will soon provide synthetic data on what we might expect human eyes to see.
- **Neuroscience** has been adapted to measure brain responses through electroencephalograms (EEGs) or galvanic skin response tools (GSR). The response changes when the stimuli put in front of the respondent changes.
- **Social listening** provides observations from social media posts. How many people are talking about the brand or product or service in a specific time frame and what they are saying.
- **Facial recognition** technology is beginning to be used to identify the age and gender of people who stop in front of a display and to measure positive and negative reactions.
- Even standard surveys should now fit onto the **smaller screens** of mobile devices, tablets, and even smartwatches as younger consumers, in particular, spend less time with the full desktop or laptop computers.

In countries with high internet penetration (particularly among desirable consumer groups), most quantitative surveys today use self-reporting, **web-based surveys**. **Telephone** and **mail** surveys are used to a much lesser degree but are still used when they suit the research objectives. **Door-to-door** surveying has mostly fallen out of favour, given access and security challenges.

Observational techniques can be used to track the behaviour of shoppers in supermarkets. Strategically placed researchers or unobtrusive cameras might capture the number of times shoppers stop in front of a shelf, how long they spend, how many products they pick up and examine before making a choice, and whether or not they put a product into their shopping cart. An additional qualitative or quantitative component could be added once the shopper has made their selections, approaching them to ask a few questions.

Artificial intelligence will have a significant impact on marketing research, leading to better research design and faster insight development. It will enable those without formal research training to do more themselves; it will keep track of and analyze secondary research, prepare questionnaires, speed up coding, spot contradictions and propose edits, and automate report preparation.

Types of Quantitative Research Approaches

Personal interviews can take place in the home, on the street, in shopping malls, in pre-arranged locations (e.g., a test facility where respondents can participate in a taste test), or in places where people congregate for a specific purpose (e.g., a voting station or hockey game). Electronic methods, particularly tablets, are often used to conduct 'personal' interviews, particularly when respondents are still 'in the moment.'

For **in-home personal interviews,** interviewers visit the respondents in their homes. Traditionally the advantages have been:
- Generally, more co-operative respondents
- A higher degree of rapport between an interviewer and respondent
- Easier to administer a more complex and longer questionnaire
- More effective prompting and probing,
- More effective use of visual aids

There are significant barriers to this approach, particularly in more developed countries:
- increasingly suspicious respondents who won't let interviewers they don't know into their homes
- areas in many cities that interviewers either cannot get into (e.g., secure condominiums or gated communities) or would not want to go into (less safe neighbourhoods)
- higher costs for travel to target communities and time spent searching for respondents
- difficulty finding sufficient respondents, particularly in specific age groups because they are rarely at home during interviewing times
- potential distortion of responses, particularly on sensitive topics, if respondents are not comfortable sharing the information, or interviewers distort responses when recording them
- lack of supervision, difficulty in ensuring interviewers are accurately following instructions
- interviewer bias, as simple as a change in voice or expression, could impact the way questions are heard or create social pressure to change an honest response
- open-ended responses are funneled through the interviewer and may be altered or pigeon-holed because there is limited time to record them in detail

If an interviewer does not understand the proper questioning process, this might not be caught until several of the completed questionnaires have been reviewed by their supervisor later that day. Even then, subtle problems might never be identified.

Generally speaking, in-home quantitative interviewing is no longer used in the most developed western countries (Europe, Canada, the United States).

In **central location** interviews (e.g., **mall intercepts**), respondents are invited to a designated interview site to complete an interview.
- They may be **intercepted** in a shopping mall, sports facility, theatre or 'on the street.'
- They may be interviewed immediately or asked a few screening questions and then asked to move to a special interview room nearby. Some research companies have permanent mall-interviewing facilities.
- Alternatively, they may be **recruited** by a telephone or online screening interview and asked to come to the interview facility. This might be the offices of the research company, a mall facility or a special product testing facility.

Increasingly, personal interviews are conducted using '**CAPI**' (computer-assisted personal interviewing) in which a questionnaire is programmed onto a laptop computer or mobile device and the interviewer or respondent can read the question on the screen and enter their response directly into the database. With wireless connections to the internet, the questionnaire and response need not sit on the interview device but can be entirely web-based with immediate uploading.

Central location interviewing offers all the same advantages of personal interviewing but are less expensive than in-home interviews. They are **advantageous** when:
- a relatively fast turn-around is required, particularly with harder-to-find target groups (e.g., specific ethnic populations, teens, parents of infants, consumers of a low incidence category)
- testing bulky or elaborate material or devices (e.g. appliances, cell phones)
- tasting products, particularly if they must be served at a particular temperature (e.g., beer) or prepared according to specific protocols (e.g., French fries and poutine)
- showing alternative advertising commercials
- employing simulated shopping behaviour
- combining interviewer-administered and self-administered questionnaires
- statistical accuracy is less important

The main **disadvantages** of central location mall intercepts are:
- Respondents are seldom representative of a larger population in a statistical sense. Unless they are the largest regional malls, they are visited only by residents of the surrounding neighbourhoods.
- Not all mall visitors will want to participate in a lengthy test when they are in the middle of their shopping. This may further diminish the representativeness of the sample.
- Online shopping is growing, and certain sectors of the population can no longer be found in malls.

Pre-recruiting can overcome many of these disadvantages but adds to the costs.

Telephone interviewing remains a relatively common way to collect information from a widely dispersed and somewhat representative sample.

It is an evolving methodology. Not long ago, in many countries, every household had a 'landline' and was listed in a phone directory. Randomly selecting phone numbers from the directory yielded a representative probability sample of the population.

But the move to mobile phones in *traditional "developed"* countries, and the fact that many in the *developing* world skipped landlines and went straight to mobile means that directories don't exist and that pulling a representative telephone sample can be a real challenge.

Researchers often sampled a population by **random digit dialing**. This means that we do not have, or need, a list of telephone numbers for every person who could be selected to participate in the study. Using a list of known exchanges, i.e., the first three integers of a 7-digit phone number, the rightmost four integers to complete phone numbers are randomly generated to bring in respondents who might have 'unlisted' numbers or might have only mobile phones. **Customer lists** are another source of sample for phone surveys, but due to ethical privacy rules in many countries, they can only be used when the customers have explicitly agreed to be contacted for the purposes of research and that is called informed consent.

Telephone interviews are generally conducted from centralized call centers where the interviews are monitored by field supervisors who ensure that interviewers are consistent in the way they read the questions, record answers, probe, present visual and audio stimuli, and so on. These call centers are equipped with "**CATI**" (computer-assisted telephone interviewing) where the questionnaire is programmed into the computer, interviewers read the questions from the screen and enter the results directly into a database. Unit 8 provides a more detailed description of CATI.

Though not ideal, and often frowned upon, some research companies use fully-automated telephone survey techniques in which respondents answer pre-recorded questions by saying 'yes' or 'no' (voice-activated) or by pushing numbers on their telephone ('1 for yes, 2 for no'). These fully automated systems are increasingly employed by fraudsters, tainting those who would use them for legitimate research purposes.

Telephone interviews have several **advantages**. They:
- are fast and can collect reactions to breaking news (e.g., political polling, new ad recall);
- collect spontaneous reactions – leaving respondents no time to plan answers;
- are better controlled when using a central call centre;
- have less restricted sampling frames; and
- can administer complex questionnaires easily when programmed into CATI.

However, as with all methodologies, there are some **disadvantages**:
- respondents can pre-screen their calls and choose not to answer a call from a number they don't recognize (increasingly common as the number of fraudulent contacts increases);
- it is easier for respondents to refuse to participate or to hang up partway through (versus when facing a live interviewer);
- it is hard for an interviewer to gain trust and build rapport with a respondent;

- there is, so far, limited ability to show visual stimuli consistently (e.g., FaceTime)
- interviewer bias could impact the way questions are heard; and
- open-ended responses are funneled through the interviewer and may be altered or pigeon-holed because there is limited time to record them in detail.

With the growth of fraud calls (from those trying to steal identity or defraud consumers), phone companies are beginning to offer a functionality that will let calls through only from a list of 'acceptable' phone numbers (designated by each phone owner). This could have severe consequences for telephone interviewing.

Mail surveys were, until the advent of the internet, the classic example of a self-completion technique. Paper questionnaires are mailed out to a target respondent audience who are asked to complete and return them within a specified period. Today, they are used primarily for more restricted target audiences, such as membership of an organization, subscribers to a magazine, identifiable customers of a company. "**Hand out**" **surveys** are a variation where respondents are physically present and accessible.

The approach is fairly low cost and may seem deceptively simple to execute. But a great deal of care must be taken with the development of self-completion questionnaires. Remember, respondents see the questionnaire itself, and so not only must the questions and answer choices be perfect, but the physical placement of the questions on the page and the overall visual appearance of the questionnaire must motivate the respondent to begin, continue, complete, and return the questionnaire. (The procedures for developing and executing successful mail surveys will be presented in a subsequent chapter.)

The **advantages** of a mail or hand-out questionnaire include:
- the questionnaires are printed, so each respondent sees the same format;
- respondents can move at their own pace and provide more considered answers;
- respondents may feel that without an interviewer present, they can be more honest, particularly with sensitive questions; and
- there is no concern about interviewer bias from inconsistent interviewing styles, verbal or visual cues or interpretation and pigeonholing.

There are **disadvantages** as well, many stemming from the lack of an interviewer:
- less depth in responses because there is no interviewer to clarify and probe;
- lack of control over skip patterns (e.g., if 'no' in Q4, skip over questions 5, 6 and 7);
- no ability to withhold something from the respondent to be revealed later, because they may read the full questionnaire before beginning to answer. For example, *unaided* brand awareness should be asked first ("Please tell me the names of all the brands of chocolate bars you are aware of") then followed by an *aided* awareness question ("Have you ever heard of Skor chocolate bars?");
- no guarantee the respondent has not consulted with others before responding;
- any stimuli (e.g., new product concept) are out in the public domain as soon as the questionnaire is mailed out;
- longer timelines for the survey (mail out, complete, mail back) because it is entirely in the hands of the respondent; and

- low response rates, depending on how 'involved' the respondent is ... it could be as low as 1 or 2 percent among a disinterested audience.

Response rates could be increased by:
- pre-screening by phone to gain permission to send the questionnaire;
- making the questionnaire more visually appealing and not over-crowding the page;
- offering a benefit for responding early (your name will be entered in a draw for a $1,000 prize);
- penalty for not responding (your name will not be included in the membership directory if you respond after Oct 31st);
- financial (guilt) incentive inserted with the questionnaire (lottery ticket or gift card); and
- reminders sent out (more effective if follow-up phone calls are used).

Hand-out questionnaires are particularly well-suited for intercept situations when a respondent has just completed an experience that you want to probe and might have some 'downtime.' A few examples might include:
- intercepting air travelers as they are waiting to board their flight or waiting for their luggage;
- questionnaires attached to a restaurant bill provided after a restaurant meal;
- economic impact questionnaires handed out to those who are attending a street festival, concert or sporting event; and
- reaction to a new car design collected at car clinics or industrial shows.

Web-based or **online surveys** are now the standard approach to self-completion studies. The methodology provides fast turn-around access to large samples of respondents with data collection that ranges from the most straightforward, single-question polls to the most complex and sophisticated computer programmed questionnaires.

Random sampling is not possible in this environment (there is no directory of users), so the sample is often drawn from **customer access panels** of recruited and pre-screened respondents who have agreed to participate in research. The panels are refreshed from a variety of recruitment methodologies, including follow-ups from telephone or personal interviewing, social networks, community sites, ad networks etc. Of course, client lists are also a source of sample for online surveys. Panelists are offered incentives to participate, ranging from draws for cash prizes to points that can be redeemed for merchandise. [More information on Consumer Access Panels is included later in this unit.]

Targeted respondents generally receive invitations to participate in the survey. The invitations include links that take each respondent to a personal version of the questionnaire and serves as the password to ensure no unauthorized entry.

The *online* questionnaire is created in the same way as a self-completion *paper* questionnaire, with many of the same advantages and disadvantages of that methodology. It is then 'scripted' or programmed into a web-based platform. The scripting builds in the skip patterns and logic that controls the flow of the questions like CAPI or CATI questionnaires.

The **advantages** of a web-based or online questionnaire include:

- the ability to target particular sub-groups of the population (e.g., parents of babies under nine months) because panels are generally pre-profiled;
- fast turn-around for even the largest sample sizes (just send out more invitations);
- the same control over sequencing as any computer-assisted questionnaire;
- the ability to increase engagement in the questionnaire with stimuli, animations and visually engaging formats; and
- the elimination of *data entry* errors because respondents' answers are captured directly into the database

Some of the **disadvantages**:
- limited access to harder-to-reach populations who may not tend to join panels (e.g., high-income earners, the oldest respondents, immigrants who have not yet gained fluency in the survey's language);
- challenges adapting the questionnaire to different systems (Microsoft, Apple) and different screens (desktop/laptop versus tablet versus mobile phone);
- the need to 'hide' the intent of a survey so that those intent on collecting participation points don't 'self-select' regardless of whether or not they qualify; and
- in less developed countries, only the upper echelons of society may have access to the internet, although smartphone technology is changing that.

Technology is evolving quickly, and the leading research firms are working hard to integrate useful advances into their field methodologies. Web-based research provides a platform not only for standard quantitative surveys but also for online focus groups, qualitative journaling, diaries, citizen reporting and new approaches that are being created every year.

Perceptual methods provide data by reading the physiological reactions of the body when exposed to stimuli. A typical and easy-to-understand example is **eye-tracking.** A respondent is seated in front of a large screen. His head may be held in place by a chin support. A computer program with a laser reader is calibrated to the respondent's eye movement so it can read where the subject is looking. Then an image of a shelf, package design or advertisement is positioned in front of the respondent. The computer can record the initial glance, the optical path over the image, the time spent on each element and even how long it takes for the subject to find something in particular (e.g., the client's new package design on a store shelf). The output from this type of data collection would show which of several alternative pack designs is more likely to attract visual attention, or where a specific claim should be positioned on a pack to maximize impact.

A **tachistoscope** is a research device that varies the timing of exposure to stimuli (e.g., ½ of a second, 1 second, 2 seconds) to measure how long it takes a respondent to recognize a product, logo, ad or package. An element that is faster to 'register' in a respondent's mind is more likely to be effective on the shelf or screen. Web-based questionnaire programming can also strictly control the length of time that an image is exposed, so the tachistoscope is no longer strictly required.

Technology is developing rapidly in neurological measurement. **Electroencephalograms** read brain activity when different stimuli are shown. A **psychogalvanometer** measures mental reaction by determining changes in the electrical resistance of the surface of the skin using electrodes. Both can be used to measure consumers' sub-conscious responses that they themselves are not aware of.

Omnibus Studies

A different way of approaching a study is to use an omnibus. This is generally a "shared cost," quick turn-around research vehicle run as a telephone or online survey.

This can reduce the cost of a study because its fixed costs (sample management, screening and demographic data collection, data processing) are shared over several clients who run their questions at the same time in a shared questionnaire.

The **costs** are set as a fixed fee per question, so the economics work well for very short questionnaires, say under 10 questions. The **sample** is generally very broad – 1,000 adults aged 18 or older from which specific target groups can be screened or boosted. For example, if you want to interview only mothers of young children, approximately 200 would 'fall out' naturally from the standard omnibus sample. A client may want to 'boost' this to 300 by drawing an additional sample (at an incremental cost, of course).

There are **incremental costs** as well for open-ended questions, for long statement battery questions, for grid questions, etc. Results are often delivered as a set of statistical tables with standard banners, or as a simple, top-line report.

The key **advantages** of an omnibus approach are:
- Speedy turn-around;
- Lower cost if the survey is a short one; and
- Consistent high quality because of the formulaic and repetitive process.

The principal **disadvantages** are:
- Much less flexibility in questionnaire layout and design;
- Less flexibility in sample definition;
- Less flexibility in timing;
- Restrictions on the types of questions, visual stimuli and programming logic; and
- Minimal analysis, modelling and interpretation of the results.

Online omnibuses are increasingly flexible and are now able to show visual stimuli and are often able to jump into fieldwork as soon as a client has questions ready to go (rather than waiting for a prescribed timeline).

Consumer Access Panels

A **consumer access panel** is a pre-recruited pool of people from whom information is collected regularly. They are explicitly recruited to provide input periodically and repeatedly over time. Members typically complete an initial screening or profiling survey to provide information about their demographics so that subsequent studies can target the specific people required for a project. Members can be **recruited** through internet advertisements or email recruiting messages. Proprietary panels (owned by one client) can be recruited from the client's customer lists. After being recruited, respondents are regularly offered opportunities to participate in surveys. The offer may arrive as an email containing a link to the study, a notice on the member's unique panel page, or a message on a mobile app.

Most research panels are "pools of potential respondents" and are not designed to be representative of any specific population. They are 'overstocked' with demographics that are in high demand (e.g., female principal grocery shoppers or younger consumers).

Each research project has its own unique needs, so a representative sample can be drawn from a consumer access panel by creating a sampling frame and searching profiles of panel members to pull together the appropriate respondent sample from the pool.

Consumer panels can be:

- used as a pool for a series of one-off surveys from a wide range of clients;
- created specifically for one client who can use them over a period for their own information-gathering needs; and
- set aside for longer-term longitudinal studies that provide the capacity to track the behaviour of the same group of people over subsequent waves (e.g., quarterly consumption diaries).

Consumption *diaries* are of interest to the industry because they become the standardized measures of consumer behaviour. Panel members record the details of all purchases of relevant products in a pre-printed diary or by using an electronic bar code scanning device. The printed diary is returned periodically (e.g., weekly) by mail to the auditing company, whereas the electronic diary is instantly uploaded via the internet.

Substantial efforts are made to **maintain panel members' interest** by sending regular surveys, engaging them in a reward points program, sending them newsletters, and including them in contests. Because of the initial agreement to co-operate and because their panel membership is reinforced, the response rates in panels can be very high. Response rates are further increased by systematic 'cleaning' – removing non-responders and those displaying suspicious responses (e.g., changing demographics from one survey to the next).

A key concern about panels is that members may be **conditioned** over time to respond to questions in a specific way. Most panel companies work diligently to 'refresh' the panel on a regular basis by dropping longer-term panelists and recruiting fresh panelists to minimize the 'experienced' or 'conditioned' respondents.

Retail audits provide a continuous measure of the effect on consumer purchases, retailer stocks, and distribution of short and long-term sales and marketing activities. This is done through auditing retail outlets (stores) for inventories, purchases, and sales. The rationale for retail audits is that company sales records and wholesale figures are somewhat out of step with actual consumer purchases.

Most audit data are derived from large, national samples of retail outlets operated on a syndicated basis. Test audits may be syndicated and shared among many clients, or exclusive to just one client. Large, national audits use stratified samples so that all types of retail outlets are adequately reflected. They usually represent distinct product groups like confectionery or tobacco. Retail audits are based on panels of stores that are audited on a regular basis. Those stores provide data that are accumulated and projected to the population within each stratum.

The major problem associated with retail audits is obtaining the co-operation of selected, representative stores, especially retail chains, and other large organizations where additional record-keeping would be considered an arduous task. Other limitations include the sample becoming out-of-date over time, the introduction of new nonconventional outlets, and auditing errors.

With the restrictions on face-to-face and telephone interviewing and the growth of online or web-based surveys, consumer panels provide samples for the bulk of marketing research studies in much of the world today.

Hybrid Data Collection Methodology

Sometimes combinations of methodologies are needed to properly access the correct sample and provide those people with the best opportunities to respond to the questions. These are referred to as **hybrid field methodologies**. For instance, a study may begin with a telephone survey through which people who meet additional requirements are invited to participate in a central-location taste test or eye-tracking study.

Often, extensive global studies require mixed methodologies. For example, an online survey may work well in North American and Europe, but personal interviewing is necessary for countries that don't have the same level of internet access. Parallel designs might have to be constructed for a single study that covers, for example, Canada and the U.S. (online) and Brazil and India (face-to-face).

What is an RFP, and Why is it Important?

One of the client's most important roles in the design of a marketing research study is the creation of the request for proposals. A request for proposal or RFP is an invitation to a research house to bid on a project.

At some point, the marketing and/or insight staff decide that they need to bring in a research supplier to begin work on a project. The first decision will be whom to invite to bid. Several scenarios are possible:

- A long-term relationship may exist, and the project is sole-sourced to that research partner who has built up a knowledge of the category and products, has established a comfortable working relationship and level of trust with the client team, and is well-respected by senior management.
- The company may have a procurement policy that all projects over a particular budget value must "go out to bid." Generally, three or more companies are identified as preferred suppliers or are recognized experts for this type of research.
- Government bodies are required to publicly post requests for proposals on websites so that anyone who feels they are qualified can bid.
- Occasionally, the client doesn't know who should be invited and sends out requests to every research company that they can identify.

That last scenario above is less than ideal. A great deal of business resources is dedicated to writing proposals, and the probability of winning a bid from a large pool of bidders might be seen to be too low to justify the investment. In the last scenario above, the client might be wasting the time of a lot of talented researchers who will never win the project. Even worse, highly qualified researchers may choose not to bid because of the perceived low probability of winning.

If a client is entering a bidding situation for the first time, it pays to do a little research and identify the best prospects, such as asking colleagues who may have done similar research before, or senior managers who might have worked in research functions in the past. Networks of insight managers from other companies are always helpful. Joining a research client council of your national marketing research association is a good way to create this network, and to learn about others' experiences with research suppliers.

> Example (contd.) In our Big Juice scenario, Stella is new to the company but has been in marketing research for eight years. There are a few research suppliers she has worked with in the past and a few that she has seen present at industry conferences. She checks in with those who have been around longer than she has to ensure there is no 'bad blood' between any of these potential suppliers and Big Juices' senior management (e.g., from a past project gone wrong). In the end, she creates a short-list of three prospective bidders who have good reputations in the specific type of research she and Richard are planning.

When issuing a request for proposals, the following components should be included.
1. A clear **statement of the marketing problem** that will help your potential research suppliers understand what decisions you need to make and what information will help you make those decisions.
2. Detailed **background** on the marketplace as you currently understand it. Penetration or incidence rates and target population descriptions are crucial for your bidders in working through costs. Lists of competitive products or companies help define the scope.
3. A summary of **previous research, both primary and secondary,** to highlight the knowledge gaps that the current study will have to fill.
4. A clear statement of **research objectives** (which is very important to bidders). Those objectives must be focused on information that is needed from the target audience being researched. While less than ideal, you may choose to compile the entire wish list of all stakeholders, but be prepared for proposals that will tell you what elements of this wish list might not fit into a single study.
5. Set out expected **timelines**. If a critical decision milestone has already been specified, make sure this is spelled out in the RFP. The schedule should include when the proposals must be submitted and when the selection will be made.
6. **Do not be too specific about the methodology**, sample definition or size. Doing so might remove the possibility of receiving a creative or leading-edge solution that could be more effective, more powerful and even more cost-effective.
7. **Specify the budget**. Some clients prefer to be coy but then receive bids that are either *over-designed* (and too expensive) so that time is lost by having to cut back to what the client can afford, or *under-designed,* and they don't get the best solution the budget can buy. It's better to have each bidder show you what they can do within a set budget than to get widely divergent proposals with very different price tags and have to choose between them.

Providing these details in the RFP will ensure similar proposals from all bidders that can be compared more easily. Before it goes out to bidders, a draft RFP should be reviewed and approved by everyone who will be using the results of the research. This should include key decision-makers in the organization while thinking about who will be in the room when the results are presented.

> Example (contd.) Stella runs her draft RFP not only by the brand manager Richard and his direct manager Alice but also by the company's Vice President of Marketing and Vice President of Sales. Both will be at the final presentation and will be directly impacted by the research findings. Alice has pointed out that a senior brand manager in another division had worked on Richard's brand in the past and should be asked for her input. Finally, she includes the company's CFO and legal department to ensure all the requisite contract details are covered.

If you are working with a sole source supplier, or have a trusted advisor, feel free to bounce key details off them before you circulate the RFP to your internal stakeholders. They will tell you if your budget and timeline expectations are reasonable. If not, you can scale back internal expectations from the start.

Even before you are ready to send out the request for proposals, give your potential bidders a heads up. They may have a lot on their plates or may be about to leave on vacation. Knowing that your RFP is coming will help them line up the resources they need to respond on time.

Finally, when you send out the RFP, invite your bidders to make requests for clarifications and ask questions. In the sense of fairness, let them know you will be sharing the questions and answers with all bidders.

If you are diligent in providing important details, have buy-in from your internal stakeholders and are open with your bidders about your process and expectations, you are likely to get well-written, competitively priced proposals that are focused on your specific needs.

Why is the RFP so Important?

The most critical function in any area of consulting is clear and effective communication. The attractive message gets attention, the clear message gets read, the message containing the right promise gets acted upon, and the author of the message that gives accurate and sound advice gets asked back to do another project. This is what we seek through a research proposal, and the purpose of this section is to help improve the writing of proposals.

When a client has successfully worked with a research consultant several times, the communication process between the two parties becomes easier and more natural. This is because of the client's increased familiarity with the role of marketing research and the researcher's work. Similarly, the research consultant has become more familiar with the client's category and brand, as well as with the client's internal processes.

When a client is considering their first marketing research project, the research consultant has a responsibility to inform the client about both the general practice of marketing research and the specific task to be performed.

Regardless of whether it is the client's first project, or their fifteenth project with the same researcher, documents should always be written in a style that clearly informs the research buyer of the exact nature of what is being proposed and of the researcher's qualifications.

The proposal should also provide clues about the **style** in which the final findings will be communicated.

- A client who receives a dense, detail-heavy proposal would quite rightly expect a similar thoroughness in the report.
- A client who receives a high-level, design-conscious proposal that offers the key reasons to choose the supplier in as few words as possible should quite rightly expect a concise, management-friendly report.

What are the Different Types of Proposals?

The request for a proposal may come in several different forms:
1. An expression of interest
2. A simple price quote
3. A letter proposal
4. A formal proposal
5. A proposal to formalize or Statement of Work

An **expression of interest** is a screening process whereby an extensive list of potential bidders is provided with a simple outline of the marketing problem and objectives and are asked if they are interested in bidding. Some will choose not to prepare a proposal if they feel that the study is not within their area of expertise or if they currently have too much on their plate to take on another project. This step can save many people a lot of time.

From time to time, a supplier will be asked to submit a **simple price quote** (i.e., the price for conducting the study) rather than a full proposal. A brief description of the research design is necessary to ensure everyone understands the scope and assumptions clearly. This often happens when the client is preparing the budget for the coming year, when the project replicates a study that has been conducted in the past (e.g., a subsequent wave) or when it is part of an ongoing program (e.g., another wave of concept testing).

The **letter proposal** is a simple outline of the nature of the project that will be undertaken, the methodology, sample, deliverables, timelines and price. The client doesn't need to be convinced and doesn't need to be educated about the approach or benefits of the deliverables. We see this often in a non-competitive situation when the client and supplier are about to enter into a project that they both understand well and are comfortable executing. The letter proposal simply ensures that everyone is on the same wavelength.

The **formal proposal** is more of a sales document. It might be written in a highly competitive situation, where the supplier must explain why their approach and team is superior. Or it may be appropriate when preparing to embark on a type of research that the client has never done before, to ensure they have a comfortable understanding of what will occur. The primary intention is to outline category knowledge, express a clear understanding of the marketing problem and research objectives, provide appropriate project design, illustrate the utility of the deliverables and convince the prospective client that the research team is fully capable of delivering what is needed. The formal proposal might include full team biographies and even testimonials from past clients.

Finally, the **Proposal to Formalize** or **Statement of Work** is written after the researcher has been selected from among competitive researchers and the basic parameters of the project have been informally agreed upon by the researcher and the client. This document formalizes the points agreed upon and states the specifics of the project, such as the sample size, the sampling procedure, the field methodology, any special analysis procedures, the completion date, any intermediate reporting dates, and the budget for each portion of the project. This is an important reference document against which all players can measure the project's progress and success.

How to Decide on Which Projects to Bid

If you are a research supplier and have been asked to bid on a project, you can assume that the client holds you (or your firm) in high standing and would welcome the opportunity to work with you. It may be very tempting - to meet sales targets, to gain experience, to work with a prestigious or fun new client. However, there may be reasons why you might give it a pass.

- **Strategic focus.** Many research firms consider themselves to be all-purpose firms and will bid on a wide variety of projects. Others have a more targeted approach and have identified the niche that they intend to occupy. This leads them to turn away from projects that might not fulfill this strategy.
- **Lack of expertise or experience.** The old Hollywood adage "when asked if you can ride a horse, say yes, then go out and learn" may not be easily adapted to marketing research. Some techniques require specialized training, access to sophisticated models and specific sampling sources. You cannot bluff your way through this. If you don't have the requisite knowledge and experience, you might consider bringing in a bidding partner who does, or you might simply pass on the opportunity. In any event, it is to your benefit to be honest with the client.
- **Financial feasibility.** Some projects are just not worth bidding on for financial reasons. The RFP may be so full of research wishes that no firm within a reasonable budget can meet the objectives. Beyond the cost issue, research firms must be cautious of their reputations. If it takes on every project offered, it might be taking on more work or more complex work than it can handle within timelines. The risk of earning a reputation for not delivering, or for delivering poorly or late, is not worth the extra revenue.
- **Impossible timelines.** In a business world increasingly focused on speedy decision making, the deadlines required in the RFP may be impossible to achieve. It is not worth damaging your (or your firm's) reputation by agreeing to a schedule you know you cannot reach.
- **The price check.** A client who has a strong relationship with a regular supplier may be required from time-to-time to put a project out to bid as a way to check pricing. They may have no intention of changing suppliers, and you may feel that it is a waste of your time to write a proposal, but you might also consider this a 'foot in the door' – your opportunity to show the client that you might be the better supplier.
- **Difficult-to-work-with clients.** There are clients who, through temperament or training, are simply too difficult to work with. They may be poor communicators, distrustful, or

mean. They may never grasp what you are trying to do or require more hours in meetings than you could ever charge them for. They may argue over every budget item (and undervalue your team's work) or escalate to senior management to gain leverage. It may be a chemistry issue, or you may simply have encountered a 'monster.' It is best for your firm and your team, to leave this client to someone who may be better equipped to handle them.

Sometimes the RFP is a 'fishing' expedition. The client or their senior management may not be firmly committed to conducting the research. They may just be testing the waters to see what is possible and what it might cost. The client should be honest enough to inform prospective bidders that the project may never see the light of day. In any event, a well-written proposal may motivate the client to action or, at the very least, consider you for a more certain project down the road. It's definitely worth bidding in this situation if all other elements fall into place.

Regardless of your first impression of the RFP, it is always helpful to ask the client for an opportunity to discuss and ask questions. This would be your opportunity to point out some of the concerns you may have around overly ambitious objectives or too tight timelines. The client may be willing to clarify or alter the RFP to address your concerns. Even if they are not, you will show yourself to be a willing partner, even if not for this study.

How to Write a Proposal?

Many RFPs, particularly those from government or public sector clients, will outline what content the proposals are to contain. Others are much more open-ended and leave the content up to the team writing the proposals. Some research firms also have prescribed content that they instruct their teams to include in every proposal.

Here are the sections that you should consider including:

1. **Cover Letter:** Not part of the proposal, but it allows you to personalize your message to the client insight manager and draw attention to what you feel are the greatest advantages of working with you.
2. **Title Page: C**lean, simple and eye-catching. Be sure to add a date (there may be revised versions) and your firm's contact information – to make it easy to call you for clarifications.
3. **Background Information:** Show them right at the start that you understand the client, the industry, and the problem area. Include a brief description of the business environment to place the problem within its business context. This is often critical to understanding the importance of the problem and the value of the proposed research. It is worth a little extra effort to do some research and bring in pertinent facts that were not in the RFP. The best source is the client. Asking a lot of questions will reveal a great deal about the client's business, competition, and the market. Ask to see other research reports on the same or related topics. Ask about the client's strategic marketing plan. Determine if there is an industry or trade association in the sector and look for industry data and research reports. Look for government statistical sources that may be relevant. Scan social

media and use a search engine to turn up recent news stories. This knowledge will lend you credibility and provide insights that will become evident in the proposal.

4. **Marketing Problem/Opportunity:** This is a clear and comprehensive statement of the marketing problem, opportunity, or issue. Don't just copy and paste from the RFP; absorb, distill and present it in your own way to show that you understand. This will be the binding direction for the project. Remember that the marketing problem section of your proposal provides the justification to spend the budget on the research project. Make sure you are talking to the senior decision-makers in the client's organization – they will be the ones who must see the value in helping them make better marketing decisions.

5. **Marketing Research Objectives:** This should be a comprehensive list of the objectives and hypotheses for discussion and consensus. The findings will be expected to address these objectives. If the RFP is a wish list of random questions, condense them into workable research objectives, but make sure you include everything. It may be appropriate to divide up the list into those that can be addressed in the proposed study and those that are best handled in a separate study. These are the critical points on which you will be evaluated as a bidder. The final report you deliver will have to check off all these boxes. A single project might reasonably be expected to accomplish a maximum of five or fewer objectives. Be careful to indicate that the research will satisfy the research objectives but the marketing objectives will require more than the marketing research findings.

6. **Design Considerations:** You may have made assumptions and there may be some issues that remain to be discussed. Outline your thought processes straightforwardly and concisely and use this as an agenda for an early meeting with the client. Examples of your design considerations might be the definition of the target consumer or the assumed length of the questionnaire required to cover all the listed objectives or the types of analyses you wish to employ and have built into the budget. For example, some clients may focus for marketing purposes on a narrowly defined population.

Example (contd.) Richard, the Big Juice Brand Manager, wants to focus on younger, more active consumers, so he defines his ideal target audience as young males aged 15 to 25. He can clearly understand how to target this audience through sports sponsorships. However, Stella, his Insight manager, understands that the people who will be buying a Big Juice sports drink are likely to include both women and older consumers. She is pleased to get a proposal back that points out the difference between a marketing bull's-eye (younger males) and a potential market (all active adults).

7. **Proposed Field Methodology:** This should be explained as fully as possible. This section should describe in unambiguous terms:
    - the proposed sampling plan;
    - sample sources (sample frame);
    - sample sub-groups that may be subject to quotas;
    - the data collection methodology, including screening;
    - questionnaire length and number of open ends; and

- Key questionnaire sections / flow.

Unit 8 will provide a more in-depth explanation of data collection methodologies. Keep in mind that as the project develops, changes in the method may be required. Your assumptions must be crystal clear so that you can justify a budget change if needed.

8. **Proposed Analysis Procedures:** In basic projects, these are straightforward and may include only basic frequency tables, cross-tabulations and graphs. However, if special techniques are needed, they should be explained and justified. You might be using techniques such as regression, factor analysis, cluster analysis, discriminant analysis, correspondence analysis, conjoint analysis, latent class analysis, multidimensional scaling, and others. You should describe the proposed analysis briefly, the reasons for using it and the benefits it will provide. Remember that clients pay to get information that will solve problems; they rarely pay just so that a fancy statistical procedure can be used to analyze their data. Concentrate the justification of the statistical analysis on the insights it will provide. It is best to show examples of what the outputs will look like and how they will lead to actionable recommendations.

9. **Project Schedule:** Provide all the key milestones and identify whose responsibility it is that they are met. For example, the dates for finalization of the questionnaire, beginning the fieldwork, completing the fieldwork, availability of top-line findings, report submission, and presentation are likely to be listed.

    In our earlier example, Stella points out to Richard that the leading proposal for the Big Juice project specifies the number of days after the first draft of the questionnaire is completed that the final version is provided. He would need to provide all feedback and sign off on the final version if the rest of the schedule is to be respected.

    Of course, the total length of the project is important – start dates and completion dates – but consider including a critical path method (CPM) diagram, project evaluation and review technique (PERT) chart, a Gantt chart, or other timeline diagrams. These are much more impactful and informative than a simple list of dates.

10. **Project Investment:** This is the total fee quoted for the full project. It is, of course, an extremely important section of the proposal, particularly in a competitive situation. The costing process can range from very quick and easy to a lengthy process with multiple inputs. The effort depends on the size and complexity of the project, the number of subcontractors that may be involved, the requirements of the prospective client, and the researcher's experience with similar projects. On relatively routine, descriptive projects, such as concept tests, advertising copy-testing, subsequent waves of a brand or loyalty tracking study, both the researcher and the client might have good ideas of the cost after a very short discussion. Sometimes an oral quote is given and later firmed up after some detailed calculations on a few of the cost components.

    The costing of large, one-off and complex projects is more challenging. There may be more players involved, there may be different analysis techniques, and more hours to be considered. Here is a partial list of potential items that **might influence project cost**:
    - type of project;

- sample size;
- field methodology (method of data collection);
- incidence of qualified respondents in the population;
- the response rate;
- location of the research and the number of locations;
- type of respondent (average consumers versus corporate executives);
- the extent of analysis (overall sample only versus repeated runs for sub-groups);
- the sophistication of analysis desired (just tables versus full segmentation);
- type of final report (topline versus detailed sub-group analyses);
- number of results presentations;
- speed of execution; and
- special services.

You may choose to split out some components – for example, separate costs for qualitative exploratory work, a separate cost for an additional presentation or workshop and assumed travel costs.

Some clients may require more detailed cost breakdowns. Government agencies often ask for very fine costing detail in the proposals. They may ask for separate costs for professional time, fieldwork, analysis, reporting and presentations. On the other hand, research companies may prefer to provide a single project cost to avoid revealing too much about their profit margins and so that over-runs in one area can be covered with efficiencies in other areas.

It is not unusual to have every person on the consulting team listed with their responsibilities, the number of hours of work that will be provided, and their rate per hour. This level of detail is infrequent in proposals submitted to private companies.

Be sure to indicate how long the proposed cost is to be considered in effect (e.g., 90 days from the submission date of the proposal). You may not be able to honour the same price a year after you submit the proposal. You might also need to restate key pricing assumptions such as respondent incidence and length of the questionnaire if too much time has elapsed between the proposal and the project 'go-ahead.'

11. **The Terms of Agreement:** This is a section that is not always included but can be critical to continuing good relations between the parties. It would cover mutually understood contract responsibilities and project conditions for both parties and might include payment terms, cancellation policy, confidentiality and intellectual property protection. In some cases, a Master Services Agreement might already exist between the client and the research supplier that obviates the need for many of those documents. The terms of agreement might also indicate which industry guidelines and standards need to be followed, depending on where the research firm or client are located, and which country the research is taking place in. For example, researchers might reference the CRIC or MRIA-ARIM (Canada), Insights Association or AAPOR or QRCA (USA), ESOMAR (Europe/Worldwide), MRS (UK), or The Research Society (Australia).

12. **Biographical Profiles of Principal Members of the Study Team:** Clients will want to know who will be supervising and working on the project. Provide a one or two paragraph profile

with each key team member's experience, educational background and their certifications or awards. Include a brief description of the type of projects they have worked on, any specialties they may have developed and the client sectors they have served. Focus primarily on what is beneficial to this project. It helps to outline the role that each team member will be playing on **this specific project** so they can be assured that there will be no 'bait and switch' – that it won't be handed over to a junior team member after it is sold by a more experienced researcher who then disappears from the scene. Proposals for government organizations typically require full and lengthy curricula vitae for all researchers.

13. **Testimonials and Experience:** You may be asked to provide a list of relevant projects that you or your firm has worked on in the past that are similar to the project you are bidding on. The client may consider this evidence of the experience that you claim to have. Keep in mind that you have a duty to protect the confidentiality of your other clients, so you may either ask the other clients' permission to provide details in this proposal or hide some of the specifics. For example, you could refer to "a significant market driver study of beverages for a major Canadian juice manufacturer."

Understanding the Importance of the Proposal

We cannot stress this enough: the research proposal plays a **critical role** in the relationship between the researcher and the client.

A well-written document will:
- help **clarify the information needs** of the client and how they link to the marketing problem;
- assist the client in **justifying the research** to senior management by pointing out how the information needs will be met;
- **set out** in detail the **assumptions** that form the basis of the **costing;**
- **educate** the reader about any innovative design, sampling, field or analysis techniques;
- **serve as a contract** between the client and the researcher;
- **set expectations** about what will be delivered by the end of the project; and
- provide a **master plan** for the execution and analysis of the project.

Because it serves as a master plan and sets expectations, a proposal must be **updated any time there are changes** and a 'revised proposal' submitted to the client. Any changes in scope, hours, design, deliverables, cost or timelines that might emerge through negotiation, at the kick-off meeting, or through the process of questionnaire design must be spelled out in a document that both the researcher and the client approve. This could be a revised version of the proposal or a subsequent 'statement of work.'

The **educational element** of proposals can be essential because it increases clients' comfort levels. They are investing not only their budgets but their reputations within the organization in their decision to hire a specific firm. Building trust throughout the relationship could contribute to a long-term relationship with multiple projects in the years to come.

The detailed design will provide a **template for communications** to field staff, data entry teams, analysts, subcontractors and any other marketing research staff involved.

A well-researched and well-written proposal will also **ease the report writing phase** at the end of the project. The background and objectives could easily transfer into the report. The analysis techniques and deliverables will already have been thought through. The familiarity gained with the client's business and the implications of the research will ensure your analysis and recommendations are tightly focused on solving the marketing research problems that have been so carefully crafted. In the end, you will be able to abbreviate a part of the project that often requires a third or more of the professional time on a project.

Concluding Comments

This unit has given you a general overview of how to approach the design of a marketing research project. We've outlined the importance of properly establishing the **marketing problem** and turning this into a clear definition of the **marketing research problem** and **research objectives**. We have worked through different types of research projects, and the various design alternatives that are available to you when designing a study. This has led to a discussion of the crucial role played by both the Request for Proposals and the preparation of the proposal itself.

In subsequent units, we will delve deeper into each of the key elements of a well-executed marketing research project, from the design to the logistics, to the analysis and presentation/communications.

UNIT 3

How to Carry Out Secondary Research

What's the Difference Between Secondary and Primary Research?

Secondary research means using information that is already available. Such information may have been commissioned, collected, and analyzed by someone for some other purpose in the past, or it may have been designed prospectively to fill a market need. It is any information obtained to help a researcher solve the current marketing problem, either partially or fully, whether or not custom, project-specific research will be conducted as well.

In contrast, **primary research** (which is the main focus of this book) begins fresh with the aim of designing and executing a marketing research study that will assist a marketing manager to make better decisions. It is a marketing research study designed and implemented to address a current need for additional information on which a marketing decision will be based. The information generated by nearly every primary research project can produce additional value if it is available for use as *secondary* information after its initial use.

A wealth of information is now available online. Internet search engines such as Google have provided easy, universal and increasingly faster access to constantly refreshed information. Artificial intelligence will revolutionize our approach, accessing and summarizing information from across the web. What AI is not currently doing, is judging whether the information is true or not, so its use still requires an informed review of what it produces.

Secondary research can be useful both to marketing research organizations and client organizations. Typically, however, secondary research has far greater applicability to client organizations.

Just as second-hand goods have ready markets, so does secondary information. Why? Using secondary information is less expensive than creating new information, and secondary information can often be obtained faster than new information.

There is a wide variety of secondary information available from various sources. The primary contrast among sources pertains to the cost and energy needed to retrieve the information. Secondary research is sometimes called desk research because researchers can sit at their desks without ever having to get up for research design meetings, planning meetings, or location-based fieldwork. The term desk research is perhaps more relevant now than ever before due to the relative ease of accessing monumental amounts of secondary information over the internet or intranet. The **intranet** would be sources available within an organization, for example in past project files or online libraries. In such cases, the secondary research helps us find *secondary data*. The **Internet** is an essential means of identifying external sources of information and downloading it immediately either for free or at a price. For example, you may come across data collected for the industry by a commercial organization in a standardized way (*standardized data*) that may help you solve the problem on hand. Such information is generally sold at a price.

Unfortunately, the utilization of secondary data is not as extensive as it should be. One of the main reasons for this, apart from simple oversight, could be that many people are unaware of the existence, sources, and value of such information. Artificial intelligence may change this by compiling sources for us.

Another reason is that secondary information does not usually solve the marketing research problem directly and sometimes it is not in a readily usable format. It requires experience to identify and organize such data. Sometimes, one may have to "stretch" the secondary data since some questions that need answering for the current project might not coincide with the format in the secondary database. Recent advances in scraping data from almost any Internet source have made that information more accessible and more quickly usable.

In practice, secondary data may be relegated to a supporting role. There are few attempts to solve crucial strategic marketing problems in large organizations solely based on secondary data. However, when budgets are tight, and the research question is less strategic, we do see secondary research playing a more significant role.

For example, a food company that might want to add product flavours that have more 'ethnic' spices could turn to census data to see how large that ethnic community is in the market. Or, they may want to change the sweetener in a product and would do a search to find news articles and blog posts that have mentioned their intended sweetener to find out if it is viewed positively or negatively by influencers. Marketers often use secondary research to keep track of what their competitors are up to.

In some instances, such as store location research, secondary research is used extensively for the initial stages of a feasibility study to understand local neighbourhood demographics and the extent of potential competitors. It is also used by companies who are planning to expand into a foreign market to develop a foundational understanding of customers and competitors in that market.

When considering the use of secondary information, several important decision steps need to be addressed and adequately solved. Using secondary or standardized information is part of the overall design task of marketing research. Consequently, all the considerations of Unit 2 need to be addressed when the use of secondary or standardized information is being contemplated.

Where to Find Secondary Data?

Search Engines: Until recently, the most common way to start secondary searches was to type keywords into a search engine such as Google, Bing, Yahoo or DuckDuckGo. These internet searches can be overwhelming because of the sheer number of articles they can turn up. They can also be misleading because few searchers look at anything beyond the first page. With paid prioritization and 'reputation management' activities, some sources force their way onto the first page. "Reputation management" involves flooding the internet with positive commentary and searches mentioning a company, product or article to make it appear popular. The result is that false, biased or misleading information appears early in many if not most, searches. It is up to the searcher to discern the quality and reliability of the information they uncover.

Wikipedia deserves mention as an open content online encyclopedia created through the collaborative effort of a community of users. Anyone registered on the site can create an article; registration is not required to edit articles. The collaborative nature means many eyes on the content to judge and update its veracity. There are no guarantees, but it can be a good stepping off point.

Artificial Intelligence: We are on the threshold of completely different ways of conducting secondary research. AI is developing at a tremendous speed and is already being used to search, gather and summarize information in response to simple and complex requests. It is important that the user investigate the quality and currency of the information being used by the generative AI platform and determine its accuracy and relevance to the task.

Sources: Most secondary data come from five main sources:
Internal
1. Company's internal records

External
2. Government and government agencies
3. Geodemographics
4. Syndicated research
5. Published material (trade organizations, journals, magazines, blogs etc.)

Many marketing problems can be answered very adequately through the analysis of secondary data. For example, suppose the sales of your brand have been going down. You may find the following types of secondary data:

- Company records (private secondary information) might indicate that your distribution has become weak over the past several years.
- A syndicated study (external standardized information) might indicate that less expensive products are gaining ground at the expense of your brand.
- Government figures (external secondary information) might indicate that the current population trend is such that there are fewer younger people (your target market) today than there were ten years ago, which goes against the targeting of younger people for your brand.
- A private source of geodemographic data indicates that the profile of the neighbourhoods that your retail store targets has shifted substantially.

One way of categorizing secondary information is to distinguish between private secondary information and external secondary information. (See the next exhibit).

Naturally, census data (e.g. Statistics Canada, the U.S. Census Bureau) are external secondary information to all research users except government staff. On the other hand, while last month's study of customer satisfaction with Coke Zero is internal information to Coca-Cola, it is external to everyone else. There is no hard rule that allows one to discern which type of secondary information is more valuable to an organization, or whether primary or secondary research is more useful. It depends on the objectives of the study, the decisions that need to be made, the amount of information currently held by the organization, the intensity of competition within the business sector, the penetration of the market potential and, of course, the cost.

Most companies have at least some information that was obtained in the past for some specific reason and then stored. This storage might have been designed so that the information could be easily accessed and effectively manipulated at some later time. Ideally, the information would have been stored in an electronic data format that can be searched and manipulated. Other information may be stored only as an analyzed report with charts, but with no link to the actual data, making further analysis difficult. It is rare these days to find older documentation in paper format that is relevant and usable.

The accompanying exhibit shows some common secondary sources of information that may prove useful.

How to Carry Out Secondary Research

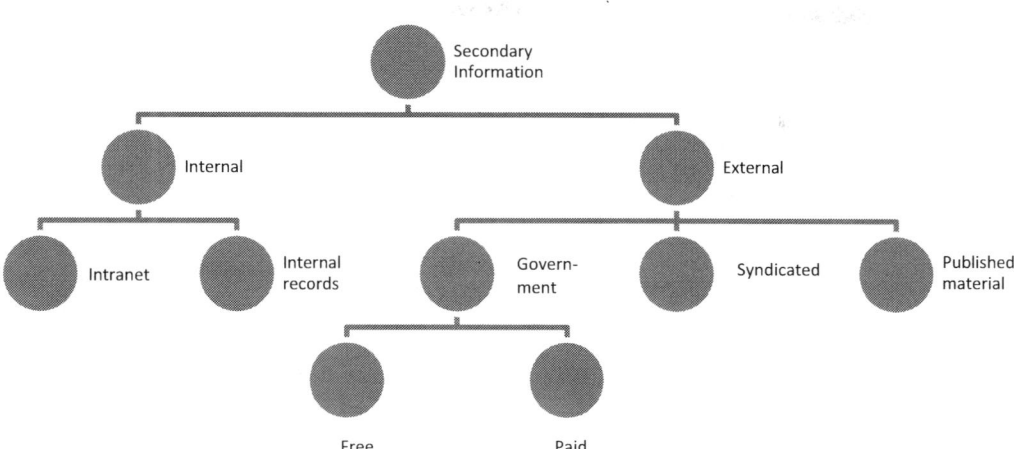

If a company does not curate its information with easy access in mind or in a storage format accessible to the department needing it, accessing and using the data might be as difficult as obtaining it from an organization outside of the corporate umbrella. Several commonly used external sources of information are listed below. While the information needed might be readily accessible from one or more of the following sources, it is just as likely that no combination of these sources would be able to produce exactly the information needed to support a future marketing decision.

1. Company – Intranet and Reports

Many companies warehouse their marketing research information on their **intranet**, their internally accessible electronic filing system. This information includes data about the host organization, including marketing plans and objectives, and financial performance, as well as other market and customer information that has been acquired over time. Past research studies that include reports, tables and raw data may also be relevant.

When a company's information warehouse is abundant, it can provide valuable background information that may significantly enhance the perspective gained by primary information. Or, it can provide continuing direction when markets are slow to change or when the cost of acquiring primary information is prohibitive.

One of the potentially richest sources of secondary data is the information obtained through Customer Relationship Management (CRM) programs. A CRM database includes information that customers have provided directly (e.g., during a registration process) and indirectly through tracked purchase behaviour. Typically, these data come from multi-channel sources and can often be integrated with other internal and external data sources.

Analysis of secondary data may sometimes provide a complete solution to a marketing problem. Basic feasibility studies sometimes use secondary data only. For instance, suppose you are in the retail business selling expensive imported perfumes and would like to open a store in a specific town. Geodemographic analysis of published data (e.g., government sources such as Statistics Canada or Prizm profiles marketed by Environics Analytics) may alert you to the fact that the income level of the people in that town is too low to support such a store.

One of the most common needs is to compare this year's sales against those of the past five years. This type of information is typically readily available internally. However, the need might arise to track sales alongside spending on marketing initiatives and the findings of two usage and attitude studies conducted three years apart. For this information to be readily analyzed, explicit decisions must have been made in the past to organize the information in specific, convenient, and congruent formats, and to store the data in ways that can be conveniently accessed and processed.

"Can I have the data from the segmentation study Anastasia did five years ago?" The answer could very well be, "No," probably because no one thought of asking the research consultant to provide both the research report and the raw data. Perhaps by the time someone thought to ask for the data, it was no longer available from the consultant. The critical point is that someone should remember to ask for the project data early in the process. When the project was being commissioned, a requirement that the project data be one of the deliverables should have been built into the request for proposal (RFP). This would have permitted the establishment of a data warehouse that would provide a steady stream of useful historical data. It would also have allowed the consultant to build in any costs at the start.

Marketing and marketing research libraries exist in some organizations. But in many firms, the person who commissions the study keeps the report, and it never goes into a formal centralized marketing research library. This is particularly problematic when staff frequently move between positions. A brand manager may not be in their role for more than 2 or 3 years. Consequently, those who assume that all past information and research studies are available, even in report format, should be prepared for disappointment. Very often, reports are mislaid several months after primary use, and if a client obtains the data from the studies, it is the exception, not the rule. This remains the case even though intranets that allow widespread sharing of general information are standard in many companies. Indeed, every acquisition of marketing information should be archived in a marketing/ marketing research library and catalogued adequately.

An important consideration is the format in which a client wants the project data. This will not be consistent across client organizations, and the typical format of the data used by consultants varies. If both the client and research consultant use the same software, the data file can simply be shared. Otherwise, the file can often be shared as a raw data file, e.g., comma-separated values (CSV) or Excel files, which are easily readable by most statistical programs.

2. Geodemographics

How does a bank identify the next location for its new branch? How does McDonald's give you a source of coffee, doughnuts, and quick meals so close to your home or office? Many companies use some type of geodemographic analysis to help decide on-site locations.

Similarly, have you noticed that the advertising and flyers that you find in your suburban mailbox are quite different from those your parents receive in their smaller town a few miles away? Geo-demographics is used by direct mailers to identify neighbourhoods that are likely to be most receptive to their offer.

Geo stands for geography. It represents the need to determine the ideal place to locate a retail outlet to provide the best opportunities for customers to access the company's products and services. Demographics refers to data based on the characteristics of the sample respondents such as residence location, work location, travel patterns, age, sex, education, household type and size, income, marital status, and several other variables.

Geodemographic analysis is typically used to micro-target a population that will be most likely to use your product or service. That's why it provides information to locate physical operations optimally. This is accomplished by analyzing information about customer location and movement, and demographic information such as family size, education, and income.

This is a crucial decision for companies. Distribution or place in the 4 Ps of marketing is one of the core marketing activities necessary for the success of an organization. Ad hoc rational analysis will often provide the right answers to the question of where to locate the next outlet or where to send your flyers. However, many organizations have found that formal geodemographic analysis provides an additional level of precision that can make the difference between getting by and being successful.

The geodemographic analysis relies heavily on secondary data, the core of which is collected by the government through the census. This information is available at a granular level (about 250 or 300 contiguous households) at the 6-digit postal code level or 5-digit zip code level; it is not available at the individual level. Firms that specialize in geodemographic analysis take this information and many more layers of other information gathered from different sources into account. Geo-demographics refers to the marrying of demographic and other characteristics with geographic areas.

Vendors of geodemographic data can identify areas of the country on several variables such as income, age, gender etc. They often combine this data with attitudinal or psychographic profiling to give clients insight into what motivates geodemographic clusters of consumers. Geodemographic data can also be linked to the clients' customer databases (e.g., through postal / zip codes on file) to add a layer of insight. For example, a bank can understand where consumers are most likely to be looking for mortgages rather than retirement fund tools.

Some prominent vendors of geodemographic data are:
- Acorn by CACI
- CAMEO by Callcredit
- C-Australia by Pathfinder Solutions
- Censation by AFD Software
- C-Japan by Pathfinder Solutions
- CLOUD CLIENT by Cloud Client Ltd
- C-New Zealand by Pathfinder Solutions
- Crucible by Tesco
- geoSmart by RDA Research
- HomeTypes and ZoneTypes by Arvato Services (Bertlsmann)
- MicroVision by NDS/Equifax
- Mosaic by Experian
- OAC by ONS/University of Leeds

- P2 People & Places by Beacon Dodsworth
- PRIZM by Claritas (US) and Environics Analytics (Canada and USA)

2. Government and Governmental Agencies

Governments and governmental agencies in most countries collect a large amount of information by way of the census, sample surveys, trade figures, income, expenditure and so on. Much of this information is available online to a researcher, either free or for a fee. Some significant providers of such information are listed below.

i. USA

These federal agency programs collect, analyze, and disseminate statistical data and information:
- *Bureau of Economic Analysis.* Economic indicators, national and international trade, accounts, and industry.
- *Bureau of Justice Statistics.* Justice systems, crime, criminal offenders, and victims of crime.
- *Bureau of Labor Statistics.* Labour market activity, working conditions, and price changes in the U.S. economy.
- *Bureau of Transportation Statistics.* Data on airline on-time performance, pirates at sea, transportation safety and availability, motorcycle trends, and more.
- *Census Bureau.* Data about the people and economy of the United States.
- *DAP Public Dashboard.* How people are interacting with the government online.
- *Data.gov* U.S. Government's open data: Federal, state, and local data, tools, and resources to conduct research, build apps, design data visualizations, and the like.
- *Economic Research Service.* Public and private decision making on economic and policy issues related to agriculture, food, the environment, and rural development.
- *Energy Information Administration.* Data on U.S. use of coal, natural gas, nuclear energy, renewable energy, and more.
- *Internal Revenue Service* Tax Statistics examines tax returns to report on such things as sources of income, exemptions, use of medical savings accounts, migration, and geographic data, tax information on foreign corporations controlled by U.S. parent corporations, exports, international boycotts, and investments and activities in the U.S. by foreign persons.
- *National Agricultural Statistical Service* Data on food production and supply, organic sales, chemical use, demographics of U.S. producers, and more. Every five years, it conducts the *Census of Agriculture* that provides agricultural data for every county in the United States.
- *National Center for Education Statistics.* Publishes the _Digest of Education Statistics,_ which includes international comparisons of students, and the annual report to Congress, _The Condition of Education,_ which reports the progress of American education.
- *National Center for Health Statistics.* The primary health statistics agency for improving the health of the American people.

- *National Center for Science and Engineering Statistics.* Data on the American science and engineering workforce and the progress of science, technology, engineering, and mathematics (STEM) education in the United States.
- *Office of Personnel Management.* Statistics on the Federal civilian workforce through data sources such as FedScope.
- *Social Security Administration Office of Research Evaluation and Statistics.* Data on social security program benefits, payments, covered workers, and more.
- *USAspending.gov.* The official source for spending data for the U.S. government. Learn about the size of the federal budget, and how the government spends that money on a national level and around the country.

You can also search a federal agency's website to see what types of statistical information it provides. Similarly, state, territorial and local governments compile and maintain their own statistical information. The National Map offers mapping products from federal, state, and local partners on a variety of topics, such as recreation, environmental resources, scientific analysis, and emergency response. Other maps cover:

- Demographic data
- Local environmental data and water resources
- Current weather
- Agricultural information by commodity
- Recreational places and activities

ii. Canada

In Canada, Statistics Canada collects and keeps detailed information on many subjects.

- Agriculture and food
- Business and consumer services and culture
- Business performance and ownership
- Children and youth
- Construction
- Crime and justice
- Economic accounts
- Education, training and learning
- Energy
- Environment
- Families and households
- Government
- Health
- Housing
- Immigration and ethnocultural diversity
- Income, pensions, spending and wealth
- Indigenous peoples
- Information and communications technology

- International trade
- Labour
- Languages
- Manufacturing
- Population and demography
- Prices and price indices
- Retail and wholesale
- Science and technology
- Seniors and aging
- Society and community
- Statistical methods
- Transportation
- Travel and tourism

iii. Other Countries

Similar information is generally available in most countries. For example, in the United Kingdom, the Office for National Statistics, and the Australian Bureau of Statistics in Australia maintain and disseminate extensive statistical information. Statistical information on OECD countries can be accessed online. However, not all countries maintain such comprehensive data.

iv. Healthcare-specific

Extensive health information can be found at the global and national levels. Some examples of these sources include:
- The Canadian Institute for Health Information (CIHI) provides data, reports and news about health in Canada (https://www.cihi.ca)
- The World Health Organization (WHO) which provides information at the country and global levels (https://WHO.int)
- The U.S.-based Center for Disease Control (CDC) provides information and statistics related to the health of Americans (https://cdc.gov)
- The Commonwealth Fund offers extensive information and statistics on the UK healthcare system. (http://www.commonwealthfund.org/)

3. Syndicated Data

Syndicated data refer to information collected by an organization to sell it in a standardized format to several clients with similar information needs. Such databases can be based on one or more sources such as surveys, consumption diaries, or electronic scanners. It is typically provided for a fee, which sometimes can be quite substantial, although considerably less than what it would cost for a proprietary study. Syndicated studies are often supported by membership.

Syndicated studies are built around three different methodologies:

1. **Surveys**. Shared cost studies, advertising evaluation, psychographics/lifestyles.
2. **Diary Panels**. Consumer purchase or consumption diaries, media panels.
3. **Passive Data Collection**. Household grocery scanning, Point-of-sale scanning data, monitoring of online activity, video monitoring.

Most major syndicated studies are offered in many countries by multinational companies such as Nielsen, IRI, Ipsos and IQVIA. The specifics in different countries may differ, but you can expect to find products like these in almost any country where the market is large enough. The best way to find what may be available in your country is to search company websites.

Shared-cost Surveys

Many research companies fund and conduct large scale data collection surveys with the intent of writing up one report and selling it to multiple clients who are interested in the same topic. The costs are shared across many clients, so it is much less expensive than a custom project. But because anyone can access the results, there is no exclusivity. These shared cost surveys have large samples so that they can give marketers a robust overview of the marketplace. Trends can be tracked because the studies run regularly (quarterly to annually). And because data is collected across an industry, competitive intelligence is readily available. Some examples include:

- Environics Institute's Focus Canada Report – which has been tracking Canadian public policy since 1976
- Ipsos' Affluent Study – providing profiles of affluent consumers in 50 countries
- GfK's Automobility Auto syndicated study
- Ipsos' Canadian Financial Monitor – tracking Canadian households' financial behaviours and attitudes

Omnibus studies are often considered syndicated research because they are shared cost studies. Different clients put their questions onto a single questionnaire and pay a fixed cost per question. The shared nature makes them very cost-effective for very short questionnaires, but the results are not shared. Only the client who has paid for a question will see its results. So omnibus services are not secondary research.

Syndicated Media Measurement Studies

Advertisers, advertising agencies, as well as other businesses, need to know the size of their viewing audience, their characteristics, purchase habits and patterns. This is so important to marketing that billions of dollars have been spent on this in the past several decades, continuing to this day. One of the most prominent companies doing this kind of measurement is the Nielsen Company, which has a worldwide presence. Media measurement companies not only provide information on the audience size for TV, radio, Internet and print media, but they also offer details on consumer demographics and even consumer purchase behaviour. This field has seen significant evolution over the past few years with the growth in digital advertising, for example, on social media sites. The standard performance indicators have been adapted to cover online dynamics. The new frontier is measuring advertising across all platforms.

Syndicated Sales and Market Measurement Studies

Many businesses have information on how much they sell, where they sell, and even to whom they sell but don't have such information on their competitors. Many companies are willing to pay for this information. Syndicated studies fill this gap. They are particularly well-developed in the Fast-Moving Consumer Goods (FMCG) market, although they are also available for other types of products.

The Universal Product Code was first developed about 50 years ago to help retailers track their inventory of goods and replenish products as and when they needed them. These codes are printed on products and can be electronically scanned. Now one of the significant uses of UPCs is to collect market information.

Point-of-sale Scanning

Point of sales (POS) data collection involves collecting UPC scanning data on products that are purchased at the check-out counter in a representative sample of stores. For example, there are approximately 300,000 grocery stores and supermarkets in the US, with over $2 million in annual sales. Nielsen randomly samples around 3,000 stores to represent the entire country. Similarly, in Canada, there are 15,500 stores from which Nielsen draws a sample of stores. The store identities are kept secret to avoid possible data tampering.

The data can be analyzed down to the individual product level and can be tracked over time to show minute movements in share and basket contents.

Nielson collects data from over 900,000 stores around the world. While each vendor may have their own criteria, in general, all of them try to minimize bias in their samples and strive towards their data being representative of the population.

Point-of-sale scanning information tracks the movement of goods, and this, in turn, can be related to marketing activities such as price, promotion, and inventory. Organizations such as IRI InfoScan, the Nielsen Scantrack service, and NPD use retail scanning data to syndicate sales information in several sales channels for many product categories.

Household Purchase Panels

While sales data give information on actual sales, they shed no light on buyer behaviour. For many products, a relatively fewer number of buyers account for a large volume of sales. The best way to understand this pattern is through household purchase panels. A panel of households is recruited to provide information on their purchase behaviour on an ongoing basis. The data may be gathered by scanning barcodes with a portable handheld UPC scanner (Nielsen and IRI), by store loyalty card usage (retailers such as Shoppers Drug Mart/Loblaw Optima cards in Canada or similar programs at Tesco, Kroger, Carrefour, in the U.S.) or by recording sales receipts by taking a picture with a smartphone (NPD) and posting it to a website. By tracking households over time, we can understand the dynamics and structure of the transactions. This will help marketers to structure marketing programs tailored to different purchase patterns. For example, if you know on what days your heavy buyers shop, you can structure your promotions to coincide with those days.

Syndicated Healthcare Panels

The healthcare industry is a large buyer of marketing and healthcare research. This is one of the more specialized branches of the field. Research in healthcare includes gathering information on doctors, patients, consumers in general, and healthcare products, both prescription and non-prescription.

Pharmaceutical products are not typically coded for automatic tracking. However, because of the importance of the industry, it has been supported by large syndicated studies over the years. Pharmaceutical syndicated services track sales, price, and distribution of most pharmaceuticals.

Most pharmaceutical data come from patient billing and processing at every point of the drug supply chain. However, unlike most CPG products, the pharmaceutical sales and distribution chains are mediated by government regulations (particularly around privacy issues), physicians, other providers, insurance companies, and other interested parties.

Here is an example of what data might typically be collected and available through syndicated sources. Of course, regulations vary from country to country. It is a simple enough task to find out what is available in a specific country by searching the Internet.

Let's consider prescription medication. The demand for a prescription drug depends on how many prescriptions are written by physicians and how many were dispensed by pharmacies to patients. As with household data, such measures can be used to detect and measure underlying market dynamics.

Here is a list of some vital information commonly collected:
1. **Prescriptions**. How much was prescribed for how many days, new or refills, number of authorized refills, pharmacy reimbursement fee.
2. **Patient Data**. Type, demographics.
3. **Doctors Data**. Doctor's specialty, geographic information, and demographic profile.
4. **Fulfilment Records**. Organization, location, payment type.

Relevant data are provided by individual physicians. In many countries, physicians are issued unique identifiers. National medical associations maintain databases of physicians, residents, and students with information on demographics and businesses. Pharmacies and intermediaries for insurance benefits also provide data.

Syndicated service providers gather all such information, remove all identifiers, connect the various sources through the distribution/sales chain and sell the consolidated data to marketers.

This process is quite complicated and poses several methodological and logistic challenges. For several decades, the company that has coped with such complexity and challenges to provide syndicated information has been IMS Health (now IQVIA). IQVIA is a giant in the healthcare data industry: it covers 85 percent of the world's prescription sales revenues and information on as many as 400 million patients. It has tracked the prescription trends in more than 70 countries, has gathered individual-level prescription data in 50 countries, and offers eight different sales monitoring and consulting services.

Other Syndicated Studies

Most syndicated studies described above are complex, require specialized knowledge and substantial upfront investments. Consequently, these companies offer their services in many countries.

However, there may also be nationally based organizations offering syndicated services as well. While some of the syndicated services are very dominant in many countries, they are not monopolies.

For example, in Canada, Vividata is a major source of audience data, print and digital, for magazines and newspapers. Its single-source survey provides cross-platform audience measurement for 50+ consumer magazines and 50+ daily newspapers. The annual national sample of 35,000+ Canadians (age 14+), surveyed 365 days a year, across 50+ markets, is released quarterly as rolling 52-week data. In addition to providing readership metrics, Vividata delivers a comprehensive database of consumer demographics, media usage, lifestyle and attitudinal data, and product usage across 150+ categories. The data collection procedures are based on a combination of telephone, cellphone, and online interviews. The database includes a range of questions for all media, product consumption, and opinions. Starting with the Winter 2020 Study, their releases also provide insight on evolving consumer trends such as plant-based diets, ethical consumerism, mobile food delivery services, click and collect, use of crypto currency, and other topics.

Numeris, on a less ambitious scale, provides broadcast measurement and consumer behaviour data.

5. Published Material (Newspaper, Magazines and other Publications)

Information obtained from media such as blog posts, newspaper and news service articles, editorials, and classified advertising is abundant. The important question pertains to its relevance for the purpose at hand and whether the expense of retrieving and extracting the information is justified by the value of that information.

Astute competitive intelligence professionals have fairly precise objectives imposed on their research. To maximize the opportunities to obtain relevant information, they will cast their information nets wide and then filter until they receive some key pieces that will help to enlighten their clients and point them in more productive directions.

Classified ads. Competitive intelligence experts creatively look for information in a wide variety of places. One of these can be in the classified ads. For example, a company that produces technical goods and wants to increase its product line might advertise for new employees in newspapers, job search websites and other media. This information can be found by diligent hunters who spot the company and the ads and link the two to the new technical areas.

Publications of trade and industry associations. These are associations of companies within an industry or business sector that provide a source for sharing information and promoting the industry. Most trade and industry associations publish regular reports for their members. Often, these organizations conduct marketing research on behalf of their members and publish the findings. For members, this information establishes an excellent base level of knowledge across the business sector. Sometimes these reports are available to those who are not association members. This information may help individuals seeking entrance to the sector gain significantly important data.

Evaluating the Quality of the Data

Marketing and market information received from any source must be scrutinized in detail before it is included in any reports provided to marketing decision-makers. Secondary information is more of a concern than standardized information (i.e., where the definitions of respondents and of other variables are fairly widely known and accepted). Since standardized information is usually produced for association members or for regular clients, much more care is devoted by the producing organization to ensure that all users, and potential users, are aware of how the data is collected and organized. Remember that the focus of those who created the secondary information was on the original objectives of the study before it became secondary information. While organizations such as Statistics Canada and Environics Analytics are conscientious about the form and content of their data products, they cannot anticipate all the uses that their data might be required to perform.

Secondary and standardized information should be scrutinized using the following questions.
1. What organization conducted the original research?
2. When was the original research conducted? When did the data collection take place? What else was happening in the world at that time that might have influenced the responses?
3. What were the details of the survey sampling, for example, the population from which the sample was drawn, whether the sample was randomly drawn from the population, the sample frame (see Unit 5), the sample unit, the sampling method, etc.?
4. Was the total sample used to produce the information being considered, or was a sub-sample used?
5. What was the response rate? (where applicable)
6. Was the sample representative of the population? On which characteristics was this tested? What was the source of the population characteristics?
7. Was the sample weighted in any way?
8. What method was used for eliciting information?
9. If a questionnaire was used, does it pass the basic requirements for good design, such as being understood by all respondents, unambiguous, easy to answer, having proper sequencing, reasonable skip patterns, not being too long, etc.? (see Unit 6.)
10. When was the survey conducted? What else was happening in the world at that time that might have influenced the responses?
11. Which organization paid for the original primary research?
12. What was the reason for conducting the original primary research?
13. Under what conditions did the original client allow the information to be made available to the public?
14. For each table and chart being considered, what was the original question, the allowable answer categories? For open-ended questions, how were the codes derived?
15. For each table and chart being considered, what is the base size on which the calculations were performed? Never re-use a graph unless the base size is provided on the graph.

16. What is the accuracy of the estimation based on the sample? (Assuming that a random probability sample was drawn.)
17. Do you have access to the complete study? Is only some of the information available? Why is the full study not accessible? Was any information withheld that might disagree with conclusions based on the released information?

The list of questions that need to be answered is extensive, and these 17 questions are not exhaustive. While secondary information might be free or less expensive, unchallenged use of that information could lead to significant exposure to error. This error might lead to inappropriate marketing decisions that could cause considerable loss of business and subsequent loss of jobs.

Most larger marketing research companies now maintain a 'news' space on their official website. If a client or media wants to release the results of a study, the research company will insist on reviewing the release to ensure accuracy, will publish their own analysis of the data on the side and will provide access to all data tables for the information in the release. This helps preserve the reputation of the research company but also ensures secondary researchers have answers to most of the questions above.

Secondary Data Providers: Roles and Responsibilities

Suppose that the 17 questions in the previous section were all answered satisfactorily. Someone will then take the secondary information, manipulate it in some way, and pass it along. The person who retrieves and passes along secondary information has a responsibility to all eventual readers. These responsibilities mimic the care taken when documenting primary information and including the documentation described below.

Provide the proper and complete citation for the originating source of the data or information. Including this information in your translation and presentation of the secondary information gives credibility and shows others that you have thoroughly researched the issue.

State the purpose of the original research that produced the information. Every research project works to achieve specific objectives. The resultant product reflects those objectives, and this information is necessary for proper translation of the secondary research into usable information for the next application.

State the name of the organization that executed the original research, along with:

- **The date of the original report.** While secondary data is not necessarily expected to be current, it is important to know when it was gathered to decide whether it is too old to be relevant. Also, due to the cyclical and seasonal modulations of some business sectors, the date can help users identify when the data should be used during business cycles.
- **The sample size in total and for all subsamples.** This information is just as vital for secondary data as it is for primary data. Unsuspecting users of secondary information might put extreme importance on statements that are based on very small samples. Make sure that sizes are provided for the overall study as well as for all reported subsamples and ensure that you know whether the data you use is from the total sample or a subsample. Ensure that the base size is provided on every graph.

Explain the sampling methodology used to obtain the information. Was the sample obtained randomly, or was some other procedure used? For example, some marketing research projects use samples of people intercepted while shopping at malls. When this field methodology was first used, the client and the consultant had agreed that mall-intercept samples were best for the study. However, this methodology might not be best for someone using the information as secondary data a few months or years after the study was completed.

For each graph or table based on a questionnaire, state the actual questions that were included in the survey. Questions can often be translated into good descriptive titles for figures and tables, but sometimes these translations can be misleading. Don't take chances when you are interpreting secondary information. Getting the original questions is the most foolproof action to ward off disaster through misuse.

Identify the organization that paid for the original research. Users of second-hand information typically have no idea of the actual purpose of the original study. We tend to assume that the data was commissioned to be captured for ethical and worthwhile objectives. This is not always the case. Getting accurate information that realistically reflects the attitudes and behaviours of consumers is a difficult task that requires a high level of expertise and substantial experience. Lack of these qualities can produce inferior information. Also, it is easy to fabricate information based on surveys. If the original data, questionnaire and people are no longer available to query, it might be impossible to judge the real value of that information correctly.

If any differences are referred to, for example, differences in purchase rates between high- and low-income households, make sure to indicate whether the difference is statistically significant and whether the difference is large enough to be meaningful. As we will see later in this book, there is a difference between having two statistics (e.g., sample averages) and being statistically different but not substantively different in a business sense. Many reports written by experts for general consumption will refer to "significant differences" between, for example, two means or two percentages without mentioning whether they are statistically different. This level of writing is designed for audiences that want to focus on the business implications of the information without continually encountering statistical jargon. The report might state that significantly fewer (45 percent) light users definitely intend to buy this product during the next 30 days compared to heavy users (64 percent). This is more readable to the non-researcher audience than, "This difference is statistically significant at a 5 percent level of risk." While some readers will demand this additional detail, many will want to read the report without having to stumble over more detailed statistical terminology. However, whoever produces material based on secondary data should know whether the statistics are significantly different.

Are the acquisition price and speed acceptable? The answer to this question needs to be answered by each organization separately. What might be inexpensive for some could be prohibitively expensive for others. However, if the 17 questions in the previous section do not produce answers that agree with good marketing research practice and ethics, the price cannot be low enough to offset the risk of making bad marketing decisions by using erroneous information.

How to Integrate Secondary Information

While information from secondary and standardized sources can be interesting on its own, it must add value to the marketing decision-making process. For this to happen, the outside information must be integrated with the primary information, if any exists. The result must be a valuable increase in the understanding of the marketplace and better marketing strategies and tactics for the organization.

There are two parts to this procedure: storing the information in a form that can be easily used for the immediate purpose and for future purposes; and integrating the information into the analysis, often through some calculations of market potential or competitive activity.

Transforming the Data and Storing it in a Usable Format

Some secondary data is valuable in the form in which it is retrieved. It can be useful, insightful and visually appealing. However, often, it is cryptic, poorly prepared and hard to decipher. The same diligence is needed to work with secondary information as with primary data.

Primary marketing research can require a significant investment. These funds need to be respected and, accordingly, the research results should be retained for later use as secondary information. Unfortunately, some companies don't realize that their studies could have a secondary purpose and care is not taken to organize them and store them properly to ensure they have extended lives. They might be stored in a random location or stored only with those who originally commissioned them, and after a relatively short time, they are lost. This happens when these individuals leave the company, or move on to another role, or simply decide to clean out their files. Proper storage requires that reports be catalogued and become part of a marketing research library, at a minimum.

Data Warehousing and Data Mining

Data mining is a term that has been applied to the activity of gleaning important information from large databases using sophisticated and robust data analysis techniques. In many cases, this involves the analysis of information about the customers of an organization. The purpose of this analysis is to understand these customers better so that the products and services of the firm can be more effectively marketed to them.

It is essential to understand the potential benefits derived from data mining. It is even more important to develop the data mine. The data mine itself may be referred to as a data warehouse. Data warehouses are established to archive both internal information and external secondary information in a logical and easily accessible manner.

As with any dataset, the quality and relevance of the information that is stored in the data warehouse are important. Sorting and accessing information can be reasonably fast, but the data as it stands is relatively meaningless. It takes much more time to pull this low-value information into a statistical analysis, properly investigate the data, and simmer it down to a meaningful and digestible amount. As mentioned earlier, it is often easier to assess the value of primary information that was designed with your specific purposes in mind than it is to determine the value of secondary information. However, using the two types of data together can be a wise decision when the strengths and weaknesses of each are properly outlined.

Very often data mining is used as the second main procedure in market segmentation. These projects usually start with a survey to collect primary information from hundreds of respondents. The end result of the segmentation is typically the identification of several groups that are internally homogeneous even though the groups themselves are heterogeneous. For example, a research study for pens might identify one segment of people who want inexpensive disposable pens. In contrast, another segment might be people who prefer to buy high-quality luxury pens. The preferences for pen characteristics within each of the two groups are homogeneous. However, there are significant differences between the two groups. Activities, interests, and opinions (AIO) of the respondents are often used to discover the groups, describe why the groups are different, and how the segmentation can help the client organization.

The *second* main procedure comes in when we want to correctly identify individual members of each segment within the broader population, say, customers of the client organization. The task is to extend the survey segmentation based on a sample of customers to all customers of the organization. This is sometimes called tagging, scoring or linking the database.

For tagging to be successful, there must be variables in the full customer database that link each individual to one of the identifiable segments that emerged from the survey. For example, if the critical segmentation variable was the family size, that variable must be part of the full customer database so that Marg Browning living in Red Deer can be assigned to the proper segment.

Spreadsheet Collection, Organization, and Analysis

For many analysts, obtaining data in a spreadsheet format is the first step in the analysis process. Usually, secondary data is available in some published form on the internet. In very rare cases, if the information is absolutely essential, you may have to enter it manually or by scanning, for example, from very old printed reports. Besides, data appearing in various forms, such as PDF and JSON, on websites can often be scraped into formats that can be used in standard analysis applications.

When you secure useful secondary data, the next challenge is to determine how to use it. There are two main actions to take with the secondary data: reformat it for more effective graphical or tabular presentation to others within your organization and use the data as-is to support projections of future market positions through statistical analyses.

If the desire is to base projections on the secondary data, a spreadsheet program like Excel or a statistics program like R, Python, SPSS, or SAS will make multiple iterations and test situations easier and quicker.

The presentation of marketing research information will be handled later in this book. At this point, we will just state that it is imperative to faithfully translate the information from its previous format to whichever format is most effective for the intended new users. Understanding how to present graphs and tables to maximize the ability of users to understand the information and to move on to the next stage of usage is a tremendously valuable skill. Entire careers are based on effective data visualization.

When the secondary information is used as a basis for projections of future market conditions, the marketing decision context must be fully understood. In many cases, an initial estimate of the market size is needed for a product before spending substantial amounts of money on primary marketing research. Often, this information is required to determine whether a company should move into new territory, product category, or acquisition. The information could also be used by an investor to judge whether to extend funds to an enterprise that wants to expand its business.

For example, suppose that a company has developed a line of health products for travellers and needs to secure bank financing or prepare a prospectus for an initial public offering. Both sources of funds would be very interested in the potential size of the market for the product and the likely annual sales during the first five years of this new endeavour. However, the firm is small and cannot afford a consumer survey. It hires a consultant to obtain relevant secondary data, develop market projections based on the data, and produce reasonable estimates of the opportunities for the new product in the market. The company cannot afford to purchase and analyze raw data from Statistics Canada. So, the consultant uses the data that appears for free on the StatsCan website as the base for calculations.

A spreadsheet or statistics application would typically be set up to use the freely available census data. This spreadsheet could be manipulated to allow a basic understanding of the secondary data. It should not be used for actual market estimates. More detailed information can be obtained, but the cost of access and processing will be higher.

Estimates can then be made for the percentage of this market that the new entrant expects to attract at equilibrium (i.e., when the market settles with the original product) and during the time up until the stability is achieved. These estimates should be provided with at least three levels: realistic, optimistic, and pessimistic. When the financial estimates seem reasonable, they can be provided and explained to prospective investors.

Naturally, this is a straightforward example of how secondary data can be used, but it is not unrealistic. Many small companies or start-ups have few, if any, funds to develop primary sources of data and must rely wholly on secondary sources. Also, the need for objective market information often sneaks up on companies that have never needed such information before. Consequently, secondary data fit into these tight timelines as well as budgets.

Concluding Comments

In this unit, we learned about the importance of secondary research in laying the groundwork for a more comprehensive understanding of the marketplace. Using data that has already been collected is a cost-effective way to get answers to many of the issues marketers need to resolve. At the same time, syndicated or standardized data are an excellent way to stay up-to-date and gain competitive intelligence quickly and without the expense of primary research. The ideal situation is where diligent, well-planned and executed secondary research provides a solid foundation that can then be built upon by primary research. If this is to happen, organizations must make a concerted effort to capture, organize and store all forms of market intelligence that they have access to, including their own research, government and other secondary sources, and information shared through industry associations

UNIT 4

How to Draw Samples

Sample surveys, usually called surveys, are the most common form of collecting data in marketing research. They are the mechanism we use to get a trustworthy, projectable answer to marketing questions.

Suppose, for example, we want to know the proportion of Canadians who might consider visiting the U.S. in the next year. We could, in theory, ask every single Canadian whether they thought they might, but this would be exceedingly expensive. In practice, it is never done. Instead, we collect the information from a sample of Canadians, perhaps 1,000 or so, and use their responses to estimate the percentage of Canadians who are considering visiting the U.S. next year. Most marketing research surveys use samples to collect data. However, if we need valid and reliable information, we need to follow specific procedures. Otherwise, the results can prove to be misleading.

Even though online surveys do not abide by strict sampling principles, it is important to understand those principles and any restrictions on reporting due to not following them. Many of the sampling principles are best explained assuming that we are conducting face-to-face, in-home interviews or telephone interviews. If you are involved only with online surveys you may find some of the following outside your experience. However, it is important that you learn the principles of sampling, many of which can only be explained by going outside of online interviewing. It is critical for any marketing or social researcher to understand the principles of sampling, because the validity of any survey is related to the way the sample is chosen.

What is a Sample Survey?

Unlike a census, a sample survey collects information from *some* members (called the sample) of the target audience (called the universe or population). To do this properly, we should use sample surveys that are based on well-defined concepts, methods, and data analysis procedures.

If we were to get information from all members of the population (whether we are talking about inhabitants of a particular city or a specific target group like cardiologists), we would be conducting a census.

Why Use Samples?

Conducting a **census** in many market research contexts is neither feasible nor desirable for several reasons:
- The target audience, in most cases, is too broad and too widely dispersed. For instance, if we want to carry out a census of all users of breakfast cereal, we may have to carry out millions of interviews.
- Many people may be unavailable when we try to contact them.
- Some of the interviewees may be in remote areas of the country or not easily reachable.
- It would take a very, very long time to collect responses from everyone.
- The research project may cost more than the potential gain would be from obtaining such information.

What if we did have the time and resources to carry out a census? Contrary to what you may think, a census is not necessarily more accurate than a properly conducted sample survey. There are several reasons for this.

For a general population target:
- Research panels, currently the source of most samples, do not include the full population, so we would have to find some other method to contact the entire population – perhaps by mail or telephone.
  - Many segments of the population are not used to filling out online surveys, and some have no access to the technology required to do so. So, there would be a need to hire personal interviewers.
  - We may not be able to find and train enough people to be high-quality interviewers in the timeframe required.

- Given the timing required, the data may be outdated by the time we complete its collection.

On the other hand, statistical theory assures us that, for a given level of accuracy, it is not necessary to interview everyone in the population. So instead of a census, we resort to a **sampling of people** from the target audience. We can restrict ourselves to a portion of the population and conduct a sample survey to obtain reliable results in a much shorter period and with far less expense.

As you would expect, there are rules that we need to follow. We cannot merely interview 100 beer drinkers who pass through the downtown corridor of a city and assume that the results can be applied to all beer drinkers in the city. Sample surveys will be valid only if the sample represents the population according to logical and relevant criteria.

Do we have any reason to believe that beer drinkers who pass through the downtown corridor will have similar drinking habits as those in the rest of the city? In fact, how can we know that any sample is representative of the target audience? What is a representative sample? How do we choose a representative sample? How large should a sample be? What happens when a large number of people who were contacted refused to participate in the survey? What is the relationship between sample size and accuracy of results? This chapter helps to answer these questions.

What are the Steps in Drawing a Sample?

Drawing a sample starts with the sample design. We must first describe the sample characteristics: the population, the sampling unit, the sample frame, the type of sample, the methods for selecting the sample, and the sample size. These are described in detail below.

1. Define the Relevant Population (Universe)

Each marketing research study is interested in a specific group of people, the **target audience**. For example, we may be interested in all beer drinkers in the country or undergraduates in a particular city who hold part-time jobs or households in rural areas that own one or more SUVs. The group of interest is called the **relevant population** or the **universe**. Definitions of the relevant population can be broad (e.g., all adults 18 years of age or older living in Canada) or narrow (e.g., high worth households who are in the market to buy a luxury vehicle in the next six months).

In practice, the target population (for which information is required) and the survey population (from which data is obtained) may be different. A researcher should make sure that they are as similar as possible. For instance, you may want to know about the behaviour of all adults in the country. However, the researcher may have neither the time nor the resources to conduct interviews in the northern territories of Yukon, Nunavut and the Northwest Territories and excludes them from the survey population, even though the results will be projected to the entire population of the country. Wherever such gaps arise, they should be specifically pointed out to the client and mentioned in every report.

Defining the population is not always straightforward for these reasons:

- For instance, if you set your target audience as adults, what defines an adult? Those who are over their driving age, drinking age or voting age? Any of these definitions can be considered valid, depending on your purpose. And what about residents of the country who are not citizens?
- Consider another example. You want to interview a sample of students who go to a particular university. Do part-time students qualify? Do distance learning or online students qualify? It may depend on whether the topic of the survey is the amenities and accessibility of the physical campus or the quality of instruction.

Since the way you define your population determines who will be included in your sample, it is important to identify your population precisely.

2. Define the Sampling Unit

A sampling unit is the smallest, individual element that you will analyze.
- If you are studying the penetration of refrigerators, your sampling unit is the household (since it is unlikely that each member of a household would own a refrigerator).
- If you are assessing how many schools have a lunch program, your sampling unit is a school.
- If your objective is to estimate how many adults in the country drink beer, an "adult" (as defined in your population) is your sampling unit.
- If you measure voting intentions, your sampling unit is a voter (an adult with the right to cast a ballot in that particular election), not an adult, not a household, since members of the same household may vote differently.

As these examples show, a sampling unit can be anything you choose it to be: an individual, a household, or an organization. The definition of a sampling unit entirely depends on the purpose of your survey.

3. Select a Sample Frame

The sample frame is how the population is accessed for the survey. Marketing research studies depend on various sample sources such as consumer access panels, on-site intercepts (e.g., in malls), client databases, and business directories.

Several considerations influence the selection of a sample frame.

Comprehensiveness. A good sample frame ideally includes everyone in the relevant population. In practice, this is seldom the case. Telephone directories were once used as a frame to reach households, even though they excluded households with unlisted numbers, those who had recently moved and those who didn't have a telephone. Over time, consumers gave up their landlines for mobile phones, which are not listed in directories. Telephone books are no longer comprehensive and have fallen out of use.

The usefulness of any frame depends on the nature and size of the omissions (those who are left out). For online surveys, the sample frame is the provider's panel or the list of customer names and contact information provided by the client. We must ask ourselves if this panel or list excludes an identifiable group within the target population (for example, older consumers, or those whose first language is not English or French).

The precision of definition. While *comprehensiveness* refers to including everyone who should be included, *precision* refers to excluding everyone who should **not** be included. For instance, if you are trying to sample members of a particular profession, you may use the membership directory of the professional association as your sampling frame. However, some associations may not have well-defined membership requirements and may admit anyone who can pay the membership fee. This might be administrative employees, suppliers or head-hunters specializing in that profession. If you are interested in doing a survey among members of a profession, using the association's membership list as your frame may result in including some respondents who are not truly in your target group. Precision would require a mechanism to identify and remove them; this is called screening.

Practicality. In many cases, it is simply not possible to list the target audience. We may have, for instance, no list of hard-of-hearing people, or people whose net worth is over $5 million, or those who saw a foreign movie in the past month. In other cases, listings may be inaccessible due to privacy regulations. And even when a listing may be available, such as homeowners listed in a city's tax rolls, the list may be too unwieldy or dated to be of use. This list wouldn't include the names of those who hide their ownership behind numbered corporations or have put their home in someone else's name, for example.

The same is true if we want to interview 2000 representative women; we may not have an up-to-date sample frame that lists all women. In such cases, we must accept this is a known weakness, discuss and get approval from the client, modify our sampling methods as appropriate and mention this in the report.

For online surveys, the sample frame is the panel from which the sample is drawn. However, the panel is not the relevant universe. A panel may have one million potential respondents, but the country may have fifty million people. So, there is a huge gap between the universe and the sample frame. While this is one of the major theoretical issues around online surveys, it is one we must accept out of practicality in an increasingly digital world.

In the end, the sample frame should be as similar to the relevant population as possible. If we use a list, we should ensure it is accurate, current and consists of unduplicated units.

For example, if we are selecting a sample of bank customers, we should make sure that the list we use does not include the same customer more than once. Duplication of names could occur if the bank has a separate list for each product (such as chequing account, savings account, investment account) owned by the customer. If the same customer is listed more than once (under different products), it will give some customers, perhaps those who have more financial resources, a greater chance of being included in the sample.

Understand that there is always an "if." What if the bank wanted to sample based on wealth rather than individual customers? Then that sampling method over several account types might provide opportunities to include sample units based more on wealth than on simple account presence. A sampling procedure similar to this exists in auditing and is called dollar-unit-sampling.

4. Choose a Sampling Method

There are two types of sampling procedures: 1) probability or random sampling methods, and 2) non-probability sampling methods.

Strictly speaking, only when we select a sample using a **probability** or random sampling method can we measure the *accuracy* of the results by using methods of statistical inference. However, practical considerations such as cost and time often make it necessary to use samples that are non-probability based.

Even though **non-probability** samples are generally accepted as a reasonable way of carrying out survey research, the marketing researcher must still ensure that the sample is representative of

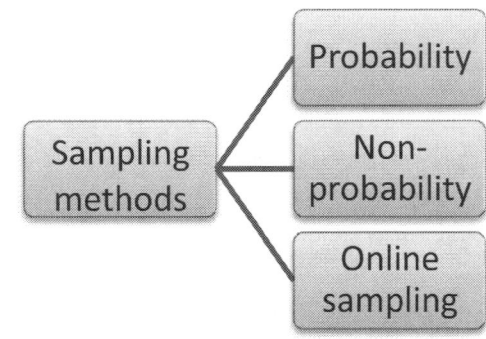

the population and that there are no obvious or subtle biases in the selection of respondents.

What is the most significant **difference between a probability and a non-probability sample**? Probability samples are based on the principle of **randomness**. Random means that each unit in the population has an equal or at least measurable chance of being included in the sample. The principle of randomness provides a sound theoretical basis for projecting the results to the general population, which is called **statistical inference**.

- For instance, if you want to sample 10 students from a class of 100 randomly, you can write each person's name on a small card, put all the cards in a hat and draw ten cards. To make sure that no one has any particular advantage, you would also make sure that the cards are of equal size, weight, and colour and you would shuffle the cards before drawing. This way, all 100 students have an equal probability of being included in the sample.
- On the other hand, a non-random or non-probability method may entail you standing by the exit and choosing the first ten students who come out. In this instance, not everyone in the class has an equal opportunity of being included in the sample. Students who are eager to get out, students who sit near the door, students without disabilities, students who attend a particular class on the day you choose to draw a sample have a much higher probability of being included than others in the same class. Such exclusions can potentially introduce biases in the sample.

Even this simple example shows that randomness automatically takes care of many potentially biasing factors and supports statistical inference to the relevant population.

Strictly speaking, **online samples** are typically non-probability samples. However, the results from a sample drawn from good access panels (as judged by polling results) could resemble those obtained from a probability sample, i.e., it might be a representative sample while not having been randomly selected. For this reason, we are treating online samples as a separate category. Comprehensive lists of sample units provided by the client may support random sampling. For example, if Company Y provides a file containing all customers who have bought directly from Company Y during the past year, that list would be the relevant population and random sampling can be conducted on that list.

Probability (Random) Sampling Methods

Probability samples can be either single-stage or multistage.
- In *single-stage* sampling, we directly sample from our sampling frame. This would be the case if we randomly select ten students from a class list of 100 students.
- In *multistage* sampling, we go through intermediate samples before sampling the final respondents. This could include selecting a few cities rather than all cities, selecting a few blocks in each selected city, and then selecting one person to be interviewed in each household in the selected blocks.

Simple Random Sampling

Simple random sampling is a procedure in which every member of the population has an equal chance of being selected and included in the sample. If your objective is to collect information on customer satisfaction among bank customers who have more than $3000 in their chequing accounts (this is the relevant population), and you have a complete list of such customers (this is the sample frame), you could use a simple random sample. Random number generators are the most common way to produce random samples, though random number tables can still be found online.

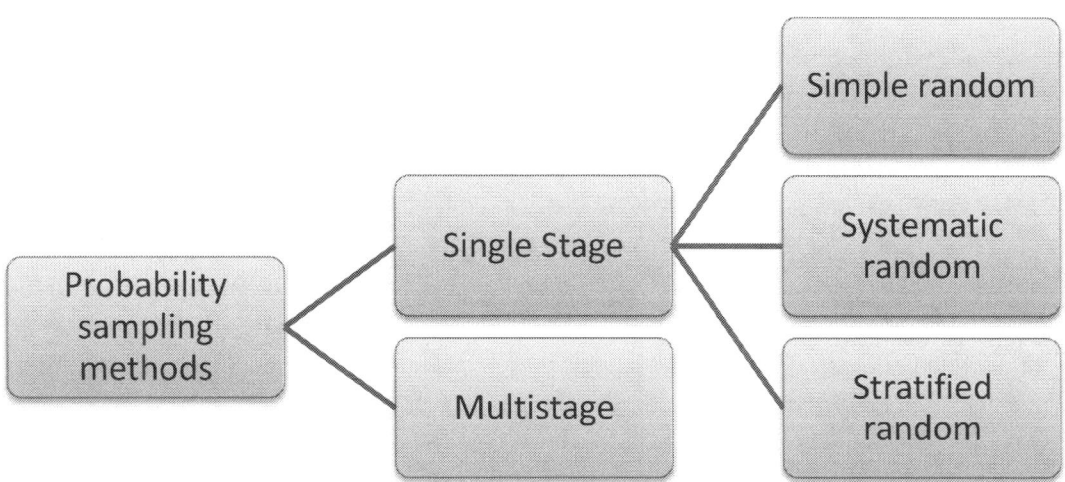

Random Number Generators. Random number generators are computer programs that produce numbers in a random sequence. Suppose we want to select 100 customers out of 3000. We can number the customers 1 to 3000 and tell the computer to generate 100 numbers within that range randomly. We then choose the 100 customers whose numbers correspond to those produced by the computer.

From a statistical point of view, random does not mean haphazard. Rather, random means that the non-generated numbers have as much probability of being included in the list as the generated numbers, and that the generated numbers do not have any common characteristic (such as all numbers being even) except through coincidence. Good random number programs are tested to make sure that they generate numbers that fulfil the requirements of randomness. Most research that requires the use of random numbers uses a random number generator. Telephone surveys, for example, use random digit dialing (RDD) with random numbers generated automatically by the computer.

Random Number Tables. Random number tables are the low-tech versions of random number generators and are used only rarely these days. These tables contain long lists of preselected random numbers. (An example is shown below. A book of random tables will contain several hundred pages.) Here, if you want to select 100 respondents out of a list of 900 customers, you can begin at any column, row, or page of the table. For instance, let's say you decide to start from the second block and go down the column. The three-digit number here is 163, so you choose customer number 163. Moving down, you note the second customer is 990, but you only have 900 customers. So, you move down one row and choose customer number 67, then 655, 19 and so on. From here, you can consistently move up, down, or sideways. Let's say you decide to move down. The next numbers that are 3000 or less are 715, 482, 011, and 515, all in block three. You accept these numbers and continue the search until you get 100 respondents.

Table of Random Numbers

53 75 23 99 07	61 32 28 69 84	94 62 67 86 24	98 33 41 19 95	47 53 53 38 09
63 38 06 86 54	99 00 65 26 94	02 82 90 23 07	79 62 76 80 60	75 91 12 81 19
35 30 58 21 46	06 72 17 10 94	25 21 31 75 96	49 28 24 00 49	55 65 79 78 07
63 43 36 82 69	65 51 18 37 88	61 38 44 12 45	32 92 85 88 65	54 34 81 85 35
98 25 37 55 26	01 91 82 81 46	74 71 12 94 97	24 02 71 37 07	03 92 18 66 75
01 63 21 17 69	71 50 80 89 56	38 15 70 11 48	43 40 45 86 98	00 83 26 91 03
64 55 22 21 82	48 22 28 06 00	61 54 13 43 91	82 78 12 23 29	06 66 24 12 27
85 07 26 13 89	01 10 07 82 04	59 63 69 36 03	69 11 15 83 80	13 29 54 19 28
58 54 16 24 15	51 54 44 82 00	62 61 65 04 69	38 18 65 18 97	85 72 13 49 21
34 85 27 84 87	61 48 64 56 26	90 18 48 13 26	37 70 15 42 57	65 65 80 39 07

Similarly, if your population consisted of 20,000 customers and you had to select a sample of 2000 from it, you would choose a five-digit number from the table (because 20,000 has five digits and will accommodate the outermost limit of your population) and proceed in any direction from that number until 2000 numbers under 20,000 had been chosen. The numbers correspond to customer numbers on your list. While selecting these 2000 names, you would automatically discard numbers that exceeded 20,000 because your population does not have any customer with a number greater than 20,000.

Systematic Random Sampling

Systematic random sampling is similar to simple random sampling. However, in a systematic random sample, instead of using a random sequence to choose sampling units, we choose units at *given intervals*. If we want to select 200 doctors from a list of 4000, we will select every twentieth doctor on the list.

A *sample interval* is the number of units in the sample frame divided by the desired sample size. Our sample interval would be 20 (i.e., 4000 ÷ 200 = 20).

In practice, this formula is modified to account for the fact that we may not be able to contact every person in our sample, or that some people we contact may refuse to participate in our survey. Suppose we expect that a maximum of 45 percent of those in our sample either will not be reachable or are likely to refuse to participate. Therefore, the expected *participation rate* is 55 percent (100 percent − 45 percent).

This leads to a modified sample interval equation: *Sample Interval = units in the sample frame ÷ [sample size X expected participation rate]*

So in our example,

Sample frame	= 4000 doctors
Required sample size	= 200
Expected participation rate	= 55%
Therefore, Sample Interval	= 4000 ÷ [200 X 0.55] = 11

In other words, we will draw every 11th name on the list to create a sample of 364 respondents (4000 ÷ 11 = 364). If only 55 percent of these people respond, then we will achieve our objective of 200 completed interviews (364 X 0.55 = 200).

Since we can never be sure how successful we will be, it is better to use a conservative estimate. For example, we may assume that participation is likely to be only 50 percent when we actually expect it to be 55 percent. However, we should not assume an artificially low participation rate, such as 10 percent, when we expect it to be 50 percent. Such unreasonable assumptions can create problems of representativeness in the sample if you stop gathering interviews once the required number of completes is obtained.

As long as the list does not have a pattern (e.g., every eleventh doctor is a surgeon), systematic sampling will yield results comparable to random sampling. Usually, systematic samples will have a random start; the first person will be chosen at random and then the sample interval will be added to that number repeatedly to select the rest of the sample. Thus, in our example, if we choose a random start number such as 3, we will select doctor number 3, and then keep adding 11 until we get the required number: 3, 14, 25, 36, 47, 58, 69, and so on. The advantage of using systematic sampling over random sampling is that it is less cumbersome and involves less work if done by hand. Random sampling using a computer can be less work.

Obviously, for practical reasons, you would choose the first random number that is less than the sampling interval. Otherwise, you may run out of units to sample.

Stratified Random Samples. There are times when you want to be sure that your research sample represents several segments or subgroups of your population. If you use a random sample, it is possible to miss an entire subgroup or not have enough people in a subgroup for it to be adequately represented. This is especially true if the total size of the sample is rather small. Just as a simple random sample allows everyone an equal chance of being chosen, it also allows an equal chance of being excluded.

Consider the following example. In a city, businesses are distributed as follows:

Large businesses	50
Medium businesses	1,000
Small businesses	20,000
Total	21,050

If we draw a simple random sample of 100 businesses, it is possible that none of the large companies would be included, and no guarantee that we would include a reasonable number of medium businesses. To avoid this, we may decide to first divide the list into large, medium, and small (i.e., stratify by size) and then sample a certain number of businesses from each stratum. This way, we can be sure that businesses of different sizes are included. This is known as stratified sampling.

Stratification can be done with any variable that we may consider relevant. For instance, we can stratify consumers as high, medium, or light users of a brand and select independent samples from each. Or we can stratify the country into several regions and select independent samples from each region. The following examples describe situations in which a stratified sample might be used.

> Example 1. A research survey of the perceptions and needs of the staff of a multi-level organization. You might choose to group interviews into tiers based on the different levels: high-level management, middle management, and lower-level employees. You do this because the different groups will not likely see things the same way, and there are fewer high-level managers, so you need to ensure you hear from them.

> Example 2. Surveying different ethnic groups. Whenever a survey relates to special characteristics of the population—be it ethnicity, education, age or income—it is more efficient to stratify the population according to the characteristic of interest first to ensure that each group of interest is adequately represented in the final sample. Canadian general population samples often start by stratifying the sample for English speaking and French-speaking Canadians. A U.S. sample might need to ensure that Black, Latino and Asian consumers are included in the sample by stratifying the frame along these lines.

In these examples, we have used what is known as stratified random samples. In a stratified random sample, we first divide our universe into a few (more) homogeneous subgroups and then draw random samples from each subgroup separately. Stratification can be of two types: probability proportional to size (PPS), and disproportionate sampling.

Probability Proportional to Size (PPS) Sample. In PPS samples, we keep the relative size of each stratum in a sample the same as it is in the population. Suppose we want to assess how a bank's customers react to the bank's services.

The bank has 800,000 customers distributed as follows:

Stratum	Number of Customers	Percent of Bank's Population
a. Customers with a balance of less than $50	80 000	10
b. Customers with a balance of $50 to $499	560 000	70
c. Customers with a balance of $500 to $999	80 000	10
d. Customers with a balance of $1000 to $1999	40 000	5
e. Customers with a balance of $2000 plus	40 000	5
Total	800 000	100

Let us assume that we want to interview 1,000 customers. If we want our sample to be similar to the population in terms of their proportions, we will distribute our sample according to the bank's population, as in the 4th column below.

Stratum	Number of Customers	Percent of Bank's Population	Sample Proportionate to Size	Disproportionate Sample	Percent of Disproportionate Sample
a. Customers with a balance of $50 or less	80 000	10	100	200	20
b. Customers with a balance of $50 to $499	560 000	70	700	200	20
c. Customers with a balance of $500 to $999	80 000	10	100	200	20
d. Customers with a balance of $1000 to $1999	40 000	5	50	200	20
e. Customers with a balance of $2000 plus	40 000	5	50	200	20
Total	800 000	100	1000	1000	100

Each stratum of customers is represented in the sample by the same **proportion** of respondents as they represent in the full customer base. For example, those with a balance of $2,000 and over is 5% in both the entire population of customers and in the sample.

However, if the bank wants to dig deeper into the behaviours or attitudes of each stratum of customers, they may have a challenge.

- They would have no difficulty doing extensive analysis on those with a balance of $50 to $499 – there are 700 respondents in this group.
- But with only 50 respondents in the $2,000 plus group, there may be little analysis that can be done.

If the subgroup analysis is an important objective, the bank would need to build a 'disproportionate' sample. We see this in the two rightmost columns in the table above, where a disproportionate sample allocation has resulted in 200 respondents for each category. This is large enough to allow us to carry out the same level of analysis on each stratum of customers.

However, the findings are distorted when disproportionate sub-samples are combined into a total sample. For instance, in our example, only 5% of the bank's customers have balances of $2000 or more, but they make up 20% of our sample. This means their responses carry far more weight in the final results than they should. The results obtained using our sample are not representative of the population-as-a-whole.

In practice, this is not a problem. A statistical procedure known as **weighting** is typically applied to the data to correct for disproportionate sampling. This procedure will be discussed later.

From a statistical point of view, Proportional Probability Sampling has no particular advantages. The use of the *disproportionate* sample is widespread in marketing research. Once the sample is less than 10 percent of the population (which is the case in almost all consumer research surveys), it is the actual *sample size* and not the size of the population that determines the accuracy of the results. A sample size of 2000 Americans will have the same margin of error as a sample size of 2000 Canadians, even though Canada is $1/10^{th}$ the size of its neighbour. So, we do not have to be concerned that we reduced the sample of a larger group when a disproportionate sampling scheme is used.

Oversampling. Oversampling is a particular case of proportionate sampling. In this approach, initial sampling is done using the Proportional Probability Sampling method. We then increase or *boost* the sample size of groups that we are interested in but for which we do not have an adequate number of respondents.

Let us return to the bank example. We first use a PPS sample and then notice that there are only 50 customers with a balance of $2000 or more. We can add another 100 respondents to this group for a more comfortable sample of 150, and the total sample size increases from 1,000 to 1,100. These additional 100 customers will *not* form a part of the main sample of 1,000, but whenever users of the $2000 group are analyzed, the 100 additional customers will be added in with the 50 in the main sample. What more typically happens is that those 150 customers are weighted down to reflect their fair share of the population when total figures are presented. In this case, oversampling is a particular case of disproportionate sampling.

Multistage Sampling

The single-stage sampling procedures described thus far can work very well when we have a reasonable and manageable sample frame, such as customers of an insurance company or students in a university. However, in survey research sampling, we face many practical problems. For instance:

- We would like a national sample of 2,000 adults, but there is no sampling frame that lists all citizens, suitably numbered, from which we can select the sample.
- Even if such a sample frame were to exist, it is quite possible that contact information such as a phone number, e-mail or physical address is not available or is out-of-date for a significant proportion of the list.

To avoid these problems, we use a procedure known as multistage sampling. **Multistage sampling** is the drawing of random samples at different levels, with each sample level becoming the population for the next level. For instance, if we want to draw a sample of 500 high-school students in Montreal, we first take a random sample of 10 high schools in the city and then randomly sample 50 students from each school. The ten high schools are the first level of sampling, and then each one becomes a new universe for the second level when we draw a sample of 50 students from each school.

Similarly, in a typical survey using random sampling procedures across the country, the country is first divided into several regions. Each region is then separated into cities of different population sizes. Then within each region, community areas representing each size group are drawn at random. Interviews could then be conducted in these selected cities/towns/rural areas.

Multistage sampling reduces the survey complexity by narrowing our focus to fewer units at each stage. Once again, when we analyze the results, we need to weight the data (described later) to account for the fact that we did not sample proportionally from a population sample frame.

Cluster Sampling

In some cases, strict random sampling may prove to be very expensive and impractical. Suppose we want to carry out 300 in-home product testing interviews with the person in the household who conducts most of the grocery shopping. For example, we want to test reactions to a new drinking water filter that requires some instructions upfront and a follow-up interview after a week of usage.

If we randomly choose 300 households in a city, those households will be very widely spread out. For instance, two randomly chosen households can be four or five kilometres apart. It can become even more frustrating if the respondent is not available in the selected household, and the interviewer has to travel four or five kilometres to find the next respondent, who may also be unavailable.

In cluster sampling, we use a larger unit as our *primary sampling unit* (PSU). In our example, instead of choosing 300 households, we may choose 30 city blocks randomly and interview ten grocery shoppers in each chosen area. This reduces interviewer travel time and the frustration associated with it. Care should be taken to determine that those city blocks are representative of the city and not highly biased towards lower or higher social strata.

A more practical solution, and one that is generally now the standard in North America, is to intercept a potential respondent in a shopping mall, qualify them and provide instructions, and then send them home with the product. The follow-up interview can then be conducted either by phone or online. Because the malls where recruitment takes place are centralized in different parts of the city, this can be seen as a form of cluster sampling, although, strictly speaking, it is a non-probability sample. This is mainly because we cannot randomly choose our respondents in a mall and those shoppers might not be representative of the relevant parent population.

Cluster sampling can approximately follow the principle of randomly selecting respondents so that researchers can generalize results from a sample to the population, but it cuts down the final costs of interviewing. Due diligence must be exercised throughout the cluster sampling process to ensure randomness and representativeness.

- The composition of the clusters should be done to mimic the composition of the relevant parent population. That means that specific key criteria should be selected that are important to the study and the physical boundaries of the clusters should be developed to be representative of that relevant population.
- After randomly selecting the sample clusters, each successively smaller sampling frame should be randomly selected. At the first stage, 30 clusters may be defined for Toronto, each representative of a specific neighbourhood. All 30 neighbourhoods

could comprise the highest-level sample frame, or a sample of say ten neighbourhoods could be randomly drawn as the second level.

- Then, several city blocks can be randomly selected from each of the randomly selected neighbourhoods. Either all residences on the city blocks could be included or a randomly selected number of houses from each city block.
- After approaching a randomly selected residence from a randomly sampled city block from a randomly chosen cluster, a respondent must be randomly selected from the household who qualifies for the study.

Following this procedure, the interviewer approaches the first randomly selected residence and attempts to complete one interview from each household. That's much more efficient than using simple random sampling across the city to conduct in-person or face-to-face interviews.

However, cluster sampling potentially increases the margin of error. This is because it is likely that those who live in the same neighbourhood share some common characteristics compared to those who live in a different neighbourhood. To adjust for this, statisticians sometimes apply a correction known as the **design factor**.

Replicated Sampling

Replicated samples are a variation of random sampling. Sometimes it is desirable to split one large sample into two or more smaller samples, each representing the population fully. For example, we want to carry out a random telephone survey of 1,000 adults who travelled to a destination that is over 100 km from their residence during the previous 90 days. Assume that we do not know the proportion of adults who would qualify to be interviewed. We might guess it is about 20 percent. This means we need to contact 5000 people to get 1000 who would qualify. Since random samples of telephone numbers may include business numbers, numbers not in service, and other numbers that are not eligible (in addition to respondent non-availability and refusal to cooperate), we may have to start with as many as 30,000 numbers to get 5,000 contacts to interview 1,000 qualified respondents eventually.

However, if the proportion of people who qualify turns out to be 40 percent instead of 20 percent, by the time we dial 15,000 numbers, we would have interviewed the desired sample of 1,000 qualified respondents. If we assume that we started interviewing from one end of the country to the other, we may have covered only half of the country, leaving the other half unrepresented in our final sample.

To avoid problems like these, we may choose to divide the estimated 30,000 numbers into six replicates of 5,000. Each 5,000 must be fully representative of the country. We start interviewing with one replicate and move on to the next only if our interview completions were not achieved. This enables us to stop our interviews with the completion of any replicate and retain the complete randomness of our sample.

For example, if, by the time we get to 15,000 numbers we had already interviewed as many as needed, we should still have a sample that is representative of the whole country. However, randomness does not guarantee representativeness. So, the completed sample should be checked for representativeness before we close the survey.

Probability Samples in Specific Contexts

Probability samples are often modified to suit the specific requirements of different data collection methods. For instance, if we use telephone surveys, it is relatively easy for an interviewer to interview 20 consumers in one evening even if they live in different parts of the country. On the other hand, when we carry out in-home interviews, doing even 10 in a single city would be difficult because the interviewer may have to travel from one location to another. Many modified random sampling procedures address these issues.

In-home (door-to-door) interviews: If **in-home (door-to-door) interviews** are carried out, interviewers must physically visit potential respondents in their homes. In such cases, strict random sampling may prove to be expensive and impractical. Let's go back to our earlier example: we want to carry out 500 in-home interviews with principal grocery shoppers. If we randomly choose 500 households, they may be too widely dispersed. To avoid this problem, we use cluster sampling, as explained earlier. Please note that while door-to-door interviewing is essentially no longer in use in most of the developed world, it is still is an important methodology in some developing countries.

Telephone interviews: Telephone interviewing does not have the same restrictions as in-home interviewing. Calling a number next door is the same as calling a number across town or across the country. In this sense, telephone samples can be superior to door-to-door (in-home) samples. However, telephone samples pose their own problems as follows:

- **Mobile Devices**: The majority of potential respondents in many countries do not have landlines; moreover, there is no directory of mobile numbers. Although random digit dialling will still enable access to cellphones and tablets, it is not unusual for those with more wealth to have more than one phone—all of these challenges the requirements of strict probability sampling.
- **Wastage:** Many randomly selected phone numbers are not assigned, belong to businesses or may be hooked up to non-telephone devices.
- **Non-availability of Respondents:** Many people have apps that block unknown callers or use voicemail and caller ID as screening devices.
- **Refusals:** Many people find it easier to refuse or discontinue an interview when the interviewer is an anonymous voice at the other end of the phone. They find it harder to say no or to discontinue when the interviewer is seen in person. Further, some people on cellphones may discontinue a call to avoid paying phone charges.

There are three common ways in which telephone interviews are carried out. (Please note, these procedures are much less common these days, especially in the most developed and some developing countries. They are still used in many countries though.)

These are:
1. telephone directories as the sample frame
2. random digit dialling (RDD)
3. seed samples/*Plus n* procedures

Telephone Directories. Telephone directories are generally a thing of the past. Most mobile devices are not listed, as many would refuse to have their numbers listed, and numbers frequently change as people switch providers for a better plan. However, this approach is a useful theoretical model for understanding other sampling techniques.

In the telephone directory dialing method, we choose the sample from the telephone directory (i.e., the white pages is our sample frame). A few pages are randomly chosen from a directory, and then a number from each selected page is randomly chosen. Even when telephone directories were commonly available, this procedure had several drawbacks. First, people who had unlisted numbers could not be reached. Second, most print directories had a lag ranging from 6 to 18 months. Even electronic databases have a lag. This is an example of a mismatch between the population and the sample frame, which may or may not be a serious problem. At the time, it was estimated that the average North American moved every five years. If people had to change their phone number as part of that move, and we assume an average lag of 12 months between a directory's data collection, up to 20 percent of the population could not be reached by this method. Online directories could mitigate this problem because they can be continually updated.

Random Digit Dialing. With telephone directories in decline, random digit dialing becomes the most appropriate approach. In the random digit dialing (RDD) method for telephone interviewing, all live exchange numbers (the area code plus the first three-digit section of seven-digit telephone numbers) are input into the computer. The computer randomly selects the last four digits, thus providing a completely randomized sample. While RDD is an excellent method from a statistical point of view, it is wasteful. It does not eliminate business numbers and numbers used on other types of devices.

There is also the additional problem that this method can include unassigned numbers. Suppose 923 is a live exchange currently in operation, but a few numbers starting with 923 have not been assigned yet. The computer has no way of knowing how many, or even whether any, numbers are actually assigned. Therefore, RDD will consist of numbers that are not assigned to anyone yet. In fact, a very high proportion of numbers selected by the RDD procedure tends to be wasted. While this does not affect the integrity of the sample, it does add to the cost of the study considerably.

Besides, phone numbers are becoming less associated with geography and more associated with individuals, making exchange numbers less useful in selecting people in specific regions. Many procedures are available to reduce such wastage, but RDD continues to be the most wasteful, although theoretically the best, method of selecting telephone samples.

Seed Samples/Plus n Dialing Method. This is a compromise between the theoretically less defensible directory sampling and the potentially wasteful RDD sampling procedures. In seed sampling procedures, we make up a set of telephone numbers that are known to exist (they can come from the telephone directory). Then, instead of using the numbers chosen, we add a number (e.g., 100). For example, if our seed number is 555-1483, we add 100 to this number, and it becomes 555-1583, which is the number we dial. This procedure has several advantages:

- We get potential access to unlisted numbers and numbers for mobile devices.

- It might be a number that was not in existence when the database was updated and thus could include people who have recently moved.

- Because we are merely adding a number to existing numbers, we are not likely to find too many unassigned numbers. For example, if exchange 555 has assigned only 1000 numbers, adding 100 to the number selected within this range is likely to pick up newly assigned numbers. If only the first 1000 numbers are assigned in this exchange, the "Plus n" method will not generate numbers in the 2000 to 9000 series.

While the "Plus n" method is not theoretically the same as RDD, it is very similar. Given the cost savings, "Plus n" should be seriously considered as an effective alternative to RDD.

Choosing a Respondent Within a Household. For the latter half of the 20th century, a telephone belonged to the household. Since the household was the smallest sampling unit that we could identify, rather than interviewing whoever answered the phone, it was necessary to select a member within the household to be interviewed randomly. When we used in-home sampling, we also had the task of selecting a member of the household to be interviewed.

There are many methods of doing this. In the grid method, we list all members of the household, and on a predetermined random basis, choose one. Since the grid method asks questions about members of the household before the interview starts (the respondent could be suspicious of the researcher's motives for asking questions), the last birthday method might be used instead. In the last birthday method, the interviewer simply asks to speak to the person in the household who had his or her birthday most recently.

Since the turn of the century, the growing use of cellphones has meant that the telephone number has increasingly become an individual contact point rather than a household contact; everyone has their own phone. This reduces the need to select someone to be interviewed other than whoever answers the phone.

Non-probability Sampling Methods

A large number of marketing research surveys use non-probability sampling procedures, mainly for cost and timing reasons. Furthermore, in some diagnostic regions of research—such as the acceptability of a proposed product's taste or the offensiveness of a new commercial—it may not be critical to have probability samples. The reasoning is that there is some cultural homogeneity in what is considered offensive or what tastes bad; if something is offensive to many people, it is likely to be offensive to a large number of people even though we cannot precisely know for how many or to whom. We don't necessarily care about the exact percentage of people who find it offensive, but rather that a large proportion find it offensive or distasteful. Some non-probability samples are described in the chart below.

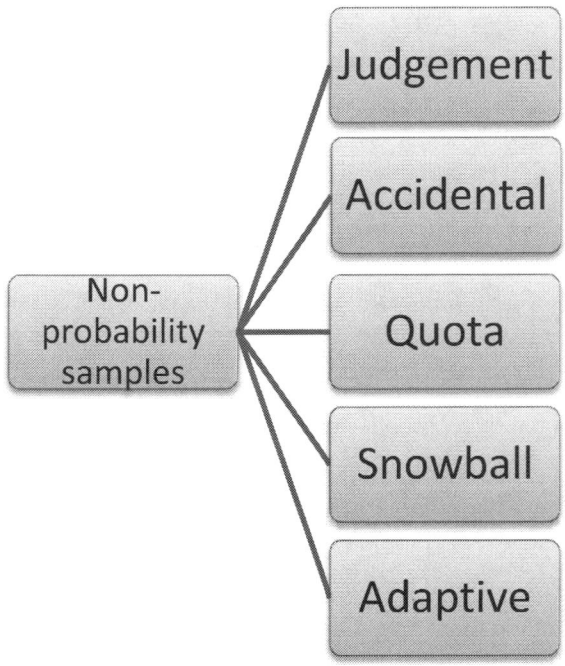

Purposive (Judgment) Sample

A purposive sample is a relatively common way of selecting people to be interviewed. In purposive samples, the choice of a respondent depends on the researcher's judgment of who is and who is not a typical representative of the population. Sometimes, people are selected because of their reputations, or because they are publicly visible or because they hold a specific position in an organization. For instance, if we want to interview 300 "influential community members," we may define "influential community members" to include judges, academics, religious leaders, artists, business leaders and political figures. A sample drawn based on this definition will be a purposive sample because the definition is based on the researcher's interpretation.

Another example of judgment sampling is the test market. Historically, when a company wanted to introduce a new product, it first introduced the product in one or two small markets to determine whether it had a chance of succeeding if it were to launch nationally. The markets were chosen on the basis of their ability to reflect the reaction of the country as a whole. In Canada, London, Peterborough, Jonquiere and Victoria were often chosen as test markets because they were relatively isolated from major markets (and inquisitive competitive eyes) and had their own media outlets for targeted advertising. All the marketer can say is that, in his or her judgment, these markets resemble Canada as a whole.

Test markets have largely fallen by the wayside, especially in North America, to be replaced by simulated test markets, but this judgmental thinking is behind sampling decisions for in-home product testing or taste-testing – carried out in a few selected markets for practical reasons, but the markets chosen because they are judged to be representative.

Purposive samples can result in invaluable information. While our judgments of the representativeness of the sample may be valid, no formal claims can be made of their accuracy. Respondents are chosen because of their perceived representativeness, which may or may not coincide with their actual representativeness.

Accidental (Haphazard or Convenience) Sample

The accidental sample is the weakest type, but it is the easiest to achieve. In accidental samples, we interview people who are easy to find; "people-on-the-street" interviews are typical of accidental samples. For instance, the researcher simply asks the first five people who pass by them if they would be willing to talk. A TV reporter stopping people on the street to get their reactions to the latest event is an example of accidental sampling.

There are enormous chances for bias in accidental sampling. For example, suppose you were doing a survey of community recreational needs, and you decided to interview 100 households. If your interviewers went to selected addresses and talked to whoever answered the door, the sample would be accidental. Children, mothers, cleaning staff and babysitters could have answered the door and been interviewed. It is even possible that the majority of respondents would have been children or teenagers (neither represents the whole of the community).

Another example of an accidental sample is to interview passersby in front of a stock exchange to assess people's reactions to a government social program. The views of people who happen to be in the financial district may not represent the views of the community at large. Internet surveys that are left open to anyone who stumbles across them and answers them, or that are featured as 'polls' on media websites, also fall under this category. Accidental sampling produces results that can easily be manipulated and can lead to errors in drawing conclusions and making decisions. Statistical inferences about population characteristics should not be based on accidental samples.

Quota Sampling

Quota sampling is the most common form of sampling these days, used extensively in online research to ensure the sample mirrors the population as closely as possible. Its great advantage is that it makes good use of limited resources.

On a small scale, you may decide that your research budget will allow interviews with a sample of only 60 people. Let's say you are interested in the views of a group of recent immigrants about recreation opportunities in their neighbourhoods, and you are also interested in the views of specific subgroups. Even though you cannot afford to do a stratified random sample of the size required to make precise generalizations, you can construct a sample of 60 people in which you specify how many persons of different characteristics should be included.

On a larger scale, you may need a sample of 500 Canadian seniors to get their reactions to changes in government pension programs. If you are drawing a sample from an online access panel, you would set quotas for men and women in their late 60s, 70s and 80s, and allocate a share of interviews to each of the country's five regions. The quotas would be set to reflect the actual population share of each group based on census data.

Quota sampling is not without its difficulties, particularly when incentives are involved. Sometimes, it can be difficult to fill each quota even when the quotas seem to be reasonable. Consider the following example. For a project requiring 100 completed questionnaires, we have tallied the demographics from 90 completed questionnaires received so far, as shown in the table below.

According to our quota requirements, we still need questionnaires from ten people aged 18 to 34 whose income is $100,000 or more and who have a 2-year college degree or less. Of course, people with these demographics exist, but they are exceedingly rare. That leaves us with two alternatives. First, we could continue to allow people to complete the questionnaire until ten more young people, and ten more high-income people, and ten more lower education people complete the questionnaire. Unfortunately, the incentive budget would have to be increased to allow for these extra interviews. Since budgets are rarely unlimited, this is often not possible. The second alternative is that hundreds of people might have to be screened before ten people with those specific demographics are found. Unfortunately, this entails disappointing hundreds of people by screening them out and not giving them an incentive. Screening also carries interviewing costs.

Demographics		Quota	Obtained
Gender	Male	50	45
	Female	50	45
Age	18 to 34	40	30
	35 to 54	40	40
	65 plus	20	20
Income	Under $25 000	20	20
	$25 000 to $44 999	20	20
	$45 000 to $99 999	30	30
	$100 000 plus	30	20
Education	Less than 2 years college	45	35
	Bachelor's degree	45	45
	Graduate degree	10	10

Snowball Sampling

Sometimes the researcher is faced with the problem of sampling respondents from a population that is rare or small. A pharmaceutical firm may be interested in contacting those who have an ailment that afflicts less than 0.01 percent of the population. It would be extremely costly and time consuming to find a sample of even 100 people who have the ailment. To reduce the cost and effort involved in finding such a rare population, the researcher might work very hard to contact a few people initially, say 10, who have the ailment and ask them if they know anyone else who also has it. The assumption—likely to be valid in general—is that a person who has a rare ailment has a good chance of knowing other people who also have it. There are many instances where snowball sampling is the only way to sample rare populations. For example, snowball sampling might be appropriate to find a sample of people who are gay in a country where being gay is punishable by imprisonment.

Adaptive Sampling

Adaptive sampling is based on the premise that people who have certain characteristics tend to be found in clusters. For instance, if we want to interview owners of expensive cars, we might first choose several areas in the city at random. When we find a respondent who owns an expensive car, we include the adjoining household in our sample. If the adjoining respondent also owns an expensive car, we again include the next adjoining household in our sample. This is known as adaptive sampling.

Online Sampling

In most of the developed world, most surveys these days are carried out online. Globally, online research accounts for 26 percent of all quantitative studies (ESOMAR 2019); its popularity can be attributed to its cost-effectiveness, efficiency and speed.

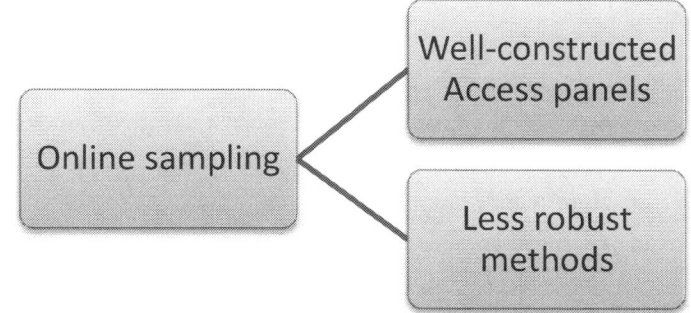

Although online samples are non-probability samples, a properly drawn sample from a well-constructed custom access panel (see below) can potentially resemble the results obtained from a probability sample. Many election polls carried out using online access panels predict the actual results as closely as a probability sample. So, most survey users give the same weight to a good custom research panel sample as they do to a probability sample.

Not all online samples are non-probability samples. When an online sample is drawn from a complete list – such as student lists in a university, client lists of a company and the like – a probability sample can be drawn from that list. In such cases, all principles we discussed under probability samples will apply. In this section, we focus our attention on online samples based on panels that do not include everyone in the universe.

Access Panels

What is an Online Access Panel? An online panel or Internet access panel is a group of pre-screened respondents who have expressed a willingness to participate in surveys. Typically, a panelist would agree to complete a certain number of surveys during the year. In return, panelists are given an incentive whenever they participate in a survey.

Respondents become "panelists" by completing a profiling questionnaire and agreeing with panel requirements. The profiling would include demographics, media habits, and other information about respondents. Because this information will be a part of the respondent's profile, in future surveys, these questions need not be asked again. This also helps the researcher to choose respondents with specific profiles, such as "unmarried females between the ages of 25 to 35, residing in a rural area, and having an income above $50,000."

Because access panels are expensive to build and difficult to maintain, most research houses do not have their own panel. They buy samples from panels maintained by a few vendors who maintain such panels. Access panels vary in size and quality. Some panels have just a few thousand respondents, while a large access panel can have over a million respondents. Some of these panels are deliberately constructed by contacting randomly chosen respondents and inviting them to join the panel. In contrast, some are constructed less systematically by contacting visitors to a website or people who participate in a contest etc. So, in buying a sample from an access panel, one should be careful to investigate the quality of the panel.

Most panel vendors go through thousands of different websites to recruit panelists. They may use apps, ads, online communities and other means to attract the attention of potential recruits. Vendors may also provide incentives to the current panelists to bring in additional recruits.

Specialist Panels. These are panels aimed at a specific group as opposed to the general population. For example, there might be panels whose members are only doctors or senior executives of different companies. In general, specialist or B2B samples are more expensive, and, in some cases (such as doctors), you may have to pay substantial compensation to each participant.

Custom Panels. Some client organizations are interested in having their own custom panels that only they can access. In this case, a supplier will recruit according to the company's exact requirements. For example, a running shoe manufacturer may want a custom panel of competitive runners; an airline may want a custom panel of frequent business travellers; a pharmaceutical company may want a custom panel of frequent migraine sufferers. The supplier can set the client up to script and run their own surveys with their panelists or may provide this service for them.

Why are online samples (from panels) considered non-probability samples?
- Even in technologically advanced countries like Canada, about 4 percent to 5 percent of the population does not have internet access. That number is about 15 percent in the U.S. In countries like Brazil and China the proportion is much higher. Therefore, not everyone has an equal opportunity to be on an online panel. (In comparison, telephone penetration in North America, at 97 percent, is near-universal.)
- There is no master email list from which an online sample can be drawn. While some providers attempt to create a panel by randomly dialing telephone numbers, they eventually all resort to multiple methods to recruit panelists.

How to buy from a customer access panel? Buying samples from an access panel is relatively straightforward. All you need to do is specify the type of respondents you want and the number of completed interviews you would like. For example, you may want your sample to resemble the demographic profile of all residents in your country. Or you may want to interview 600 adult males residing in cities with a population of 500,000 or more. Whatever your specification, you can buy a sample accordingly.

What is a sampling matrix? A sampling matrix is an outline of the demographic characteristics sought in a specific research study. For example, let's say your target population is all adults in the country. You would first need to discover the demographic characteristics of the country, likely using government sources such as census data, and then seek to replicate those characteristics within your sample.

A typical way to do this is by creating what is called a sampling matrix. At a minimum, sampling matrices outline the percentages of a sample that need to be represented by age, gender and region groups. Panels that collect a wide range of pre-screening data and which are sufficiently large to permit such subtle distinctions may also outline percentages for language, household size, race and ethnic origin.

		Male	Female
		50%	50%
Age	18 to 24	30%	30%
	25 to 44	30%	30%
	45 to 64	30%	30%
	65 plus	10%	10%
		100%	100%
Region	Ontario	30%	30%
	Quebec	30%	30%
	West	30%	30%
	East	10%	10%
		100%	100%

The panel company would input this desired sampling matrix into their automated sampling system, and this system would subsequently identify a sample of potential respondents who match the desired criteria. (Many traditional panel companies include this matrix in a publication called the panel book that they present to potential or existing clients.) This sampling matrix would also be perfectly suited to be used as a weighting strategy should the demographics of *completed* questionnaires not precisely match this matrix. This could happen if the response rate for one quota group turns out to be very different from that of another quota group.

Sometimes, a panel may not have sufficient panelists who meet a client's targeting criteria to complete a project – for example, if the incidence of the target group is low, or the number of completed interviews is very high. In such cases, the panel company may choose to collaborate with a second, or even a third, panel company to generate a large enough sample. In this case, the original panel company must perform additional analytical procedures to attempt to avoid generating duplicate completes from people who may be members of more than one panel.

Another reason that a panel may have difficulty finding enough potential panelists to fill out a sampling matrix relates to panel rules. For instance, if the panel has a rule that panelists can only be invited to participate in a maximum of ten questionnaires per week, and all the 18 to 24-year-old men on their panel have already received ten invitations, there may be no available men in this quota group. The alternatives include waiting until the panel rule expires (i.e., seven days have passed), recruiting more 18 to 24-year-old men to join the panel, or collaborating with another panel. All of these options have the potential to delay a project.

Online Targeting. Respondents are generally selected for a survey based on characteristics that they report themselves. This includes profile questionnaires administered by the sample company and real-time targeting questions that are shown to participants before the start of the study. In addition to what is provided by the respondents, other information can also come from cookies used to track online behaviour, and geolocation information such as retail establishments visited identified through mobile devices. It is important in these scenarios to understand what information is going to be used for targeting and when it was collected.

Survey Routing. When several surveys are happening simultaneously, panelists who are willing to do the survey at that time should be matched to the most appropriate survey in the most efficient manner possible. The term "router" refers to the technology that matches the two. Different routers work differently, but they all have a built-in random component to optimize the opportunity of every willing respondent to participate in a survey at that moment. Sometimes when there are too many surveys competing for the same audience, the router algorithm can introduce bias. For example, a large survey that requires French-speaking men aged 19 to 24 years may take up all of that sample, leaving a blank space for this age group in other surveys that don't have a specific quota for this group.

Online Mobile Sampling. Online surveys are not usually dependent on devices. Any device – laptops, desktop computers, tablets, and smartphones – can be used to complete the questionnaire. However, there may be instances where smartphones may be unsuitable. For example, we may need the respondent to see the visuals for two different products side-by-side, and a smartphone screen may be too small for this purpose. However, if this is known beforehand, it can be so arranged that those who are known to complete surveys only on smartphones are excluded from this study.

The Main Advantages of Access Panels. The main advantage of sampling with an access panel is that panelists have agreed in principle to participate in future surveys. This does not mean that they *will* complete every questionnaire that is made available to them, but the completion rates will be higher than merely emailing anyone who has an email address. Indeed, because of the depth and breadth of information in the panel database, it is possible to know the approximate completion rate a questionnaire will generate even before the questionnaire is launched.

A second significant advantage of online access panels is that very detailed demographic and psychographic information is available for every person. This allows the panel company to determine whether they can meet client demand for a specific survey, and subsequently to target particular people depending on their prescreened demographics.

The third advantage is, if we don't have enough respondents of a particular type in the panel, we would know it before we field the survey. For example, if you are looking for 500 people belonging to a certain ethnic group and if the panel has only 200 of them, even if all of them respond (a highly unlikely scenario), you still won't have enough respondents. Knowing this in advance can save a lot of time and money.

The Main Disadvantages of Access Panels. The main disadvantage of sampling from online access panels is that most of them are non-probability, self-selected, accidental samples. Their large size of often hundreds of thousands of panelists or more, makes it seem as though random sampling from the population is taking place, but the panelists did self-select to be members. It is impossible to apply a margin of error to these data when generalizing beyond the panel is desired.

Sometimes, researchers are concerned that the volunteer status of panelists means they do not represent the *online* population or that panelists have 'learned' how to take surveys such that their responses are no longer generalizable to people who aren't panelists.

Another disadvantage is what is known as **prior survey exposure**. This can happen if panelists are allowed to take different surveys in quick succession. Consider a panelist who answers questions about a less well-known brand of refrigerators. If she receives the following day a different questionnaire asking her the brands of refrigerators she's aware of, the lesser-known brand is more likely to be recalled than if the panelist had not answered the survey the previous day. Even if the same panel company does not send two questionnaires in succession, there is nothing that prevents panelists from enrolling in several panels, thus doing more than one survey at the same time.

Less Robust Online Samples

Although even well-constructed access panel samples are non-probability samples, because of their increasing ability to approximate probability samples in marketing research contexts, we would like to differentiate good access panels' samples from other weaker online samples that are of unknown quality (closely resembling the sample types we discussed under the heading "Non-probability samples.")

Online River Sampling. River sampling is a form of accidental sampling that involves inviting people as they browse the internet to participate in research. For instance, while perusing an online shopping website or viewing friends' pictures on a social network, a pop-up may be shown asking the person if they'd like to answer a questionnaire. A river sampling company may have partnered with as few as one or as many as thousands of websites to provide their sampling services. Of course, a broader range of people can be targeted if many websites are used.

Because river sampling does not involve pre-screening of demographic information, there is often no way for the website to target people who have specific demographics with the survey invitation. It is possible that a research study for mortgages could be presented to teenagers or that a study about learning to drive could be presented to senior citizens. Typically, people with inappropriate demographics would be screened out early in the research process, but this is still an annoyance to people who have volunteered their time only to be rejected. Further, river sampling can result in a very biased sample because only people visiting the websites that are partners in the research program can be asked to participate in research. Quota sampling is typically applied to river samples.

Domain Sampling. Domain sampling is another form of accidental sampling that involves selecting internet users to participate in research based on the internet domain they are visiting. One version of this method involves identifying people who have incorrectly typed a web address and then redirecting them to a research website. Because typing errors are not random, this sampling method is not random and does not create a probability sample. For instance, people who pay close attention to detail may never make typographical errors when entering a web address and, therefore, may never end up being redirected. Other people who prefer to use generic web searches instead of typing addresses into the browser also might never be invited to such surveys.

However, domain sampling may have more promise than some other online sampling methods. As with river sampling, the demographic characteristics of people who are invited to participate in research are unknown. These questions must then be asked as part of the research, which can lengthen the research process and annoy people when the target group does not include them. Quota sampling is also typically applied to domain samples.

Mixed Access and Mixed Mode Sampling

While most research studies are carried out using one of the above methods, sometimes we may need to use more than one way to reach the respondents. It is not always possible to reach all the respondents we want to reach through a single-mode. For example, some people in our target population may be reachable only by telephone and others only by e-mail. Or they may have a definite preference for one over the other. These considerations become critical when we research a particularly small target audience.

Ideally, we would aim for a sample frame that would include everyone in our target population, with a way to contact them – street address, e-mail, telephone, social media etc., and their preferred mode of contact. More often, samples are developed from completely different frames such as mailing lists, e-mail lists etc., and each list requires a different mode of contact.

Mixed modes of contact can help us in two ways: one, they help us to increase response rates for our study and two, they help us to increase the number of participants, especially if it is a hard to reach target group.

> Example 1: Mixed Access to Increase Response Rates
>
> We first send out a letter announcing a forthcoming study. Then we mail a postcard with their user ID along with the URL link. Next, we call them over the telephone to remind them about the study. Thus, in the same study, we are using different access points using different modes.
>
> Example 2: Mixed Mode to Reach a Wider Audience
>
> We may want to carry out an online study. However, because many in our target audience are only infrequently online, we may first call them or contact them by some other means to alert them about the online survey. Even though we use only one mode of data collection, we use more than one mode to reach potential participants.

Both approaches will increase the costs with no guarantee that it will significantly increase respondent participation. A third strategy is to apply different modes to different respondents. When we use this strategy, for example, we let those we reach via the phone complete the survey over the phone and those we reach online to complete an online version of the survey. It is generally observed that interview modality will have some influence on responses. Given that one version is over the phone and the other online, one is with the interviewer and the other without, we should expect some differences that can be attributed to the interview mode. We need to be aware of this challenge, even though there is no definite solution to it.

A mixed mode strategy is generally used to save money. Online interviews are cheaper, and so they are preferred. But there may be instances where online interviews may not yield a sufficient number of target respondents to complete the interviews on time. It is in these instances that we use the multiple mode approach.

However, this approach may sometimes result in respondents appearing in both samples. If this is a risk, we should take steps to avoid reaching the same respondent twice or ensure that we catch repeated respondents in the screening questions.

Which Sampling Method to Use?

Given that there are so many sampling methods, which one should we use? As with all marketing research decisions, choosing a method will depend on time and cost constraints. However, there are some guidelines.

When there are no special requirements, the primary mode of the interview – online, telephone or personal – is most likely determined by the 'default mode.' For instance, if you are in North America or Europe, the chances are that your survey mode is online unless you have some specific reason to use some other mode. In many countries of the world, especially in Asia, the preferred mode is door-to-door interviews.

As a general rule, the more critical the study results are to you, the closer you want to get to probability sampling procedures. Any decision that requires a significant degree of investment, or where the cost of failure is high, would require results that provide a high degree of certainty.

For instance, if you want to estimate the potential demand for a new product that requires increased plant capacity to produce or if you need to set the price for your product based on what consumers are willing to pay for it in a competitive environment you will want to feel comfortable that sampling procedures will allow you to generalize the results to the population.

In practice, very little research uses strict probability sampling. The choice of the actual sampling method will depend on practical considerations.

With so much research conducted using **online panels** today, non-probability sampling may be the only feasible alternative. Using quotas, we can assemble a sample that resembles the demographics of the target population as closely as possible.

Taste tests are sometimes done in central locations like a mall so that the quality and temperature of the product can be controlled. In a mall survey, the best we can achieve is a quota sample with some possible random selection of shoppers. The assumption in such tests is that the taste judgments of people found in the mall are unlikely to be substantially different from those who do not usually visit a mall, or who visit different types of malls.

When probability sampling is practical, the method will depend on research design considerations. If you are doing national door-to-door interviewing, you would consider multistage sampling; if you are sampling an industrial company whose customers are similar to one another, you may do a simple random sample or a systematic random sample. If you are doing a survey among consumers who vary vastly in their purchase habits, you may want to consider a stratified sample.

Choosing a specific type of sample depends on:
- what's possible given the sampling source (quota sampling is the only option if using an online consumer panel);
- the importance of the sample for decision making (the more critical the study results are to us, the closer you want to get to probability sampling procedures);
- the questions being asked;
- constraints imposed by cost and timing;
- the suitability of the method to the problem at hand (e.g., multistage sampling for door-to-door interviewing, snowball sampling for finding members of rare populations, or seed sampling for telephone sampling).

5. Setting the Sample Size

We mentioned earlier that sample surveys could provide valid estimates of the "true values" of key indicators, i.e., the results we would have obtained if we were able to contact everyone in the relevant population.

Most of us would intuitively guess that a larger sample would give us more reliable estimates—a survey based on 2,000 interviews is likely to reflect the opinions of the target population more closely than a survey based on 200 interviews. This intuitive assessment is mostly correct. But there is more to choosing a sample size. To understand the effect of sample size on survey results, we must first understand what factors affect the accuracy of our estimates.

Estimates and Parameters

Suppose you are interested in knowing how many adults use your product. You conduct a study using a sample of 1,000 adults. Your results show that 33 percent of those surveyed use your product. This result (33 percent of users obtained through a sample survey) is called an estimate or statistic. What would the result be if you had collected this information by asking *every* adult rather than a sample of just 1,000? Intuitively, we feel that the results obtained by asking everyone in the population (called the parameter) are likely to be somewhat different from the sample estimate that we obtained. But how different are they? How close are our results to the true values or parameters? We try to estimate parameter values through sample estimates. The primary sampling questions are:

• How well does a sampling estimate represent the parameter values?

•What factors can distort the relationship between a sample estimate and the corresponding parameter values?

Sampling theory, which is based on statistical principles, provides answers to these questions.

Sample Representativeness

Sampling provides good estimates of parameter values if two conditions are met:
1. The sample is chosen using a set of procedures known as probability sampling.
2. The sample size is large enough. When a sample is chosen according to statistical principles, the closeness between sample estimates and parameter values is a function of the sample size.

What is a "large enough" sample? This will depend on how precise you want your results to be. In some cases, you may want more precise results (e.g., trying to predict the results of next week's election). Here a large error may result in an incorrect prediction. At other times, you may accept less precise results (e.g., trying to get a rough estimate of the proportion of adults who attend church every week) if the study is of less importance.

Factors that Affect Representativeness

Two factors, "non-sampling error" and "sampling error," directly affect how close our estimates are to the "true values" or parameters.

1. **Non-sampling Errors.** Non-sampling errors are errors in our estimates that are not the result of the sample size. Non-sampling errors will persist even if we use a large sample size and they bias our estimates. **Biases** are distortions that affect our estimates in a given direction, for instance, they overestimate a number, or they underestimate a number.

Uncontrolled or uncontrollable factors often enter a study and can create biases. A respondent's refusal to answer the questionnaire, language problems, respondent fatigue, a high level of non-response, incorrect data collection procedures, incorrect sample frame, misunderstanding of questions posed and poorly designed questionnaires are examples of factors that can create biases and distort survey results. Even incorrect data analysis and misleading reporting of findings are classed as non-sampling errors.

Biases, even when they are avoidable, are not always easy to spot. Unlike sampling errors, non-sampling errors can be eliminated in theory. In practice, eliminating bias is not an easy task, and you should assume that every research project contains at least some bias.

Non-sampling errors are non-statistical and cannot be easily measured. Neither can we reduce bias by merely increasing the sample size since bias will distort the results in a given direction regardless of the sample size.

For example, let's say you are trying to estimate how people would vote in the next election. If we assume that many immigrants tend to vote Liberal, and if a significant portion of new immigrants are not proficient in English or French and therefore not interviewed, then we would underestimate the proportion of voters who would vote Liberal. Increasing the sample size will not solve the problem because we will not necessarily bring more new immigrants into the sample. As a result, we would only consolidate the existing bias. Therefore, it is imperative to identify and, to the extent possible, eliminate bias, in this example, by consciously adding in a sub-sample of new immigrants.

Response Rates. When we attempt to contact potential respondents for our survey, several things may happen: the respondent may not be available, may refuse to participate, or may discontinue participating partway through the questionnaire (break-offs). Those who are not readily available or are not willing to participate may be different from those who are readily available and willing to participate. This can bias our results.

For example, suppose we want to find the average income of consumers who own homes that cost over two million dollars. If people with the highest income levels refuse to participate in the study, the results will underestimate the income levels of those who own expensive homes. This can bias our study since we do not know the incomes of those who refused to participate. We cannot even assume that those who refused necessarily have high incomes. It is also possible that those with low incomes refused to participate.

Those who are not readily available may have different characteristics than those who are easily available. Suppose a manufacturer is trying to estimate the demand for athletic goods. If the people who are likely to buy the products tend to spend more time outdoors using their athletic goods, they may not be interested in spending time completing online surveys or be available when the interviewer calls. And people who spend more of their time at home or online may be less likely to buy athletic goods. This will result in an under-estimation of the demand.

Given the importance of response rates, the researcher should try his or her best to keep the rates as high as possible. However, nowadays, high response rates are very difficult to achieve. There are several reasons for this.

When it comes to *telephone research*, many consumers fail to distinguish telemarketing calls (where the caller is attempting to sell them something) and fraud calls (where the caller is trying to steal personal information or money) from marketing research (where the interviewer is only collecting information).

A major problem here is "sugging" or selling under the guise of research, and "frugging" or fund-raising under the guise of research. Some telemarketing companies and charities (presumably only a minority) pretend that they are conducting research and then attempt to sell a product to the respondent or convince them to make a donation. Such practices make consumers suspicious of all research. Phone apps that let through only approved callers, call display and voicemail make it even easier for the respondent not to pick up the phone at all.

Further, many consumers avoid answering surveys because it is an inconvenient time, the questions are dull or irrelevant, the interview is too long, or there is nothing in it for them.

Online research also suffers from low response rates for several reasons. For instance, online research opportunities now have to compete with many other online activities that are far more enjoyable – online gaming, social media, and shopping. Also, research companies that rely on e-mailed invitations have to compete with inboxes filled with e-mails from friends and family, newsletters from a person's favourite retailer, and increasingly, a lot of unwanted spam e-mails.

Three Ways to Reduce/Account for Non-response. If we cannot achieve a high response rate, we should at least attempt to reduce the level of non-response. There are three primary ways this can be done:

- Callbacks/reminders
- Statistical adjustments
- Non-responder surveys

Call-backs are attempts to contact respondents who were not available when they were first called. Call-backs are standard in telephone marketing research. Most telephone surveys routinely carry out at least three call-backs at different days and times before giving up on a respondent. Government researchers may carry out up to ten call-backs, but this is not recommended for commercial researchers as potential responders may be deliberately not picking up the telephone. Chances are their phone will tell them you have called ten times, and they won't appreciate that.

Reminders are typically used for online or text surveys where the respondent initially received the questionnaire but did not yet complete it. Reminders are usually used a maximum of two times as respondents may choose to block emails and texts from researchers who are perceived to be annoying.

Statistical adjustments are made through a procedure called **weighting**. Suppose our final survey tally shows the sample is 70 percent women, while we know that they represent only 52 percent of the population. We statistically adjust the results so that they represent the equivalent of only 52 percent of the sample. Weighting does not compensate for poor response rates or unacceptably low sample sizes for a specific group of people. Instead, it reduces the impact of differential responses among subgroups, which is particularly critical when low response rates are not uniformly distributed among subgroups.

When the characteristics of the non-responders are not evident, and the results are important, we may carry out a **non-responder survey** –intensive attempts to survey people who have been difficult to access.

For instance, suppose we do a door-to-door survey and succeed in contacting only 30 percent of the intended respondents. We may then attempt to contact some of the non-responders by phone instead and collect information using that mode. We would then compare the information from the non-responders with the information in the original survey to assess how different non-responders are from responders. This is a fundamental attempt to validate the survey among responders. These non-responder surveys add substantial expense to studies and are not conducted very often.

Response rates in marketing research are low and getting lower. Is there any reason to believe that responders are likely to be different from non-responders, especially on critical variables in our survey? The answer to this question, while subjective, is the criterion applied to assess the soundness of the sample. This does not absolve the researcher from the responsibility of making sure that the highest possible rate of response has been achieved, given the constraints of cost and time. It is only after this that the researcher subjectively evaluates the risk of bias because no objective method is available to estimate it.

2. Sampling Errors. Sampling errors result from interviewing only a small portion of the population rather than everyone in the population. For instance, suppose we interview 1,000 adults in Montreal to estimate the proportion who read a weekly magazine. Our results show that 45 percent read a weekly magazine. What if we could collect information from every adult in Montreal? It is unlikely that the result of this census would also be exactly 45 percent, but how different would it be? Sampling error is an estimate of this difference.

We can intuitively guess—and confirm through statistical theory—that the larger the sample, the higher the precision of the estimate. This means that you can reduce the sampling error by merely increasing your sample size. (Remember that we cannot reduce non-sampling error bias by using a larger sample.) This is a significant difference between sampling and non-sampling errors.

Without repeating the study using random sampling, the sampling error can be mathematically estimated using statistical formulas. These formulas apply only if the sample is chosen using probability methods. A survey, for example, may show that 40 percent of the people favour the Liberal party, but the actual figure (if we measured everyone in the relevant population) could be somewhere between 35 percent and 45 percent (40 percent ± five percentage points). This is called the

confidence interval (margin of error or precision of the estimate), and it can be estimated using statistical formulas.

Every confidence interval has a **confidence level** attached to it. Thus, we can make statements such as "Results are accurate within ± five percentage points (p.p.), 90 percent of the time." Our confidence interval or margin of error is ± five p.p. and the confidence level is 90 percent. In other words, if the study were repeated, the resulting confidence interval would include the true population parameter within plus or minus five p.p. in 90 out of 100 times. We shall see how to calculate the margin of error in Unit 9.

If an actual census were achieved of all people in the relevant population, there would be no sampling error. But if bias was present, for example, a question was phrased to have a double meaning, the study might have a non-sampling error and might not be valid.

Reliability and Validity. Another way to look at survey errors is in terms of reliability and validity. **Validity** means that we are *properly* measuring whatever it is we are trying to measure. For instance, a watch may be a valid instrument for measuring time. But a ruler is not a valid instrument for measuring time, and neither is a barometer.

Reliability, on the other hand, means that we measure whatever it is that we measure *consistently*. A reliable measure might or might not be valid. A broken watch is reliable—it shows the same time whenever we look at it. But it is not a valid measure of time.

Applying these concepts to sampling and non-sampling errors, we can say that non-sampling errors affect the validity of the study because they distort the findings. Sampling errors, on the other hand, affect the reliability of the study. We know that the results are valid, but they can vary within a known range (i.e., be more or less consistent) depending on the sample size. That defined range of accuracy, the confidence interval, specifies what is meant as the reliability of a study. Surveys that use larger samples provide more reliable results compared to ones that use smaller samples.

In deciding how large a sample should be, researchers use two sets of criteria: non-statistical and statistical.

Non-statistical Criteria. Sample sizes are often decided based on non-statistical criteria.

Although "non-statistical" sounds unscientific, many of the *non-statistical criteria* used to decide sample size are, in fact, very important. For example:

- The *importance of the study for decision making*: A study upon which multimillion-dollar decisions are to be based warrants a larger sample size than one that is a general fact-finding study.

- *Convention*: the *range of sample size* generally used for such studies. Many shopping mall studies use a convenient sample size of 100, while a national, full-scale usage and attitude study is likely to use a sample size in the region of 1,000 to 2,000 respondents. These are robust round numbers that in themselves instill confidence. This can be compared to the typical reporting of national political polls where findings based on probability samples are stated to be accurate within ± four percentage points 19 times out of 20. That level of accuracy requires a sample size of 601 respondents.

- *Resources available* for the study: The actual sample size, to a large extent, depends on the resources available for the study. Though calculations may determine that a sample size of 600 is necessary, you may only be able to afford 400 and be forced to accept a lower level of accuracy.

- *How many subgroups* are to be studied and in what detail: If your conclusions must be valid for each subgroup (such as each region of the country) rather than for the population as a whole, then you would need a larger sample size.

Statistical Criterion. When we use the statistical criterion to estimate the required sample size, we are trying to achieve one thing only: to identify only the sample size necessary to providing the acceptable size of sampling error. Simply put, the larger the sample size, the smaller the sampling error.

Assuming that our sample is chosen using a simple random sampling, we can use a simple formula to calculate the required sample size. To understand the formula, we will need to understand the statistical theory behind it. This will be developed in Unit 9. Here we will simply describe the formula that will enable you to calculate the sample size.

In commercial marketing research, the statistical criterion is less routinely used than the criteria listed above. The main reason for this is cost. For instance, if you specify that your results should be within ± two percentage points at the 95 percent level of confidence, you would need a sample size of about 2,400. (Note that this formula assumes an incidence parameter. This will be introduced in Unit 9.) For most marketing research studies, that sample size may be unrealistically large. Consequently, even when the sample size is calculated using statistical formulas, in practice, they are often drastically reduced to accommodate budget constraints.

To choose the sample size according to statistical criteria, we need to specify three parameters: the acceptable margin of error, the likely variance and the degree of certainty or confidence required.

Let us assume that a marketer wants the results to have a margin of error of no more than four percentage points at the 95 percent level when estimating the percentage of people who say that they will buy a brand. What does this mean? It means that the results should fulfil two requirements:

1. *The results should not have a margin of error greater than ± four percentage points*. This means that if our survey results showed 30 percent of respondents using our product, the range between 26 percent and 34 percent (30 ± four percentage points) would include the true percentage in the population (the parameter) that used our product. The margin of error is also called the **confidence interval**.

2. *The above requirement will be met with 95 percent certainty*. This means that if we carried out a large number of surveys with the same sample size and made a similar statement concerning each survey result thus obtained, the margin of error, or confidence interval, would include the true percentage who would buy the brand in 95 percent of the surveys. This specification is known as the **confidence interval**. By convention, the most commonly used levels of confidence in marketing research are 90 percent (less rigorous) and 95 percent (more rigorous)

A Quick Short Cut Formula for Calculating Sample Size. There is a quick formula that closely approximates the sample size required for a given margin of error at the 95 percent level of confidence (95 percent is the most commonly used level of confidence).

$n = 2500 \div [\text{Acceptable margin of error} \div 2]^2$ (where n is the sample size)

Example 1. Suppose we want our results to have a maximum margin of error of 4 percentage points at the 95% level of confidence. (The 4 percentage points is what you or your client specifies as the maximum margin of error acceptable for this study.)

Acceptable margin of error = 4 percentage points

Insert the figures in the formula:

n = 2500 ÷ [4 ÷ 2]²

= 2500 ÷ 2²

= 625

In other words, if we are willing to accept a maximum margin of error of ± four percentage points, then we need a sample size of about 625. As mentioned earlier, the actual sample size needed is 601 if the complete formula was used instead of the short-cut formula above.

Example 2. Suppose we want our results to have a maximum margin of 2 percentage points at the 95% level of confidence.

Acceptable margin of error = 2 percentage points

Insert the figures in the formula:

n = 2500 ÷ [2 ÷ 2]²

= 2500 ÷ 1²

= 2500

In other words, if we are willing to accept a maximum margin of error of ± two percentage points, then we need a sample size of about 2500.

The above two examples illustrate an interesting relationship. For a four percentage point margin of error, we need a sample of 625, but for a two percentage point margin of error, we need a sample of 2500, four times as many. This relationship is consistent: *to halve the margin of error, you have to quadruple the sample size.*

[A note on the shortcut formula above (optional)]. You might wonder where the 2500 in the simplified formula comes from and why we divide the acceptable margin of error by two. The actual formula for calculating the sample size is

n = $z^2 \cdot [p \cdot (100-p)] / [e^2]$, where z is the confidence coefficient for a specified level of confidence, p is the actual proportion of the population that is thought to have the attribute and e is the desired margin of error.

The p-value refers to the percentage we expect obtain in the survey, such as the percentage of citizens who would support a candidate. But we face two challenges: First we don't know this percentage ahead of the survey and second, we may have many estimates within the survey that may require different sample sizes.

These problems are elegantly solved if we use p=0.50. When we do this, p*(1-p) is the largest value possible and so it assures that our sampling error is the most conservative estimate possible. In addition, we have no need to know what p we are likely to obtain from the actual survey.

Why we divide the acceptable margin of error by two: The most common confidence used in research is 95% and it has an associated confidence coefficient of 1.96 (see the unit *How to Analyze the Data*). A value of 2 is close enough to 1.96 and therefore we divide the acceptable margin of error by two in the short-cut formula.]

You might have noticed that all our formulas are based on expected percentages rather than on expected means. Formulas are available if you want to set your sample size based on an expected mean (e.g., mean income of those who live in Edmonton). However, to do this, you have to know the variance of the estimate before doing the study. One could, of course, get an idea by looking at a previous survey, but that would imply the whole study is designed to test just one single variable, in this case, income. This is a highly unrealistic situation in marketing research. Besides, there is no reasonable upper limit to variance as it relates to the mean. For these reasons, sample size estimates in marketing research are almost always done using the above formula.

Do we need a larger sample for a larger population? You might have noticed that in the above formula for setting the sample size, we did not consider the size of the population at all. Does that mean that to have a 4 percentage point margin of error, we need the same sample size in a small town with a population of 20,000 as we do in a large city with a population of 2,000,000? The two sample sizes are very close, 583 for the town and 601 for the big city. Similarly, a survey of 2,500 respondents in Canada will have virtually the same margin of error as a survey of 2,500 respondents carried out in the United States, even though the U.S. has a population that is ten times larger than Canada's population.

However, when the sample is significant in relation to the population (e.g., when the sample is about 10 percent of the population or higher), we can apply the **finite population correction (FPC)** to the sample size. This will result in a smaller sample size for the same margin of error.

Suppose an industrial company has 300 customers. We want to sample from this list and still have a four percentage point margin of error at the 95 percent level. We note that the sample calculated using the formula is 600. Since 600 is larger than the population size of 300, it is possible to sample fewer people and achieve the same accuracy. To do this, we use the FPC formula:

Finite population corrected sample size = n' = n ÷ [1 + (n ÷ N)] Where

n' = Sample size corrected for the small population size

n = Sample size set as per the original formula (in our example, 600)

N = Size of the population (in our example, 300)

Applying the formula to our example:

n' = 600 ÷ [1 + (600 ÷ 300)]

= 200

This means that we can use a sample of 200 instead of 600 to achieve a four percentage point margin of error because our sample is a substantial proportion of our universe.

As we said earlier, all these formulas (or their variations) apply only if the sample is chosen according to probability procedures. When a sample is chosen according to non-probability procedures, these calculations do not apply, and the margin of error is virtually unknown. In practice, it is common to find margins of error computed on samples that cannot be strictly considered as probability samples. You should know when it is and isn't appropriate to use the margin of error and only apply it in appropriate situations.

Is There an Ideal Sample Size? As we saw, the larger the sample size, the smaller the margin of error. We can make the margin of error as small as we like by simply increasing the sample size. However, *a properly selected sample of 300 respondents can be as valid as a similarly selected sample of 600 as long as both studies were conducted correctly*. The only difference between the two samples is that the estimates obtained from a larger sample will have a smaller margin of error or accuracy. In marketing, precise estimates are not always necessary.

For instance, you may be interested in knowing the proportion of your customers who also use a competing product. Here, your purpose may be to get an approximate idea of multiple usage occurrences. You may not need to know, for example, if multiple-use occurrence is 23 percent or 25 percent but whether it is very high (e.g., over 60 percent) or very low (e.g., less than 10 percent). In this instance, it will be a waste of resources to choose a sample size that would yield results with a margin of error of ± two percentage points.

We should not, of course, stretch the concept of validity to absurd limits. Although a randomly chosen sample of 30 people to represent in the entire country's population may be a technically "valid" sample, the margin of error at 95 percent level of confidence for a sample of 30 [± 18 percentage points] makes the results too inaccurate to be of any practical value.

We can summarize as follows: validity is essential in all studies, and given that a study is **valid it will be reliable.** The key question now is, how accurate do you want the results to be?

An ideal sample size is one that is accurate enough for your purposes and large enough to allow sub-group comparisons if they are important to your business or research question. If additional resources are available, they are better spent on improving the quality of sampling by controlling non-sampling errors and increasing the response rates. Increasing the sample size is not always the best way to use additional resources.

Concluding Comments

As survey research has moved from face-to-face to telephone to online interviewing, the principles of probability sampling have become increasingly difficult to apply to sample selection. It is still a work in progress, and, in the next few years, things may change. In any case, the principles of sampling described in this chapter provide a basis for understanding the logic of survey research. When you read Unit 9 on analyzing data, you will see the importance of sample selection even more clearly.

UNIT 5

How to Conduct Qualitative Research

Introduction

Qualitative research is focused on exploring, challenging and digging deeper into consumer understanding. It is an opportunity to push beyond marketers' current understanding and preconceptions and offers a consumer-centric perspective.

Qualitative study results may provide invaluable insights into consumer beliefs and behaviour, but they cannot be projected numerically onto the broader population. The end-product of qualitative research is the researcher's reasoned interpretation of the oral statements of several people. It is inappropriate to state the findings in any form of measurement language (for example, 80% of participants said …).

The aims of qualitative research are to:
- obtain insights rather than draw precise conclusions;
- generate hypotheses that can eventually be quantified further through quantitative research;
- develop an understanding of the breadth of opinions;
- identify new or confirm existing perspectives and motivations;
- capture consumer language;
- provide colour commentary on quantitative results;
- allow in-depth probing after a survey to help explain the findings.

Qualitative research is particularly useful when dealing with sensitive topics, when consumer motivations are complex, when decisions are made more on an emotional level than rational, and when consumers themselves are not aware of their motivations.

In those situations, asking a direct, quantitative question like "what do you like about this coffee?" might result in a superficial answer: "I like the taste." But what does this mean? They like the strong taste, the mild taste, the taste that lingers, the bitterness, the flavour, how it compares to competing brands? This degree of probing is generally not possible in quantitative surveys, particularly given the need for increasingly shorter surveys. (That said, Artificial Intelligence Chatbots are emerging that can tailor an automated probe to a response in an open-ended question.)

Qualitative can serve as a source of insights and direction for decision-makers, not just as a precursor to an obligatory survey.

> Example 1. Finance Corp. is interested in launching a new 'reverse mortgage' service that will allow older consumers to use the equity in their homes to improve cash flow. It is the company's first offering in this area, and management is aware that emotions can run high when the family home is slowly turned over to a bank. They want to understand if consumers actually understand the idea, what they think about it, and how reactions to different approaches might vary across different socioeconomic levels. They also want to identify any potential risks to the company's reputation if this service is launched. Because so much is unknown, the insight department is recommending a qualitative approach.

> Example 2. Costa Coffee Company believes that it has a superior tasting product, but it's not entirely sure what 'taste' means to consumers. It makes sense to the marketing team to explore the meaning and emotional impact of taste among coffee consumers so that they can fine-tune its communications and speak directly to consumer needs. The marketing team will need some qualitative work to hear a variety of consumers talk about what taste means to them.

> Example 3. The Ministry of Citizenship has conducted an extensive public opinion survey and uncovered a degree of discomfort with current refugee policies. The numbers indicate that an identifiable demographic group is interested in seeing a significant reduction in the number of refugees

that the country accepts per year. The Minister would like to know more about the motivations and concerns of this demographic group and has asked her department to organize some qualitative work to probe beneath the surface for possible explanations.

Qualitative Research Techniques

There is a wide range of qualitative techniques available to marketing research professionals. Each has its strengths and weaknesses.

The most widely used qualitative methodologies have been in-person focus groups or In-depth Interviews (IDIs). Many of these techniques now have digital or online equivalents.

Here is a shortlist of qualitative techniques that are commonly used.

In-person Techniques
Traditional Focus Groups
In-Depth Interviews (IDIs) (Live or via video links)
Ethnography/Observation
Mystery Shopping

Online Techniques
Virtual or online Focus groups
Online Ethnography
Bulletin Boards
Online Communities

Secondary Qualitative
Semiotics

The Qualitative 'Team'

While qualitative research may be seen as a 'one-person show,' the researcher/moderator is actually backed up by several collaborators. The whole team can consist of:

- the **moderator** who designs, leads, analyzes and reports on the findings
- the **recruiter** who recruits consumers to participate in the research, often from databases that they maintain, but also through referrals, cold calls and other techniques
- the **facility** such as focus group rooms, intercept locations, sometimes the consumers' own homes
- **hosting** companies or organizations that provide software for online qualitative techniques and host online 'events'
- **simultaneous translators, note-takers, and transcript typists** who participate in the real or virtual backroom to capture participants comments
- the **client** who can observe the proceedings from a real or virtual backroom and provide the moderator with on-the-spot direction and feedback

The skills and techniques are very different from those in quantitative research, and few researchers do both. Moderators must be multi-talented: curious, confident, gregarious, quick-thinking, well-spoken, analytical and diplomatic.

While many full-service marketing research firms offer many or all of these services in-house, this is one branch of the field where the independent researchers/moderators can operate comfortably.

1. Traditional Focus Groups

Focus groups have traditionally been the most frequently used form of qualitative research. The approach involves an extended discussion (usually 1.5 to 2 hours) between a moderator and a group of participants (typically eight to ten).

The discussion follows a carefully constructed plan focused on getting the insights required by the marketing decision-makers. It may start with a free-ranging review of current behaviours, then narrow to deep dives into motivations and emotional reactions. Debate and disagreement are encouraged to ensure a range of perspectives is heard.

The moderator's role is to focus the discussion and move it along, encouraging quieter respondents to participate, challenging easy answers and encouraging participants to reveal more than they normally would in simple conversations. The moderator performs a balancing act: ensuring that the client's issues are addressed while allowing the conversation to flow naturally so that unanticipated but valuable discussion can occur.

The influence of focus groups has been more pervasive than most people realize. For example, political parties regularly conduct focus groups to find out how people would react to a particular issue or how to word an unpalatable message so that it is more acceptable to voters. Hollywood producers use focus groups to help assess which of two possible endings for a movie would appeal more to moviegoers. Food and beverage manufacturers use focus groups to identify emotional motivations that they can use to fine-tune their messaging.

Given the visible and invisible roles focus groups play in our lives, it is important to understand how they work.

In most cases, 8 to 10 consumers are recruited to a central location. These participants are selected to participate because they represent a particular demographic, psychographic, or behavioural group. Once assembled, the moderator will introduce the topic and lead a discussion, loosely following a discussion guide, and will record and interpret the discussion. At the end of the project, a report is issued to the client, a formal presentation takes place, and, in many instances, guidance is given in designing a questionnaire for a quantitative phase of research.

Selecting the moderator: As with most research projects, clients can invite proposals from several qualified moderators. However, qualitative research often requires a lot of interaction between the client and the moderator. Clients generally attend the groups to observe from behind a one-way mirror. As a result, many clients have developed close relationships with moderators whose style they are comfortable with. Because of the degree of trust that develops, it is not unusual for qualitative projects to be 'sole-sourced.'

Briefing the moderator: Because it is difficult to determine in advance the direction that group discussions may actually take, a moderator must have a thorough understanding of the client's needs, the marketing environment, the display materials and other stimuli and any particular exercises that will be used. This allows him or her to make ad hoc adaptations intelligently and to sense when an unexpected comment should be probed, or tangents followed. The poorly briefed moderator will be ill-equipped to adapt. Naturally, the more familiar the moderator is with the category, the less he or she will need a more general briefing.

When the moderator is being briefed, clients should avoid revealing what results they are hoping to get. This may put pressure on the moderator's essential role of impartiality and may bias her. The briefing should be used to test the relevance of the topics the client wants to discuss against the objectives. A good moderator will challenge the client to exclude marginally relevant topics and 'nice to know' questions. A group discussion is usually limited to two hours due to scheduling needs, respondent fatigue and patience. Marginal topics reduce the amount of time available for discussing important ones.

How to Set Up a Focus Group

Defining the Objectives: The objectives of a focus group project must be clearly defined upfront. Because topics can be added or deleted right up until the group discussion starts, sometimes even in the middle of a focus group, it might be tempting to neglect the primary objectives of the study. This can be unwise because if the objectives are unclear, even the best moderator cannot direct the discussion effectively.

For instance, a focus group to assess the corporate image of a company could have a discussion guide with content that is very similar to one designed to assess the competitive structure of the market. However, the specific objectives of the two different focus groups will dictate the order in which topics are discussed and the amount of emphasis placed on each topic. Because the time is limited in focus groups (generally 1 ½ to 2 hours), we have to be careful not to introduce too many topics.

If the topic to be discussed is very technical, if participants are likely to have a lot to say and if the moderator has to push hard to get respondents into deeper emotional spaces, the number of participants should be reduced to 3 to 5 (a mini-group), so each participant has more time to talk.

The objectives will also help determine how many groups are required. Is the objective to understand how opinions might differ between markets? Then you will need to ensure there are groups in each market. If the target audience is relatively narrow, you may be able to minimize the number of groups. If the target is broad – for example, men and women across a wide range of age groups, then you will need more groups. If the objective is to contrast the opinions of users versus non-users of a product or service, then you will have to add corresponding groups.

How are Participants Recruited

The process of recruiting participants starts with the recruitment guide, prepared in collaboration by the moderator and the client. The recruitment guide clearly spells out how many groups and the composition of each group, with specific questions used to identify the right individuals and invite them to participate.

For example, a recruitment guide might start by specifying:

- Total of 9 groups: 3 in city A, 3 in city B, 3 in city C (For each group, recruiting 10 participants so a minimum of 8 might show.)
- All must be adults who make the coffee brand buying decisions for their homes and drink hot coffee at home at least four times per week.
- In each city, 1 group with "value brand instant" buyers, 1 group with those who buy and drink premium instant coffee, and 1 group with those who buy and drink percolated or press coffee.

This example covers multiple markets and different brand users while keeping them separate. Alternatively, the recruitment guide might choose to mix users of different products to see how they interact and try to convince each other of the merits of their product. On more sensitive topics involving "social identity," it might be more critical to divide men and women into separate groups or to divide participants by age to ensure everyone feels comfortable in the group.

With the groups defined clearly, the guide then focuses on finding the right people to participate.

Who to include? Criteria for respondent selection are usually specified by the client, working in collaboration with the moderator, and then passed on to professional recruiters who specialize in assembling participants for qualitative studies.

Example 1

Possible criteria for focus groups for a manufacturer of an expensive perfume aimed at young women could include women between the ages of 25 and 39 who have a household income of at least $75,000 and who are receptive to the idea of using perfume.

Example 2

An auto manufacturer interested in reactions to potential design improvements might need to recruit male owners of high-end cars (e.g,. over $75,000 new purchase price) who are likely to be looking for a new vehicle in the next six months.

While determined recruiters can usually find respondents who fulfil almost any set of criteria, complex recruitment criteria should be avoided whenever possible because they prolong recruitment time, increase cost, and may result in erroneous respondent selection. It is essential to carefully consider and challenge *each* criterion and restriction to make sure it is important and relevant for the study.

The broader the defined universe that is the source of recruitment, the more successful the recruitment process is likely to be. Recruitment procedures can take a week or two or several weeks if the criteria are complicated. This should be taken into account when deciding on the lead time required for focus groups.

All participants should pass a test to ensure they are capable of independent thinking and can express their thoughts clearly and in the language of the group.

How to Conduct Qualitative Research

Who to avoid? Qualitative research is not bound by the same rigorous sampling rules that govern quantitative surveys. Respondents are not expected to be as statistically representative of the population as they would be for a quantitative survey.

However, this doesn't mean that participants are recruited haphazardly. Recruitment procedures must be designed to control the introduction of unintended recruitment-related bias.

Proper recruitment processes follow several guidelines.

- **Strangers**: Participants in any group should be strangers to the moderator and to each other. Friends tend to act as a social unit, which can inhibit broader group interaction. Within reason, people who know each other may take part in back-to-back groups on the same day but not on different days in case the first participant briefs the second. There are exceptions, of course. Bring-a-friend groups are found to work for specific "chatty" issues such as cosmetics where friends may regularly communicate and share ideas as part of their everyday lives. Also, when recruiting in small communities or among rare populations, finding participants who do not know each other might be almost impossible.

- **Inexperienced:** Respondents should *not* be regular participants in focus group discussions. Respondents who have participated in too many groups, sometimes with the collaboration of an unethical recruiter and sometimes as a consequence of their own intent, are called "professional respondents." They become wise to the ways of the moderator and learn to guess the intent of certain lines of questioning. Some even come to see themselves as amateur moderators and try to help out the moderator by asking their own probing questions.

  The general rule is that participation is permitted just once per year, or five times in total, and never twice on the same topic. In some countries, there is a qualitative research registry that recruiters can use to check on participation rates of individual people and also identify people who do not wish to be contacted.

- **Disrupters:** An experienced moderator can fairly quickly get the feel of a group and identify a participant who is likely to be uncooperative, or dominating, dishonest or even threatening. Where registries exist, participant names should be checked against a list of 'trouble' participants far enough in advance of the groups that they can be replaced. Moderators should add the names of disruptors to the registry to ensure they do not inhibit other moderators.

Guidelines

Several guidelines are generally used when recruiting:
- **Unaware**: Participants are generally unaware of the discussion details. In many cases, a primed respondent is thought to be less representative of a typical consumer.
    - In these cases, recruitment questionnaires can include questions unrelated to the topic to keep respondents from guessing what the discussion will be about. For example, a focus group on coffee might screen candidates on whether they drink milk, soft drinks, coffee, tea, beer, and wine

- o   However, there are exceptions when the respondents are asked to do pre-work, for example, taking a photo of the products in their pantry, or bringing in examples of books that their children like to read.
- **Professional exclusions**: Participants should not be closely connected (personally or through family members) with advertising, marketing research, or industries related to the topic of discussion. This helps ensure (a) the discussion represents lay consumers rather than those who are particularly well informed, and (b) helps guard against revealing confidential information to competitors.
- **Established residents**: Participants should not be recent arrivals in the country or the city because, until they get used to their new environment, their point of reference continues to be the point from which they moved. The exception, of course, is if 'recent immigrants' is the particular target group.
- **Language**: Participants should be sufficiently skilled in the language of the focus group, so they don't misunderstand the moderator and vice versa. Linguistically disadvantaged respondents are usually non-participatory and can also inhibit the free flow of dialogue.
- **Able to see, hear, read**: Participants should be literate and told to bring glasses or hearing aids if they use them. Many qualitative techniques involve responding to physical stimuli, questions in writing, or projective image techniques. Respondents may also be asked to respond to audio-visual stimuli such as concept statements or television commercials.
- **Articulate**: Respondents should be articulate and comfortable speaking in a group. Many recruiting companies include a standard screening question to ensure that potential respondents can express themselves clearly.
- **Homogeneity**: If some participants might restrict the willingness of others to participate, they should be separated into different groups. For example, if a teen group were composed of respondents ranging from 13 to 18 years old, the younger ones could easily be intimidated by the older ones and defer to them. Users and nonusers may also feel conflicted or that they need to defer to the other group, and ought to be kept separate. There are times when men and women might be included in separate groups, for example, if the topic is socially sensitive (e.g., personal hygiene products such as deodorant.)
- **No Need for Continuity**: Remember that focus groups are intended to uncover a range of perspectives. It's not necessary to cover every identifiable sub-group. For example, you might create a group of "20 to 29-year-old" and a group of "45 to 54- year-old" to understand broad generational contrasts; there may be no need to include the middle age group.

These points are not rigid rules, but guidelines to be used when no specific criteria are set.

Whenever the budget permits, the study structure should include at least two focus groups with each identified target sub-group. This is to guard against any one of the groups being atypical and leading the researchers astray. In the earlier example, each of the three markets had a group with consumers of each type of product, so there are three groups with each target sub-group.

Mixing respondents of opposing views (e.g., in political or social matters, or even brand loyalty) to create a confrontation has theoretical appeal but may not work very well in practice. Strong disagreement as a starting point for discussion among a group of strangers may lead to silence and discomfort rather than to a spirited and constructive debate.

How to Recruit Participants. Participants *could* be recruited through a statistically **random selection method** like those used in quantitative studies. This may be considered an ideal procedure because it eliminates human judgmental errors that may result in bias, but in practice, this method is seldom used. It would require a great deal of *over*-recruitment because of the high refusal rate and high rate of 'no-shows.' You can imagine that someone who is approached and asked to come to a gathering at an unknown location might doubt the legitimacy of the invitation and could have real concerns about their safety. Those who do show up may have their guard up and not be open to sharing details of their lives.

Some of these concerns can be alleviated by recruiting randomly through access panels, where every candidate has *already* agreed to be contacted about potential research opportunities. Because focus groups are very location-specific, it may be challenging to find enough people who qualify for the recruitment specifications through a panel in a specific location. Besides, this relatively expensive and time-consuming approach has not been shown to produce better participants than the referral method.

The most commonly used method is the **referral method**. It is a snowball or pyramid technique in which others refer to potential participants. Recruiters build up lists of willing participants – those who have participated in the past and those who are recommended for future studies. This technique is relatively inexpensive, and participant reliability is usually good. Those approached are less skeptical because someone they know has participated in a study before and has recommended them. Potential participants can quickly and independently verify that the invitation is genuine. The referring friend will probably encourage them to take part.

Participants tend to enjoy the experience. Indeed, many are flattered to know that someone values hearing their opinion, they learn from the exchange with others, and they like the sense of having been admitted to the inner sanctum of the marketing world.

In many countries, industry associations will offer guidelines for recruitment. The Canadian Research Insights Council (CRIC) and Marketing Research has a Code of Conduct based on ESOMAR and international guidelines that outline:

a. All respondents must meet usage/trial/ownership standards, including category, brand, frequency of use/trial or other time limits specified for the study. Also, demographic specifications for the study such as marital status, age, sex, income, occupation, and household composition must be achieved.

b. No respondents (nor anyone in their immediate families or households) may work in an occupation that has anything to do with the topic area (whether wholesale, retail, sales, service or consultant) nor in advertising, marketing, marketing research, public relations or the media (e.g., radio, television, newspaper, film/video production) nor may respondents themselves ever have worked in such occupations.

c. No respondent may be recruited who has attended, in the past two years, a focus group discussion or in-depth interview on the same general topic as defined by the Moderator.

d. No respondents should be recruited who know each other for the same study unless they are in different groups or interviews that are scheduled separately.

e. No respondent may be recruited who has attended a group discussion or in-depth interview within the past six months.

f. No respondent may be recruited who has attended five or more focus groups or in-depth interviews in the past five years.

g. At least one-third of the respondents recruited for each group/study must never have attended a group discussion or in-depth interview before.

h. All respondents must have been living in the specified market area for at least the past two years.

i. All respondents must be able to speak, read, and write in the language of the group or study being conducted.

j. Recruiters should not use advertising to recruit respondents for a particular project unless authorized to do so by the moderator (or client). The moderator (or client) must approve both the ad copy and the selection of the medium/media in which the proposed advertisement would run.

To guard against fraudulently recruited participants, 'switchers' or imposters, they are often 'rescreened' as they arrive at the facility.

Incentives. While traditional marketing research ethical guidelines preclude payment to respondents for their opinions (to avoid 'professional' respondents), there has always been space for qualitative 'incentives.' These are payments that are meant to cover the expenses required to get to the focus group facility – transportation, child care, parking etc. A fee per participant is set at the beginning of the project and can vary depending on market expectations (they may be higher in bigger cities) and the target group's degree of specialization. For example, when professionals are assembled to discuss a professional issue (e.g., health care professionals to discuss a new drug or lawyers to explore new citation technology), the incentives can be much higher than for consumers who are brought in to discuss food and beverage shopping habits.

Preparing the Discussion Guide. With the recruitment underway, the moderator and client have time to plan, write and fine-tune the discussion guide.

Rather than using a strict set of questions to elicit responses, the moderator works from an outline of topic areas that need to be covered. This 'guide' is a 'best guess' of how the discussion should flow. Often, a better way of exploring the topic emerges once the discussions begin, and moderators (and observers) have to be willing to adapt as required.

A discussion guide is not a hard and fast rule in the same way a questionnaire would be. It is a jumping-off point into possibly uncharted waters. The ongoing adaptability of qualitative research is what makes it conducive to *exploring* issues. As Langer (2001) put it, "Each focus group has its own rhythm, and the moderator follows it up right away. To cut respondents off and move on to another question can dissipate the energy that the group may not regain."

Like questionnaires, focus groups tend to follow a funneling structure: the discussion starts with broader issues and becomes more and more narrowly focused as the discussion continues. For example, in a focus group discussion about insurance, we would start very generally: current plan versus former plan, motivations for buying the current plan, how good the plan is, why it is satisfactory, why it is superior. Such topics are impersonal and easy to comment on. This ease, in turn, creates rapport among participants and the moderator. Then we move along to more specific and personally involved topics such as communications, decision-making, and customer satisfaction.

The spontaneity of live focus groups allows for changes throughout the fieldwork. Topics may be removed or added between groups, even part-way through the group. It is essential, however, to keep in mind that the purpose of multiple groups is often to compare different target subgroups. Removing or adding topics between groups might make this impossible.

The Setting. Typically, a focus group takes place in a specialized focus group facility. It may be set up in a **boardroom style** with participants sitting around a large table. It may be more of a **'living room' set up** with a more casual arrangement of sofas and comfortable chairs around a coffee table. More 'emotion' based research may require consumers to break down social barriers – and might involve sitting in bean-bag chairs, or on the floor. When conducting focus groups with teens or younger children, the less-formal setting is more likely to put them at ease.

A good focus group location should have a neutral and relaxing decor. There should be a **host or hostess** to control comings and goings, look after hospitality including snacks, attend to the recording equipment, and ensure that all respondents are on the attendance list. Sometimes, respondents will try to bring along friends to join in the experience not realizing that they have been chosen very carefully. Of course, only those specifically recruited for the group are allowed into the room.

One common element of most focus group facilities is a **one-way mirror** between the room where the participants are meeting (mirror side) and an observation room (window side) where clients, note-takers, simultaneous translators and collaborators may watch and listen to the proceedings.

Microphones and cameras discretely positioned in the room carry the discussion into the observation room and permit **audio and video recordings** that are used in preparing transcripts, coding, analyzing the results and capturing verbatim comments. Many facilities can **live stream** the audio and video images to observers in other locations (including other cities) over the internet.

Participants must always be made aware of both the recording and the presence of observers behind the one-way mirror. But for evident reasons of bias prevention, the specific identity or connections of the observers are not divulged. Observers usually are only described as people relevant to the topic and eager to hear the respondents' comments firsthand. Even when respondents do not object to being recorded, images and sound may not be used in other contexts (such as advertising) without obtaining specific permission from the respondents involved.

In areas where there are no formal observation facilities, two adjoining meeting rooms in a hotel or conference facility can be used where the group is conducted in one meeting room, and clients observe the group in the room next door by way of a closed-circuit video link.

If it is impossible to have adjoining rooms, and depending on the arrangement of the space, one or two observers can sit off to the side in the group room. Such observers must remain quiet and unobtrusive and do nothing to interfere with the moderator's control of the group. The moderator customarily introduces such observers as research colleagues who will collaborate on the final report.

Focus Group Interactions. Once the observers are settled in behind the one-way mirror, and the back-room lights are dimmed, the focus group participants are seated around the table, drinks poured, sandwiches selected, the moderator is seated, and the group begins.

The ambience of a focus group is intended to be informal, a friendly conversation about a product or service and how it makes them feel. It is essential to build rapport and put the participants at ease. Unless there is a specific reason to do otherwise, participants in a focus group discussion are generally compatible with one another demographically and through shared, topic-related interests.

The discussions generally last between 1½ and 2 hours. The moderator must discretely keep control of the group, sometimes directing the order of participation, sometimes letting it flow naturally. Body language (a gesture, a look, a swivel of the shoulders, inhaling of a breath) can invite someone to speak or tell a talkative participant that their time is up. Everyone needs to participate.

Individual tasks can be assigned to measure personal beliefs *before* discussions begin. Group exercises can be worked in to allow participants to *build off of each other*. *Exercises like collages, role play, projective techniques* can open up consumers and get beneath the surface.

The moderator generally takes a break half-way through the group and another just before the end to check in with the observers in the back room and find out if they want further probes on a topic that was covered. Occasionally, the observers can send a note to a moderator with a question or a request for a consultation. But this can be disruptive to group flow if it happens too often.

The Role of the Client-Observer. As with any research, the client plays a crucial role in setting objectives, providing timely feedback and ensuring the research team understands the study requirements. For focus groups, it is generally desirable for clients to observe the sessions as they happen. This is one of the main spin-off benefits of qualitative research. The opportunity for marketing people to play "fly on the wall" and to learn first-hand what their customers (or those of the competition) are thinking can provide invaluable insight.

Having the client present is also invaluable to the moderator, at least for the first few sessions, to ensure that she or he is working to the ends the client desires. Frequently, modifications to the flow and content of the discussion are made as a result of client observation.

It is better to limit observers to people who have a direct reason for being present. The more observers there are, the more they interact among themselves, and the less attentive they are to the job of observing. For example, including the client's director of marketing and the senior account person from their ad agency might lead them to discuss other business or compare past collaborations. The client insights person may not be in any position to ask them to pay attention to the group.

The observers should view the proceedings with a completely open mind and not be quick to judge the participants or the moderator. The respondents may not say what the observers expect them to say, and the moderator may not ask the questions observers think should be asked. Nothing can be learned by being critical of the participants or the moderator.

Observers should make it a point to be respectful of the participants (as they may be drawn from a very different social stratum than the observers) and of the moderator (who may have deviated from the discussion script for reasons not evident to the observers). If the participants say what the observers want to hear, and if the moderator asks the questions exactly as the observers want him or her to ask them, there can be little additional learning.

Remote Viewing. It is often not possible for all client stakeholders to attend the focus groups. Many facilities now offer live streaming of the video and audio feed to remote observers. Video conferencing connections allow two-way interaction so remote observers can relay additional questions to the moderator during breaks or seek clarifications.

How to Determine the Number of Groups

Determining the number of groups required to meet the research objectives is a crucial design issue because it will

- impact how comfortable the participants feel, and as a result, how much they reveal of themselves;
- reveal where there may be variations in opinions, between markets, demographic and behavioural groups;
- ensure the findings reflect real consumer perspectives and not just the view of what may be an aberrant individual or group;
- have a possible direct multiplier effect on the cost of the project.

The goal should be to provide as many dimensions and safeguards as possible, with a *minimum* number of groups. The starting point should be to understand how many unique segments you would need to hear from to get the full range of perspectives.

Obviously, the more diverse the target group, the larger the number of groups required. At the same time, the law of "diminishing returns" also applies. Increasing the number of groups may improve the chances of finding new insights, but at some point, you will have heard all of the main perspectives, and it would be counterproductive to add more.

There is no magical number of groups beyond which you won't hear anything new. The number of groups required could depend on:
- significant regional variations in attitudes toward the product
- different socio-economic groups that may buy the product for different reasons
- distinct age segments with different needs
- incompatible motivations between segments
- differences between heavy users and light users
- any need to separate users of the client's product from users of the competitors'
- the point at which you run out of budget

There is a real danger that including a very large number of participants, over many groups, might lead clients to begin interpreting the findings quantitatively rather than qualitatively.

> Example 1. Martindale Fine Chocolates has commissioned groups on 'gifting' to understand better how to position their products. Their research partner suggests that they need to hear from households with children versus those without – because buying patterns and motivations are likely to be influenced by the presence of children during Easter and Halloween. It's also recommended that they hear from men and women separately because their views of the category, particularly

around gifting on Valentine's Day, are likely to be very different. Men might be shy to admit their motivations with women present. In the markets where Martindale operates, different ethnicities may have different views of gifting chocolate that would be worth capturing.

Example 2. Sure Strong Inc. manufactures garbage bags and is about to introduce a new, almost unbreakable product to the market. They need to understand the language around 'failure' in this category because their dominant positioning will be the elimination of this risk. They suspect that men and women use trash bags in different locations, throw out different things, and have different perspectives on taking out the trash. So clearly, they need to separate the sexes. They also suspect that families with young children might have specific garbage concerns. But perhaps this can be covered by ensuring at least a few parents in each gender group. The brand will face different competitors in different regions of the country so that a regional dimension would be required.

Besides, other considerations will impact how smoothly the focus groups will function. Many are unwritten rules and may differ from moderator to moderator.

Age Range. Separating groups for younger and older people increases the sense that you are among peers. Among teenagers, an age span of two years is advisable; among those under 30, five to ten years, among older adults, 20 to 25 years is an acceptable span. Studies often focus on consumers under 50 years old, but this is due to marketing target definitions and not to any inherent age-related impediment. When their input is pertinent, groups of older people are just as productive as younger segments.

Demographics. It is best to keep white/blue-collar, higher/lower educated, upscale/downscale groups apart. People tend not to open up when social gaps are evident.

Gender. It may not be productive to mix males and females in the same group, although it is often done when budgetary constraints deem it necessary. Mixed groups tend to be less relaxed and less productive. Moreover, gender-related issues will usually not emerge because both genders will avoid the risk of possibly demeaning or stereotyping the other (although such stereotypes can provide highly valuable insight). These are, of course, general suggestions. Whether to mix genders or not will depend on the context and content of the research questions at stake.

Research design can be creative across dimensions to keep costs down. It may not be necessary to hit all demographic breaks in all markets. For example:

Market 1	Market 2	Market 3	Market 4
Young males		Older males	
	Young females		Older males
Older females		Younger males	

Key Moderating Skills

Because of the nature of qualitative research, the skills required to be a good moderator involve a high degree of sensitivity to others, lateral thinking, and the ability to be a catalyst rather than an influence. Without being exhaustive, this section aims to familiarize you with some of the skills and tools that are available to moderators. Almost all are also relevant to individual depth interviews. In fact, some of the skills (e.g., creating rapport using matching and mirroring) are much more effective in individual depth interviews than in focus groups.

Overall a moderator needs to be:
- capable of maintaining a firm but quiet control;
- non-critical and non-judgmental of the opinions expressed and able to keep their own biases out of the discussion entirely;
- alert and interested without showing emotion;
- able to think laterally;
- even-handed in seeking equal participation;
- encouraging to respondents, notably the reticent who may need special attention and stroking to be forthcoming;
- able to keep the topic reasonably on track;
- credibly naive to induce discussion of key fundamentals that respondents may otherwise assume are self-evident;
- sensitive to undercurrents and disagreements;
- flexible, adaptable, and able to improvise;
- observant of cues from body language;
- able to interact, probe, and bring out feelings and emotions.

Putting Respondents at Ease: Putting respondents at ease is the priority of the moderator. It is done by first explaining the purpose of the discussion in an informal and non-technical way, and then by establishing a relaxed and permissive climate. The moderator should adapt the way he or she speaks to match that of the participants. The moderator should also be dressed accordingly. Moderating a group of blue-collar workers while wearing a business suit may signal that the moderator wants them to know he is not one of them. This won't increase comfort levels.

Creating Rapport: Creating a feeling of rapport requires the ability to enter someone else's world and to communicate to make the other person feel that she or he is understood and that his or her views (mainstream or not) are important to the moderator. This leads the person to trust the moderator, which in turn results in an uninhibited flow of information. When rapport is established, the respondent becomes less self-conscious and guarded, and thus is in a position to provide valuable information more openly.

Most good qualitative researchers do this intuitively, even subconsciously. Developments in the fields of sociolinguistics, hypnotic patterns, psychology, and neuro-linguistic programming (NLP) have identified specific patterns that can help the researcher establish rapport with the respondents.

Of course, maintaining rapport does not mean surrendering control of the group to the participants. If this happens, the moderator will have failed in one of the most critical tasks.

Controlling Group Dynamics: Whenever two or more people interact, two conflicting motives propel their interaction power and solidarity. A person may want to be heard (power), but that person is socialized to make room for others' views (solidarity). Different people have different balances of power and solidarity. Most people balance the two well, although an imperfect balance is to be expected. When a group has one person with an extreme power orientation and seven others with a high solidarity orientation, the power-oriented person will tend to dominate the discussion. The main danger, in this case, is that the acquiescence of the remaining participants for reasons of solidarity will limit the range of the discussion. In other words, they may simply agree with the dominant person, although they have their own different opinions on the topic.

The challenge of moderators is to control the dominant person(s) without appearing to do so and, at the same time, enhance their communication links with the others. Whether or not power-solidarity conflict is a problem, it is essential for moderators to keep all their links open and always make it clear that conflicting views are not only welcome but also essential to their purpose in learning about all facets of the topic.

Understanding Surface Messages and Meta Messages. When people are together in groups, two types of messages are sent out: surface messages and meta-messages. Suppose you ask your colleague, "Have you finished the report?" The surface message is the information that is sought in the literal sense: whether the report is finished or not. The meta-message might be, "I don't think you have," implying incompetence.

Meta-messages are conveyed through the intonation, pitch, and facial and bodily expressions that accompany the words. They carry or are perceived to carry an implied message within the surface message. Because meta-messages are so important in communication, it is quite common to observe people reacting to meta-messages. For example, if you ask your colleague if he has finished the report, he might not say no, but he might respond, "It's almost finished," or "I would have finished it by now, but the network was down for a couple of hours this morning." Similarly, a person who buys a notably non-prestigious brand may offer a defensive explanation of her or his purchase without even being asked.

Meta-messages are essential in all forms of human communication. They become particularly critical in face-to-face situations between strangers, i.e. focus group and depth interview participants. A straightforward question such as, "What wine do you drink?" can send out any of the following meta-messages to the respondent:

- I expect any normal person to drink wine.
- The wine you drink will tell me how sophisticated you are.
- You look like a person who would drink wine.
- I'll bet you drink cheap wine.

The participant's answer will vary depending on the meta-message he or she received, based on the tone and context in which the question was asked, body language, facial expressions and even the previous line of discussions. There may be no more important skill for a moderator than knowing how to ask a question without appearing to make a statement or suggest an appropriate response. The moderator should be aware of the meta-messages he or she might be sending.

Maintaining Rapport: Sociolinguists, psychologists, hypnotists, and neuro-linguistic programming specialists have identified many ways in which rapport is created between people and have offered several guidelines for creating and maintaining it in the shortest possible time.

One major premise in creating rapport is that we have a higher affinity with people who are similar to us. Similarity can be created through three main methods: physical similarity, speech patterns, and framing. The techniques described here can be used effectively in focus groups.

Matching and Mirroring: If we observe people in a social setting, we find that close friends tend to mirror each other. If one of them leans forward, the other tends to lean forward as well; if one tilts his head, so does the other. This process can be used deliberately to create rapport.

Rapport is created to make the participants feel that the moderator is one of them. In terms of physiology, oneness is created by the moderator, mirroring the physical behaviour of the participants.

You can mirror things such as the body posture, breathing pattern, and tonality of the voice of the other person. If the person you are dealing with is a slow talker, talking to him fast will not be conducive to establishing rapport. If most participants lean forward, a moderator who leans back in his or her chair is not likely to create rapport. Using a tonal up-lift at the end of a sentence might work in a room of young women, but not among older professionals.

Of course, there are situations in which there is no consistent pattern in the group, so the moderator may not be able to use his or her physiology to create rapport. However, there are other means.

Neuro-linguistic programming holds that we use a dominant modality when we communicate. The dominant mode may be visual, auditory, kinesthetic, or even olfactory or gustatory. Better rapport is created when we follow the speaker's modality. Let us review the following brief conversation: (It should be noted that although the theories of Neurolinguistic Programming often seem to conform to common sense, there is no hard evidence to confirm them.)

> Participant: I don't see how this new concept fits into the whole picture.
> Moderator: Listen to this carefully. I was saying...
> Participant: It's still fuzzy to me.

The participant is using words suggesting a visual perspective (the word see), picturing a mental image and trying to make sense of that. The moderator, however, is coming from an auditory perspective and merely repeats himself, which at this point is like speaking to the participant in a foreign language. Moreover, in this example, there is a concealed meta-message from the moderator that the respondent is either imperceptive or not very bright. Neuro-linguistic programmers hold that such a mismatch is destructive to maintaining rapport. The moderator could have matched the participant in the following way:

> Participant: I don't see how this new concept fits into the whole picture.
> Moderator: Let us look at it this way. If you observe...
> Then perhaps the participant might have responded:
> Participant: Oh, I see what you mean.

The second conversation, in which the moderator matched the participant's dominant modality, would have created a powerful rapport between the moderator and the participant.

When the conversation is not one-on-one as described above, the moderator may have to use the dominant modality of the group while also reiterating his or her talk in other modalities.

Even when participants do not use modality-specific words (such as see, hear, think), it is possible to know how they are processing information. Interestingly, our eye movements correlate with the mode in which we operate. For example, when we try picturing something, our eyes go up; when we feel angry, we look down to the right. Observing the eye movements of the participant is one way to get a better idea of how she or he has processed the information.

Speech Patterns: The second method of creating rapport is through following the speech patterns of the participants. Speech patterns vary in different dimensions:
- speed
- tempo
- tonality
- words

To someone who is a slow speaker, a fast speaker may appear rude and self-centred. A fast speaker, in turn, may perceive a slow speaker as less intelligent. Whether a given tone is perceived to be firm and friendly, or bossy and offensive, depends on the background of the participants. What is bossy and offensive to people from one part of the country may simply be normal to people from another part of the country. Extensive use of colloquial expressions may be perceived as coarse by members of some socio-economic groups, while the absence of colloquial expressions may be perceived as stuffy and pompous by other groups. A good moderator is aware (consciously or subconsciously) of such speech patterns and adjusts his or her speech to suit that of the group's.

When the groups are distinct, it is sufficient to identify suitable speech patterns. However, good sensory awareness is needed to assess the physiological and language patterns when the groups are not very distinct. Some rapport almost always develops within the group and with the moderator (assuming that she or he is competent). This might happen in the waiting room prior to starting the group. The real challenge to the moderator is to elevate the level of rapport as much as possible by being alert of the subconscious signals generated by participants through the course of the discussion.

Framing and Reframing: *Framing* is a way of creating a context. This is done to guide participants to change the topic or to give up their current orientation while maintaining rapport. Sometimes, framing can also be used to create rapport.

Consider a situation in which the discussion has moved into areas that are outside the scope of the study, and the moderator's attempts to steer the conversation back onto the desired topic have not been very successful.

Perhaps the moderator wants to know which of the two products under consideration the participants are more likely to buy. Still, for some reason, the discussion animatedly moves on to the colour of the packages. In such cases, *reframing* the mindset of the participants can be accomplished by the moderator by saying something like, "That is very interesting. Now suppose you are in a store and you have only $5. Which brand of Product X would you buy? Assume that the colours of the packages are switched. Now, which brand would you buy?" These new frames are specific and therefore require the participants to abandon their earlier frames. Yet they are non-offensive as they do not ask them to stop the original discussion. However, the indirect result is that the participants have no logical way of returning to their earlier frame.

Reframing can also be used to change someone's orientation while maintaining rapport. Consider a situation in which a participant believes that he has superior knowledge and is bent on exhibiting it by straying into areas that are of no consequence either to the moderator or to the other participants. (This, by the way, is one of the key reasons for screening out respondents who have inside industry knowledge.) The moderator may reframe the participant's orientation by saying something like: "That is a very sophisticated view. We may even have another group discussion on that topic. Now, if you were to deal with the issue at a more general level, what would you say about...?" Here, by acknowledging the participant as sophisticated, the moderator maintains rapport by patting the respondent on the back while making it clear that another frame is required. The respondent cannot ignore the fact that his previous frame of reference and that of the moderator are at odds.

Breaking Rapport: While a moderator must create and maintain rapport, she or he may also want to break the rapport from time to time by not following some of the procedures described above. For example, the group rapport may be so high that participants start interacting with exuberance. To regain order, the moderator may temporarily break rapport with the group by reframing. One must also remember that the group is being recorded and observed. When the proceedings break down into crosscurrents of chatter, the conversation will become unintelligible, and the observers will be lost. The moderator's challenge is to maintain rapport with participants without losing control of the group itself or becoming personally involved in the discussion.

Being Specific: When a moderator asks a question, he or she does not settle for the first answer but probes over and over again to get at deeper levels of perception. The ability to uncover such material is one of the most important differences between qualitative and quantitative research. (This is also a key reason why moderators must control the number of topics covered in a discussion guide – too many topics means not enough time to probe beyond the first, top-of-mind responses.)

The moderator achieves this in several different ways:
- by encouraging the respondents to expound on their views in greater detail,
- by feigning non-comprehension,
- by deliberately playing the devil's advocate,
- by reframing,
- by questioning body language, and
- by questioning without words (e.g., with looks, gestures).

A good moderator never takes anything for granted. She must think on her feet as, unlike survey researchers, she does not have the luxury of pre-testing questions to refine their effectiveness. Every moderator miscue or error may potentially impact the respondents and influence results.

The moderators' toolbox consists of a wide variety of tools that enable them to achieve their objectives.

Writing Exercises: During the discussion, a moderator can make use of writing exercises. Writing exercises are used when the moderator would like to know the uninfluenced opinions of each member of the group on a pivotal point. For example, after viewing a commercial, each respondent may be asked to complete a simple questionnaire before the open discussion begins. There is no intent to tabulate the answers. The questionnaires are collected and scanned by the moderator as an opinion snapshot of the group, and they guide where to proceed with questioning.

When less precaution is needed, a close equivalent of a show-of-hands may be used. The round-robin question is a similar technique in which each participant's bottom-line response is obtained serially (e.g., for a yes or no, for ratings from one to ten). Although serial questioning tends to make the respondents passive, a few round-robins done quickly cause no harm and aid the goal of equal participation.

Hypothetical Scenarios: If the discussion is about alcoholic beverages, the moderator may introduce several scenarios such as dinner at home, dinner in a restaurant, relaxing in the afternoon. Such scenarios put the participants in theoretical situations that can make the discussion more realistic and shed light on how different products are perceived under different usage circumstances.

Regression: When participants get stuck in a part of a discussion, removing them from the present and putting them in a different context in the past might help the discussion to move forward. A question such as, "What did you think about smoking cigarettes when you were young?" may also be used to gather additional information about participants' attitudes toward a product.

Silence: In Western cultures, a long pause in conversation can create a *level* of discomfort. The moderator could use this pause to ask another question, but, with a little patience, someone in the group is bound to speak up, if only to fill the gap. Forcing respondents to fill the vacuum when the group seems to be running out of steam is one way to induce a fresh approach. However, the moderator should be careful not to let the silence go on too long in case someone says, "I guess we're done, then," when this is not the case.

Negative Questions: These can be used to elicit less apparent distinctions that exist in the participant's mind. Suppose a participant says that she never goes to supermarkets. The moderator might simply ask, "What would happen if you did?" This type of negative questioning is likely to focus the participant's thinking on the specific reasons for a given behaviour.

Display Materials: Many discussions involve display materials such as package or ad designs, product samples, or concept statements. When the goal is to assess the *relative* impact of these materials, they are presented all together at the same time. When the relative impact is not important, but the moderator needs to understand reactions to each design in depth, it is more appropriate to show the display material one after the other. However, this may introduce a degree of order-effect bias. A moderator can minimize this impact by carefully working out the sequencing of the materials when designing the discussion guide and by rotating the order of the material between groups.

After the Group

At the end of each focus group, it is useful to have a 'backroom discussion' with the observers, particularly if clients are present. Each individual may have heard something different from the discussions, and it can help the analysis to collect these impressions. Keep in mind that backroom distractions – the serving of a meal, checking e-mails, side-bar conversations – may mean that observers missed important revelations in the focus group room. It may help to identify and correct misapprehensions before the observers leave the facility and spread their view, or worse, make decisions based on an incomplete understanding of what happened.

Once everyone leaves the facility, the analysis phase begins. Approaches to analysis may be very similar across all of the qualitative methodologies, so we will cover off other approaches and speak about analysis later in this unit.

2. Mini Groups, Dyad, Triad and IDIs

There are times when a conventional focus group is too cumbersome. The topic may be inherently sensitive, or the target audience may be particularly expert. In those instances, when an individual may have a lot to say, a smaller group can provide extensive insights with fewer participants.

Mini Groups, Dyads, Triads

Mini groups generally have four or five participants. Triads would have three, and dyads would have two. Dyads and triads can be set up as an 'interview with friends', where the first recruit is asked to bring a close friend (or two) who share(s) the same characteristics. This allows each participant to build off the others, and for the friendship, dynamics to reveal more profound truths as they talk about each other.

> Example: A major manufacturer of baby wipes wants to hear about what drives new mothers to buy specific brands of the product over another, and why they may or may not buy a generic version. The incidence of mothers of infants in diapers is very low among the general population, and the topic can be a very emotional one, and for both pragmatic and revelatory reasons, it makes sense to set up a triad with a primary participant bringing two friends with babies – perhaps from a "mothers' group."

Most of the details that apply to traditional focus groups would also apply in these smaller group interviews. The critical difference is the potential for more in-depth, revelatory discussions, but covering less breadth in terms of types of respondents.

Individual Depth Interviews (IDIs)

The **individual depth interview or IDI** is conceptually similar to a focus group except that the moderator talks to one respondent at a time rather than to a group of people. The interviews tend to be more structured than with groups and need more moderator involvement. At the same time, there's no need to manage group dynamics. They last about 20 to 40 minutes, or longer if necessary.

It would be preferable to conduct individual interviews instead of focus groups when others can easily colour an individual's opinion in a group environment, or when certain opinions are not likely to be expressed in a group because they are too personal, sensitive, or embarrassing in nature.

> Example. Incontinence is a concern that affects not just older members of our society. A variety of conditions might lead a younger consumer to need an adult diaper daily. This fact can be very embarrassing and awkward to discuss in front of others. IDIs would be the best approach to probe needs, expectations and fears around brand choice.

IDIs might also be more appropriate when it is more important to learn what people do *not* know about a topic than what they do know. In a group setting, more knowledgeable respondents quickly teach less knowledgeable ones, making it very difficult to explore areas of ignorance or misperception.

> Example. The Ministry of Health has been directed to implement a new policy that will significantly affect health care options for those who have diabetes. This is a relatively common condition, and a great deal of information is available about living with it – not all of it scientifically based. In a group situation, one reasonably well-informed (or ill-informed) participant could become the group expert who influences what others say. Probing current understanding and reactions to the potential new policy is likely to be more productive with individual interviews.

IDIs might also be the best choice when participants risk being reminded of issues that they *usually do not have* because someone in the group expressed strong concerns. An issue that is minor or even non-existent in an individual's life can take on impressive proportions in a group setting resulting in a temptation to offer comments to impress others.

> Example. As part of their manufacturing process, a manufacturer of condoms hoped to explore the real need for specific product features, like colour or texture. There was concern that in a focus group situation, some participants would be too shy to offer their real opinions. In contrast, others would try to impress their fellow participants with invented situations.

Sometimes, there is simply no choice but to conduct individual interviews. An example of this would be when executives from competing firms are interviewed. They will not open up in front of each other and may even intentionally make misleading statements. Similarly, medical specialists are unlikely to travel across the city to attend a focus group, even with a very high incentive. It's best to go to them to conduct an individual interview.

Although there are differences between focus groups and individual depth interviews, the skill set required of the moderator is common for both techniques. However, some approaches lend themselves particularly well to an individual interview.

3. Projective Techniques

Several techniques can be used in any of the qualitative methodologies. Projective techniques are perhaps the most common. While they are useful tools, they are not automatically part of every focus group. Some moderators use them a lot, others less often.

Projective techniques are an indirect way of gaining insights into human behaviour. These techniques are based on the work of psychoanalysts who claim that while we may not want to admit to our less socially acceptable feelings, emotions and motives, we can comfortably attribute them to others. For example, we may be too embarrassed to admit (or may not even know at the conscious level) that we are highly concerned about our appearance. Yet, if we are asked to write a story based on a photograph that we pick out of a pile, we may freely project our concerns onto that person in the story and state that he or she seems highly concerned with his/her appearance.

Personification. Personification is a commonly used projective technique in which respondents are asked to assume that a product is a person and then describe this person. For example, if two vehicles, perhaps a Toyota and a Jaguar, were people, what human characteristics would you attribute to them?

Personification is widely used because of its common reference points and because it is relatively easy to interpret and to understand. However, it really lends itself only to situations where the products have a well-established and distinctive image. Trying to personify products such as two obscure brands of laxatives might be asking too much.

To determine whether a projective technique is appropriate, the researcher must ask herself whether she could respond reasonably to the question herself. If she is uncertain about how to answer, the question is bound to leave respondents scratching their heads. Here are a few projective techniques relevant to qualitative researchers.

Some Common Projective Techniques

Transposed Vocabulary. The transposed vocabulary technique is similar to personification. Participants are asked to assume that a given product is actually in a different category and then are asked to describe them. For example, what if Ivory Liquid and Palmolive Liquid were not detergents but clothing stores? What would they look like? What lines would they carry? How would they arrange their displays? Who would shop there? How would they advertise?

Such transposition is expected to remove the participants' mental blocks and release them from rational and linear thinking, thereby providing valuable insights to the researcher.

Transference. Transference has similar psychological roots but is particularly suitable for socially sensitive issues. Participants are asked to explain the viewpoint of another person who might not agree with the socially acceptable position. An example of the use of this technique would be: "That is very interesting, but I bet you know people who wouldn't share your viewpoints. What do you know of the way others think about this?" By removing the participants' responsibility for the opinions expressed, the researcher may be able to obtain a less inhibited view of the underlying motives behind their behaviour. There is a danger here: it may be impossible to know whether the respondent shares the transferred views or is merely being a good reporter.

Sentence Completion. With this technique, the moderator gives participants an incomplete sentence and asks them to complete it. The theory is that the participant will reveal her or his biases, preferences, and hidden motives. An example of the sentence completion technique is: "From what I've seen, people who only fly with Air Canada are...." (The respondent is expected to complete the sentence.) There are several variations of this technique.

Participants may be quick to recognize this for the manipulation it is. More sophisticated participants may refuse to play along by pointedly doing little more than reiterating what they have said before to dissuade the moderator from trying again. Excessive use of this technique may also become annoying. However, these drawbacks can be true of any projective technique.

Half Questions. The half-questions technique is a variation of the sentence completion technique—except that the respondents do not know they are filling in a sentence or a question. For example, the researcher may say, "If I understand you correctly, this commercial is getting at..." and then draws a blank. As the researcher seems to fumble for words, the participants hopefully try to help out with a suitable completion, not realizing that the researcher had no intention of finishing the sentence in the first place. This approach is much less likely to be problematic with sophisticated participants who may even think their wisdom has come to the rescue. Here, too, discretion is called for. Some moderators are very skilled at working this into their conversational tone. However, there is a risk that if used too often, it can convey the meta-message that the moderator might be daydreaming, has trouble understanding what is being said, or is merely faking it, to the detriment of rapport. At the same time, a participant with a dominating personality may be the only one to jump in, and subsequent discussions could be focused only on his or her perspective.

Cartoon Test. In a typical cartoon test, two characters are shown. One of them may say something like, "I heard that John bought a Ferrari." The balloon for the other character is empty, and the respondent is asked to fill it in. The response thus elicited (such as, "John loves fast cars," "John is always trying to show-off," or "John could have got a good sports car for a lot less money") is expected to provide clues to underlying motivations.

Photo Sort. The photo sort technique provides participants with a deck of photographs and asks them to sort them into groupings based on a specific question. This technique is often done as a group exercise, so the discussion that they have while working out the groupings is as important as the final result.

For example, they may be given a deck containing photographs of people (e.g., a business person, student, homemaker, and manual worker) and asked to group them into users of different brands of a product (e.g., what car they drive, or what brand of iced tea they drink). The set of photographs associated with each brand is expected to reveal that group's image of the brand.

A photo sort can also be done with photographs that have no relationship with the research topic (a tightrope walker, an orchid, a hammer) to elicit respondents' emotional, non-rational responses to the subject at hand. It is critical, in this case, to probe respondents to understand the associations each photo holds for them. For example, the moderator might assume that the tightrope walker represented a complex and challenging life. However, for a respondent, the tightrope walker could conjure up the sheer joy of a childhood circus visit.

The exercise can also make use of the actual product. For example, respondents might be asked to use actual packs of different brands of cookies and be asked to group them into neighbourhoods in "cookie city." The neighbourhoods can then be named. So, a grouping of thin or dark-chocolate cookies might end up in "Sophisticate Town," and a grouping of colour sprinkled and sweet cookies might be in "Kiddie Treat Heights." The descriptors that the group offers of each neighbourhood, the style of architecture, the people that work there, the jobs they do, how they entertain themselves, provides invaluable insight into the cookie brands.

Free-choice Rankings. Free-choice rankings of products provide participants with an assortment of related products that are to be arranged according to *any* criterion chosen by a given respondent; subsequent rankings by others are to be based on *different* criteria. One can even use masking tape to create a product segmentation grid on the discussion table and allow the group to place actual products on it as a reflection of how the products are perceived.

Other Projective Techniques. There are projective techniques that may be more helpful with certain groups of people than with others. For example, techniques based on **drawings** and **cartoons** can be helpful when dealing with children. **Fantasy** or **hypothetical scenarios** may help re-organize perceptions when participants are locked into some form of linear thinking and are not providing new insights into the problem.

Role-playing techniques ask participants to 'act out' a particular scenario. They may be an ideal way to probe inherently interactive situations such as customer-salesperson relations or patient-doctor interactions. They work particularly well with teenagers who can be very shy and hard to motivate.

Risks in Using Projective Techniques

There are several things that one should bear in mind when using projective techniques.

First, the interpretation of what the respondent says is not always clear-cut. The statements may be open to more than one interpretation, and there is a possibility that the moderator may project his or her own biases onto the respondent.

Second, some respondents may not want to respond to projective technique type questions and may even be dissuaded from further participation.

Third, projective techniques leave room for client observers to overlay their own biases in the way they interpret the responses, resulting in conflict later when they try to decide what it all means.

Notwithstanding all these limitations, projective techniques can be very useful if used properly.

4. Ethnographic Studies

There are times when it is best to 'embed' the researcher in the consumer's life, so an activity can be observed and questioned as it takes place. This is particularly useful when a consumer might be an unreliable reporter. Perhaps the activity is so routine that consumers do it without thinking. Perhaps it occurs in a highly socially interactive situation, and it's important to see the reaction of others involved.

Example 1. A manufacturer of showerheads was interested in providing a 'lower flow' option for their product but did not want to diminish the public's enjoyment of this very private activity. It was important to understand the biomechanics of showering and to identify sources of pleasure and of frustration. This is very much a habitual behaviour, and consumers would not be able to replay what happens in their shower to a focus group several hours later.

Example 2. A manufacturer of luncheon meats is on the verge of an innovation process to create products specifically for children. Little is known about how mothers prepare lunches for their children. What role do the children play both in influencing brand choices, but also in how the lunch is prepared?

Example 3. A brewery believes that future growth for its brands is most likely to occur in 'away-from-home' occasions. It's important to understand the role of the bartender or server and others in the environment.

Each of these situations calls for an ethnographic investigation. Instead of inviting consumers to come to a central location, the researcher goes to the locations where consumers are using or buying the product to observe movement patterns, interaction and conversations carefully and to question decisions made. Observations might involve looking for specific actions, but the process has to be open to picking up the unexpected.

The study can be purely observational; the observer makes sure that his or her involvement in no way influences the behaviour of the consumer or participant. Or the observer can interact with the consumer to question actions or decisions made as they occur.

In the shower study, a small camera was installed over the showerhead in the homes of volunteer participants and the users' movements and interaction with the showerhead was recorded and analyzed. After the shower, an on-site interviewer played back the video and asked the participants about what worked well and what didn't.

In the luncheon meat study, a researcher joined individual families at noon each day as lunch was prepared initially, watching interactions with the children, the choices that were made and the reactions of children to what they were served before in-depth interviews with the mothers to ask about their motivations and decisions.

For the bar study, a group of younger researchers spent a few evenings in the entertainment district looking for behavioural patterns among various demographic groups – how people order their drinks, what influences them and how patterns may change throughout the evening. They studiously avoided interacting with the subjects.

This approach has its roots in anthropology and can also be called "anthropological" or "observational" research.

Like all other methods, this methodology has both advantages and disadvantages. The main advantage is that the observations take place in the "real world" and are unprompted. The observer can notice things that even the consumer may not be aware of. The main disadvantage is that behaviour may be subject to cues that the *buyer*, but not necessarily the observer, may be aware of.

5. Semiotics

It is not always necessary to collect observations from consumers in qualitative research. Semiotic research is an example of a technique that does not require human subjects.

Semiotics is the study of signs, symbols, and communication. It is based on the concept that all human communication is a text that needs decoding. Different elements of a product (e.g., packaging, claims, advertising) develop a message that contains the information or meaning the sender hopes to convey. To understand the symbolic meaning that might be conveyed in a marketing touchpoint, qualitative researchers strive to 'decode' the different elements.

For instance, what does a brand mean to a consumer? If red is the dominant colour of the brand logo, what meaning does that colour impart to the brand? If the script is flowing and rounded, what does that say about the brand? If the pack features graphic stripes rather than a photograph, but the meaning is triggered? What is the cumulative impact of each of the elements of a pack design (e.g., illustration, font, colour, placement, relative emphasis)? How does the music in a commercial relate to the visuals and shade the message consumers are receiving?

From a semiotic perspective, every marketing message has three essential components: an object, a sign or symbol and an interpreter. The product is the object, and it is the focus of the message (e.g., canned peas). The sign is the sensory imagery that is used to represent the intended meaning of the object. The interpretation is the meaning derived (e.g., fresh, cheerful).

The message must be communicated in a way that is appropriate for the medium being used. Qualitative researchers who specialize in semiotics aim to disassemble and decode the elements of communication to map out how consumers might understand what is being communicated and identify conflicting messaging that undermines its effectiveness.

6. Other Qualitative Techniques

There are other qualitative techniques that some researchers use from time to time. Some of them are freely available, and some of them are 'proprietary.' Here is a sampling of a few of these techniques.

Laddering

Laddering is based on means-end theory (Gutman, 1982) and holds that the attributes of a product or a service can be viewed as a means to an end. For instance, one of the attributes of education is that it enables a person to get a good job (means) that leads to a feeling of security (end).

Every product or service has several attributes. The objective of laddering is to connect the various attributes of a product or a service to the underlying motivators or "ends." The means-end theory does not settle for the first reason for using a product given by the consumer; instead, it tries to explore the underlying motives or the ends.

In laddering techniques, the respondent is probed until he or she comes up with the end value. Such probing leads the participant from surface Attitudes to Consequences to end Values (the ACV model). The moderator probes the respondent until the end values are determined.

> I like this brand of shampoo. (A—Attitude)
> Why do you like this brand of shampoo?
> Because it is of high quality.   (C—Consequence)
> What does high-quality shampoo do?
> It makes my hair look good, and others notice it. (C- Consequence)
> Why is that important?
> It makes me feel sophisticated. (C—Consequence)
> So...?
> I feel good about myself.   (V—Value)

In the above example, the interviewer has led the participant from an attitude to various consequences to an end value (self-esteem). The data collected are analyzed using several techniques. Standard analysis results in a visual display such as tables and charts. The analysis steps include the following:

Step 1: Content analysis. This step involves going through the interview transcripts and identifying attitudes, values, and consequences.

Step 2: Constructing the implication matrix. In this step, the analyst constructs a matrix that shows how frequently each construct (be it an attribute, consequence, or value) is associated with every other construct.

Step 3: Constructing the hierarchical value map. This is a visual representation of the implications matrix. A typical hierarchical map shows how attributes, consequences, and values are related.

Step 4: Determining the dominant perceptual orientations. In this step, the analyst tries to understand the pathways that lead from the bottom to the top. A formal numeric table that explains the dominant perceptual orientations can be created at this stage.

Zaltman Metaphor Elicitation Technique (ZMET)

This technique was developed by Gerald Zaltman (Harvard University) and Robin Higie Coulter (University of Connecticut) and was designed to elicit the mental models that drive consumer thoughts and behaviour.

In a typical ZMET study, a small group of consumers (about 20) are recruited to take photographs and collect pictures (from the internet, magazines, newspapers, and books) to show what a brand means to them. The respondents come for a two-hour, one-on-one interview.

The interview, known as a "guided conversation," may involve several tasks such as:
- storytelling (describe the content of each picture),

- missed images (pictures that the consumer could not find along with an explanation of their relevance),
- sorting (sort pictures into meaningful groups and label each group),
- construct elicitation (produce basic constructs and their interrelationships using Kelly repertory grid and laddering techniques),
- most representative picture (picture that represents the brand),
- opposite images (picture that is opposite of the brand),
- sensory images (what does and does not describe the concept in terms of colour, emotion, sound, smell, taste, and touch),
- mental map (consumers are asked to create a map or causal model that connects all the constructs elicited in the process of the guided conversation),
- summary image (consumers create a summary image representing the core issues), and
- vignette (consumers put together a vignette or short video to help communicate important issues).

7. Qualitative Methods Online

The world of research has taken a quantum leap in the past decade and is on the threshold of an Artificial intelligence revolution. The internet has become a ubiquitous, global source of information and entertainment and a comprehensive shopping channel accessed through computers, tablets and smartphones. The Covid-19 global pandemic sped up the adoption of virtual interactions and made video links such as Zoom and MS Teams almost universally accessible and acceptable. This has opened several alternative qualitative methodologies – offering researchers the ability to pull in participants from a broader geographic distribution, and the opportunity to get much closer to the action. This has also allowed qualitative research to continue when face-to-face interactions are restricted (e.g., during a pandemic lockdown).

Initially used only for online versions of face-to-face research – focus groups and in-depth interviews -- digital technologies now offer researchers a plethora of unique opportunities to capture consumer behaviour and motivations in-the-moment, where it happens. Capturing speech and respondents' facial expressions from video links also provides extensive inputs for Artificial Intelligence analysis.

Here are some examples of the fast-evolving new research approaches.

Virtual or Online Focus Groups

Initially, online focus groups were thought of as simply an online version of the in-person focus group, with participants in a virtual room, guided by a moderator and observed by others in a virtual backroom. The video links that become common during the Covid-19 pandemic have made the two more similar than ever before, but the dynamics and outputs can be quite different.

Here is an overview of how virtual focus groups can work. With the pace of innovation in this space, new methods are continually emerging.

Recruitment. Respondents are recruited from a research panel, client list or by a focus group recruiter according to the demographic and behavioural requirements of the study. They can be geographically widely dispersed because there is no need to come together at a central facility. One essential requirement is that their connectivity be appropriate (e.g., to participate in a video link, watch videos, etc.).

Facility. Rather than a centrally located room with a one-way mirror, the focus group can take place on a video link like Zoom or MS Teams. It can also use a website designed to allow for different levels of interaction. On the website version, the moderator and participants can see and hear each other, and 'observers' can watch and post comments only in the 'backroom' where other observers and the moderator can see them. The moderator bridges both the participants' room and the backroom and follows both.

Discussion Guide. The discussion guide is prepared as it would be for any qualitative exercise, but it can be programmed into the website for both the moderator and observers to see.

Advantages. Online focus groups have several advantages: participants don't have to travel to a central facility, and are, as a result, more available to participate. Participants from a wide variety of backgrounds can be recruited quickly, and low incidence respondents can be located faster; geographically dispersed respondents can be included in the same group, some respondents may be less intimidated by other people. The full transcripts can be made available to clients and researchers instantaneously.

A key advantage, as Artificial intelligence evolves, is that voice and video images are recorded and can be analyzed using text analytics (on the transcripts), speech or facial emotion recognition and sentiment analysis.

The backroom is not unlike a face-to-face group session – observers can exchange messages to discuss what they are hearing and can send messages to the moderator. They can also be distracted by other tasks and pop in-and-out of attentiveness.

Disadvantages. The online environment may allow participants to take on a fake identity and pose as someone else in order to earn the incentive. For example, in a recent pharmaceutical study one participant falsely claimed to be at home in the Canadian target market, but the tropical bird calls and foliage in the background clearly indicated that he was not.

Because they are not in the same room with as the moderator, participants are also more easily distracted and can pop in-and-out of attentiveness.

Analysis. Interpreting the results of qualitative research in the virtual environment is undergoing a massive shift as we prepare this book. Artificial Intelligence is creating new tools and technologies that can:

- analyze transcripts to find patterns, themes and inconsistencies,
- reduce bias by giving every single data point the same weight against the same criteria, and

- identify, measure and analyze subconscious indicators of emotion e.g. facial expressions, tone of voice and language sentiment in ways that were previously only available in biometric lab settings. [1]

It is important to understand that AI can collect and analyze the data points, but it doesn't have the wisdom that human moderators bring to creating forward-focused business solutions.

Despite all of this technological change, the **qualitative report** that emerges from virtual or online focus groups still requires the researcher's wisdom and story-telling ability to create insightful and impactful business direction.

Online Bulletin Boards / Online Ethnography

While participants in an online focus group are all required to attend during the same 1 ½ to 2-hour window, those who participate in a research *bulletin board* are asked to check the bulletin board website periodically over several days.

When they do, they'll see questions that have been posted by the moderator. They may be asked to examine some visual stimuli like concepts or videos, they may see some responses posted by other participants, and they can offer their own perspectives before signing off again. Conceptually, the online bulletin board is more like a series of simultaneous, digital, individual depth interviews with little meaningful interaction between participants.

By coming in and out over time, participants can think about the subject without being influenced by other participants. They can go about their daily lives with the questions in mind and are often assigned tasks. They may be asked to photograph something relevant in their environment (the food in their fridge, the beer sold in their neighbourhood bar, the clothing stores displays that appeal to them, sponsorships they may have seen at an event), and submit those with detailed, thoughtful explanations. They can be asked to go on a shopping expedition and report back on sources of delight or annoyance.

If a mobile device is being used, participants can report on what they are seeing, hearing, feeling in real-time while it is happening. A skilled moderator can use these interactions as a form of online ethnography – observing, questioning and probing without the need to be in the same location.

The near-universal penetration of smartphones suggests that this form of online qualitative ethnography is likely to be a significant growth opportunity in this field.

---

[1] Sidi Lemine, Jade Kite's AI Insider newsletter, May 19, 2023

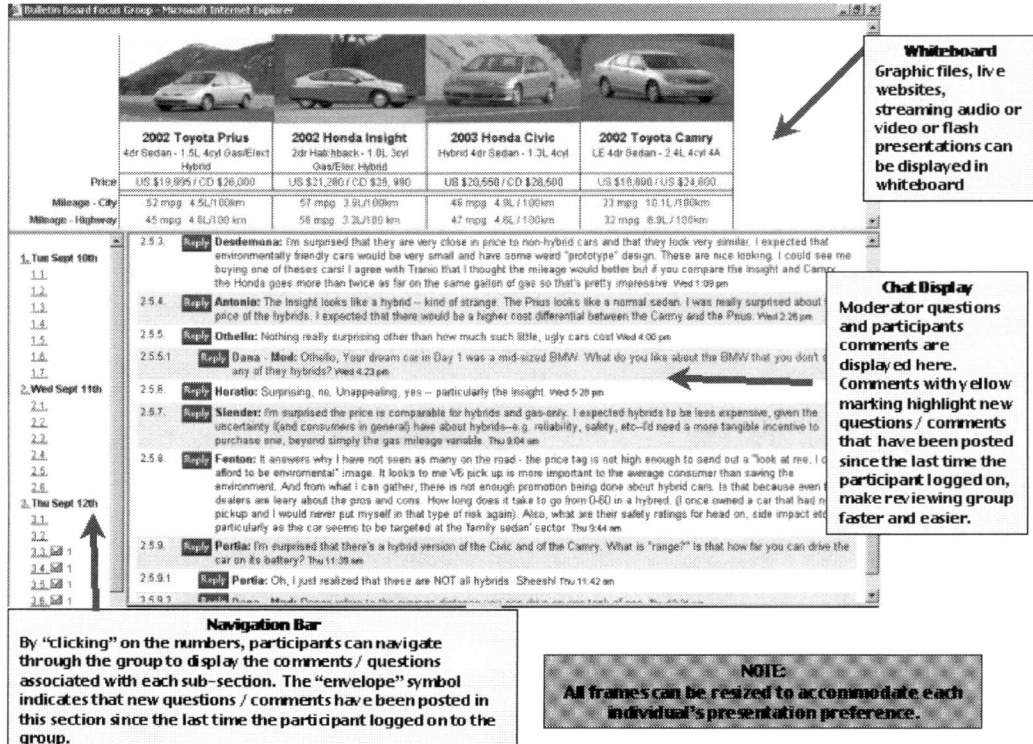

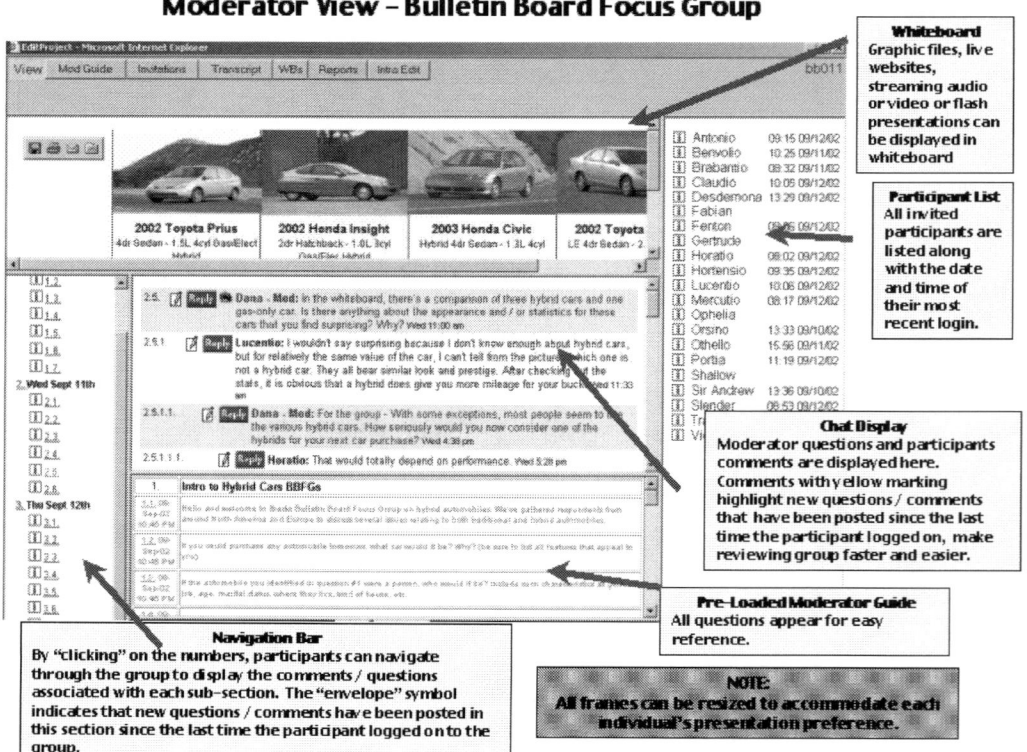

Online Communities

The qualitative research techniques described to this point are generally about two-way interactions primarily between participants and the researcher, with some controlled discussions. Online Communities are more about the exchanges between all members.

A true community is not a Panel, which is a pool of potential respondents recruited to participate in research studies. A true community is connected through several interactive tools and can communicate, not only with the researchers but also with each other.

A community can join in bulletin board discussions, post their own questions and begin chains, participate in moderated discussions, ideate and co-create and provide unsolicited feedback if the urge hits.

An online community is generally recruited because members have a common interest.

Example 1. A running shoe manufacturer has a research partner set up a community of hard-core running enthusiasts. The goal is to develop a deep understanding of and empathy with the everyday challenges, frustrations and delights of this very focused group. There may be forums to discuss how one prepares for marathons, discussions of the latest high-tech fabrics for running clothes, pros and cons of different running shoes for various climates and running conditions and discussions of unmet needs and 'ideal' sports equipment.

Example 2. A maker of baby food wants to ensure it understands the deepest hopes and motivations of young parents, using any insights gleaned as a springboard for stronger positioning and communications efforts. Recognizing the increasing role of men in caring for young babies, the research company is charged with creating a community of fathers of newborns and infants. In this safe space, they can discuss their deepest feelings with others in the same situation. Discussion spaces can be created to talk about spousal negotiations, how to find male social groups in a 'Mommy and Me' culture, dealing with stereotypes about bumbling dads, and of course, feeding practices. Members regularly upload videos of their successes and their failures to get advice, share learning and have some fun.

A community can be a short-term "pop-up," i.e., a week or two, designed to tackle a specific research question, or it could be an on-going effort over several years with regular refreshes.

Participants may be asked to log in to the custom-designed website every day or several times per week to respond to requests, upload videos or images, answer polls, or interact with other members. The website can be branded (e.g., the running shoe manufacturer puts their name on it) or 'blind' (the baby food manufacturer opted to have the market research partner act as the named host of their community).

The environment is particularly well-suited for ideation and co-creation – activities that ask participants to build on what others offer up as suggestions. As with any online methodology, it's generally not possible to hear the 'tone' of the response or to interpret body language. The key, as with any methodology, is to set expectations appropriately for the tool that is being used.

Social Listening

So much of today's interactions and information exchange takes place on social media sites: Facebook, X (Twitter), Instagram, Pinterest, WhatsApp and many, many others. Tools exist to scan these discussions, using keywords and putting geographic and time period fences around them.

> Example 1. A well-known bank has hired a celebrity as a spokesperson and wants to keep close tabs on how the 'Twittersphere' is talking about him. They ask the research company to do monthly 'Social Listening' reports, covering just the three regions where they have branches, and capturing just the commentary that was posted within the past four weeks. They are looking for an increase in associations with their brand name and want to be alerted if any of it turns negative.

> Example 2. A food manufacturer is about to launch a product with a new artificial sweetener in it. They know the science behind it but don't know what might be circulating on social media. Before they make the announcement, they commission some social listening to see what information or misinformation, if anything, is circulating so they can be ready to respond if need be.

The deliverables from social listening are generally word clouds, with the most frequently mentioned words appearing in larger fonts, and linkage networks, that show which words are used most often together when posting about the topic. Sentiment analysis is used very often.

Social listening is fast, easy and a great way to 'dip' into the consumers' mindset. It can be a one-off inquiry or set up as an on-going monitoring program. Another key advantage of social listening is "timestamp." One project can "listen in" on social media posts from *last* summer and from today to map shifts.

8. Other Technology-based Techniques

The introduction of digital methodologies for qualitative research started in the first decade of the 21st century. The considerable advantages include accessing the perspective of widely dispersed consumers who no longer have to live within a short drive of focus group facilities to participate. They made it possible to reduce travel costs for moderators and observers and made it easier to 'scale-up' projects by conducting a larger number of interactions in a shorter time frame. The automatic recording of voice and video also offer a huge advantage to artificial intelligence analysis.

From Online to Mobile

The shift from computers to smart mobile devices has had a significant impact. Increasingly, consumers are accessing the internet through their smartphones and tablets instead of through laptops or desktop computers. The advantage of being able to check-in from anywhere, anytime, is hard to resist.

What this means is that consumers are *always* carrying the tool needed to provide ethnographic feedback to researchers, in the actual moment when they are engaged in the behaviour that is under study. For example:

- Who are the event's sponsors? Take photos of any brand logos you see on-site and text them to us.
- Help us understand traffic patterns in the supermarket by downloading an app that will track your movement from when you enter to when you exit.
- Anytime you take a drink of a beverage, open an app and tell us where you are, what you are feeling, what you ordered, why you made that choice, how satisfied you are with your choice. Then send us a photo of the scene.
- Making lunch for your kids? Take photos of the ingredients you are using and the finished product and post them to the study's Instagram or Facebook page.
- Make a short video of you and your friends at your favourite bar, talking about what you are ordering and why.

Mobile technology is already ubiquitous. The next wave of mobile connectivity will include wristwatches and eye-glasses that will be able to embed researchers right into 'the moment.' AI will help us deconstruct and analyze anything that is picked up through these new technologies.

Overall, remote qualitative research is bound to become more common.

Virtual Reality

Another emerging technology is virtual reality. Rather than setting up different store layouts in a real space, instead of building prototypes of new cars for consumers to sit in, designers are using computer programs and body-wear (headsets, gloves etc.) to create artificial environments that can be activated with a few keyboard clicks.

Participants can walk through the environment, reach for and pick up products on the shelf, turn them over to read the back, put them in a shopping cart and move on to a new section. Their physical movements are captured by motion sensors and translated into the visuals that they see through the headsets.

This methodology can be used for both quantitative and qualitative research. The latter might involve consumers talking through what they see, how they are reacting, what their decisions are and the reasons behind them.

For now, the virtual reality methodology requires a visit to a central location. Still, if VR gaming systems become more ubiquitous, it would not be a significant leap to use these home-based games for research purposes by building a program that can be downloaded when needed by potential respondents.

Artificial intelligence is capable of learning the behaviours of participants in these environments, leading to the emergence of 'synthetic data' – predictive models of how consumers would react to a stimuli without actually involving participants.

9. How to Analyze, Interpret and Report the Findings

Regardless of the qualitative methodology used, the thought processes that go into analysis and reporting are very similar.

Independent qualitative researchers often handle the analysis process themselves from analysis to interpretation to reporting and presentation. In larger organizations, the efforts may be shared with 'apprentices' and other colleagues.

Qualitative analysis can include a wide variety of techniques and tactics. As the groups or interviews are happening, the discussions are captured in audio and video recordings or by note-takers. Moderators often discretely make analytical notes to capture critical phrases and note dynamics and non-verbal cues.

Organizing

As a first stage, the moderator or a trained analyst re-reads the notes, watches the video recordings or reads transcripts of the recordings. As they do, they may apply two standard modes of analysis: classification and pattern identification.

Classification. Every quote and every analytical note is examined and classified under various categories derived from the study objectives. A study outline may yield ten or more main classifications, each divided into sub-classifications.

Pattern Identification. The moderator or analyst looks for patterns among groups and tests the data with the following questions:
- Which groups reacted one way, which another? Why?
- Were there correlations by group structure? Why?
- On what did the groups agree or disagree? Why?

AI Technology. Emerging technologies can now be applied to analyze the videos and transcripts from qualitative groups or interviews to identify common and variant themes. This fast-developing field, including 'natural language processing, can perform sentiment analysis, and speech and facial emotion recognition in minutes, saving a lot of professional time. The experience, wisdom and foresight of a human qualitative researcher is still required to extrapolate the findings, apply it to the business problem and develop impactful insights and strategic recommendations.

From this process, which seeks not merely to describe the responses but to explain them, come the hypotheses that qualitative research generates for helping to confront the key marketing objectives.

Analysis and Interpretation

Although there is no generally agreed-upon format for reporting qualitative research findings, there are different levels of understanding that the research report should reflect.

The following levels of understanding are important:

1. **Reporting (what happened):**

At this level, the analyst looks for what people actually said, using their verbatim comments or video clips extensively to bring the findings to life.

This can be useful in understanding the "language of the consumer" as well as establishing the difficulty people may have relating to the language used by marketers and advertisers. Does an average investor really know what a "fixed-income instrument" is? Would they recognize 'pralines' as boxed chocolates?

The goal at this level is simply to summarize the salient points of the discussion with supporting verbatim comments from the participants.

2. **Analysis (what it seems to mean):**

At this more profound level, the analyst can go beyond what was said verbally by interpreting body language and tone of voice. For instance,
- If a participant simply smiled and commented that it was good when shown an advertisement, was she being polite, or did she really like the ad?
- Did the body language of the respondent who agreed with others consistently indicate that he was doing so only to be agreeable?
- Did participants' positive comments indicate simple acceptance or great enthusiasm?
- Which words or phrases did a respondent emphasize?
- Did the participant simply echo a cliché or genuinely comment on the topic at hand?
- Was the participant saying things simply because they were socially acceptable?

At this phase, the analyst, perhaps with the help of AI, pulls the pieces together and identifies areas of apparent consensus and dissent, looks for contradictions that reveal surface responses rather than deeply held feelings, draws lines of meaning between different areas of probing, attempts to decipher what may be demographic or cultural differences and simply put, thinks through what the potential answers to the research questions might really mean.

By thinking deeply about the patterns of discussion, the analyst can pull out insights into deeper meanings and motivations. It is a creative process grounded in careful reflection and built on experience.

The client also has a role in the analysis phase – offering commentary and interpretation that is filtered through knowledge of their company, the industry, and their own experience in the field.

3. **Targeting (identifying market segments):**

As the moderator or analyst organizes the themes and insights, he or she gains an understanding of how consumers might differ from each other. Framing this analysis in terms of underlying market segments can help identify a sub-market that may respond to a specific message or be motivated by a specific benefit. Qualitative research can create the hypothesis that they exist but cannot extrapolate their size or their value to the client.

4. Trend Context (what it means today):

Qualitative research is a relatively open forum for participants; the comments they make can provide insight into societal shifts. If the same unexpected comment is made in several different interviews, groups or bulletin posts, a researcher might identify this as an emerging trend.

> Example. During a qualitative project about all-inclusive resorts, several participants across several groups volunteer their fears about being in public spaces, mentioning terrorist attacks and kidnappings in popular destinations. The researcher suggests that this may be a trending concern that could affect the destinations travelers include in their consideration sets.

5. Implications (so what?):

A good moderator does not simply lay out the problems but offers solutions as well. To do this, the moderator needs to be familiar with the client's marketing and communication objectives to ensure the solutions do not sound unrealistic. In fact, the more a moderator knows about the context of the problem, the more effective he or she will be in outlining solutions.

The Report

Even if the client observes all the groups, listens in on all interviews or reads all the bulletin board posts or transcripts, a report is still needed. The interpretation and conclusions that come from careful reflection, connecting the dots and rolling in knowledge and experience, will not be apparent from simply being aware of what was said. Remember as well, that the "backroom" may hear things differently than the moderator who is in the room with the participants.

Besides, many people who did not observe or read the proceedings will need to use the findings: senior managers, brand managers, the sales team, communications specialists, the advertising or packaging design agencies, a new employee who will be hired six months from now. It's important to have a carefully constructed report that these people can refer to.

It may take as long as two to three weeks to complete an analysis and prepare the comprehensive report, which includes participants' verbatim comments and the moderator's interpretation.

In many cases, a client will ask for a topline report with the moderator's 'impressions' that can be produced within a few days. These reports are not substitutes for comprehensive reports since they lack the careful analysis and reflection and wouldn't have the very revealing verbatim comments.

There are two thoughts to report styles. Traditionally, the qualitative report has been a text-heavy Word document that painstakingly builds the analysis into a comprehensive revelation of findings and conclusions.

Today, clients have little time to read long, wordy documents. They need a direct line from the evidence, through the insights, to the recommendations. Increasingly, qualitative reports are short PowerPoint (or similar) presentation decks, heavy in illustrations and headlines, with bubble verbatims built in at appropriate moments. These have the benefit of being appropriate to present summaries to senior management and other stakeholders.

If focus groups have produced collages or product sorts, photos of them help illustrate the observations. If online methodologies result in photo or video submissions, illustrative examples can be rolled into the report. The report can also be illustrated by images of people or products that are mentioned. Increasingly, the report includes compelling, edited clips of participants voicing key phrases that were central to the conclusions drawn.

The goal today, as with any research report, is to communicate the findings and provide direction that is as painless as possible, even entertaining for the client. The 'video' report is emerging as a popular deliverable – skillfully piecing together key clips from recorded interviews, respondent submissions, even 're-enactments' with the researcher's voice-over, will make a point that a client will never forget.

Regardless of the format, a comprehensive report might include the following elements:

1. Introduction
a. Background and purpose
b. Detailed objectives

2. Method
a. General approach
b. Where and how conducted

3. Executive Summary

4. Discussion
This section should not be organized in the order of the discussion guide, but in a way that clearly responds to each of the original objectives. Headlines should contain the critical insights that emerged, and evidence should be provided through illustrations, carefully composed analysis and selected verbatim comments. It's important to understand that different people will approach the report with different intentions: a quick skim to get the general flow and conclusions, more in-depth reading to capture the nuances, and with great detail to capture language and brand or product-specific reactions.

5. Conclusions and Recommendations
The research must lead to some conclusions. So, what are the hypotheses that emerge for the research objectives? What are the insights that can inform decisions or that can be validated and sized in quantitative research? A researcher should know enough about the client's business to be able to make some recommendations about future business decisions.

6. Additional material
The report may also include other supporting materials such as discussion guides, audio, video, or images. When the audio is transcribed, the transcript is often provided to the client as a separate document.

Avoiding Numbers

It is imperative to understand that qualitative findings should not be reported with numbers. Participants have been chosen to represent the target population, but they are not a representative sample of the full population.

As a result, it is not appropriate to report that "8 out of 10 participants agreed with this statement" ... or "half reported this behaviour" ... and certainly not that "90% liked this proposed service". The reaction of qualitative participants provides insight into how the broader population thinks and reacts, but their reaction cannot be quantitatively projected onto the broader population.

Instead, it is appropriate to say that "some participants felt the statement sounded pretentious," or "the discussion revealed a degree of enthusiasm for this proposal," or "the general tone was more negative towards X than Y because it was felt Y did not fit with the company's image."

Natural language processing, including word clouds and sentiment analysis, has introduced more quantitative interpretation of the findings. Care must be taken to ensure that rich qualitative insights are not overshadowed by the graphs and tables provided by natural language processing.

The Presentation

Not all qualitative studies lead to a personal presentation. A skillfully crafted report may be sufficient to communicate the findings, and a client may need to move quickly with the results.

But a presentation is an excellent opportunity to discuss what has emerged from the research and to clear up any potential misunderstanding. It's also when other stakeholders – the client's management or agencies, the brand managers, any quantitative researchers who may be undertaking the 'next phase' of research – can be in the room and align their understanding with the client's.

It is also an important opportunity for the qualitative researcher to build on the relationship with the client and set themselves up for the next project.

10. How Does Bias Arise in Qualitative Research?

There may be three types of bias in qualitative research:
- study-related,
- moderator-related, or
- client-related.

Study-related biases arise out of incorrect problem definition, improper recruitment, poor display material, restrictions on the proper rotation of display material, an inappropriate research location, excessive subject matter, inappropriate use of AI and other technology and unrealistic timing provisions.

Moderator-related biases arise out of factors such as the moderator's inability to remain dispassionate, moderator incompetence, inability to control and insensitivity to crosscurrents and subtleties.

Client-related biases arise when the client inadequately or incorrectly briefs the moderator or when the client introduces his or her expectations and biases into the briefing. Clients can also insist on adding or removing lines of questioning while the groups are in progress, eliminating the ability to make key comparisons or to gather broad enough evidence to create hypotheses.

If the research team is aware of biases in a study, they can adjust for them, as long as these biases are not overwhelming.

11. When to Use Qualitative Research

Qualitative research can be a powerful tool if used appropriately and carried out by a competent researcher. However, it can be misused. It is a common misperception that one does qualitative research when the budget isn't big enough for quantitative research; that it can answer all of the same questions but on a smaller scale.

A related misperception is that if more groups or interviews are added, it can be treated like quantitative research, counting the number of hands raised and projecting to the broader population. This leads to overblown designs that attempt to cover all possible combinations of demographics and markets.

Some research buyers shy away from quantitative research because of its technical nature and feel more comfortable with qualitative research, even when it is not appropriate or adequate. They like to hear the consumers' voices and believe that is all they need to understand them.

What this means is that decisions that may require more quantitative solutions are being made on qualitative insights and hypotheses. Such misuse eventually diminishes the power of qualitative research by forcing it to do things that it is not designed to do.

Qualitative research should be used when it is the correct approach to the problem at hand. Some of the specific applications to which qualitative research is well-suited include:
- brand or service positioning exploration;
- new product or advertising concept reaction and refinement;
- assessment of the competitive environment and brand or corporate imagery assessment;
- packaging, and graphic design development.

Generally, qualitative research works when:
- there are information gaps that need to be filled before quantitative methods can meaningfully and effectively used;
- there is a need to understand the basis of consumer motivations, priorities, anxieties, hidden agendas, patterns of perception, desires, and so forth that may not fully emerge when investigated quantitatively;
- many initial possibilities need to be narrowed down to a more workable and promising short list;
- the language consumers use when dealing with a product or service needs to be understood;
- it is used as input to the creative process;

- the subject matter is too subtle to create efficient direct questions for use in standard survey research techniques.

Qualitative research is **unsuitable** when the objective is to obtain a quantitative estimate of any parameter such as market share of a brand, the extent to which a brand is liked or disliked or the extent to which consumers have changed their perceptions. It is also unsuitable when generalizations to the population are required because we cannot know whether the people in a focus group represent anyone other than themselves. This is because the "sample size" is too small, and they are not chosen using a scientific probability approach. Plus, a focus group of 8 people might transform into three subgroups that have different perspectives and react in different ways.

While qualitative research may provide many valuable insights, its results cannot be generalized to the population without support from quantitative research. It is crucial to bear this in mind because errors in this regard can prove to be expensive for the company commissioning the research.

Here is a summary of when qualitative research **is and is not** appropriate.

Examples of Business Issues that Can be Addressed by Qualitative Research

- We're not sure who our market is. Who uses the category, and why? What are their lifestyles, and how do our products fit into it? Are we pigeon-holed into a specific use?
- We don't know how to speak to our market. What language and images would resonate with consumers? Which are appropriate for our brand?
- We don't know how consumers might react to our new product idea. What selling points and barriers would they see? How might we improve the idea to make it resonate more?
- We don't know why they've stopped buying our product. What flaws are they seeing? Where are we falling short when compared to competitors? We want to uncover the real reasons, not just superficial responses.
- We need to create new products that target unmet needs. Where do we start? What are consumers really looking for and where are current products on the market falling short?
- We need new ideas for an ad campaign. A good starting point is to listen to consumers talk about their deepest dreams and aspirations, something that we can realistically latch onto, so we are speaking the same language.
- We need to understand what various alternative approaches to our new advertising campaign are going to communicate with consumers. Is there a risk that it might be misunderstood?
- We want to know if consumers are having difficulties with our current packaging and how we might correct them. Are there some new ideas that could give us a competitive advantage?
- We want to know how consumers are thinking of our brand compared to the competitors. Is there an emotional reaction that is holding us back? If so, what are the elements of this and how might we correct them?
- Can we gain some insights into who our audience is for media so we can sell them to our advertisers in human terms?

- Is there any risk in taking the strategic shift that we are planning? Might it be misunderstood? (disaster check)
- We've uncovered something in our quantitative research that we hadn't expected. What beliefs or behaviours might be behind it?

Examples of Business Issues that <u>*Cannot*</u> be Answered by Qualitative Research

Any sizing or measurement question:
- How many people will subscribe to this service?
- How often will they buy the product?
- Which of the new concepts is a bigger idea?
- How big are the different segments in this market?

Any profiling question:
- What are the demographics of our customers?
- How do our customers compare to those of our competitors?

Ranking or prioritization questions:
- We want a definitive answer on the top-three reasons why people buy our product.
- Which policy platform are voters going to respond to?

High-risk decisions that should be made on economic feasibility:
- Is this idea big enough to justify the acquisition of a new manufacturing facility?
- Will we increase our sales if we reposition our brand?
- Is this new product idea a breakthrough that will pay off?

Any finding that needs to be projected to the parent population.

Concluding Comments

Qualitative research provides the colour commentary that brings market research to life. It gives us the ability to hear and integrate the voice of the consumer, to listen to and understand nuances in language and perception, to follow the consumers' thought processes and study how they are impacted by discourse. Qualitative is increasingly 'in the moment,' allowing us into consumers' lives as they are experiencing our products and services and allowing us to observe, probe and challenge them. Qualitative makes quantitative research more efficient by narrowing our focus, building a solid foundation of hypotheses and zeroing in on language that we know consumers will understand and use. And not surprisingly, qualitative helps us bring clients on board – allowing them to hear what they need to hear directly from the consumers' mouths. Qualitative research is not an alternative approach or a sideline. It is an integral component of the marketing research toolbox.

UNIT 6

How to Design a Questionnaire

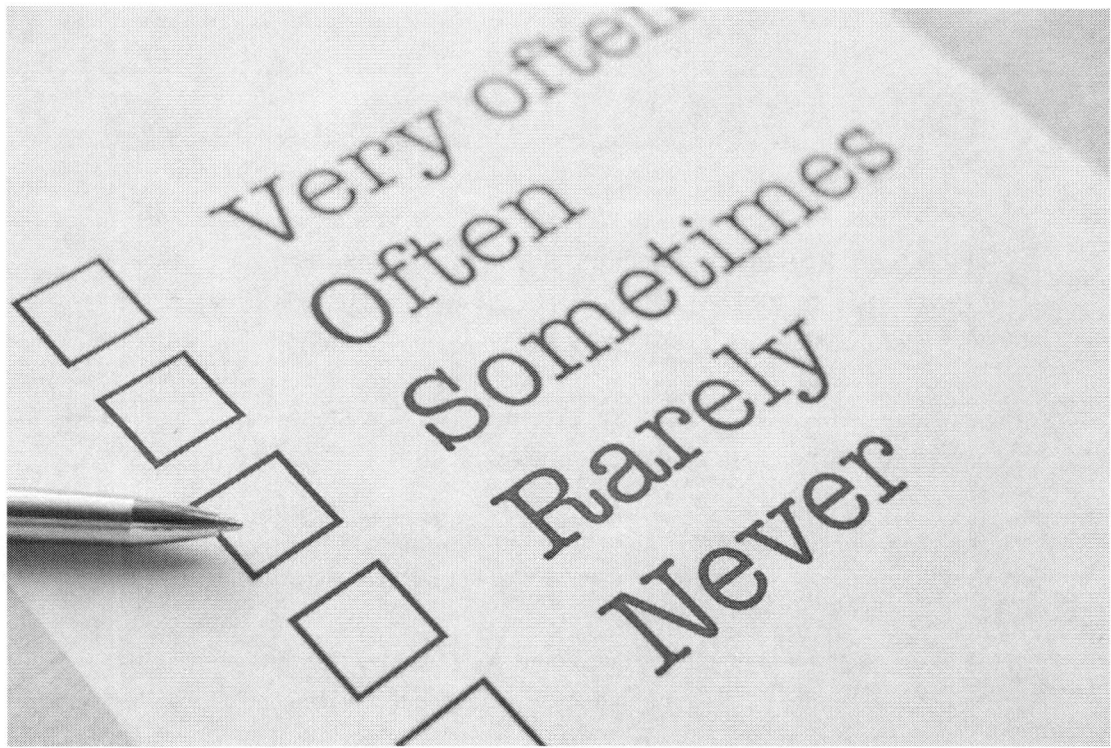

The survey questionnaire has been the primary quantitative work tool for generations of marketing researchers. It is how clients' information requests are translated into words that consumers will understand, and how we collect the information that consumers offer in a consistent and interpretable manner.

In a world of do-it-yourself "polls," the skill required to construct a useable questionnaire is often underestimated. It is, in fact, one of the most important things a marketing researcher is expected to do. Poorly constructed questionnaires generally produce erroneous results.

Writing a good questionnaire is part art and part science. It requires strong language and logic skills and a degree of creativity. These come with experience, and this **chapter** will give you the foundation that you need to get started – the principles, techniques and knowledge of potential pitfalls.

Artificial intelligence can be an important questionnaire development tool. It can assemble questions used in the past, put them into a format that has worked in the past, spot redundancies and ensure instructions are comprehensive. What it *cannot* do is ensure that the client's information requirements are translated into questions that will provide predictive insights and strategic direction.

Why is Questionnaire Design Important?

A **questionnaire** is comprised of a standard set of questions, asked in a consistent order and asked of all people who participate in a survey. Questionnaires are vehicles that help support better marketing decisions based on information collected from samples drawn from the relevant study populations.

A well-written questionnaire will:
- collect the specific information we need to achieve each survey objective;
- minimize the effort required by respondents;
- be suitable for the methodology used (e.g., interviewer conducted, online, mobile);
- ask questions that are interpreted the same way by all respondents; and
- produce results that can be interpreted clearly and precisely with no confusion.

The same questions are to be asked, in the same manner, and generally in the same order for all respondents. This is critical because the responses are combined and analyzed as a database, there is no room for *respondents* to **interpret the question in different ways**, and no space for the *researcher* to **interpret individual responses separately**.

For example, suppose you want to find out how many basketball games a person attended during the past 12 months. You can ask directly: *"How many basketball games did you attend in the past 12 months?"*

It looks straightforward, but the question is likely to provide misleading results.
- It starts with the assumption that the respondent *has* attended a basketball game in the past 12 months. Some respondents may accept this and make up a number, perhaps because they don't want to disappoint the interviewer, perhaps because they want to appear 'cool.'
- It does not specify what level of basketball we are interested in hearing about. Is it professional basketball like the NBA, or might it include college or high school teams? What about a pick-up game at the local park?
- Does 'attend' also include watching a game on TV? What about shooting hoops with family members on the driveway?

A more experienced questionnaire writer may instead write the question this way:

a. *Which of the following, if any, have you done in the past 12 months? (Select all that apply)*
- *Attended a professional basketball game in person*
- *Attended a college or high school basketball game in person*
- *Watched basketball on TV*
- *Played basketball on a team or in a league*

- *Played informal basketball with friends or family members*
- *None of these*

[If professional basketball game selected (Code 1), ask b.]

b. *How many professional basketball games have you attended in the past 12 months?*

The second version does not imply that respondents have been to a professional game and is very clear about different 'attendance' options. By introducing more everyday activities such as watching on TV or playing with friends, the researcher has made it easier for respondents to select at least one thing from the list. Finally, 'none of these' means that *every* respondent has an answer to select.

In designing a questionnaire, the marketing researcher has to keep track of two parallel components: the standardized **question wording**, and the **programming logic** that determines how each response might affect the order of the questions that follow. This would be the same whether the interview is conducted by an interviewer or self-completed by the respondent. Nothing must be left to individual interpretation.

The Impact of Current Trends on Questionnaire Design

The increased growth of **mobile technology** and **social media** is a significant societal shift that has a big impact on how questionnaires should be designed. Researchers must take into account the following developments:

- With mobile devices like smartphones and tablets, consumers can be continually connected to the internet.
- With the growth of social media, consumers not only have a good reason to connect continually, but they are also addicted to the continual stimulation that it provides.

The result is that attention spans are shorter than ever, consumers get bored quickly, and more engaging stimulation is only a tap away. It is more important than ever that we minimize the burden involved in completing a questionnaire and engage respondents in varied and exciting tasks.

At the same time, mobile technology gives us the ability to capture consumer feedback any time, 'in the moment,' when they are experiencing the activity we want to understand. For example, using cellphone cameras, we can capture images of what subjects are seeing and doing and use video analytics to provide quantified data.

Social media has also created a culture of self-exposure. Many consumers are more than willing to open up about their most intimate behaviours and deepest motivations.

Passive data capture technology will continue to develop rapidly. Passive observation methods such as eye-tracking glasses can capture what consumers look at as they walk through stores (although not necessarily what they 'see'). Cookies can relay what users are doing on specific sites or in social media. Sensors can capture details from digital devices as people walk by them. As technology develops, ethical considerations around permission based on informed consent become more important than ever.

Unfortunately, **fraudulent respondents** are also a growing concern. They complete surveys for which they don't qualify to earn incentives that may be only tokens in developed countries but can be a significant source of income in developing countries. "Click farms" exist to complete surveys fraudulently on a large scale. It is unfortunate, but modern marketing research must take this into account when designing good questionnaires, e.g., building in traps that will identify fraudulent respondents.

What are the Steps in Designing a Questionnaire?

There are six steps in designing a good questionnaire:
1. Decide what topics the questionnaire should cover. (Scope based on Objectives)
2. Decide how the topics will be sequenced. (Sequencing the questionnaire)
3. Decide how each question will be worded. (Questionnaire wording)
4. Test and fine-tune the logic and flow. (Programming logic)
5. Decide on the layout, the design, and then edit. (Layout)
6. Pre-test the questionnaire and revise it. (Refinement)
7. Translate and adapt to different cultures. (Translation)

1. How to Define the Scope of the Study?

What Should We Include?

The primary purpose of a questionnaire is to gather information that can be used to **meet the objectives** of the study.

The first step in designing a questionnaire, therefore, is to make a list of items to be covered based on the research objectives. This is a crucial phase both in creating the outline of the questionnaire and in setting the expectations of the client who has specified the project objectives.

Given both clients' **tight research budgets** and respondents' **short attention spans**, care must be taken from the start that this list of topics is driven by what you **need** to know. Anything that is just a "**want**" to know or is prefaced by "**while we are at it**," should be put on a secondary list and included only if there is space.

For example, let's say that you are working for the manufacturer of a brand of laundry detergent called Dazzler. You are charged with understanding the health of the brand and its current positioning in the marketplace and determining what weaknesses must be addressed and what strengths can be exploited to provide growth.

We begin with a list of what will help us answer the research question. It might look something like this:
- How many people have heard of Dazzler?
- Where did they first hear about Dazzler?
- How many have they bought Dazzler?
- How often do they buy Dazzler?
- What incentives spur a purchase?
- How many packs do they usually buy at each purchase?
- How often do they use Dazzler?
- How many consider Dazzler their favourite brand?

How to Design a Questionnaire

- What brand might they consider buying instead of Dazzler?
- How do Dazzler and the alternative brands differ on important characteristics?
- Which brands are considered Dazzler's main competitors?
- What characteristics of detergent are important in driving the choice of a brand?
- What temperature of water do they use Dazzler with?
- What types of clothes do they wash with Dazzler?
- How do they measure the amount of detergent they put into a wash?
- What other laundry products do they use at the same time (softener)?
- What format of detergent do people prefer?
- What scent do they prefer?
- How often do they wash clothes?
- What do they do differently for various types of clothes (e.g. whites, colours, children's, heavily soiled, etc.)?
- How do they dry them?
- What does Dazzler's packaging communicate about the brand?
- How convenient is Dazzler to carry home/ store/ open/ reclose? Are they satisfied with Dazzler?
- Will they buy Dazzler in the future?
- Will they recommend Dazzler to others?
- Do they encounter any problems when they use Dazzler?
- How interested would they be in some new innovations that are in the pipeline?; etc.

It helps if the topics are arranged in **logical groupings**. Once a list similar to the one above is compiled, we might see the following groupings emerge:

- General laundry behaviours;
- General detergent shopping behaviours;
- Importance of characteristics in choosing between detergent brands;
- Detergent brand health (awareness, trial, preference, future intent);
- Detergent brand perceptions;
- Packaging reactions; and
- Innovation testing

At this point, it may become evident that we have **too many topics** for the maximum length of the questionnaire (based on budget and respondent endurance, a maximum engagement time of 20 minutes might be the limit). Some topics may need to be split for another study. Use logic to make this decision. For example, the detergent shopper and the person who does the laundry may be different people. So, might there be separate "shopper" and "user" studies? Reaction to the innovations might be biased by preceding questions on what is important in choosing between brands. Perhaps the innovation topic should be split out into a separate study. Packaging reaction might require sophisticated shelf testing to determine if Dazzler stands out from the competition. This, too, could be a stand-alone piece. So, at the core, perhaps this questionnaire has to focus on shopping, the importance of characteristics, brand health, perceptions, demographics and nothing else.

This scoping topic is, at times, a **challenging conversation** to have with a client, but the goal driving both the researcher and the client is high **quality** research – ensuring the most accurate and insightful findings. The questionnaire cannot overly burden the respondents and whittling down the number of topics is the first and most important step to ensuring a quality instrument.

How to Fine-tune the Scope

With the list of topics in hand, it will be necessary to gain some more precision in the scope of the questionnaire.

For example, one of the key objectives in the Dazzler example is understanding the brand health within the context of competitors. **Which competitors** should be included in the study must be addressed? There may be ten major detergent brands on the shelf, but when you take into account different formats, pack sizes, scents and formulations (e.g., for cold water), there may be 100 or more products (Stock Keeping Units or SKUs) that could be included in the study.

At this stage, we would want to discuss options with the client – do we focus only on the master brand level? Do we include formats but not scents? Perhaps we include all products, but only for a shortlist of the three largest competitors?

Understanding Dazzler's **brand health** is an objective. The first step in brand health is awareness. But awareness can be measured in several different ways:

- Top-of-mind ("When you think of detergents, what brand comes to mind first?")
- Unaided ("Name all the detergents you can think of. Anything else?")
- Aided ("Have you ever heard of Dazzler before now?")

Which of these questions should be included in the study? The answer may depend on the brand's current situation. If Dazzler is an established, top-three brand, then 'top of mind' might be the measure that has the most significant impact on future growth as they do battle with other well-known brands. If Dazzler is new to the market and just beginning to get a foothold, then aided awareness might be a better measure of growth as they try to get consumers' attention. An unaided awareness question can be followed by an aided awareness question.

Similarly, the highest measure of brand health might be measured in several different ways: use most often, favourite brand, would recommend to others, etc. It is essential to use the measure that is most relevant to the client's organization. We might want to consider:

- What have they used in the past to track a brand's strength? Consistent measures are crucial for comparability over time.
- Is there a measure that is used to judge the performance of brand managers, perhaps tied to a 'management by objective' or bonus plan?
- Does the organization have a performance measurement philosophy? For example, some have adopted the "Net Promoter Score" as the measure that is used across the organization to determine success. If so, this measure should be integrated into the list of topics. The Net Promoter Score (NPS) measures customer loyalty, satisfaction and enthusiasm with a company that's based on one question: "On a scale from 0 to 10, where 0 indicates that you definitely not recommend Dazzler to a friend or colleague and 10 signifies that you would definitely and always recommend Dazzler, how likely are you to recommend Dazzler to friends and colleagues?"

How to Map a Topic to Objectives

At every stage in the design of a questionnaire, it is important to keep an eye on how each topic, and eventually, each question, will **answer the specific objectives** of the study. This is important as topics are removed or added to ensure the design remains focused on what is 'needed.' It also ensures we don't lose the ability to answer an objective.

Not all objectives require an explicit question. Some **can be 'modelled'** from the results. For example, a topic that we need to cover in the Dazzler study is to determine what drives brand choice. Rather than explicitly asking "why do you choose one brand over another" (consumers may not know), we can model drivers by correlating what brand they buy most often with what characteristics they associate with that brand.

There will be some explicit hypotheses that have been formulated in advance and need to be tested in the study. For example, the brand manager may be concerned that consumers are not buying the brand because it is expensive. This is the stage in the design process when you determine what questions are needed to test those hypotheses.

Mapping the topics (and eventually the questions) back to the objectives and hypotheses is as simple as creating a 3-column chart that lists each topic, then each specific question and then the objective/hypothesis that each is intended to address.

Consider the following question map for investigating the hot cereal market. Each objective must be satisfied and this table identifies which questions will provide the needed information in the right-most column. The actual questions should be checked again to ensure compliance.

Topic from brief	*Analysis planned*	*Questions*
Objective #1: To determine the size of the current market		
Incidence of current hot cereal consumers	Make inference based on those screened into survey back to the general population. Compare the demographics of consumers to non-consumers.	Call Record
Incidence of potential consumers	Use 'never' in S.2 and Yes to 'would consider' among those screened out. Calculate on the base of the general population before the screening.	S. 2, T.1
Incidence of instant vs. standard preparation	On the base of the general population before the screening	S. 3
Volume calculation	Incidence x frequency x household size	Call record x S.3 x D.3
Objective #2: To understand the barriers to hot cereal consumption		
Barriers among rejectors	Question asked of those screened out (never in S2)	T.2
Why not eating more		Q. 16
Objective #3: To develop a clear picture of how hot cereal is consumed		
Who normally eats	Chart consumption by age group/gender	Q.11
Where, when,	Show daypart / meal-snack type/house plan	Q.12, 13
How prepared, What is added	Describe "typical" bowl	Q.14, 15
Objective #4: To uncover the motivations that drive consumption		
Drivers for category usage	Dependent variable: likely to eat hot cereal in the next few weeks.	Q.3

How to Design a Questionnaire

	Independent: category attributes / benefits	Q.5, 6
Drivers for product choice	Dependent variable: the brand most likely to **buy** in the next few weeks	Q.22
	Independent: Brand association w. attributes	Q.23, 24
Objective #5: To understand shopping behaviours		
Frequency of purchase, mission	# times/year, stock up/ regular/emergency	Q.28, 29
Influencers, coupons, sales		Q.30, 31, 32
Shopping list, in-store influences		Q.33, 34
Loyalty	What if stock out	Q.35

This table can be updated at every stage of the design process to help keep track of the objectives for both researchers and clients. If a question is inserted at some point that cannot be related to any of the hypotheses or objectives, discuss whether it is superficial and can be removed. It is often tempting to include additional questions due to curiosity, but this adds to the questionnaire length and could potentially fatigue and annoy respondents. An ideal questionnaire contains only questions that serve the objectives and hypotheses of the study.

2. How to Sequence the Questions

One of the most common errors made by inexperienced researchers is to order the questions in the same way the objectives are written. If you do this, it's unlikely the questionnaire flow will make sense to the respondents. There are several things to think of when structuring the questionnaire:

- Ordering the sections to achieve the tasks each is designed to achieve
- Following a line of thinking that respondents are comfortable with and that increases their comfort in revealing themselves
- Being careful not to reveal information that will influence how respondents answer subsequent questions

Generally speaking, questions follow this sequence, but it may be changed to suit the needs of the study.

Section	Content and examples
Screening quotas	Questions to establish that we are interviewing the appropriate participants
	Do you do all, almost all, about half, less than half or none of the grocery shopping for your household?
Main section	Questions that may be easy or complicated. It contains all questions that relate to different objectives and hypotheses of the study. An historical sequence may be best, e.g., what did you do in the past, what are you thinking now and doing now and what do you intend to do in the future.
Behavioural questions	[What they did] *How did you get to work yesterday: drive, take transit, ride a bike, walk, other?*

Attitudinal questions	[What they think] *In your opinion, should it be legal or illegal to use cannabis for recreational purposes?*
Lifestyle questions	[How they live] *Do you generally check the ingredient labels on food items before you buy them or not?*
Classification	*What is the total annual income of your household before taxes during this past year?*
	What is the highest level of education you have completed?

Each of these sections plays an important and distinct role in collecting respondent data and there are good reasons for following this order.

Screening and Quotas

Screening questions to fulfill quotas determine whether a consumer is eligible to take part in a survey and ensure the sample has the desired mix of respondents (through quotas). They are always the first to be asked.

Common screening questions include age or gender, recent use of a particular category of products, and responsibilities for decision making. Sometimes people in only a specific income range should be included in the survey. These questions about income, age, gender and education can be very sensitive to some respondents. If there are no quotas imposed on the study, those questions are typically asked last in the survey. Otherwise, people sensitive to those questions might leave the survey prematurely. When quotas are needed, ask only what is absolutely needed to qualify respondents.

For example, if we need to speak only to those aged 18 to 69 years who have bought a cough or cold medicine for the household in the past six months, the first question would ask about age, the second might ask if the respondent does all, most, half, less than half or none of the shopping for over the counter medications for their household and the third might ask if they have bought a cough or cold product within the past six months.

When asking that screening age question, ask only if the respondent is between 18 and 69 years of age and don't ask a complete age question; that should be left for the end of the questionnaire. Also, think about ways of asking sensitive questions in ways that might get more responses. People are more prone to answer an "age" question when asked if they were born between two years rather than when asked the actual age range or asked for the year-of-birth rather than the age.

If the person is outside the age range or does less than half of the shopping or if they have not bought a product in this category, they are excused from responding to the rest of the questions. This ensures that as little as possible of the respondent's time is wasted.

A typical screening need is to exclude all 'rejecters' of a category or service. For example, a vegetarian probably shouldn't be required to complete a survey on deli meat products. Someone who doesn't have a driver's license would not be helpful in a survey of car purchasing behaviour.

Quotas are also set to ensure that the final sample has the right mix of respondents. For example, it is usually important that a sample be representative of a specific parent population. This means that it should include a very specific number of men and women and the right share of people across different age groups. Once the targeted quota number for a group is achieved, the screening question will not let any more of that group into the survey.

For example, if the survey is to include 100 men and 100 women, the quota will only allow the first 100 men to continue into the main questionnaire. The screening questions can continue to admit women until 100 have completed the survey.

'Non-screening' questions mustn't find their way into the screener. For example, while asking about their responsibility for grocery shopping, it might be tempting to ask how often they shop. If this is not the screening criteria, then save it for the main questionnaire and ask it only of those who have qualified.

Screening questions must be written very carefully so that you do not offend or annoy a respondent at the very beginning of the interview. For example, you may want to include only those respondents who have a high net worth. Asking a personal wealth question at the very beginning of the survey can lead to many drop-outs. In this case, it might be better to ask less sensitive questions first to gain trust before asking the important financial screener. If high net worth is defined as personal income last year above $100,000, ask, "Was your total personal income before taxes for [insert last full year date] less than $100,000 or not?" Don't ask a long list of income categories at the beginning if that is not needed. A more detailed income question can be asked at the end of the questionnaire.

Was your total personal income before taxes in {insert last full taxation year} less than $100,000 or not?

○ Yes, less than $100,000

○ No, $100,000 or higher

When respondents do not qualify for a survey, because they don't have the right behaviour, or because the quota group they fit into is full, they are thanked for their interest in participating. They might be asked a few additional questions – to help them feel they've not wasted their time and have contributed.

Main Section

The main section of a questionnaire contains all the critical information we need to know to answer the study's objectives. This section can potentially contain three types of information, generally in the following sequence:

Behavioural and Attitudinal Sequencing

Behaviour. Questions that relate to what respondents do: where they go, what they own, how they make decisions, etc. For instance, what brands of hot cereal they bought last month, how many bags they bought, what they paid, whether they used coupons or a loyalty card, where they bought each bag, how often they eat it, whom they serve it to, etc.

Attitudes. Questions that relate to what respondents think or feel. For instance, how they rate the hot cereals they bought, how they rate the hot cereals they did not buy, how reasonable they think the prices are, and why they like or dislike different brands, what characteristics an ideal hot cereal would have, and so on.

Lifestyle. This is a specialized section that many questionnaires do not include. These are questions that relate to the respondent's lifestyle and not necessarily directly to the category or brand. For instance, whether they consider themselves a gourmet, whether they focus on health above all else, if they like being outdoors, participating in spectator sports, playing musical instruments, painting, spending time with friends, or fixing things around the house.

Behavioural questions generally come before attitudinal questions because it puts the respondents in the right frame of mind. We want to understand the attitudes behind the behaviour we have just asked about. For example, *"Which brand of shampoo did you buy last?"* (behaviour) and *"How would you rate it overall?"* (attitude) relate closely to one another and follow naturally.

Behavioural questions are also generally asked first because they are easy. The respondent knows the answer and doesn't have to work too hard. For example, *"Which brand of shampoo did you buy?"* is merely asking them to remember a recent action. The follow-up attitudinal question, *"How would you rate it overall?"* requires more work to think about the product and to understand and apply the scale they are asked to use. Attitudes often ask respondents to think about something they've never thought about before.

Although this is a common way to think about sequencing the questionnaire, not all questionnaires need to be ordered this way. There might be many instances where you want to ask about attitudes first and behaviour later. For example, you might need to ask about attitudes towards food early in the questionnaire because you are going to ask "gourmets" a different series of behavioural questions than you are going to ask people who merely consider food to be fuel. Or you might need to capture attitudes before you ask behavioural questions that would lead them to alter what they want to tell you about their attitudes.

Questionnaire sequencing is a mix of hard logic and creative storytelling. The more you think it through, the more experience you gain, the better you will be at it.

Funnelling. Within each sub-section—especially in the behaviour subsection—the most common way to sequence a questionnaire is by funnelling—starting with generalized questions and moving on to more and more specific questions. For example, if you would like to find out which consumers use brands of anti-dandruff shampoo, the questionnaire is not likely to start with, "Which brand of anti-dandruff shampoo do you use most often?" Several questions are leading up to the targeted information. We would first ask about hair care in general, then about shampoos in general, followed by questions about medicated and anti-dandruff shampoos.

This provides context for the respondent and valuable background information for the researcher. It may also help the respondent feel more comfortable sharing information about a topic that could be potentially embarrassing.

The main advantage of the funnelling approach is that it leads each respondent through the same scene-setting context in a logical way to the point that they are all going to interpret each question the same way. It helps put all respondents' answers into the proper, common perspective.

There are, of course, situations in which the use of the funnelling approach is inappropriate. For example, when a general question might change how people respond to the questions that follow.

An example might be if you need an overall rating, such as "satisfaction," "willing to recommend," or "intention to return."

If you ask it **at the beginning**, in keeping with the funnelling approach, and then ask specific aspects about the product or service, respondents might alter their answers to appear consistent (and therefore justify) the overall response they had given. The effect is a cleaner, top-of-mind read on satisfaction but perhaps altered reads on the specifics.

If you run through the specific aspects first, you will get a cleaner read on them. Then ask the **overall measure at the end**. In this way, the overall is most likely to be a summary of all the other, specific questions. You are telling respondents what aspects you want them to consider when giving the overall impression. But what if overall impressions are actually judged on specific aspects that you have not included on your list?

The latter approach can be referred to as an **inverted funnel**, where specific questions are asked before the general question.

Here is a live example.

QuickFix, a national chain of auto repair shops, is establishing a satisfaction tracking program to ensure it can spot and correct any shortcomings across its franchises. Compensation is based on the degree to which each location leaves customers "willing to recommend" the chain to others. There is a distinct list of services offered and apparent performance standards.

The protocol asks respondents to complete a questionnaire after each visit. Here's an outline of an inverted funnel:

a. Specific Factual Questions
When was your most recent visit to QuickFix?
How did you make your appointment for this visit to Quickfix?
What work did you have done on this visit?
How long did it take from when you arrived to when you left with your car?
Did you make use of the shuttle service to take you somewhere while your car was being serviced?
What was the approximate cost of all work done?

b. Specific Evaluative Questions
On a 7-point scale, where 1 is terrible, and 7 is excellent, how would rate each of the following aspects of your visit?
The ease of making the appointment.
The comfort of the waiting area.
The promptness of the attention you received.
The availability of the shuttle service.
How well the service needed was explained to you?
How long it took to complete the work?
How courteous were the staff ?

How confident the service manager made you feel?
The length of time it took to get your car fixed?
How reasonable you felt the bill was?

c. General Evaluative Question

How likely are you to take your car back to Quickfix in the future for servicing or repairs?

[ ] Definitely would
[ ] Probably would
[ ] Might or might not
[ ] Probably would not
[ ] Definitely would not

Beyond the attitude/behaviour and funnelling principles, other factors should be taken into consideration when designing a questionnaire.

Building rapport and confidence. Standard practice is to start with questions that are simple and easy to answer. They tend to be factual, for example, about the respondent and what they do. These require little effort and little personal investment on the part of the respondent and help them feel that the task is going to be easy.

If we ask difficult or potentially embarrassing questions at the beginning, there is a risk that the respondent will become frustrated or annoyed, and not continue with the interview. It is more likely that a respondent will be willing to answer questions that require mental effort once they have invested some time into the questionnaire. **Rapport is established** through an initial series of carefully designed questions.

The look and feel of the first few questions are critical. If they are short and straightforward, they can build respondents' trust and encourage them to continue. A few quick questions establish a rhythm that will move the respondent along until they feel they have invested in the process. It is usually not a good idea to include grid questions or repetitive statement batteries at the beginning.

Simple and easy formatting is particularly important if the questionnaire is to be answered on a small screen, like a mobile phone or tablet. Try to minimize the amount of "ink" on the page or screen.

The principle is that, wherever possible, more straightforward questions should precede the difficult ones, less personal questions should precede the more personal and sensitive ones, and factual questions should precede questions that require judgment. This is generally true whether we use the funnelling or inverted funnelling approach.

The following survey of people attending a music festival is an example of a flow that could build rapport by easing a respondent into more difficult questions:

Easy recall

Is this your *first-ever* visit to Jazz Fest, or have you been here before?
How long have you been on the Jazz Fest site today?
Did other members of your family come with you today? Who came?

Have you bought anything from any of the concession stands? If so, what?

Which acts have you heard so far today?

Harder opinions

How would you rate each of the acts you heard on a 7-point scale?

How would you rate the variety of acts? The cleanliness of the grounds? The parking?

How would you rate the admission price?

Hardest – asking for creativity

What are your suggestions for making JazzFest more interesting?

The first four questions deal with factual items that are easy to answer. The respondents are experts. The remaining questions ask for opinions and creativity and therefore require respondents to think more deeply.

The principle is that the sequencing should draw respondents in, make them feel that the task is going to be easy, that they know the answers, and that the information they are providing is interesting and important.

Avoiding Fatigue. At the beginning of a questionnaire, you need to build rapport. Towards the end, you must be careful to avoid inducing fatigue. A questionnaire that tires out respondents because it is too long, is too repetitive, requires too much effort, or confuses them with hard-to-understand questions will not yield useable results.

Keeping our questionnaire and our questions short is an important way to minimize fatigue, but we can also do this by building **variety** into the sequencing. Occasional changes in topics, varied types of questions, and using more interesting response scales can help keep a respondents' interest. Many of these are covered in later sections.

Classification

When surveys collect questionnaire responses, it's often essential to understand how different groups of respondents answered the questions. Do women like our product more than men? Is the Millennial generation more motivated by a specific claim on the pack than the Baby Boomer generation? Do residents of one region see it as a replacement for a specific local product?

To do this type of analysis, we need to collect background information on our respondents. If it is a **consumer** survey, the background or classification information will be mostly demographics and can include items such as age, gender, income, education, household composition and place of residence.

For **non-consumer** surveys, the classification information we need might depend on what role the respondents are playing. For instance, if it is a business survey, classification information would relate to the characteristics of the company, such as industry sector, number of employees, annual sales etc.

For consumer questionnaires, classification information is almost always asked at the end because age, income, and education are considered private, and many would be hesitant to reveal it to strangers. When those sensitive questions are asked at the very end of the questionnaire, respondents are likely to feel more trust since they invested so much up to that point, and they often feel that they might as well just finish it. In a person-to-person interview, the interviewer is less of a stranger by the end of the interview.

Even so, particularly in this era of data breaches and heightened **privacy concerns**, the respondents must be assured that the answers to personal questions will not be revealed to anyone, will not be connected directly to the respondent, and will only be used to group data into demographic categories. It may also be necessary to reassure the respondent that the information they provide will **not be used to sell them anything**. The issues of informed consent and survey ethics are particularly relevant here.

It is a very important duty of the questionnaire author to carefully consider what demographics they need to provide the required insights. We often throw in the "usual" questions without thinking. But do you really need to know the respondent's marital status (married, divorced, separated, widowed, single, common law), or do you just need to know how many adults are in the household? Will your client actually make decisions based on religion, race or ethnicity? (There may be specific reasons for collecting such data. For example, religion or ethnicity may have some bearing on food preference or on health issues. However, if no decision is going to be made based on this information, collecting such unnecessary data should be avoided.)

If you are not going to need a classification question, don't include it.

3. How to Word the Questions

The actual wording of the questionnaire is crucial to the quality of the data we get back. We must write carefully to:
- Encourage respondents to read or listen to the full sentence carefully.
- Transmit the same meaning to all respondents.
- Make them feel comfortable answering truthfully.

This is best accomplished by ensuring the questions are worded simply, directly, and include the cultural lens through which the respondent is reading or hearing it. The cultural lens might be national, cultural, or age or gender-based.

People are not obliged to answer any of our questions. They do so to help us. We should encourage them by creating questions that are not unnecessarily boring, irritating, embarrassing or complicated while ensuring that they are not biased.

Keep in mind that the most motivated respondents, the ones most likely to make it to the end of even the most poorly written questionnaires, maybe fraudulent respondents – the ones intent on earning the incentive. The more concise and better written the questionnaire, the more likely it is that your sample will be populated by authentic respondents.

We can offer many guidelines to make it easier for the respondent to engage and answer our questions. We will deal with some of the basic principles in this section, but of course, the actual wording will depend on the objectives, information requirements, sequence, and context in which the question is asked.

Use Simple Words

The first rule is never to use a "big" word when a small one will do. Here are some examples:

- How many incumbents in your establishment work in administrative assistant functions?
- **Versus:** How many of your employees are administrative assistants?

- What is your total per annum remuneration from all sources combined?
- **Versus:** What is your total annual income from all sources?

- Do you have a preference for purchasing your soup in retortable pouches, polypropylene bags, tetra-pak cartons or mason-style bottles?
- **Versus:** Do you prefer to buy soup in pouches, bags, cartons or bottles?

- Please estimate the number of caffeinated hot beverages you have consumed in the past 24-hour period
- **Versus:** How many cups of coffee or tea, or did you drink yesterday?

- How many sticks, pellets, or pastilles of chewing gum have you used in the previous seven days?
- **Versus:** How many pieces of gum have you chewed in the past seven days?

A respondent is seldom impressed by convoluted questions or questions that use complicated words. In fact, it is very likely to be irritating: "Buy" is more straightforward than "purchase"; "eat" or "drink" is simpler than "consume." A large proportion of respondents rarely understands technical jargon.

One way to write simply is to ask yourself how you would ask it if you wanted the same information from a friend. You would probably not ask, "What is your total per annum remuneration from all sources combined?" You would be much more direct: "What do you make?" or "What's your income?"

You can't always write a question in *exactly* the same way you would ask it when talking to a close acquaintance. But it is a good starting point to ensure it is as direct and straightforward as possible. We can always alter it to ensure it is grammatically correct and precise enough.

Be Specific, Avoid Ambiguity

We may think we say what we mean, but words and phrases are not interpreted in the same way by everyone. You should be very aware of this when you write a questionnaire. It is incredible how many meanings one word can have depending on the context and usage, cultural background of the subject, and so on.

For example, think about this fundamental and straightforward question requiring an open-ended text response: "In what state do you eat oranges?" Now, look at the range of legitimate answers you could receive:

In response to "In what state do you usually eat oranges?", you might get the following answers:
- Usually, Florida because you can pick them right off the trees (state meaning geographic divisional unit or province)
- Half-asleep in the morning (state of mind)
- Sitting down at the table (state of physical being)
- As a juice (state or form of the fruit)

To avoid the problem of respondents interpreting the same question differently, we have to make it unambiguous and specific.

Generally, **this means providing the list of acceptable responses**: "*How do you usually consume oranges? As a fresh fruit, as a juice, from a can or baked into a recipe?*"

Even this doesn't always work correctly. For example, you might ask someone where they live. They might wonder if you mean what country, what city, what neighbourhood, what building. So, you offer more precision by offering the options: a single-family home, a duplex, a triplex, an apartment. Depending on where you live, each of these options may mean a very different housing format. And in many cases, a single-family could live in each of the options. In this case, it **might be helpful to include an icon thumbnail image** of the building type.

We might want to ask 'how many people are in your family.' But the consumer might wonder, "do I include my parents who live across town? What about my siblings who live in another city? Does it include my grown children who have moved out on their own? Does it include my partner's children who now live with us?"? It would be far more precise to ask, '*how many people currently live in the home in which you live*". **It is best to think of the consumption unit (a household) rather than a relationship unit (a family)**. If the survey purpose is actually to understand the number of people who are in each respondent's family, then a definition of what is meant as a family for survey purposes must be included. For example, the question may include a definition such as, "When you count the number of people in your family, include only any spouse you may have at this time and any children for whom you are the biological, or natural, mother or father or legal guardian." Then ask the question.

It is important to understand that we may not use the same words a consumer uses in everyday language. In marketing and market research, we get so used to using jargon that we think it is common language. For example, we talk about a unit or a SKU. We might think in terms of penetration and frequency, usage cycles and use-up rates. **It is best to use plain everyday consumer language**. If you are ever in doubt, fully pre-test your questionnaire in face-to-face interviews.

It's also important to avoid short forms and acronyms. They can easily be mistaken for something unknown to you. For instance, does E.D. stand for eating disorder, educational dysfunction, the name of a familiar jam manufacturer? Does B.P. stand for blood pressure, basis points, Boston Pizza, British Petroleum, or Brad Pitt? **It is good practice to spell out all words in full.**

The risk is that we will never know that a respondent has not understood our question the way we intended. In a person-to-person interview, they might not want to embarrass themselves by asking for clarification. In a self-completion questionnaire, there's simply no feedback loop to let researchers hear from respondents.

We need to **spend time with consumers,** get out of our offices, conduct qualitative interviews and listen carefully to the language that is used. At the very least, we should read the questions out loud to ourselves and colleagues to hear how they sound.

Avoid Difficult-to-Answer Factual Questions

We often need to collect factual information to meet our study's objectives. We can ask respondents to give us the facts of their lives and behaviour. Sometimes the request is easy to answer, and sometimes it is almost impossible.

Several factors make a factual request difficult. The respondent:
- may never have had the information requested;
- may not recall details for the full-time frame that's relevant;
- may have to work too hard to give you the details being sought;
- maybe hesitant or embarrassed to share what's being asked.

Much of what we do in life is **done automatically** or slips quickly out of our memories. For example, our electricity bill may be automatically taken out of our account every month, and we don't see it happen. So, we may never fully understand how much electricity we've used in our household. We are exposed to advertising billboards continually as we drive through a city, or ride public transit, but we are not involved enough to keep track of what we are seeing and would not be able to report an accurate count. We may always have a bottle of water on our desk beside us and simply lose track of how many times we fill it over the course of the day. It is sometimes said that these types of activities are subliminal or slightly below the surface of our active cognitive focus.

The **time frame** that is of interest to the study may not be the same as a respondent's ability to recall. For example, we might need to report on monthly television viewing habits. We could ask "How many hours of TV did you watch last month," but this would be nearly impossible for most people to answer precisely. A far more reasonable time frame would be "How many hours of TV did you watch yesterday?". Recall would be more precise, and over the full sample, you will get a clear read of longer-term viewing habits.

The time frame depends on the activity being measured. For example, "How many times did you get your car serviced last month" would be difficult to answer for someone who has it serviced 3 or 4 times a year. Car servicing is relatively infrequent, and the event can be quite memorable, so it would be fine to ask for the number of service calls over the year.

Asking them to recall **too much detail** can be a problem as well. If we aim to collect precise factual information, rather than impressions, we have to make sure the questions are within the respondent's recall capabilities.

For example, respondents may recall how many units of canned meat they bought last month, but it is an added layer of effort to identify the number of units by specific types of meat. Then asking them to estimate how many of each can was consumed by each member of the household drives the task into the territory of the impossible.

Respondents may be able to recall the behaviour we are asking about, but **may not organize it in the way the question is asking**. For example, we can estimate how much we spend on groceries every month with some accuracy, but don't have the awareness to answer:

- How much of this was spent on meat?
- How much on vegetables?
- How much on impulse purchases?

This task is particularly complex because we are asking for **fractional division** on the original difficult task.

Anything that increases respondents' sense of frustration and fatigue must be identified and purged from the questionnaire. Otherwise, increasing numbers of respondents will refuse to participate, either providing unhelpful 'don't know' responses or abandoning the survey altogether. This is particularly true of self-administered questionnaires.

The key is to write the question in a way that is within respondents' spheres of knowledge. If we want to estimate how much a consumer spends on groceries per year, as accurately as possible, we can ask how much they spent on groceries *the last time* they went grocery shopping. This is easier to remember, and their response is likely to be more accurate. If we then ask how many times a month they go grocery shopping, we get a relatively accurate multiplier to extend to the whole year. There will be some projection errors, but remember that aggregating responses over the whole sample rather than looking at the results of one respondent are what will give you a relatively full picture of the behaviour you are seeking to describe.

Of course, focusing on a shorter time frame might introduce seasonal influences. If the study is conducted in January, "last month" would include the holiday season. Likely, purchases made during that season are not representative of purchase patterns for the rest of the year. One solution could be to avoid periods that are non-typical. Another solution could be to extend the data collection period over several months if memories can recall that information.

The use of mobile technology makes it easier to overcome some of these recall issues by giving respondents the ability to report their behaviour in-the-moment. For example, asking respondents to download a 'diary' app and have them scan or record their purchases on a typical shopping trip can yield far more accurate shopping data than even day-after recall questions.

Problems like these can be handled in any number of ways as long as we give sufficient thought to underlying problems. Remember that there is no all-encompassing correct way to ask the question, but there are more specific and precise ways to ask the question.

Avoid Double-barrelled Questions

Double-barrelled questions are those that have two question parts but ask for only one answer.

For example, the question, *"Would you say that this product is expensive but good value for the money?"* is double-barrelled. "No" *could* mean:

- "the product is expensive but not good value for the money," or
- "the product is not expensive *and* is good value for the money," or

- "the product is not expensive and not good value for the money."

Each of these very different responses has significant marketing consequences. Yet the fact that the question is double-barrelled has wholly obscured the interpretation.

Here are some more examples of double-barrelled questions:
- Would you say that this product tastes and smells good?
- Do you generally agree with the government's domestic and foreign policies?
- Should the government spend more on education and less on the military?
- Do you believe that the rich and the famous prefer to vacation in Europe?
- Should students take more art and music classes?
- How satisfied are you with your pay and benefits?

It is a simple solution to separate each double-barrelled question into its separate components and ask them as two (or more) separate questions. For example, "Would you say that this product tastes and smells good?" can be broken into "Would you say that this product tastes good?" and "Would you say that this product smells good?" Of course, if you only need to ask one of the two questions, a shorter questionnaire will be the result, and that is a good thing.

Avoid Ambiguous Questions

Ambiguous questions are those that can be interpreted in different ways by different respondents. For example, "How much money did you spend on groceries for your household in the last month?" is potentially ambiguous. Do groceries include cleaning products and pet foods? What about items that were not bought in a grocery store?

If our purpose is to estimate how much money people spend in grocery stores, we might ask, "How much money did you spend in grocery stores last week?" On the other hand, if our purpose is to estimate how much money people spend specifically on grocery products, we may first define "grocery products" and then ask the question.

"Grocery products" include food and beverages that your household eats and drinks, e.g., bread, meat, butter, soda.
- *How much money did you spend on grocery products for your household in the last month?*

Here are some more examples of ambiguous questions:
- *How many movies did you watch during the past 30 days?* – Only those seen in a movie theatre? Do movies on TV qualify? How about movies from streaming services like Netflix? Or movies on DVDs?
- *Do you read the* Globe and Mail *newspaper?* – Should we answer yes if we only read it on Saturdays? What about if we don't actually buy it, but read it in the library? How should we answer if we skim the headlines and look at the pictures? Is that considered reading?

A potentially false comparison will also make a question ambiguous. For example, if we ask, "Would you be more interested in commuting to work by bike than by bus?" we are leaving committed car drivers with no option to choose, and they must pick one they would not otherwise choose.

As you write a question, pause and ask if there are any other ways that someone might interpret the question. Also, ask if every qualifying respondent can provide their particular answer to the question. Or better yet, bring in another set of eyes and request feedback for possible ambiguity.

Avoid Leading and Loaded Questions

A **leading question** is one that leads a respondent to a specific answer because of the way it is phrased. "How many charities do you support?" is a leading question because it assumes that the respondent supports one or more charities. This assumption *leads* (but does not force) the respondent to provide a number in response. Leading questions commonly end up in questionnaires unintentionally in a format like this: "Do you agree that the blue package is more attractive than the red package?" Because this question makes a mild suggestion that the responder ought to 'agree,' responders may be more likely to select 'yes.' That question should read, "Do you agree or disagree that the blue package is more attractive than the red package?" Or, "Which package do you feel is more attractive, the red package or the blue package?" A leading question is often the result of carelessness and improper wording.

A **loaded question** is similar to a leading question. Loaded questions imply that certain answers are socially and emotionally more desirable. A question like, "Do you agree or disagree that the government needs to spend money on healthcare to save children with curable diseases?" is likely to elicit more "agree" than "disagree" responses simply because of the way it is worded. By focusing on 'children' and 'curable,' the researcher has made it very difficult for the respondent to disagree with this government initiative. Who would disagree with a policy that doesn't help sick children? Unless the respondent has strong views on healthcare, the chances of answering no to this question are minimal.

Another way of loading a question is by providing a reason to choose one response and not the other. For example, "Would you choose the first bank service to reduce the fees that you pay, or would you choose the second bank service?"

Adding the weight of "experts" is another way to create a loaded question: "Nutritionists have suggested that removing soft drink vending machines from schools will improve our children's health. Do you agree or disagree? Unscrupulous researchers could get any desired answer by loading the question with bias or leading the respondent.

Here are some more examples of leading and loaded questions:

- *Nowadays, more and more people are going on expensive holidays. Could you tell me if this is true of you*? Here, the answer is likely to be biased because of the *bandwagon* effect. Many people would like to say that they are just as financially sound like other people by agreeing with what seems to be the current trend. Instead, you could simply ask whether they plan to holiday this year and whether they plan to spend less, the same, or more than last year.
- *Do you believe that Procter and Gamble makes the detergent Protector*? Research has shown that many people would answer yes to this question even though there may be no detergent called Protector. This is because some respondents will assume the researcher is sharing correct information and go with their suggestion. If the same question is rephrased as '*Which of these detergents have you heard of?*' and then follow it up with '*Who makes these detergents?*', the answers could be very different.

- *What kind of fiction do you read? (e.g., mysteries)* More respondents are likely to mention mysteries because they are reminded of them by the question-wording. A better question would offer several suggestions to the responder like '*What kind of fiction do you read? (e.g., romance, fantasy, mysteries, adventure, graphic novels)*'

A question can be made less 'leading' by permitting respondents to say 'no.'

- "Which of the following, if any, have you done in the week"? – the phrase 'if any' permits respondents to say, 'none of these.'
- "Have you heard of this brand before today, or not"? – the phrase 'or not' gives equal legitimacy to a negative response.
- "Do you agree or disagree with each of the following statements?" – Both options are given equal weight.

Avoid Black-and-White When the Answer May be Grey

Consumers often have opinions that cannot be covered by a stark 'yes-or-no' or 'agree or disagree' choice. The answer often lies between the two extremes.

For example, "Do you agree with the government's foreign policies or not?" The respondent may agree with some foreign policies and not others or may agree with the foreign policies with some qualifications. The black-and-white nature of the question is very frustrating when respondents really want to provide an accurate answer.

Respondents often want to let you know when they don't have an opinion. Forcing them to choose an agree or disagree answer creates a false view of the situation.

For example: "Are you satisfied or dissatisfied with the service you receive from your phone/data provider?" A consumer might feel that she or he is "mostly satisfied" or "neither satisfied nor dissatisfied," and may be unable to choose between "satisfied" and "dissatisfied."

During the questionnaire design phase, a proper technique is to try to answer every dichotomous question with a neutral or grey answer and see if that is a valid answer. If it is, then redesign the question and/or the answer choices.

Be Careful when Wording Sensitive Questions

Where possible, avoid sensitive and personal questions. However, if it is necessary to ask such questions, develop a proper context so that the question sounds logical and not offensive.

Suppose we need to know how much a consumer spends on alcohol. Asking this point-blank at the beginning of the questionnaire might create some protective hedging or even distorted answers. We are more likely to get a truthful answer if we establish some rapport with the consumer first and then frame the question in the context of another household spending. "Please tell us roughly how much you spent last month on (a) gasoline, (b) restaurant meals, (c) alcohol?"

Establishing rapport with the respondent and developing the context can be very useful in eliciting more accurate responses to sensitive questions.

In some cultures, almost anything can be asked of strangers, while in others, great care must be taken not to scandalize the respondent. Researchers who have a better understanding of the cultural environment and human nature, in general, are often able to avoid writing questions that are unacceptable to many respondents.

Embarrassment is more likely to ensue during face-to-face interviews. For instance, consider a man and his 15-year-old son who have been stopped in a shopping mall. If the interviewer were to ask the man to indicate his income, he might not want to answer because he does not want his son to know. This problem can be overcome by using a *response card* that lists the different income categories of interest. Each category has a random letter next to it, and the respondent can provide an answer by reading out the letter.

F. Under $25 000

A. $25 000 to $49 999

S. $50 000 to $74 999

J. $75 000 to $99 999

The embarrassment has significantly been reduced, and the correct answer is much more likely to be provided.

Response cards can be used for many sensitive questions in face-to-face interviews. They are also effective when the respondent must keep track of a response scale with many descriptors or when they have to keep track of several brands as they go through a battery of questions.

Anticipate and Counter Respondent Bias

Even when the questions are correctly worded, taking all the principles into account, a questionnaire can still give biased results. Respondents generally want to make a good impression to appear informed, be socially acceptable and provide what they think is likely to be the "right" answer.

For instance, respondents naturally tend to over-report *socially acceptable* behaviours and under-report *socially unacceptable* behaviours. As an example, a much higher percentage of consumers say that they voted in the last national election than actually ever vote, and a much lower percentage report after an election that they voted for a losing party.

Similarly, very few people say that they have cheated on their income taxes and that they drive while intoxicated.

This tendency to offer a 'better' answer is a typical manifestation of human behaviour. Researchers must be aware of this when developing questionnaires and shouldn't assume that people are deliberately lying or trying to mislead.

Respondents may, at times, provide answers that are consciously or unconsciously distorted. Such distortions arise out of motivations such as:

Social correctness bias. The question, "Did you give any money to the local children's hospital campaign this past Christmas season?" is likely to be answered "yes" by many more people than those who actually did donate.

Politeness/suggestion bias. Consumers often give higher brand ratings or say they are more likely to purchase a product because they want to please the interviewer. They might assume that the interviewer has a stake in the product and would like them to buy it and answer 'yes' to avoid disappointing them.

Mind reading bias. The question, "Which brand of coffee did you buy *last* time?" might prompt respondents to provide the name of the brand that they buy most often, not necessarily the one they bought the last time because they think that is what you want.

Perceived importance bias. The question, "How often did you eat a meal in a restaurant last month?" might be interpreted by the respondents to mean eating out in a "good" restaurant and not in a fast-food outlet. However, the researcher may be interested in *any* restaurant.

The researcher should take steps to reduce the potential for distortion in the following ways:
- Make the purpose of the question less obvious;
- Make negative answers just as socially acceptable as positive answers;
- Explicitly define the information that is required;
- Clearly define the scope of the answer.

Here are a few examples of how questions may be reworded to account for possible biases.

Making the Purpose Less Obvious

Did you give any money to the local children's hospital campaign during this past Christmas season? could be changed to:

Which of the following did you do during the past Christmas season?

- ○ bought gifts
- ○ gave to the children's hospital campaign
- ○ sent cards to friends
- ○ spent time with my family
- ○ travelled by car

Making Negative Answers Acceptable

Do you intend to buy this product? could be changed to:
- *Do you intend to buy this product or not?* (Simply making the negative alternative explicit reduces the politeness/suggestion bias. This should always be done.)
- *Which of these products do you intend to buy?* (And then, along with the target product, include several products that someone would be expected to buy.)

Making the Intention of the Question Explicit

Which brand of coffee did you buy the last time? could be changed to:
- *Which brand of coffee did you buy the last time, even if it is not the one you usually buy?* Or,
- *Thinking of the last time you bought coffee, which brand did you end up buying?*

Making the Scope of the Question Clear

How often did you eat a meal in a restaurant last month? could be changed to:

- *How often did you eat a meal in a restaurant last month?* Please consider any type of restaurant, such as fast food, casual, and fine dining restaurants.

This does not exhaust all the ways that we can reduce or eliminate biases. There are many other biases, even though they may be less frequent. Other methods of reducing biases are:

- Changing the sequence of the questions to minimize the impact of a given question.
- Changing the wording to make the question neutral and precise.
- Eliciting the information through indirect questioning.
- Collecting comparative data and such other means.

Consider Numeric Responses Carefully

Questions that require a number for a response (e.g., "How many...") seem simple enough to write, but there are several important criteria to keep in mind. The following guidelines will help ensure that every respondent can find an appropriate answer and that respondents can find the right answer quickly.

- Include zero. Even when skip logic has been used to ensure that every respondent ought to buy or use something, be prepared for some respondents to require a zero answer.
- Include an opportunity to provide the largest possible number. This is often best accomplished by using a phrase such as "20 *or more*."
- Include every possible number. Surprisingly, this is a common error in questionnaires. For instance, if a respondent is 20 years old, how are they to respond to a question that asks whether they are "under 20 years old" or "over 20 years old."
- Do not include any number twice. This is another common error on questionnaires where the response options might include both "1 to 20" and "20 to 30."
- Where appropriate, each response should start with an even or common number such as 2 or 5 or 10. For instance, response options like 10 to 19, 20 to 29, and 30 to 39 are easier to read than options like 11 to 20, 21 to 30, and 31 to 40.
- Use 'or' and 'to' appropriately. The answer options 2 *or* 3 and 2 *to* 3 do not mean the same thing. Consider whether you have 2 to 3 cans of peaches in your cupboard as opposed to 2 or 3 cans. Similarly, consider whether you have 2 to 3 cups of sugar in the cupboard as opposed to 2 or 3 cups of sugar.

Be Spare, Edit to Precision

The more extended and more complex a question appears the less likely a respondent is to read every word. Every subsidiary phrase adds complexity. Keep the questions as spare and to the point as possible.

It's relatively common to see a question with a lead-in like this: "Thinking now of the last time you visited your bank, how many different transactions did you do on this last occasion?" Removing the initial phase does not remove any precision: "How many different transactions did you do the last time you visited your bank?"

It's also unnecessary to repeat the same qualifier on every subsequent question: "How long did you have to wait to see a teller *the last time you visited your bank*?" "Were you greeted by name by the teller *the last time you visited your bank*?" "Was the main transaction completed promptly *the last time you visited your bank*?

The respondent doesn't need to be reminded on each screen which visit you are talking about. This sparseness is particularly important when a questionnaire is going to appear on a small screen like a mobile phone or a smaller tablet. It's important to avoid scrolling, so the whole question and all of the response categories should fit onto one single cell phone screen. It is in writing for mobile devices that we truly learn how to edit questions to their most basic language.

Additional Observations

In addition to the principles discussed, several additional considerations will lead to better quality questions and answers, and consequently, better quality data.

- Focus on using common, *understandable* grammar and punctuation instead of perfect grammar and punctuation. For instance, though it may be correct to ask, "Into which of the following age groups do you fall?" it sounds better to ask, "Which of these age groups do you fall into?"
- Use the active voice rather than the passive voice to give your question more immediacy and make it more personal. Rather than "How many bottles of water have been consumed by your household in the past week" (passive), ask "How many bottles of water have you and any other members of your household consumed in the past week" (active).
- Keep in mind that every 'question' on your questionnaire may not actually be a question but rather a statement or command. Commands such as "Please indicate which option reflects your opinion" is a statement and should not be punctuated with a question mark. However, it is best to phrase most 'questions' as questions.
- When providing examples to questions, take care to use, i.e. (in other words), e.g. (for example), and etc. (and so forth) in the right situations. It is never appropriate to use both, e.g. and etc. in the same listing. For example, this is not an appropriate way to list categories (e.g., soap, shampoo, conditioner, etc.)
- Remember that respondents are doing you a favour when they complete your questionnaire. In comparison to their regular job, incentives are only enough to be viewed as a small token of gratitude. They are not compensated for time. Questionnaires ought to be friendly and polite. Just as you will thank respondents for completing the questionnaire, occasional use of the word 'please' within the questionnaire is desirable.
- It is a good idea to include an optional open-ended text question at the end of every survey. This allows respondents to share any final opinions, whether those opinions are about the design or the content of the survey. Either way, it is a respectful way to let respondents share their unique voice after the researcher has been the sole director of the conversation.

How to Use Different Question Formats

The **layout of a questionnaire** refers to the physical way in which questions appear to the respondent. Different types of questions require different layouts. For instance:

If the question is, "Did you drink Coke yesterday, or not?", only three possibilities exist: Yes, No, Do Not remember. These three options will appear on the questionnaire with checkboxes or "click boxes," also called "radio buttons," so that the answer can be recorded quickly.

If the open-ended question is, "What do you like about the car you drive?" respondents can say just about anything they want, and the questionnaire should provide space to record the answer.

The **layout of a questionnaire** may differ depending on the medium: whether it is a self-completion (on paper or on a computer screen) or interviewer-administered (face-to-face or by phone).

The bulk of marketing research surveys in North America and Europe are conducted using **web-based surveys**. This medium is growing quickly in other parts of the world as well. Web-based surveys can be completed on computers, tablets and smartphones.

A sizable proportion of surveys are still conducted using the **telephone**, which is usually computer-assisted. **Mall intercept** interviews and **recruitment** of respondents **to a central location** for a personal interview are still common everywhere in the world. A small proportion of **in-home** interviews are also being carried out, but they have become much less common in many countries. A few surveys are still conducted by mail, especially longer surveys such as the census in Canada and many other countries.

Regardless of the medium, the questionnaire should be laid out in a very clear and attractive way to enable natural, fast, and correct responses. The questionnaire must be designed so that the least capable qualified respondent can successfully provide responses to all of the questions and navigate into and out of the survey.

While there are many commonalities in questionnaire construction among the different media, there are also significant differences. These will be pointed out as we continue our discussion.

A questionnaire may contain several types of questions.

Closed-Ended Questions

Closed-ended questions have predefined answers. A question like, "Are you eligible to vote in a federal election, or not?" is a closed-ended question because the only possible answers are "Yes" and "No" (or refused). The researcher defines the scope of both the question and the answers.

For comparison, open-ended questions let the respondent define the scope of the answer. "Why did you buy that brand of computer?" is an example of an open-ended question. Respondents are free to answer the question in any way they like; some possible answers are, "it was reasonably priced"; "It's a trustworthy company"; "They have good tech support," "My spouse works for the company"; or "The salesperson recommended it."

Closed-ended questions can take many forms. The following are some common types of closed-ended questions.

Simple Dichotomous Pre-coded Questions. These questions are among the simplest of all questions and can be answered with a *yes* or *no, have* or *have not*, etc. **Simple dichotomous pre-coded questions** are easy to administer and work well for non-sensitive, factual items. Here are a couple of examples:

Did you buy any meals at a restaurant last week, or not?

◯ Yes
◯ No

Do you currently own a motorcycle, or not?

◯ Yes
◯ No

These dichotomous questions offer two possible answers, with radio buttons to indicate the answer.

A good questionnaire design requires that the minimal amount of "ink" is put on the page so that respondents do not become distracted from the questions and answers. Sometimes, extraneous numbers, figures, and designs can bias responses. Each answer provided by respondents becomes a code in the computer. That happens immediately when a respondent clicks a radio button in an internet survey. Sometimes with self-administered paper-and-pencil questionnaires, number codes are assigned to the responses to help the coders enter the correct numbers into the computer. Entering answer codes by hand is prone to error, and special methods of quality control have been developed to minimize errors.

There is no hard and fast rule about how to number answer options though sometimes it is helpful to use 1 for yes and 0 for no. But whatever numbers are entered can be changed easily when in the computer. However, stringent guidelines for data entry and data interpretation must be kept in what are called data dictionaries or data glossaries. Every question and answer code resides in those documents.

Some questions require just simple Yes or No answers with no other options, such as the two questions above. The respondent either bought a meal or did not. He or she either owns a motorcycle or not. No other options are needed.

Some questions are such that a "Do not know" category should be provided. Such as the following.

Did you encounter anyone over the age of 75 yesterday in any way, or not?

◯ Yes
◯ No
◯ I don't know

Although the question is dichotomous (chose one of two responses), space is provided for "I don't know." Even if it seems like a simple 'yes/no' question, there may be some circumstances when it's not as clear. Some people may not know.

While space is provided for "DK/NS/Refused," it often doesn't show up on a self-administered paper survey because it might encourage some people to use it to avoid the question. If the question is left blank, it can be coded as a 'don't know' after the fact. It can be printed on an interviewer-administered survey, and just not read aloud. It is generally needed on web-based surveys because a respondent may not be allowed to proceed to the next survey if a response is not given.

Traditionally, the so-called "missing" responses of "refused," "don't know," and "not applicable" have been coded as "7 = refused", "8 = don't know" and "9 = not applicable". Or, 77, 88 and 99 if there are many answers to a question.

In some cases, it may be necessary to distinguish among people who did not answer the question (due to lack of knowledge or oversight) from people who refuse to answer the question. Refusals may occur when the question is sensitive in nature. For instance, a question like, "Do you have a Swiss bank account, or not?" may result in many refusals, especially among people who hold such an account. When the researcher expects the refusal rates to be high, it is common to create a separate category for refusals rather than combining it with "Do not know" responses.

Software for designing internet surveys allow the survey designer to require each question to be answered before moving ahead or allowing the respondent not to answer and move ahead. Often, answers are required for all questions except those that might be sensitive, such as age, income and some others. While there might be no refusals in an Internet survey, many people may have refused to answer a question by leaving the survey altogether. Each survey methodology has its peculiarities, and it is important to understand the pros and cons of each.

Multichotomous Pre-coded Questions work exactly like dichotomous questions, except there are more than two possible answers. The researcher must take care to ensure that all appropriate answer options are included in the list, and this is dependent on the research objective.

Here is an example:

During the past week, how many issues of The Globe and Mail newspaper did you read?

○ 1 issue
○ 2 issues
○ 3 issues
○ 4 issues
○ 5 issues
○ 6 issues
○ 7 issues

This is very similar to the dichotomous question, and no new principles are involved. It merely is a longer list.

Although the list may seem exhaustive, with allowances made for one newspaper every day, the researcher should determine whether the newspaper regularly publishes additional issues. If the newspaper published a morning edition and an evening edition, the answer list might require an '8 or more' option. It's also possible that a respondent read some back issues during the week. Of course, the respondent may not have read any issues, and that response option needs to be provided. And what does "reading" an issue mean to a respondent? Does it mean every word or just glancing at the headline on the first page? Once again, the objective must be achieved by the wording of the question.

Multichotomous Pre-coded Questions—Multiple Answers. Consider the following question:

Which news site did you read at least one article from last week? (Please select all that apply.)

- ☐ Huffington Post
- ☐ Google News
- ☐ CNN
- ☐ The New York Times
- ☐ Yahoo! News

☐ Other, please specify below

☐ Didn't read from any news sites last week

In the case of an interviewer-administered questionnaire, the interviewer reads the list of newspapers, and the respondent says "Yes" or "No" to each newspaper. For a self-completion questionnaire, the respondent would be presented with the full list of newspapers at once. Either way, this type of question is known as a "prompted" question because the respondent is given a list of possible answers. This type of questioning is used when the researcher believes that respondents might not remember without prompting all of the possible relevant answers. Prompted responses are also known as **aided recall** or **recognition** questions.

Rotating Prompted Lists: When and Why. When the researcher is sure that all the important responses have been identified, a good option is to 'randomize' the order of the responses when they appear on the questionnaire. This means to present the responses in a different order to different respondents to avoid potential order bias.

The image below is of the "response options" tab for a question being constructed using Lighthouse from Sawtooth Software. Notice the "Randomize Response Options" in the right centre of the image. Also, option 6, "Other ..." is indicated as "Respondent Specify," and that option will not be part of the randomized list; only options 1 to 5 will be randomized.

How to Design a Questionnaire

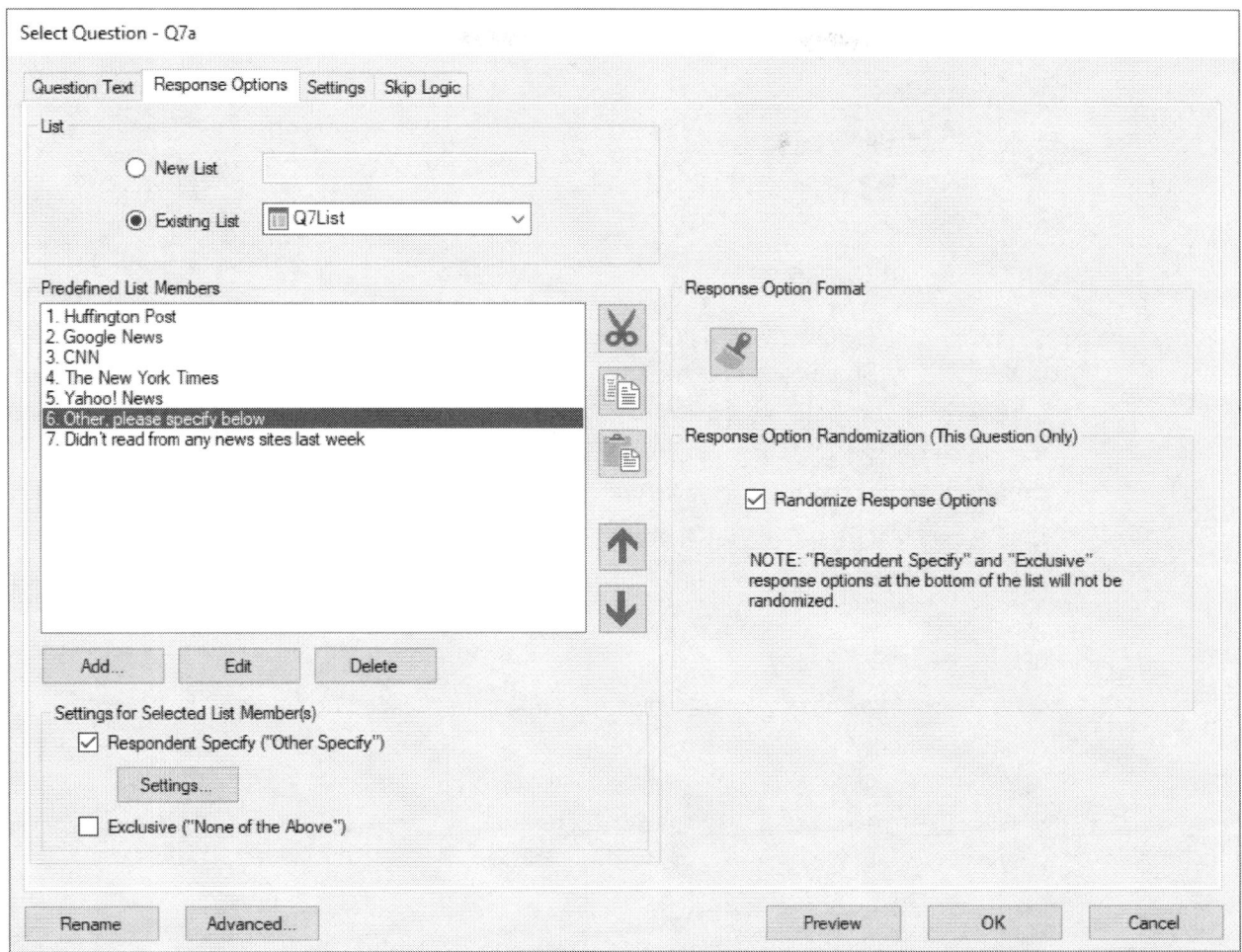

It has been shown, for example, that respondents often prefer the first-mentioned (primacy effect) and the last-mentioned (recency effect) option. Randomizing order can be problematic and expensive for printing paper questionnaires. However, any response list that is programmed for a mobile device or computer can now be easily randomized, ensuring respondents are shown the responses in different orders. Of course, the computer keeps track of the actual orders of responses.

Although prompted lists are generally randomized, there are exceptions, for instance, when the responses have an inherent or logical order. Counting questions do not have randomized response codes. Any set of responses that have ordinal properties should not be randomized or rearranged. For example:

How many cups of coffee did you drink last week, if any?

- ○ 0, none
- ○ 1 to 4 cups
- ○ 5 to 9 cups
- ○ 10 to 14 cups
- ○ 15 or more cups

But let's think about those answers. A numerical answer was requested. As those answers are listed, the information content of the answers has been reduced from being ratio-scaled, the highest level of information content, to ordinal, a lower level of information content. Perhaps the numeric quality of information is not important. If not, then the question and answer are fine. But if the level of analysis of that question is not fully known at the questionnaire design phase, construct the answers to provide the highest level of information. One option is below.

How many cups of coffee did you drink last week?

[   ]

A pull-down menu of numbers could have been used instead. Of course, is last week the appropriate period? Or is it yesterday.

Questions about dayparts, days of the week or months of the year would never be re-ordered because there is a strong chronological order. Mix them up, and respondents will find it challenging to find the answer they want.

On which day of the week do you go grocery shopping most often?

- ○ Monday
- ○ Tuesday
- ○ Wednesday
- ○ Thursday
- ○ Friday
- ○ Saturday
- ○ Sunday
- ○ I never shop for groceries.

Rating scales are also never randomized. They should always follow the same gradient order.

How would you rate the quality of this product?

	Very poor	Poor	Average	Good	Very good
Quality rating	○	○	○	○	○

We can minimize potential bias in a rating question like this and still retain the natural order by reversing the order for every other respondent. Each respondent must see the same order throughout their questionnaire. Starting with a negative rating on the left as in the above example, then switching part-way through the questionnaire to put the negative rating on the left will only create confusion.

Similarly, response options that make more sense when presented in alphabetical order would not be rotated. We might do this with long lists of brands or countries. If we keep them in alphabetical order, respondents can more easily find the answer they are looking for.

As questionnaire writers, we should do our best to ensure that any response list is not *too* long. Some guidelines call for a maximum of twelve to fifteen items in a self-administered questionnaire and five to seven for an interviewer-administered telephone survey. In a face-to-face interview, prompt cards or screens may be used to make the process easier for the respondent.

It is best to minimize scrolling for any questionnaire on a screen. Respondents can be tempted to choose a response from whatever appears on the screen initially and not make an effort to scroll down a long list.

Multichotomous Pre-coded Questions—Unprompted Multiple Answers. When an interviewer is involved, we have the option of NOT reading the full list of possible responses and allowing the respondent to respond with no prompting. In the case of the question about news sites, the interviewer would not read the names but would record only those sites volunteered by the respondent. This is known as an unprompted, spontaneous, or **unaided recall**. Another common term for this is the **top-of-mind recall**.

Unprompted questions are preferred when:

1. There are too many alternatives to list all of them, e.g., 20 or more possible answers and reading the entire list is tedious for both the interviewer and the respondent.;
2. We want to know what is spontaneously remembered by the respondent;
3. We believe that reading the list will make it easy for the respondent to say yes (falsely) to one of the alternatives.

Multichotomous Pre-coded—Single Answer (Prompted or Unprompted). In the above examples, respondents were allowed to give more than one answer. A respondent could have read an article from both the *Huffington Post* and the *New York Times*. But there are situations when we need a single answer. For example, a consumer may have accounts in three different banks, but we might want to know which one is his or her main bank for retirement planning. Single-answer questions are useful when a respondent is likely to buy more than one brand per year (e.g., toothpaste) but may consider only one as his or her main brand. When only one answer is allowed, this should be clearly specified in the question. For example:

Which one of the following is your favourite type of movie? (Please select only one)

- ○ Horror movies
- ○ Romantic comedies
- ○ Adventure films
- ○ Documentaries
- ○ Other [_____]
- ○ No particular favourite type

Some questions, such as income level or attitude scales, are, by definition, single-answer questions. It would be illogical for a person to belong to more than one answer category on a question like this:

How likely are you to buy a new car in the next six months?

	Very likely	Somewhat likely	Somewhat unlikely	Very unlikely
Likelihood	○	○	○	○

A common type of multichotomous single answer question is a **grid question**. Grids are an efficient way to collect a large amount of information in a small space. However, long grids and many grids can be very taxing on respondents and can quickly become boring for them. This may lead them to take short-cuts – such as straight-lining (choosing the same answer all the way down the grid) or randomly selecting any response without reading the question. This results in poor quality data.

It is advisable, therefore, to use as few grids as possible and to ensure that they are as short as possible. For a short questionnaire, we might suggest no more than two or three grids and aim for no more than eight lines in each grid.

There is some debate about whether to include both positively and negatively worded statements in a grid to ensure that respondents read the questions carefully. However, this does introduce double-negatives (**dis**agree with **not** doing something) that makes interpretation difficult.

Do you agree or disagree with the following attributes about packaging?

	Strongly agree	Somewhat agree	Slightly agree	Slightly disagree	Somewhat agree	Strongly agree
I always read the ingredient labels of food	○	○	○	○	○	○
It is important to me that packaging is recyclable	○	○	○	○	○	○
I prefer smaller resealable packaging	○	○	○	○	○	○
I never pay full price for this type of product	○	○	○	○	○	○

The last item is a negatively worded statement. If we find 80 percent strongly disagree that they never pay full price, does that mean that they always pay full price?

Notice that there is no neutral or "neither agree nor disagree" point on that scale above. This is a somewhat contentious point. Research has shown that people tend to take the neutral category when it is included in the scale while they will express an opinion when there is no neutral category. Since attitudinal questions seek attitudes, it is generally better not to provide neutral categories in opinion questions. If pretests show that respondents are uncomfortable not having a neutral category, increase the number of positive and negative points until they feel comfortable. Of course, neutral categories might be necessary for questions that pertain to a fact rather than an opinion.

Multichotomous Partially Pre-coded Questions. Sometimes, the researcher may only be interested in certain answers. In other instances, there may only be two or three dominant brands on the market, followed by several brands with minimal usage. In such instances, it will be wasteful (and tedious) to list all potential responses. Here, we may use a partially pre-coded list. For instance:

Which is your preferred cola drink? (Please select only one)

○ Pepsi-Cola
○ Coca-Cola
○ Other (Please specify.) [   ]
○ None in particular

If we are interested only in Coke or Pepsi, and no other minor brands, we can group all other cola drinks under "other" and not record the specific brand. If we are interested in knowing what other brands consumers drink, we can ask the interviewer (or the respondent if it is a self-administered survey) to record the cola brand under "other" if it is not Coke or Pepsi. Coca-Cola and Pepsi-Cola should be rotated while the Other and None categories stay fixed.

Multichotomous Non-Coded Questions. Suppose we want to know the makes and models of cars that people drive. There are hundreds of models, each of which has specific and known names. It would not be practical to list them all in a prompted question. Consequently, the researcher simply asks an open-ended question, the answers to which can be coded later. Examples may be provided, such as BMW for the first question below and X3 for the second.

What is the make of your car? [   ]

What is the model of your car? [   ]

Open-Ended Questions

Open-ended questions let the respondent decide the scope of the answer. The answers given by the respondent are typed into a textbox on a web-based survey, written into the lines provided on a paper questionnaire or recorded verbatim by the interviewer.

The first response might be somewhat superficial. For example, if we ask, "Why did you buy that brand of smartphone?" the initial response could be, "because I liked it." That is too general and does not give us much to work with.

- In a person-to-person interview, the interviewer is required to **probe** the respondent for more detail, usually with a simple question such as, "What else?" or "Anything else?" Interviewers do vary in their ability to probe effectively, and without sufficient training, the data may not be consistent.
- In self-administered questionnaires, respondents can easily ignore open-ended questions or enter a single word or even nonsense data (e.g., dunno, asdf). However, **Artificial Intelligence probing tools** like NEXXT Intelligence's Inca have appeared that can listen, understand and probe appropriately based on participants' answers and the research objectives. For example, it might respond to a nonsensical response with "your response doesn't appear to answer the question, could you tell me [repeat question]". Or it might respond to an overly simple response with "it is interesting that you say [repeat answer], could you tell me more about your thinking behind this?".

The exhibit shows how a simple AI probe might look to a survey respondent.

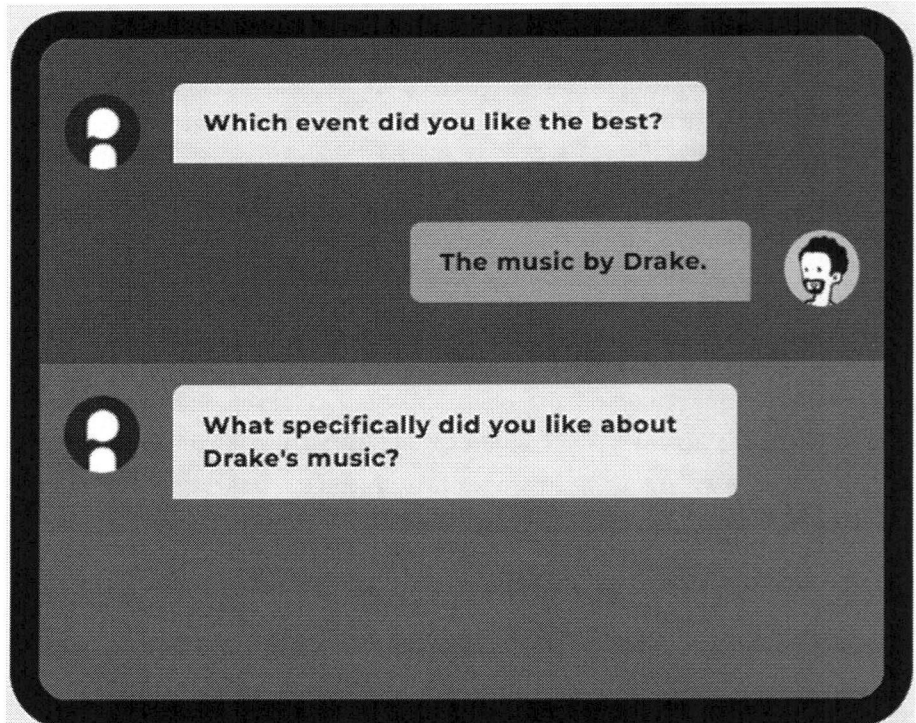

Regardless of the methodology, respondents vary in their abilities to verbalize or capture their thoughts in writing. It may be difficult to draw consistent conclusions from open-ended questions.

To get more precision, we often follow open-ended questions with follow up questions covering specific reasons. For example, we might include a grid asking the importance of several alternative options. For example, asking, "How important were each of the following in your decision to buy that brand of cellphone?" after the open end would add a numeric rating grid of the responses we had anticipated.

Open-ends are an excellent way to find insights that we hadn't anticipated. We might concentrate on product attributes such as size, weight, colour, speed when asking about a smartphone. Still, we might not have anticipated that the real problem is the complicated procedure to turn off the alerts when in public places quickly.

In many studies, open-ended questions give us the "aha" moments that help give meaning to the statistical analysis.

Responses to open-ended questions have traditionally been coded by teams of coders who read every written response and assignment to a theme. Tables can then be run using the themes as response codes. This can be a time consuming and expensive task. Often, to reduce costs, the responses, or verbatims, are simply listed for researchers to review and qualitatively understand what respondents are telling us.

However, artificial intelligence tools such as text analytics are now offering automated approaches to create coded responses from open ends, bypassing the human interpretation stage. This may make it faster but might also create errors that miss the local or cultural meaning. Research on text analysis, aka, natural language processing, has moved along from simply counting words to investigating the relationships among words that appear in sequences while attempting to discern the sentiments behind the words and phrases.

a. Image and Video Capture

Not all data need to be collected with a question.

In today's 'always in touch' culture, most respondents carry with them a device that is capable of capturing images of what they are seeing and experiencing – a smartphone. The old saying 'a picture is worth a thousand words' is absolutely true in marketing research.

Increasingly we are asking respondents to take photos of the contents of their refrigerator, of the shelves they are shopping from, of how they prepare their meals or even pack their suitcases. We can analyze these images to understand purchasing and shopping behaviour, create common inventories, check for opportunities when gaps are spotted, and so much more.

Even having respondents video record their answers to standard questions will provide insights into the tone, context and environment that can add layers of understanding to consumer interpretation.

Video analytics are increasingly able to code the images and words in video clips and give us statistics we can use to write our reports. Images and video clips can also be used to communicate and illustrate the findings and recommendations from our research studies.

An excellent example of a video capture project is one in which a company wants to learn about the effectiveness of their sponsorship material at a music festival. A group of festival-goers are asked to capture images of things that catch their attention during the day and feed it back with explanations about what they saw (no mention of the sponsor is made). The images and videos that are returned are analyzed for images of the sponsor's activation or advertising, and to see how many were exposed to it and how many saw it. Follow up questions can measure conscious recall.

Using a video recording for an open-ended response opens the door for artificial intelligence to analyze speech patterns, facial expressions and other images to determine in great detail, the emotions that underlie responses.

b. When to Use What

Although there are different types of questions, the way a question is asked depends on the context. With a little practice, it will become obvious which type of question will provide the required information.

Prompted versus Unprompted Questions

Consider a question like, "What toothpaste brands are you aware of?" Should we prompt the respondent by providing the names of different brands, or should we let the respondent answer spontaneously?

- If we aim to understand what brands come to a consumer's mind when we mention toothpaste, the question should include no prompts. These responses are called "brand recall" or "top-of-mind response."
- On the other hand, if we want to make sure that we obtain a complete reading on brands that people are aware of, we may use a prompt list. These responses are called "brand recognition."

Recall is a more stringent measure than recognition. Sometimes, the recall question can be more practical because there may be many brands with no one brand dominating the market.

It is also possible to combine recall with recognition to gather both types of information. In a self-administered interview, this is as simple as beginning with an open-end recall question on the first screen and following it up on the next screen with a closed-ended multichotomous question. Of course, it is important to disable the back button so that respondents cannot change their response to the open end after having seen the full list.

In a person-to-person survey, the interviewer might present the question in two stages:

When you think of smartphones, which brands come to mind first?

(DO NOT READ BRAND NAMES. RECORD FIRST MENTION ONLY. PROMPT THREE TIMES.)

- ○ APPLE
- ○ ASUS
- ○ DELL
- ○ IBM
- ○ GOOGLE
- ○ HTC
- ○ HUAWEI
- ○ LENOVO
- ○ LG
- ○ MICROSOFT
- ○ NOKIA
- ○ PHILIPS
- ○ SAMSUNG
- ○ SHARP
- ○ SONY
- OTHER ○ [   ]

○ NONE MENTIONED AFTER PROBING

This is an interviewer-administered question. It is common to provide instructions to the interviewer directly on the questionnaire, whether it is computer-assisted or paper-and-pencil. Interviewers are told to read out everything that is in lower or sentence case but not read out anything that is in upper case. In the question above, the interviewer reads the question and waits for the first answer and records only that first answer. It is important to have the most viable alternatives pre-coded for speed of recording. If the respondent does not mention a brand, the interviewer will gently probe to draw a brand name from the respondent without biasing the answer.

Have you heard of ... (ASK EACH BRAND BELOW NOT MENTIONED IN LAST QUES

- ○ APPLE
- ○ ASUS
- ○ DELL
- ○ IBM
- ○ GOOGLE
- ○ HTC
- ○ HUAWEI
- ○ LENOVO
- ○ LG
- ○ MICROSOFT
- ○ NOKIA
- ○ PHILIPS
- ○ SAMSUNG
- ○ SHARP
- ○ SONY

If the survey is computer-assisted, that brand that was mentioned in the recall question would not appear in the brand recognition question.

Closed-Ended versus Open-Ended Questions

Closed-ended questions are relatively easy to ask, easy to answer, easy to record, easy to interpret, and inexpensive to implement.

Open-ended questions, on the other hand, can be difficult to record (the respondent may give a rambling answer), challenging to interpret (different respondents may interpret the question differently), and expensive to implement (may require extensive coding). It is also possible that open-ended questions will leave us with highly superficial answers. For instance, "Why do you like this brand?" may elicit answers such as, "I like it," "It's good," or "Someone said I should." Such responses are so nonspecific that they are useless to marketers. As a general guideline, unless there is a defined reason and unless there are follow-up probing questions, closed-ended questions are preferred to open-ended questions.

Open-ended questions can be useful in exploratory studies and in areas of investigation for which we do not have a great deal of information. A common reason for asking an open-ended question is to ensure that we do not limit the possible answers to the ones that we are aware of or think are relevant.

An open-ended question such as, "What do you like about this product?" can provide unanticipated answers such as, "It's made in Canada" or "It reminds me of my mom," which may prove to be very useful to the marketer.

While there are many situations in which open-ended questions provide useful insight, they can also elicit trivial answers and add to the cost of the survey. It is for these reasons that they should not be used indiscriminately but rather only when necessary.

A vast majority of marketing research survey questions tends to be closed-ended, with only a small proportion of questions being open-ended.

Care should be taken when applying the guidelines given in this chapter. Not every guideline applies to all situations. Although the basic principles of questionnaire construction do not change, specific details may vary depending on several factors. For example, it is not practical to provide a prompt list to a respondent in a telephone interview; and, it is not practical in a mail survey to dissuade the respondent from looking through the whole questionnaire before answering the first question.

4. What you Should Know about the Questionnaire Layout and Design

So far, we have reviewed what a questionnaire should contain, how the information should be sequenced, and how the individual questions should be worded.

To ensure that the well-developed questions are communicating properly to respondents and that the answers are recorded accurately, we need to pay careful attention to the physical appearance of the questionnaire.

The 'look and feel' of the questionnaire has a significant impact on the respondent experience and, as a result, on respondents' willingness to participate and complete all of your questions. A visually appealing questionnaire can increase attention, build trust, reduce boredom and, as a result, improve the quality of the data collection.

Of course, each researcher will have his or her own preferred layout. This discussion is intended not to set rigid rules but to offer guidelines that can form the foundation for a proper question and answer communications.

Group Questions about the Same Topic

A well-designed questionnaire should read like a story. It should have a beginning that draws in the reader, a logical flow that carries them along, and a comfortable ending that leaves them feeling satisfied. The reader should not be unsettled or confused by sudden jumps in the plotline. Along the way, it should be pleasant, informative, and enjoyable.

Although the respondent should not be able to guess what the next question will be, there should be a natural flow to the interview. It should seem to the respondent that he or she is participating in a structured conversation, not in a linguistic tug-of-war.

A couple of guidelines for grouping questions:

1. Follow a respondent's logic – for example, if talking about shopping practices, start with how a shopping list is made, then how the destination store is chosen, then what priority purchases might be, then how decisions are made in a specific aisle, then if coupons are used when paying. It's easier for the consumer to walk through the process in order.

2. Where possible, place questions that the respondent would consider useful or important early in the questionnaire. This gives the respondents a sense that the study is not frivolous, helps build rapport and gives them a reason to continue participating.

3. Ensure that earlier questions do not give respondents information that they should not have before asking later questions (e.g., making it clear too soon that a particular brand is the prime concern of the study).

4. Group questions that are similar in content together to create a natural flow. Once the respondent's mind is focused on a particular theme, it is easier to answer related questions. For example, anything to do with past purchasing behaviour can be grouped together; a series on typical shopping trips can be grouped together; perceptions of the competitive set of products should generally be together; the demographic questions are generally grouped in the last section of the questionnaire, and so on.

5. Place questions that are likely to be complicated or objectionable as late in the questionnaire as possible. At this point, they have invested time in the interview and are less likely to quit. Even if they do quit, we have already collected the bulk of the information we need.

Earlier in this chapter, we included an example of how objectives can be mapped to the questions. But this should not determine how the questions are grouped. The flow of the questionnaire can be very different from the flow of the final objectives-based report.

Signal When You Change Direction

When passing from one distinct section of questions to another, it is often helpful to the respondent if there is a short sentence or two to explain the next set of questions. This creates a smooth transition into a state of mind suitable for answering those questions.

For example, after a section in the questionnaire that deals with the respondent's ownership of automobiles, you may want to ask about his or her experience with the automobile. The "experience" section could be introduced by the following:

Now we would like to better understand your experiences with your vehicles, and your opinions about those experiences.

Or, if the following section is about the respondent's opinions about automotive service in general, we can preface it by saying:

We are also interested in opinions about automotive services. Please share your thoughts on this topic now.

One transition that is common to most questionnaires is the demographic section at the end in which respondents are asked about their age, income, and other personal questions. You do not want to start this section with an apology. This acts as a red flag to respondents, and their guard will be up, and their mouths closed.

A better approach would be to state the reason for asking such questions professionally:

Now, just a few more questions to help us understand how groups of people differ in their opinions.

or

Now, I have just a few more questions to make sure that we've heard opinions from a wide variety of people.

Format for Impact

The physical format of the questionnaire can have a genuine impact on the willingness of potential respondents to participate in a **self-completion** questionnaire, and on the accuracy and ease of recording for an **interviewer-administered** questionnaire.

The look-and-feel is particularly important for **online or web-based surveys** because the questions have to fit onto different sizes of screens – from full-sized desktop monitors to smaller smartphone screens. Different interfaces are needed if the respondent is navigating with a mouse and keyboard, or with a touchscreen.

There are substantial differences between the layout for self-completion versus interviewer-administered questionnaires. In interviewer-administered questionnaires, we would have a (hopefully) well-trained person who can ensure the questions are asked correctly, in the right order and that the response alternatives are well understood.

For self-completion questionnaires:
1. we depend on the respondent's goodwill, so the effort they must devote to answering must be minimized with a straightforward design, relevant content and brevity;
2. instructions and flow must be completely self-explanatory and easy to follow;
3. design so that all qualified respondents can read, understand, and respond to all the questions;
4. paper questionnaires must have only very simple, easy to follow skip patterns (i.e., questions to be answered by a respondent dependent on answers to previous questions);
5. on paper, we have to accept that respondents can skip back-and-forth through the questionnaire so that information revealed part-way through can influence responses to earlier questions.

Points 4 and 5 are not generally applicable to web-based or online surveys in which software can ensure that respondents see one question at a time, that skip patterns are correctly followed, that going back through the questionnaire can be restricted, and that information is provided at the right time.

Several basic principles should be followed to ensure the question formatting works in our favour.

Prefer Vertical Format

Do not make respondents try to figure out how to answer the question physically. Their only job should be to determine their answer mentally and record it effortlessly. Here is an example of a very inferior format for a question:

How would you rate the general health of teenagers today?

Very good health _____ Good health _____ Fair health _____

Poor health _____ Very poor health _____

This horizontal answer layout makes it hard to figure out where the response should be recorded. If teens are in "fair health," should the check be on the right or the left of the words? Respondents should be able to figure it out intuitively, but it is not their job.

A much better layout lists the alternative responses vertically with an obvious place to select one answer:

How would you rate the general physical health of Canadian teenagers today?

- ○ Very good health
- ○ Good health
- ○ Fair health
- ○ Poor health
- ○ Very poor health

This vertical format has several advantages:

- Respondents can clearly see where to record their answers. In the first version, the respondent might have to study the sequence of answers and spaces carefully before figuring it out.
- While it is quite obvious where the answers lie in most online questionnaires, that might not be true for paper-and-pencil questionnaires. It is a good practice with paper-and-pencil self-administered questionnaires to have the answers in a font different from the question. For example, the answers may be in capital letters or italics. As the respondent progresses through the questionnaire, it becomes more evident that when a specific font appears, it is time to check a box to answer a question.
- The vertical column of answers establishes a flow that helps the respondent move more quickly through the questionnaire and feel a sense of accomplishment. The look is also much less cluttered.

Ensure Skip Patterns are clear

Often, a particular response to a question will mean we want the respondent to skip a few questions and pick up again later on.

With any 'programmed' questionnaire – web-based or online, self-completion on a tablet or computer, or computer-assisted telephone (CATI) – the skip takes place in the background, and the respondent doesn't know it is happening. Instructions to those who are programming the questionnaire must be clear and detailed.

However, on paper-and-pencil questionnaires, the respondent must see and understand what to do next. The vertical placement of the answers allows for a much more unambiguous indication of which question(s) should be skipped. Here is an example:

How would you rate the general physical health of Canadian teenagers today?

- ◯ Very good health ➡ GO TO Q3
- ◯ Good health ➡ GO TO Q6
- ◯ Fair health ➡ GO TO Q6
- ◯ Poor health ➡ GO TO Q6
- ◯ Very poor health ➡ GO TO Q6

If, for example, the respondent checks the box for "Fair health," she or he is asked to go directly to Question 6. The way the answers are laid out minimizes any potential confusion.

The interviewer-administered version requires that the response choices are read aloud by the interviewer. Here's how it would look:

Would you rate the general physical health of Canadian teenagers today a very good, good, fair, poor or very poor?

- ◯ Very good health ➡ GO TO Q3
- ◯ Good health ➡ GO TO Q6
- ◯ Fair health ➡ GO TO Q6
- ◯ Poor health ➡ GO TO Q6
- ◯ Very poor health ➡ GO TO Q6

Provide Instructions for Answering/Recording Answer

While questions should be as self-explanatory as possible, it is often necessary to give instructions to the interviewer (if interviewer-administered), to the respondent (if self-administered) or to the programmer (if digital) to minimize any risk of misunderstanding.

Here are a few examples of using instructions in questionnaires. This next question is for an interviewer-administered questionnaire.

Which of these cities, if any, have you visited in the past year? (INTERVIEWER: READ EACH CITY)

- ◯ London
- ◯ Paris
- ◯ Shanghai
- ◯ Tokyo
- ◯ Moscow
- ◯ New York
- ◯ Toronto
- ◯ Rome
- ◯ Sydney
- ◯ None of these

The following question is for a self-administered questionnaire.

Which one of these beverages do you drink most often? (PLEASE SELECT ONLY ONE.)

- ○ Water
- ○ Juice
- ○ Carbonated Soft Drinks
- ○ Coffee or Tea
- ○ Beer or wine
- ○ Other [_____]

How many people live in your household? (Including yourself.) [____]

PROGRAMMERS: RANDOMIZE ORDER & REPEAT HEADING EVERY 6 LINES

How likely are you to recommend each of the following websites to a friend or family member? (SELEC EACH ROW)

- ○ YouTube
- ○ Instagram
- ○ Facebook
- ○ Tumblr

MANY OTHER SITES WILL FOLLOW

Minimize Clutter

A standard uncluttered format will always speed up the work and minimize errors. Whether you are formatting a self-completion questionnaire, or preparing an electronic questionnaire for programming, keeping the script clear and easy-to-read should be a goal.

One way to do this is to use a different font size or colour for a specific function. For example, programming instructions (which a respondent will never see) can be included in bold, blue font. Anything the respondent sees will be in black font – the questions and answers can be in regular font and instructions to the respondents in italics.

Interviewer-administered questionnaires would follow similar protocols and formats – the blue font in capitals, making it easy for interviewers to know what to read and what not to read out loud. Often "READ" AND "DO NOT READ" instructions are added to the tops of the response lists.

On paper questionnaires, data entry instructions (e.g., numeric codes to enter for each response) can be included down the right column to keep it clear of the question and answer. With the answers right-justified and the inclusion of this "coding strip," the tasks of editing, coding, and data entry are simplified. The editor reviews the answers that are checked or circled by the interviewer. The data-entry staff can then key in the data directly from the edited and coded questionnaires. Not only are costs reduced, but a potential source of error can be avoided.

The following is an example of an interviewer-administered question. The answers in the upper case mean that this is a recall question, i.e., the types of accounts are not to be read out, and the ability of the respondent to recall the types of accounts is the key focus. Aligning the answers to the right of the page allows the coders just to read down the right margin, see the answers and type the answers into the appropriate fields as specified by the computer data entry protocol.

73. Which types of accounts do you now have at this bank?	YES	NO	
REGULAR SAVINGS	1	2	Q.73a
REGULAR CHEQUING	1	2	Q.73b
MORTGAGE	1	2	Q.73c
LINE OF CREDIT	1	2	Q.73d
CREDIT CARD	1	2	Q.73e
AUTO LOAN	1	2	Q.73f

Simple tasks like aligning the response columns, consistent spacing between questions and between answers, go a long way towards making questionnaires look clean, easy-to-answer and easy to code.

Minimize Scrolling

When questionnaires are on **paper**, they are generally always printed on the same size of paper. There is not usually a risk of a question running off the side of the page.

However, respondents are now using a wide range of screen sizes to participate in **web-based** or **online** surveys. The questions must be formatted so that they wrap around on any screen that could possibly be used. It is a significant effort for the respondent to '**scroll across,**' and if they don't, they will miss part of the meaning of the question.

Similarly, if the question has multiple **columns**, they could quite easily choose an answer from amongst whatever is on the screen and remain unaware that there are more options off the screen to the right. To avoid this, we can use other formatting options, like progressive grids and drop-down boxes that can be employed. These are described a little later.

Scrolling down also requires some effort, but because the "next" or "submit" button that allows a respondent to move to the next question is generally below the question, respondents are going to see that there are more options. That said, there is still a tendency to choose from what appears on the screen with the question, so response lists that are going to appear on a small screen should be kept as short as possible.

On **paper-and-pencil** questionnaires, do not start a question on one page and then continue it on the next page. Keep each question and its corresponding answers on one page. When a question spans two pages or the space for the answer is on a different page, it makes additional work for the respondent in self-administered questionnaires, and it interrupts the conversational style in interviewer-administered questionnaires. If a question is very long, break it into two parts, each of which fits on one page.

Columns, Progressive Headers, Drop-downs and Sliders

It is common to use a **column format** when you are confident that a questionnaire will be completed on paper or on a larger computer screen. For example, the following format makes it easy for a respondent to see all the options and provide comparative responses.

Which of the following brands would you associate with each of the characteristics listed below? (Select all that apply for each row)

		Brands			
Characteristics	SuperClean	Slick Soap	SnowWhite	Zorax	None
Great Value	○	○	○	○	○
Removes tough stains	○	○	○	○	○
Keeps colors bright	○	○	○	○	○
Does not leave residue	○	○	○	○	○
Works in cold water	○	○	○	○	○

When the questionnaire is to be managed by an interviewer, space can be saved by arranging multiple questions into columns, as demonstrated in the example below. However, this is often difficult for respondents to use on a self-completion questionnaire and can result in recording errors.

 a. Which brands of toothpaste have you tried in the past year? (*Select all that apply*)

 b. Which of these brands have you heard of? (*Select all that apply*)

 c. Which brand do you use most often? (*Select only one.*)

	a. Tried in past year	*b. Aware of*	*c. Main Brand*
Colgate	_____	_____	_____
Aquafresh	_____	_____	_____
Crest	_____	_____	_____
Other	_____	_____	_____

There are more options when a questionnaire is programmed for a digital environment (computer, tablet, phone). In fact, columns are virtually impossible to manage when the questionnaire is to be completed on a smartphone.

Several other options are available that take care of this situation. One is the **progressive header** which has the column headings appear on each screen with a single statement:

How to Design a Questionnaire   221

Which of the following brands do you associate with Good Value?

	SuperClean	SlickSoap	SnowWhite	Zorax	None
Good Value	○	○	○	○	○

Which of the following brands do you associate with Removes Tough Stains?

	SuperClean	Slick Soap	SnowWhite	Zorax	None
Removes Tough Stains	○	○	○	○	○

Another option that works well on a small screen is a **drop-down box**. This might put several statements on a single screen and feature a box beside each one. When the respondent taps the box, the response options "drop-down," and when the respondent chooses one of them, it rolls up again.

Initial Screen:

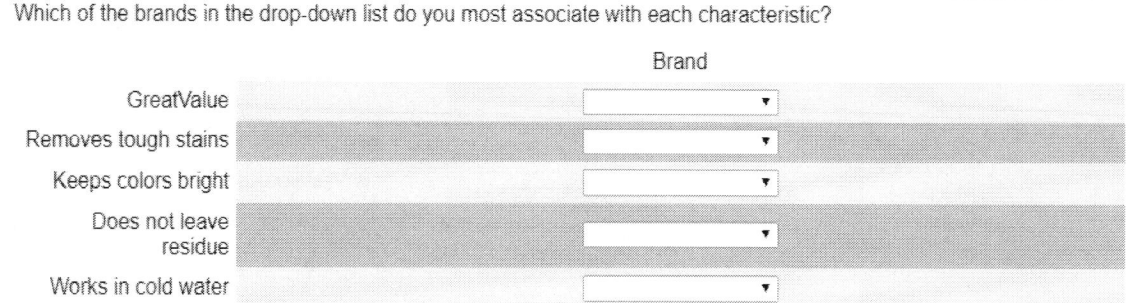

After GreatValue is tapped:

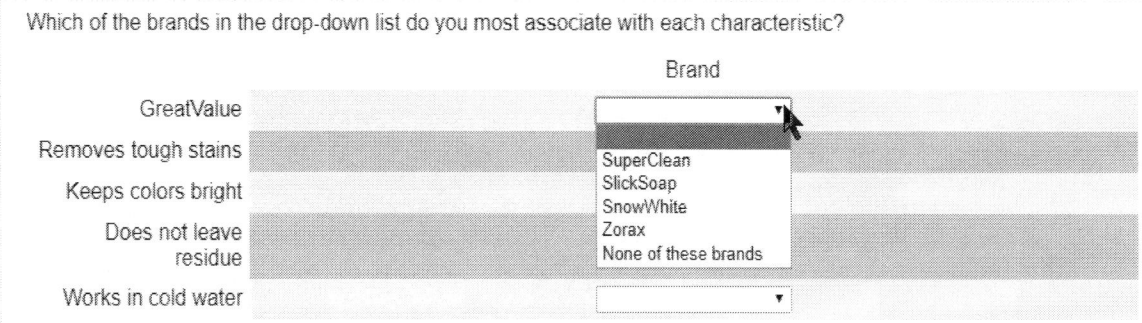

A **slider** scale also works well on tiny touch screens, and when tapping and dragging a finger is how responses are recorded. The slider can also be more fun than a list or scale because the dynamics of the visual can change as the icon is dragged – perhaps changing colour from red to green, or having the smile on a happy face shift from a downward frown to a smile. Here is an example.

All of these provide essentially the same exposure and response patterns as a column layout but can be easily read and answered on a small smartphone screen.

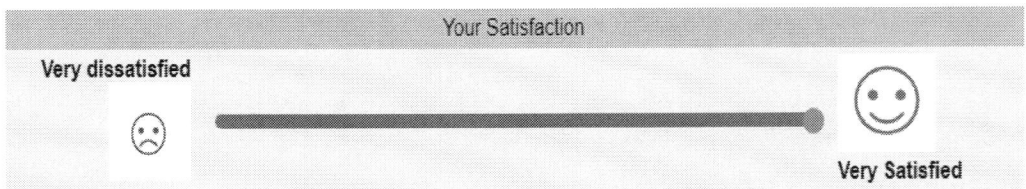

Use Images Effectively

In self-completion questionnaires, we can use photos, brand logos, or icons for several reasons:

a. **Accuracy**. Respondents may not always be thinking of the same product you are when you list a brand name. For example, Black Diamond cheese may be a brand that you are asking about, but respondents may mix it up with another brand of cheese that uses a lot of black in its pack design. To reduce the risk of error, we would show an image of the pack or the brand logo next to each brand name.

b. **Speed**. Respondents can more quickly absorb and process an image than a few words. The image is quicker to conjure up associations and emotions that form a respondent's view of the brand, making it faster for them to respond to your questions.

c. **Engagement**. Images are the currency of internet engagement. Facebook posts without images are rarely read. Instagram and Pinterest are all about images. Some suggest that we are entering a 'post-writing' world. In this environment, the more visually appealing your survey, the more attention respondents are going to pay to complete it accurately.

Use Progress Bars

In an online environment like a web-based survey, boredom can be resolved in a split second by clicking off your survey to find something more interesting. One way to keep respondents engaged is by showing them that they are *almost* finished the survey.

How to Design a Questionnaire 223

How satisfied or dissatisfied are you with how long it took to resolve your complaint?

Your Satisfaction

Very dissatisfied ☹ ────────────────────● 😊 **Very Satisfied**

Back   Next

0% ▬▬▬▬▬▬▬▬▬▬▬▬▬▬▬ 100%

A progress bar appears at the top or bottom of the screen and shows what proportion of the questionnaire has been completed and how much more there is to complete. The progress bar at the bottom of the question above shows that the survey is almost 100% complete.

Make sure, if you can, that the "progress" is proportional to the **time** spent and not the **number of responses** recorded. This is because the grid questions that respondents can move through quickly are often 'click heavy' and located towards the end of the questionnaire. So, the bar shows little progress until well into the questionnaire. A progress bar that doesn't move quickly can be more detrimental than helpful.

5. How to Improve Data Quality in Self-administered Surveys

Regardless of the method used for data collection, every researcher must be concerned with data quality. When an **interviewer** is asking questions, careful training and monitoring are usually enough to ensure that the question is asked correctly, the respondent understands, and the answer is recorded accurately.

However, we are much less confident when the questionnaire is **self-completed** by respondents. The truth is that *most* respondents are happy to tell you what they think and do want to answer accurately. They will do their best in a world that is full of distractions (child care, TV or radio, e-mail notifications, social media). But when a questionnaire is visually dense, hard to understand, or asks for too much effort, some will not consider it worth the effort. That's why this book is focused on making the task as easy and enjoyable as possible for our respondents.

A small proportion of respondents will *deliberately not* take the time and effort to complete the questionnaire accurately. Generally, this is because they are intent on earning whatever incentives are offered in as short a time as possible, so they will lie about who they are to qualify, and then speed through the questionnaire to complete and repeat.

In the worst cases, "click farms" are set up to complete surveys in large numbers so that the incentives earned become substantial, but data quality is clearly compromised.

Catching Poor Quality Respondents

Several techniques have been developed to identify completed questionnaires that may not include the best quality data. Some of the more common techniques include the following.

- **Red Herrings**. When building a list of brand names, consider including one or two brands that don't exist. Search for these red herrings online first to be sure they don't actually exist. While you might pull anyone who clicks on a 'red herring' out of the data set, be careful. A 'made-up' name may seem plausible, and you might be eliminating a legitimate respondent who just thought the name 'sounded familiar.'

- **Straightlining**. When a rating question includes several questions in a grid, look for cases where a respondent has chosen the same response for every question. For example, in a question with 25 statements, and the respondent 'Strongly Agrees' with every one, they may be suspect. You can be sure of this if you have statements that are polar opposites, and they agree strongly with both. This might be something like:
  - I carefully read all nutrition labels on food products before I buy them.
  - I don't worry about nutrition; I just buy what I like.

- **Setting Traps**. Within the battery of statements may be a trap to catch those who are speeding through without reading. For example, the 7th statement might always be: 'Please select the number 2 here'. Anyone that selects another response should be suspect.

- **Text Responses**. When respondents are asked to type out an open-ended response, identify whether the response is valid, e.g., responses with profanity, or nonsense text such as 'asdf.' If your survey has no text responses, you might consider creating one just for this purpose. Of course, open ends require even more effort, and a nonsensical response may only mean they didn't want to make an effort to think on this one question, and all other responses are legitimate.

- **Speeding**. There are no standard calculations to identify speeding, but a helpful indicator is to flag the fastest 5 percent of completion times. Keep in mind that skip patterns and logic may result in some respondents having legitimately fast completion times.

- **Overly Easy Recruiting**. One trick of fraudulent respondents is to try to qualify for a 'hard-to-reach' respondent group. For example, young males are notoriously difficult to recruit for online surveys. If a large proportion of your sample suddenly qualifies for this group, you may have a problem. Similarly, families with children in multiple age groups are more likely to qualify for many surveys. Raise a flag if you identify a large group of young males in their 20s with children in a wide range of age groups.

- **Inconsistencies**. Sometimes, the data just doesn't make sense. A childless household is unlikely to report buying diapers every week. Respondents with no driver's license should be driving over 100 kilometres every week. Those who live in apartments are probably not buying lawn fertilizer. You can bury cross-checking questions like this into a questionnaire, preferably spaced far apart, so fraudulent respondents don't realize they are being tested.

Improving Data Quality with Paper-and-Pencil Questionnaires

Here are some tricks of the trade that you may find useful for self-administered paper-and-pencil questionnaires.

- Consider *not* numbering the questions sequentially from the beginning to the end of the questionnaire. The respondent might balk at the large number of questions, even though the time needed for completion might be quite short. This problem can be avoided by numbering questions sequentially *within* each section or not numbering at all.
- Use a high-legibility font (e.g., Calibri, Arial, Times or Helvetica) so that even people who have poor vision can read it. Do not use small font sizes.
- If the paper-and-pencil questionnaire is longer than five pages, consider formatting it as a booklet in a size smaller than the standard 8.5-by-11-inch sheet of paper. Often, a standard sheet of paper folded in half and turned sideways makes a good size for a booklet. Both sides of the page would be printed.
- Use clean and generic images to enhance the attractiveness and heighten interest.
- Do not crowd the questions together. Some open space, or 'white space,' makes for a more appealing questionnaire—one that will be more inviting for respondents to complete.
- Reduce the amount of ink on the page. Only the questions, the answer categories, and instructions to the respondents should be on the page. If any coding information appears on the questionnaire, reduce it to a bare minimum by using smaller and lighter fonts.
- Keep open-ended questions to a minimum. People are usually reluctant to record lengthy responses, which may lead to superficial or scattered answers.

Increasing Response Rates

The higher the response rate (the proportion of people invited to participate who do), the better the data quality if everything else is well done. The lower the response rate, the more likely you are to have a biased sample rife with poor quality or fraudulent respondents. Only those intent on earning the incentive, at any cost, will make it through to the end of a poorly designed questionnaire.

Of course, our main objective is to design a questionnaire properly. But incentives and reminders can also improve response rates.

Incentives

Virtually all surveys now offer incentives for participation. With the move to online or web-based surveys, respondents must belong to a panel (there is no 'random probability sampling' in the online environment). The incentive to join and remain on a panel might be a token payment, an entry in a regular cash draw, or the ability to collect points that will eventually allow you to select an item from a catalogue.

Qualitative research such as focus groups or in-depth interviews may offer more substantial incentives, perhaps $60 to $100 for the general population and as high as $250 or more for a specific profession (e.g., medical practitioners or accountants).

Small incentives are not feasible in telephone studies because the postage, labour, and administrative costs involved in mailing might far exceed the cost of the incentive itself. If it becomes necessary to offer incentives for telephone studies (e.g., if it is a lengthy questionnaire extending more than 20 or 30 minutes), a common practice is to offer a substantial prize (e.g., $1000 or a smart TV or several smartphones) based on a draw.

In some jurisdictions, offering prizes through a draw requires a government permit and requires stringent regulatory guidelines.

In the online environment, the initial invitation to participate is sent out by e-mail to selected members of a panel. If the panel is well managed, its members are kept engaged by regular contact (either invitations to continue with the panel, newsletters or games and prizes).

Ongoing Engagement

Most online research participants are members of a **panel**. They have been recruited to complete surveys. They are more likely to stay on the panel and to participate in surveys if they feel a sense of connection, of community. Panel managers create on-going communications plans, including newsletters, updates on the points they've earned and fun surveys to keep them connected if they have not recently completed a real research survey. A well-managed panel monitors the response rates of its members and refreshes regularly by removing those who are not responding frequently, or appropriately, and recruiting fresh members to fill the gaps.

Specific sub-groups may need more active engagement efforts:
- Some sub-groups are in high demand – packaged goods companies do a lot of research, so 'principal grocery shoppers' are invited to more surveys than those who are not. Because of the attention on products for families, parents tend to be in high demand. Researchers must be careful to limit the number of surveys respondents complete or response rates will drop.
- Some sub-groups are hard to recruit – young un-married males, for example, are less interested in joining research panels (they may have other things to do), and extra effort may be required to ensure those who are on the panel are engaged in ways that make them stay and participate.
- Some respondents may be very important but only surveyed infrequently, such as members of specific professions or those who speak a minority language. We may need them for specialized research that does not happen very often. Engagement efforts are needed to ensure they stay on the panel and are ready to respond when they are needed. For example, medical oncologists are very difficult to recruit and they require very high incentives, often $100 to $500 per questionnaire.

When working with a research firm that uses a panel, it is important to ask members their opinions about the panel management and engagement protocols.

Reminders

Response rates for online and other self-administered surveys can almost always be increased by sending out reminders. For online surveys, one or two email reminders several days apart are common. Any more than this and potential respondents may become annoyed.

In mail surveys, a three-wave technique is often used.

- **Wave 1:** The cover letter, questionnaire, stamped self-addressed return envelope, and incentive are mailed.
- **Wave 2**: Follow-up reminders are mailed one-and-a-half weeks after Wave 1 to encourage co-operation.
- **Wave 3:** Reminder letters, questionnaires, and stamped self-addressed return envelopes are mailed one-and-a-half weeks after the Wave 2 reminder.

---

6. What are the Benefits of Online Questionnaires

Online questionnaires made the entire process of self-administered surveys much easier for both the respondent and the researcher. We can:
- include complex skip patterns that are invisible to the respondent
- make the questionnaire more engaging with different response methods, like sliding scales, click-and-drag sorting exercises, icons that change colour or expression based on which answer you select, drop-down boxes, even animations etc.
- personalize questionnaires by including responses in subsequent questions
- do a better job of hiding questions that the respondent is not yet supposed to see
- provide more careful, customized explanations, including links or pop-ups to let respondents see the instructions or stimuli a second time if desired
- make it easier to change one's responses
- allow piecemeal completion of a questionnaire (e.g., come back and finish it later)
- provide an environment for artificial intelligence to probe based on a respondent's initial answer
- is capable of capturing voice and video that can be analyzed using AI
- obtain respondents' answers immediately

In the early days, most online questionnaires simply recreated the printed questionnaire page for page and question for question, formatting and instructions included. However, this approach is not engaging and ignored the unique advantages that the internet offers. This section discusses some of those unique advantages in some detail.

Skip Patterns

Online or web-based surveys allow us to display one question per screen. This makes it very easy to use complex skip patterns: their response to a question will determine which question is seen next. If appropriate, more than one question can be shown per screen.

For example, if a respondent reports having consumed Green Yogurt in the past week, we might ask which brand. If they have not, we will skip over the brand question, and the respondent would be completely unaware that the brand question even existed. This enables different sets of respondents to see different subsets of the questionnaire that are relevant to them.

Response Piping

This allows us to incorporate the answers of earlier questions into later questions.

For instance, if a respondent indicates that, among other purchases, she had recently signed up for a new data plan for her phone, a later question may refer to this by piping in (bringing forward) her previous response: "You said that you recently signed up for a new data plan. Which of the following features does it include?"

Response piping allows for intricate skip patterns—answers can be filtered through several questions before they are "piped" into a subsequent question. Piping is particularly useful when you want to prompt a responder about several different brands or products that they said they use, instead of going through a long list all over again.

Another benefit of piping is that it can personalize the questionnaire experience.

For example, in the initial screening question, we may ask for the ages and gender of members of a respondent's household, so that later in the questionnaire we can ask about the behaviour of a specific member. We can personalize this by asking for each household member's first name or nickname so that later on, we could ask about "your son Nicholas" rather than "your male child aged 5 to 9".

Response Rotation

Rotation is used in response lists to avoid order bias effects. This can easily be programmed into online questionnaires, so every respondent sees the list in a *fully* randomized order.

It is even possible to ensure that a specific answer always appears in the same position, a feature called 'anchoring,' even though every other response has been fully randomized. For example (note that these are directions to the questionnaire programmer, not the actual text seen by respondents.):

- when you want particular options always to appear side by side to avoid confusion
    - whole bean coffee
    - ground coffee
    - instant coffee
    - coffee in single-serve pods [ALWAYS SHOW NEXT TO DISC OPTION]
    - coffee in single-serve discs [ALWAYS SHOW NEXT TO POD OPTION]

How to Design a Questionnaire

- when you need blocks of responses to rotate together so respondents can easily find what they want to select without sifting through the entire list
    - Randomize brands, but keep all variants of a single brand together
        - A&W Root Beer
        - Brio
        - Coca-Cola.
        - Diet Coke.
        - Coke Zero Sugar.
        - Coca-Cola Life.
        - Cherry Coke.
        - Caffeine-free Diet Coke.
        - Vanilla Coke.
        - Coke Zero Sugar Cherry
        - Dr. Pepper
        - Fanta
        - Kinney
        - Pepsi Cola
        - Diet Pepsi
        - Pepsi Zero Sugar
        - Pepsi Wild Cherry
        - Pepsi Real Lime
        - Royal Crown Cola
        - Tab
- when a catch-all 'other' response must always follow the full list of specific brands that you don't want to be included in the "other" category
    - grocery store
    - club store
    - discount department store
    - convenience store
    - drug store
    - other types of stores [ANCHOR AT END]

responses that are escape valves that allow respondents to move on to the next question, even if they can't find a response that fits their situation.
- Swimming
- Running
- Skiing
- Working out
- A team sport (baseball, hockey, football/soccer, etc.)
- None of the above [ANCHOR AT END]

Logic

Logic is an important advantage of online questionnaires. By transferring the application of skip patterns to the software instead of the interviewer or the respondent, far more complex questionnaires can be designed. Specific questions, and sets of questions, can be presented to people dependent on any combination of prior answers.

For example, people who have different degrees of involvement with a brand can be tagged and directed on different pathways through the questionnaire. We may identify:
- frequent users – and have them answer a series of questions on the full range of usage patterns;
- occasional users – and ask them the same usage questions, but also ask why they don't use more often and identify their 'most often' product;
- non-users who would consider using – and direct them into a series of questions to explore usage patterns of what they are using and identify barriers for the usage of our product;
- aware rejecters and ask them what the barriers to consideration are; and
- not aware to terminate their participation in the survey.

Complex logic requires precise programming instructions. As much care should be taken in writing the logic for online questionnaires as is spent composing the questions themselves. Rigorous testing of the questionnaire once programmed is also required to ensure the logic is capturing the data as required. Once launched, an online questionnaire can't be altered without drawing a new sample – an expensive proposition. However, a small pilot sample can be used to help identify any problems with the questionnaire.

Look and Feel

Marketing research questionnaires are now competing for the attention of respondents with very engaging social media, slick videos, and other forms of constant stimulation. A questionnaire with standard fonts and tables will not hold a respondent's attention for long.

Questionnaires now have to be more engaging. The marketing research industry is increasingly upgrading the look and feel of their online questionnaires and panel engagement efforts. This is done by creating more interactive, fun elements, taking the cues from video games etc.

Increasingly, questionnaires include audio and video as stimuli. This might be using full ads as stimuli rather than storyboards, providing instructions in the form of animations, offering voice recordings to ask the questions, etc.

Response scales can incorporate movement and colour changes and sliding scales. Respondents can drag-and-drop images into different spaces on a screen and can provide responses by recording a video of their family using the product or incorporate images of advertising they've seen to illustrate their point.

Ultimately, it should be as enjoyable and engaging to complete an online questionnaire as it is to watch or participate in other leading-edge online activities.

7. What are the Challenges of a Multi-country Questionnaire Design Study?

The largest marketing research clients are international in scope. They seek consistent methodologies that provide comparable results across all their markets. Marketing research suppliers are asked to meet these expectations without losing sight of each market's unique character.

Global consistency requires an awareness of the challenges that this presents:
- Even countries that speak the same language and seem to be culturally very similar to each other have **unique words or phrases**. Some expressions may mean different things in different cultures. For example:
  - An elevator, truck and trunk in North America are a lift, a lorry and a boot in the UK.
  - The store where over-the-counter medications can be bought might be called a pharmacy in one country, a drug store in another and a chemist in a third. In some counties, peddlers can supply these medications out of baskets or carts.
  - A single-family home may, in one country, mean any dwelling in which a family can live, while another more specifically uses the term to describe a detached house surrounded by property.
- What may be considered a straightforward question in one culture could be considered **offensive or inappropriate** in another. For example
  - Income is not an appropriate question in every country.
  - Race may be a commonly-asked classifier in the United States but might lead to discomfort and anger elsewhere
  - Gender questions that go beyond male/female classifications are increasingly required in many markets but would be considered offensive in more traditional societies.
  - Questions on marital status and household composition can include a more extensive list of options in more liberal societies.
  - Social roles might be handled differently. In some cultures, "Are you the head of your household?" might be considered inappropriate because it suggests that one person is in charge of others when in fact, two spouses share equal responsibility for a household.

Some concepts simply **don't exist** in every culture. For example:
- Socio-economic classes might be easily defined in Europe, but in North America, income might be the only appropriate measure.
- Professional or occupational categories might be very different from country to country, including the status that they imply.
- Second homes might be common in some parts of the world, and might be called cottages, cabins, camps, dachas, country or weekend houses. Elsewhere the concept might be unimaginable. This is important when we are asking people to describe their living conditions.
- Brand lists, retailers, channels are all appreciably different from country to country.

Even within one country, regional variations present a challenge to effective question-wording. This is particularly true in countries that have regions or populations that speak a different language or belong to different ethnic groups.

It is important to understand that these challenges exist and to be open to adapting our methodologies to local market realities. Any team that manages a multi-country study from a central location should get someone with an in-depth knowledge of the language and culture of *each* target country to proof-read the questionnaire before it is fielded in that country.

Translations

It is often necessary to translate a questionnaire into another language when working internationally, or in countries with more than one common language.

Translating the questionnaire *accurately* is just as crucial as getting the wording right in the first place. An accurate translation will not only carry the same meaning as the original version but the same tone.

Ideally, the researcher who wrote the original version speaks both languages and can ensure both versions reflect the same meaning and intention. However, that is not often the case, and a third party is required to do the translation and check accuracy. Here are some essential tips to increase the chance of success.

- Use an *experienced translator* who specializes in questionnaires and has the appropriate questionnaire design training. At the very least, buy them a copy of this book.
- Have a *research colleague* who understands the second language review the translation. Sometimes this is best done side-by-side where the author reads the original version out loud, and the colleague follows along with the translation, stopping to ask for clarifications on intention.
- Pay particular attention to *subsidiary phrases* in the questionnaire wording that are important and often lost in a translation. Some key examples are: 'if any,' 'or not,' 'or another member of your household,' 'in the past 12 months', 'on this one occasion,' etc. The question may still make sense if these are missing, but some fundamental meaning and permission may be lost.
- Simple tests like comparing the *number of response options* in each version will reveal if something as been inadvertently missed.
- Pay special attention to *respondent instructions* like 'please choose all that apply' or 'select one only.' If something has been block copied as a starting point for translation, these instructions are often overlooked.

In a case where no-one in the organization can check the translated version of the questionnaire, you may have to ask for a '**back translation**' in which *another* translator re-translates the questionnaire back into its original language. The idea is that if the first translation was well done, the back translation would recreate the original questionnaire. Unfortunately, language is so complex, and there are so many ways to say what we want to in each language, that a back translation rarely returns to exactly the same starting point. We then have to judge which attempt created the gap. We would be well advised to have a discussion with both translators after the exercise to work through anything that makes you uncomfortable in the back translation.

One thing is certain, NEVER use automated translation programs like Google Translate for something as important as questionnaire wording. They are not yet at a point where they can understand and recreate meaning and tone.

8. How to Review, Refine and Pretest

Throughout the questionnaire design process, there are several checks and balances required to minimize the risk of errors in the data.

Keep Close Tabs on the Questionnaire Length

The length of a questionnaire impacts respondents' willingness to participate, the time required to complete, analyze and report and, as a result, the cost of the project. Throughout the design process, you must keep track of the questionnaire length, checking it each time a series of questions is added or removed. It is too late to make significant cuts after client approvals have been received.

That said, a final check of length is a wise disaster prevention check. It is often stated that a telephone interview should last for 10 to 15 minutes at the longest. An online questionnaire should be no longer than 15 minutes but can stretch to 20 minutes if the content and look-and-feel are entertaining.

In rare cases, interviews of 30 minutes can be conducted with good response rates when the subject matter is of particular interest to the respondents and when the questionnaire is well-written and exciting. Substantial incentives are required for questionnaires that take this long to complete.

If the questionnaire is found to be overly long at any point in the design process, some tough decisions must be made:

- Each question should be justified relative to the objectives of the study. If a question is not essential to achieving one of the objectives and consequently would not be used to test one or more of the hypotheses, it should be seriously considered for elimination.
- The questionnaire flow might be altered so that at one point, respondents are divided into balanced samples – each of which sees a different series of questions. For example, half the sample may answer the shopping questions, and the other half may answer the meal preparation questions. This would result in a shorter completion time for each respondent without actually reducing the length of the questionnaire. However, the programming and analysis time is not reduced, and there are challenges cross-tabulating data when different people answered different questions.
- At the very least, the client may have to cover the costs of additional incentives required to keep respondents answering through to the end of a longer questionnaire.

Edit Rigorously

The first draft of the questionnaire may contain several superfluous questions which not only waste resources but can make the interview process more difficult. Rambling questionnaires reduce respondent co-operation, but they may also affect the analyses and the report. The final report may lack cohesion because the responses to non-relevant questions won't be related to the objectives of the study. Be careful of "wouldn't it be nice to know" questions. They often serve no purpose other than unnecessarily lengthening the questionnaire. Superfluous questions should be rigorously edited or omitted.

The fundamental criterion that determines whether a question should be included is the usefulness of the response to the decision-maker. Can the answer to this question, either by itself or in combination with other information, help the decision-maker arrive at a better marketing decision? If you cannot think of the right way in which the specific response can be used in decision making, the question is probably redundant.

The questionnaire should also be checked for redundant questions. On occasion, more than one question might be used to investigate one particular point or objective. However, redundancy will create an unnecessarily long questionnaire that might bore or annoy the respondent and result in a reduced response rate.

At this point, it makes sense to go back to the Objectives Map and revise it to ensure all of the objectives of the study have been fully met, or that you have alignment from the client on objectives that will not be fully covered.

Pre-testing and Soft Launches

Once a questionnaire has been finalized, it should be pre-tested, i.e., subjected to an interview-like situation to gauge how well it works. This is less important for any survey that is part of an on-going tracking program in which few changes are made between waves or part of standardized procedures like concept testing. However, it becomes more crucial for longer, complex, sensitive, technical or any other 'out-of-the-ordinary' questionnaire.

Pre-testing should be both informal and formal.

Informal Pretesting

Informal pretesting is used to make sure that the questionnaire has no obvious problems with flow, understandability, and length. The questionnaire is completed by a colleague, an acquaintance, or even a few randomly chosen people to identify such problems. It might be a '**swivel chair' pre-test** where you read the questionnaire out loud so both you and the respondent can hear what it sounds like. The ear can often pick up a problem that the eye didn't catch. It might be a '**protocol' pre-test** in which the respondent completes the questionnaire himself or herself while speaking their reactions out loud. Or, it might be a **'debrief' pre-test** in which the respondent sits down with the research professional after having completed the questionnaire and points out any issues faced in understanding the questions or flow.

Informal pre-testing is <u>unlikely</u> to identify less obvious problems with the questionnaire.

- For example, testing a questionnaire on investing with a colleague might suggest that it is understandable and problem-free. However, your colleagues may have experience with investments and may have a better understanding of the terminology used in the questionnaire. The actual targeted respondents might be less familiar with some of the words used and run into roadblocks that the informal pre-test did not uncover.
- Colleagues may also be more forgiving of a tedious questionnaire because they are used to reviewing them, but a live respondent may simply terminate the interview.

The tendency is to forego informal pre-testing when a more formal test is scheduled. But this may be a mistake. The human interaction, the conversation that takes place in an *informal* pre-test, can provide more profound insight into meaning and understanding and ultimately result in a more sensitive research instrument than a larger scale formal pretest.

The most common form of informal pre-testing in online research is '**link testing.**' The questionnaire is already programmed onto the web-based platform, and the research team is sent links to the questionnaire. Just as a respondent would, they follow the link to their own questionnaire and complete it as if they are respondents. By working their way through a variety of scenarios and testing what happens when every response in the questionnaire is selected, the researcher can spot programming errors, identify inconsistencies and check for layout problems (e.g. left- or right-scrolling to see all response options, items trimmed, etc.)

Links must be tested on devices with different sized screens. What works well on a full-sized monitor screen might be incomprehensible on a smartphone screen.

Formal Pre-testing

For **formal pretesting**, a small sample of respondents (20 to 50, depending on the size of the study) is surveyed in exactly the same way as they would be in the main study. This means that telephone interviewers start calling potential respondents to interview them over the phone, that mall intercept interviewers go out into the field to find a few 'real respondents' to interview them. And in an online survey, a questionnaire is launched with invitations sent to a small sub-sample of the full sample. This is often referred to as a '**soft-launch.**'

The formal pretest will give an accurate read on completion time and data capture and whether the program or interviewer is picking up the responses appropriately. Only if follow up interviews are conducted with respondents will we know if there are comprehension issues or moments of confusion or frustration that reduce respondent engagement.

If the survey is conducted in more than one language, it would be appropriate to have each translated version pre-tested by someone who speaks that language fluently.

Any deficiencies encountered in the pre-test must be corrected before the full survey launch takes place. If the pre-test requires no (or only minor) changes to the questionnaire, the pre-test questionnaires can be rolled into the main study sample. This is usually done for practical reasons because some pre-tests can be expensive, and it is unnecessary to waste useful data. If the changes are more substantial, the pre-test sample is abandoned.

Final Approvals

Once all versions of the questionnaire are fine-tuned and finalized, it is important to get the client's final sign off. This is important to ensure they are on-board with the version that is about to go to field and provides a highly visible signal that no more alterations can be made.

Once the client signs off and the study is launched, any further changes would require pulling it out of field, wasting samples and causing significant delays. The client must understand the implications.

It is important to get sign-off from the major stakeholders. You don't want to be standing in a final presentation of the results and have an important decision-maker in the client organization question the methodology.

Concluding Comments

We cannot hope to get valid answers if we don't ask the right questions. If you are only using online questionnaires, you may find some of the materials referring to interviewer-administered or paper questionnaires superfluous. But remember, even now, around the world, fewer than one in three surveys is done online. In any case, the important thing is to understand the critical nature of questionnaires. We hope this chapter provided you with a solid foundation.

UNIT 7

How to Measure Attitudes, Behaviour, and Traits

In the last unit, we saw how to design a questionnaire in general. However, there is more to writing a good questionnaire than knowing the general principles. We also need to know how to ask specific questions that relate to consumer attitudes, behaviours, and traits. Different information requirements may call for different types of questions.

General Overview of Measurement and Scaling

A standardized questionnaire can be viewed as a measurement tool. In broad terms, a questionnaire measures attitudes, behaviours, and traits. Measuring each one of these categories involves unique challenges. A non-researcher may not notice the impact of subtle differences wording can have, but the way a question is asked or phrased can lead to a wide variety of sometimes unexpected interpretations. Even a simple question like "How many people work in your company?" may produce a wide variety of different responses depending on how people interpret it. For instance, some people may include part-time employees and job sharing in the headcount while others may not, counting only 'full-time-equivalent' positions. Some people may include employees in all locations, and others may include only employees in a particular location.

There are also many ways to measure attitudes. Some attitudes are held firmly, others less strongly. For this reason, when we measure attitudes in marketing research, we often use scales. Scales can be classified in many ways: numeric or semantic (verbal), comparative (such as paired comparison and constant sum) versus non-comparative, and so on, depending on the perspective. Here we begin with nominal (Yes-No) types of scales, discuss ranking scales, and then move on to rating scales. We also discuss other related scales, such as semantic differential and Likert scales.

There are literally hundreds of scales and several theoretical frameworks for classifying them. The scales that we have chosen to describe are those that are most frequently used in marketing research. As each scale is described, we also point out when that particular scale should be used.

How to Measure Attitudes

Attitudes deal with consumer awareness, knowledge, perceptions, preferences, motivation and judgments.

- Which brands are considered healthier?
- How much does the consumer like product A?
- What triggers the search for a new car?
- How important is safety to a consumer who is about to buy a car?
- What impact do tariffs have on consumers' lifestyles?
- Would consumers support lowering trade barriers?

Attitudes exist in the mind of consumers and cannot be directly observed. They are assumed to be relatively enduring (i.e., attitudes change slowly). This means that a person who has an attitude (i.e., he or she favours more open trade or likes a fast car) is likely to hold on to that attitude for a while—perhaps for months, years, or even forever.

Attitudes are assumed to influence behaviour. For example, if you like a product very much (attitude), you are likely to buy that product (behaviour). In marketing research, the term attitude is not used as a purely psychological construct. Instead, it is used as a convenient shortcut to include a wide variety of cognitive (perceptual), affective (emotional), and conative (behaviour motivating) aspects of the respondent, which are self-reported. It includes consumer evaluations of products and services, intent to purchase and more. Since one of our aims is to understand how a consumer would behave—for instance, what they would buy, how much they would buy—we measure attitudes to help us predict behaviour.

Sometimes it is enough to know that consumers hold individual attitudes (e.g., The attitude may be 'companies are not concerned about the community'.). But in most cases, we need to know how strongly they hold their attitudes as well. So, there are *existence* and *intensity* components to attitudes.

1. **Existence**. Does a consumer hold a given attitude?
2. **Intensity**. If so, how strongly does the consumer hold that attitude?

The following exhibit illustrates one theory of the stages that consumers pass through when considering and buying products. The following exhibit shows 'the hierarchy of effects." This and other renditions of the hierarchy of effects may be good models to use when developing questionnaires, analyzing data and interpreting the findings. Although the theoretical sequence shown in the exhibit probably happens much of the time, it does not always happen. Think about when this does not occur. For example, you're in a bar with friends, one of whom buys you a pint of beer, and you take a sip when it is handed to you. You've already behaved by drinking before developing any opinion of the brand.

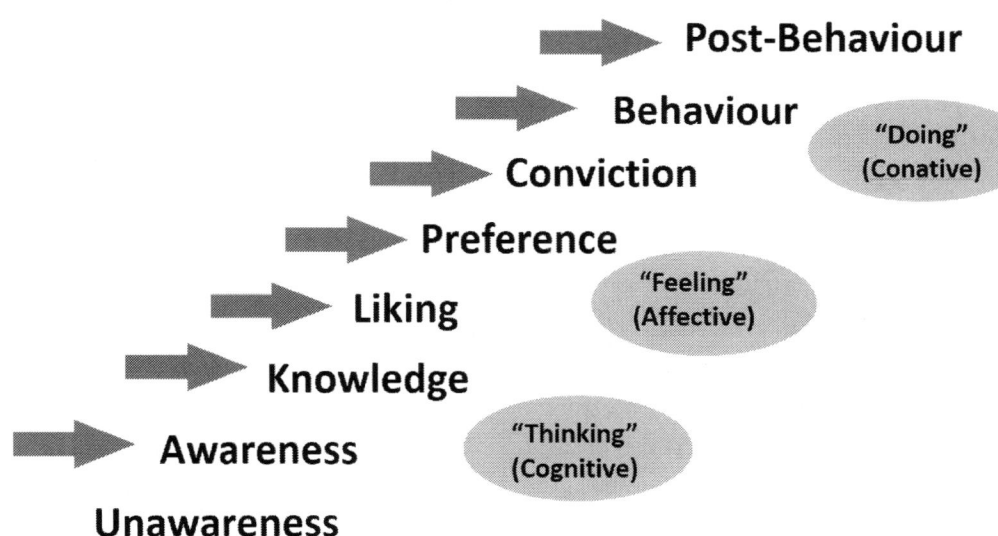

Because attitudes are not directly observable, we must depend on consumers to tell us what attitudes they hold and how strongly they hold them. As a result, we can never be entirely certain about the accuracy of our measurements. However, experience shows that attitudes can be measured in ways that are useful *enough* for making marketing decisions. Marketers know that there is no one-to-one correspondence between attitude and behaviour. If 100 consumers state that they would buy Brand X, it is doubtful that all of them will indeed do so. However, some relationships are bound to hold, such as the following:

- A certain proportion of people who say they would buy Brand X would indeed buy it. For example, if 100 consumers say that they would buy Brand X next time, 40 might actually buy it. This is often called a conversion.
- The proportion may vary by product category. For instance, among car owners who say that they would repurchase the same model, only 30 percent actually do so. For users of a certain brand of toothpaste, the equivalent percentage might be 90 percent. Conversion proportions have been shown to vary between cultures as well.
- The intensity of attitudes can also help project to related behaviours. For instance, larger proportions of people who say that they would "definitely buy Product X" are likely to buy it than people who only say that they would "probably buy Product X."

In practice, this means that attitudes can be measured in standard ways, usually using some type of numeric scale. Scales attempt to quantify the *existence* and the *intensity* of attitudes. In marketing research, both the existence and the intensity of an attitude are generally assumed to be the same as that reported by the individual. Even though we assume this, it is still our responsibility to make sure that attitudes are measured correctly.

Reliability and Validity Revisited

Measurement of attitudes should be valid, reliable, accurate and sensitive. As long as the consumer holds a specific attitude, we should get the same measurement when measuring in repeated or parallel studies. When the consumer changes her or his attitudes, it should be reflected in the measurement.

Although reliability and validity were dealt with in an earlier unit, let's review it with the following two examples.

1. **Validity**. Suppose two similar studies are carried out among salespeople in a specific industry. Participants were randomly selected, randomly assigned to each study, matched between samples and representative of the parent population. Assume that the sales estimates in the two studies are very close. This means the sales estimates are reliable. But the estimates may not necessarily be valid. Suppose salespeople in this industry tend to exaggerate their sales figures by about 20 percent. Therefore, the sales estimates are not valid because they are higher than actual sales by 20 percent. There must be some way of externally validating answers to the questions against objective sales data. (A subtle point: if the aim is to measure what salespeople actually say about their sales volume, then the estimate may be valid. However, if the intention was to measure actual sales, then they are not valid despite being reliable.)

2. **Reliability**. Consider a large-scale study using 2500 respondents. A strict probability sample of this size will have an estimated margin of error of ± 2 percentage points at the 95 percent level of confidence. If we repeat the study with another probability sample of 2500 respondents, we will get similar results if the study is reliable. On the other hand, if our study had only 100 respondents, our margin of error would be ± 10 percentage points (at the 95 percent level of confidence). If the study is repeated with another sample of

100, the results may be statistically close, i.e., with a 95% confidence limit, but will perhaps not be materially close. Assuming that all these studies were carried out correctly in all ways, all studies should be equally valid. However, studies with smaller samples are less reliable.

3. **Reliable and Valid**? Many people will say, "reliable and valid" very quickly and may believe that they mean the same thing, but they don't. A reliable study might or might not be valid. However, for a study to be valid, it must be reliable. Reliability is said to be a necessary but not sufficient condition for a study to be valid. This implies that attitudes should be measured so that their validity (Do they measure what they are supposed to measure?) and reliability (Do they measure what they measure consistently?) can be tested or, at least, defended. Testing reliability is easier than testing validity.

The fourth condition, **sensitivity**, is a critical concept of measurement but, like reliability, depends on the measurement context. Consider the question, "Were you satisfied or not satisfied with the service that you received the last time you stopped at a Shell gas station?" Is this question sensitive? It is if our purpose is to assess the overall reaction. However, it is quite insensitive if we aim to understand the degree to which a customer is satisfied with the service offered. A person who says that he or she is not satisfied can be mildly dissatisfied or completely unhappy with the service received. If the aim is to understand the level of satisfaction, then the question as phrased is insensitive. To construct attitudinal questions, we need to ask ourselves these three questions:

1. **Validity**. Does this question, battery of questions or study measure what we intended to measure?
2. **Reliability**. Will this question (or battery of questions) provide consistent measurements among similar studies?
3. **Sensitivity**. Is the measurement scale that we use sensitive enough to detect the shade or intensity of meaning that we need?

Attitudinal Scaling

The topic of attitude scaling is actively debated in social sciences. It amounts to creating different numeric and verbal scales to identify the existence and intensity of consumer opinions that are assumed to be relatively stable. Exhibit 7-2 shows the framework used in the discussion that follows. When developing questions and scales to measure attitudes, think forward to how those answers may be analyzed. Uninformed question and answer design can lead to significantly limited analysis options that may prevent achieving study objectives and/or make the analysis much harder, more expensive and less productive.

Exhibit 7.2 A framework for attitude measurement

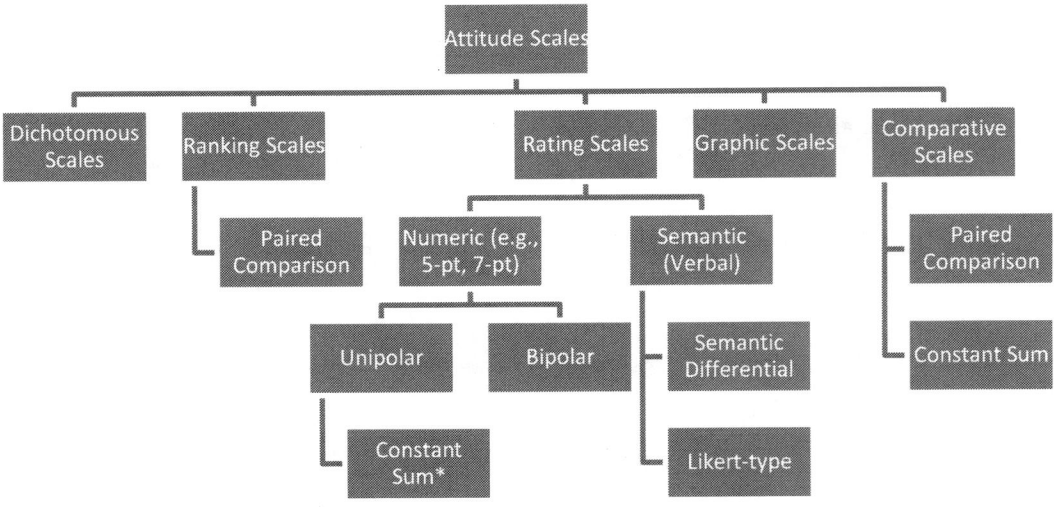

Nominal Scale

The most straightforward scale may not even seem to be a scale since it involves naming things. Following the hierarchy of effects (see the exhibit earlier in this unit), a survey often starts by asking respondents to name any brands they are aware of in a category (unaided awareness). Respondents answer with all of the names they can think of. This is nominal information.

When writing a questionnaire, it is essential to keep in mind the statistical analyses that will be performed once the data is available. Nominal data will only tell us the response that got the highest number of votes or mentions, i.e., the mode.

Dichotomous scales are often used to assess the existence of an attitude and typically provide only nominal information. The respondents are given only two options: "Yes" or "No," or "Like" or "Don't Like," "Agree or Disagree." They are used to count votes or preferences. Dichotomous questions can be used to obtain ordinal information when judgement questions are asked, such as, "Do you like Breyers or President's Choice vanilla ice cream better?"

An unaided awareness question is used to describe respondents' cognitive states, e.g., their awareness of ice cream brands. In an online survey they might appear as follows.

Please type in the names of all **ice cream brands** that you can **think of** at this time. (Just the brand name, not the type or flavour. One brand on each line, please.)

[   ]

This is a dichotomous scale, although it might not appear to be. Twelve brands are of interest to the client. If a respondent were to type "Chapman's," that would translate into a "Yes" for Chapman's. If "Haagen-Dazs" is not typed into the box, the answer for that brand would be "No." So, this is a dichotomous question with a variable number of brands. But the data file would show 12 brand columns for each respondent, each containing a "Yes" or "No" or a 0 or 1. Each column can be considered separately as a univariate question, or the 12 columns can be combined as a multiple response question.

When we consider the hierarchy ladder in the earlier exhibit, our next question would likely seek the aided awareness for the relevant brands. This question would remain hidden from respondents until the unaided question was answered. There are 12 brands, and the answer to each is, "Yes, I've heard of that brand before." or "No, I have not." Again it is a set of 12 dichotomous questions while it does not appear as such.

Which of the following brands of ice cream had you **heard of before** participating in this survey? (Please click all that apply.)

- ☐ Breyers
- ☐ Chapman's
- ☐ Ben & Jerry's
- ☐ Haagen-Dazs
- ☐ Halo Top
- ☐ Natrel
- ☐ President's Choice
- ☐ Nestle
- ☐ Kawartha
- ☐ Scotsburn
- ☐ Farmers
- ☐ Magnum

A logical next question would be to ask about past behaviour, i.e., which brands of ice cream have been purchased. This is also a cognitive question since it pertains to a supposed higher level knowledge of brands. Depending on the intention of the study, respondents may have been asked which brands they had consumed or both bought and consumed. Again, this is a set of 12 dichotomous questions that could be combined and displayed as a multiple-response question.

Which of the following brands of ice cream have you **purchased** during the past six months?

- ☐ Breyers
- ☐ Halo Top
- ☐ Magnum
- ☐ President's Choice
- ☐ Nestle
- ☐ Farmers
- ☐ Kawartha
- ☐ Haagen-Dazs
- ☐ Natrel
- ☐ Chapman's
- ☐ Ben & Jerry's
- ☐ Scotsburn

When to use Dichotomous Scales

To measure attitudes, we use dichotomous scales in three contexts:

1. **When the attitude being measured is clear-cut.** For instance, did you buy the ice cream or not? Are you against the death penalty for any reason or not against it?
2. **When the attitude being measured has shades of meaning, but the researcher is not interested in that granularity.** For instance, the researcher may like to know whether a consumer is against higher taxes but not how strongly. The objective of the ice cream study might have led to a question about the quantity consumed of each brand.
3. **As a prelude to asking the strength of attitudes.** For example, if a consumer says that she or he is against higher taxes, then we may ask whether the consumer is "somewhat strongly" or "very strongly" against higher taxes.

Ordinal or Ranking Scales

Ordinal scales or ranking scales are one step above dichotomous scales. Here the respondents are asked to state their order of preference but not their intensity of preference for each object. Consider the following question:

People are concerned with health care, the environment, and jobs. Of these three, which one is of the greatest concern to you?
- Health care
- The environment
- Jobs

Which one is next?
- Health care
- The environment

- Jobs

Suppose the respondent says that the environment is of the greatest concern, followed by health care. There is now an order for the three items, the environment then health care and lastly jobs. It highlights that the environment is of more concern than health care for this respondent, but not by how much.

A ranking of the brands on relative liking is often relevant and fits into the next step in the hierarchy of effects. Liking is part of the affective aspect of attitudes. The following question provides a full ranking of the brands after earlier questions have screened out brands that the respondent had not heard of or had not bought (because he or she would have little or no knowledge of them).

How much do you like each of the ice cream brands listed below? Please drag that brand that you like best into the box at the right first. Then, drag that brand that you like second best into the box and so on. You can change the order by shuffling brands up or down in the box.

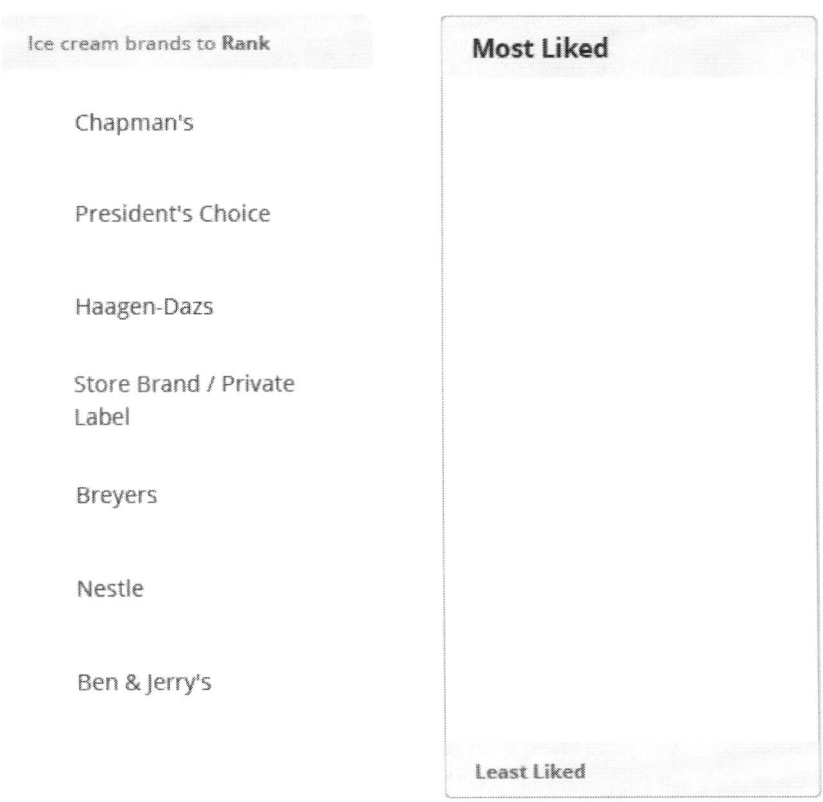

Answers to this question provide a rank order of the 'liking' of ice cream brands. While this is an easy question for respondents to understand in a self-completion survey and to answer in an online survey, it might be too complicated to ask in a telephone survey.

Another example of a ranking scale is paired comparison. Paired comparison questions hide the fact that they are ranking scales. Consider the following question:

Which of these two fast food restaurants do you go to more often, Swiss Chalet or Chicken Deli?

For the ice cream example, one paired comparison is shown below. Of course, many more of these questions must be asked to provide meaningful information for analyzing the paired comparisons for all relevant brands. Each would be on a separate screen of the online survey.

Please consider how much you like each brand of ice cream.
Considering only these 2 brands, which one do you Like **Most** and which one do you Like **Least**?

(1 of 15)

Like Most		Like Least
○	Chapman's	○
○	Haagen-Dazs	○

Click the 'Next' button to continue...

Although similar to a dichotomous scale, this is indeed a ranking scale because the consumer is implicitly asked to rank a lengthy design of pairs. Answers to all the paired comparisons would be used in the analysis. If many brands are being studied, the MaxDiff or Best/Worst scaling methods can be used.

When to Use Ranking Scales

Ranking scales are useful when we are interested in knowing respondents' perceived orders of importance or preferences or concern among several choices. For example, the importance of ranking of a list of ice cream attributes (creaminess, fat content, sugar content, lactose-free).

Just before an election, a political party may be interested in knowing the issue that is the most important to voters: Is it the economy? Is it leadership? Is it the environmental policy? The fact that an issue is considered "most important" to voters is of utmost importance to the party. If the voter considers the economy as the most important issue, then this is the issue that the party may want to concentrate on as an election issue. Similarly, in consumer research, a manufacturer may be interested in knowing how consumers rank factors such as price, quality and service. Or the manufacturer may simply want to know whether the competition is perceived to be better or worse on different attributes.

A ranking scale is assumed to be easier for consumers to use because it is more in line with how people think. For instance, people tend to think of a brand as the most or least preferred, not as a 6 on a 7-point scale. However, this assumes that they are not asked to rank too many items. Ranking is not effective when there are too many alternatives, especially when the survey is conducted over the phone.

Rating Scales

On a ranking scale, there is no information about the "distance" between one rank and another. If a respondent says that his first-ranked brand is Tim Hortons and his second-ranked brand is Country Style, we do not know whether the respondent would readily accept a Country Style donut if a Tim Hortons donut is not available, or if he would only accept it very reluctantly. In other words, Country Style can be a close second or a distant second. And, while Tim Hortons might be first, it might be a weak first, i.e., the best of a bad lot.

To overcome this limitation, we can use rating scales. Suppose we ask the respondent to rate Tim Hortons and Country Style on an 11-point scale where 10 is 'a perfect choice' and 0 is a 'terrible choice'. Thus, a respondent who rates Tim Hortons as a 10 and Country Style as a 9 considers Country Style to be a close second; a respondent who rates Tim Hortons as a 10 and Country Style as a 3 considers Country Style to be a distant second. Rating scales, unlike ranking scales, provide information on the distance between scale points and can provide measures of intensity.

Any scale that has three or more points can be considered a "rating scale." An interval scale is one in which the distance between any two contiguous points on the scale is perceived by respondents to be the equal of the distance between any other two contiguous points. Consider the following examples:

Example 1. How much are you willing to pay for a litre of Haagen-Dasz ice cream if it were available in the store where you usually shop?
$5 $10 $15

Here, the distance between $5 and $10 and the distance between $10 and $15 are the same: 5 dollars. While it is evident that those dollar differences are equal, this scale is more than just interval. It is a ratio scale, which we'll see a bit later. Not only are the intervals identical, but there is a natural zero point, and we can say one group is willing to spend twice what another group is willing to spend (a ratio).

Example 2. What is the highest level of education that you have completed?
1. B.A.   2. M.A.   3. Ph.D.

Here, can we honestly say that the distance between B.A. and M.A. is the same as the distance between M.A. and Ph.D.? Probably not in terms of prestige and the commitment needed. The distance between a B.A. and an M.A. can be very different from the distance between M.A. and Ph.D. Therefore, we cannot really say that these educational ranks are interval scaled. Rather, it is probably an ordinal scale.

It is important to focus on the perceptions of respondents, not on the assumptions of the researchers when evaluating the traits of scaled answers. There are methods for analyzing whether the perceptions of respondents among points on rating scales constitute interval properties or only ordinal properties. However, typically, if the researcher perceives that the scale has interval properties, it will be analyzed as such. It is important to develop good scales and scrutinize them before deciding to use them as having interval properties.

Semantic scales. Semantic rating scales use words instead of numbers to measure the strength of an attitude. For example, consider the following satisfaction question for ice cream. Satisfaction is another aspect of the affective dimension of attitudes.

How satisfied or dissatisfied are you with each of the following brands of ice cream?

	Extremely Dissatisfied	Very Dissatisfied	Somewhat Dissatisfied	Slightly Dissatisfied	Slightly Satisfied	Somewhat Satisfied	Very Satisfied	Extremely Satisfied
Chapman's	○	○	○	○	○	○	○	○
Ben & Jerry's	○	○	○	○	○	○	○	○
Breyers	○	○	○	○	○	○	○	○
Store Brand / Private Label	○	○	○	○	○	○	○	○
Haagen-Dazs	○	○	○	○	○	○	○	○
President's Choice	○	○	○	○	○	○	○	○
Nestle	○	○	○	○	○	○	○	○

This scale uses descriptive words rather than numbers to describe scale points and is called a semantic scale. A semantic scale like this one is often assumed to approximate an interval scale. However, it can be argued that the distance between "Very Dissatisfied" and "Somewhat Dissatisfied" may not be the same as the difference between "Very Satisfied" and "Extremely Satisfied."

Numeric scale values can be assigned to each of the verbal descriptors at the coding stage or automatically in the questionnaire program. For example, we can treat the above semantic scale as an interval scale by assigning numeric scale values, as follows.

8 = Extremely Satisfied
7 = Very Satisfied
6 = Somewhat Satisfied
5 = Slightly Satisfied
4 = Slightly Dissatisfied
3 = Somewhat Dissatisfied
2 = Very Dissatisfied

1 = Extremely Dissatisfied

But does that make the semantic scale an actual interval scale? Provide that question to several researchers, and arguments will be split. In practice, the semantic scale is typically assumed to have interval properties and is rarely analyzed to determine if it does have interval properties.

Remember that when those numeric assignments are made, the differences between scale points are assumed to be at least approximately the same. We can then make statements like, "Bank of Patagonia received an average quality rating of 4.8 on a 5-point scale." A benefit of having a semantic scale with interval properties is that averages can be calculated and assigned a semantic descriptor. For example, if the average turns out to be 7, we can say that respondents are, on average, "Very Satisfied." If only the two endpoints had semantic descriptors, the average would be stated as "7 on a scale where 8 is Extremely Satisfied, and 1 is Extremely Dissatisfied". In this example, the 7 average could not be described as "Very Satisfied" since that term would not have appeared on the questionnaire.

Numeric scale values cannot be assigned to a semantic scale when there is clearly no measurable distance between the choices. For instance, suppose the categories were as follows:

What is your highest level of formal education?
- High school, not graduated
- High School, graduated
- Bachelor's degree
- Master's degree
- Ph.D. degree

We cannot assign numeric scale values to the categories because, for example, the distance between a Master's and a Ph.D. degree cannot be judged—even approximately— to be equal to that of High School and bachelor's degrees. It does not make sense to say that the average level of education for people is 2.9.

Likert-type Scale. The Likert scale is used in psychology to measure the strength of attitudes based on a battery of questions. In marketing research, we use the structure of the Likert scale but not necessarily the other methodological trappings that go along with it. Therefore, the Likert scale used in marketing research can be more appropriately called a "Likert-type" scale. Although the Likert scale is a semantic scale, the scale points are converted into numbers for computing averages.

The Likert-type scale technique asks respondents to express agreement or disagreement with each of a set of attitudinal statements, usually using a 5-point or 7-point scale. Each degree of agreement is given a numerical value from 1 to 5. For example:

To what extent do you agree or disagree with the following statements?

	Strongly disagree	Disagree	Neither agree nor disagree	Agree	Strongly agree
When you are on holiday, you worry about work.	○	○	○	○	○
Money is no object when you are on holiday.	○	○	○	○	○
Taking a break from work makes you more efficient.	○	○	○	○	○
Workaholics are always stressed.	○	○	○	○	○

Likert-type scales are extensively used in marketing research, especially in measuring psychographics/lifestyle statements (discussed later in this chapter). While the agree/disagree scale is used often, other semantic scales can be used.

Semantic Differential. Semantic differential, like the Likert scale, has some methodological trappings that are not generally used in marketing research. So again, what we use in marketing research is a "semantic differential–type" scale. In semantic differential, the respondent is presented with a word (e.g., a brand name like Ford Escape) and a variety of adjectives that could be used to describe it. The adjectives are presented at either end of a 7-point scale, ranging from, say, "good" to "bad" or from "fast" to "slow." The respondents are asked to indicate where they would place the brand on each scale (see the following example).

A semantic differential scale is very visual, so it works well on paper or in an online survey. But they are challenging to use in a telephone survey.

Semantic scales have an advantage over numeric scales because a word is assigned to each point, giving it meaning. But this is a disadvantage when administering the questionnaire over the phone. Semantic scales are rarely used when we have more than 7 points because it can be confusing for respondents and is very difficult to find that many descriptor words that clearly communicate gradations. (See the second example on the following page).

How would you rate [INSERT BRAND] on each of the following scales?

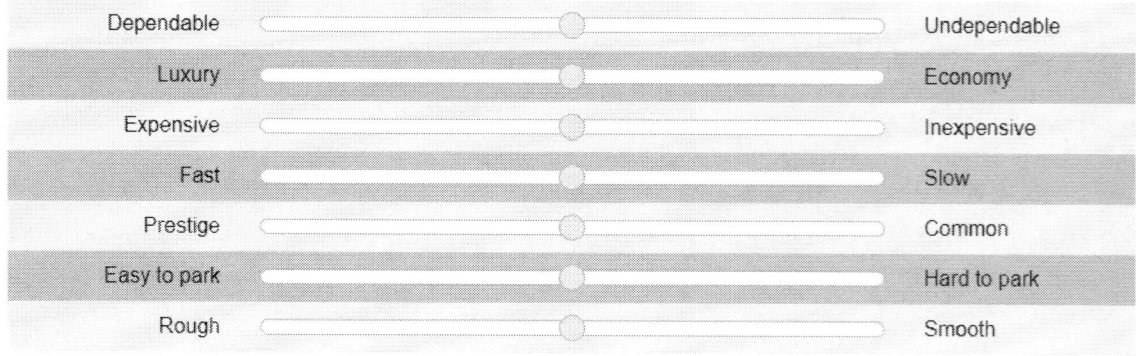

How efficient are the following airlines in your opinion?

	Extremely Inefficient	2	3	4	5	6	7	8	9	Extremely Efficient
Air Canada	○	○	○	○	○	○	○	○	○	○
Porter	○	○	○	○	○	○	○	○	○	○
West Jet	○	○	○	○	○	○	○	○	○	○

b) How reliable to you think Air Canada is?

Extremely Reliable	○
Very Reliable	○
Reliable	○
Somewhat Reliable	○
Slightly Reliable	○
Slightly Unreliable	○
Somewhat Unreliable	○
Unreliable	○
Very Unreliable	○
Extremely Unreliable	○

Question [a.] above is a numeric scale and can be asked over the phone without causing any confusion to the respondent. Question [b.] is a semantic scale. It cannot be answered unless the interviewer reads all the possible options available over the phone to the respondent, and even then, the chances are that the respondent would not remember all ten categories. Moreover, the question must be repeated all over again for Porter and WestJet separately. Either question could be asked in online surveys, but the issue of understanding so many fine gradations in the words remains.

The second issue with semantic scales has to do with having neutral midpoints, a problem semantic scales sometimes share with numeric scales. Consider this question:

How would you rate the quality of service you received the last time you visited Bank A?
- **Very good**
- **Good**
- **Neither good nor bad**
- **Bad**
- **Very bad**

Some researchers believe that the presence of a neutral midpoint encourages some respondents to choose it indiscriminately because it requires the least intellectual effort. If we eliminate the midpoint and give respondents only four choices, they are forced to choose either a positive adjective or the negative adjective.
- **Very good**
- **Good**

- **Bad**
- **Very bad**

Research has shown that a very high number of people choose neutral categories rather than indicating their attitudes. But those people will provide their attitudes if the neutral point is eliminated and a broader range of points is provided. Moving from a 4-point scale to a 6-point scale may make those who feel just a little positive or a little negative a bit more comfortable with their decisions.

This argument is plausible, and removing the neutral midpoint is likely to force people to reveal their true attitudes, provided they are leaning one way or another (positive or negative). But what happens when respondents have no genuinely positive or negative attitudes about the issue at hand?

It has been found that when people do not have genuine opinions, they tend to choose a positive response rather than a negative one. (See "The Art of Scale Development" in *Marketing Research*, Vol.15, No. 3, Fall 2003, pages 10–29; also refer to the BackTalk section in the Winter 2003 issue of the same publication.) In other words, if a respondent is forced to choose between "good" and "bad," he or she would choose "good." This means that leaving out a legitimate midpoint can potentially inflate the score. To counter this possibility, some researchers assign more positive points on a scale than negative points. But this can cause other problems.

Graphic rating scale. Graphic rating scales use neither numbers nor words to describe scale points. Graphic rating scales use pictures as scale points. For instance:

How to Measeure Attitudes, Behaviour and Traits

Happy Face Scale
How would you rate your level of satisfaction with our service the last time you were in our store? (Choose a picture that matches your satisfaction level.)

Like it very much   **Don't like it at all**

Similar to the semantic differential, the graphic rating scale is visual and therefore is limited to self-administered questionnaires. While many may consider this as just an ordinal scale, it is often used in practice as an interval scale.

Consider the following purchase intent question from the ice cream study.

Among the ice cream brands you have purchased during the past six months, how likely are you to **purchase** each brand **again**? Please use a scale from 1 to 7, where 1 means "not at all likely to purchase again" and 7 means "extremely likely to purchase again". You may use any number from 1 to 7.

	1 Not at all likely to purchase again	2	3	4	5	6	7 Extremely likely to purchase again
Breyers	○	○	○	○	○	○	○
Chapman's	○	○	○	○	○	○	○
Ben & Jerry's	○	○	○	○	○	○	○
Haagen-Dazs	○	○	○	○	○	○	○
President's Choice	○	○	○	○	○	○	○
Nestle	○	○	○	○	○	○	○
Store Brand / Private Label	○	○	○	○	○	○	○

The above is an example of a conative component of attitudes since it provides evidence of the respondent's future behaviour.

Or the following question and answer scale could be used.

How likely are you to buy Breyers ice cream the next time you buy ice cream?

| Extremely Unlikely | 1 | 2 | 3 | 4 | 5 | 6 | 7 | 8 | 9 | 10 | Extremely Likely |

Do respondents perceive that the difference between a rating of 1 and 2 is the same as the difference between 6 and 7? The answer here is not clear. Although the difference in both cases is one point, people who gave ratings of 1 and 2 are probably not going to buy; people who gave a rating of 7 are more likely to buy than people who gave a rating of 6. The perceived distance between 1 and 2 by one respondent can be different from the distance between 6 and 7 for that same respondent.

In the ice cream study, we need to understand the perceptions of each brand on each of the ten attributes to map the cognitive understanding of ice cream brands. Those questions could take the form of a grid shown on the following page.

The 7-point numeric scale on the next page is anchored at each end and is bipolar. Notice that these ten questions would be asked for each ice cream brand that the respondent had said that he or she had heard of. Any respondent who has heard of all seven brands will be asked 70 questions just in this battery. Will that cause fatigue? Will the rate of completion decline? Designing and executing marketing research surveys entail many trade-offs for the researchers.

Interval scales can support advanced statistical analyses. In practice, a scale that has five or more points that appear to be interval is typically considered "interval scaled." Sometimes, 4-point scales are treated as if they are interval. Although those assumptions may not be 100 percent appropriate, many statistical methods can accommodate some deviations from what is strictly true. However, those who design questions and those who analyze the answers should be fully aware of the relevant statistical assumptions and the risks that accompany inappropriate analyses.

From what you have heard or experienced, please indicate how well each statement describes [INSERT BRAND FROM AWAREAIDED].

	1 Does NOT Describe at all	2	3	4	5	6	7 Describes extremely well
Buy as a special treat but not regularly	○	○	○	○	○	○	○
Offers a wide variety of flavors	○	○	○	○	○	○	○
Absolutely delicious	○	○	○	○	○	○	○
Best value for the price	○	○	○	○	○	○	○
Tastes better than most brands	○	○	○	○	○	○	○
Wholesome	○	○	○	○	○	○	○
Great for the whole family	○	○	○	○	○	○	○
Premium – uses better quality ingredients	○	○	○	○	○	○	○
Low calorie	○	○	○	○	○	○	○
Great for guests	○	○	○	○	○	○	○

As mentioned earlier, a numeric rating scale is one that measures the intensity of an attitude as a number. Such a scale can have any number of points. Scales with 5, 7, or 10 points are common, although other rating scales—such as scales with 100 points—are also possible. Identical questions can be worded to fit any of these scales. For example:

Please rate the overall quality of Haagen-Dasz ice cream on a 10-point scale, where 10 means Excellent and 1 means Terrible?

Excellent 10   9   8   7   6   5   4   3   2   1   Terrible

Please rate the overall quality of Haagen-Dasz ice cream on a 7-point scale, where 7 means Excellent and 1 means Terrible?

Excellent   7   6   5   4   3   2   1   Terrible

Please rate the overall quality of Haagen-Dasz ice cream on a 5-point scale, where 5 means Excellent and 1 means Terrible?

Excellent   5   4   3   2   1   **Terrible**

The three questions above are called bipolar adjective questions. There are also agree-disagree scales that can be used in this way.

If all these questions are designed to capture the intensity of attitudes, which one should be used? Is there an ideal number of points for a scale in marketing research? There is no definitive answer to these questions. Different scales might be suitable in different contexts, and no general guidelines can be given. However, certain observations can still be made.

1. Ratings on the same scale tend to be consistent over time. For instance, an insurance company may want to assess how customers evaluate its services on an ongoing basis. If they collect data consistently with the same scale (let's say a 5-point scale), the results will have much greater comparability than if the scale is changed from one survey to the next.

2. The 5-point scale is often used because it is easier to attach descriptive words such as "Very Good," "Good," "Average," "Poor," and "Very Poor" to each scale point (see the discussion on semantic scales below). This makes it easier to administer the question over the phone: "How do you evaluate the service you received— was it "Very Good," "Good," "Average," "Poor," or "Very Poor?" This scale is also better when online surveys are answered on mobile devices. These are called semantic scales since every point is described semantically.

3. The 10-point scale is sometimes favoured because it gives greater freedom to respondents to make finer distinctions. It is also easier to administer since a 10-point scale is intuitively understood (e.g., a "perfect 10") by many respondents, perhaps because we use the decimal system in our daily lives. Due to the many points, usually only the endpoints are anchored with descriptions. When bipolar adjectives anchor the endpoints, this scale is more likely to have interval properties. One challenge with a 10-point scale is that there is no mid-point (it's actually 5.5). Respondents looking for a neutral choice may choose '5', but that actually tips towards the lower end.

4. We cannot assume that data collected using one scale can easily be mapped onto another scale. For example, if a respondent rates a product as a 4 on a 5-point scale, we may not be able to translate this successfully to an 8 on a 10-point scale. Both a '4' on a 5-point scale and a '9' on a 10-point scale could be seen to be one tick down from the top score. For this reason, when research is repeated or 'tracked,' it is better to use the same scale so that the results can be compared. And it is beneficial to use the same scale or the same number of points on scales within a questionnaire. This makes the thought process easier for respondents and promotes easier analytical comparability among attitude measures.

5. Many potential respondents, particularly younger ones, now primarily use mobile devices to access the internet. It is important, therefore, that questionnaires be formatted so they can be accessed, read and responded to on the smaller mobile screens. This means that rating scales with few points are more comfortable for respondents to read. Hitting a small

number to respond to a question can be difficult. As a result, sliding scales are often used in online surveys instead of numbers or semantic points.

Which way should the scales run? When numeric scales are used, you are free to assign scale values in either direction—ascending or descending.

a) How would you rate this product on a 5-point scale, where 5 means Excellent and 1 means Poor?

Excellent   5   4   3   2   1   Poor

b) How would you rate this product on a 5-point scale, where 1 means Excellent and 5 means Poor?

Excellent   1   2   3   4   5   Poor

From a technical point of view, it does not make any difference in which direction the numbers go—ascending or descending. But it is good practice to assign higher numbers to more positive responses (as in "a" above) because this is in line with the general conventions of communication. An average person is likely to interpret a rating of 4 on a 5-point scale as "better" than a rating of 2 on the same scale. By following this general convention, we can avoid our results being misunderstood. In any case, it is important to avoid scales going in different directions in the same questionnaire.

While best practice is to use the same scale consistently within a questionnaire where possible and to assign higher numbers to more positive constructs, combining questions that are phrased in the positive with some phrased in the negative within the same battery can help to catch "speeders," those respondents who click in the same pole of a question just to get through the questionnaire faster. This technique, if used, should be handled with care.

Issues with Numeric Rating Scales

One major problem with numeric scales that are anchored only at the two poles is that intermediary numbers do not have a definite meaning. For instance, if a 7-point scale is used, what does a 5 mean? Good or just a bit above average? If a person rates a product as a 5 on a 7-point scale, how would that person rate the same product on a 10-point scale? There are no clear-cut answers to these questions.

The second problem with numeric scales relates to the way different respondents may interpret the same scale. Since numeric points do not have any intrinsic meaning, a 7 on a 10-point scale may be interpreted as "good" by some respondents and "above average" by others.

The third problem has to do with cultural differences. While the meaning of scale points might vary from person to person, there may also be cultural differences in the way rating scale questions are answered. Certain cultural groups tend to give routinely higher ratings. This is often referred to as the "politeness bias."

Another bias may stem from the schooling system in which the respondent was raised. Homework and tests may have been graded on 10-point scales where a 6 (or 60 percent) is judged to be a failure. As a result, they may use the mid-points on a survey's 10-point scale to indicate failure rather than the lowest end of the scale.

In addition to the straightforward numeric rating scales discussed above, there are also other kinds of numeric scales, some of which are described below.

Bipolar (positive/negative) rating scales. When attitudes range from negative to positive, some researchers use negative numbers to indicate negative opinions and positive numbers to indicate positive opinions. For example,

Some people believe that the current level of taxation in our country is too high. How much do you agree or disagree with this statement?

Strongly Disagree	−3	−2	−1	0	1	2	3	Strongly Agree

Scales like these are likely to be challenging to understand for many respondents because negative numbers are not often used in our daily lives. Many consumers may find it difficult to visualize the difference between −3 and +2. Another problem with bipolar scales that use negative numbers (also known as the Stapel scale) is that it is very difficult to administer over the telephone. For these reasons, unless there are special reasons, it is best not to use this type of scale.

Ratio Scales

Nominal questions provide names only with no implied order. *Ordinal* questions indicate when one item is above or below another. *Interval* scales provide an equal weighting of points on the scale.

Ratio Scales reflect their name; ratios between two points on the scale are easily interpretable. Ten dollars ($10) is twice 5 dollars ($5). Convert dollars to euros, and the ratio is still valid. Besides, there is always a natural zero point in ratio scales. When you're broke in Canada, you're broke in the U.S. and in Belgium. Ratio scales contain the highest information content among measurement scales.

Typically, there are very few ratio-scale questions/answers in marketing surveys. Questions about money, the quantity bought of a product, age, years of formal schooling, actual income and frequency of purchase are some examples. Another is the constant sum method. Those questions would require respondents to provide exact numeric values. While that might be possible with the quantity bought of a product last week, it is not likely for income, which is typically categorized.

Constant Sum Method. The constant sum method is a special type of numeric scale. Suppose consumers are asked to rate three products on a 10-point scale where 1 means "Do not like it at all" and 10 means "Like it a lot." There is nothing that prevents the respondent from assigning 9 to each of the three products. This may indicate that the respondent likes all three products, but it does not tell us her or his preferences. It does not tell us what the consumer would do if she or he were to choose one when all alternatives are available, as is the case in real life. To obtain a better reading on customer attitudes concerning the three products, we may use the constant sum method.

The constant sum method asks respondents to divide a given number of points among all alternatives. This is another example of a question that helps interpret respondents' conative attitudinal dimension.

If you had **$100 to spend on ice cream** over the next several weeks, how much would you spend on each of the brands listed below? Type in the number of dollars that you would likely spend on each brand.

[ ]	Breyers
[ ]	Nestle
[ ]	Haagen-Dazs
[ ]	Ben & Jerry's
[ ]	Chapman's
[ ]	President's Choice
[ ]	Store Brand / Private Label
[ ]	Total

In the earlier ice cream purchasing question, a respondent may click "Extremely Likely" for several or all brands. That would not be very helpful. In the constant sum, a respondent would be less likely to apply exactly the same amount to several or all brands. It is much more likely that the respondent would think through the exercise more carefully and supply more useful information.

The constant sum method can be an effective method of "forcing" respondents to reveal their preferences. The constant sum method is likely to be less effective as the number of alternatives increases—for example, it is much more difficult to divide $100 among 17 brands than it is to divide $10 among three brands.

However, the constant sum is an excellent method for measuring attitudes and is used frequently. Analysis methods provide ratio-scaled metrics.

A variation on this approach is 'chip allocation' in which respondents are offered 11 chips and are asked to allocate them among a list of items. The prime, odd number ensures there can never be a tie.

How to Assess Behaviour

The term behaviour refers to what people do rather than what they think. The conative dimension of attitudes is thought to indicate likely future behaviour but does not directly measure behaviour itself. Sometimes direct questions are asked about behaviour (e.g., "How much did you spend on clothing last time you went shopping?"), and at other times we ask indirect questions (e.g., "Do you think you spend too much on your clothing?"). Research objectives should influence the actual question used in the survey.

Measuring General Behaviour

The reliability of behavioural measurement is central to marketing research. What do consumers buy? When do they buy? Where do they buy? How do they buy? How often do they buy? How much do they buy? Answers to questions like these provide rich information to the marketer.

Let's start with a problem to illustrate the issues involved in measuring behaviour. We want to estimate the number of meals that people eat in restaurants. We may start with two assumptions:

1. The frequency of eating in a restaurant will vary from person to person; and
2. Each person will have an average frequency of eating out that is likely to stay consistent over a period of time. Consumer A might eat out every other day, Consumer B twice per month, Consumer C once per week, and so on.

The assumption that each consumer has a characteristic behaviour frequency (also known as the rate or the base rate) is important in marketing. This is what drives market share and is often the target of marketing efforts. However, how exactly do we measure behaviour such as frequency of eating out? There are at least three ways of asking the question: as a rating question, as a manifest behaviour question, or as a latent behaviour question. For example:

a. **As a rating question:**
How frequently do you eat out?
   1. Very infrequently
   2. Infrequently
   3. Frequently
   4. Very frequently

b. **As a latent variable question:**
   On average, how often do you eat out in a typical month?

c. **As a manifest variable question:**
   How many times did you eat out last month?

Question [a] **How frequently do you eat out?**

This is the weakest of the three if we are trying to estimate how often a person actually does eat out. There are two problems with this question. First, what is meant by frequently? Does it mean every day, every other day, once per week, or once per month? Second, does 'frequently' mean the same thing to every respondent? Consider two respondents, Jane and Bill. Both eat out once per week. For Jane, very 'frequently' means more often than once per week, while for Bill 'very frequently' means every week. Although one person eats out as frequently as the other, Jane may choose somewhat frequently, while Bill may choose very frequently. Does that mean we should avoid asking such questions? Not necessarily. Questions of this nature are useful in understanding how consumers view themselves and their habits. Question [a] is an attitudinal question. It tells us what consumers think of their behaviour rather than giving an accurate reading of their behaviour itself.

Question [b] **"On average, how often do you eat out in a typical month?"**

This question assumes that there is a "characteristic rate" associated with the behaviour. This is a reasonable assumption—some may eat out once per month, some twice per month, and so on. In mathematical modelling, this characteristic rate of behaviour is called the latent variable[2]. Latent variables are challenging to measure directly.

The question may be interpreted differently by different people:

- Some may think back to the recent past (the previous month or so) and, on that basis, may estimate their average rate.
- Some may think back to the previous 12 months or so, and on that basis, may estimate their average rate.
- Some may think back to the previous 12 months or so, but exclude December (i.e., not an "average month" because of the holiday season) and, on that basis, may estimate their average rate.
- Some may look forward to what they intend to do in the future and answer accordingly.
- Some respondents may select a month that they think is "average" and report what they did in that month.
- Many respondents will mentally round the numbers. For example, a respondent who eats out 20 times per year is more likely to say twice per month rather than 1.67 times per month.

Therefore, question [b] is also an attitudinal question with different people interpreting the same question differently, although [b] gives answers that are easier to quantify than [a].

Question [c] **"How many times did you eat out last month?"**

This question is a true behavioural question. The time frame is precisely defined in the question, and the respondent is not asked to estimate the rate but to report on what he or she actually

---

[2] The term *latent variable* is also used in attitudinal measurement to describe constructs (e.g., customer satisfaction or customer loyalty) that cannot be directly measured. They are generally derived with the use of advanced statistical techniques such as regression, factor analysis and structural equation modelling.

did. For this reason, the variable being measured is called the manifest variable. In measuring behaviour questions, type c should be preferred.[3] In fact, in measuring newspaper or magazine readership studies, or in food consumption diaries, manifest variables are used almost exclusively.

While this is a better way to ask a behavioural question, we should be aware of the problems associated with this type of question. For example, we want to estimate the frequency of drinking. If we conduct the survey in January and ask respondents, "How many drinks did you have last month?", we are likely to overestimate drinking because many people drink more during the holiday season than at other times of the year. Similarly, if we ask in February, "How many times did you eat out last month?", we may underestimate the frequency of eating out since people may go out less often immediately following the holiday season.

Of the three, question c is the best behavioural question. However, we should make sure that no special factors are affecting the outcome.

Thus, behaviour can be measured as an attitudinal variable (least precise), latent variable, or manifest variable (most precise). Each type of measurement has its own uses. In writing a questionnaire, we should first determine how the information will be used and ask the question accordingly. To give an example, if we want to know how people *perceive* their alcohol consumption levels, we can ask:

How frequently do you drink alcoholic drinks?
- **Very frequently**
- **Somewhat frequently**
- **Somewhat infrequently**
- **Very infrequently**

If we aim to know how much people *actually drink*, a question like the following will provide more useful answers.

How many alcoholic drinks did you have last week, either at home or elsewhere?

Lifestyle Measurement

A commonly-accepted model is that attitudes influence behaviour. For example, if consumers like a product (attitude), they will likely buy it (behaviour). If they do not like it (attitude), they do not buy it (behaviour). It is for this reason that attitude measurement is given a central role in marketing research.

However, an attitudinal statement by itself is not very insightful. For example, a statement such as, "I prefer to watch a movie at home rather than at a theatre" tells us very little about the person and provides only limited information to the marketer. A person may prefer to watch at home

---

[3] If we want to determine the underlying rate of consumption, we can do so by applying mathematical models to the manifest behavior question.

because she or he (a) does not want to spend the extra money to go to a theatre; (b) prefers to watch movies in bed; and (c) prefers to be able to pause the movie to use the bathroom or get a snack.

We can ask respondents why they watch movies at home. But, doing so is less likely to elicit answers such as, "I cannot really afford to go to see movies in theatres," even when this is the real reason, because they are afraid it would show them in a poor light.

Another reason why direct questions may be less helpful is that they have limited explanatory power. For instance, "prefer to watch it at home" does not really tell us whether it is because the respondent is a homebody or whether the theatres are not convenient to get to in that person's neighbourhood, or because they are nervous about being in a crowded space.

In many instances, we may need to go no further than merely asking an attitudinal question, followed by asking 'why.' There are instances where we need to really dig into the motivations behind what a consumer does. This is commonly done with groups of consumers who have similar underlying patterns of attitudes. The process of grouping consumers based on how similar they are on several attributes is known as market segmentation. One can segment the market based on any set of relevant characteristics such as demographic similarities (e.g., older, wealthier, better-educated consumers versus younger, working-class, blue-collar consumers), similarities of benefits sought from a product (e.g., people who buy cars purely to get from point A to point B, versus people who want to be admired because of what they drive), attitudes or lifestyle similarities.

Lifestyle or "psychographics" refers to a combination of a person's self-reported behaviour (e.g., I go to movies often), self-reported personality traits (e.g., I'm easily excited), and attitudes (e.g., I always plan for my future). Usually, the respondent is asked to what extent she or he agrees with a number of statements. Although there are theoretical models for measuring lifestyle, the questions are constructed by the researcher, taking into account the product being studied and the relevant motivational and personality traits that may be related to it. Here is an example of a few lifestyle questions that deal with organic foods:

Please indicate your level of agreement with each of the following statements regarding organic food products. There are no right or wrong answers.

	Agree Strongly	Agree Somewhat	Disagree Somewhat	Disagree Strongly
I am willing to pay a little more for organic food	O	O	O	O
Organic produce does not look as appealing as non-organic produce	O	O	O	O
If there were more organic food choices available, I would buy more organic products	O	O	O	O
I find that organic produce is often not as fresh ~~or long-lasting~~ as non-organic produce	O	O	O	O
Organic produce tastes better than regular produce	O	O	O	O
There are certain items for which I always buy organic.	O	O	O	O

I do not understand why organic food usually costs more than non-organic products.	○	○	○	○
In the future, I expect to purchase organic products more frequently than I currently do.	○	○	○	○

Lifestyle or "psychographics" refers to a person's self-reported behaviour, personality traits, and related attitudes. When we analyze a battery of lifestyle questions, we are more interested in the pattern of their responses rather than their answers to any particular question. A statistical technique known as cluster analysis is designed to group people who answer many questions similarly. For instance, consumers who disagree with question 1 but agree with question 7 may be identified by cluster analysis as belonging to the same segment. After examining the statements, we may conclude that consumers in this segment are price sensitive or particularly open to online shopping. (Most lifestyle segmentation studies will contain a large number of statements, typically between 20 and 50.)

Not all questionnaires will contain lifestyle statements. In general, only those that aim to segment the market on lifestyle will. If you are faced with writing a questionnaire aimed at producing a lifestyle battery of questions, consider the following:

- The **benefits** of the category. For example, if the product is a car, the benefits might include dependable transportation, impressing people, and excitement of moving fast.
- what might **influence the purchase** of one product over another? For example, being practical, being concerned with other people's opinions, the desire for the highest level of safety, the need for performance in bad weather.

Peoples' lives are very complicated, so focusing on lifestyles that pertain specifically to the product being investigated will be more effective at reaching study goals than more general lifestyle questions. The following questions may help to understand better how people relate to ice cream specifically.

We would like to understand your ice cream opinions in general. Please indicate how well each of the following statements describes you.

	Does not describe me at all	2	3	4	5	6	7	Describes me extremely well
I eat ice cream only on special occasions.	○	○	○	○	○	○	○	○
I eat ice cream almost every day.	○	○	○	○	○	○	○	○
I buy ice cream only when it is on sale.	○	○	○	○	○	○	○	○
I buy the ice cream I want, regardless of price.	○	○	○	○	○	○	○	○
I buy the same flavour of ice cream all the time.	○	○	○	○	○	○	○	○
I buy the same **brand** of ice cream all the time.	○	○	○	○	○	○	○	○
I buy ice cream in bulk.	○	○	○	○	○	○	○	○
I prefer smaller containers of ice cream that may be more expensive.	○	○	○	○	○	○	○	○
I look for ice cream every time I go to the store.	○	○	○	○	○	○	○	○
I always buy low fat ice cream.	○	○	○	○	○	○	○	○
I look for the healthiest ice cream on the shelf.	○	○	○	○	○	○	○	○
I avoid artificial colours and flavours.	○	○	○	○	○	○	○	○
I prefer to buy all-natural or organic ice cream.	○	○	○	○	○	○	○	○
If a store does not have the brand and flavour that I want, I'll go to other stores until I find it.	○	○	○	○	○	○	○	○
I serve ice cream to guests as dessert.	○	○	○	○	○	○	○	○
None of the above.	○	○	○	○	○	○	○	○

Measuring Demographic Traits

As mentioned in the last unit, the demographic section is typically placed at the end of the questionnaire. Demographic questions usually include variables such as age, gender, income, household composition, education, and region. Because these are personal questions and may be considered very sensitive by some, asking them upfront is likely to elicit suspicion and higher termination rates. The only exception to this is when we use a demographic trait for screening purposes.

For instance, if we are interested in interviewing only people having personal incomes of $100,000 or higher, we may make our purpose explicit and ask the following screening question at the beginning of the interview:

Was your total personal income before taxes in 2022 less than $100,000 or not?

○ Yes, less than $100,000

○ No, $100,000 or higher

A screening question identifies whether the person contacted is eligible to participate in the survey.

The demographic section at the end of a questionnaire should start with a reassuring introduction like this:

Demographics

We would prefer not to pay a coder to categorize something that can be checked off a list. Our standard gender demo would read:

Do you identify as:

○ Male

○ Female

○ Other

Are you:

○ Married, common law or co-habitating?

○ Single, separated, divorced or widowed?

■ NEXT SCREEN

With respect to your current marital status, are you...

○ Married

○ Cohabitating with a partner / living common-law

○ Single

○ Separated/ Divorced/ Widowed

- **NEXT SCREEN**

    How many people in total, including yourself, are living in your household? (Please select from the pull-down list.)

    How many of those people are adults 18 years or older?

    How many of those people are children 17 years or younger?

    - 1 (one)
    - 2 (two)
    - 3 (three)
    - 4 (four)
    - 5 (five)
    - 6 (six)
    - 7 (seven)
    - 8 (eight) or more

-

- **NEXT SCREEN**

What is the highest level of formal education that you attained?

- ○ Some high school
- ○ Graduated from high school
- ○ Some/ completed technical school
- ○ Some / completed community college or CEGEP
- ○ Some university
- ○ Graduated from university
- ○ Some or completed graduate school

- **NEXT SCREEN**

How many people in your household are employed full-time?

- ○ 0, none
- ○ 1
- ○ 2
- ○ 3
- ○ 4
- ○ 5
- ○ 6 or more

■ NEXT SCREEN

What is your occupation?

[   ]

■ NEXT SCREEN

Which language did you first learn to speak in childhood and still understand?

Which language is spoken in your home most often now?

	Language **First Spoken**	Language **Spoken Now** in your home
French	○	○
English	○	○
Indigenous language	○	○
German	○	○
Spanish	○	○
A language from India	○	○
Mandarin or Cantonese	○	○
Italian	○	○
Other	○	○

■ NEXT SCREEN

Which of the following categories includes your total annual household income for 2022 before taxes?

○ Less than $20,000
○ $20,000 to $39,999
○ $40,000 to $79,999
○ $80,000 to $99,999
○ $100,000 to $149,999
○ $150,000 or higher

■ NEXT SCREEN

In which year were you born? (4-digit year please) [   ]

■ NEXT SCREEN

Thank you for taking this survey.

You've been very helpful.

0% ▰▰▰▰▰▰▰▰▰▰▰▰▰▰▰▰ 100%

Some questionnaires contain more demographic information than others. Some principles of writing demographic questions are as follows:

1. There is a general reluctance among many people to reveal their exact income. Show the income question last in most cases. Use categories similar to those shown above and similar to those used by Statistics Canada unless other categories are needed.
2. Even when you use categories, use as few as needed for your purposes. For instance, people are more likely to respond to an age question with fewer categories (34 and under, 35 to 49, 50 and above) than questions with many categories (19 and under, 20 to 29, 30 to 39, 40 to 49, 50 to 59, 60 to 69, 70 or older). It is better to use categories that coincide with those used by Statistics Canada so that the sample can be compared to total population data to measure representativeness. Respondents are more likely to divulge their age when asked for their year-of-birth.
3. People do not want to belong to the lowest category in variables like income. It is sometimes useful to include a low-income category to which most people are unlikely to belong.
4. Unless we specifically need to know personal income, it is better to ask for a person's household income because, in many cases, household income is larger than personal income, and so is less embarrassing to reveal and might better reflect purchasing power. It may also be more useful.
5. Although we ask for demographic information, we should remember that many respondents might refuse to provide some or part of the information. Refusals can be particularly high for income-related questions. It is common in online questionnaires to require respondents to answer all of the questions. However, it is typically best **not** to require answers to sensitive questions such as age and income and perhaps other demographic questions as well. This can be accomplished by offering a 'refusal' or 'prefer not to say' response code.

Concluding Comments

In the last unit, we talked about writing questions that are clear and unambiguous. In this unit, we have discussed how to design questions to elicit different types of attitude information.

Writing a questionnaire is both a science and an art. These two chapters will give a reasonable grounding in science. As you gain experience, you will learn that the rules are not hard and fast.

Once you understand the basic principles, the actual question, as well as the wording of it, depends on the context in which it is asked, the respondent from whom the information is needed, the precision of the answer required and the statistical analysis methods to be used.

Unit 8

How to Manage the Mechanics of Quantitative Research

In earlier units, we discussed the role of a researcher in all the stages of a project up until fieldwork. We described the work needed to define the business issue, set the objectives, identify the target group and create the questionnaire.

Once the design elements are all in place and all involved parties have given their approvals, the project is ready to go to field. This chapter will walk you through what comes next.

If you work for a large research firm, you *may* simply 'hand over' the questionnaire to the field operations team at this point, and do nothing more than wait for field management, programmers, interviewers, coders and data processing to do their work and deliver the results to you.

But often, you have a continued role to play in:
- instructing the operations teams/programmers/interviewers,

- monitoring their work and solving any problems that arise,
- monitoring the results as they come in, and
- determining how you want the results processed and delivered to you.

There is still much that you can and should do.

How do Different Methods Impact the Researcher's Role?

The researcher's specific roles may depend on the methodology, but a good researcher will always understand the mechanics of what goes on behind the scenes, monitor these activities, and make sure that things are done properly and as expected.

The key dichotomy in managing research projects is whether interviewers are involved. At a very high level, the key differences are:

- The human interface between interviewers and respondents in both **telephone** interviews and **face-to-face** interviews requires:
  - clear *interviewing instructions* that will be understood without interpretation by a wide range of individuals
  - careful supervision and
  - 'on-the-go' problem resolution.

The instruction and monitoring are likely to differ if the interviewer is using:

- a **digital questionnaire** programmed onto a tablet or smartphone (referred to as Computer Assisted Personal Interviewing, CAPI), where the programming takes care of questionnaire flow and leaves less room for interpretation or
- a **pen-and-paper questionnaire** that may require more data cleaning and interpretation.

On the other hand, a **self-completion** questionnaire requires special attention to written instructions that will be perfectly clear to the respondents who will be reading them – respondents who are likely to vary widely in age, education and cultural background, etc.

- For a **digital version** of the self-completion questionnaire – online or web-based – the researcher will provide programming instructions that leave nothing to chance. But it also offers the opportunity for a researcher to test the questionnaire to ensure it is working properly before it is launched to the respondents.
- **Paper questionnaires** are more heavily dependent on respondents understanding skip patterns and other instructions as they go. This places more emphasis on pre-testing – asking non-researchers to complete the questionnaire before it is launched and checking that the instructions are easily understood and followed.

Who Are the Players?

Field Managers

The starting point is always the researcher. He or she may act as the field manager and oversee all aspects of the field operations themselves or will have a relationship with another individual who will serve as field manager. In this case, the field manager may be a colleague inside the researcher's own firm, particularly with the larger research suppliers, or a sub-contractor in a field services firm. Field managers will:

- provide feedback on the questionnaire when it first arrives,
- ensure the proposed schedule is feasible,
- instruct their team,
- oversee the work that occurs at each phase of field operations,
- conduct quality checks throughout the process, including the programming of the questionnaire, the collection of the data and the logic in the tabulated results.

Field managers must have a solid understanding of research principles and strong project management and problem-solving skills. They must keep all parts of the field machinery working smoothly on several projects simultaneously to ensure none of the deadlines slip. They must be organized, diplomatic and have good people management skills.

The field manager oversees several distinct roles within a field team.

Scripters / Questionnaire Programmers

This is the role that takes the final questionnaire from the researcher and turns it into a smoothly functioning interviewing experience. Among their responsibilities are:

- turning all the instructions into logic (e.g., skip codes) to ensure all potential pathways through the questionnaire flow as they should;
- allowing each respondent to see only the questions that they are supposed to answer;
- ensuring each question accepts a single response or allows multiple responses as intended;
- capturing every legitimate response choice made and everything entered in open-end text boxes;
- minimizing or eliminating scrolling (particularly side-to-side) on any device the respondent may be using;
- optimizing the look and feel of the questionnaire including any images, video or concepts that are to be seen.

With digital interviewing now using mobile phones, the last two points – minimizing scrolling and optimizing the look and feel – are more important than ever before. Each brand and model of mobile phone has a different screen size and configuration, and the questionnaire must be fully functional on each. If those who have a specific type of phone can't experience the questionnaire as designed, we risk introducing sample bias. This will drive up research costs when these respondents must be replaced. Even worse, if we are not aware that different respondents experience the questionnaire in different ways, we may also end up with inaccurate results.

The final result of a scripter's work will be an accurate, efficient and pleasing data collection program. In fact, there is so much competition for a respondent's attention from social media, games and other online content, questionnaires should be as interactive and entertaining as possible. Scripters should have a range of interactive response scales, images, scripts, videos and sounds in their toolboxes.

For example,

- an ad testing study might use a 'joystick' that respondents could manipulate to show how they are feeling in real-time while watching a version of the advertisement;
- a corporate image question might employ a sliding scale with a heart that grows in size as it moves from negative to positive;
- respondents might be offered photographs of people showing different emotions and be asked to choose which was closest to how they felt after seeing a new product description;
- a behavioural study might ask respondents to take a short video of their lunch and ask them to explain how they prepared it, giving us insight not only into the meal but the location and context.

Questionnaire scripting tools are constantly evolving, and new, interactive approaches are an important growth area for the industry. Scripters generally come out of computer science backgrounds and are increasingly benefiting from game programming experience.

Interviewers

Professional interviewers have long been the mainstay of marketing research. With the growth of digital questionnaires, there are fewer of them, but they still play a crucial role when telephone or face-to-face interviews are required.

The interviewer's role is to:
- make contact with respondents, induce them to participate and keep them engaged to the end of the interview;
- ensure the questions are asked as consistently and accurately as possible without interpretation or biasing influences; and
- record responses accurately and completely.

For example, an interviewer conducting a product taste test in a mall must approach shoppers walking by, invite them to spend 15 minutes to help a food manufacturer make their product more appealing, and offer them a small incentive to put whatever they were doing on hold for a little while. She might direct them into a small storefront interview facility and follow questionnaire instructions accurately to ensure each respondent is exposed in exactly the way prescribed by the interview guide. She must be careful to ensure her own personal feelings or opinions are not evident and must record each respondent's reactions accurately.

Similarly, a telephone interviewer might work his way through a long list of phone numbers (or react when an auto-dialer gets a live respondent on the line) and has a few seconds to convince the respondent to spend 15 minutes answering a few questions that will benefit the marketplace in some way. Once he convinces someone to participate, he must read all the questions clearly, and accurately record responses, without introducing any of his own personal biases. At some point, the respondent may express impatience, and the interviewer may encourage them to stay on the line and ask 'just a few more questions' to complete the interview.

Interviewers must be confident, patient, friendly and speak the language of the interview. It also helps to have a thick skin because rejection by potential respondents is a regular part of the job.

Research with specialized populations will require interviewers with particular skills. For example, interviewing "executives" and senior managers in large companies or government requires very confident, experienced and highly proficient senior interviewers.

Interviews with doctors, pharmacists and nurses will require interviewers with health care knowledge because they will need to understand the questions they are asking and, more importantly, capture the responses including names of medicines and procedures that would be hard for most of us to pronounce.

Supervisors

Supervisors are responsible for training and monitoring the interviewers and ensuring they know how to ask each question and record each response. In central location telephone facilities, they can listen in on each interview and watch how responses are recorded on shared screens, providing feedback if anything is done incorrectly.

For example, when a large project starts up, the team of interviewers might include a few experienced staff and a few first-timers. The supervisor can conduct training sessions with the newbies, a few trial interviews pairing the experienced and new interviewers, listen in on each of the first few interviews of those starting out and, after each interview, go through the questionnaire in detail providing feedback on wording, emphasis, flow and tone.

Interviewers come from a wide range of backgrounds and are often part-time employees working on contract on specific projects. It's not uncommon to find students, seniors, and individuals who need workplace flexibility (e.g., actors, writers, etc.) staffing the phones. The last section of this chapter offers more detail on interviewer training and procedures.

Data Entry Professional

With digital interviews (also known as online or web-based interviews), when the responses are recorded directly into the questionnaire program by either the respondent or the interviewer, there is no need for data entry. This may eliminate one potential source of error in the research process.

However, when interviews are conducted by pen and paper, the completed questionnaires are sent to the data entry team, who are responsible for accurately entering the responses into a **database**.

A key part of this process is **data cleaning** – ensuring multiple responses are not entered when only one is needed, removing responses from questions that should have been skipped, cleaning up the language of open-end responses, etc.

Accuracy checks might include spot-checking individual responses to ensure they have been entered in the right location, or 'double entry' where each questionnaire is entered into the database twice with errors identified when the two entries don't correspond.

Data entry clerks must be very detail-oriented and need to be able to focus and stay engaged during long and often tedious tasks.

Coders

Regardless of the data collection methodology, open-ended questions allow respondents to answer using their own words. They may provide one or two words or whole paragraphs.

These can be entered into the data file and provided directly to clients as "**verbatims**" – the actual words of the respondent – but with large samples, few clients would have the time or the inclination to read through them all.

More often, the open-ended responses are "**coded**," grouped into response categories so that the frequency of mentioning certain themes can be recorded.

For example, a question on a survey might have asked, "What is your favourite vacation destination?". Responses may list destinations as diverse as Disneyworld, Bali, Mykonos or Paris. They may offer environments such as the beach, cottage, cruises or mountains. They may offer activities such as hiking, shopping, theatre or scuba diving. It's up to the coders to identify the themes, gain the researcher's approval, then group responses into these themes so they can be tabulated in the data processing phase.

Coders are also required to '**clean**' the data, for example, removing responses that are not relevant or useful to the study, perhaps filling in abbreviations and removing insulting or offensive language. This is particularly important if the verbatim file is to be given to the client.

Coders must speak the language(s) of the questionnaire fluently and be able to recognize the nuances and cultural references.

Text recognition technology, text analysis and natural language processing (NLP) are currently coming on-stream to automate the coding function. Substantial advances have been made in this area. However, the many subtleties of language usage, including capturing tone, sarcasm, specific cultural references, or colloquialisms, are challenging those involved in research to improve these methods. Humans are still superior with some of these tasks.

Data Processing Professionals

Once the data is entered, cleaned and coded, a **data file** is delivered to the data processing team. They work with a **tabulation plan** that the researchers provide. This plan will detail how the data is to be tabulated:

- which population groups are to be split out (e.g., men versus women, younger versus older respondents, east versus west);
- how scales might be 'netted' (e.g., combining very important and somewhat important)
- where averages are to be calculated;
- which questions are to be cross-tabulated (e.g., satisfaction with an experience crossed with a specific type of experience);

and use this as a plan to create computer tables with all the required data breaks.

For example, an important point of analysis for the study might be to understand if men and women make travel decisions differently, or if desired destinations differ by household income levels, or if those who take beach vacations are looking for different types of lodging than those who want to spend their vacation in big cities. It is important that these breaks, i.e., breakdowns, appear in the final data tables.

Data processing is essentially a series of mathematical and logic equations, so it's not uncommon for practitioners to have strong math and programming skills.

Marketing Science Team

Sometimes more advanced types of data analysis are required, such as segmentation, driver analysis, discrete choice, market landscape mapping, etc. In these cases, a specialized marketing science unit can be called in. These are often people with advanced degrees in statistics and can provide creative and insightful analyses.

For example, while those who take beach vacations all prioritize safety, warm water and clean sand as the factors that drive them to take this type of vacation, these are not factors that would determine which tour operator they book with. They perceive real differences in 'quality of food' and 'cleanliness of rooms.' A straight crosstab of the results won't reveal this, but a 'key driver analysis' provided by marketing science will.

The marketing science team must work very closely with the researcher to ensure each understands the others' needs.

All these players work together to get a research study from the final questionnaire through to the point where a researcher can begin to write the report. Here's how that might work.

How is Fieldwork Organized?

The fieldwork process is designed to ensure:
- **Allocation**: That the right people are recruited and ready to go when their involvement is required and that all field materials that will be required have been identified and are in place;
- **Alignment**: Every member of the team knows exactly how the interviews are to be conducted, that there is no room for interpretation or bias;
- **Accuracy:** That the survey instruments, interviewer and programming instructions, tab plans and coding manuals are carefully vetted and reviewed to ensure there are no errors and that each player understands exactly what he or she must do; and
- **Flow:** That each phase of the process is lined up and ready to go when the previous section is completed and that each player knows what has to be passed on when the next team steps in for their component.

The actual activities may vary between interviewer-administered interviews and self-completions and between digital questionnaires and paper-and-pen questionnaires, but the flow and principles will remain the same. This section looks at each step and what might be required to ensure fieldwork is successful.

1. Preliminary Checking

Generally, once the client and researcher agree that the questionnaire is final and both parties 'sign off', the field manager is asked to review it. With an experienced eye from overseeing many studies, the field manager can spot potential programming and fielding problems.

For example, she or he might offer suggestions on:
- improving the wording for programming, interviewer or respondent instructions,
- adding "escape" response codes such as "don't know/no answer" or "none of the above" that would make it easier for respondents to make their way through the questionnaire;
- improving the overall look and feel of the questionnaire;

For digital questionnaires, the field manager might:
- recommend alternative response mechanisms like slider scales, progressive grids or colour shading;
- identify locations for recurring column headers on long statement batteries;
- insist on adjustments to remove horizontal scrolling, for example, when a grid question has too many columns, or an image is too large.

As more and more questionnaires make the transition to '**mobile-friendly,**' making it possible for respondents to complete them on small, smartphone touch screens rather than on larger computer screens with keyboards – questions must be more concise, scrolling must be minimized or eliminated, and complex grids are unusable. However, game-derived programming, like slide bars, evolving icons, etc., can make responding more fun.

These 'mobile-friendly' measures should be built in from the start, but the field manager is best positioned to ensure all are in place before questionnaire programming begins.

Ultimately, responsibility for correction doesn't lie with the field department. It is the sole responsibility of the researcher.

2. The Kick-off Meeting

Once the questionnaire is ready to be handed off to the fieldwork team, the researcher must meet with representatives from each of the teams involved—programming, interviewing, coding, data processing—to ensure everyone understands the study's overall objectives and expected process. This is the opportunity for each group of field specialists to review the questionnaire and any documentation, ask questions and ensure they are comfortable with what is expected of them.

If everyone is in the same location, a face-to-face kick-off meeting is ideal. However, increasingly such meetings are held by phone or visual meeting app, particularly when the different players are based in different locations and even different countries.

3. Digital Questionnaire Programming

With a **digital** (as opposed to pen-and-paper) questionnaire, once everyone is comfortable that content and flow are final, it is sent to the questionnaire programmers, or 'scripters.' They follow the programming instructions that were built into the questionnaire when it was written, creating the interface that the interviewers or respondents will see on their screen.

If there is any uncertainty, there should be some back and forth between the researcher and scripters (often through the field manager) to clarify the intent and expected functionality.

Questionnaire programming is an exercise in logic, keeping track of all potential pathways through the questions, ensuring the right questions show up at the right time, in front of the right respondents. In many cases, a supervisor or separate quality control group would check the accuracy of the programming.

Programmers can spot potential logic errors, may suggest 'no opinion/no answer/none-of-the-above' options that ensure respondents aren't frustrated and may have suggestions for improving the look and feel of the digital version of the questionnaire.

For example, if respondents are expected to be able to complete the questionnaire on a cellphone, the scripter may realize that a grid question set up by the researcher is too wide to fit onto the small screen without scrolling across. Respondents are unlikely to scroll across, so this will skew results towards responses on the left-hand side of the screen. It's appropriate for the scripter to recommend another format – perhaps a sliding scale or a drop-down box for each statement.

4. Testing Digital Links

Once the questionnaire is scripted, the links are sent to the researcher to test. These links are very similar to what a respondent will receive when invited to complete the survey. The links are embedded in an e-mail, and when the researcher clicks on one of them, it will take her to the questionnaire where she can answer the questions as if she were a real respondent.

Testing involves going through every possible pathway in the questionnaire to ensure the right questions appear after each response. To do this, the researcher must 'role play.'

For example,
- if the screening question is designed to ensure respondents have travelled by airplane on vacation in the past 12 months, the researcher will try to respond as a non-traveler to ensure they are not let into the questionnaire;
- If the response options for a specific question are to be randomized, for example, the list of airlines that respondents might consider, the researcher must run through the questionnaire numerous times to ensure the order is different every time they go through the test questionnaire;
- If a shortlist of responses is to appear in a question based on what was selected in a previous question, for example, if the respondent prefers to vacation in the south of Spain, only those hotel chains with properties in that region should appear, the researcher would pretend to prefer different destinations and check to see that the right hotel chains are showing up;
- If a block of questions is to appear only if a pattern of previous questions is selected, for example, if cultural vacations are on a respondent's wishlist, the block of questions about museums, art galleries and performance venues is to appear, the researcher tries different combinations to make sure this is working correctly.

Not surprisingly, this can be a lengthy and even tedious task, but it is crucial to ensuring that the questionnaire form is working as it should. In some situations where there are multiple cells, multiple qualifications, extensive rotations, etc., it might mean testing dozens of links. A researcher might enlist the help of colleagues to ensure fresh eyes are doing the testing. Any corrections are passed back to the scripters, changes are made, and a *new* set of links are ready for testing.

Adjusting the questionnaire program can create new problems, so the researcher must keep testing revised links until she or he is certain that the questionnaire programming is flawless. Once the questionnaire goes 'live,' it is next to impossible to make changes without disrupting fieldwork and losing sample.

5. Quality Checking for Paper Questionnaires

If the questionnaire is on paper (*not* digital), there won't be links to test, but it is still important to test the logic and flow of the questionnaire for accuracy and intent. This starts with a careful 'proof-read,' ideally including a second set of eyes that would be seeing the questionnaire from a different perspective. Running through the paper questionnaire a few times, different role-playing identities, and testing a full range of possible answers to ensure all the correct termination and skipping instructions are in place is very important to the quality of the survey instrument.

Quality checking also involves pre-testing by real respondents – whether the questionnaire is digital or on paper.

6. Translating

If the fieldwork involves *more than one* language, the questionnaire will be translated once everyone has signed off on the original language version. This process would be the same for digital or pen-and-paper questionnaires.

Because questionnaire wording is very specific and must carry consistent meaning to all respondents, questionnaire translators must be proficient in the principles of questionnaire design. A translator can introduce biases that don't exist in the original version simply by choosing a different set of words.

A translator should also be comfortable with the nuances and colloquialisms of the local version of the second (or third, or fourth) language used in a study. An English-to-Spanish translator in Spain is less likely to produce an appropriate version for Chile than a translator in Chile; the French spoken in Canada or West Africa is very different from the French spoken in France.

The researcher may speak only the original language, but that does not absolve them of the responsibility for ensuring the translation carries the same meaning as the original. Different techniques are possible:
- Asking a colleague who speaks the second language to read the translation aloud and explain what it is saying – the discussion may reveal subtle variations in meaning;
- Having the questionnaire 'back-translated' – employing a second translator to translate the second language version back into the original language;
- In desperation only, using an online translation program like Google Translate to do a 'back translation' yourself, phrase by phrase.

It is crucial that translation programs NOT be used to *create* a second language version. Current technologies are not yet able to capture all the nuances that exist between languages.

In the case of digital questionnaires, the translated version is "poured" into the programming set up for the original language. It does not have to be programmed separately. However, it is still important to test the links for the second version to ensure everything is in the right place and working as it should. This task should fall to the researcher.

If the study involves the use of interviewers, follow the guidelines below:

7. The Interview Manual

When data collection is a person-to-person interview, the researcher and the field director will want to make sure all interviewers are acting consistently. An interviewing manual is created to provide administrative instructions, sample selection requirements, interviewing instructions, and respondent management directions.

There would be two parts to the manual:

a. **General guidelines**: covering general interview etiquette and standard answers to common respondent queries.

For instance, here are some questions that interviewers are commonly asked:
- "My phone number is unlisted. How did you get it?" *The manual would explain random digit dialing if that technique was used.*
- "Why do you want to know how many people live in this household?" *The manual could suggest that this is important to understand how behaviour might differ among households of different sizes.*
- "You asked for my income. Does that include my bonus?" *The manual will probably suggest that any earnings that impact spending power should be included.*

b. **Instructions specific to the study**: covering off the purpose of the study and specific instructions for each question, particularly those that can be problematic. More sensitive questions (e.g., sexual habits) might require more instructions than more 'everyday' topics (e.g., detergent usage), but it's important to anticipate problematic scenarios.
- *For example, perhaps you are doing a media study and ask a question like, "Yesterday, how much time did you spend reading the newspaper?" The respondent may say, "Yesterday, I read the paper for 45 minutes, but it was not yesterday's paper. It was the day-before-yesterday. Do you want to know whether I read any issue of the paper yesterday or yesterday's paper yesterday?" A good interviewer manual should anticipate a question like this and provide answers.*

In digital surveys, explanations can often be provided with the question so that a respondent can get added clarity. For instance, such a question might look like this:
- *Yesterday, how much time did you spend reading the* Vancouver Sun? *(Please include all the time you spent reading the* Vancouver Sun *yesterday, whether it was yesterday's paper or not.)*

Of course, not all potential problems can be anticipated, but a proper pre-test will uncover the most common issues.

8. Briefing the Field Staff

The kick-off meeting at the *beginning* of the fieldwork period would have provided instructions for the various field management teams, but a *separate* briefing should be held with <u>interviewers</u> on a person-to-person interview study.

Remember that each project is unique—even if only in a minor way—so each field venture must be treated as a stand-alone project. This means that each project must be preceded by a **briefing** to familiarize the supervisors and the interviewers with the special requirements of the study and with the questionnaire. This is particularly important if new interviewers are joining the team.

Having more carefully prepared and tested questionnaires and clearer built-in instructions will reduce the time required for briefing. Most briefings take an hour or less. But in more complex situations, a half-day may be required for preparation and practice interviews. In general, the field director briefs all supervisors (including supervisors from different call centres or different central location sites), and the supervisors, in turn, brief the interviewers. However, it is not uncommon for the field director to brief all interviewers directly.

All interviewers must work the same way, asking each question exactly as written. There must be no paraphrasing, no additional explanations, no variations in emphasis. Some response codes are to be read out loud, and some used only if volunteered by the respondent. Rotations of response options must be followed exactly.

The researcher (indirectly), the field director (directly), and the field supervisor (operationally) are responsible for the quality of the interviews. As with any job, some interviewers can be less competent than others, but it is the supervisor's job to minimize this source of bias.

The supervisor will read through the questionnaire step-by-step and brief the interviewers who will then practice interviewing. If questionnaire problems arise at this stage, they are reported to the researcher immediately.

In modern call centres, supervisors can continue to monitor interviews once the fieldwork is underway and provide directions and further instructions as needed to ensure the highest quality of interviews. Live supervision is more of a challenge in intercept interviews (stopping people in malls or on-the-street) or in door-to-door interviews (interviewing people in their homes).

The latter part of this chapter provides more details on training and supervising interviewers.

9. Receiving and Preparing Samples

In **online or web-based** surveys, the sample preparation is a separate function from the fieldwork. Specialists who manage panel databases will create a sampling program that selects potential respondents from the panel who fit the target definition provided by the researcher. The "sample frame" ensures those with different characteristics appear in the right proportions.

For example, if the survey is designed to interview parents of young children aged 2 to 11, the database will be combed for qualified households and their contact information programmed into a sample file that will eventually be sent invitations to participate. The researcher should specify what proportion of the sample should be parents of children aged 2 to 6 and 7 to 11 and how many she wants from each of the market's regions.

The process would be similar for **client-supplied** samples. The client will provide the contact information for the employees or customers that are to be invited to participate from their database.

In **telephone interviewing**, the phone numbers to be dialed are sourced from databases (like phone books or panel lists) or are randomly generated within existing exchanges.

For example, in North America, most phone numbers within a geographic area start with an area code and then the same three digits (e.g. 416 555-xxxx or 212 954-xxxx). Randomly generating the last four numbers rather than the whole number will create more 'real' numbers.

These numbers can be dialed by the interviewer or by an automated dialer that then passes an answered call over to a live interviewer.

In **face-to-face interviewing**, however, the field staff will have to be instructed on how to create the sample themselves.

- **Door-to-door** interviewing will require maps and sampling plans so each interviewer can be given a specific path through a neighbourhood that is orderly, and verifiable. This ensures a broad and randomized sample.
- *For example, an interviewer might be asked to go to a specific intersection in a specific part of the city, to start at the north-west corner and begin knocking on doors, moving clockwise around the block. Each time the door is answered, they would find out the demographics of the household and then consult a sample plan to see who in the household they would need to interview.*
- **Intercept interviewing**, for example, in a mall, would require interviewers to stop people who are passing by, follow a screening questionnaire to qualify them before beginning the interview. They are likely to have age, gender and behavioural quotas that must be checked before they can begin the interview.

Mail surveys require addresses that are drawn from databases – perhaps city directories, client lists or panels. The mailing lists and labels are provided to clerical staff who prepare the packages that are sent out. This approach is best suited to in-home product tests (often following an online screening questionnaire). The mailed or delivered package contains the product to be tested, instructions, and a self-administered paper questionnaire or instructions to go online to complete a digital questionnaire.

Participation and response rates have fallen over the years for all these methodologies, so the samples that are required initially are generally much larger now than they have been historically.

Feasibility is an important concept when dealing with large samples or very narrowly-defined respondent qualifications: are there even enough people in the database or panel to fill all the quotas, given expected qualification and participation rates?

For example, testing a dozen new pet food concepts designed specifically for very small dogs might be challenging because only a small proportion of pet owners have this type of dog. A quick calculation multiplying the known incidence of these breeds, the size of the sample required and the expected response rate by the size of the overall panel may indicate that the panel can supply only enough qualified respondents to test 6 concepts at a time. As a result, the study would have to be redesigned with two waves.

10. Pre-test / Pilot Test / Soft Launch

Pre-testing involves conducting a few interviews before going ahead with full-scale interviewing.

Just as rehearsal is required for successful plays, pre-testing is required for successful interviews. Even the best questionnaire writer can create a question that is not clear to a respondent. For example, the word 'funds' in the question "Do you have sufficient funds to retire comfortably?" may well be interpreted by a respondent as "investment funds" rather than simply 'resources' or money.

A simple typing error can lead interviewers to the wrong question. For example, instead of going to question 3 as required, the interviewer may go to question 8, skipping five questions that need to be asked, all because of a typographical error.

Or a question might be out of sequence. For instance, early in a questionnaire, there might be a question that asks, "How many miles did you drive last year?" and then later in the questionnaire, the question "Do you drive?" appears. Anyone who doesn't drive and answered zero miles initially might be annoyed by the latter question.

There are simply too many ways to go wrong, especially when the questionnaire is complicated. Pre-testing is a relatively inexpensive way of making sure that the questionnaire is sufficiently accurate for use in the study. In fact, even when there are no major problems with the questionnaire, pre-testing may still be used to refine it.

From a practical position, many questionnaires are so basic that, with proper attention from an experienced, capable, and sensitive researcher and field director, and perhaps someone else in the office, they can often go into the field with no formal pre-testing.

Pre-testing does not have to be expensive nor very time-consuming, but sometimes the crunch of meagre budgets and demanding time schedules do not leave any time for this important function.

Whether the project design calls for telephone interviews, face-to-face intercepts or self-administered questionnaires on paper or digitally, it is always a good idea to **initially test all types of questionnaires through personal interviews**, in addition to testing it in the actual medium for which it is intended. Thus, a telephone questionnaire should be tested using personal interviews *as well as* telephone interviews.

Personal interviews are used so that when the respondent is sitting in front of you, you can see the smile on his face that means the question is silly or the frown that means he can't find the correct answer in the list of alternatives. In a personal interview, the respondents can tell you what they are thinking as they read through and respond to the questions in front of them.

After the face-to-face test of the questionnaire, a small sample pre-test should be conducted to test the refined questionnaire through its **natural medium** (e.g., if it is a telephone questionnaire, telephone is the "natural medium").

Why test a telephone questionnaire in its natural medium? The face-to-face situation helps both the researcher and the respondent by using visual cues and explanations, but other questionnaire deficiencies will become apparent only when it is being used as it will in the study. When we test the questionnaire over the telephone, we find out how effective the questionnaire is when the respondent must understand and respond to questions with only *verbal* cues.

Pre-tests are **monitored** by supervisors (sometimes even by the researcher) to detect subtle problems that might be missed by the interviewers.

If the study is complex or particularly important, we should conduct a **pilot test** – a live, small-sample day-or-two of fieldwork, using a variety of interviewers and the actual methodology, to create a microcosmic version of the main study. The pilot test collects actual data that can be analyzed to ensure the questionnaire is collecting and delivering what it should.

Pilot tests can be expensive. For this reason, major problems are first eliminated through pre-tests and dry runs (interviewers interviewing each other or other readily accessible people). But once it is considered final, the first 10 percent of the interviews may be designated for a "pilot test." If there are no problems or only minor issues (too insignificant to affect the overall results), the completed pilot test interviews may be added into the main survey.

In the digital environment, this 'pilot test' is often referred to as a '**soft launch**' with a small portion of the full sample. The soft launch should also be used to confirm that the responses are being captured by the program properly and are showing up as expected in the database.

Many aspects of a questionnaire should be reviewed during pre-testing, pilot testing and soft launches to ensure they meet some basic quality criteria. These include:

- **Questions.** Questions should be clear and understandable; there should be no biases, errors, ambiguities, or offensive questions.
- **Answers.** Pre-coded response options should be relevant, exhaustive and mutually exclusive (to avoid overlap). Closed-ended and open-ended questions should be properly laid out, especially in self-administered questionnaires.
- **Flow.** The questionnaire should flow logically, topics should not abruptly jump around.
- **Skip patterns.** There should be no improper skip patterns.
- **Screener.** Screening questions should accurately eliminate all non-qualifying respondents and retain all qualified respondents.
- **Format.** The format should be conducive to the interviewer's presentation style and be natural and interesting to the respondent. In self-administered questionnaires, the format should be attractive, even fun, and easy-to-follow.
- **Overall length and general feasibility of the questionnaire.** The overall length should be acceptable to the respondents and conform to the agreement between the client and the research firm.
- **Boredom.** This can be gauged by respondent drop off, "straightlining" (simply selecting the same answer through an entire battery without reading the statement) or impatience in answering the questions.

Following the pre-test, pilot test or soft launch, the field director gives the researcher **feedback** needed to refine the questionnaire. In most cases, the revision of the questionnaire is a quick process of rephrasing a few questions. However, in some cases where questions just did not work, a substantial revision might be necessary, perhaps even with another pre-test.

Some research firms will encourage the client to attend the pre-test debriefing of interviewers so that suggestions for changes are communicated directly by people who had to administer the less-than-perfect questionnaire. This practice can be very helpful to the whole field process.

11. The Invitation to Participate

There is a crucial moment at the beginning of each interview when the respondent must be convinced to participate. It is the 'elevator pitch' of the introductory statement that plays a critical role in ensuring the robust and representative sample, timely completion and a positive image for the marketing research industry in general.

In **online** or **web-based consumer surveys**, the current sample source is a pre-recruited **panel** of potential respondents who have already agreed to participate in research. For the most part, they are kept engaged by regular newsletters and frequent invitations to complete a survey. The incentive to participate may involve collecting points that can be used to acquire products or draws for cash prizes. In these cases, the invitation is a simple alert that another survey is ready to be completed.

If the sample is **client-supplied** rather than from a consumer panel, the invitation must be carefully worded to maximize willingness to participate. This may be more readily achieved if the invitation comes from the client directly, explaining that the research company has been brought in to conduct a dispassionate third-party evaluation. In many jurisdictions, privacy legislation requires that people who are in a client database cannot be contacted by a third-party unless they had explicitly agreed to that in advance. So, companies that wish to use their customer or prospect databases for research should ensure that all those on the list are *offered the choice to opt in* to being contacted for research purposes.

It is extremely rare and relatively ineffective to invite participation in an online or web-based survey with a **"cold call" e-mail invitation**. In this era of e-mail spam, viruses, malware and ransomware, consumers are understandably reluctant to click on a link embedded in an e-mail from someone they don't know.

Regardless of the sample source, an invitation to participate in an online or web-based survey would be more effective if it followed these principles:

   a. Doesn't look like spam: Email invitations should look professional and be free from spelling and grammar errors. They should be clear and to-the-point. It is important to avoid overly effusive language (e.g., "win big today") – one of the key triggers for spam filters.
   b. Do not reveal the survey topic: To prevent respondents from further self-selecting, use generic subject lines that won't attract or detract people from completing a specific survey.
   c. Use the subject line to indicate the person is being invited to a survey.

d. Provide the salient points immediately, including the type and value of incentive as well as the estimated time requirement.
e. Ensure potential respondents know they may not qualify to complete the entire survey and receive the incentive.
f. Provide contact information for help or more information. Include an e-mail address, as well as a toll-free telephone number and physical address, in case potential respondents have concerns or questions.
g. Include a confidentiality statement and a link to the privacy policy on your website. This will help to reassure people who are not intimately familiar with the research organization. Privacy concerns center primarily around: *Are you going to sell my contact information? Is there a risk of identity theft? Might this expose me to a computer virus/malware?* Two pervasive fears also express confidentiality concerns: "Who is going to see my answers?" and "Will I be confronted by someone if my reactions are negative or be approached by direct-marketers based on the information provided?"
h. Ensure your privacy policy is detailed, specific and up-to-date. Over time, more and more people are checking formal corporate privacy policies before entering any type of personally identifiable information. If you have not published a formal privacy policy, there are numerous sources for templates and definitions.

Many international organizations subscribe to the ICC/ESOMAR International Code on Market, Opinion and Social Research and Data Analytics. The code can be found on their website.

Other potential reference points include:

- The British Marketing Research Society (www.mrs.org.uk)
- The American Insights Association, formed by the merger of the MRA and CASRO in 2017 (https://www.insightsassociation.org/issues-policies/insights-association-code-standards-and-ethics-market-research-and-data-analytics-0)
- The Canadian Research Insights Council (https://www.canadianresearchinsightscouncil.ca/home/)

a. Provide an opt-out e-mail address and toll-free number: Emails must contain a free opt-out mechanism for removal from lists. This is a legal requirement in many jurisdictions. Ideally, this should be a one-click system such that the person does not have to re-enter their email address or write a separate email.
b. Industry affiliations and ethics standards: A great deal of comfort comes from affiliation with a national or international industry group with a broader mission for ethical standards and the enforcement of those standards. If your company or department is a member of such an industry association, we recommend that you provide the name of the organization (with a hyperlink) in your invitation, and within your e-mail invitation:

When contacting a potential respondent by phone or in-person, many of these principles are also relevant. Initial contact for phone surveys is often a 'cold call' so the initial 5 to 10 seconds is crucial to get a potential respondent into the survey. Careful attention to wording is critical. Some principles might include:

- Explain the purpose of the call immediately (to conduct a survey) and expected length (don't ask someone how they are today)

- Identify the research organization by name
- Promise that you will not try to sell them anything
- Assure confidentiality
- Offer a phone number they could call to verify the validity of the survey
- Mention any incentive

If the respondent is still on the line, additional information can be provided as per the questionnaire introduction.

12. When the Study is in Field

Once the questionnaire is finalized and "in field," it's time to wait for the results to come in. But that doesn't mean that there is nothing for the researcher to do. **Quotas** can be tracked to ensure they are filling properly, a **new sample** may have to be ordered if response rates or 'completes' are lower than expected, some **troubleshooting** may be necessary if unexpected problems arise, preliminary data can be pulled to do a **trial data run** or give a client a preliminary glimpse of the results.

More importantly, this is a good time to make plans for the next stages of the project. It's time to:

- create the tab plan,
- order a data file (e.g., SPSS, SAS, R or Python),
- map out any modelling or advanced analysis that the marketing science will need to do,
- prepare the report template,
- write the background and objectives sections for the report, and
- begin story-boarding the full report.

How does Data Management Work?

As soon as the study is 'out-of-field' – when the last interview has been completed, and the data collection closes – the data preparation can begin. This is the phase that molds the responses into a form that the researcher can analyze and use to prepare a report.

1. Cleaning the Data / Data Entry

When dealing with **pen-and-paper** questionnaires, a field supervisor will read through each questionnaire, checking that it has been answered correctly and completely and editing for clarity. If important information is missing, the supervisor may choose to call the respondent back to fill in the gap. Questions answered when they should not have been (e.g., skips missed or used incorrectly) will be crossed out.

At the same time, the supervisor will keep an eye out for suspicious response patterns that may suggest an interviewer filled out the questionnaire *without* interviewing a respondent. If she does become suspicious, she can 'validate' by contacting the respondents to ask if they were, in fact, interviewed. Names and phone numbers are collected in pen-and-paper questionnaires specifically for this purpose.

Once a questionnaire is 'clean,' data entry clerks enter the results into the data program. This can be a significant source of error in marketing research, so quality control is an important consideration. Questionnaires may be 'double entered' (entered twice) to help identify a 'misplaced' entry.

In **programmed** or **digital questionnaires**, the interviewers or respondents are entering their own data as they respond to questions. If the questionnaire programming is flawless, the data should be clean. Spot checks and a careful eye on logic is still necessary, but cleaning is much less important and the potential source of errors that data entry may present has been eliminated.

2. Coding Open Ends

Computer tabulation of data requires that all responses be numerical rather than verbal (except when verbatim responses are all that is needed). As a result, most questions are "pre-coded" – meaning that the researcher will create a list of anticipated responses and assign a number to each response.

What is your favourite hot drink? (Select one only.)

○ Coffee
○ Tea
○ Hot chocolate

The responses are pre-coded, and the response of "tea" is entered into the database as a "2".

Although most questions will have pre-coded answers, there are some situations in which pre-coding is either not efficient or not possible. These are:

When There are Too Many Alternatives

In an automotive survey, we may need to know the make, model, and year of the car driven by the respondent. There are hundreds of possibilities, many of which may never be selected in any one survey. Precoding all possible combinations is difficult and cumbersome. Imagine how time-consuming it would be for a person-to-person interviewer to scroll through the makes and models to find the correct answer. It would be better to record the make, model simply, and year of the car on the questionnaire and code (i.e., assign a numeric value to each response) later.

On a questionnaire, it would look like this:

What is the make of your car? [ ]

What is the model of your car? [ ]

What is the year of the car you drive? [ ]

Where a Few Alternatives Dominate

Where a few possible responses are expected to dominate, even if the list is relatively long, we may want to pre-code the dominant responses and then wait to code the lesser-known alternatives later.

For example, we'd see this type of question with a reduced coding task:

What is your favourite soft drink? (Select one only.)
- ○ Coke
- ○ Pepsi
- ○ Dr. Pepper
- ○ 7-Up
- ○ Other (Please specify.) [ ]

If we assume that most of the respondents will choose Coke, Pepsi, Dr. Pepper, or 7 UP, then we will already have pre-coded most responses. This not only makes the recording of answers easy, but it also minimizes the amount of coding that will be required. We ask that they be specified because we do expect a few additional brands to emerge with significant counts. The risk with this 'partial open-end' is that lazy respondents will choose one of the pre-coded options rather than make an effort to write in their true answer.

Where the Answers are Unanticipated

In more exploratory work, there are times when we don't know how respondents are going to answer. These would be true open-ended questions that allow us to hear the 'why's behind consumer opinions' without prompting or biasing from us.

For example, an open-end might ask:
- <u>Why</u> is tea, your favourite drink?
- What do you <u>like most</u> about the car you drive?
- What is the <u>most important issue</u> facing your country today?

Because the potential responses are so broad and generally unknown, the question is asked as an open-end, responses are recorded verbatim and then coded later.

The actual coding process starts with the question verbatims – the full responses provided by the respondents, written on paper, typed into an online questionnaire, captured by the interviewers or by an audio/video download application. Those responses may be sent directly to the coding team, but increasingly they are initially processed by an artificial intelligence platform that quickly finds themes in the word and phrase patterns. AI does this by 'learning' how coding has been done in the past, so it may not anticipate the needs of the client or the researcher on a specific study. The human filter is still required.

Traditionally, with a pen-and-paper survey, the actual paper questionnaires might arrive before data entry takes place, and the coders write the actual 'codes' onto the questionnaire for the data entry clerks. Alternatively, the data entry team may have typed the actual, full verbatim response into the database, and this database is sent to the coders.

With a digital survey (online/web-based), the verbatim responses are already in the database, entered by the respondent or interviewer.

As the responses are being are being reviewed, a **coding manual** is created.

The researcher may already have a series of codes that are to be used, based on past studies or the client's objectives, and would give the coding team this list before they start their work. If there are no anticipated codes, the researcher may leave it to the coding team to propose an approach.

A senior coder looks through a limited number of responses to each open-ended question looking for response patterns and develops a list of potential codes that could be used. These are shown to the researcher for approval. The researcher will want to ensure that the codes will be helpful in meeting the client's objectives and may choose to combine codes, relabel them or break some apart into more detailed breaks.

For example, if the open-ended question was "Why is tea your favourite drink?", the responses may begin to show common references to:

- Like the taste
- Less expensive than other hot drinks
- Lower caffeine
- Has anti-oxidants
- Healthier than alternatives
- Hydrating
- Reviving
- Calming
- Habit
- What my family has always had
- Other

The researcher may decide to combine 'lower caffeine,' 'anti-oxidants,' and 'healthier than alternatives' into one code labelled 'healthier' and might relabel 'what my family has always had' as 'tradition.'

The preparation of this initial coding manual is one that can be shifted to artificial intelligence, but it must still be reviewed and adjusted by a human researcher to ensure it is focused on the clients' needs.

Once the coding manual has been finalized and the researcher signs off on it, the coding team gets to work coding the open-ended responses across all completed questionnaires.

Throughout the coding process, answers that would have gone into 'other' may begin to show interesting patterns, and new codes are added to the manual. Once the coding has been completed, the data is ready for processing.

3. Data Processing (DP)

The first step in processing the data is to evaluate the **quality** of data. This can be particularly important in the case of self-completion interviews where no interviewers or supervisors were present to keep an eye on consistency and check quality. Data quality checks may not be a separate part of the process but will certainly be built into the tabulation of the data.

The data processing team 'tabulates' the data – turning raw data into 'tables' - following instructions provided by the researcher in a **tabulation plan**. This is a document that outlines how the data is to be organized into computer tables that the researcher uses to write the report.

The tabulation plan may ask that the data be **weighted**. The results should reflect the intended population profile and correct for differing response rates among subgroups of respondents.

For example, women may be more likely to participate in a survey than men. If the final sample is to be 50% male and 50% female to reflect the true balance in the population, and if the lower response rate among men means that only 40% of the final sample are male, they should be 'weighted up,' meaning each individual male respondent is given a weight of 1.25 in the data (.40 x 1.25 = .50) and each female respondent is given a weight of .834 (.6 x .8334 = .50).

Weighting is often applied for sex, age and region and less often for education or income. In some countries, 'social class' weights combine education and income. It can also be applied for other household characteristics (e.g. presence of children) and behaviour (e.g. brand users) if a target weight is known.

The **target weight**s are generally sourced from a reliable profile of the target population – most often government census data.

In the tab plan, the researcher will also specify what breaks they want in the data. Generally, each table will start with a 'total' column. Common **demographic breaks** include:
- Region (specific to the country)
- Gender identity: male, female, other
- Age group: generally 3 or 4 groupings (e.g. 18 – 29, 30 – 45, 46 – 64, 65+)
- Household composition: 1, 2 or more adults, presence of children
- Education achieved: primary, secondary, university
- Employment status: student, working full time, working part-time, retired, stay at home full time
- Income level: generally 2 to 4 groupings

Depending on the country, the plan may also ask for language spoken at home, race or ethnicity, social class, urban/rural or community size and marital status. What is important is that these breaks be generated only if they help target a useful sub-population with marketing communications.

Behavioural or **affiliation breaks** specific to the study can also be included in the tab plan. Depending on the topic of the study, these might include:
- Heavy, moderate, light category users
- Brand used most often, current or lapsed users
- Decision maker/influencer
- Organization membership
- Program participation
- Homeownership, etc.

Finally, there are opportunities to specify **cross-tabulations** between questions within the survey in the tab plan. These might include:
- Simple cross tabs between two questions, for example:
    - Frequency of usage of different over-the-counter pain remedies, cross-tabulated by the type of pain suffered
    - How long until the next anticipated car purchase, cross-tabulated by the current make of car owned
    - Opinion of proposed government policy, cross-tabulated with the party voted for in the last election
- Breaks for any consumer segments that emerge through modelling or by combining the results of multiple questions

Traditionally, the study results are tabulated so that each response code is listed down the left side (known as "the **stub**"), and subgroups or 'breaks' are listed across the top (known as "the **banner**").

If you are doing a project on your own, then you would export the data into an Excel format or into a format suitable for the computer program that you are likely to use to analyze the data, such as SPSS. Software such as SPSS will allow you to prepare your own data tables.

It is important, once the data tables are received, to **check their accuracy**. The data processing team will have done their best to ensure quality, but the researcher should undertake a few quick checks before beginning the analysis.

For example: Compare the stubs in the demographic section with the banner points that are derived from those demographic questions. Are the gender identity, income, education and region breaks all falling into alignment?
- If the banner shows 300 completed high school, 250 have undergraduate degrees, and 50 have post-graduate degrees, go to the table for the question that asked about education and look at those banner points. Are 100% of those who offered each of these answers in the right column? Continue investigating from the basic frequency distributions through several of the crosstabs.

Are the sample sizes in the tables for any questions that were asked only of a sub-group of the population correct?
- Check the frequencies in the questions that led to the 'streaming' in the questionnaire. If a question separates people who travel to work by car, by public transit, or under their own power (walking, cycling), and 500 people identified 'transit' as their mode of travel,

make sure that the sample size for follow up questions about transit (have to transfer? Buy a monthly pass?) have the same 500 sample.

Once the data tables are received and have been quality checked, the researcher's work kicks into high gear again. All the work up until this point—designing the questionnaire, choosing a sample, carrying out the fieldwork, and producing computer tables—are a prelude to the task of understanding what consumers say and what impact it has on marketing decisions.

The first step toward understanding the consumers is data analysis, which will be covered in the next chapter.

What are the Principles and Best Practices?

1. Respect

An absolutely key part of the researcher's role during the fieldwork phase is to ensure that we respect the respondents and the role they play in our profession. Without their active involvement, we would not be able to provide the insights that our clients need to make effective marketing decisions. In this era of rampant identity theft, the public's trust is particularly fragile.

Many of the professional marketing research associations and societies around the world have prepared guidelines in their codes of conduct covering our responsibilities to our respondents. One good example comes from ESOMAR and followed by MRIA and CRIC also. Their code is based on three fundamental principles:

i. When collecting personal data from data subjects for research, researchers must be transparent about the information they plan to collect, the purpose for which it will be collected, with whom it might be shared and in what form.

ii. Researchers must ensure that personal data used in research is thoroughly protected from unauthorized access and not disclosed without the consent of the data subject.

iii. Researchers must always behave ethically and not do anything that might harm a data subject or damage the reputation of market, opinion and social research industries.

The articles in marketing research codes of conduct cover our responsibilities to our data subjects (respondents), to our clients, to the general public and to our own profession. Those documents, and others like it in your jurisdiction, should be required reading for all professional researchers, at regular intervals during their career.

The full ESOMAR text can be found at this link: https://www.esomar.org/uploads/public/knowledge-and-standards/codes-and-guidelines/ICCE-SOMAR_Code_English_.pdf. The CRIC standards are at this link: https://canadianresearchinsightscouncil.ca/standards/por/.

2. Confidentiality

One of the primary responsibilities we have as researchers is the maintenance of our *respondents'* and our *clients'* right to security, confidentiality and anonymity.

Protection of confidentiality and privacy is very important in marketing research. Although the professional regulations do not and cannot cover every possible contingency, the rules are near-universal in their applicability and must be followed.[4]

The **client's identity** should not be disclosed to anyone unless prescribed by the client. On some occasions, it might seem to the field staff that the client's identity is obvious. However, this assumption is often incorrect, and no information should be provided to a respondent that is not specified in the questionnaire or in the interviewer manual.

In a *personal interview* situation, the interviewer shouldn't know the client's identity to avoid any conscious or subconscious biasing. The interviewers can honestly say that they do not know when asked.

Maintaining a client's anonymity is important because:
- the information may reach a competitor, and the client may not want this to happen;
- the respondent may intentionally or unintentionally alter his or her response depending on who the client is; and
- the information may reflect poorly on the marketing research company.

Equally important is protecting the **respondent's identity**. Participation in research is entirely voluntary, and those who are interviewed must be made to feel comfortable and free to express their honest opinions without fear that any personally identifiable information (e.g., name, address, contact information) will be released. All information given by a respondent is held in confidence between the respondent and the marketing research company. No one other than those who have a legitimate reason to see it (e.g., interviewer, coder, data entry team) will have access to any individual respondent's replies.

Clients may be allowed to review a live link to a digital survey and see 'preliminary' data downloaded from portals, or they may be allowed to listen in on phone interviews remotely. In either case, steps must be taken to ensure they cannot see or hear any personal information that may identify individual respondents.

Clients are also to be discouraged from 'dropping in' on telephone or face-to-face interviewing when it is in progress because:
- there may be other studies underway for other clients and the confidentiality of those studies must be respected;
- the respondents' identities may be revealed in an interview; and
- interviewers or respondents may recognize the client or determine their identity (logos on clothing are common).

Clients may occasionally want to access respondents to ask follow-up questions or for such non-research purposes as educating them (to change their opinion or behaviour), or to offer a product or service or to use their responses as testimonials. This is <u>not</u> the purpose of research and, in many jurisdictions, violates codes of conduct and privacy legislation.

---

[4] There might be situations in which other considerations may override the confidentiality rule. Such conditions could include slander, legal issues, or other deeper ethical issues. It is a good policy to assume that stated professional rules are applicable under all conditions. Should a truly unusual situation arise, it is a good idea to seek the applicability of the code of conduct to the situation.

Clients can be given data tables and a report that shows the results in aggregate – so no individual responses are identified. Rarely would a client see (or want to see) the individual completed questionnaires. Should a client request to see the actual completed questionnaires, personally identifiable information such as names, phone numbers, or e-mail addresses should be removed and replaced with an ID number.

An interviewer must not reveal to anyone except the field staff what an individual said during the course of an interview. Each interviewer is responsible for the confidentiality of the respondents they interview.

The only circumstances in which re-contact is possible is when the respondent is explicitly asked permission to do so and provided with the reasons (e.g., to ask additional questions) in the initial interview by the research company. This is deemed to be the case if the respondent is part of a recruited research panel and therefore has agreed to be contacted multiple times to participate in research.

3. Unethical Practices

Sugging (selling under the guise of research), **Frugging** (fund-raising under the guise of research), **Push Polling** (using the flow of questions and information introduced in question-wording to change respondents' opinions) are all considered unethical and should never be undertaken by a professional researcher. **Lead generation**, while perfectly legal and ethical, is not a marketing research function and should never be included in a marketing research study.

Here are some examples of these code violations:

- **Sugging.** Consumers are invited to participate in a survey on water quality and are asked for their reactions to a long list of contaminants frequently found in city drinking water. The survey leads to a 'concept' description of a residential water filtration kit and a hard sell sales pitch based on the participants' obvious concern about what they are drinking.

- **Frugging.** An animal rights charity mails out a survey questionnaire to its mailing list of current and past donors and prospects, asking for their input in this 'important research.' The questionnaire asks a series of questions to elicit opinions on how important animals are in their lives, and how they would react to scenarios of mistreatment. At the end of the questionnaire is a pitch for donations. The opinions are never aggregated and analyzed; the sole purpose of the questionnaire is to put participants in a frame of mind to donate willingly.

- **Lead generation.** The phone rings at dinner time, and the voice on the other end asks permission to conduct a survey on travel habits for an important national survey. The questionnaire elicits behavioural information about past travel patterns, future travel plans and household characteristics, and the participant is thanked for their input. It seems very legitimate. But a week later, the phone rings again. This time it is a travel company offering the household a special deal on a cruise. The offer seems tailor-made to the interests of the household, clearly based on the results of the previous call.

4. Quality Control

When dealing with **digital, self-completion questionnaires**, quality control focuses on the programming of the research instrument. The specific quality control measures that can be taken include:

- "Swivel-chair" pre-testing – running through the pre-programmed version of the questionnaire as if you were a respondent, perhaps reading it aloud to a colleague. Hearing the questions can reveal problems that are not evident when you run through them in your head.
- Link testing – once it is programmed, running through live versions of the questionnaire (following invitation 'links'), role-playing every possible scenario to ensure the right questions come up when required and that all potential response patterns are accounted for.
- Soft launch – releasing invitations to participate to a small proportion of the sample a day or two before the actual launch to ensure the data is being collected as required. If adjustments are required, they can be made before the full launch, and only a small portion of the sample is "lost." If no adjustments are required, the soft launch data can be added to the completed surveys.
- Monitoring returns – involves downloading the data at intervals during fieldwork to check quotas and responses to designated questions. If they are not coming in as expected, an investigation can be conducted and, if necessary, adjustments made and replacement sample added.

Some research firms have formalized the quality control function – with a separate team reviewing all programming created by the scripters to ensure logic and functionality. Whether formalized or not, the most beneficial step is to have a second set of eyes review the questionnaire before it goes to programming and to test the links before it goes to field. The author of a questionnaire knows the intent of the questions and may not see potential flaws that a fresh perspective would uncover.

Quality control has another dimension when **interviewers** are involved. In that case, interviews are either *monitored* as they occur or *verified* after the fact.

5. Monitoring

With telephone surveys, field supervisors continually **monitor** interviewers to ensure they are doing their jobs properly. In central location facilities, this involves listening in on the interviews on a muted connection and watching on a separate monitor to see how the responses are entered into the Computer Assisted Telephone Interviewing (CATI) program. Monitoring is often conducted from an adjoining room, but remote monitoring is also generally possible – from any phone anywhere.

Industry standards suggest how many of each interviewer's interactions are to be monitored (e.g., 10 percent). If a particular interviewer is experiencing problems, then all or most of their interviews should be monitored. If problems persist, the interviewer should be retrained or fired.

6. Verification

When monitoring interviews is not possible, **post-interview verification** becomes the primary quality control measure. In this situation, a supervisor will call back a respondent to make sure the interview was actually conducted. Verification includes the following three steps:

1. **Obtaining the Respondent's Permission.** During the normal interviewing process, each respondent is asked for his or her name and telephone number so that a verification call can be made. The phone number is requested even if the interview was conducted by telephone in case the number was dialed incorrectly or was 'call forwarded' to another number or is not the best number to reach them on. Today, many people have work, home and a cell number or two. A typical request might be worded as follows:

My supervisor may want to call you to verify that I conducted this interview. At what phone number can you usually be reached?

Or

My supervisor might have to check over some of my work. So, she can do that, would you please give me your name and the phone number to reach you on?

At the end of each interview, the interviewer is to sign a statement certifying: "that this interview was conducted according to the questionnaire and the instructions for this study, and that the answers recorded are as given to me by this respondent. I also realize that a proportion of my work will be checked for verification."

2. **Verifying the Interviews.** Respondents selected for verification (a proportion of *each* interviewer's work) are called back by a supervisor or a separate team of senior interviewers. They are asked (a) if the interview was actually carried out, and (b) if the interviewer was professional and polite. A few questions from the survey may be repeated to make sure all the questions were asked, and all the answers recorded properly.

3. **Reconciling the Records.** The verified interviews for each interviewer are reconciled with the original interviews. If problems are identified, the likely causes are recorded and followed up with the interviewer as soon as possible.

7. Maintaining the Schedule

There are many moving parts to a survey, and careful scheduling and tracking are required to ensure each stage happens when it must and that none begin until the previous stage is properly concluded.

Each project is different. It is crucial to build a "Critical Path" that sets deadlines for all phases. The critical path ensures that the assumptions are visible to all stakeholders and ensures discussion and corrections can take place at the beginning of the process rather than when the project is already off track.

The researcher creates this 'critical path' with the input and co-operation of the field manager and the directors of other key functions – field preparation, sample selection and preparation, pre-testing, questionnaire scripting and testing, translation, data cleaning, data entry, coding, data processing, analysis and modelling. Once the questionnaire is ready for field, the field director has to ensure that all these operations are executed within the agreed-to timelines.

The researcher must check on progress throughout the process, questioning any delays, finding solutions to problems that arise, and, if necessary, reporting scheduling issues back to the client with notes on implications and possible solutions.

For example, consider the following.

A project is in field with a 25-minute questionnaire to be completed with mothers of very young children. It's a well-constructed questionnaire, a clearly defined and identifiable target group, and a standard timeline for fieldwork to be completed. However, returns are coming in much slower than expected. After the first few days, only half of the expected completions have happened.

The field manager decides to contact a few of the respondents who clicked through to the survey, but either didn't start or didn't complete the questionnaire. She determines that the 25-minute length, clearly spelled out in the introduction, meant that they had decided to put it aside for a time when they knew they would have 25 uninterrupted minutes. In a very busy young mother's life, those free periods of time are hard to find.

The researcher is informed. He decides, with the client, to cut a lower priority section from the questionnaire and reduce the length to 20 minutes. They also decide to increase the incentive. The next day, returns start to come in at the expected rate.

Scheduling is an important project management role, and the techniques used varied and well documented.

8. Monitoring Response Rates

It is important to *monitor* survey operations and to evaluate the data collection methodology as it takes place. One way to do this is to track response rates – the cumulative proportion of respondents who agree to participate are not dropped off at each phase of screening and complete the full interview. Each of these phases is important.

> The higher the proportion of those targeted who agree to participate, the greater the chance that the final sample will reflect the full target population. This often pertains to:
> - the quality of the panel or sample source, their past experience with completing surveys as part of this panel and the incentives offered;
> - the quality and tone of the approach/invitation;
> - the incentive offered; and
> - the task required.
>
> Tracking the proportion who **drop off at each phase of screening** will ensure that the final results can, if desired, be projected back to incidence levels within the full population. The higher the proportion making it to the end of the survey without abandoning, the more likely the final sample is to reflect the behaviour and opinions of the target population. Completion is impacted by:
> The relevance of the topic to each individual respondent;
> The quality of the questionnaire design (readability, appropriateness, ensuring each question has a response for every respondent, etc.);
> The length; and
> The complexity of the tasks demanded.

If each of these steps in the process is reasonable and appropriate, we can consider the basic principles and best practices "covered."

What the Interviewers Should Know

Training Principles

The key interface between a researcher and a respondent in a self-completion environment is the questionnaire – which can be tested and re-tested to minimize the risk of misunderstanding. However, in interviewer-administered surveys, an intermediary is introduced over which we have less control. Not even a brilliant research design or sophisticated interpretation of results can compensate for incompetent interviewing.

In these situations, interviewers are the eyes and ears of marketing research. It is their job to make the respondents understand what is needed from them, to ask the questions properly and to report accurately, without bias or personal opinions, the respondents' answers.

When an interviewer is **first hired**, she or he is usually trained by a supervisor on the <u>general principles of interviewing</u>. This may involve some role-playing to help recognize scenarios that might arise and how to handle them. Examples cover how to handle difficult respondents, how to identify a respondent who is 'playing' and not providing appropriate answers, what techniques to use to keep a respondent engaged, what an appropriate speaking tone and speed sound like, etc.

Then, just **before a study goes into field**, the interviewers are instructed on what to do and what not to do (e.g., whether to probe or not probe, to clarify or not clarify, which codes to read and which to leave as 'volunteered') for the <u>particular questionnaire</u> that they are using. At this stage, training would include "dry runs" in which the interviewers interview each other to develop a level of comfort with the questions and response options and to spot any potential problems.

When a new interviewer starts to interview, he or she is generally closely monitored so that any potential problems can be spotted quickly and remedial training provided. On-the-job training ensures interviewers have the skills they need to succeed.

Each study is different in some way, even the most routine tracking programs, so **continual monitoring** is the norm. Even experienced interviewers can have 'off days,' so everyone is monitored at least 10 percent of the time to ensure high quality.

Here are some <u>**principles**</u> that need to be covered in interviewer training and recognized during monitoring.

1. Interview as a 'Live' Exchange

Interviewing is more an artistic activity, like acting, than a mechanical or scientific activity. It is the art of carrying on a structured conversation that is recorded after each verbal exchange. While most theatre audiences do not participate in the performance, a respondent's answers during an interview are needed to complete the script that the interviewer speaks.

Every respondent is different. They may not understand the words in the question the same way it was intended or may not grasp the overall intent of the question. They may be distracted, hard of hearing, or simply need a little more time to absorb what is being asked.

Interviewers must:
- be able to think on their feet;
- listen to themselves as well as to the respondents;
- be capable of self-discipline; and
- have the ability to adjust to many different types of respondents.

After a half-dozen repetitions of the questionnaire, interviewers can too easily switch into 'auto-pilot.' We might see them:
- increase their reading speed;
- lose any emphasis in their voices and fall into an uninteresting monotone;
- automatically record the first impression they get from the respondent without listening to everything said;
- alter what they hear, so it fits easily into a popular response code, rather than listening for important nuance;
- 'push' a reticent or slower respondent to answer faster rather than carefully consider their answers; and
- even suggest responses to respondents in the interest of completing the interview quickly.

Interviewers should read each question as if it is being read for the first time, using an interested and energetic tone and making it sound conversational rather than mechanical.

Target populations and interviewing staff can be very diverse. The language of the interview may not be the first language of either player. Some respondents may be older, hard of hearing or dealing with background noise. In _any_ interview, it is crucial to enunciate carefully and ensure each respondent has the time he or she needs to absorb the meaning of the question.

Of course, it is a fine line between adapting an interviewing style to each respondent and biasing the interview with unnecessary emphasis or added explanation.

2. Understanding the Intent

Competent interviewers are trained to use judgment that is based on both a thorough understanding of the *interviewing function* and of the project questions. The competent interviewer should be able to answer the following questions for each project:
- Do I understand **why** I'm asking this question?
- Do I understand the **meaning** of this question, that is, the type of information I'm seeking?
- Do I understand why I am asking the questions in this **order**?
- Do I understand how all of these **questions fit together** to make a meaningful interview?

Interviewers who understand the questionnaire and the nature of the project conduct more effective interviews.

3. Understanding the Respondent's Mindset

Even though the interviewer asks the same question in the same way in each interview, respondents may hear different things. An experienced interviewer will know the following to be true:
- Respondents have different frames of reference from that of the interviewer.
- The same word may mean different things to different people.
- Respondents may try to please the interviewer by giving the answers they think he or she wants to hear.
- Respondents have pride and do not want to give the incorrect answer, so they may intentionally misunderstand the question rather than give a 'wrong' answer.
- Respondents may not want to appear uninformed, so they may make up answers rather than admit that they don't have one.
- Respondents may want to get rid of the interviewer and will say almost anything to be let off the hook.
- Respondents may lose interest in the interview and start to answer mechanically without much thought.
- Respondents are sometimes confused by survey questions and guess at answers rather than seeking clarification.

A key element of success is **building trust** with each respondent. This will allow the respondent to open up and provide more honest and detailed responses. A good interviewer would acknowledge and anticipate the respondents' mindsets, striving to build rapport in each interview by:
- Being sensitive to the **verbal** (or visual) **cues** from respondents at the beginning of the interview;
- Adapting speaking **speed** and **enunciation** to suit the respondent's listening and comprehension skills – but never changing the language;
- **Actively listening,** so the respondent feels that their response is valued;
- Providing **feedback to the field supervisor** if comprehension issues are surfacing consistently; and
- Making the effort to **record responses** as **accurately** and in as much detail as possible.

The personal connection that is created during the interview – primarily by showing respect for the respondent – goes a long way to improving the quality of the experience for both parties, and ultimately, the quality of the data collected.

4. Correctly Asking Closed-ended Questions and Recording responses

In a structured interview, *closed*-ended questions provide the response codes that a respondent is to choose from. The interviewer must simply read the question clearly, with the right pacing, without skipping or adding words and record the response accurately.

The questionnaire will indicate whether all, some, or none of the response options are to be read out loud. Because all the options are provided, there should be little chance for misinterpretation. The respondent is *only* allowed to choose one or several of the pre-coded responses or say that he/she does not know the answer or refuse to answer. Interviewers should make sure respondents hear *all* the response options before choosing one.

There are differences of opinion around the inclusion of "don't know" and "refuse" options on a questionnaire.

- Some researchers feel that there must be a space in a pre-coded question for any possible, reasonable answer. If someone says they don't have a response, there should be a place on the questionnaire to record this.
- Others feel that providing a "don't know" code allows the interviewer to accept a *lazy* response without at least trying to elicit a thoughtful or true opinion. Sometimes two or three specific probing questions are used by the interviewer to elicit a response before recording "don't know."

There is no clear-cut best practice on this issue. The general practice is to have "don't know" available as a response code, whether it is offered to the respondent by reading it aloud or not.

5. Correctly Asking Open-ended Questions

Open-ended questions do not have pre-coded responses. The interviewer must read the question with great care and accurately capture the true essence of what the respondent says, without interpretation. A clumsy or unskilled interviewer will undermine the integrity of the survey results.

Here are some interview guidelines for open-ended questions that should be part of any interviewer training:

Reading Accurately and Consistently

Interviewers should read the questions word for word as they are written, without variation from interview to interview. If the respondent does not seem to understand a question, it should be repeated exactly as it was written on the questionnaire. If the respondent says, "What do they mean by...?, the reply should be, "Whatever you think it means." Or "Whatever it means to you."

Interviewers must make no changes in the phrasing and must not add, skip or change any words even if it seems to make the question clearer. Every respondent must hear the same question-wording.

Example
a. Question read as worded
Question:
Where do you get the majority of your news about current events in this country—from social media, internet news sites, the radio, newspapers, TV, or talking to people?
Response:
TV

If the question is not read out as it is printed on the questionnaire, the respondent may provide answers that do not coincide with any of the pre-coded choices.

b. Question with the list of choices omitted

Question: *Where do you get the majority of your news about current events in this country?*

Response: *From others*

c. Question with 'current events' omitted

Question: *Where do you get the majority of your news— social media, internet news sites, the radio, newspapers, TV, or talking to people?*

Response: *Depends if it's celebrity news, industry news, or just current, local stuff.*

c.   Question 'interpreted' by the interviewer

Question: *Where do you get the majority of your news about current events in this country – social media, internet news sites, the radio, newspapers, TV, or talking to people? That is, which one do you rely on the most?*

Response: I think the newspapers are the most accurate

By changing the wording of a question, the current respondent may be answering a different question than all the other respondents of the survey. The information given by that respondent, therefore, is worthless.

Using Consistent Tone and Emphasis

The tone and emphasis of the interviewer's voice should be absolutely matter of fact with no indication of feelings or opinions about the question or the expected answer. The interviewers are to be impartial recorders of opinions.

Example (Impact of emphasis)
Question: Do you think the United Nations is doing all it can to help keep peace in the world, or not?

If interviewers use a very **even**, **matter-of-fact tone** with every respondent when reading the **question**, a consistent and more accurate range of responses should be the result. However, a slight change in inflection can change response patterns. If the word "*all*" is emphasized, a higher than normal percentage of negative responses might result because it is setting an 'absolute' goal. If "*United Nations*" is stressed, it is likely to elicit a higher percentage of positive answers because they are comparing it to other organizations.

When reading a list of **potential responses**, the interviewer must maintain an even voice tonality throughout. Otherwise, an emphasis on one of them might suggest an answer the interviewer wants to hear and would bias the response. The interviewer must also read the **complete list** of possible answers even if the respondent indicates an answer partway through.

Not Assuming Responses

Sometimes a respondent will offer a detailed and lengthy answer that seems to cover several questions in the survey. However, it is the interviewer's responsibility to ask each question even if it seems some points are being repeated. In the context of the questionnaire flow and response options for each question, the actual responses may be different than what the interviewer felt they heard earlier.

6. Probing and Clarifying Open-ended Questions

Open-ended questions allow the respondent to provide a complete and rich answer to the question. They can reveal respondents' thoughts much better than can closed-ended questions. But because there is no structure for responding, there can be a great deal of variation in information provided. In some interviews, respondents will go to great lengths to answer the question and then to explain or justify their answers. In other cases, answers may be cryptic and uninformative.

Answers to open-ended questions are recorded in the questionnaire exactly as the respondent phrases them (i.e., verbatim). By their very nature, open-ended questions are answered *in the words of the respondents*. Unfortunately, not all respondents provide *complete* answers. Some open-ended questions contain additional instructions to probe for more detail or to ask for clarification. This should allow the respondent to communicate more fully about how they feel or what they know, i.e., to turn a general response into a detailed response.

Probing is the technique of asking "What else?" until the interviewer feels that he or she has the respondent's complete answer, or of asking the respondent for *more* answers until she indicates that there is nothing more to add. For example:

Question:	What do you like about this cheese?
1st answer:	It tastes good.
Probe:	What else do you like about this cheese?
2nd answer:	It doesn't cost a lot.
Probe:	What else do you like about this cheese?
3rd answer:	The package is easy to open because it has the zip-open strip
Last Probe:	What else do you like about it?
4th answer:	That's about it.

Some examples of general probe questions are:
- What else?
- Please tell me more.

- What other reasons?
- Any other reason? (This probe should be used only at the very end because it tends to solicit a "no other reasons" response.)

Clarification is the technique of asking a respondent to explain an answer, previously given, in greater detail. The interviewer wants to know specifically what the respondent meant by an answer. It is necessary to make the respondent's answers more precise so that they can be used for marketing input.

Question:	What do you like about this cheese?
1st answer:	It tastes good.
Clarification:	What do you mean by "It tastes good"?
2nd answer:	I like the taste of this cheese. It's just the way I like it.
Clarification:	What do you mean "it's just the way I like it"?
3rd answer:	It has just the right amount of salt in it.

An interview with a different respondent might proceed as follows:

Question:	What do you like about this cheese?
1st answer:	It's good.
Clarification:	What do you mean by "good"?
2nd answer:	It tastes good.
Clarification:	It tastes good in what way?
3rd answer:	It tastes smooth, not biting and has a nutty flavour.

From a general answer, "It's good," the interviewer has been able to extract a specific answer "tastes smooth, not biting" and "has a nutty flavour" by requesting clarification.

Respondents wouldn't realize that "It is good," "I like it," or "It's a nice idea," can mean different things to different people, the interviewer will need to ask for clarification to make respondents' opinions useable.

Only neutral, unbiased questions should be used when clarifying. Interviewers should **never suggest answers** to the respondent because those will almost always be played back by the subject as her or his own answer. Respondents want to be helpful and might formulate an answer that they feel will please the interviewer. However, we need the respondent's answers, not the interviewer's interpretation of the respondent's thoughts.

Examples of neutral probing questions are:
- What do you mean by that?

- Why do you say that?
- What are your reasons for saying that?
- How do you mean [*repeat respondent's exact words*]?
- In what way would it be [*repeat respondent's exact words*]?
- How did you notice it was [*repeat respondent's exact words*]?
- Please describe what you mean by [*repeat respondent's exact words*].

Why, what, when, where, and how should be used in the same manner as they would be by a newspaper reporter trying to get the details of a news story or by a detective trying to pick up clues about a crime.

What follows are two examples of how to probe *and* clarify using two different techniques. The first is to clear up incomplete answers before asking probing questions.

Question: What did you dislike about your new [Brand M] automobile?

Respondent: I don't know. It's really terrible.

(Too general; she has not told you anything specific.)

Clarification: What do you mean by "it's really terrible"?

Respondent: It sounds like an old tin truck.

(Better, but still not detailed enough.)

Clarification: In what way does it "sound like an old tin truck"?

Respondent: It rattles a lot and is very noisy.

(Good, now you have some specific details, move on to probe)

Probe: What else do you dislike about your new [Brand M] automobile?

(Asking for more answers to the original question.)

Respondent: Nothing else.

(Stop probing because the respondent has stated all her reasons.)

The second way is to ask all the probing questions before clarifying any incomplete answers.

Question: What did you dislike about your new Brand M automobile?

Respondent: I don't know. It's really terrible.

Probe: What else do you dislike about your new Brand M automobile?

Respondent: Nothing else.

Clarification: What do you mean "It's really terrible"?

(Go back to clarify the incomplete answer.)

Respondent: It sounds like an old tin truck.

Clarification: In what way does it sound like an old tin truck?

Respondent: It rattles a lot and is very noisy.

Interviewers cannot take it upon themselves to probe or clarify an open-ended response. If it is required, they should be specifically directed to do so on the questionnaire or instructed to do so during the briefing meeting. If you, as a researcher, want a question probed or clarified, you should make sure that your instructions appear on the questionnaire itself, next to the appropriate question. Remember, instructions to interviewers should appear in capital letters.

Probes and clarifications introduce an element of risk into the interview because they can be leading and introduce bias if worded inappropriately. Respondents may feel they have to make something up to please the interviewer to "get them off my back."

Leading questions should not be asked when probing or clarifying since respondents may be led in directions they would not normally take. For example:

Incorrect: You say you don't like it? What is it about the taste that you don't like?

The respondent has not mentioned taste, but the interviewer has steered her towards this. It would have been better to ask:

Correct: You say you don't like it? Why is that?

The interviewer might also take the respondent off track by providing an example when asking for clarification:

Question: How do you think things are going in the world today, specifically our relations with other countries?

Response: Well, I don't know too much about our relations with foreign countries. *(Question has not been answered and requires clarification.)*

Correct Clarification: There are no right or wrong answers on things like this, I'm really just interested in hearing your opinion. *(Repeat the question here.)*

Response: Well, it seems as if most other countries look at us as a constant source of financial and military support.

Leading/Incorrect Clarification:

You mean like in our relations with Latveria?

The respondent will now consider any answer that she might give in terms of our relationship with Latveria, a subject she herself has not mentioned at all but was introduced by the interviewer.

It will be impossible to find out what the respondent really thought about "our relations with other countries" in general. It would have been much better to ask for clarity without an example:

> **Correct Clarification**: Please tell me more about that.

It's also too easy for an interviewer to suggest a response, particularly if he or she feels she senses what the respondent intends to say. For example:

> **Incorrect**: You don't like the taste? Is that because it tastes too strong?
>
> **Correct**: You don't like the taste? What is there about the taste that you don't like?

Here is another example of a 'leading' clarification request:

> **Question**: What was the major *benefit* of buying your [Brand Z] car rather than [Brand Q]?
>
> **Response**: Really, both cars were comparable in style, comfort, gas mileage, and standard factory-installed features.
>
> **Suggestive/Incorrect Clarification**: Do you think the *price* was too high on Brand Q?
>
> **Correct Clarification**: And what do you feel was the major *benefit* of purchasing?

It is considered "leading" if the interviewer puts words into the respondent's mouth. If the respondent does not have an answer, that is still an answer. (Record as "don't know" or "no answer" "DK/NA.")

Here are some more examples:

> **Incorrect**:   You don't like the taste? Oh, you mean the strong taste?
>
> **Correct**:   You don't like the taste? What is it about the taste that you do not like?
>
> **Question**:   What do you like least about your new [Brand T] car?
>
> **Respondent**:   Well, the apple red isn't exactly the shade of red I was expecting from the colour chart.
>
> **Suggestive/Incorrect Clarification:** Oh, I see... You mean the colour red was more like tomato soup red than like apple red?
>
> **Correct Clarification**: What was there about the apple red that was different from the colour chart?

The interviewer should never insert her or his own ideas or otherwise bias the interview. Care must be taken by the interviewer *not to encourage* the respondent with reactions to answers such as "that's good" or "that's right."

Incorrect reaction:	You don't like that taste? I don't either.
Correct reaction:	You don't like that taste… let me record that.
Question:	And what do you dislike about live stream TV?
Response:	There are never any commercials during the movies, so I don't get a chance to raid the refrigerator without missing a part of the plot.
Incorrect reaction:	Oh, I know what you mean. I've solved that by turning the television around so I can see it from the kitchen.

The interviewer must not introduce unrelated information because it will disrupt the respondent's train of thought or bias the answers. The sequence and wording of questions have already been planned for continuity and must remain consistent from interview to interview. Earlier questions have been structured so that they will not affect the respondent's answers to later questions.

Probing is part of the interviewing process where artificial intelligence is making early in-roads. Chatbots can be programmed to ask probing follow-up questions based on the initial response provided by the respondent and on the study's objectives. (See NEXXT Inca example in the Questionnaire Design Unit, How to Use Different Formats, Open-ended Questions).

7. Dealing with Interviewer Embarrassment and Hesitation

Sometimes interviewers can be uncomfortable asking a personal question or interviewing on a **personal topic**. In today's marketing community, manufacturers of very intimate products (e.g., anti-diarrheal products, condoms, yeast infection kits, sexual aids, etc.) need consumer research as much as others. So, studies that ask sensitive personal questions are not uncommon.

Interviewers must be comfortable asking personal questions on these topics exactly as scripted. If they are hesitant in any way, they should be moved off the project. Hesitancy might cause an interviewer to change the emphasis of certain words – dropping their voice to a whisper, for example. That would clearly reveal the interviewer's bias as they communicate their own values to a respondent who may not feel the same way.

Similarly, asking **personal demographic questions** – such as about race, ethnicity, age or income – might embarrass some interviewers. These are very important when grouping respondents together for analysis, and they should be treated as carefully as the rest of the interview. Embarrassment or hesitation about asking these potentially sensitive questions may lead the respondent to refuse to answer.

For example: in an on-going study on racism, an older interviewer told the supervisors that she couldn't say 'this' (pointing to the word 'Jew') out loud because it was a bad word. Had she been allowed to continue the study, she would have certainly introduced a biasing element to the interviews she conducted.

In all cases, carefully worded questions, answers and instructions assure *both* the respondent *and* the interviewer that these questions are being asked to understand groups of people better or to ensure that a wide range of people have participated.

Obtaining and confirming the **respondent's name and contact information** for validation purposes is a requirement of many person-to-person studies. Such procedures also allow incentive prizes to be awarded for all types of studies. The interviewers and the respondents should be assured that this personal information will not be put on a mailing list and that no further contact other than those specified will be made.

Concluding Comments

After the design work covered in earlier chapters, this chapter has walked you through the important tasks of preparing a study for fieldwork. We've

- outlined the various players involved and their responsibilities,
- covered the tasks that need to be undertaken to ensure the fieldwork design is implemented flawlessly,
- touched on data collection, processing and quality control
- covered recognized best practices and ethics governing the logistics of a marketing research study, and
- ended with a section on interviewer training.

With this new knowledge in mind, you should now be ready to participate in fielding a marketing research study. While you have read about principles, processes and several examples, the best learning comes from working alongside experienced practitioners on real studies.

In the units that follow, we will get into greater depth on key marketing research roles and functions.

UNIT 9

How to Analyze the Data

Once the tasks of fieldwork, coding, and tabulation are complete, the data must be analyzed, the findings must be interpreted, insights for better marketing decisions must be drawn from the findings, and those insights must be effectively communicated to the marketing client and decision-makers.

One of the traditional outputs from data analysis has been "stub and banner tables." Those large tables *could* contain hundreds of pages, scores of worksheets, and contain thousands of numbers and percentages. What do you do with them? Stub-and-banner tables are rather old-school but are still used and you need to discern their value.

Marketing analytics and data science have pushed insight-seeking far beyond stub-and-banner tables. What types of information and insights do the client expect, how and where do you start, and where do you finish? This may look intimidating at the beginning. Once we understand the basics, marketing analytics can be fascinating.

In the end, these numbers contain information that can lead to important marketing insights—information and insights that will help tell your clients how to solve their marketing problems and how to exploit marketing opportunities. This chapter begins the journey of understanding how probability and statistics leads into marketing analytics to support better marketing decisions.

What is Numeracy?

As a marketing researcher, you are expected to interpret the information contained in data.
- If 20 percent of the people use your product, what does it mean?
- Is an overall rating of 8.6 on a 10-point scale good or bad?
- If a competitive brand scores an overall average rating of 8.9, should you be worried?

In order to interpret these numbers, marketing researchers make use of the tools of their trade. These tools include prior knowledge, background information, reviews of the literature, insights from experts, knowledge of statistics and understanding how to communicate technical information effectively.

Many people think that they need to be mathematical experts to understand and communicate the implications of data. This is not true. What we need is **numeracy** or a "number sense," **the ability to understand and communicate what numbers mean**.

While mathematics and statistics play a significant role in the interpretation of numbers, it is possible to gain a sophisticated understanding of *numbers* with only a rudimentary knowledge of *statistics*.

Knowledge of basic statistical principles is a prerequisite for any marketing researcher; however, a blind application of statistics may do more harm than good. You must be able to interpret what the statistics are saying. In this unit, we will review the bare minimum of statistics that you need to know. If you want to be a career marketing researcher, you should be comfortable with more than what is covered here. We suggest that you read a good basic book on statistics, marketing analytics and data science and take the corresponding courses, whether online or in-person.

Develop Focal Points

Marketing research data are most commonly presented in data tables produced by some computer program. Quite often, these tables are overwhelming. Because of this, there is a tendency among researchers to go through each table one by one, commenting on any interesting or significant differences. This approach usually results in weak reports.

When each table is looked at individually, there is a tendency to miss significant patterns that may be present in the data. Statistics used in this way will often obscure any possible underlying patterns. Further, because marketing research data tables tend to be voluminous, it may not be possible to summarize all data onto one single page to understand the patterns. The first step in data analysis is to develop focal points.

As an example, let us assume that one of the objectives of your study is to understand the attribute ratings of your brand compared to other brands. This can be your first focal point—understanding the ratings from a broad perspective.

Suppose you have just completed a study in which consumers rated ten stores (A, B, C, ...J) on a 10-point scale on 15 attributes such as 'Satisfies customer' and 'Convenient location.' The higher the rating, the greater the agreement with the statement. A basic early step involves organizing the average ratings of different attributes for different brands, as shown in the following exhibit. Do not worry about breaking down the data by demographics at this point. Look at the ratings to see if anything stands out – whether it's because a number is very different from other numbers, or not different when you expect it to be. If something looks exceptional, can you explain it? Is it logical? Is it consistent with earlier studies?

You may want to identify some major patterns in the data. To do this, you may want to go through each attribute ratings (rows) and identify the stores that scored much above or much below the overall average. Even casual scanning of this table indicates some clear patterns. For example, Stores A and B score high on "Satisfied Customers," while C, E, and F score low on the same attribute. You can also observe a similar pattern for the next attribute "Convenient Location." At this stage, you may form a preliminary working hypothesis that customer satisfaction may have something to do with the store being conveniently located. (Throughout this chapter, you will learn a variety of techniques to help you interpret these numbers and draw quality conclusions.)

Summary of Average Ratings

Attributes	A	B	C	D	E	F	G	H	I	J	Mean
Satisfies customers	7.1	7.3	**3.2**	6.1	**2.8**	**3.6**	4.0	6.8	5.3	5.7	5.2
Convenient location	7.6	7.9	**3.7**	6.6	**3.3**	**4.1**	4.5	7.3	5.8	6.2	5.7
Items easy to locate	7.8	8.1	3.9	6.8	3.5	4.3	4.7	7.5	6.0	6.4	5.9
Meets overall needs	7.6	7.8	3.7	6.6	3.3	4.1	4.5	7.3	5.8	6.2	5.7
Convenient hours	8.6	8.9	4.7	7.6	4.3	5.1	5.5	8.3	6.8	7.2	6.7
Meets expectations	8.1	8.4	4.2	7.1	3.8	4.6	5.0	7.8	6.3	6.7	6.2
Prompt refund	8.3	8.6	4.4	7.3	4.0	4.8	5.2	8.0	6.5	6.9	6.4
Fast checkout	8.3	8.5	4.1	7.0	3.7	4.5	4.9	7.7	6.2	6.6	6.2
Low-interest credit	8.1	8.4	4.2	7.1	3.8	4.6	5.0	7.8	6.3	6.7	6.2
Friendly staff	8.5	8.2	4.3	7.2	3.9	4.7	5.1	7.9	6.4	6.8	6.3
For specialty prod.	6.2	7.8	3.1	6.0	2.7	3.5	3.9	6.7	5.2	5.6	5.1
Knowledgeable staff	6.7	8.2	3.6	6.5	3.2	4.0	4.4	7.2	5.7	6.1	5.6
Variety of items	7.9	6.9	3.3	6.2	2.9	3.7	4.1	6.9	5.4	5.8	5.3
For everyday shopping	8.4	7.2	3.8	6.7	3.4	4.2	4.6	7.4	5.9	6.3	5.8
Attractive layout	8.8	9.1	5.5	5.9	4.5	5.3	5.7	8.5	7.0	7.4	6.8
Mean	7.9	8.1	4.0	6.7	3.5	4.3	4.7	7.5	6.0	6.4	5.9

Understand Sub-group Analysis

The analysis described above is a good starting point, but it is not enough. Scrutinizing each row in the table is called univariate analysis, an essential beginning, but life is more complicated. Multivariate analysis involves two or more variables and may better reflect real life. We may need to understand the data at the sub-group level to add texture to our understanding.

For example, if consumers like your product overall, does that necessarily mean men and women like the product to the same extent? Is it possible that people from some regions of the country thoroughly dislike the product? Does the same geographical pattern hold for men and women? Do Francophone or Hispanic consumers feel differently about your product?

The two exhibits on the following page break down the data by gender. For most attributes, it is clear that men and women react similarly. The difference between men and women is within a range of ±0.3. However, on some attributes (for example, 'items easy to locate' and 'meets expectations,' women rate all stores higher than men.

A high-level analysis cannot answer questions posed above. From a marketing point of view, if we understand the data only from a broad perspective, we may arrive at erroneous conclusions. For example, assume that younger women (who form 10 percent of the sample in our example) dislike our product and the remaining 90 percent of consumers like our product. When we look at the overall data, we conclude that almost everyone likes our product, and we miss a small but significant group that dislikes the product. Consequently, we miss the opportunity to increase the attractiveness of the product among younger women.

Problems like these are widespread when we fail to do sub-group analysis. So, while an analysis always starts with the overall understanding of the data, this understanding should be extended, refined, and modified through more detailed sub-group analyses.

What sub-groups should you use for your analyses? This depends on your objectives. For example, if your research deals with fashion, then variables such as age, gender, and income are likely to be relevant. If you are researching computers, then variables such as the type of user (business versus personal) and purpose for which the computer is to be used (communications, scientific calculations, computer-aided design) are likely to be important. The researcher must decide which variables are likely to be important and then test their level of importance.

It is important to note that to do subgroup analyses, you need a sufficient number of respondents in each subgroup. If the overall sample size is small, it can restrict your ability to analyze your data by subgroups. So, in choosing a sample size for a study, you must not only calculate the appropriate size for the overall sample, but you must also consider whether the sample will yield a sufficient number of respondents in each of the sub-groups of interest.

Summary of Average Ratings (men)

Attributes	A	B	C	D	E	F	G	H	I	J	Mean
Satisfies customers	7.4	7.0	3.5	6.4	3.1	3.3	4.2	6.6	5.0	6.0	**5.3**
Convenient location	7.9	7.6	4.0	6.9	3.6	4.4	4.7	7.1	5.5	6.5	**5.8**
Items easy to locate	**7.5**	**7.8**	**3.6**	**6.5**	**3.2**	**4.0**	**4.4**	**7.2**	**5.7**	**6.1**	**5.6**
Meets overall needs	7.8	7.6	3.9	6.8	3.5	3.9	4.6	7.2	5.6	6.4	**5.7**
Convenient Hours	8.7	8.8	4.8	7.7	4.4	5.0	5.6	8.2	6.7	7.3	**6.7**
Meets expectations	**7.8**	**7.9**	**3.9**	**6.8**	**3.5**	**4.3**	**4.7**	**7.5**	**6.0**	**6.4**	**5.9**
Prompt refund	8.4	8.5	4.3	7.4	4.2	4.6	5.2	8.0	6.4	7.0	**6.4**
Fast checkout	8.2	8.6	4.0	6.9	3.8	4.4	4.8	7.8	6.3	6.5	**6.1**
Low-interest credit	8.0	8.5	4.0	7.0	3.9	4.5	4.9	7.9	6.4	6.6	**6.2**
Friendly staff	8.4	8.3	4.1	7.1	4.1	4.5	4.9	8.1	6.5	6.7	**6.3**
For specialty prod.	6.0	8.0	2.9	5.8	2.6	3.6	3.8	6.8	5.4	5.4	**5.0**
Knowledgeable staff	6.8	8.1	3.9	6.3	3.1	4.1	4.1	7.5	5.6	6.2	**5.6**
Variety of items	7.7	7.1	3.6	6.0	2.7	3.9	3.8	7.2	5.6	5.6	**5.3**
For everyday shopping	8.7	6.9	4.0	6.4	3.1	4.5	4.3	7.7	5.6	6.6	**5.8**
Attractive layout	9.1	8.8	5.7	5.6	4.2	5.6	5.4	8.8	6.7	7.7	**6.8**
Mean	**7.9**	**8.0**	**4.0**	**6.6**	**3.5**	**4.3**	**4.6**	**7.6**	**5.9**	**6.5**	**5.9**

Summary of Average Ratings (women)

Attributes	A	B	C	D	E	F	G	H	I	J	Mean
Satisfies customers	7.6	7.9	3.7	6.6	3.3	4.1	4.5	7.3	5.8	6.2	**5.7**
Convenient location	7.3	8.0	3.4	6.3	3.0	3.8	4.3	7.3	5.9	5.9	**5.5**
Items easy to locate	**8.1**	**8.5**	**4.2**	**7.1**	**3.8**	**4.7**	**5.0**	**8.0**	**6.3**	**6.7**	**6.2**
Meets overall needs	8.6	8.9	4.7	7.6	4.3	5.1	5.5	8.3	6.8	7.2	**6.7**
Convenient Hours	7.7	8.0	3.8	6.7	3.3	4.5	4.7	7.5	6.1	6.3	**5.9**
Meets expectations	**8.4**	**8.7**	**4.4**	**7.6**	**4.0**	**4.8**	**5.2**	**8.1**	**6.5**	**6.9**	**6.5**
Prompt refund	8.3	8.5	4.1	7.0	3.7	4.5	4.9	7.7	6.2	6.6	**6.2**
Fast checkout	8.1	8.4	4.2	7.1	3.8	4.6	5.0	7.8	6.3	6.7	**6.2**
Low-interest credit	8.5	8.2	4.3	7.2	3.9	4.7	5.1	7.9	6.4	6.8	**6.3**
Friendly staff	6.2	7.8	3.1	6.0	2.7	3.5	3.9	6.7	5.2	5.6	**5.1**
For specialty prod.	6.7	8.2	3.6	6.5	3.2	4.0	4.4	7.2	5.7	6.1	**5.6**
Knowledgeable staff	7.9	6.9	3.3	6.2	2.9	3.7	4.1	6.9	5.4	5.8	**5.3**
Variety of items	8.4	7.2	3.8	6.7	3.4	4.2	4.6	7.4	5.9	6.3	**5.8**
For everyday shopping	8.8	9.1	5.5	5.9	4.5	5.3	5.7	8.5	7.0	7.4	**6.8**
Attractive layout	7.9	8.0	4.0	6.6	3.5	4.3	4.6	7.6	5.9	6.5	**5.9**
Mean	**7.9**	**8.2**	**4.0**	**6.7**	**3.6**	**4.4**	**4.8**	**7.6**	**6.1**	**6.5**	**6.0**

Dependent and Independent Variables

Any numerical information that changes from one subject to another (such as age, product ratings) can be defined as a **variable**. (A 'subject' can be, in this context, any entity such as an organization.) Each question in a survey becomes a variable in a dataset. Thus, a subject's age, the overall rating of a product, and the number of magazines read in the previous week are all examples of variables.

An **attribute** is the absence or presence of specific characteristics (e.g., young, old, male, female). Thus, "female" is an attribute of a subject and is one of the levels of the variable called "Sex" or "Gender". The dollar amount a subject spends on electronics is a variable. In marketing research, we are primarily interested in the relationship between attributes and variables:

- Is purchase intent related to gender (male/female)?
- Is age related to smoking behaviours?
- Is readership related to socio-economic characteristics?

Suppose we try to examine the relationship between purchase intent and product ratings. In this case, our hypothesis states that purchase intent *depends* on how a consumer rates a product. Purchase intent is, therefore, the **dependent variable,** and the product attributes are the **independent variables**. Dependent variables are sometimes called response variables or criterion variables, and independent variables are often called predictor variables. Other examples of hypotheses are:

- Expenditure *depends* on income: Expenditure is dependent, and income is independent.
- Smoking *is related to* lung cancer: Lung cancer is dependent, and smoking is independent.
- Higher education *leads* to higher-paid jobs: Higher-paid jobs are dependent, and higher education is independent.

According to the context, the same variable may be a dependent or independent variable. For example, a person who has a better job may have enough financial resources to enroll him/herself in an evening course to obtain an MBA. In this case, the better job is the independent variable, and higher education is the dependent variable.

When we plot the relationship on a graph, the independent variable should be placed on the horizontal axis and the dependent variable on the vertical axis. Thus, to demonstrate the pattern that sales are related to a dependent of price of the product, we can plot a graph where price of the product (the independent variable) will be on the *x*-axis and sales (the dependent variable) will be on the *y*-axis, as shown below:

In marketing research data tables, the independent variables are generally presented in the columns as **banners**. Dependent variables are presented as rows called **stubs**. Notice that the percentages in the table below sum down the columns to 100 percent. This is usually the best way to configure the table when trying to identify dependence relationships between the variables. It is easy to see that as income increases, the percentage of respondents having private cars increases. This table presents a bivariate analysis where the Income variable is shown relative to the Mode of Transportation variable. Within the Income variable, Low, Medium and High are attributes of respondents' incomes. Of course, Mode of Transportation chosen is much more complex than relying only in Income. These stub-and-banner tables, or crosstabs, present bivariate relationships. Multi-variate relationships where there is more than one predictor variable begin to explain the complexity of human attitudes, attributes, behaviour and lives.

Mode of transportation and income (fictitious data)

Mode of transportation	Low income	Medium Income	High Income
Private car	20%	65%	85%
Public transportation	50	15	9
Bicycle	12	10	2
Walking	12	5	3
Other	6	5	1
Total	100%	100%	100%

Three Factors to Consider in Developing a Story

In practice, there are three bases of good data analysis: *prior knowledge, background information,* and *statistical analysis.* Suppose your organization is a large bank, and the average customer satisfaction rating on a 10-point scale in a recent survey is 8.3. How do you interpret this number?

- **Prior knowledge.** Past research shows that the overall rating for large banks tends to be between 8.0 and 9.0. Our result of 8.3 is neither above nor below this, so it is what was to be expected.
- **Background information.** Last year, our rating was 9.0. The decrease from 9.0 last year to 8.3 this year seems to align with the presence of corporate scandal stories that appeared in the news recently.
- **Statistical analysis.** Compared to our main competitor, we have not gone down that much. Our major competitor's rating declined by 1.5 points compared to last year, while our decline is only 0.7 (from 9.0 to 8.3). Our statistical analysis will tell us if that 8.3 rating is significantly below 9.0. And what is the significance to the business of having the rating drop from 9.0 to 8.3?

It is important for organizations to archive their research so that current information can be compared to prior knowledge and background information. Archiving information and insights has become more clearly recognized during the age of data science and marketing analytics. And marketing analytics has made the archiving function easier and can expedite the integration of prior information with current insights.

The purpose of this chapter is to provide the reader with a quick and basic working knowledge of the most frequently used statistical measures in marketing research. We won't explore the theoretical underpinnings of these measures except at an intuitive level. Once again, marketing researchers should take a formal university or college level course in statistics.

Measured (metric) vs. Counted (non-metric) Variables

In marketing research, we use two types of variables: *counted* and *measured.*

Counted variables answer the question *how many.* How many adults smoke? How many consumers earn over $100,000? How many students enroll in a university graduate degree programme? The basic summary measure we use for counted variables is the percentage (e.g., 15 percent of adults smoke; 80 percent of the students who enroll in a university graduate). Counted variables can be nominal variables with no inherent order (e.g., gender, place of residence) or ordinal variables with inherent order (e.g., the product liked the best, the second-best).

Measured variables or *metric variables*, on the other hand, measure something and can be *interval* variables or *ratio* variables.

- Ratio variables have definitive *zero points* (e.g., How much do people earn? How many bottles of beer did you drink last week?). Also, ratios between the measured values have *real meaning*. For example, $2 is twice as much as $1. It means $2 will buy twice as much as $1.
- While interval variables are considered to be metric also, they do not have the above two characteristics of ratio variables. For example, if we consider an

agree-disagree scale, 0 doesn't have any real meaning. Again, a rating of 8 is not twice as much as a rating of 4 when it comes to the liking of a product. A rating of 4 may mean that you don't really care for the product while a rating of 8 may mean that you do care.

When we summarize a measured variable, we often use the mean as an indicator of central tendency. It is important to remember that the choice of which statistical measure to use depends on whether we use counted variables or measured variables. Most statistical analyses that can be performed on ratio-scaled variables and be used with interval-scaled variables.

How to Summarize the Data Using Averages?

The purpose of data analysis is to understand and interpret the information contained in numbers. To do this effectively, we have to reduce a large set of data to a few summary numbers that can be more easily processed mentally. This principle applies to both simple and complex data analysis.

The summary measures we use are generally referred to as averages in everyday language and as "**measures of central tendency**" in the statistical literature. The three commonly used summary measures of central tendency are the *mean*, the *median*, and the *mode*.

Averages are an important tool used in analyzing statistical data. We use them constantly: the average income of computer programmers, the average age of MBA graduates, the average amount spent on alcoholic beverages, and so on.

Arithmetic Mean

Averages are the most frequently used statistical measure. They are so common that most people already know how to calculate them. Here are the ages of six students.

| Joh | 19 | Jane | 21 | Brenda | 20 |
| Li | 22 | Joe | 21 | Marisa | 23 |

What is their average age? It is 21, of course. We calculated this average by adding the ages of all the students and dividing that sum by the number of students.

	Age
John	19
Li	22
Jane	21
Joe	21
Brenda	20
Marisa	23
Total	**126**

Average = Total/Number of Observations = 126/6 = 21

What we generally call "average" is only one of the many averages used by statisticians. This type of average is known as the **arithmetic mean** or simply the **mean**.

We expect that an average is a representative number. In our example, the average age was 21 years. From this, we assume that this group of young people is mostly in their early 20s or late teens. This assumption is likely to be valid in most cases, to a lesser or greater extent, but we could also be very far off the mark, as we shall soon see. When we decided that the mean fails to represent the underlying numbers, we can use a different type of average or other statistical measures to understand the numbers.

In statistics, we use symbols and formulas. While their seeming complexity may discourage some students, they are meant to make life easy for us as we continue to study statistics. So, let's start with some notations.

Marketing and research data deal with **variables** such as age, gender and attitude ratings. In the age example above, age is the variable: John's age is different from Li's; age varies from person to person. Traditionally, statisticians refer to variables by the last few letters of the alphabet (e.g., x, y, z.) This is only a tradition, and you can indicate a variable by any letter if you so choose. We can let the letter x stand for the variable *age*, but how do we represent the age of a specific person, say John? We can use a subscript, for example, x_{john}. In more general terms, x_i would stand for the value of x for respondent i. Now we are ready to define the mean.

The formula for arithmetic mean is

$$\bar{x} = \Sigma x/n$$

Where,
$\bar{x}$ (pronounced x-bar) = mean
Σ (pronounced sigma) = the sum of
x = an observation (in our example, the age)
n = the number of observations (in our example, 6)

When should we use the mean as a summary number? The answer is practically all the time with measured data unless we have some specific reason for not using it. You will see some of those reasons soon.

The Median

The mean is a widely used and widely understood statistical measure, but it is not always the best measure. There are times when the mean can be misleading. Consider the case of a business tycoon (let's call him Mark Gates) working out of a small office with eight other people.

Here are their annual incomes:

	Income
Mark Gates	$5,000,000
Amanda Argyle	$80,000
Laura Arts	$90,000
Bryn Slayer	$105,000
Joseph Geronimo	$60,000
Abel Aronchuk	$85,000
Dilbert Hulbert	$101,000
Cain Cuthbert	$93,000
Gloria Duckson	$87,000
Mean	**$633,444**

The mean income of those who work in this office is $633,444. Yet, except for Mark Gates, no one makes even one-sixth of this amount. Mark Gates, on the other hand, makes more than seven times the mean income. In this case, the mean does not correctly represent the group because the mean of $633,444 does not come even close to anyone's income, including that of Mark Gates. The problem, of course, is the one exceptional number (referred to as the *outlier*) that is far removed from the other numbers in our dataset.

Whenever we deal with small sets of numbers and have reason to believe that some numbers could be outliers (i.e., too far removed from the other numbers in the dataset), we can use another type of average, known as the *median*. The **median** is defined as the middle observation when the observations are arranged in order of magnitude.

	Income
Mark Gates	$5,000,000
Bryn Slayer	$105,000
Dilbert Hulbert	$101,000
Cain Cuthbert	$93,000
Laura Arts	**$90,000**
Gloria Duckson	$87,000
Abel Aronchuk	$85,000
Amanda Argyle	$80'000
Joseph Geronimo	$60,000
Median	**$90,000**

In the above example, we have arranged the income values from the highest to the lowest and taken the middle value, $90,000, as the representative number. (It is the middle value because there are four employees whose income is above this level and four employees whose income is below this level.) As you can see, an average of $90 000 is a more representative income for this group rather than $633,444. One advantage of using the median is that it is not affected by extreme numbers or outliers.

In our example, there were nine people, so we took the income of the fifth person, $90,000—four people had incomes above this amount, four people had incomes below this amount, but what happens if there are an even number of observations? Let's say we have ten people instead of 9, as shown below:

	Income
Mark Gates	$5,000,000
Bryn Slayer	$105,000
Dilbert Hulbert	$101,000
Cain Cuthbert	$93,000
Laura Arts	**$90,000**
Gloria Duckson	**$87,000**
Abel Aronchuk	$85,000
Amanda Argyle	$80'000
Joseph Geronimo	$60,000
Bob Barro	$59,000

We take the mean of the two middle values:
Median = (90,000 + 87,000)/2 = 88,500

When we have an even number of observations, we identify the middle two observations from the ordered list and compute the mean of these two observations.

When should we use the median instead of the mean? The median should be used only in specific cases, such as when we expect extreme values (outliers) to be present in a small dataset. Note that when the dataset is large, outliers will have a much smaller effect. For instance, if Mark Gates worked in an office that had 2500 employees, the impact that his income would have on the mean would only be $2000 ($5,000,000/2500). If the data suggest that we could use either the mean or the median, we should prefer the median only when two conditions are met:

1. The dataset is likely to contain outliers; and

2. The outliers are likely to be of such magnitude that it would make the mean so unrepresentative as to be meaningless.

The Mode

There are situations where our interest is very specific: we would like to know what the most common value is. In these situations, we ask questions like the following:

- What is the typical number of cars owned by a rural household?
- What is the typical age of a first-year university student?
- What is the starting salary of most business school graduates?

In the above examples, we are not interested in the mean or the median. We are asking what is *typical*. If 53 percent of rural households own two cars, two is the *typical* number of cars owned by rural households, irrespective of the number of cars owned by the remaining households. Here *typical* refers to the most frequently encountered value. If most first-year university students are 19 years of age, it is the typical age, even though there might be students who are older or younger. Such typical values are called the *mode*. The **mode** is the most frequently occurring value.

As an example, here is the age distribution of a group of people.

	Age (in years)
John	19
Li	22
Jane	21
Joe	21
Brenda	20
Marisa	23
Chris	21
James	21

What is the mode? Since the mode is the most frequently occurring value, it is 21 because more people in this group (four) are 21 years old than any other age. Some data sets do not have a mode because each value may be different. In some cases, we may have more than one mode. For instance, if a product is either liked a lot or disliked a lot, a large number of people may give it a rating of 8 (like a lot), and an equally large number of people may give it a rating of 2 (dislike a lot). In this case, we will have two modes.

When should we use the mode? The mode is useful when we expect a *typical* value to be present in the data, a value that would apply to many people. In the above example, the mode of 21 is not any more informative than a mean or a median because either of these measures would have been close to 21. On the other hand, if a builder is looking to build houses for affluent people with children, the mode may be an excellent measure: how many bedrooms would a typical affluent family with children want? Here the mode would make the most sense rather than either the mean (such as 2.6 bedrooms) or the median (which ignores all values except the middle ones).

The Supremacy of the Mean

Although the median and the mode have their special uses in specific circumstances, their usefulness is limited by the fact that they do not use all the available data. For instance, consider the median:

	Income
Mark Gates	$5,000,000
Bryn Slayer	$105,000
Dilbert Hulbert	$101,000
Cain Cuthbert	$93,000
Laura Arts	**$90,000**
Gloria Duckson	$87,000
Abel Aronchuk	$85,000
Amanda Argyle	$80,000
Joseph Geronimo	$60,000
Median	**$90,000**

What happens next year if Mark Gates' salary increases to $10 million instead of $5 million in the following year while the incomes of the others remain the same? Or what happens if Gates' salary drops to $91,000? or if the incomes of Duckson, Aronchuk, Argyle, and Geronimo drop by 50 percent? In all these examples, the median income will not change. This insensitivity to changes in data points is a significant drawback of the median.

The mode suffers from similar problems. Since the mode is not concerned with any other value except the one that occurs most frequently, it simply ignores all other values. Here is our example again:

	Age (in years)
John	19
Li	22
Jane	21
Joe	21
Brenda	20
Marisa	23
Chris	21
James	21

The mode will be 21, even if the age distribution is like the one shown below because 21 is still the most frequently occurring value. What is the mode income from the income data?

	Age (in years)
John	53
Li	54
Jane	38
Joe	51
Brenda	37
Marisa	48
Chris	21
James	21

So, the median and the mode are of limited value, especially when we use the data to calculate more advanced measures such as variance and standard deviation. The main weakness of both these measures is that they ignore many values. When we continue learning about statistical measures for variability, such as correlation, we will seldom encounter the median or the mode. (When we use nonmetric data, we may have no choice but to use the median or the mode. Here we are discussing cases where we do have a choice of using any of the three measures.) You may wonder what happens to the outlier problem since the mean can be sensitive to outliers. First, you must always be aware that any of these problems could arise with your data. Second, advanced statistical measures include ways of detecting and dealing with outliers in ways other than using the median or the mode. The median and the mode have their uses in specific contexts and with specific types of data. Sometimes, the median is the preferred measure. Outside of these limited contexts, the mean is clearly the most useful measure of central tendency.

How to Understand the Variability of your Data?

The summary measures discussed so far (the mean, median, and mode) are essential for understanding and analyzing the data. However, in many cases, they may be of limited value because they do not tell the whole story. Consider the following ratings of four brands by ten respondents on a 10-point scale.

	Respondents										
	1	2	3	4	5	6	7	8	9	10	Mean
Brand A:	5	5	5	5	5	5	5	5	5	5	**5.0**
Brand B:	1	1	1	1	1	9	9	9	9	9	**5.0**
Brand C:	1	2	3	4	5	5	6	7	8	9	**5.0**
Brand D:	3	4	4	5	5	5	5	6	6	7	**5.0**

The mean rating for each brand is 5. Yet the implications of the non-aggregated ratings are quite different. For example, Brand A is perceived to be an average product by all respondents, while Brand B evokes only extremely high and extremely low reactions among consumers. On the other hand, Brands C and D evoked a wide variety of responses. Therefore, we need measures that will give us information about how the scores are distributed.

Several measures are available to describe the variability in our data. These are called **measures of dispersion or variation**. In marketing research, five such measures are commonly used. These are:

1. range
2. mean absolute deviation
3. variance
4. standard deviation
5. standard error.

The Range

The **range** is the difference between the largest and the smallest score. Thus, in the above example, for Brand A, the range is 0 (5 − 5), for Brands B and C, it is 8 (9 − 1), and for Brand D, it is 4 (7 − 3).

The range is not a very useful measure for two reasons:

1. It is extremely sensitive to one single large or small score. For example, if 100 respondents earn approximately $25,000 and one single respondent earns $150,000, the range would be $125,000. If this one person with the high income were not in the sample, the range would be much smaller.

2. The scales used in marketing research are such that, in most cases, all the scale points would be used by at least some consumers. For instance, if you use a 5-point scale, it is almost certain that at least one person would use one, and at least one person would use 5. Therefore, we are likely to end up with a range of 4, no matter how variable the scores are.

An early task in data analysis involves checking to ensure that the data conform to what is expected based on the questions and the source of data. If a question uses a 7-point scale from 1 to 7, the data must conform to that range. So, an initial step is investigating the ranges of all the variables to confirm that they match expectations or to investigate the process if they don't conform.

The Mean Absolute Deviation

The **mean absolute deviation** is a slightly more sophisticated measure of variability. To calculate the mean absolute deviation:

1. Calculate the mean.

2. Subtract the mean from each score to generate deviations.

3. Add all the deviations obtained in step 2, ignoring the negative signs, i.e., use the absolute values of the deviations.

How to Analyze the Data

4. Divide by the sample size.

When you ignore the sign of a negative number, you are converting the number into an absolute number (positive value). If you want to indicate an absolute number, you write it between two vertical lines. Thus:

$|-3| = 3$

$|\ 3| = 3$

The formula for the mean absolute deviation is:

$$\Sigma |x - \bar{x}|/n$$

The mean deviation is a useful measure of variability, but it has some limitations. The most important limitation of the mean absolute deviation is that it treats different numbers differently; if a number is positive, it is left as it is, if a number is negative, it is changed into a positive number. This treatment, along with the fact that absolute values are somewhat awkward to manipulate mathematically, makes the mean absolute deviation unsuitable for many statistical uses.

The Variance

The **variance** overcomes the problem of positive and negative numbers by simply squaring each deviation from the mean.

To calculate the variance:

1. Calculate the mean.

2. Subtract the mean from each score. (These are called *deviations*.)

3. Square each deviation. (These are called *squared deviations*.)

4. Add the squared deviations. (This is called the *sum of squared deviations or just sum of squares*.)

5. Divide it by (sample size – 1).

(Unlike the formulas we have encountered thus far for calculating the sample variance, we divide the squared deviations by $n - 1$ rather than by n. This is based on statistical theory, and it will not be explored any further here. If you are interested, you may want to look up 'degrees of freedom' in any standard statistical text to understand the theory.)

The result is called the variance. The variance of a set of data points is usually symbolized as s^2. The formula for calculating the variance is:

$$variance = s^2 = \sum (x_i - \bar{x})^2 / (n - 1)$$

The squaring of the deviations causes values very different from the mean to dominate the variance more than they would influence the mean absolute deviation. This means that the larger the deviation, the greater the weight assigned to that large deviation. Variance is one of the most useful measures in statistics.

Standard Deviation

Because the deviations are squared to obtain the variance, the variance is on a different scale compared to the mean. So, while the variance is an extremely useful measure, it cannot be directly related to the mean. This is because variance is based on squared values and therefore is on a different scale and magnitude. This problem is solved by simply taking the square root of the variance, bringing the measure back to the same scale as the mean. The square root of the variance is called the **standard deviation** (symbolized as s).

$$standard\ deviation = s = \sqrt{\sum (x_i - \bar{x})^2 / (n-1)}$$

How do we interpret the standard deviation? According to statistical theory and several key assumptions, the mean and the standard deviation, taken together, summarize all the important information that is contained in the data. For instance:

- Mean ± 1.00 standard deviation will contain 68 percent of all observations.
- Mean ± 1.96 standard deviations will contain 95 percent of all observations.
- Mean ± 2.58 standard deviations will contain 99 percent of all observations.
- Mean ± 3.00 standard deviations will contain *almost* all observations.

(Note that the statements that follow are based on the assumption that the scores (income in this case) are normally distributed. We will explore what this means later in this unit.)

For example, suppose you do a survey of 1,000 respondents and find that the average income of the respondents is $42,000 and the standard deviation is $10,000.

- 1 standard deviation   = 1.00 * $10,000 = 10,000
- 1.96 standard deviations = 1.96 * $10,000 = 19,600
- 2.58 standard deviations = 2.58 * $10,000 = 25,800

Since we know that that the Mean ± 1 standard deviation will contain 68 percent of all observations, we can now state that 68 percent of all observations will fall between a mean, for example, of $42,000 ± 10 000. To put it another way:

- 68 percent of all our respondents earn somewhere between $32 000 ($42 000 –10 000) and $52 000 ($42 000 + 10 000).
- 95 percent of all our respondents earn somewhere between $22 400 ($42 000 – 19 600) and $61 600 ($42 000 + 19 600).
- 99 percent of all our respondents earn somewhere between $16 200 ($42 000 –25 600) and $67 800 ($42 000 + 25 800).

The size of the standard deviation in relation to the mean tells us how widely the scores are spread out. For instance, in the above example, if the standard deviation is 13,000 instead of 10,000, then 68 percent of all our respondents earn somewhere between $29,000 ($42,000

− $13,000) and $55,000 ($42,000 + 13,000), rather than between $32,000 and $52,000. The smaller the standard deviation with relation to the mean, the less the scores are spread out.

The standard deviation is the most frequently used measure of dispersion for reasons such as the following:

- Unlike the variance, the standard deviation is on the same scale as the original measurement. This makes it easier to interpret.
- The standard deviation enables us to make specific statements about how widely the scores are spread out.

Coefficient of Variation (CV)

Suppose we have a study in which men and women rated a brand of chocolate on a scale where 10 was "I like it a lot" and 1 was "I don't like it at all". The mean ratings and standard deviations are given below.

Gender	Mean rating	Standard deviation
Men	8.8	2.2
Women	5.7	1.9

Whose scores are more spread out: the men's or the women's? If we just look at the standard deviations, it looks as though men's scores are more spread out because they have a higher standard deviation. However, they also have a higher mean. Standard deviation can only be interpreted in relation to the mean. To understand the standard deviation, we may find it helpful to calculate another measure called the coefficient of variation. The **coefficient of variation** expresses the standard deviation as a percentage of the mean.

$$\text{Coefficient of Variation (CV)} = (\text{Standard Deviation} / \text{Mean}) \cdot 100$$

To answer the question in our example above, we calculate the coefficient of variation for men and women:

Gender	Mean rating	Standard deviation	CV
Men	8.8	2.2	(2.2/8.8) * 100 = 25%
Women	5.7	1.9	(1.9/5.7) * 100 = 33.3%

Although the absolute standard deviation is higher for men than for women, the coefficient of variation shows that, in relation to the mean, the variation is higher for women (CV = 33.3 percent) than for men (CV = 25 percent). In other words, we can conclude that not only do women rate the product lower (5.7 as opposed to 8.8 for men), but their responses vary more widely than that of men.

The following exhibit summarizes the procedures for calculating the mean, the variance, the standard deviation and the coefficient of variation.

Calculating mean, median, variance, standard deviation, and coefficient of variation

Consumer	Rating (x)	Deviation (x − x̄)	(x − x̄)²
(1)	(2)	(3)	(4)
A	8	(8–5) = 3	3² = 9
B	7	(7–5) = 2	2² = 4
C	7	(7–5) = 2	2² = 4
D	5	(5–5) = 0	0² = 0
E	5	(5–5) = 0	0² = 0
F	5	(5–5) = 0	0² = 0
G	5	(5–5) = 0	0² = 0
H	4	(5–5) = −1	−1² = 1
I	4	(5–5) = −1	−1² = 1
J	3	(5–5) = −2	−3² = 4
K	2	(5–5) = −3	−2² = 9
$n = 11$	Sum (Σx) = 55		$\Sigma(x-\bar{x})^2 = 32$

How to Calculate the Mean ($\bar{x}$)

1. Calculate the number of respondents n. $n = 11$
2. Sum the scores (x) to obtain $\Sigma x = 55$
3. Find the mean = $\Sigma x/n$ = **5**

How to Calculate the variance (s^2)

1. Calculate how each score deviates from the mean (Col. 3)
2. Square each deviation (col. 4)
3. Add the squared deviations. (Total of Col. 4) = 32
4. Divide the results by n-1. $\Sigma(x-\bar{x})^2 / (n-1) = 32/(11-1) = 3.2$

How to Analyze the Data

How to Calculate the Standard Deviation (s)

Calculate the square root of the variance = sqrt(3.2) = 1.79

How to Calculate the Coefficient of Variation

1. Divide the standard deviation by the mean. =1.79/5 = .358
2. Multiply the result by 100. = 358 X 100 = 35.8%

Standard Scores (z)

In marketing research, we may be required to compare numbers that cannot be compared directly. For instance, Peter lives in City A, where the cost of living is low while Paul lives in City B, where the cost of living is high. They are paid different salaries.

	Salary paid	Ave. salary (city)	SD (city)
Peter (City A)	$40,000	35,000	$5,000
Paul (City B)	$38,000	32,000	$3,000

Paul claims that, although his salary is $2000 lower than Peter's, in relative terms, he is better off than Peter. How do we resolve this?

The main problem here is that these salaries are not directly comparable because they relate to two different cities and different pay structures. One dollar in City A may not be the same as one dollar in City B because of the different costs of living. To make them comparable, we need to bring them to the same unit of measurement. This can be done by calculating how much each person earns above (or below) the average and converting it into standard deviation units (called z-scores). This brings all measurements to the same scale so they can be directly compared. **Standard scores** or **z-scores** are measurements expressed in standard deviation units. The formula for z-scores is given by

$$z_i = (x_i - \bar{x})/s$$

Where

   z = standardized score for respondent i

   x = respondent's score

   $\bar{x}$ = the mean

   s = standard deviation

Applying the z-score formula:

Peter: z = (40 000 − 35 000)/5000 = 1

Paul: z = (38 000 − 32 000)/3000 = 2

Peter's z-score is 1, and Paul's is 2. In other words, Peter is 1 standard deviation above the average income for his city, while Paul is 2 standard deviations above the average income for his city. In relative terms, Paul is paid better than Peter even though, in absolute terms, Peter earns more.

Standardized scores can also be used when we need to compare data collected in different units (such as dollars and pounds, or height and weight).

The Normal Curve

We have made several inferences about standard deviations such as
- Mean ± 1.00 standard deviation will contain 68 percent of all observations.
- Mean ± 1.96 standard deviations will contain 95 percent of all observations.
- Mean ± 2.58 standard deviations will contain 99 percent of all observations.

What is the basis for these inferences? To understand this, we need to understand the normal probability curve or the normal curve.

The **normal curve** is a mathematical curve that looks like the one shown below. It appears that many physical variables in nature, such as height and weight, and **measured variables** such as income and product ratings tend to approximate this distribution. Let us take a variable such as the height of each of 1,000 people and plot them on the x-axis and the number of people who have that height on the y-axis. If, as we expect, height follows the normal curve, the average height will fall precisely in the middle. Let us say the average height is 5'6". Most people will be close to that mean. As we move away from the mean, there will be fewer and fewer people with the corresponding height. If the average height is 5'6" and if the height is normally distributed, then only a small proportion of the sample will have extreme values such as well below 5'0" or well above 6'0".

The Normal Curve

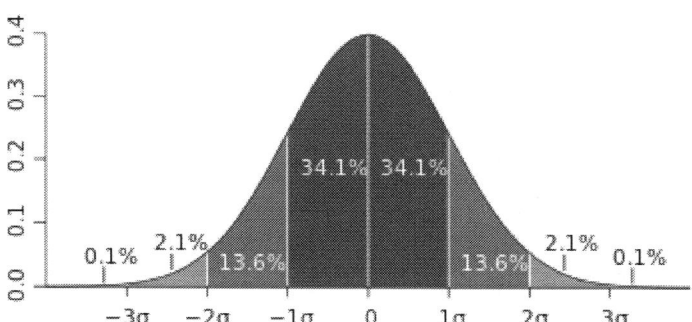

The normal curve is generally shown in a standardized format and is called the *standard normal distribution*. This makes it easier to understand. Standard normal distribution is a distribution that plots the standardized scores (z-scores) rather than the actual scores. Because the z-scores are obtained by subtracting the mean from each score and dividing the result by the standard deviation (as shown in the previous section), the standard normal distribution has a mean of 0 and a standard deviation of 1.

The normal curve has the following additional properties:

- Fifty percent of a normal distribution lies on either side of the mean since the mean marks the centre of the distribution, which is perfectly symmetrical. In our example, 50 percent of the people will be taller than 5'6," and 50 percent of the people will be shorter than 5'6". In other words, the median is the same as the mean.
- Sixty-eight percent of a normal distribution is contained between 1 standard deviation below the mean and 1 standard deviation above the mean.
- Ninety-five percent of a normal distribution lies between 1.96 (or 2) standard deviations on either side of the mean.
- Ninety-nine percent of a normal distribution lies between 2.58 standard deviations on either side of the mean.

Nearly 100 percent of a normal distribution is enclosed within 3.00 standard deviations on either side of the mean.

Not all distributions are normal. However, some variables do follow the normal curve, and in many cases, we implicitly assume that they do.

So far, we discussed how to calculate averages and measure the variation around the mean. In other words, we were *describing* our data. So, measures of central tendency and measures of dispersion are called **descriptive statistics**. However, we also want to know how generalizable our results are. Suppose we survey 1,000 adults and find that 35 percent of them read at least one newspaper every day. How accurate is this estimate of 35 percent? Could it be, for instance, as high as 45 percent or as low as 25 percent if we measured everyone in the population? If we find that 37 percent of men and 34 percent of women read a newspaper every day, can we be sure that the difference is *real* (i.e., the difference of 3 percentage points will persist if we measured all adults in the country)? In other words, we want to infer something about the population based on our sample results. Methods that are used to draw inferences about a *population* from a sample are known as **inferential statistics**. But first, we need to understand the difference between sampling and non-sampling errors.

Sampling and Non-Sampling Errors

Marketing research data are subject to two types of errors—sampling and non-sampling errors. These were discussed in Unit 4.

When our questionnaire is not clear, when our interviews are not done correctly, when we interview the wrong people, and so on, our results are subject to **non-sampling errors**. These errors do not depend on the sample size. They can be as large as or even more extensive than sampling errors. They are there because the research was not carried out the way it should have been. There is no easy way of consistently measuring the impact of all non-sampling errors.

On the other hand, **sampling errors** are not avoidable, but they are measurable. They come about because we survey only a few hundred respondents and try to generalize the results to several million people. We can make the sampling error as small as necessary (by taking larger and larger samples), but we cannot eliminate it unless we survey everyone in our target group or relevant population.

How to Calculate the Margin of Error

When only a small fraction of the population is sampled, we sacrifice some accuracy. But how much accuracy is sacrificed? To understand this, we need another concept—*the margin of error*. The **margin of error** refers to the range within which the "true result" (the value we would have obtained if we had measured everyone in the population) is likely to fall. Such ranges can be specified to any given level of probability. The *true* value is called the **parameter**. The value obtained from the data is called the **estimate**. The margin of error is a statistical term. This concept might be more palatable if it were called the precision of the estimate.

For example, based on statistical tests, we can state that 25 percent of all adults in the country smoke cigarettes; the margin of error on this estimate is ± 3 percentage points at the 95 percent level of confidence. This statement means that if we repeated the study several times with the same sample size and calculated the proportion of the sample that smoked and calculated the margin of error each time at the 95 percent level of confidence, such margins of error would include the true proportion of adults smoking 95 percent of the time.

When we talk about the margin of error, we refer strictly to the sampling error and not to other errors that may occur in our data. Questions concerning the margin of error are posed as follows:

- In a survey of 1,000 adults over the age of 18, 56 percent said they would vote for the Conservatives in the next general election. What is the margin of error?
- Although the survey said that 56 percent would vote Conservative, if we had interviewed all adults in the country over the age of 18 years, we might have received a different answer. Given that we interviewed only 1,000 adults, to what extent can we be incorrect?
- In a product test with 300 consumers, the average rating for sweetness was 6.5. What is the margin of error?
- If we had carried out the product test on every consumer in the target group instead of just 300, how far off would we be from our current results?

Let us start with an example. Suppose we want to find out the percentage of teenagers who smoke. We can survey 1,000 teenagers in the country. But how do we know that our results, based on just these 1,000 teenagers, are representative of all teenagers in the country? How do we know that the results obtained through a sample will represent the population? This is the fundamental sampling problem.

To make any statement about the population from a sample, we must first make sure that our sample is drawn using random sampling procedures: it can be a simple random sample, stratified random sample, multistage random sample, or cluster sample using random sampling procedures.

Provided we choose our sample using random procedures, we can make certain generalizations. It can be shown that if we plot all the means of all possible samples of any size (provided it is not too small) from a population, it will also follow a bell-shaped curve, the *normal probability curve*. This result is called the *central limit theorem*. The practical implication of this finding is that it is possible to estimate how close our results are to the true mean by using a well-

How to Analyze the Data

established and relatively straightforward procedure that relies on the normal probability distribution.

This, in turn, generates what are known as confidence intervals and margins of error.

Standard Error

At this stage, we need another measure called the *standard error*. The standard error is the standard deviation of the means of large samples of a specific size from the same population. While standard deviation tells us how many observations are included within a range, the standard error tells us how many sample means are included within a given range.

The **standard error** is simply the standard deviation divided by the square root of the sample size.

$$\text{Standard Error (SE)} = s_x = s/\sqrt{n}$$

Example:

In a survey, it was found that $7 per week was spent on milk by households with one or more children between 1 and 18 years old. Therefore,

Sample mean (x) = $7 ;

Standard Deviation = 1.5;

Sample Size = 100

What is the standard error?

Standard Error (SE) = sx = s/√n

= 1.5/√100 = 1.5/10 = 0.15

Confidence Intervals

The interpretation of the standard error is given below:
- Mean ± 1 Standard Error range will contain the true mean 68 percent of the time.
- Mean ± 1.65 Standard Error range will contain the true mean 90 percent of the time.
- Mean ± 1.96 Standard Error range will contain the true mean 95 percent of the time.
- Mean ± 2.58 Standard Error range will contain the true mean 99 percent of the time.

The above multipliers, such as 1.65, 1.96, 2.58, are called confidence coefficients and the corresponding percentages, such as 90 percent, 95 percent, and 99 percent are called confidence levels. By applying the confidence coefficients to our standard error, we can now obtain the margins of error (confidence intervals) for our mean of 7.
- We can be 90 percent confident that the true mean will be between $6.75 and $7.25.
- We can be 95 percent confident that the true mean will be between $6.70 and $7.30.
- We can be 99 percent confident that the true mean will be between $6.61 and $7.39.

The standard error for **percentages** is calculated using the following formula:

$$\text{Standard Error of Percentages} = \sqrt{\frac{P(100-P)}{n}}$$

where P is percent obtained in the survey.

Example 1

In a survey of 100 respondents, 30 percent said that they had bought Brand A last week. What is the standard error of this percentage?

P = 30%

100-P = (100-30) = 70%

n = 100 (sample size)

$$SE = \sqrt{\frac{P(100-P)}{n}} = \sqrt{30 * \frac{100-30}{100}} = \sqrt{21} = 4.6$$

The half-width of the 90% confidence interval = 1.65 * 4.6 = 7.59

We can then say that we are 90 percent confident that the true percentage of the population that bought Brand A was 30 percent ± 7.59 points.

Example 2

In an election poll of 400 respondents, 38% said that they would vote Conservative. What is the standard error?

$$SE = \sqrt{\frac{P(100-P)}{n}} = \sqrt{38 * \frac{100-38}{400}} = \sqrt{5.9} = 2.4$$

The half-width of the 95% confidence interval = 1.96 * 2.4 = 4.7

We can then say that we are 95 percent confident that the true percentage of the population that would vote conservative would be somewhere in the range of 38% ± 4.7 points (2.4*1.95) at the 95% level of confidence.

Calculate Statistical Significance

The researcher is quite often interested in finding out whether two groups are different in their responses. Do men like baseball more than women do? Is a brand of soap preferred more in Montreal than in Vancouver? As before, our concern is to make sure that the observed difference is the result of genuine differences between the groups under consideration and not the result of the size of the samples chosen. We need to calculate one more statistic called the standard error of the difference. The formula is:

$$\text{Standard Error of Difference } (SE_d) = \sqrt{SE_1^2 + SE_2^2}$$

Where

SE₁ = Standard error for group 1
SE₂ = Standard error for group 2

How to Analyze the Data

To assess whether the obtained differences in means between the two groups are significant, we calculate what is known as the t-test. (As the sample size gets larger – say over 100, the t-values approximate z-values of the normal curve.) For the difference between two proportions, the z-test is performed. For small samples, there will be differences between z-values from the normal distributions and t-values from the Student-t distribution. There will be minimal differences when the sample sizes grow to 100 or higher, which is quite typical in a practical marketing research survey.

$$\text{For percentages, } z = (P_1 - P_2)/SE_d$$
$$\text{For means, } t = (\bar{x}_1 - \bar{x}_2)/SE_d$$

Where,

P_1 = percent in group 1; P_2 = percent in group 2; SE_d = standard error difference

$\bar{x}_1$ = mean of group 1; $\bar{x}_2$ = mean of group 2; SE_d = standard error difference

Example 1

In a survey, 40 percent in London, Ontario and 35 percent in Hamilton, Ontario said that they would start saving more next year. The sample size was 400 in London and 325 in Hamilton. Is the difference in results statistically significant (i.e., likely real and not the result of random sampling variations) at the 95 percent level?

p_1 = 40%

p_2 = 35%

Standard error for London = $\sqrt{(40*60)/400}$ = 2.45

Standard error for Hamilton = $\sqrt{(35*65)/325}$ = 2.65

Standard Error of Difference (SE_d) = $\sqrt{(SE_1^2 + SE_2^2)}$ = $\sqrt{(2.45^2 + 2.65^2)}$ = 3.6

For percentages, $z = (P_1 - P_2)/SE_d = (40 - 35)/3.6 = 1.39$

The above formula is for the percentages. If you are working with means, substitute $\bar{x}_1$ and $\bar{x}_2$ for P_1 and P_2, respectively. The standard deviation for ratings must be used here. All other calculations and interpretations are identical. See Example 2. (Note that these formulas assume unequal variances.)

Is this z-value of 1.39 significantly different from zero? If it is significantly different from zero, it would mean that the expressed level interest in starting a savings program is different between the two cities.

Standard Normal Table

Z	0.000	0.010	0.020	0.030	0.040	0.050	0.060	0.070	0.080	0.090
0.000	0.000	0.004	0.008	0.012	0.016	0.020	0.024	0.028	0.032	0.036
0.100	0.040	0.044	0.048	0.052	0.056	0.060	0.064	0.068	0.071	0.075
0.200	0.079	0.083	0.087	0.091	0.095	0.099	0.103	0.106	0.110	0.114
0.300	0.118	0.122	0.126	0.129	0.133	0.137	0.141	0.144	0.148	0.152
0.400	0.155	0.159	0.163	0.166	0.170	0.174	0.177	0.181	0.184	0.188
0.500	0.192	0.195	0.199	0.202	0.205	0.209	0.212	0.216	0.219	0.222
0.600	0.226	0.229	0.232	0.236	0.239	0.242	0.245	0.249	0.252	0.255
0.700	0.258	0.261	0.264	0.267	0.270	0.273	0.276	0.279	0.282	0.285
0.800	0.288	0.291	0.294	0.297	0.300	0.302	0.305	0.308	0.311	0.313

0.900	0.316	0.319	0.321	0.324	0.326	0.329	0.332	0.334	0.337	0.339
1.000	0.341	0.344	0.346	0.349	0.351	0.353	0.355	0.358	0.360	0.362
1.100	0.364	0.367	0.369	0.371	0.373	0.375	0.377	0.379	0.381	0.383
1.200	0.385	0.387	0.389	0.391	0.393	0.394	0.396	0.398	0.400	0.402
1.300	0.403	0.405	0.407	0.408	0.410	0.412	0.413	0.415	0.416	0.418
1.400	0.419	0.421	0.422	0.424	0.425	0.427	0.428	0.429	0.431	0.432
1.500	0.433	0.435	0.436	0.437	0.438	0.439	0.441	0.442	0.443	0.444
1.600	0.445	0.446	0.447	0.448	0.450	0.451	0.452	0.453	0.454	0.455
1.700	0.455	0.456	0.457	0.458	0.459	0.460	0.461	0.462	0.463	0.463
1.800	0.464	0.465	0.466	0.466	0.467	0.468	0.469	0.469	0.470	0.471
1.900	0.471	0.472	0.473	0.473	0.474	0.474	0.475	0.476	0.476	0.477
2.000	0.477	0.478	0.478	0.479	0.479	0.480	0.480	0.481	0.481	0.482
2.100	0.482	0.483	0.483	0.483	0.484	0.484	0.485	0.485	0.485	0.486
2.200	0.486	0.486	0.487	0.487	0.488	0.488	0.488	0.488	0.489	0.489
2.300	0.489	0.490	0.490	0.490	0.490	0.491	0.491	0.491	0.491	0.492
2.400	0.492	0.492	0.492	0.493	0.493	0.493	0.493	0.493	0.493	0.494
2.500	0.494	0.494	0.494	0.494	0.495	0.495	0.495	0.495	0.495	0.495
2.600	0.495	0.496	0.496	0.496	0.496	0.496	0.496	0.496	0.496	0.496
2.700	0.497	0.497	0.497	0.497	0.497	0.497	0.497	0.497	0.497	0.497
2.800	0.497	0.498	0.498	0.498	0.498	0.498	0.498	0.498	0.498	0.498
2.900	0.498	0.498	0.498	0.498	0.498	0.498	0.499	0.499	0.499	0.499
3.000	0.499	0.499	0.499	0.499	0.499	0.499	0.499	0.499	0.499	0.499

To find out if the obtained z-value is significant, we look up the z table or standard normal table provided above. So, we find above that for a 90 percent confidence level, we need a minimum z of 1.65, for a 95 percent level, the z-value is 1.96, and for a 99 percent level, it is 2.576.

- In the table body, search for 0.90/2 or 0.45.
- That number appears in the row labelled 1.60.
- That number appears in the column labelled 0.05, this provides the second decimal value.
- Add 1.60 and 0.05 and you get 1.65 which furnishes the z-value.

The z-value of 1.39that we obtained is much lower than any of the above. Therefore, we conclude that there is no evidence to support the conclusion that the claimed levels of interest in starting a higher savings program are different in the two cities. (To find the exact probability level of 1.39, first go down the z column to get 1.30 and then go across until you get to the column with a z value of 0.09 to find the value of 0.418. Multiply this value by 2 to get 0.836, which is less that 0.90, so the value is not significant at the 90% level.)

Example 2

In an in-home test, respondents were asked to try a new detergent and rate it on a 10-point scale where 10 is excellent cleaning and 1 was very poor cleaning. The following results were obtained.

How to Analyze the Data

	City A	City B
Mean	6.30	5.70
Standard error	0.17	0.23
Sample size	20	20

Can we state, with 95 percent confidence, that the observed difference between the two cities is real and not due to sampling error? Since we are working with means, we use the t-test.

We need to calculate $t = (\bar{x}_1 - \bar{x}_2)/SE_d = (6.3 - 5.7)/\sqrt{.17^2+.23^2} = 2.1$

As with the previous example, we first calculate the degrees of freedom:

$df = [(20 + 20) - 2] = 38$

Since t values are not provided in the table below for n>40, we use the last row of the table and look up for the value for 40 that for a 90 percent confidence level, we need a minimum t of 1.684, for a 95 percent confidence level, 2.021 and for a 99 percent confidence level, 2.704. The t of 2.10 we obtained is higher than that needed for significance at the 95 percent confidence level (but not at the 99 percent confidence level). Therefore, we conclude that consumers in City A rate the product more differently than do consumers in City B at the 95% level of confidence.

Table of t-values

df	90%	95%	99%
1.	6.314	12.706	63.657
2.	2.920	4.303	9.925
3.	2.353	3.182	5.841
4.	2.132	2.776	4.604
5.	2.015	2.571	4.032
6.	1.943	2.447	3.707
7.	1.895	2.365	3.499
8.	1.860	2.306	3.355
9.	1.833	2.262	3.250
10.	1.812	2.228	3.169
11.	1.796	2.201	3.106
12.	1.782	2.179	3.055
13.	1.771	2.160	3.012
14.	1.761	2.145	2.977
15.	1.753	2.131	2.947
16.	1.746	2.120	2.921
17.	1.740	2.110	2.898
18.	1.734	2.101	2.878
19.	1.729	2.093	2.861
20.	1.725	2.086	2.845
21.	1.721	2.080	2.831
22.	1.717	2.074	2.819

23.	1.714	2.069	2.807
24.	1.711	2.064	2.797
25.	1.708	2.060	2.787
26.	1.706	2.056	2.779
27.	1.703	2.052	2.771
28.	1.701	2.048	2.763
29.	1.699	2.045	2.756
30.	1.697	2.042	2.750
40.	1.684	2.021	2.704
∞	**1.65**	**1.96**	**2.58**

What Happens as your Sample Size Becomes Larger?

You might have noticed that the t-table does not provide values for large samples. You might have also noticed that the value of t required for significance does not change appreciably once the sample size is larger than 30 or so. Once the sample size becomes larger (as is the case in most survey research), the t distribution approaches the normal distribution, as discussed earlier. (The values of the standard normal distribution are referred to as the z values.) Therefore, whenever our sample size is large (say 100 or more), we can simply use the following coefficients:

1.65 (for a 90% confidence level)

1.96 (for a 95% confidence level)

2.58 (for a 99% confidence level)

In our first example, we had a sample size of 725 and a t-value of 1.39. Since this is lower than 1.65, which is needed for the 90 percent confidence level, we conclude that there is not a significant difference. (By convention, the most frequently used confidence levels in marketing research are 90 percent and 95 percent. A confidence level of less than 90 percent is virtually never used.)

What is Hypothesis Testing

In the above examples, we tried to find out whether the difference between two means or two percentages is real or came about just by chance, because of sampling errors.

For instance, consumers in Vancouver rated the detergent 6.3, while consumers in Montreal rated it 5.7. Apparently, the product is better rated in Vancouver than in Montreal. However, it is also possible that the difference in rating between the two cities could have been the result of sampling error.

If our results are statistically significant (using statistical significance tests such as those shown above), then we can conclude that the differences are not due to chance but because consumers in Vancouver indeed liked the product better than consumers in Montreal.

When we do this formally, it is known as hypothesis testing. As we mentioned above, there are two possibilities: the difference is due to chance, or the difference is due to real differences between the two groups. These two possibilities correspond to two hypotheses:

Hypothesis 1. (Null hypothesis): There is no difference between the two groups.

Hypothesis 2. (Alternative hypothesis): There is a difference between the two groups.

You will note that the first hypothesis says that there is no difference. Traditionally, this hypothesis is always stated first. It is called the null hypothesis or the hypothesis of no difference. Only when our statistical tests show that the null hypothesis is false, do we reject it and accept the alternative hypothesis that states that the observed difference is not due to chance. In other words, we reject the null hypothesis when we find the results to be statistically significant. In applied marketing research, these hypotheses are not spelled out. However, in academic research, traditionally, they are explicitly stated. But, hypotheses are always present while not always expressed.

Type 1 and Type 2 Errors

Suppose we reject the null hypothesis because a significance test shows that there is a difference between the two groups at the 95 percent confidence level. It follows that there is a 5 percent chance that the two groups are indeed not different, even though we have rejected the null hypothesis. So, we have a 5 percent chance of making an error, and this is known as a type 1 error or an alpha (α) error—concluding that there is a difference between the two groups when, in fact, there may not be.

We can, of course, set the level of significance to the 99 percent level and thereby decrease the value of alpha (α) error to just 1 percent. However, by doing so, we have increased the probability of concluding that there is no difference between the two groups when, in fact, there might be. This is known as the type 2 error or beta (β) error. These errors are summarized below.

	If the null hypothesis is	
	True	False
Do not reject the null hypothesis	Type 1 error	Correct
Reject null hypothesis	Correct	Type 2 error

	True	False
Do not reject the null hypothesis	Correct	Type 2 error
Reject null hypothesis	Type 1 error	Correct

Ideally, we would like to reduce both the alpha (α), Type 1, and beta (β), Type 2, errors. However, for a given sample size, reducing the value of α will increase the value of β and vice versa.

If the Vancouver mean rating is significantly different from the Montreal mean rating, it means that residents of the two cities really do feel differently about the detergent. However, this does not mean that the difference necessarily has any marketing significance.

In this example, suppose there are two large organizations, A and B, that pay very similarly for similar work. The mean salary at A is $38,865, and at B is $38,875. The difference may be statistically significant. Yet, a difference of $10 on a salary of $38,865 would not be considered by most people to have any practical significance. Therefore, you should always bear in mind that just because something is statistically significant (i.e., the difference between the two groups is not due to chance), it does not follow that the difference has any marketing significance.

Hypothesis testing is not a substitute for thinking about a problem critically and understanding what type of differences would be significant from a marketing point of view. Mechanical significance testing should be avoided, and so should marketing decisions based purely on significance tests. Be aware that some important statistical assumptions underlying the use of t-tests have not been mentioned in this discussion.

A Note on How Significance and Confidence Levels are Reported

In applied fields such as marketing research, we talk about 90 percent, 95 percent, and 99 percent levels of confidence. However, in academic literature and statistical packages, these levels are referred to as 0.10, 0.05, and 0.01 levels of risk or significance. The following shows how these levels are derived:

90% level of confidence: 100 − 90 = 10% risk; expressed as a proportion, this becomes 0.10.
95% level of confidence: 100 − 95 = 5% risk; expressed as a proportion, this becomes 0.05.
99% level of confidence: 100 − 99 = 1% risk; expressed as a proportion, this becomes 0.01.

Again, while these are the most-commonly-used levels of significance, the level of significance can be determined for any z or t value.

What to do When There are More Than Two Groups

In the previous example, we saw how to compute the significance of the difference between two means if we had two groups: in the first example, we compared London with Hamilton, but what happens if we have many groups? Suppose we need to compare five cities. What do we do then? One alternative would be to compare each city to every other city. If we call our five cities A, B, C, D, and E, then the following comparisons are possible:

A versus B	B versus C	C versus D	D versus E
A versus C	B versus D	C versus E	
A versus D	B versus E		
A versus E			

This poses two problems
- we have to do a large number of significance tests, and
- as the number of tests is increased, we increase the chance of finding something to be of significance when it is actually not.

To avoid problems like these, when more than two groups are involved, we use overall tests of significance. These tests tell us whether there are any significant differences between any of the groups at all. As with other tests, we will have to use two different tests, depending on whether we are dealing with counted data or measured data.

How to Analyze the Data

Chi-squared Tests (for Non-metric Data)

Let us first consider nominal variables (Yes/No type questions). Here the appropriate test is the chi-squared test.

Example 1 (One-way tables)

Consumers were asked to indicate a preference among three flavours of a soft drink. Their preferences were as follows.

Prefer	n
Flavour A	62
Flavour B	46
Flavour C	42
Total	150

If we assume that there is no reason to believe that one flavour is preferred to any other (null hypothesis), the preferences would be expected to be equal for all three flavours—in this case, 50 preferences for each flavour (expected frequencies). Our objective is to assess whether the obtained frequencies (62, 46, and 42) are sufficiently different from expected frequencies (50, 50, and 50) such that the null hypothesis can be rejected, and it can be concluded that all flavours are not equally preferred.

To do this for each set:

1. Calculate how much each set of preferences deviates from the expected value.
2. Square this difference.
3. Divide it by the expected value for the set.
4. Sum all the values obtained. This is called χ^2 (chi-squared). $\chi^2 = \sum[(O - E)^2/E]$

Treatment (Flavour)	Observed (O)	Expected (E)	O-E	$(O-E)^2$	$(O-E)^2/E$
Rosemary	62	50	12	144	144/50=2.88
Mint	46	50	-4	16	16/50=0.32
Pine	42	50	-8	64	64/50=1.28
Total	150				c^2=4.48

$\chi^2 = \sum[(O - E)^2/E]$, where O = Obtained result; and E = Expected result.

To evaluate whether χ^2 is significant or not, we use the χ^2 table. We need two values to use the table: The χ^2 value and degrees of freedom for χ^2. The degrees of freedom for a one-way chi-squared value is simply:

df = Number of Groups – 1.

In our example, only one variable is considered—soft drink preference. We have three groups. Therefore, the df = 3 − 1 = 2.

To find out if this Chi-square statistic is significant, we refer to the χ^2 table below:

Values of the Chi-Squared Distribution

df	90%(0.10)	95% (.0.05)	99% (0.01)
1	2.7	3.8	6.6
2	4.6	6.0	9.2
3	6.3	7.8	11.3
4	7.8	9.5	13.3
5	9.2	11.1	15.1
6	10.6	12.6	16.8
7	12.0	14.1	18.5
8	13.4	15.5	20.1
9	14.7	16.9	21.7
10	16.0	18.3	23.2
11	17.3	19.7	24.7
12	18.5	21.0	26.2
13	19.8	22.4	27.7
14	21.1	23.7	29.1
15	22.3	25.0	30.6
16	23.5	26.3	32.0
17	24.8	27.6	33.4
18	26.0	28.9	34.8
19	27.2	30.1	36.2
20	28.4	31.4	37.6
21	29.6	32.7	38.9
22	30.8	33.9	40.3
23	32.0	35.2	41.6
24	33.2	36.4	43.0
25	34.4	37.7	44.3
26	35.6	38.9	45.6
27	36.7	40.1	47.0
28	37.9	41.3	48.3
29	39.1	42.6	49.6
df	90%(0.10)	95% (.0.05)	99% (0.01)

We find that we need at least a Chi-square value of 4.6 for significance at the 90 percent level for 2 degrees of freedom (d.f.). Since the calculated Chi-square value of 4.48 is less than the critical Chi-square value of 4.6, we should conclude that we do not have sufficient evidence to suppose that the flavour preferences are anything other than even among the three flavours.

We are not restricted to the assumption that the preferences are equal. For instance, in the above example, the marketing manager may believe that, traditionally, Flavour A is preferred by

50 percent of the consumers, B by 25 percent, and C by 25 percent. In this case, the expected frequencies would be 75, 37.5, and 37.5. χ^2 can be calculated on those values using the same formula as used above.

Example 2 (two-way tables)

A test was run to obtain the appeal of a new magazine cover format among a random sample of 300 subscribers. The results are tabulated below.

Gender	Preference		Total
	Old	New	
Men	122	38	160
Women	88	52	140
Total	210	90	300

The Problem. Is the preference related to the sex of the subscriber? Our null hypothesis is that these two attributes (sex and preference) are statistically independent (i.e., that men and women have similar preferences).

To compute the expected frequencies for each cell, we calculate:

(Row total * Column total)/Grand total

For example, the expected value for row 1, column 1 is as follows:

(210 * 160)/300 = 112. This is based on the formula for the joint occurrence of two events when those events are statistically independent.

Similarly, we can compute expected frequencies for each cell in the new magazine cover format preference test, as shown below.

Row/Col.	O	E	(O – E)	(O – E)²	(O – E)²/E
11	122	112	10	100	0.893
12	38	48	–10	100	2.083
21	88	98	–10	100	1.020
22	52	42	10	100	2.381
					$\chi^2 = 6.377$

For a two-way table, χ^2 has a d.f., which is calculated as follows:

(Number of rows – 1) * (Number of columns – 1)

In our example, there are two rows and two columns. Therefore, (2 – 1) * (2 – 1) = 1 df.

Referring to the χ^2 table, we find that a χ^2 value of 3.8 for 1 d.f. is significant at the 95% level. Since the calculated Chi-square value of 6.377 is larger than the critical value of 3.8, we should conclude that the preferences of men and women differ.

To use χ^2, we need to satisfy the following conditions:

- The raw data for χ^2 must always be frequencies (actual numbers) and not percentages or proportions.
- All χ^2 analyses require that each respondent be counted once and only once. All respondents should be accounted for (for instance, we should include both "Yes" and "No" responses).

If the samples are very small, or if some expected events are infrequent, χ^2 may not be appropriate. (Guideline: For 2 * 2 tables or less, each expected value should be five or more; for 2*3 tables or larger tables, E should be two or more. Plus, no expected value should be less than 1.0. If these requirements are not met, there are still ways to perform this test.)

Analysis of Variance (for Metric Data)

If we want to compare more than two groups when our data are metric, analysis of variance (ANOVA) can be used. Suppose consumers rate four different products. To assess whether any product is rated differently than any other product, we first need to use an analysis of variance test, as the example illustrates.

Twelve respondents are divided into four groups of three. Each group rates a different product, A, B, C or D on a 10-point scale. (*In real life, ANOVA should not be performed on such a small sample. This is being used to illustrate the procedure. As with the t-test, several important requirements for proper statistical testing are being ignored to keep the presentation simple.*)

Their ratings are shown below.

	Product				
	A	B	C	D	
	3	10	6	7	
	6	6	6	6	
	3	8	3	8	
Total	12	24	15	21	$\sum X = 72$
$\overline{x} =$	4	8	5	7	$\overline{x} = 6$

We note from the average ratings of the four products that different products are rated differently. However, how can we tell that the average differences we see between different products are genuinely due to product differences? After all, the same product is rated differently by different respondents—for instance, product A is rated as a 3 by one respondent and as a 6 by respondent 2.

ANOVA attempts to answer this question by calculating:
1. The total variation in our data (Total Sum of Squares or SS_T). SS_T tells us how much variation is in our data in total.
2. The variation in average ratings between the products (Between Groups Sum of Squares or SS_B).

How to Analyze the Data

3. The variation in ratings for each product (Within Groups Sum of Squares or SS_W). SS_W tells us how much variation can be attributed to individuals rating the same product.

a. Compute the **total Sum of Squares (SS_T)**.

$= \sum(\text{Each value} - \text{Overall mean})^2$

$= (3-6)^2 + (6-6)^2 + (3-6)^2 + (10-6)^2 + (6-6)^2 + (8-6)^2 + (6-6)^2$
$+ (6-6)^2 + (3-6)^2 + (7-6)^2 + (6-6)^2 + (8-6)^2 = 52$

The degrees of freedom for SST = (Total number of values – 1) = 12 – 1 = 11.

b. Compute the **within the sum of squares (SS_W)**.

$= \sum(\text{Each value for the group} - \text{Group mean})^2$

$= (3-4)^2 + (6-4)^2 + (3-4)^2 +$
$(10-8)^2 + (6-8)^2 + (8-8)^2 +$
$(6-5)^2 + (6-5)^2 + (3-5)^2 +$
$(7-7)^2 + (6-7)^2 + (8-7)^2 = 22$

The degrees of freedom for SSW = (Total number of values – Total number of groups) = 12 – 4 = 8

The Mean Sum of Squares for SSW (MSW) = SSW /degrees of freedom = 22/8 = 2.75.

c. Compute between groups sum of squares **(SS_B)**.

The formula for the between-groups sum-of-squares is:

$3*(4-6)^2 + 3*(8-6)^2 + 3*(5-6)^2 + 3*(7-6)^2 = 30$. Notice that this investigates the variation of the group means around the total or grand mean. That calculation can be simplified to the following.

Between groups sum of squares = Total sum of squares – Within sum of squares

= 52 – 22

= 30

The Mean Square for between groups = 30/3 = 10. The Mean-Squares are variances.

Finally, we need to compute one more quantity, the F-ratio.

F = MSB / MSW = 10/2.75 = 3.64

These values are filled in below.

Source	Sum of Squares	Degrees of Freedom	Mean Square	F
Between	30	3	10	3.64
Within	22	8	2.75	
Total	52	11		

Now we have everything we need to evaluate to answer the question of whether respondents rated the four products differently. The table above shows that:

1. The F ratio, the statistic is 3.64.
2. The degrees of freedom for the numerator (SSB) = 3.
3. The degrees of freedom for the numerator (SSW) = 8.

Is F = 3.64 statistically significant? To answer this question, we refer to the F table on the following page. Notice that the comparison or critical value from that table for 3 degrees of freedom for the numerator and 8 degrees of freedom for the denominator is 2.9. We find that the calculated value of F = 3.64 is larger than the critical value of 2.9 with d.f. of 3 for the numerator and 8 for the denominator. Therefore, we can state that ratings for the four products are not the same and that at least one is different from the others. This finding is significant at the 90% level of confidence or 10% level of risk of a Type 1 error.

Now, consider the second table below for the 95% level of confidence or 5% level of risk of a Type 1 error. The critical value in that table for 3 and 8 degrees of freedom is 4.1. Since the calculated F value from the ANOVA is 3.64 and less than the critical value of 4.1, the correct conclusion is that the null hypothesis of no difference among the four ratings should not be rejected at the 5% level of risk. Therefore, whether we consider the results to be significant or not depends on how stringent we want our inference to be.

F table: Alpha = 0.1 (90%)

Degrees of freedom (Numerator)

	1	2	3	4	5	6	7	8	9	10	12	15	20	30	60	120
1	39.9	49.5	53.6	55.8	57.2	58.2	58.9	59.4	59.9	60.2	60.7	61.2	62.0	62.3	62.8	63.1
2	8.5	9.0	9.2	9.2	9.3	9.3	9.3	9.4	9.4	9.4	9.4	9.4	9.4	9.5	9.5	9.5
3	5.5	5.5	5.4	5.3	5.3	5.3	5.3	5.3	5.2	5.2	5.2	5.2	5.2	5.2	5.2	5.1
4	4.5	4.3	4.2	4.1	4.1	4.0	4.0	4.0	3.9	3.9	3.9	3.9	3.8	3.8	3.8	3.8
5	4.1	3.8	3.6	3.5	3.5	3.4	3.4	3.3	3.3	3.3	3.3	3.2	3.2	3.2	3.1	3.1
6	3.8	3.5	3.3	3.2	3.1	3.1	3.0	3.0	3.0	2.9	2.9	2.9	2.8	2.8	2.8	2.7
7	3.6	3.3	3.1	3.0	2.9	2.8	2.8	2.8	2.7	2.7	2.7	2.6	2.6	2.6	2.5	2.5
8	3.5	3.1	2.9	2.8	2.7	2.7	2.6	2.6	2.6	2.5	2.5	2.5	2.4	2.4	2.3	2.3
9	3.4	3.0	2.8	2.7	2.6	2.6	2.5	2.5	2.4	2.4	2.4	2.3	2.3	2.3	2.2	2.2
10	3.3	2.9	2.7	2.6	2.5	2.5	2.4	2.4	2.3	2.3	2.3	2.2	2.2	2.2	2.1	2.1
11	3.2	2.9	2.7	2.5	2.5	2.4	2.3	2.3	2.3	2.2	2.2	2.2	2.1	2.1	2.0	2.0
12	3.2	2.8	2.6	2.5	2.4	2.3	2.3	2.2	2.2	2.2	2.1	2.1	2.0	2.0	2.0	1.9
13	3.1	2.8	2.6	2.4	2.3	2.3	2.2	2.2	2.2	2.1	2.1	2.1	2.0	2.0	1.9	1.9
14	3.1	2.7	2.5	2.4	2.3	2.2	2.2	2.2	2.1	2.1	2.1	2.0	1.9	1.9	1.9	1.8
15	3.1	2.7	2.5	2.4	2.3	2.2	2.2	2.1	2.1	2.1	2.0	2.0	1.9	1.9	1.8	1.8
16	3.0	2.7	2.5	2.3	2.2	2.2	2.1	2.1	2.1	2.0	2.0	1.9	1.9	1.8	1.8	1.8
17	3.0	2.6	2.4	2.3	2.2	2.2	2.1	2.1	2.0	2.0	2.0	1.9	1.8	1.8	1.8	1.7
18	3.0	2.6	2.4	2.3	2.2	2.1	2.1	2.0	2.0	2.0	1.9	1.9	1.8	1.8	1.7	1.7
19	3.0	2.6	2.4	2.3	2.2	2.1	2.1	2.0	2.0	2.0	1.9	1.9	1.8	1.8	1.7	1.7
20	3.0	2.6	2.4	2.2	2.2	2.1	2.0	2.0	2.0	1.9	1.9	1.8	1.8	1.7	1.7	1.6
30	2.9	2.5	2.3	2.1	2.0	2.0	1.9	1.9	1.8	1.8	1.8	1.7	1.6	1.6	1.5	1.5
60	2.8	2.4	2.2	2.0	1.9	1.9	1.8	1.8	1.7	1.7	1.7	1.6	1.5	1.5	1.4	1.3
120	2.7	2.3	2.1	2.0	1.9	1.8	1.8	1.7	1.7	1.7	1.6	1.5	1.4	1.4	1.3	1.3

Degrees of freedom (Denominator)

For F-table: Alpha = 0.05 (95%), see next page)

When the results turn out to be significant, we can use multiple range tests (not described here) to find out which groups are different from which other groups. Those tests are equivalent to conducting all of the t-tests on pairs that were listed previously.

The main advantage of using ANOVA is that we partition the variance in such a way as to answer:

- How much of it is due to differences in product rating?
- How much of it is due to random variations?

These ideas can be extended to other complex designs. ANOVA is very seldom carried out manually. It is almost always carried out using a computer package, as are the other tests mentioned here. Once again, several statistical requirements for conducting ANOVA have been ignored to simplify the presentation.

F table: Alpha = 0.05 (95%)

Degrees of freedom (Numerator)

Degrees of freedom (Denominator)

	1	2	3	4	5	6	7	8	9	10	12	15	20	30	60
$df_2=1$	161.4	199.5	215.7	224.6	230.2	234.0	236.8	238.9	240.5	241.9	243.9	245.9	249.1	250.1	252
2	18.5	19.0	19.2	19.2	19.3	19.3	19.4	19.4	19.4	19.4	19.4	19.4	19.5	19.5	19
3	10.1	9.6	9.3	9.1	9.0	8.9	8.9	8.8	8.8	8.8	8.7	8.7	8.6	8.6	8
4	7.7	6.9	6.6	6.4	6.3	6.2	6.1	6.0	6.0	6.0	5.9	5.9	5.8	5.7	5
5	6.6	5.8	5.4	5.2	5.1	5.0	4.9	4.8	4.8	4.7	4.7	4.6	4.5	4.5	4
6	6.0	5.1	4.8	4.5	4.4	4.3	4.2	4.1	4.1	4.1	4.0	3.9	3.8	3.8	3
7	5.6	4.7	4.3	4.1	4.0	3.9	3.8	3.7	3.7	3.6	3.6	3.5	3.4	3.4	3
8	5.3	4.5	4.1	3.8	3.7	3.6	3.5	3.4	3.4	3.3	3.3	3.2	3.1	3.1	3
9	5.1	4.3	3.9	3.6	3.5	3.4	3.3	3.2	3.2	3.1	3.1	3.0	2.9	2.9	2
10	5.0	4.1	3.7	3.5	3.3	3.2	3.1	3.1	3.0	3.0	2.9	2.8	2.7	2.7	2
11	4.8	4.0	3.6	3.4	3.2	3.1	3.0	2.9	2.9	2.9	2.8	2.7	2.6	2.6	2
12	4.7	3.9	3.5	3.3	3.1	3.0	2.9	2.8	2.8	2.8	2.7	2.6	2.5	2.5	2
13	4.7	3.8	3.4	3.2	3.0	2.9	2.8	2.8	2.7	2.7	2.6	2.5	2.4	2.4	
14	4.6	3.7	3.3	3.1	3.0	2.8	2.8	2.7	2.6	2.6	2.5	2.5	2.3	2.3	2
15	4.5	3.7	3.3	3.1	2.9	2.8	2.7	2.6	2.6	2.5	2.5	2.4	2.3	2.2	
20	4.4	3.5	3.1	2.9	2.7	2.6	2.5	2.4	2.4	2.3	2.3	2.2	2.1	2.0	1
30	4.2	3.3	2.9	2.7	2.5	2.4	2.3	2.3	2.2	2.2	2.1	2.0	1.9	1.8	1
60	4.0	3.2	2.8	2.5	2.4	2.3	2.2	2.1	2.0	2.0	1.9	1.8	1.7	1.6	1
120	3.9	3.1	2.7	2.4	2.3	2.2	2.1	2.0	2.0	1.9	1.8	1.8	1.6	1.6	1

A Measure of Association—Correlation

Is smoking related to lung cancer? Is income related to expenditure? Do people with higher education get better jobs? Is the purchase intent related to buying behaviour?

Questions like these can be answered by calculating a measure called the correlation coefficient. A correlation coefficient is a number that summarizes the relationship between two variables. The value of the correlation coefficient can range from −1.0 to + 1.0.

A very high positive correlation means that the two variables under consideration are highly related. For example, if we find a very high correlation (0.8 or more) between the number of cigarettes smoked and the incidence of lung cancer, then it would follow that as the number of cigarettes smoked increases, so does the incidence of lung cancer; conversely, as the number of cigarettes smoked decreases, so does the incidence of lung cancer.

A correlation of 0.6 or more (but less than 0.8) would lead us to the same conclusion but with a lower degree of certainty. A correlation of 0.4 or more (but less than 0.6) would still indicate an identifiable relationship. If the correlation is less than 0.4 but greater than 0.2, we will infer a weak relationship between the variables. A correlation that is between 0.0 to 0.2 indicates that the relationship if it exists at all, is too weak. A statistical test can be calculated to determine if the correlation is significantly different from zero, i.e., no correlation.

A very high negative correlation (for example, −0.8) means that the two variables under consideration are highly—albeit negatively—related. For instance, if there is a negative relationship between regularity of exercising and the incidence of minor illness, the correlation between the two variables would be negative. The interpretation of the magnitude of negative correlations is similar to the interpretation of the magnitude of positive correlations.

The interpretation provided here is just a rule-of-thumb guideline. There is no magical difference between a correlation of 0.78 and another of 0.81. Another thing to bear in mind is that correlation does not mean causation. If smoking and lung cancer are correlated, it does not automatically follow that smoking causes lung cancer. It merely means that both these variables are related, and it is up to the researcher to find out if the relationship is spurious or real.

Relationships are **spurious** when two variables are highly correlated but not directly related to each other. For example, there might be a high correlation between the number of rats and the size of the human population. It might simply mean that, over time, both the rat and human populations have increased. The increase in the rat population did not cause an increase in the human population or vice versa. A high correlation in such instances is called spurious.

Consequently, you should avoid inferring causal relationships based purely on correlations. For instance, assuming if the group as a whole may be less well educated, that they automatically have less earning power. The relationship between literacy/level of education attained and income earned is thus spurious. (When we find strong correlations, the causality can be established by using techniques of experimental design.)

There are several techniques available for calculating correlations. One of the most widely used methods is known as the Pearson product-moment correlation, which is used on metric or measured data. Other correlation measures are available for ordinal and nominal data.

Regression Analysis

We are often faced with the problem of identifying how a critical marketing variable is affected by several other variables. How do different attributes of an organization affect customer loyalty? How do variables such as inflation, discretionary income, and advertising expenditures affect sales? Which of a product's attributes influence the overall valuation of that product? What is the contribution of different service attributes to customer satisfaction? What are the 'key drivers' of purchase behaviour? Answers to questions like these enable the marketer to deploy resources effectively and predict, however weakly, the course of future events and the potential effects of specific marketing actions.

Regression analysis answers the question, 'what sets of weights attached to independent variables will predict the value of the dependent variable with maximum accuracy?' (When we have only one independent variable, the technique is called 'simple regression'; when we have more than one independent variable the technique is called 'multiple regression.') The criterion variable is seen as a linear (weighted) combination of independent variables. Regression analysis is a metric technique. Since variables are not inherently dependent or independent, it is for the marketer to specify which variable is considered dependent and which are considered independent. (For instance, it may be considered equally valid to say that satisfaction with price leads to satisfaction with the company, and that satisfaction with the company leads to satisfaction with the price.)

Why do the Regression Analysis?

Let's start with this question: how do we increase customer satisfaction? To know the answer to this question, we need to know what contributes to customer satisfaction. Is it *quality? Price? Availability? Prestige?* If many variables contribute to customer satisfaction, which are the most important ones? How important is each attribute compared to others in contributing to customer satisfaction? Questions like these can be answered by multiple regression analysis. In regression analysis, we try to understand the relationship between one single variable (for example, customer satisfaction) and several other variables (such as *price, quality, availability* and *prestige*).

Regression analysis is used in several contexts in marketing and research. Some of these are:

- What variables affect customer satisfaction? How much does each of the influencing variables contribute to customer satisfaction?
- What are the key drivers (the most critical variables) that influence how likely a consumer is to buy our brand?
- What would happen to my sales if we increase the price by 10%?
- What will our sales be under different possible scenarios?

Here are some examples of marketing problems that attempt to relate several independent variables to a dependent variable, making them suitable for tackling using regression analysis:

1. Customers rate a company on a 10-point scale on several characteristics such as *customer service, price competitiveness, product quality*, and *responsiveness*. The marketing manager would like to know whether these ratings will enable her to predict how a customer would rate the company overall. She would also like to know the exclusive effect of each one of these attributes on the dependent variable.
2. A luxury goods manufacturer would like to forecast their sales for the next 12 months. Experience has shown that factors such as *inflation rate, interest rate* and *discretionary income* affect the purchase of luxury goods. The manufacturer has data for the past 20 years on these variables and would like to understand how they affect sales, so the relationship can be used to predict sales for the next 12 months.
3. A marketer has a database with a wealth of information on customer demographics and a score for loyalty (self-rated *intention to buy again*). The marketer would like to know which of the demographics influence loyalty.

Examples - where regression analysis may be used

What we want to predict (Dependent variable)	What we want to predict with (Independent variables)
Customer satisfaction	Price, quality, service, etc.
Customer loyalty	Customer satisfaction, value etc.
Sales	Price, distribution, etc.

How to do Regression Analysis

1. Decide what variable you are interested in as your primary focus. For example, your primary focus may be *Overall Customer Satisfaction.*
2. Decide the variables that are likely to influence Overall Satisfaction. These could be variables such as *Product Quality, Durability, Price,* etc.
3. Collect data. In our current example, you may ask customers to rate their satisfaction and evaluate product quality, price etc. Typically, customers would be asked to rate these attributes on a scale (such as a 10-point scale).
4. Submit the data to multiple regression analysis. (All statistical applications such as SAS, SPSS, R and Python have simple functions that perform regression calculations.)
5. Interpret the results.

For example, in a survey, 2,500 customers rated a shopping mall. The rating covered their total experience – including the experience of driving to the mall, parking etc. Customers rated the mall on 11 variables and their *overall satisfaction* with the mall. The variables were ease of parking, the heaviness of traffic, friendliness of staff, efficiency of staff, cleanliness, safety, *quality of food (food court), overall experience, customer service, price, variety,* and *overall satisfaction.*

The research question is which of these attributes are "key drivers" or the variables that have the highest leverage on customer satisfaction.

To answer this question, we submit the data to multiple regression analysis. Here are some of the critical things that the analysis provides.

The correlation matrix. Exhibit 7.3 shows how each variable in our analysis is related to every other variable. Following this, the analysis typically provides the information shown in the exhibit below.

Exhibit 7.3: The Correlation Matrix (All columns are not shown)

Variables	Traffic	Parking	Friendly	Efficient	Clean	Safety
Traffic	1.00	0.51	0.23	0.24	0.28	0.22
Parking	0.51	1.00	0.15	0.16	0.20	0.18
Friendly	0.23	0.15	1.00	0.55	0.51	0.43
Efficient	0.24	0.16	0.55	1.00	0.43	0.40
Clean	0.28	0.20	0.51	0.43	1.00	0.41
Safety	0.22	0.18	0.43	0.40	0.41	1.00
Food	0.20	0.15	0.36	0.35	0.35	0.28
Experience	0.16	0.10	0.31	0.31	0.28	0.21
CustService	0.18	0.16	0.35	0.38	0.33	0.31
Price	0.13	0.07	0.24	0.23	0.21	0.19
Variety	0.10	0.07	0.19	0.19	0.19	0.20
OverallSat	0.16	0.10	0.32	0.34	0.31	0.27

Regression Analysis Results

Variable	B	Std.Err.	t	Pr > |t|	Beta
Intercept	0.37	0.09	4.16	< 0.0001	
Price	0.30	0.02	16.73	< 0.0001	0.29
Food	0.13	0.01	9.28	< 0.0001	0.16
Variety	0.10	0.01	9.84	< 0.0001	0.18
CustService	0.08	0.01	5.73	< 0.0001	0.10
Experience	0.08	0.01	6.77	< 0.0001	0.12
Efficient	0.08	0.02	4.43	< 0.0001	0.08
Clean	0.07	0.02	3.23	0.00	0.06

R-Squared: 0.67 (67%)

The table is interpreted as follows:

Predictive Model (The 'b' coefficients)

The first column of the table is the "predictive model." It shows the impact each variable has on *overall satisfaction*. For example, *price* has a b-coefficient to 0.30. This means, if we improve price perception by one point, the overall satisfaction should go up by 0.30 points. If we improve the *food* perception by 1 point, the overall satisfaction should go up by 0.13 points and so on.

However, it does not tell us how important a variable is compared to another. *Food* has a 'b' coefficient of 0.13, and *variety* has a coefficient of 0.10. This does not mean the *food* is more important in relation to *overall satisfaction*. There are other factors (such as scale value and variance) that help explain the influence of each predictor on the response variable.

The third and fourth columns indicate which variables may be significantly related to Satisfaction. The null hypothesis is that each independent variable is NOT related to the dependent variable, Satisfaction. If the p-value, or Pr > |t|, is 0.05 (5% risk) or smaller, it is likely that the independent variable is significantly related to Satisfaction. A common procedure is to execute the regression on all of the independent variables and then eliminate those that have p-values larger

How to Analyze the Data

than 0.05. However, due to some of the complications mentioned below, i.e., multicollinearity and outliers, this can be a complicated process.

The Relative Importance of Variables (The beta coefficients)

If you want to know the rank order of importance of these variables, you need to look at 'beta' coefficients (the last column). The 'beta' coefficients are standardized 'b' coefficients. (Please note that while the beta coefficient is most often used, there are other measures of importance that may be better.)

Standardized regression coefficients. The beta coefficient tells us the rank order of the importance of different variables. For example, we have a beta coefficient of 0.18 for *variety* and 0.16 for *food*. So, *variety* is more important than *food*, although it was reversed with 'b' coefficients. Similarly, 'b' coefficients are the same for *experience* and *efficiency* (0.08), but the 'beta' coefficients indicate that *experience* is more critical than *efficiency*. Standardized beta coefficients are one of many metrics for identifying the relative importance of the independent variables for predicting the dependent variable.

R-squared Underneath the table, you also see another value, "R-Squared = .67". R-squared shows how well the key drivers taken together predict customer satisfaction. In our example, it is .67 or 67%. This means that these six key drivers account for two thirds (67%) of all variability in customer satisfaction.

What Else Should You Know?

Be careful of highly correlated variables. A problem known as *collinearity* occurs when two or more independent variables are highly correlated among themselves. This is known as *multicollinearity* or simply *collinearity*. Multicollinearity makes the regression coefficients unstable, making the analysis unreliable. This problem is not always easy to identify by examining the correlation matrix. However, most computer programs provide diagnostics to identify collinearity. When we encounter multicollinearity, we can combine the collinear variables; use alternative techniques such as ridge regression, or apply principal components analysis to the original data and substitute component scores for the values of measured variables.

Look for possible 'influential observations.' Sometimes we get some data points that are not typical and commonly known as 'outliers.' These outliers affect the dependent variable in a way that is very different from other data points. These atypical observations can be so influential that they can change the regression line substantially. The most common reasons for influential observations are (1) atypical behaviour of some individuals in a sample; and (2) mistakes in data entry. Since influential observations change the regression line such that it fits less well for the remaining observations, it is important to spot and eliminate influential observations. Influential observations exert a much stronger influence when the sample is small than when it is large. In marketing research, the sample tends to be large, so this problem is not as common as other problems such as multicollinearity. However, there are cases where it can be a major concern and, therefore, cannot be ignored.

Be careful about extrapolating the results. Regression analysis is often carried out for predictive purposes, such as sales forecasting. For example, by using regression analysis, we can identify the relationship between *sales* and other variables (such as *inflation rate, interest rate* and *price of the product*) over the past several years. We can then use this equation to predict sales in the future. This extrapolation of the equation of data outside the range can be risky. This is because the validity of the equation outside the range is not tested and cannot be taken for granted. Relationships that worked for the period 1980-2000 may not work very well if applied to 2000-2020. In general, extrapolation of the equation to points that are closer to the model range is less risky than those that are farther away. For instance, applying a forecasting equation developed on data for years 2010-2015 to the years 2016 and 2020 is likely to be less risky than applying the same equation to 2020 and 2025.

Make sure the relationship is a straight line. Regression analysis assumes that the relationship between the dependent and the independent variables is a straight line. This may not always be the case. For instance, if we relate actual income to the percentage spent on luxury items, we may find that the more you earn, the more you spend on luxury goods. However, the overall relationship may not be linear. For instance, the highest income group may spend less money on luxury goods (as a proportion of their income) than the middle-income group. Yet within each of these income groups, there may be a linear relationship between income and proportion of income spent on luxury goods. Non-linearity can be identified by looking at the residuals. If residuals exhibit a non-random pattern on either side of the mean, then the relationship may be non-linear.

Make sure your sample is not too small. If the sample size is not substantially larger than the number of variables, then it is possible to get large R^2 values even when there is no relationship. A rule of thumb in applied research would be to have at least ten respondents per variable so that in the above example, we should aim to have a minimum of 200 respondents. It is true that in many cases, this is not possible. For instance, in forecasting sales using ten variables, we may not have 100 years (or even 100 quarters) of data. Even if we had, the relationship of these variables to sales might have changed over the years. In such cases, R^2 values that do not exceed the expected value, as computed above, should be used with extreme caution.

Remember, you specify the model. Consider a regression equation in which the investigator tries to predict overall customer satisfaction through variables such as customer evaluation of the company's *product quality, service quality, price*, etc. On the face of it, the model looks reasonable. But is the customer satisfied overall because of price acceptance, or did overall satisfaction with the company lead to price acceptance? Marketing actions will depend on the nature of such relationships. If satisfaction leads to price acceptance, then the marketer would attempt to increase customer satisfaction. If price acceptance led to satisfaction, then the marketer might find ways to ensure that the price is acceptable to customers and abides by corporate and competitive constraints. Identifying the nature of relationships is not a statistical problem. So, the researcher should pay a lot of attention to the reasonableness of the model as specified.

Modelling and Analytic Techniques

Modern research relies heavily on advanced modelling techniques such as correlation analysis, factor analysis (principal component analysis), segmentation and predictive analytics. These techniques are becoming increasingly important in research. The following paragraphs provide a sketchy description of these techniques. It is important that you supplement your knowledge by reading a basic book on analytic techniques. (A non-technical book that is specifically aimed at marketing researchers is *Analytics for Customer Insights: A Non-technical Introduction* by Chuck Chakrapani.) At a minimum, you should have a good knowledge of analytic techniques at least at a non-technical level

Predictive analytics. Predicting the future, even if it is only five minutes away, is as natural as eating and drinking. Humans are driven to predict. Marketers continually strive to understand how they can change the pricing, design, communication and distribution of their brands to increase sales, market share and profit. That involves prediction. And that type of prediction relies on the many tools of marketing and is called marketing mix analysis. In marketing analytics, prediction is the central purpose and regression is the main technique. While prediction may be the most important objective, predictive models can and usually should be used for explaining the reasons for why high values of certain predictor variables lead to high values of the response variable while low values of other predictor variables lead to high values of the response variable. This interpretation function of predictive modeling is very important so that marketing decision makers understand the reasons for making specific marketing mix decisions and not just what values to specify.

Example. An online retail sales and delivery company needs to better understand how to increase its sales in the Atlantic provinces. Those provinces are a substantial distance from the company's main distribution centres and the population is relatively low. What will increase the volume of sales to make shipping to that region more worthwhile? The company conducts a marketing research survey on a random sample of online shoppers across the Atlantic provinces. Many questions are asked, including measures of customer satisfaction, expectations, intentions to buy and intentions to recommend the company to acquaintances. Those measures are all attitudes. The survey asked about past sales and that is a behavioural characteristic. Questions are asked about pricing, advertising, internet usage, delivery preferences and types of products that subjects like to buy online. Customer perceptions and preferences about the company itself, its image, are also retrieved. As part of the company's online policy, it asks and received permission to collect sales and other information about its customers and then warehouses that data. After completing the survey, the company has a comprehensive profile of its customers and, perhaps, non-customers. The marketing director commissions its analytics group to develop a model for predicting customers' likely purchasing responses to various alterations to the marketing strategy. This is likely to become the justification for making changes to pricing, delivery practices and other marketing activities that promise to increase sales and profit. Such a predictive model can have a lengthy shelf-life and be revised periodically based on regular surveys and data collection.

Correlation Analysis

Correlation analysis measures the degree to which items are related. This is a word that most people naturally understand. We often hear comments such as people being in good spirits and the amount of sunshine are highly correlated. In marketing, the strength of correlation between buyers' satisfaction with a brand and their incidence of purchasing that brand might provide valuable insights. Correlation between an attitudinal or perceptual measure and an outcome behavioural measure to understand what is driving that behaviour may provide useful marketing insights. This is helpful in uncovering what perceptions or attitudes are likely driving behaviour. But correlations analysis does not work in a directional manner; it just describes how two things move together in the same direction or in different directions, whether strongly, weakly or not at all in sync.

> **Example.** A questionnaire is designed for a toy manufacturer to understand what factors motivate parents (and grandparents) to buy one toy rather than another for a child. The factor analysis reveals that key themes are value, 'up-to-date', educational impact, status, participation of both child and parent, durability and link to favorite cartoons. The correlation analysis might reveal that the most important driver is participation of both child and parent. This can help the manufacturer find ways to include adults in design, decision making and to be featured in marketing campaigns.

Factor Analysis and Principal Component Analysis

Factor analysis and principal component analysis are data reduction techniques that use response patterns to group together statements or attributes data from a survey in order to identify common underlying themes. They basically identify semantic similarities among concepts.

> **Example.** In a study about laundry detergent, consumers were asked to check off the characteristics that they would use to describe several brands. Invariably, those statements that spoke to good value (lower prices, often on sale, more value for the money) were used to describe one or two products and not others. Statements that pointed to strength (works on tough stains, removes 'ring-around-the-collar', removes even the toughest dirt) are used to describe one or two brands and not others. Statements that talk about cleaning well (gets clothes clean, removes everyday dirt, keeps whites white, etc.) are used to describe one or two. These groupings are likely to emerge from principal component analysis as "themes".

The groupings of descriptors or statements into themes, principal components or factors, helps us understand the underlying commonalities in the data. This is particularly useful if there are many descriptors for the same theme (e.g., getting clothes clean). Factor analysis would group them all together allowing other themes to emerge.

The principal components derived in this way can provide input into other consumer understanding analysis. This can lead to reducing the number of questions asked if several tend to mean the same thing.

Cluster Analysis (segmentation)

Segmentation is both a key marketing strategy for an organization as well as being a type of analysis that extends consumer understanding. Deciding to follow marketing strategies built on segmentation is a serious decision for organizations. There must be convincing evidence that marketing differently to several diverse target segments will produce greater corporate returns than will mass marketing.

Not all consumers react the same way to products, advertising, pricing or positioning. Every consumer is a unique individual. Previously, marketers could not tailor their messaging to the hundreds of millions of North Americans who are shoppers 18 years and older. Currently, personalization strategies are being developed that provide for targeting each subject differently. At the other end of the scale, marketing in the same way to the entire population of a market, i.e., mass marketing, might mean that the marketing is directly relevant to very few consumers.

Segmentation analysis divides the population into manageable *clusters* of the relevant market population. Those within each segment share behaviour, attitudes and demographics – making them more homogeneous. A well-executed segmentation creates several segments each of which is distinctly different from the others.

Marketing segmentation identifies and characterizes each segment so that the marketing managers can determine to which segments they should market and which may be bypassed. While there may be an overall predictive model, most marketers will develop predictive models for each of the segments it decides to target.

> **Example 1.** A cellphone company commissions a segmentation study to understand how it can best target identifiable groups of consumers with different plans. The segmentation study reveals that there are needs-based segments characterized by how people like to interact with others.
> - One group are very family-focused and really use their phone only to connect (calling as much as texting) with the same 3 or 4 or 5 people all of the time – likely spouses, children and other family members. For this group, it makes sense to offer a family-and-friends package on a very simple phone.
> - Another group is characterized by a desire to be the nexus of a very large social circle. They love to organize, post photos of gatherings and find last minute events to attend. They are heavy texters and rarely make a phone call. They are generally younger and unmarried. For this group, the company can design a plan with free connections to a defined group of friends.
> - A third group uses their phone as a mini-computer, a constant companion that they always have with them. They do research, watch videos, play games, but rarely connect with others by phone. This segment would respond well to a data-only plan.
>
> **Example 2.** A liquor conglomerate has a wide range of beverage alcohol and liqueur brands. Their segmentation research has found that there are identifiable groups who have different needs and

motivations when they are drinking. By focusing on these motivations, they can align different products with different groups. They identified:

- A younger, largely female group who use alcohol to signal that it is OK to let their hair down and go a little crazy. Coolers (a wine/alcohol mix) have a lower price point, a lower alcohol content and fun, sweeter flavours. They would be ideal for an all-night party.
- A largely male group with higher incidence among specific ethnic groups who use alcohol as a badge of sophistication. Higher end beverage alcohol like Scotch whisky or cognac fit the bill and can target these consumers.
- An older group, equally male and female, in higher income brackets are showing a growing interest in older mixed drinks, Manhattans, Martinis, Highballs, etc. These consumers are interested in the authenticity of the products they consume and gravitate towards older, well-known brands of vodka, gin and rye.
- An adventurous group, spanning all age groups, are interested in exploring new and interesting products. They might be tagged by unusual flavourings or beverages that come from other parts of the world (e.g., sake from Japan, or Amarula from South Africa).

By identifying differentiating characteristics that are important to different groups of consumers, segmentation can ensure a company's varied services don't cannibalize each other.

Sometimes, a marketer will want to understand how people make their decisions; in what order they consider product characteristics when choosing between a number of offerings. With this knowledge, retailers can understand how best to organize products on a shelf (planogram), manufacturers can decide what to emphasize in their broader advertising and what to focus on in the store.

The tool that is often employed is a **decision tree.** It would determine, for example, if consumers first decide what 'brand' they want to buy. Then once they are certain about the brand, they may choose a product that offers that pack size they are looking for. Then the final branch may be to seek out a specific flavour.

There are many ways to do a decision tree study. Most involve a simulated shopping exercise where consumers are shown a shelf and then are asked to make a 'purchase'. That product is then taken away and they pick their 'second choice'. The characteristics that are similar between these two products can be considered the first branch in the decision tree. The exercise is repeated for successive branches.

Discrete Choice Experiments (Conjoint Analysis)

Conjoint analysis (especially in its most popular version, Discrete Choice Experiments or DCE) has become an extremely important method for designing new products, redesigning existing products, determining pricing, measuring brand equity and many other tasks. Because of its importance in marketing research, we describe this technique in greater detail here.

DCEs are true experiments that randomly recruit respondents and randomly assign them to different stimuli. This process involves showing respondents several **variations in the design** of the product in which different attributes are switched around at the same time (conjointly). The respondents' experiences are similar to real-life repetitive shopping in that they simply view the product offerings and choose the one option they like the best or decide not to buy any.

The information is then analyzed to determine the relative importance of each of those attributes in driving the purchase decision and respondents' relative preferences for each level of each attribute.

One of these attributes can be price – making conjoint analysis a highly effective type of pricing research.

Example. Swish is at an earlier stage in the design of their condo-sized laundry detergent. They can still design a different sized product (800 ml, 1 litre, 1.2 litres), launch it initially with 'unscented', morning fresh or lemon scents, price it at $8.95, $9.95, $11.95, $14.95 or $15.95, and add a drip proof lip or not. We have 4 attributes at play (size, scent, price and lip) and each attribute has between two and five levels. Each respondent is shown 8 choice tasks where they are shown three different variations of the product, each one mixing together a different combination of the variables and levels and is asked which of the three they would likely buy. They might see an 800 ml, unscented product with no lip for $11.95, and then a 1.2 litre morning fresh scented product with a lip for $14.95 etc. When analyzed, the results will show the utility of each level of each variable and guide us to the optimal combination of attributes that will attract the most potential buyers.

Prohibitions or rules can be established so that 'impossible' combinations are never shown. In the example above, the 'no drip lip' on the bottle may be impossible to include if the product is sold for less than $11.95, so it will never be shown in combination with the $8.95 and $9.95 price points.

As in all conjoint studies, the product must be broken down into its main attributes (e.g., size, price, brand, ingredients, etc.). For each attribute, a range of alternative levels is defined so that each alternative level spans the range of realistic offerings of the product in its intended markets. However, in this case, the product formulations are shown on a shelf *with similar products* and a 'none of these' or opt-out option. Rather than asking how likely each respondent would be to buy the product, they are asked which product they would buy (if any) multiple times as the test product shifts attributes and levels.

Example. An internet provider is defined by three attributes: speed of connection, monthly cost, and activation/installation fee. This is an unusually small example comprised of only three very simple attributes. Speed is expressed by multiples of dial-up speeds and range from 10 times faster to 100 times faster than dial-up. The monthly cost is set at a minimum of $24.95 and a maximum of $54.95. The fee to activate and install is either $20 or $25. The respondents are shown a variation in this new internet product, with the major competitor's product and dial up next to it (along with a 'none of these') and are asked to choose an internet product. After choosing, the client's product which is shown with a speed 30 times faster than dial-up, a price of $24.95 per month for unlimited usage, and a $20 activation/installation fee over the two competitors, the next screen appears with a different formulation for the client's product, and the same competitive products. The respondent then makes another choice and moves to the next screen, and so on.

An Example of Three Attributes and Levels with Each (Internet Provider)

Speed
100· faster than dial-up
50· faster than dial-up
30· faster than dial-up
10· faster than dial-up

Monthly Cost
$54.95 a month
$44.95 a month
$34.95 a month
$24.95 a month

Activation/Installation Fee
$20.00
$25.00

A key benefit of DCEs is that respondents are asked to make totally natural decisions during the survey, picking one product to "buy" out of several shown or buying nothing. Two choice tasks are shown below. In the first choice task, subjects are asked to select one of the two product configurations shown or indicate that they would not buy either of the so-called random alternatives. That request is repeated for the second choice task and for the following eight, 10 or 12 choice tasks.

One Choice Screen of the Discrete Choice Experiment

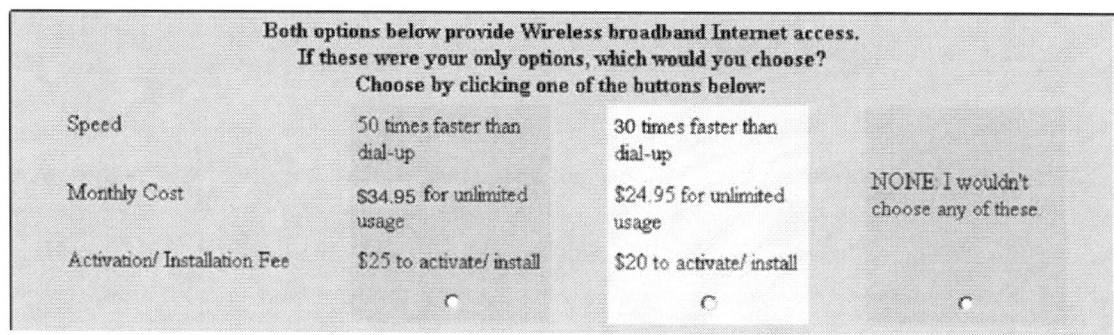

A Second-Choice Screen of the DCE

How to Analyze the Data

	Both options below provide Wireless broadband Internet access. If these were your only options, which would you choose? Choose by clicking one of the buttons below:		
Speed	100 times faster than dial-up	10 times faster than dial-up	NONE: I wouldn't choose any of these.
Monthly Cost	$44.95 for unlimited usage	$24.95 for unlimited usage	
Activation/Installation Fee	$25 to activate/install	$25 to activate/install	
	○	○	○

Highly sophisticated economic and psychological theory supports DCEs. Methods for analyzing the data are highly developed and provide for approaches that suit different study designs.

As long as the full range is covered by these prices, we can **interpolate** between levels. For example, the company could easily determine the attractiveness of a monthly cost of $49.95. However, **extrapolation** above the maximum shown or below the minimum should never be attempted.

The analysis provides the relative importance of the attributes in contributing to the respondents' decisions. For example, transmission speed may turn out to be the most important with monthly cost slightly less important, as shown below. The activation/installation fee is only slightly important to making this decision.

Importance of attributes

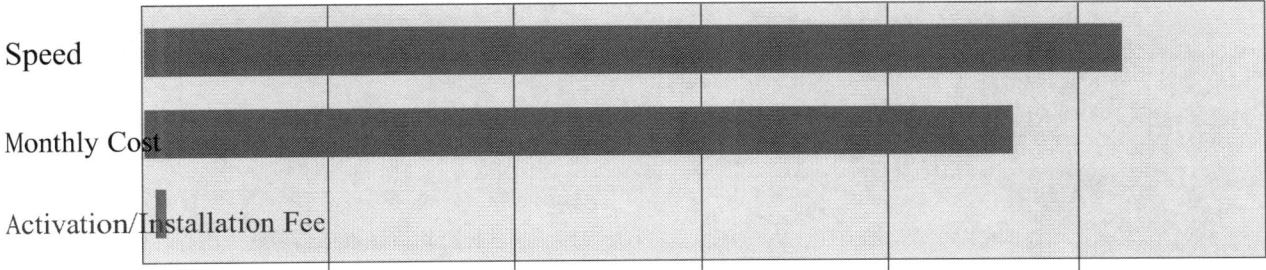

The analysis also provides the information for constructing **utility graphs** that show respondents' preferences for each of the several levels of each attribute. The so-called part-worth utilities are graphed below for broadband customers and for dial-up customers separately. The steeper the line, the more sensitive respondents are to price. If price were totally inelastic, the price utility line would be horizontal. Notice that dial-up customers are more sensitive to price than are broadband customers.

Preferences (Part-worth Utilities) for Monthly Cost

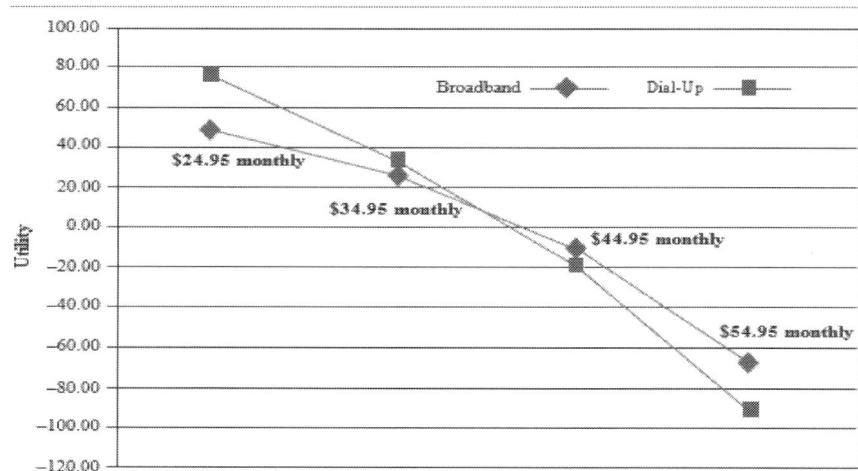

Conjoint analysis can be conducted with software from general-purpose statistical packages such as SPSS, SAS or more specialized software such as Lighthouse Studio from Sawtooth Software. There are R-code packages, such as ChoiceModelR and DisplayR, for conducting discrete choice experiments and this can be done using Python as well.

Ultimately, conjoint analysis allows the researcher to find the optimal configuration of the product, including the optimal price point that will maximize revenue for the client. That is done by running simulations to identify the degree of shares-of-preference among differently configured products. Many consider the simulations to be the major benefit of DCEs since it is somewhat like testing the market prior to actually committing to the final product.

Concluding Comments

While this unit touches only the surface of the statistical techniques used in marketing research, most researchers who are not statistical specialists tend to do only a few tests. These include calculating the margins of error and calculating the simple statistical significance tests. Statistical specialists usually do everything else. However, a highly competent research professional will be familiar with the meaning and implications of different statistical techniques that are used in marketing research.

UNIT 10

How to Present the Findings

All of the work that researchers do to collect, tabulate and analyze data is of little use if the findings are not communicated to the client in a way that they can readily interpret to help them understand and solve their marketing problem.

In this unit, we will discuss common approaches to ensuring your findings are accessible, useable and shareable within the client organization.

This unit is divided into four sections.

1. **Basic principles of communication**. The first part presents basic but important principles of business communication. A marketing research report is a type of business communication and can be improved markedly by following these principles.

2. **Writing reports in a presentation format**. The second part discusses the specifics of preparing the research reports in PowerPoint (or something similar).

3. **Presentation to an audience**. The third part deals with preparing an actual in-person presentation. The COVID-19 pandemic has accelerated the acceptance of 'virtual' presentations, and this unit includes on some pointers.
4. **Workshops**. Increasingly, research suppliers are helping their clients integrate the research findings into the client organization's corporate culture by running facilitated workshops. This section introduces some of the basic principles and approaches.

What are the Marketing Research 'Deliverables'?

There are several acceptable formats for the main "deliverable" from marketing research projects. When the contract for the project is written, the research client and the research consultant will agree on one or several deliverables. The list of deliverables can contain everything from the final research plan, the questionnaire, the sampling plan, the field plan, daily or weekly disposition reports, the tabulation plan, the data tables and data files, a topline report, a final written report, a personal presentation and a workshop.

- The **research instruments** including questionnaires, sampling and tab plans, are likely to be of interest to only the most research-focused clients with well-organized archives. They would be of interest primarily if a study will be repeated several years down the road.
- **Field disposition reports** show how many interviews have been completed and provide information on incidence and qualification rates. Not all clients will need this much detail, but they can help reassure them and help them communicate progress within their organization.
- A **topline report** is a succinct summary of marketing research findings focused on the key objectives only. Toplines are created shortly after the fieldwork is completed and may be necessary if the client has to make a quick decision or needs to show progress on the study contractually. Because they are often written before the research team has had time to reflect on the meaning of the results and make judgmental adjustments to the data, toplines should always be accompanied by a caveat that they are "an early view into the data and do not represent the final analysis."

There should always be a description or understanding of the format for the **final report**. Sometimes the primary deliverable is as basic as a set of cross-tabulated tables or as complex as a lengthy formal written report and workshop.

The most common forms of the final deliverable include:
1. Raw data
2. Data cross-tabulated against key variables
3. A report written in Word and/or PowerPoint format
4. A personal presentation

The most common format in North America and Europe is PowerPoint. A client is free to ask for and receive other deliverables as well, and that specification should be reflected in the project budget. New presentation formats are emerging that provide a more dynamic and visual presentation of the data. An engaging, even entertaining, report is more likely to have an impact.

Sometimes a presentation must be done in PowerPoint, and the final report is provided in full written format.

Structure of a Formal Research Report

Many client organizations have very specific style sheets for material that is distributed internally. Research suppliers should provide deliverables in formats that can be used with minimal changes for internal communication within the client organization. This is sometimes a delicate balance between the client's style sheet and the supplier's own brand look.

Because the report is often the researcher's only contact with the ultimate decision-maker, it could be the most critical part of the research project. So, make sure that you give careful attention to writing this vital document. While the previous sections apply to all business communications, this section contains basic principles for writing and improving marketing research reports in particular. There is, of course, considerable overlap between general business communication and written research reports.

A variety of report formats are used in marketing research. However, two particular formats appear most often; the *full report* and the *report based on the PowerPoint* presentation. The structures of these two types of reports are similar. The difference is that the full report is a more formal document containing the standard text format for headings, subheads, and paragraphs with key points illustrated by exhibits, whereas the PowerPoint report is focused on displays of the analytical findings and contains brief sidebars with further explanation. The PowerPoint reports will often include several pages of text in addition to the many pages of exhibits plus sidebar text.

If your company does not have a predetermined format for research reports, you may want to follow the following sequence.

Title or Cover Page

This page contains the title of the study, the name of the client, and the name of the research house and the date. Some clients prefer to have their corporate logo displayed while others do not; ask first to ensure that the correct protocol is followed.

The "look" of the title page is important. It sets the tone for the report and invites the reader in. Increasingly, distinctive colours and large colourful illustrations or photos are used to boost corporate identity for the supplier and to increase anticipation. The visual 'tone' established by the title page should carry through the whole report.

Executive Summary

This is a brief section that contains a summary of the study and its key findings. It is the most critical part of the report. It will be read first. It will be read intensely. In many cases, nothing else will be read.

The project sponsor has been waiting for several weeks (maybe months) for the answers that you know, but he or she will only find out after receiving the report. The yearning for information should be satisfied quickly, effectively, and painlessly in the executive summary.

One common approach is to provide the key findings as numbered paragraphs, the fewer the better. If the report is in PowerPoint, the executive summary should be one or two slides of bullet points.

More visual approaches are increasingly popular, showing the key findings as a roadmap or floor plan of different rooms in a house, to link it to the subject matter.

Begin the executive summary with a short statement of the project background, objectives and a brief statement of the methodology essentials. The writer might feel this style does not fully explain the findings – and it does not. However, the reader will get the primary information quickly and will then be able to read the findings sections for further elaboration.

You will want to make it as easy as possible for your direct client to present your work to others within the organization. You will probably be asked to present the key conclusions on one PowerPoint slide. This will likely come from the executive summary.

Executive Summary

- Repeat visits: 1.53 at time of survey
- Retention: 64% attended in 2000
  63% attended in 1999
- Event importance: Stage shows, Parade, Carnival
- Top performances: Cochrane, Oyster, Leahy, Trooper
- Already spent: $28.53 at time of survey*
- Additional spend: $36.73 more*
- Bucks for banks: $4.19 average*
- Spent in Burlington downtown: $57.85*
- $10 admission charge: 50% definitely or probably would;
  37% definitely not or probably would not

Burlington's Sound of Music Festival,

For factual findings, write clear, concise, and descriptive statements such as, "Repeat Visits: 1.53 at the time of the survey," rather than, "Of the 1077 respondents interviewed during the study, the average number of repeat visits during the 2001 Burlington Sound of Music Festival was 1.53." Alternatively, provide statements that could serve as speaking notes: "Half of all attendees make more than one visit."

Keep it simple, short, and punchy. Do not belabour points in the summary and do not feel as if all of the intricacies need to be explained there; they do not.

Background

This section outlines why the client commissioned the study and the **marketing** objectives behind it. It does not need to be long and detailed in most reports because readers of detailed reports are already familiar with the study background. It should provide a statement of the context within which the project has operated and address the organizational needs that precipitated the project. A good exercise is to write it as if you were the client organization's Chief Marketing Officer (CMO).

This section is not needed so much for the direct client within the sponsoring organization but rather for others who will not have detailed knowledge of the problem area. Consider that people may refer back to this report one or two years from the submission date, and they should be able to understand why the report exists, even if the original client is in a different department or is no longer part of the organization.

Objectives (Marketing Problems to be Addressed)

The most damning question of any marketing research project is, "Now, why did we do this project anyway?" This section of the report informs all readers of the problem context, which the project addresses and answers. Generally, this section includes just a listing of the key research objectives, but sometimes brief explanations of each objective are included as well.

The objectives that are included in the client's initial brief may have been re-worked and re-worded in the proposal. Be sure to list only those objectives that were in the proposal that the client accepted. It serves as a checklist to ensure everything is covered, and you don't want to list an objective that was removed or altered before the project started. See the Proposal Writing unit for more details on this.

Methods

This section describes the parent population, the sampling methodology, the field methodology, data cleaning methodology, analytical methods and steps to obtain approval from any relevant ethics committees.

The direct client will need this information to confirm the face validity of the project to others in the organization. Other readers of the report might view this section as an annoying diversion. If the methodology needs a large amount of detailed explanation because of its complexity, then provide that material in an appendix and give only the basics in this section.

The methodology section should include the following:
- the nature of the marketing research process (whether it included ethnography or a series of focus groups, was it an online or telephone survey, or some combination of several methodologies);
- definition of the relevant population;
- the sample frame;
- how the sample was selected and why;
- the sample size and the accuracy provided by that size and sampling procedure;
- when the fieldwork was conducted;

- where the fieldwork was conducted;
- how the fieldwork was conducted;
- the success of the fieldwork (e.g., response rate, incidence rate);
- methods used to clean the data, such as missing value imputation;

any weighting applied to sub-groups

- analytical methods used; and
- any helpful comments on the researcher's insights about the fieldwork.

Key Findings

This section is the core of the report. It will describe the key findings of the study as they relate to the objectives. The reader who becomes sufficiently interested in the executive summary and decides to read further will probably skip directly to this section. In most reports, this section should be direct and uncomplicated.

If your questionnaire was well-designed, only essential questions were included in it. Consequently, the client wants to know the respondents' answers to those questions. Satisfy the client's yearning by answering the following questions:

Who was asked?

What was asked?

What did they say?

What does it mean?

Concentrate on answering all four of these questions in the most direct way possible. Once again, remember that the person commissioning the study usually has the responsibility of communicating the research findings to others within the sponsoring organization. To aid in this communication process, plan your report around a carefully staged presentation of tables, charts, and graphs explained with succinct headlines, prose and point form comments.

Reports have traditionally displayed the key results as one-page tables. These tables consist of the question exactly as asked, written within quotation marks at the top of the page, the table of numerical frequencies in the centre of the page, and an interpretation at the bottom of the page. Naturally, not all findings, especially those from qualitative studies or those resulting from sophisticated analysis techniques, can be presented in this manner.

Today's research suppliers are using more creative presentation techniques to highlight the key findings. Considerable effort is expended to find the best presentation format for their project's findings, and the outcome is worth the effort.

It is good practice to state each objective (and sometimes the related hypothesis), the corresponding questions asked, the findings in numerical or diagrammatic form, and the interpretation of the findings.

Brief statements about statistical significance may be made for each key finding if the client requests them. This task is often handled by the use of symbols (circles, squares, arrows) to identify where differences are significant. In many reports, the more technical statistical information is better placed within the appendix.

Analysts must properly analyze the data and write or illustrate important insights so that their meanings can be recognized without resorting to statistical jargon. Most readers of research reports are not conversant with statistics, but they can recognize important research findings and then devise ways to use that information for better marketing decisions.

Do not expect the client to dig into lengthy tabulations and the detailed statistical analyses to find answers to their questions. When it is necessary to refer to statistical analyses of the data, it is often best to place this technical information in an appendix. When referring to an addendum from the body of the report, make sure that your references are accurate and that the appendix is easy to find. The reader should be rewarded in the appendix by finding explanations that are understandable and not expressed in jargon.

Most projects contain questions that needed to be asked, but either were not of primary importance during the design phase or turned out to be less important when the findings were reviewed. Treat this information in a more abbreviated manner.

The guiding principle throughout the report should be to keep the reader's interest high through clear, succinct and direct writing accompanied by well-designed tables, charts, graphs, diagrams and infographics. Again, use the appendices for the technical material.

Recommendations

Not all studies will have this section. But this is where the researcher recommends a course of action to the client based on the findings. The recommendation section can be sensitive. This is where the research supplier becomes more of a consultant or trusted advisor.

Many clients say to the researcher, "Now give us your opinions. What would you do if you were running this organization?"

In most cases, the researcher will have valuable insights based on intimate involvement with the project and the data, past experience working on other projects with the client and on an objective consulting perspective. Sometimes that is just what the client wants.

However, some clients feel that the researcher's job is simply to report on the survey findings, and that is all. Such clients might believe that any interpretive or call-to-action statements made by the researcher are based on incomplete and sometimes incorrect information about the brand, the company and the market and, therefore, are not worth hearing.

In both above situations, know and respect the opinion of the client. The researcher is paid to provide the information needed by the sponsor of the research to make his or her decisions.

Appendix

This section will contain additional materials, such as:
- more detailed methodological information such as sample profiles and weighting schemes used;
- results from the survey that were collected, but have no direct bearing on the storyline that was created (for example, regional breaks that the client had asked for, but that don't reveal any interesting trends);

- alternative views of the data (e.g., detailed tables that contain the data summarized in an infographic in the report);
- the questionnaire and detailed computer tables (perhaps only for really short surveys).

Contact Information and Project Number

Sometime after the study has been completed, perhaps years later, there may be a question that needs to be answered, or a desire to repeat the study to update the understanding of the business problem. The direct client may no longer be with the client organization or may not remember who had carried out the study. Including the **research team's contact information** in the report will help everyone and avoid the frustration of searching both organizations for the people responsible. Including the research company's **project number** will make it even easier to find the questionnaire, data and report, in the archives even if the research team has departed and someone else needs to assist the client.

What are the Basic Principles of Communication?

Write with your Audience in Mind

The key to providing an analysis that satisfies the client is to think of her or his needs. These needs are expressed by the project objectives and your knowledge of what presentation format is required.

Realize that your direct client also has clients within his or her own organization, and you must also address their internal communication needs. If possible, find out who is on the distribution list for the report or will attend the presentation and what report format is preferred within the organization. Remember that these people will be very busy. Put your report in a familiar style, and the likelihood that it will be widely read increases significantly.

Make your Reports Readable and Usable

The keys to readable and useful research findings are simplicity and conviction.

Overly long and complex reports are often not read. The secret to having people read your report is to interest them with a punchy executive summary. Use a limited number of bullet points and cut out all nonessentials. Always strive to answer the question, "What will help my client the most?" Answer this question successfully, and your future is guaranteed to be bright.

If your report is in a **PowerPoint** format,
- Make the graph, chart or infographic the focus point and ensure they clearly illustrate the conclusion you are drawing (rather than showing every data point).
- ensure the headline summarizes what the reader needs to know (rather than just naming the chart). For example, rather than headlining "Purchase Intent," write, "Majority will buy the product."
- Add a few bullet points in a sidebar to provide supporting or secondary insights, such as second-tier findings or regional differences.

How to Present the Findings

- Add the question wording, base size and any footnotes in small font at the bottom of the slide to avoid cluttering.
- Consider using the 'notes' section for more detailed commentary and speaker's notes.

If your report is a **text document** (e.g., in MS Word), find ways to generate interest by inserting tables and charts and diagrams to underscore your point and allow readers to confirm your conclusions. Readers always yearn for something to break the monotony of pages and pages of prose. Insert complete slides from the PowerPoint report into the written report. If the slide is too busy to fit well with the prose, add the graph or table that was the focal point of the slide.

Regardless of the format, here are some rules that may help you to write readable reports.

1. **Be positive.** Whenever you have a choice, make the tone of the report positive.
2. **Be clear and concise.**
3. **Use markers.** Markers such as headings, subheadings, emphasizing important words through italics or bold typeface, make it easy for the reader to locate relevant information.
4. **Limit one thought per page.** This may not always be possible, but it can be a guiding principle.
5. **Don't use jargon and technical terms** to impress. It doesn't. Use comfortable everyday language.
6. **Use active voice rather than passive voice. Say,** "*80% of consumers like the product*" rather than, "*The product was liked by 80% of consumers*".

Remember that the client decided to do the study to find answers to marketing problems, not to buy a marketing research report. Marketing research is just the vehicle that provides better problem-solving ammunition.

Basic Principles of Communication

What the writer should do
1. Use short words, short sentences, and short paragraphs.
2. Use plain language.
3. Use the active voice rather than the passive voice.
4. Use redundancy (with care).
5. Avoid over-communicating.

What impact it should have on the reader
6. Make it easy for the reader.
7. Use an attractive format.
8. Present complete arguments.

What to remember at all times
9. Write with a purpose.
10. Write with an outcome in mind.

In literature, the writer uses the content only as a vehicle to express his or her skills as a superior writer. The reader's enjoyment is derived from the way the writer expresses himself or herself and not necessarily from the content of the writing. For example, a poet can describe a tree. The reader learns nothing new in a physical sense and yet derives enjoyment from the reading because of the way a poet uses the words and imagery. This kind of writing is entirely different from business writing.

In the business world, time is precious. The reader needs to absorb the information effortlessly and in the shortest possible time. Short sentences and short words go a long way toward achieving this objective.

Compare the following examples. Which message communicates faster and better?

ORIGINAL

In the UK and throughout the Western world a rapidly growing proportion of young people appears to be faced with the almost certain prospect of periods of prolonged unemployment brought about by fundamental changes in the structure of industry and commerce. However, many young people currently in employment find that a lack of initial basic educational skills, together with a lack of access to training facilities at work, means that their ability to adapt to these changes is also very restricted. (Broadcasting for Youth)

REVISED

In the UK and the Western world, more and more people face the almost certain prospect of long-term unemployment. This stems from deep changes in the structure of industry and commerce. Even young people who have a job find that they cannot adapt easily to changes because they lack basic skills and have no access to training at work.

While the revised version can still be improved, it is much better than the original.

It is also a good idea to use short paragraphs. This is particularly true of the first paragraph of a report. Short paragraphs are likely to be less intimidating to the reader than long, wordy ones. However, rigidly following the formula, "short words, short sentences, and short paragraphs" might lead to writing that is monotonous and choppy. A good rule is to vary the length of words, sentences, and paragraphs from time to time. And insert diagrams, graphs and tables where appropriate.

Use Plain Language

Avoid jargon. Be concise. Use plain language. Here is a passage from the Canadian Income Tax Act:

Reduction of dividend tax on hand—in the case of a new corporation that has been a private corporation continuously from the time of the amalgamation to the end of any taxation year, for the purposes of computing the refundable dividend tax on hand (within the meaning assigned by subsection 129(3)), of the new corporation at the end of the taxation year, where a predecessor corporation had refundable dividend tax on hand immediately before the amalgamation, the amount by which the refundable dividend tax on hand at that time exceeds any dividend refund (within the meaning assigned by subsection 129(1)) of the predecessor corporation for its taxation year ending immediately before the amalgamation and shall be added to the aggregate determined under subsection 129(3) shall be deemed nil where, had a dividend been paid by the predecessor corporation immediately before the amalgamation, subsection 129(1.2) would have applied to deem the dividend not to be a taxable dividend.

What does it mean? Is the idea so complex that it cannot be expressed in straightforward English?

Those who use complicated language (particularly in the legal and accounting professions) tend to argue that the concepts they use cannot be precisely expressed with plain English. When we consider the fact that lawyers constantly argue over the interpretation of legal documents written in legalese and different accountants interpret the Income Tax Act differently, it is hard to believe that the use of gobbledygook somehow makes the meaning more precise.

In all business communication and most personal dialogue, the principal objective is to be exact. Otherwise, people do not value what is being said and cannot react as desired because they do not understand what is wanted.

Plain language and brevity are seldom out of place. As *The New York Times* noted:

The Lord's prayer contains 56 words, 23rd psalm 118 words, the Gettysburg address 326 words, and the Ten Commandments 297 words, while the U.S. Department of Agriculture directive on pricing cabbage weighs in at 15,629 words.

It is easy to fall into the trap of believing that jargon and complicated expressions are inevitable in your area of expertise. The fact is there is no evidence to suggest that plain language is less precise than obscure language.

In business, people often seem to prefer the use of the passive voice to the active voice. For example:

Statement. Commitments have been made for the availability of further funds. (passive voice)
Improved Statement. The management has committed additional funds. (active voice)

Statement. Two meetings were held regarding the legal implications. (passive voice)
Improved Statement. The advertising department held two meetings regarding the legal implications. (active voice)

Statement. It is suggested that the implications of this survey be considered seriously. (passive voice)

Improved Statement. We suggest that you seriously consider the implications of this survey. (active voice)

While the passive voice has its uses, for example hiding the person who is responsible for the action, using the active voice wherever possible will increase the directness and force of your writing.

Use Short Words and Short Sentences

Short words and short sentences are easy to read. They are also easy to understand. Many people seem to have difficulty expressing themselves in simple language. They may prefer to express themselves in a more sophisticated way because of their superior linguistic skills. Some may feel that unless they use an extensive vocabulary and complex sentences, their writing may be considered juvenile. However, it is essential to remember that there are two kinds of writing: one that is read for the enjoyment of the language where the content is of secondary importance and one that is read for its content where nothing else is of any great significance.

> "All big things have little names. Such as life and death, peace and war, dawn, day, night, hope, love and home. Learn to use little words in a big way. It's hard to do, but they say what you mean. When you don't know what you mean, use big words. They often fool little people." (Arthur Kudner, a copywriter, to his teenage son)

Your writing style, by definition, is yours. The problem is that it may often seem peculiar to your reader. Incorporating generally used techniques into your style enhances your writing's readability and reader experience.

Use Redundancy (or Repetition) – With Care

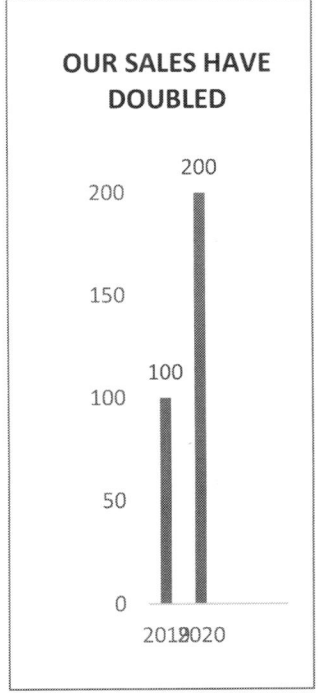

Redundancy is the communication of an idea to a person in more than one medium. For example, the communication can be through print in text, graphs, tables, or the spoken word. Redundancy reinforces one's understanding because it underlines an idea already encountered. Furthermore, the reader has a second chance to understand and retain the information.

In textbooks, redundancy is often achieved by summaries and marginal notes. In research reports, this is achieved in several ways. For example, different sections of the report, such as the executive summary, the general summary, and detailed findings present the same information, although the details differ. In a slide, a graph can be presented along with a verbal summary.

Redundancy must be used with care. If it is overused, readers may find it condescending or annoying. There are many ways in which you can use redundancy effectively. For example, you can use a headline 'Sales have doubled' and present a graph and the sales figures to support it.

Redundancy, if used well, can compensate (at least in part) for the reader's short attention span. Furthermore, different people learn in different ways. Presenting the same idea in different ways increases the likelihood that readers will find a format that appeals to them.

Avoid Over-communicating

Over-communicating is telling the reader what he or she already knows (or is likely to know). Here is an example of over-communicating:

> Stand the box in an upright position and remove the protective wrapper. Carefully open the top of the box. Pull the instrument out. Remove the cellophane wrapper. Put the instrument in a suitable place and connect it to an appropriate AC electrical outlet. Switch the instrument on.

Cut to the chase as quickly as possible. The writer could simply have said, "unwrap the instrument and plug it in." In business writing, over-communicating arises out of the writer's lack of confidence in the readers.

The problem with this approach is that by carefully traversing the steps that an average person would go through anyway; the writer might confuse the readers. Instead of simply opening the box and plugging in the instrument, the readers might spend time making sure that they have followed all the instructions. Furthermore, when the readers come to the part where they must pay close attention, they may not do so, having been conditioned to gloss over the details by the trivial instructions provided thus far. The way to avoid over-communicating is to ask yourself the question, "Is there a possibility of serious misunderstanding if this explanation is not provided?"

Over-communicating is different from redundancy. In using multiple exposures, we emphasize points that need emphasis; in over-communicating, we emphasize aspects that do not need to be explained.

Make it Easy for the Reader

The writer's job is to make it as easy as possible for the reader to find the information that he or she needs, quickly and accurately. Write in such a way that it can be rapidly read, understood easily, and acted upon effectively. Do not cloud the issues. This can be achieved in several ways.

1. Use Subheadings

While the headline advances the story, subheadings can provide more detail or alert the reader to the next idea. They make it easy for the reader to find what she or he is looking for. Where possible, use subheadings that are idea-oriented rather than description-oriented. For example, subheadings used in this chapter (such as "Use Short Words and Short Sentences," "Use Multiple Exposure") are idea-oriented and tell the reader the basic ideas behind each section. In contrast, subheadings such as "Sentence Length" and "Multiple Exposure" are descriptive titles. Idea-oriented headings serve as summaries, increase multiple exposures, and therefore increase comprehension and retention.

2. Number Items When Appropriate

When paragraphs, sections, or points are numbered, it makes it easy for the reader to follow the relationship among the ideas that are discussed. Consider the following three versions:

Version 1. We can increase our market share by lowering our price by increasing our promotional activity or by stepping up our distribution.

Version 2. There are three ways in which we can increase our market share. One, we can lower our price. Two, we can promote our product heavily. Or, three, we can step up our distribution.

Version 3. We can increase our market share in three ways:
1. Lower our price
2. Increase our promotional activities
3. Step up our distribution

Most readers would find the information they need much more readily in the last two versions (especially the last one) than in the first version.

3. Break Up (Chunk) Complex Information into Smaller Pieces

Chunking refers to the process of breaking down complex information into smaller logical units. This applies to written communication as well as oral communication. Instead of expressing complex relationships among variables in one lengthy paragraph, you should break what you want to say into smaller logical chunks.

Pay Attention to the Layout

The way the information is displayed can make it easy or difficult for the reader to follow what is being communicated. Compare the following:

Version 1 Layout as Paragraph
Most secondary data come from four primary sources: Company records of sales, advertising expenditures, special promotions, and public sources. This information is collected by large information organizations such as Statistics Canada, AC Nielsen, Forrester, and Frost & Sullivan in which information on people, products and brands, in general, is collected and distributed either free or for a fee.

Version 2 Layout in Point Form
Most secondary data come from three primary sources:
   a. *Internal records* of the company
   b. *External information* obtained from authoritative sources
   c. *Syndicated surveys* like ACNielsen, Forrester, and Frost & Sullivan in which information on products and brands, in general, is collected and distributed either free or for a fee.

The second version aids the reader by using various visual aspects of written communication, such as the use of numbering, indenting and italics. However, you should be careful not to overuse these devices.

People often make judgments about your report before they read one word of it. Most of these judgments are subconsciously based on visual appearance. An attractive looking report is an invitation for the reader to read it. Unless the reader is anxiously awaiting the information that is contained in the report, a badly laid out report is less likely to be read.

The techniques discussed in the previous section—using subheadings, using numbers, using chunking, and using suitable layouts—also tend to make the report visually attractive.

Present Complete Arguments

Many report writers—either due to writer's block or laziness—present incomplete arguments. In marketing research reports, for instance, a researcher may write something like:

> When rating quality of service, customers rate a bank based on their experiences with the person at the counter. In our survey, a large proportion of customers rated the tellers of XYZ bank very highly. Hence, we can infer the quality of service provided by the XYZ bank is high.

It is not clear whether it has been established either in this survey or in earlier ones that there is a relationship between the quality of perceived service and a customer's experience with the teller or whether it is an assumption made by the researcher. Also, what does "a large proportion" mean; an actual percentage based on the survey should replace that phrase. Incomplete arguments can mislead and frustrate the reader and, therefore, should be avoided.

Write with a Purpose

Business communication has three purposes (Sherry Sweetnam, 1986): to inform, to persuade, and to create action. To make sure your report sticks to the point, you may want to assess each paragraph by these criteria: does this paragraph inform, persuade, or aim to create action? If a paragraph is not accomplishing any of these three purposes, perhaps it should be cut.

Of the three, the most difficult to identify are statements that inform. Almost any statement can be assumed to inform. How can you decide whether you are writing information statements or conveying purposeless information?

When you are in doubt, an effective way of differentiating purposeless information from purposeful information statements is to refer to your objectives. If the sentence has information that would help achieve the study objectives, then it is a valid information statement; if not, then perhaps it is a candidate for elimination.

Every sentence in your report should have a purpose and should contribute to achieving your objectives. It should fall under one of the following categories:

1. Purpose statements
2. Problem statements
3. Benefit statements
4. Information statements
5. Solution statements
6. Feel good statements

If a sentence does not fall under any of the categories, what is it doing in your report?

Write with an Outcome in Mind

Marketing research reports must do more than just provide information to the decision-maker; they must persuade the decision-maker of the validity of the findings, the correctness of the interpretation, and that the information can help them make better decisions. The researcher is hoping for an outcome; the decision-maker is looking for a solution.

The report should be structured to make the decision-maker appreciate the validity of the interpretation. In other words, the presentation tools the researcher uses (e.g., language, style, arguments, analysis, and interpretation) should convince readers that the information is valuable and that it is safe to base major marketing decisions on the information provided.

The communicator should aim for seamless communication so that both the communicator and the receiver are involved in the outcome of the message. For example, when someone asks us what time it is, we simply respond with the time—we do not concern ourselves with things such as how well the question was asked, whether it is grammatically correct, the motives of the other party. The message was attended to, not the medium. Seamless communication (such as arguments that do not put up a barrier between the writer and the reader, writing that does not puzzle the reader, words that do not confuse the decision-maker) has a much better chance of achieving the intended outcome.

Avoid Complexity

Avoid complexity. Keep things simple. When you have a choice, use simpler words, more straightforward sentences, and simpler graphics. Complexity, even if it is impressive, soon becomes tiresome. Remember, simplicity is the ultimate sophistication.

Do not Follow the Rules Mechanically

Writing is an art. Therefore, while the general rules discussed will improve your writing, the rules may not always work. For each rule, there may be several exceptions. We would like to emphasize that while you should pay attention to all the rules mentioned thus far, you should also feel free to ignore them if it is necessary to communicate your point better.

How to Write Reports in a Presentation Format

Most research reports these days are written in a presentation format using software like Microsoft PowerPoint. To a large extent, this format has replaced the linear written format like the ones using software like Microsoft Word.

In a linear written report, a thought unit is unrelated to the number of words or the number of pages. A page may contain a single idea, several ideas, or an idea that may start half-way through one page and may continue to the top of the next page. In the presentation format, on the other hand, each page is treated as a unit and complete (unless there are markers indicating that the next page is a continuation). So, when something is not very clear, the reader goes to the next page, hoping to find something more understandable.

From the writing perspective, the most critical difference between the linear written format and the presentation format is that a linear written report has to convey information, as well as conform to rules of grammar, syntax, and flow. We cannot write incomplete sentences. The constraints for the presentation report are much less stringent.

Corporate format. In many companies, reports follow a standard, predetermined format. They are often template-based. This means that the look and feel, the sequence of topics, the colour scheme, the placement of graphics, headings and sidebars are already decided, and you simply follow the format. Sometimes, the client may specify how the report should be formatted. Even with such constraints, you may find the following suggestions useful.

Use Fewer Words

Unlike the linear written report, the presentation format report does not require that we use complete sentences. This allows us to be economical in the way we present information. Consider the following two versions, A and B:

Version A

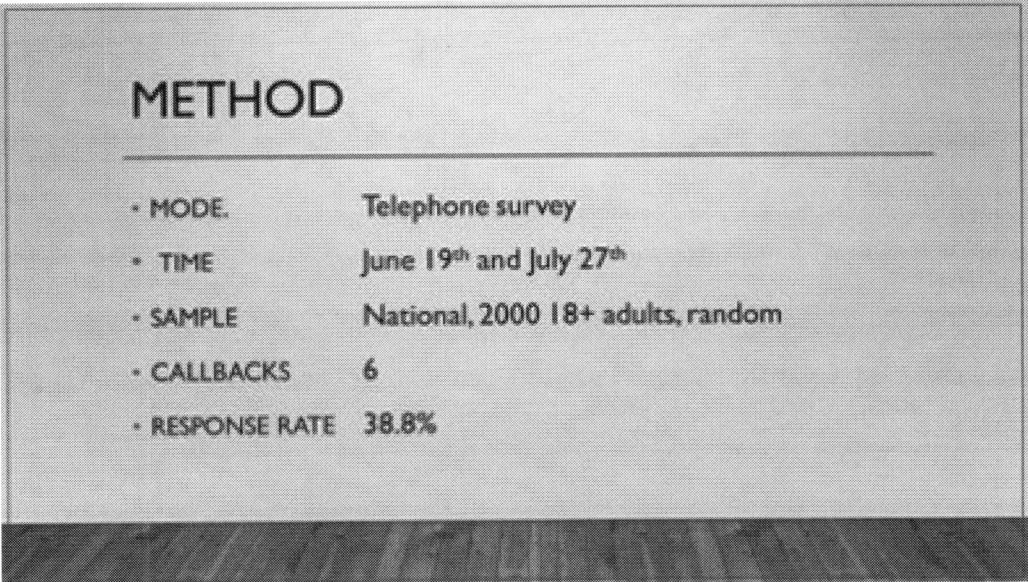

Version B

Both formats contain virtually the same information. Even though Format B uses far fewer words, most people will find format B easy to read. Readers can also find the information they are looking for more easily in Format B than in Format A.

Don't' be Afraid of White Space

Another reason why version B above is not only easy to read but also looks visually better is the amount of white space. We tend to fill up space because it is there. However, white space makes the page visually attractive and allows the eye to rest, making it easy for the reader to absorb the information.

Select a Non-Intrusive Background

You should never sacrifice ease of reading in favour of your presentation looking attractive. Select a white or light-textured background and dark text colours. The exhibit below looks visually attractive, but it is harder to read.

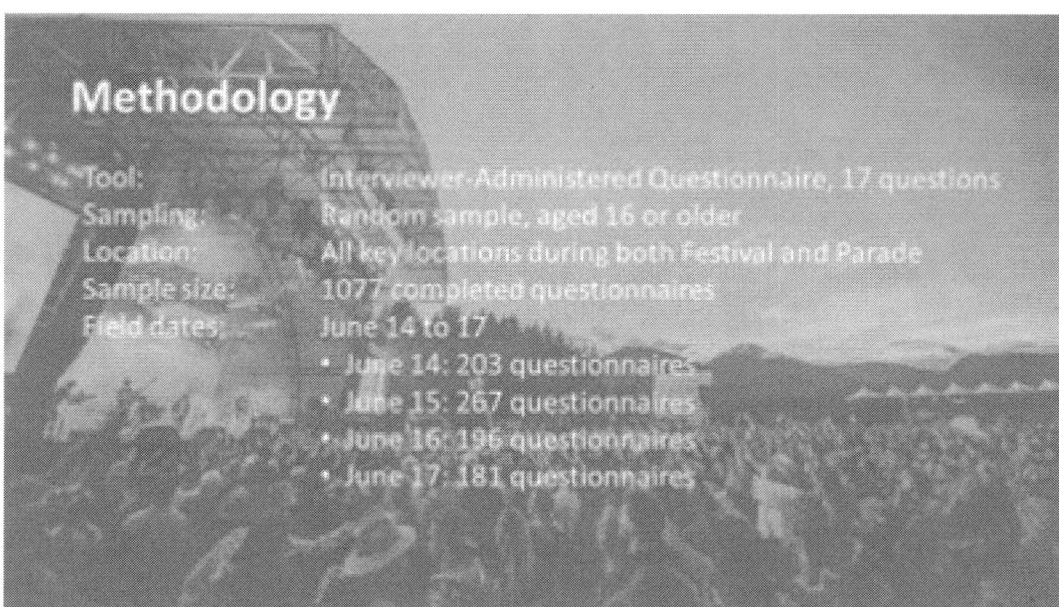

There is a great benefit in making your report visually attractive, but it shouldn't be done at the expense of readability. Some engaging, but non-intrusive, features or illustrations can be included if the audience's attention is not taken away from the information.

For example, the supplier's logo, the client's logo, or some design feature that relates to the company and/or the project can be included. The exhibit below reduces the photo of the music festival to a design element but leaves the (abbreviated) slide content against a white background. Most will find this to be far less difficult to read.

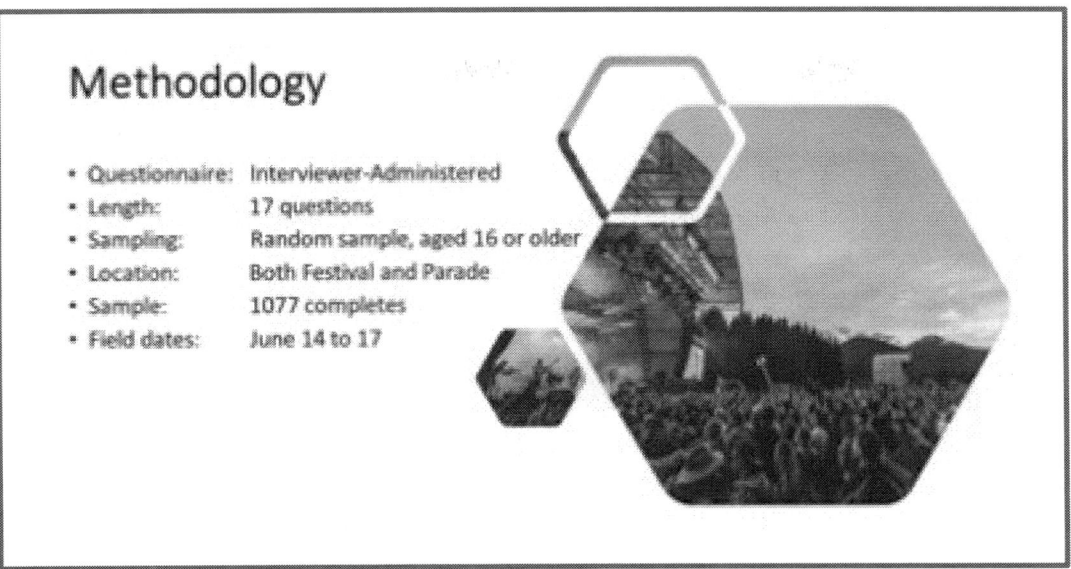

Use Clipart and Images Intelligently

Different researchers use clipart and images to different extents. Some believe that it distracts readers from the message. Others feel that it makes the report more impactful and the message more memorable. The key is to use illustrations intelligently:
- They should not crowd out or overwhelm the text
- They should be relevant and reinforce the message
- They should fit into the design of the page rather than look like a cut and paste collage
- They should be of consistent style and quality throughout the report (i.e., don't use a cartoon sketch on one page and a full-colour photo on the next).

The bottom line is that the illustration should enhance and reinforce the message, not distract from it.

The overuse or inappropriate choice of images can undermine clear communications and make the report tiresome to read. Many companies now have graphic designers on staff to ensure their finished reports look professional and attractive. Remember, the use of graphics or illustrations does not automatically improve the quality of the slide.

Use an Easy-to-Read Font

We often choose a font that looks attractive, creative, or unique. However, there is also another characteristic of fonts that is important: readability. All fonts are not equally easy to read.

Fonts can be either "serif" (with a decorative stroke that finishes off the end of a letter stem (e.g., The 'feet' of the letter) or "sans-serif" (without the extra stroke).

This is Times Roman, a serif font

This is Arial Nova, a sans serif font

In general, serif fonts are more readable than sans-serif fonts, especially when a large amount of text is involved. There are exceptions to this general rule. For example, Calibri, a sans-serif font, has clear lines and excellent readability.

If you find yourself wondering whether a font is easily readable, the chances are it isn't. A good rule that many people use is to use a sans-serif font for the headline and a serif font for the rest.

Use Colours Judiciously

Use one primary colour (mostly black or a softer dark grey) for the text. If you use two colours, use the second colour for a different element such as the heading or the dividing lines. Avoid using too many colours (unless colours are relevant as in a picture of a package) because they can have a distracting effect.

Many research companies now have professionally designed report templates with carefully selected colour palettes with prescribed uses. This ensures the corporate identity is consistent from one report to the next.

Don't Overdo Emphasis

You can call the reader's attention to important words by accenting it with *italics*, **bold typeface**, <u>underlines</u>, and other such devices. However, to have the desired effect, accents should be used sparingly.

If you compare the two versions below, you will note that version A, by accenting too many words, loses its effectiveness. Version B, on the other hand, is more effective because it lets the reader know that the accenting principles relate to techniques like italicizing, underlining and bolding of texts.

Version A

> # THE ACCENTING PRINCIPLE
>
> Call the reader's <u>attention</u> to <u>important</u> words by <u>accenting</u> it with <u>italics, underlining, bold</u> typeface and other such devices. However, <u>do not overuse</u> accents.

Version B

> # THE ACCENTING PRINCIPLE
>
> Call the reader's attention to important words by accenting it with <u>italics, underlining, bold</u> typeface and other such devices. However, do not overuse accents.

Don't Overuse Charts and Graphs

Charts, graphs and infographics should aid the comprehension of key findings, reduce the amount of written material on the page, and motivate discussion. Graphs and the labelling on those graphs must be carefully prepared so that they create nearly instant understanding.

Some researchers tend to use charts or graphs to represent every numerical table. It results in an overabundance of pie charts, bar charts, line charts etc. which may look pretty but become tedious to view and not as easy to understand as the researcher may think. Don't feel compelled to use a chart to represent every number.

How to Present the Findings   392

Depending on the context, a single number, or an infographic or word-cloud, may work equally well, if not better. Here is an example of an impactful page of findings that focuses on a single number for each question.

Prefer Simple Charts

Simple, uncluttered charts are much more effective in communicating information quickly. Where possible, eliminate unnecessary colours, shades, gridlines, 3D representations that serve no purpose and are distractions. If you compare the following two charts, you will see the one on the left is easier to read and understand.

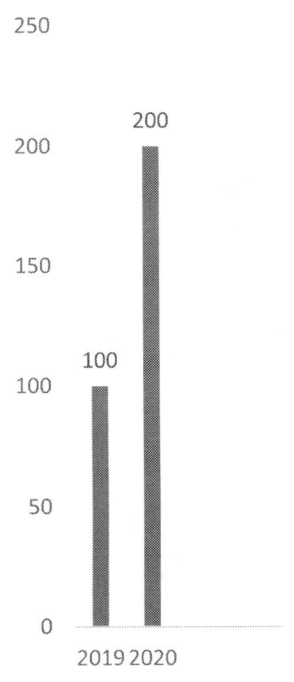 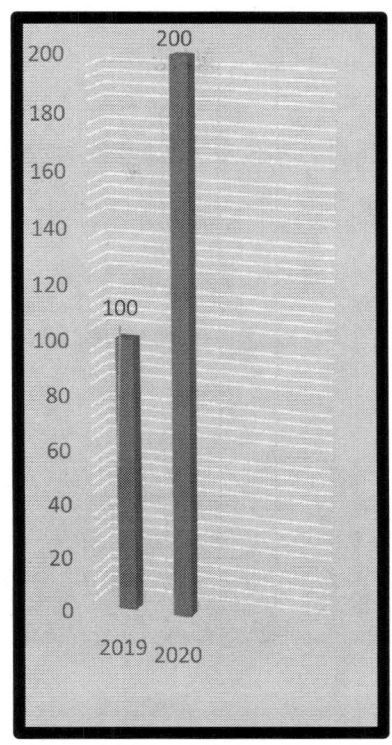

OUR SALES HAVE DOUBLED   **OUR SALES HAVE DOUBLED**

(Clear)   ('Noisy')

Make your Heading Part of your Story

Avoid using descriptive headings such as "Average Brand Ratings." When we use descriptive titles, the task of understanding what the chart means is left to the reader. A better way of presenting data would be for the researcher to understand first what is relevant and exciting about the chart and showcase it in the heading as well as in the chart.

Version A

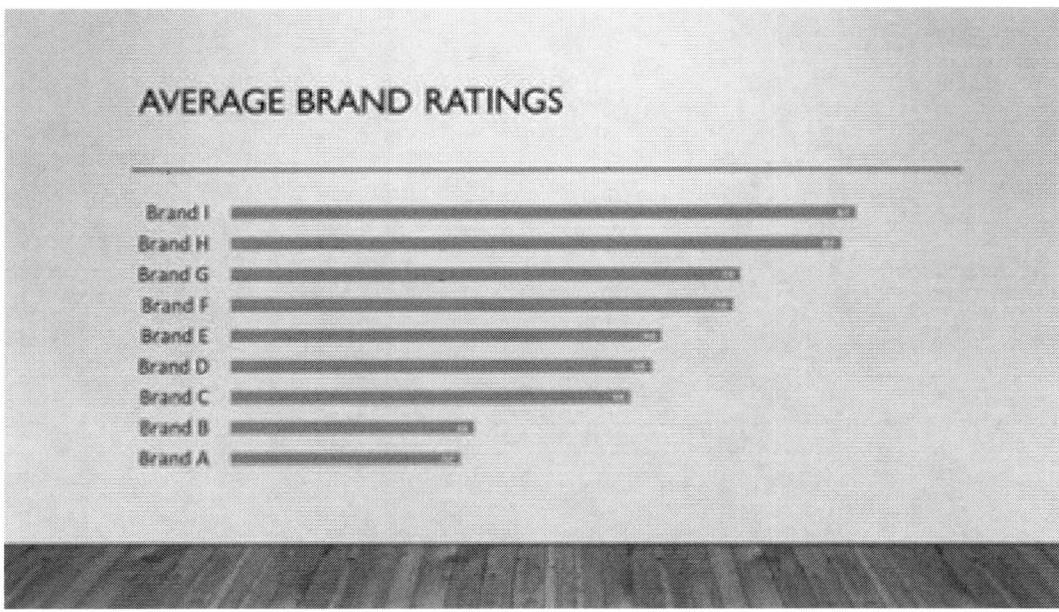

Version B

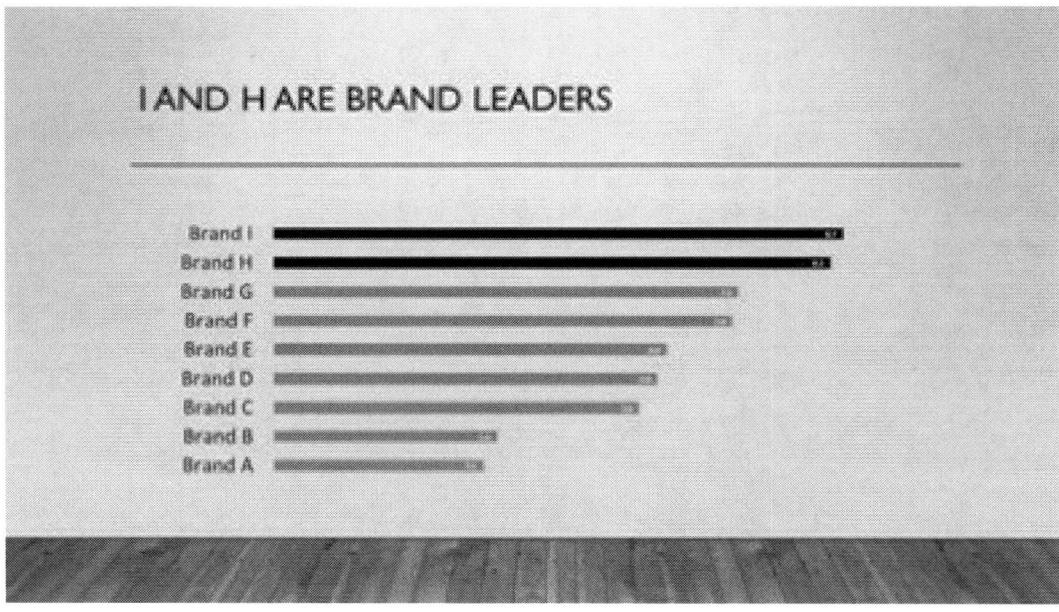

A heading like "Average Brand Ratings" (Version A) does not guide the readers, leaving them unsure what to look for and what the significance of the chart is. But a title like "Brands I and H lead the market" with the bars for the two brands highlighted immediately directs the attention of the viewers to the significance of the table to the client.

Make your Headings Tell a Story

As you become skilled at writing reports, practice making the heading of each page a sentence in your story. For instance, page headings could be strung together to tell this story:
- We are the most expensive brand on the market;
- Our competitors are gaining ground because they are cheaper;
- Consumers believe that our product is of the highest quality;
- Not all consumers are willing to pay more for higher quality;
- A small segment of the market is willing to pay more for quality

and so on.

As the reader scans the headlines, the story unfolds. This is an effective way of story-telling and can make the report enjoyable. More importantly, a senior executive in the client organization can quickly thumb through the report (or click through it on-screen) and get the full story in a few minutes.

Keep Sidebars Focused on Insights

While the headline and sub-heading are telling the story, and the graph or chart or infographic is providing the proof, it is sometimes necessary to go into a little more detail with key points in a sidebar. It is crucial that these bullet points not be simply a written version of the data in the chart. "Laundry list" analysis simply lists what is, for example, high or low on the chart. The interested reader can see that for themselves. Instead, the bullet point sidebar should identify patterns, draw attention to surprises, and focus on reinforcing the page's main story. If there is nothing further to add, don't feel you need to fill the space. Bullet points, graphs and tables can be introduced sequentially so that the whole slide doe not initially look cluttered.

Reproducible Research – An Interlude

Although most research reports in marketing research are created using Microsoft PowerPoint or Word, the emerging technical advances (as exemplified by the R and Python software environments) enable us to do more, faster. For example, in this section, we show how we can integrate an interim report with the final report, without having to redo the report. If you are only using programs like Microsoft PowerPoint or Word in your work, you may still want to browse through this section to understand what is possible.

The Problem

Suppose that a client has a large and important study in the field and has asked for an interim report half-way through data collection. Of course, that involves analyzing the first half of the dataset for the interim report and then analyzing the full dataset for the final report; and, writing two reports.

Suppose there was a way to write that interim report that paved-the-way to very easily analyzing the final dataset and automatically producing the final report. Well, almost. Wouldn't that be terrific?

That procedure is called reproducible research, and R Markdown and Jupyter Notebooks provide that type of report preparation. There are many environments for statistically analyzing marketing research data. Two of those that have gained a substantial share of usage compared to traditional applications are R and Python. Both R and Python are open-source and free environments for analyzing and manipulating data as well as for preparing several types of documents. R Markdown is R-based, and Jupyter Notebooks is primarily Python-focused but broader. However, Python code can be used in R.

Most marketing research reports include tables and graphs that are developed by statistically analyzing the study data. Of course, statistical analysis involves calculations based on equations and computer code. There are GUIs (Graphical User Interfaces) that help avoid direct interaction with code; R Studio for R and Anaconda for Python. Still, the code is at least behind the surface GUI, and many researchers and analysts use R-code or Python-code to conduct their analyses. To keep this exposition as simple as possible, only R Markdown will be discussed.

The Solution - Using R Markdown

Using R Markdown, we can produce full text-based reports or slide-based reports. A GUI for using R is R Studio and R Commander. R Commander is a statistical GUI fully based on pull-down menus, as are SPSS, SAS and other general-purpose statistical packages. A dataset can be opened in R Commander, tables produced, graphs developed and a very wide range of statistical analyses produced. While R Commander can be used fully in the menu-mode, each action in the menu produces corresponding code in an integrated R window and R Markdown window. Those two windows showing R-code can be ignored fully if a user wants to use only the pull-down menus in R Commander.

When finished conducting an analysis sequence in R Commander, the application asks if the R Markdown file should be saved. If that option is requested, an R Markdown file is saved in the desired folder. That file can be reopened in R Commander or in R Studio, the principal GUI for using R. When opened in R Studio, whose new name is Posit, the R Markdown file contains the R-code produced in R Commander. That R-code is in R-code chunks. Outside of the R-code chunks, text can be written, and images can be imported, including videos.

With a minor amount of coding, a document can be configured to produce the complete marketing research report in Word, PDF and HTML formats. The final report from R Markdown looks like a report produced in MS Word with charts and tables copied and pasted into the Word file. However, in R Markdown, the tables and graphs are produced within the document using the R-code provided by R Commander or adding R-code directly within R-code chunks in R Markdown. R Commander does not have to be used and is recommended for beginners with more seasoned users encouraged to code directly in R code chunks within R Markdown.

In most R Markdown documents, code within an R-code chunk would read a data file. Code in another chunk would produce a table, another chunk may conduct a statistical test and produce a table of those findings and a corresponding graph. Then, a YouTube video explaining a relevant component of marketing or marketing research may be accessed if the result is a report in HTML format. (HTML provides greater flexibility for formatting than do Word and PDF formats.)

Remember that interim report your client requested? That could be composed in R Markdown. All the text would be written and formatted within R Markdown. Reading the interim dataset and the analyses requested would be programmed in R and contained within a set of several R-code chunks. When finished, the production of the R Markdown document is requested, called "knitting," and the document appears on the computer monitor. If that document is rendered in HTML format, there can be a floating table of contents and that YouTube video can be played at the appropriate point within the report.

Let us assume that the interim report was fully acceptable to your client. When the final dataset is obtained from the field provider, it can be read by the R Markdown report file, all data cleaning and reshaping is done automatically as are the analyses and the production of tables, graphs and other exhibits. If the findings from the second half of the data are a bit different from those found using the interim data, some textual changes will need to be made. But, if the analysis was fine for the client in the interim report, there will be no separate analysis conducted for the final report. That analysis is fully conducted within the R Markdown document. Send off the report, and you are done.

This procedure supports reproducible research. Reproducible research means that after composing the R Markdown document, you or anyone else can reproduce the same results by clicking on the HTML file or opening that R Markdown document and executing it in R Studio.

Transmission of the marketing research report might be in one direction from the marketing researcher to the marketing client. There may be no back-and-forth. However, more than one researcher might be working on the report and the analysis. When that's the case, the report in R Markdown format can be shared and altered among the authors until fully complete. When author Two receives the report from author One, the report can be viewed immediately in author Two's browser by simply clicking on the HTML file. And, the full report can be executed in R Markdown and the same results obtained as produced by author One. Author Two may edit and add to the text and may alter the existing R-code and add other analyses to the report. Then Author One can review the changes made by Author Two.

How to Make Live Presentations: General Principles

Because most reports these days are written in a presentation format, many researchers use their full reports as presentation slides. This is not a good idea (unless your client expects you to walk them through each page of the report). There are crucial differences between a report written in a presentation (PowerPoint) format and an actual presentation itself.

Reports in a Presentation Format vs. Live Presentations

The fundamental difference between a report and a presentation is this:

- In a written report, the focus is on what the report says because there is no one else to explain it.

- In an actual presentation, the focus is on the presenter. The slides are there to help the presenter and not the other way around. In a compelling presentation, the focus is always (or should be) on the presenter.
- The other significant difference is that a report typically uses a smaller typeface – around 12 to 18 points. This is generally too small for a presentation that should never use less than 24-point font.

The written report provides bullet-pointed sentences to encourage the reader to follow the argument and reach the same conclusion the researcher has made.

There is no need for this when the presenter takes the audience through the argument. When an audience starts reading the slides, the presenter loses relevance, and the audience may wonder why a presenter is needed.

So, what is the function of slides in a live presentation? Here are a few:
- To reinforce a point made by the speaker
- To illustrate a point made by the speaker
- To add credibility (proof) to back up the speaker's point
- To add some visual interest to the presentation
- To serve as a marker – where we are in the presentation

While all the principles of communication we discussed also apply to live presentations, some additional principles apply specifically to live presentations. We will discuss later how to prepare the visuals for a live presentation. But first, let's start with some general principles.

Create a Storyboard

We all tend to create our presentations directly on our computers. But this may not be the best way. You may first want to create a storyboard. It will force you to think logically about the best way to tell the story instead of presenting the results in a way that may not be logically sequenced.

A storyboard can just be a series of post-it notes. Each post-it note will contain one topic, for example:
- Our challenge is to retain our market leadership
- Newcomers to the category challenge us
- Customers believe that price is an essential deciding factor
- Customers will stay with us if we are not more than 10% more expensive
- We are now close to this level
- Challenge: What actions should be taken if the competition drops the price
- What is a "Plan B" option?

Slides are then created to support each one of these points. Such prior sequencing of the story, followed by the creation of slides that would help the storyline, is a powerful way of creating a presentation.

In creating your presentation, you may also want to think about the audience. A general rule is that senior management usually prefers shorter, focused presentations that tell a story that leads to a course of action. When you prepare for a live presentation, think about the story you want to tell about what you found and start with this question: If you were to describe the results of the project in a conversation without any charts, what would you say?

How to Present the Findings

The following is an example of the preliminary storyboard. The first figure is the outline of the presentation and the second figure is an example of what would go in a given section. As the presentation develops, topics that did not fit the story could be eliminated, and topics that would strengthen the story could be added.

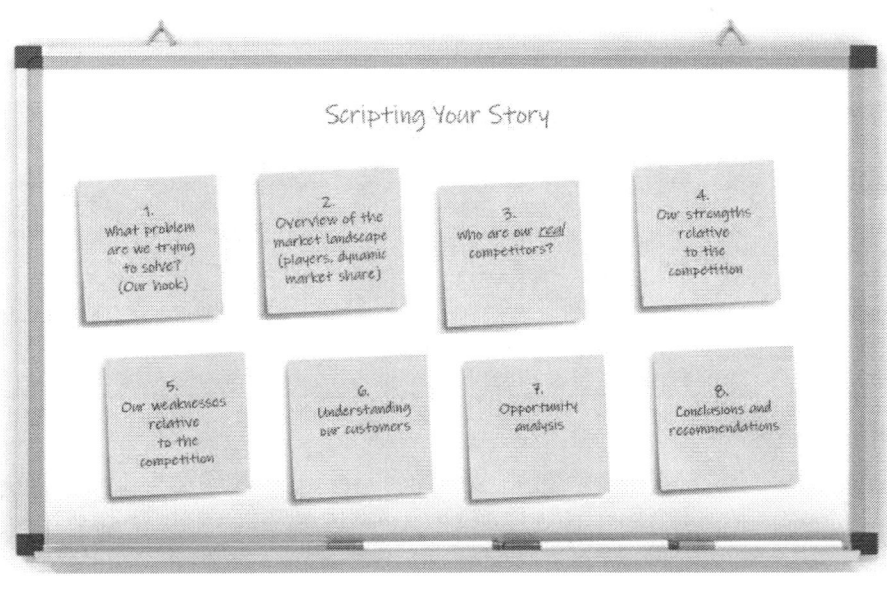

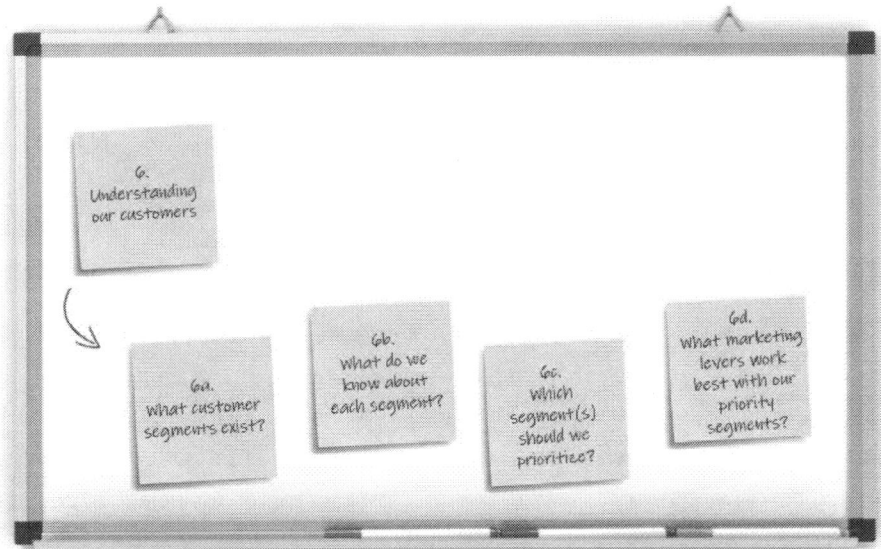

One of the advantages of using sticky notes to create a storyboard is that they can be added, removed, or changed quickly. Having a visual outline of the presentation focuses one's attention on the sequence and flow of presentations. It also helps us to see what visuals we need to make our points effectively.

Another key advantage of the sticky note storyboard is that the research team can work together to plan the presentation, each member contributing to ideas. This is particularly helpful if more than one person will be creating slides. It ensures everyone is on the same wavelength.

Don't Make your Presentations Long

The length relates directly to the amount of detail presented, so it is important to clearly understand the level of detail that your direct client wants. Unless the client specifies how long the presentation needs to be, a good principle is not to exceed 20 to 30 minutes. The purpose of a live presentation is to communicate the critical findings and not laboriously list every single detail. (That's what written reports are for.)

One tip to determining if you have too much information for the allotted time is to divide the number of slides by the number of minutes. Can you get through 30 slides in 30 minutes? That's unlikely; you'll have a minute for each slide. As soon as someone asks a question, you'll run over time.

You also have to allocate time for set up, late arrivals and discussion during the presentation. So if you have an hour-long time slot – 30 minutes worth of slides gives you some breathing room and time for an engaging discussion at the end.

Know your Audience

Know your audience. Most likely, your client would indicate their preferences: presentation format, presentation length, etc. Find out who will be attending the presentation. As a general rule, the higher up you go in the management hierarchy, the less detailed and more focused your presentation should be.

It is also very helpful to know your direct client well. They may be very detailed and would prefer to see all of the numbers that back up your finding or may trust that you have done all of the due diligence and trust your conclusions.

How to make Live Presentations: Specific Principles

Make it Easy to Read

In a live presentation, a person could be sitting 20 feet away from the screen. Make sure your slides are readable at a distance. (Even if it is a webinar, remember people could be watching it on a smaller device.) A general guideline is that the title font should be about 44 points and at least 36 points, the standard text font should be 32 points and at least 24 points, and the second level text font should be 24 points and at least 18 points. The font size can fall below 18 points in rare situations. Avoid using more than three font sizes as it likely isn't necessary. The more time people spend trying to read something that is not easy to read, the less time they have to listen to what you are saying.

A presentation will look more professional if the text on each slide follows the same conventions. For example, if you use 36-point font in your headlines, make sure every slide's heading is 36 point. You may need to shorten the text so it will fit at this 'standard' size; not a bad discipline.

Be Economical with Words

Consider the following slide that is written in a report format.

Version A (Report format)

> **Why we lead the market**
> - We are priced lower at $2 compared to our nearest competitor $2.50
> - We are distributed uniformly across the country while our competitors are regional.
> - Our product is rated of higher quality (9 on a 10-point scale). This is clearly above the rating of our closest competitor (a rating of 8)
> - Our reputation score is 91 as opposed our competitor's 85.

When you present a visual like this, the audience starts reading it. But this sets up a conflict. When the audience is busy reading your slides, it is only paying partial attention to what you are saying.

Therefore, it is critical that the slides aid your presentation and not distract the audience. The best way to accomplish this is to minimize the amount of effort needed to understand the slide. Slides should be designed in such a way that the contents can be taken in by just glancing at the slide. This means fewer words. In addition, you can sequence the bullet points one-by-one so that your audience will read only the point that is on-screen.

Version B (Presentation format)

> # Why we lead
> - Lower price
> - Wider distribution
> - Higher quality
> - Better reputation

To understand the difference between the two, compare version A with version B. Version A requires that the audience read the contents from left to right and understand it. It distracts the viewers and makes work for them. Version B requires just a brief glance.

When we present several slides containing a lot of written material, the viewers will find the presentation uninteresting and tiresome. Version B does not expect any effort from viewers. It's there to reinforce your presentation. When using a tight format such as Version B, be prepared to provide additional information, such as "What do you mean by higher quality?".

The slide can be animated to show just one point at a time. Then, the audience is not tempted to read ahead, and the presenter can comment on each point while holding the attention of the audience.

Prefer Simple Graphs

The same is true of graphics. When you present complex graphs or charts, viewers will spend time trying to understand it. Their full attention will not be on what you are saying but on understanding the graphs. Use simple graphs like bar charts or line charts, which don't take much effort to understand. Do not use complex graph just because they look attractive.

What happens if the data itself is complex, like the one below? Here, bar charts and line charts are of little help. The bar chart is even more challenging to read than the table.

How to Present the Findings

	Actuate	Arc Pln	Board	IBM	IDS Scher	Infor	Info Builders	Jasper soft	LogiX ML	Micros oft	Micro Strtgy	Oracle	Panor ama	Qlik tech	SAP	SAS	Tableau	Targit	Tibco
Doing complex ad hoc analysis	8	24	27	8	28	12	9	16	24	24	18	22	16	33	10	18	29	19	21
Doing moderately complex ad hoc analysis	43	50	57	48	52	54	59	67	60	43	41	68	29	56	41	51	51	42	38
Doing predictive analysis	3	12	18	7	12	2	5	3	9	6	2	13	7	16	4	6	20	19	16
Doing simple ad hoc analysis	8	10	8	7	14	6	4	10	11	7	11	13	20	19	11	11	18	9	14
Monitoring scorecards	19	18	26	23	24	29	22	23	25	30	33	29	38	35	20	25	42	34	49
Using parameterized reports	8	21	21	10	24	22	19	19	30	13	12	24	15	30	9	10	34	11	24
Using personalized dashboards	12	9	12	11	15	10	13	17	13	16	18	22	22	24	13	17	29	17	25
Viewing static management reports	41	38	39	38	40	64	42	59	40	37	39	39	43	37	40	42	37	39	28

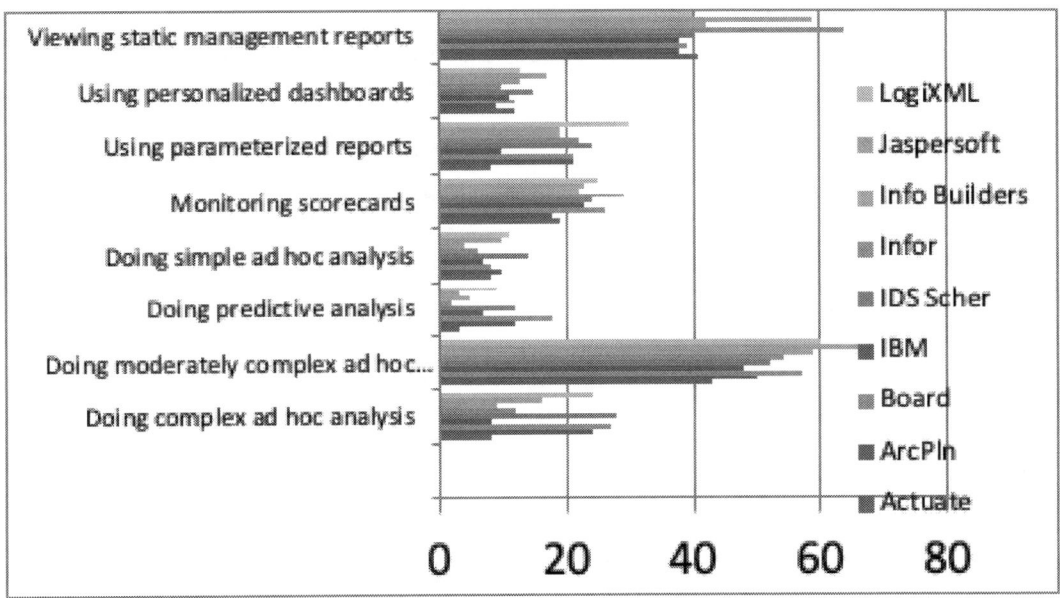

If it is essential that the profiles of different brands be compared on several attributes, and simple charts like bar charts or line charts cannot do the job, break the data down, as shown below:

How to Present the Findings

BI Tools are used for	MicroStrategy	Oracle	Panorama	Qliktech	SAP	SAS	Tableau	Targit	Tibco
Viewing static management reports	▪	▪	▪	▪	▪	▪	▪	▪	▪
Monitoring scorecards	▪	▪	▪	▪	▪	▪	▪	▪	▪
Doing moderately complex ad hoc analysis	▪	▪	▪	▪	▪	▪	▪	▪	▪
Using personalized dashboards	▪	▪	▪	▪	▪	▪	▪	▪	▪
Doing simple ad hoc analysis	▪	▪	▪	▪	▪	▪	▪	▪	▪
Doing complex ad hoc analysis	▪	▪	▪	▪	▪	▪	▪	▪	▪
Using parameterized reports	▪	▪	▪	▪	▪	▪	▪	▪	▪
Doing predictive analysis	▪	▪	▪	▪	▪	▪	▪	▪	▪

By breaking down complex data into their component elements, we can create a chart that is meaningful and effective. Instead of showing the whole graph at once, sequence parts of the graphs into the slide, say each column or each row, comment on those, then move along to the next chunk.

Make your Charts as Lean as Possible

A lean chart is one in which every unnecessary element is eliminated. The following chart is similar to what we see in many presentations.

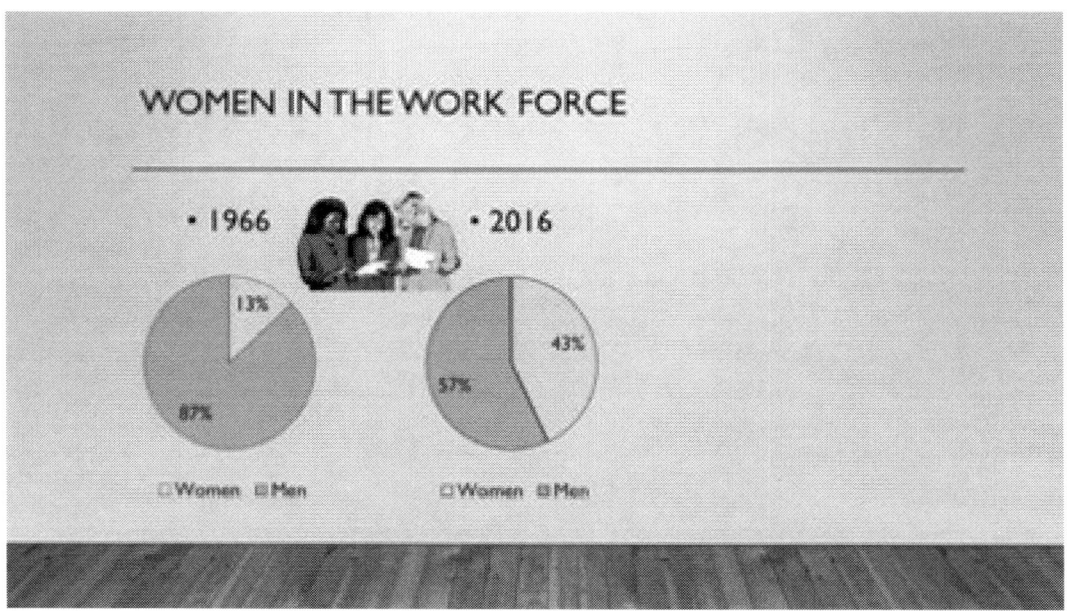

But many elements in the chart are unnecessary. For example,
- Do we really need the clipart?
    - Are the pie charts adding anything to the communication?

- Look at the pie charts. Why do we need them? If 13% are women, then clearly, 87% are men. We don't need a pie chart to know that. However, the contrast between 1966 and 2016 is the key point.
- When using pie charts, do not isolate the legend as above. Place the label and the percentage within each slice of the pie. Don't make the audience work too hard.

We can create a more powerful chart if we eliminate all that is unnecessary. Here is a more impactful presentation of the key finding.

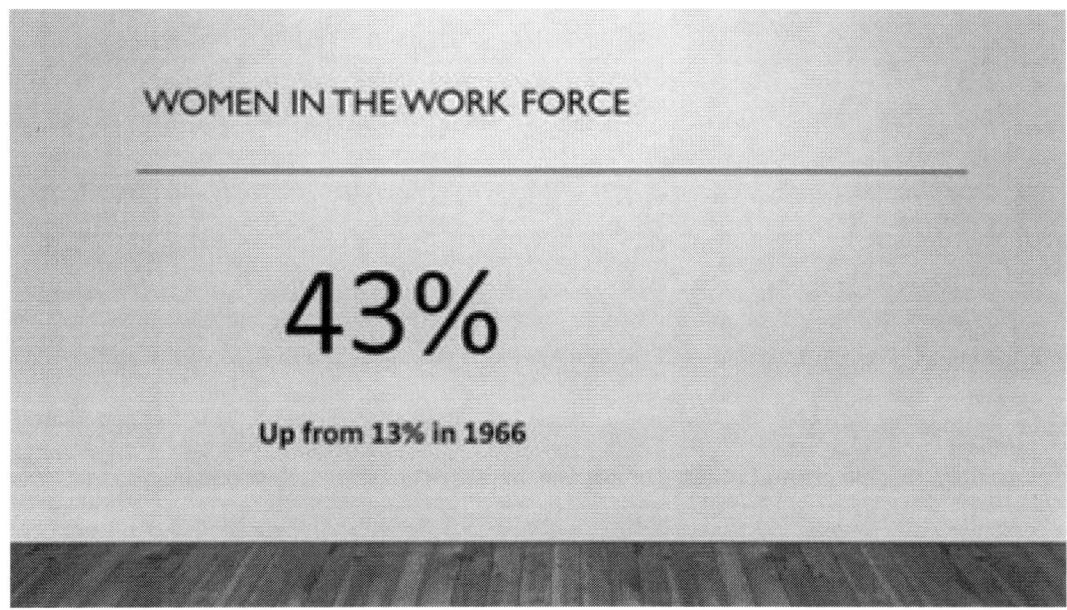

The 'lean slide' above conveys the same information as the standard slide but in a much more powerful and insightful way. Practice creating 'lean slides.'

Keep Gimmicks to a Minimum

Keep gimmicks like fancy transitions, music, and animations and video clips to a minimum. If used for no real purpose, they can become annoying and distracting. Avoid them if they are not needed.

There are exceptions. Video clips, for example, can be very useful in demonstrating how a product actually works, or to let us see how consumers reacted physically to a stimulus. Animations can help to simplify a busy slide that has already been reduced to the minimum for the topic. They also hold back details on a slide until you are ready to explain them, so the audience can focus on what you want highlighted.

Be Mentally Prepared

The old theatre adage "rehearse, rehearse, rehearse then improvise" holds for marketing research presentations as well. Make sure you know your data and analysis inside-out. Write speaker notes if it helps clarify what you want to say when each slide is up on the screen. Do a dry run speaking out loud, so you know how it will sound to the audience.

Then when it comes time to present, put your notes down, turn your back to the screen, and talk to your audience.

If you read off of the screen, with your back to the audience, they may not hear you well and may wonder why you are even needed (they can read just as well). If you read your notes, you are not making the personal connection that draws them into the story you are telling.

Here are some more tips:

Practice stillness. If you have nervous mannerisms like pacing, swaying, touching your face or head frequently, they become part of the performance and distract from your message.

Slow down. You may tend to race through your presentation. Practice speaking at a pace that feels uncomfortably slow. You will be giving your audience time to absorb and integrate what you are saying. Speaking more slowly will also help eliminate annoying interjections ("um," "like," "I mean").

Use pauses. Stop speaking for a second after you have made an important point. Give it time to sink in. Not only will the audience get your point, but it's an effective technique to bring wandering minds back to you.

Look into their eyes. You will want to create a connection with your audience. The most effective way to do this is to look directly into their eyes. The suggestion to look over the audience's heads when speaking only works in a large auditorium.

Everyone's eyes. You may see speakers focusing only on the senior people in the room. This is a mistake. Include everyone in the room when you are talking. Focus on them one-by-one. The young intern in the corner may someday very soon be the senior brand manager or an insights manager. They will remember the researcher who included them in the presentation. Move around the room if you can to ensure everyone feels they are part of the "happening."

Acknowledge questions. If you are interrupted by a question, acknowledge and answer it, or indicate that the answer is coming or suggest they bring it up again at the end of the presentation (parking it). When you get to the slide, refer back to the questioner, so they know they have been heard.

Make your point and stop. Do not ramble on. When you write your speakers' notes or rehearse, hone in on the one or two points you want to make on each slide, and say only that.

Step back when the discussion starts. If a discussion starts during the presentation, step back for a moment or two and let it happen. The commentary from the client will help them absorb the findings and is an opportunity for you to learn about how they are interpreting it. Keep an eye on the time, and step forward again when you have to get things back on track.

Be prepared to go virtual. In-person presentations have long been the standard, but webinars had been a presentation option, particularly when the client organization has stakeholders in different cities. However, when the Covid-19 pandemic hit in 2020, offices were closed, and meetings moved quickly into virtual spaces like Zoom, Skype, Google Meet or MS Teams. These meeting apps have presentation modes that allow for screen sharing and let you hand control over to other participants. The presentation can be recorded by any of those apps. Many have found this to be an efficient and comfortable way to interact. Virtual presentations will continue to be a standard option long after life has returned to a new normal.

In summary, whenever you prepare for a presentation, remember to

- Prepare fully.
- Understand your audience.
- Build rapport with the audience quickly.
- Speak clearly and be articulate.
- Have complete knowledge of the information being presented.
- Anticipate questions and answer each question thoroughly.
- Motivate your audience to use the information.

How to Integrate the Findings: The Workshop

The live presentation is the traditional stopping point for a research project. What this often means is that you are handing the report off to your client and stepping away. It is up to the client and her colleagues to ensure the findings are absorbed, integrated and acted on by her organization. Sometimes the report simply goes into the electronic archives and is forgotten.

We can avoid this by following the presentation with a workshop in which exercises help key stakeholders within the client organization apply the findings to the decisions they will have to make. Stakeholders are likely to include the insight staff and the brand management and marketing teams. Depending on the strategic importance of the research, it might also include marketing executives, research and development people, the advertising agency, etc.

The research supplier can play a key role by organizing and facilitating this exercise. Here are some tips to help set this up.

- A workshop should follow the presentation with enough time between them to allow participants to absorb the findings.
- Holding the workshop off-site will ensure the undivided attention of participants.
- A workshop can be a half-day, a full day or spread out over more than one day, depending on the complexity of the findings and the decisions to be made.
- A strong facilitator will help keep the proceedings on track and let the research and insights team participate. Bring along a note-taker as well so that the discussions and decisions are noted.
- Create a plan for the day that takes the group through the key elements of the findings, for example, spend an hour getting to know the consumer segments that have emerged, another hour on understanding how the brands align with each segment, another hour on the language that should be used to reposition the clients' brand against the key competitors, etc.
- A half-day or full-day workshop is a long haul, and smartphone messages are only a short reach away. Keep the day moving with team exercises (like collage building to flesh out the segments) and presentations, animated brainstorming and plenary discussions.
- If breakout team exercises are planned, pay attention to the personalities in the room. Ensure that others balance strong or authoritative voices in smaller groups (e.g., ensure the CMO has another confident voice or two in her group).
- Know what the final output of the day will be (e.g., a decision about which segment to pursue or a long list of potential innovation ideas) and ensure you get there.

- Use the note-takers notes, take photos of any group activities and their outputs (e.g., collages, or village groupings of products), keep track of different perspectives that are voiced and any decisions that are made, and create a compilation of the workshop proceedings. It needn't be a report but should record important decisions that were made.

At the end of the day, setting up a workshop helps ensure that the hard work that went into creating and executing the research study results in concrete actions. It also helps elevate the research function by bringing it into strategic discussions.

Workshops are time-consuming and incur hard costs like a facilitator, room rental, supplies and catering. Be sure that if you are proposing a workshop, you cost properly for it in the proposal.

Concluding Comments

Your report is what your client paid for, and it is your job to make sure that the client will be happy with it. It is also your indirect sales pitch for your next assignment from the client. A client is likely to use your services again and again if they are satisfied with your reports.

So, try and apply all principles of communications outlined in this unit. Remember, a linear written report is different from the presentation form report and presentation form report is different from actual presentation slides. The differences may be subtle, but they are critical. Making a presentation is both a science and an art. Practice them until you become proficient.

UNIT 11

How to Research Common Marketing Problems

Marketing research is used to help marketers make more informed decisions. The challenges it can address and the methodologies that can be applied are as diverse as the people and organizations they assist.

Marketers must be aware that the success of a brand or an organization

- **depends on** the proper execution of **marketing functions** that they can control – offering the right product or service, at the right price, in the right place (distribution) with the right communications (promotion); and
- is **constrained** by **market and environmental forces** that they have little or no control over, including changing consumer tastes, cultural evolution, competitive actions, changing regulations, evolving trade practices, ingredient costs and many more.

Marketing research can minimize risk in these areas by providing insights and information to help make better decisions and create additional value for stakeholders. However, it is important to know which approach is most appropriate for each issue that needs to be addressed.

In this unit, we will profile some of the more common marketing issues that can be addressed by marketing research:

- consumer understanding,
- market landscaping and brand equity,
- innovation development,
- marketing communications,
- go-to-market tactics (e.g., pricing, packaging and line optimization)
- and specialized fields including business to business (B2B), political, legal and pharmaceutical marketing research.

These topics have similarities and differences. "Consumer" understanding is similar to "voter" understanding for political polling and "citizen" research for public policy development. "Market understanding" applies as much to the motivations of *voters* in supporting a specific political party or *doctors* in prescribing a specific drug as it does to *consumers* who choose one product over another. The overall challenge is that of understanding how people make decisions in different situations.

Regardless of which area of marketing research you are working in, the general principles outlined in this book apply. But each area of specialization has its own techniques to solve its distinctive problems.

Here are a few examples of the *type*s of adaptation we will need in different marketplaces and with different targets.

- If you are interested in learning what brands of toothpaste consumers use, you can interview people on any day of the week. However, if you are interested in knowing which sections of a daily newspaper people read each day, your sample should be designed so that all days of the week are covered, and you have a large enough sample on each day.
- If you are interested in finding out people's political views, you can probably call them on the phone and administer a 15-minute questionnaire. However, if you are interested in knowing what doctors think of a new medical innovation, you may have to arrange 15-minute in-person interviews with them in their offices or face-to-face via a meeting app (e.g., Zoom, MS Teams). And if you want to capture the reaction of younger consumers to a new personal care product, you'll need a 15-minute digital questionnaire they can answer on their phones.
- If you need to understand consumers' opinions about their financial institutions, you may not need interviewers who have backgrounds in finance. However, if you want to interview investment managers, you may need interviewers with appropriate specialized skills and knowledge.
- If you interview consumers of mass-market products, you are likely to aggregate the data to understand the market as a whole. However, if you interview industry leaders, you will probably analyze each interview individually to identify the patterns and distinctiveness of their responses.

This chapter will help you appreciate the breadth of marketing research in practice and highlight some interesting differences among applications.

Consumer Understanding

An organization's brands, products or services must be relevant to consumers. They must speak to the real needs that motivate people to act – to buy a product, sign up for a service, put the garbage out on the correct day, select a medical treatment, vote for a specific party etc.

Developing an understanding of what motivates consumers is a core function of marketing research. The insights that come out of these studies give marketers a window into their target audience's mindset and give them direction in tailoring the development of their products, services and messaging. Marketers who understand their consumers can vastly improve their chances of success.

> **Example 1.** A manufacturer of canned meats is hoping to increase their share of school children's lunches. They decide to undertake research that will explore what parents prepare for their children's lunchboxes, what makes them choose one product over another, what their children ask for, what causes them concern, and what might be on their wish list that isn't currently available.

> **Example 2.** A municipal government has started a new curbside composting program. 'Green bins' have been delivered to each household in the city so they can collect food scraps separately and put them out for weekly collection. Participation rates are low. The city's insight manager decides she needs to find out what is motivating those who participate and what the barriers are for those who don't. She'll want to know if awareness is the issue, if there is confusion about what goes into the green bin, if there are concerns about smell, pests (raccoons, mice, ants, cockroaches), contamination or social stigma.

> **Example 3.** *An insurance company has been tracking its brand image for years, and despite good scores, renewal rates are beginning to drop. There is concern that consumer needs have shifted since the tracking measures were first created, and management now agrees that it is time to undertake some research to discover 'today's' motivational drivers.*

What a Market Understanding Project Can Explore

Consumer understanding research is often very exploratory, starting with **qualitative** research or **ethnography** to discover new insights, explore consumer language and develop new hypotheses. This book has an entire chapter on qualitative research and its uses, so we will not cover those methodologies in this chapter.

Quantitative consumer understanding studies will often follow the qualitative work to validate and quantify any hypotheses that emerged from the qual and to model and map out behaviours and motivations. We often hear basic consumer research referred to as Usage and Attitudes

(U&A), Attitude and Usage (A&U), or Habit and Attitude (H&A) studies. However, consumer research covers the complete spectrum of research from exploratory qualitative studies to complex causal experiments.

Consumer research has language and terminology that can provide an envelope describing behavioural patterns in general, on specific occasions and for any number of research approaches. Those include:

- *Market mapping* to create two- or three-dimensional maps of how consumers see marketplace offerings as clusters of substitutable options,
- *Key Driver analysis* to learn what motivates consumers, both consciously and sub-consciously, in the choices they make
- *Motivation mapping* to discover how consumers make decisions to meet these needs, and
- *Segmentation* (people and occasions) to uncover how motivations differ across the population

Each of these methods can focus on

- How a person *'consumes'* the product, or
- How a person *'shops'* for the product.

Many organizations formalize these two perspectives into separate **'consumer insight'** and **'shopper'** roles. It's an important distinction because *consumer* insight would inform relationships with marketing and product development departments while the *shopper* role informs the relationships with retail partners.

A *consumer understanding* study starts with a **sample** that reflects the key target population. The sample frame often starts as encompassing the entire population of the market and is narrowed to remove those who would never be interested in the product or could not be accessed.

Example 1. If the manufacturer of diapers wanted to do a usage and attitude study, they would probably include only parents of young children currently in diapers. They might try to add a sample of prospective parents expecting a baby to capture 'pre-market' perceptions.

Example 2. A manufacturer of luxury cars might consider researching all adults with drivers' licenses. Still, they could legitimately narrow the focus to those who are likely to be in the market for a luxury automobile, perhaps based on income levels, previous ownership or intention.

Example 3. A government tourism organization might research neighbouring countries to understand better what tourists from those countries are looking for in a vacation, but it would be reasonable to limit the focus to only those who have valid passports and an intention to travel within the next few years.

Questionnaires for consumer understanding research generally start with questions about past behaviour. These are easy for consumers to answer and make them feel like experts, thereby gaining their trust and warming them up for the more difficult attitudinal questions that follow.

Example 1. A usage and attitude study on soup would start by asking respondents how often they consume soup, what types of soup they generally make, which one they make most often, what occasions they make soup for and what they serve or consume it with. These are easy to answer.

Example 2. A tour operator would ask consumers how often they go on vacation, where they generally go, with whom they travel, how long they are away, what modes of transportation they use, what types of lodging they stay in, where they have their meals, what activities they participate in, etc.

Common behavioural questions for a consumer understanding study for a food manufacturer might cover:
- **Consumption patterns.** Generally, what they eat, how it is prepared, who participates, what are potential substitutes, where it is stored in the home.
- **Shopping patterns.** What are the triggers to buy, do they use a shopping list, do they stock up or wait till they run out, have they decided before they enter the store, what do they consider on the shelves, is it habitual or exploratory every time, what might change their mind at the shelf, how does the placement on the shelf impact their decisions.
- **Occasion profiling.** What do the specific consumption occasions look like, are they special occasions, everyday events, when entertaining, what is served, how is it prepared, what else is served with it, is it centre of plate or a side dish, etc.

The **attitudinal** component generally follows the behaviour questions. Attitudes are comprised of three main components: 1) cognitive, 2) affective, and 3) conative. The cognitive component pertains to awareness and knowledge. The affective component seeks to understand peoples' emotions, i.e., whether a person likes a product and prefers it to others. The conative aspect basically drives people in certain directions; for example, a shopper intends to buy a specific brand the next time that the product is needed. This part of the questionnaire can be more challenging to answer – posing questions many consumers may never have thought about. They may appear as a long battery of questions that they are asked to agree or disagree with or assigning emotions or personality descriptions to occasions or products.

Example 1. In the soup study described above, the behavioural questions would be followed by questions on the perceptions of different brands, or what they judge to be important in selecting a brand.

Example 2. In the tour operator example above, they would move on to attitudinal questions about the relative desirability of different activities when on vacation, what an ideal vacation might look like, how they would rank different potential destinations, etc.

Example 3. A perceptional study on financial services might ask how consumers relate to their financial institution's staff, ranging from 'we're on the same team' to 'adversarial' or 'I don't trust them.'

Example 4. A laxative U&A might ask consumers to agree or disagree with a list of statements that could describe how constipation makes them feel, such as I feel sluggish, I don't want to be with anyone, it's just a minor ailment, common medications easily control it, it can be avoided with a proper diet.

Example 5. A study on television viewing might ask consumers to describe an 'ideal' night of TV viewing by checking off which characteristics from a list would best describe it, for example, with close family, accompanied by popcorn, ending before 10 pm, dressed in comfy clothes, etc.

The attitudinal questions are crucial components of any modelling work that might be done, such as key drivers or segmentation. Attitudes are latent variables. This means that they are not seen but are inferred through consumers' answers and analytical methods. Attitudes are difficult to measure and challenging to confirm and follow. While people are thought to have attitudes, no one has really seen an attitude – just some physical manifestation that may or may not represent the attitude. Very clever techniques have been developed to help people adequately express their attitudes.

Sometimes the questionnaire skips back and forth between behaviour and attitude as it follows a logical pathway, for example, asking about both behaviour and attitudes related to meal *planning*, then for *shopping*, then for meal *preparation* and finally for meal *consumption*.

Market Landscaping and Brand Equity

While consumer understanding research is about learning what *motivates* consumers to make the decisions that they do, market landscape and brand equity research focuses on **how they perceive the market place** and its **products** and **services**, how these deliver against their motivations and where gaps may exist that can be exploited through innovation or repositioning.

An important foundation for any organization that wants to make better-informed decisions is understanding the market landscape: Who are our competitors? What do they offer (from the consumers' perspective), and how does that compare to what our organization can provide? How are our brands, our products and services perceived by the consumer in this competitive context?

Example 1. A manufacturer of high-end candies is about to enter a new market and needs to understand not only which competitors it will be facing, but how they are perceived, what role each plays and where there may be room for their new products to fit in.

Example 2. One of the country's leading financial institutions has seen its mortgage business lose ground in recent years as competitors develop innovative new services. They need to get a clearer picture of what needs these new services (and the old ones) are fulfilling to see if they need to begin innovating themselves, extolling the benefits of their existing products, or simply continuing with current tactics because competing innovations are a fad that is incompatible with their own equity.

Example 3. A grocery retailer has initiated some new services – integrating on-line purchasing (click and collect), providing more 'ready to serve' meals that compete with fast food outlets, and providing more community meeting spaces in their stores. They have made significant investments and need to know if they have moved the needle on how consumers perceive them – their brand equity.

A very popular market landscaping technique is the **perceptual brand map**. It is a visual representation of how consumers view the marketplace, an attempt to spatially represent consumers' perceptions of similarities and dissimilarities among the brands or their relative preferences for the brands.

The research asks consumers which brands they associate with a **list of characteristics** that might play a role in their decision to buy one brand or another. This list might come from past brand tracking research, from qualitative research, or from prior knowledge and brainstorming.

The map uses **correspondence analysis** to place the brands in a 2-dimensional space. Brands that are associated with similar characteristics appear to be close to each other in the space. Brands that are associated with a very different set of characteristics are located far from each other. This helps us identify which products are likely to be competitors.

The exercise also allows us to overlay the characteristics themselves, so we see why brands are grouped together. Two products that are associated with a specific characteristic by most respondents will appear close together and near this characteristic on the map.

(These techniques are described in greater detail along with examples in Chuck Chakrapani's *Analytics for Customer Insights,* a companion volume to this book.)

Example. "PriceCo," a retail grocer, wants to understand how consumers perceive the chain compared to its competitors, what characteristics consumers see it performing well and what it is <u>not</u> associated with. The key attributes that they want to explore include best prices, freshest produce, most attentive staff, best specials, fastest checkouts, widest range of frozen foods, freshest bakery items, best deli, best seafood, most accessible (parking/transit), etc. Respondents are asked to associate "PriceCo," and its major competitors with each of these characteristics and the perceptual brand map reveals that the chain is most closely associated with low prices and specials, accessibility and fast checkouts (which competitor "Zoey's" is also associated with), but is not identified with freshness or good service. These are the domain of the competitor, "Fresh Basics." None of the competitors seem to be associated with a variety in the frozen section.

Driver Analysis from a consumer understanding component of the survey may identify the frozen section to be a key determinant of grocery store choice. This gives "PriceCo" clear direction on what they can do to gain an edge over other competitors. They could try to own variety in the frozen section to gain an advantage over "Zoey's" or open an upscale variant with knowledgeable staff and an emphasis on fresh food to compete against "Fresh Basics."

The visualized information helps "PriceCo" learn the strengths and weaknesses of their brand in comparison to others and may lead them to change the emphasis of their communications or even completely reposition to compete better.

A **brand health pyramid** is built from data on brand awareness, trial purchasing, repeat purchasing and loyalty. Each brand's ability to convert consumers from one stage to another will help them understand where to direct their marketing dollars.

> **Example**. "PriceCo" enjoys nearly universal awareness and has converted most consumers to trial and repeat purchasing. But they claim little loyalty (it's not the 'most often' source for a wide swath of consumers). "Zoey's" also has high awareness but is much weaker on trial. However, those who have been to the store at least once are much more likely to convert to being loyal. New upstart "Farmer Jim's" has low awareness, but once consumers are aware of the brand, its conversion through trial to loyalty is very strong.

Each of these profiles or 'pyramids' dictates a different strategy to grow. "PriceCo" needs to understand why their own current shoppers are going to other stores. "Zoey's" need to figure out what's wrong with their current marketing because it is not convincing shoppers to enter their stores. Both of them need to watch out for "Farmer Jim's" because if they build more stores, or gain more awareness, they risk eating significantly into their brand shares.

Brand equity is another form of research and analysis that helps marketers understand how consumers see the marketplace. We can think of this as the value of the brand derived from consumer perceptions and preferences. There is a range of ways that this can be measured. Each research organization will have its own measures and method of presenting the result, but the most common is to measure a "share of preference." We can think of this as the share of what consumers would like to buy before they are influenced by promotions, feature pricing, stockouts or other 'passing' influences that may make them pick up another product.

The "share of preference" might be quite different from a "market share".

This market equity measure, however it is calculated, is very important for brand managers because it is what is tracked over time. Are the marketing communications and positioning work increasing preference for our brand? Are we moving the needle on brand equity? The stronger the equity, the safer the brand is from competitive attacks.

Innovation Development

Once we have a good sense of what motivates the consumer to choose a product or service over another and once we know how products or services currently in the marketplace are performing on the key components of the marketing mix, we can move on to fine-tune or develop new positionings for our offerings or to create new offerings to meet the needs we've identified.

The most successful innovations are those that are relevant to consumers in their daily lives. By conducting consumer understanding research and market landscaping research, we should have gained several new **insights** into how to market to consumers.

Example. "PriceCo" may have learned from its consumer understanding work that:
- younger consumers are increasingly motivated by a desire to try new and exotic foods,
- they don't consider frozen foods to be healthy,
- they appreciate having information at their fingertips when shopping for groceries but don't want to track down and ask an employee.

When several different insights emerge, we need to narrow our focus and concentrate on a few that will be most effective in fine-tuning our positioning or creating new products or services.

Insight Screening

A robust innovation program will include **insight screening** to ensure that the insights used as an initial point for innovation are recognized needs for their target audience and that no one else is adequately meeting those needs at the moment.

Example. A simple insight screening study for a grocery retailer might show respondents a battery of insight statements like
- "I wish someone would tell me how to tell if an exotic fruit is ripe when I'm in the store," or
- "Wouldn't it be great if I could get answers to questions I have about a product without hunting down a clerk" or
- "I'd love to know where each cut of meat comes from before I buy it."
- Respondents would be asked to what extent they identify with each statement or how motivating a solution would be for each. The various insights tested can then be ranked.

This simple method ensures the marketing or product development teams can focus on the *most* important needs when they begin to innovate.

Concept Testing

New product or new positioning '**concepts**' can then be written based on the prior research above. A concept is a simple representation of what consumers will encounter when making a purchase decision. It might help to think of it as an old-fashioned magazine ad, with:
- an illustration,
- a headline,
- the consumer insight on which it is built,
- the product description and
- reasons to believe.

The concept might also include size, price and where it can be found – retail details.

Concept testing will put trial renderings of the concepts in front of respondents and ask them a few key questions. The key performance indicators (KPIs) would produce measures that are considered indicators of how well the proposed product or positioning will do once it is available for purchase.

Depending on the concept testing system that is used, the key performance indicators may be:
- Future interest in purchasing
- Meeting a personal need
- Meeting this need in a way other products currently do not
- Credibility of claims
- Overall liking

Some concept testing systems will compare these scores to **norms** derived from databases of concepts tests conducted in the past. Some will compare the scores to **benchmark measures** (for example, another concept tested at the same time for a product that was successful), and some will set **hurdles** that have been derived from **simulated test market** research designed to model actual sales patterns.

Some concept testing programs will test new ideas **monadically** – meaning that each respondent sees only one concept and rates it in isolation. This provides the cleanest read and comes closest to replicating an actual in-store exposure. But if you are testing a large number of new product concepts, it can become very expensive.

Some concept testing programs will use a **'sequential monadic'** design in which each respondent sees several new ideas, in randomized order, and answers the same key performance indicators for each one. This is a much more cost-effective way of screening a large number of new positioning or product concepts, but there is always the risk that we will get 'comparative' measures rather than the clean replication of 'at shelf' exposure. This means that one particularly strong or appealing idea in the group would actually suppress the scores for others, even though they are potentially very appealing.

Example. "Bark 'n Meow" is a manufacturer of pet foods and treats. They are testing 26 new product ideas and have opted for a sequential monadic approach. The list will be randomized, and each respondent will see and evaluate five ideas. On the list is a breakthrough new product that will freshen a pet's breath, strengthen their teeth, help them sleep at night and facilitate the learning of new tricks. It is a terrific idea, and everyone scores it very high. However, every time it is one of the five tested by a respondent, the other four pale in comparison and get lower scores than they would when the star idea is not in rotation.

Regardless of the system used to test the alternative positionings or new products, the outcome will be a recommendation on whether the concept should proceed to the next phase of development, be redesigned or be put on the back-burner in favour of other, more promising ideas.

Many concept testing programs are linked to **volumetric sales forecasting models**. These are used to project how many units of the product would be sold with the positioning described in the concept. Sales forecasts can be created for different "go-to-market" scenarios, including alternative positioning approaches, different levels of spending on advertising, different degrees of distribution. The models will also forecast **cannibalization** of the company's existing products so they can determine the net impact across the whole business.

Marketers can input the sales forecasts from these models into their own financial models, factoring in their own costs of manufacturing and packaging, any listing fees to get it into stores and other expenses to determine whether or not they can make a profit if they go ahead.

The data that is fed into a volumetric forecasting model generally includes:
- The key performance indicators from the survey,
- The current products respondents will likely replace with the new product, and
- The marketers' best estimates of how the product or positioning will be launched, including:
    - Expenditure on advertising by month or by quarter after launch
    - Type of paid media used – TV, print, outdoor, digital
    - The extent of distribution through sales channels at the time of the advertising launch
    - The number and size of expected competitors and their anticipated marketing expenditures
    - All specific promotional activities (extent of sales pricing, the value of coupons offered, any free trial sizes offered, etc.)
    - An estimate of the impact of social media efforts on awareness and desire to purchase.

Sales forecasting at the concept stage involves several assumptions. Because the respondent has not actually tried the product, there is no feedback on performance. Will the physical product meet consumers' expectations set by the concept? Will there be some deleterious impact from extended use? Will the packaging perform well or create a hindrance?

To answer these questions, a product test is often required.

Product Testing

Marketing research will be asked to test products when:
- A **new product** or **line extension** is about to be introduced to the marketplace, and the manufacturer needs to understand if consumers will like it and what the potential market for it will be
- A **new competing product** has appeared, and the manufacturer of an existing product needs to know how the two compare from the consumers' perspective
- An existing product's **formulation** is about to change, and the manufacturer needs to know what consumers will think of it or if they will even notice
- A product's **positioning** is about to change, and the manufacturer needs to know if the existing product can live up to the claims that are being made

Product testing is a core area of marketing research focused on how people react to a physical product. It is commonly used by manufacturers of **packaged goods** (also known as fast-moving consumer goods) including food, beverages, personal care products, home care products, etc.; essentially, any product that consumers interact with physically by consuming it, putting it on their bodies, using it around their homes, as long as it is used up at some point and they go back to the store to buy more.

Companies like Campbell Soup, Kellogg, Kraft Heinz, Nestlé, Ferrero, PepsiCo or Coca Cola are continually concerned about whether the people who eat their soup, cereal, coffee, confections snacks, beverages or frozen foods appreciate those products more than the competing products.

> **Example**. MacDuff's Soup has created a new Haggis-flavoured soup and wants to know:
> - how consumers will perceive the aroma, saltiness, smokiness, after taste, value, and other characteristics
> - whether they would be interested in buying it for their households,
> - how they would use it (themselves or whole family, everyday meals, special occasions, ingredients in recipes) and
> - if it will draw business away from other flavours in the MacDuff's line or attract business away from competitors' lines.

Drawing business away from other products that the manufacturer currently has on the shelf is commonly called '**cannibalization.**' Measuring the 'net benefit' to the company must take this into account because, at the end of the day, it is the cumulative performance of the entire brand that is important to management and shareholders, not just the performance of the product being tested.

The **target respondent** for product testing depends on the product that is to be tested, and the client's strategic needs. Here are some common scenarios:
- Often an existing product is **reformulated to save costs on ingredients**. This can happen when the new ingredients are less expensive or more readily available. Consumers are generally not going to be notified of the change, and the key concern is that they do not notice the difference. Only current users are included in this test because a "quiet" reformulation is not going to attract new users.
- An existing product is **reformulated to improve its performance** compared to competitors. This might be done to increase differentiation (cleans better than the competition), adapt to changing tastes (now less salty, with added goji berry juice). In this case, consumers will be told of the change and it will be important to seek the reaction of both *current users*, to ensure they are not disappointed and abandon the product, and *non-users* who may be attracted to buy the product for the first time because of the change.
- An existing product is **reformulated to improve perceptions** or overcome perceptual barriers. This might be done in response to societal trends (now with no artificial preservatives, gluten-free, ethically sourced). Again, both *current users* and *non-users* are included in the test.
- A **new line extension** is to be added to an existing product line, for example, a new scent of laundry detergent or a new mildew-fighting 'basement' cleaner to complement a line of kitchen, bath and general-purpose household cleaners. In this case, *all consumers* who might be buying a product like this would be included in the test. It's important to identify

current users of other products in the line because they will provide a sense of potential cannibalization.
- A **brand new product** is being added by a manufacturer who has **not previously been in an existing category** and has no existing products that can be cannibalized, for example, a manufacturer of perfumes and fragrances decides to launch an underarm deodorant. All *category users* can be included in this test because cannibalization is not a concern.
- A **new-to-the-world product** is about to be launched, creating a new category where none has existed before, for example, a pharmaceutical company has developed a 'hair change' treatment that changes the colour of hair as it grows, eliminating the need for bleaching and dyeing. In this case, the sample is wide open – including *anyone who would have a realistic expectation of buying the product (those with hair who might consider changing its current colour)*.

There are two primary types of product testing:
- "**sensory testing**" - designed to get feedback on the physical characteristics of a product, often in comparison to a competitive product. This might include:
    - A soup's saltiness, thickness, aroma, aftertaste or colour
    - A garbage bag's strength, size, ease of opening, ability to contain smells,
    - A laundry detergent's scent, ability to clean, absence of residue on cleaned clothes, the scent left on the clothes, etc.
- "**simulated test markets**" – designed to replicate the trial and repeat shopping process that measures consumers' reactions to initial exposures (like advertising), decisions to purchase, in-home usage of the product, and decisions whether or not to repurchase *and* sensory testing feedback. Data from this type of test is generally fed into a volumetric forecasting model to predict first-year sales.

Sensory Testing

Sensory testing can be used to:
- determine how consumers perceive a **new formulation** of a product in comparison to the *current* formulation to see if it is considered better, the same or worse
- determine how **different formulations** of a potential product **compare** to each other to determine which is the strongest to move into development
- **compare** the **client's product** to the **competition's product** to see if noticeable advantages are perceived and can be addressed in marketing
- provide **empirical proof** to back up claims of product superiority.

We often think of sensory testing for food and beverages – the famous soft drink 'taste tests' come to mind. But it can certainly be used for household and personal care products as well.

Example 1. Oildoor Inc. makes underarm deodorants and has come up with a quick-drying, long-lasting product designed to out-perform one of the lead products in the marketplace. Consumers are unlikely to understand its superiority when first hearing about it, or even after the first application. But the company feels after several days, the product's advantage becomes very clear. A product test involving the major competition is needed to prove this and inform marketing communications.

Example 2. DrumCo makes a soy-based beverage with a texture that takes some getting used to. It may also not appeal to children. They need in-home tests with real consumers over several days to see how much of a barrier these two concerns may be.

Example 3. Lebaton Breweries believes that there is room in the marketplace for a guava flavoured beer, but they are working on alternative intensities of the flavour. They want to get consumer reaction to several different iterations of the flavour and need to ensure the test is done in a very strictly controlled environment, so the only variable is the flavour strength.

Sensory testing can take place in a central location test facility, or it might involve an in-home test.

Central location facilities are the most appropriate if, as in the beer example above, the environment must be strictly controlled.

> Every sample of the beer tasted must be exactly the same 'age' (number of days from manufacturing) and served the same number of minutes after opening the bottle and at exactly the same temperature to ensure a fair comparison. The glasses they are served in must be exactly the same size, free of any residue (soap, remnants of the last beer), and the same temperature when the beer is poured into them. The pour itself must be exactly the same for each tasting to ensure the same head on each sample.
>
> In french fry taste tests, the ovens that the different samples are prepared in must be calibrated to exactly the same temperature. Each sample must spend the same amount of time in the oven. Putting frozen fries into an oven will cool it down, so the ovens must be allowed to warm up to the desired temperature before the next batch is put in.

There is a rigour and science in sensory testing that ensures respondents are reacting to the differences in the products and not to any differences in preparing and serving them.

On the other hand, **in-home tests** make more sense when usage patterns must be taken into account. This is particularly true if the product is going to be used by or served to other members of the household if it will be used in conjunction with other products or if the true impact of the product occurs over time.

> Different people might use the soy beverage mentioned in the example above in different ways. Some will drink it straight out of the refrigerator; some will pour it over cereal; some will add it to their coffee or tea. While the initial taste may be attractive, over time, it may begin to feel overly sweet or cloying. A proper evaluation, in this case, requires that the consumer use the product as they normally would over a week or more.

Similarly, the underarm deodorant requires several days of usage, perhaps covering several activities (workday, exercise, a night out on the town) to give the respondent a true sense of how it will perform for them and whether they might be interested in buying.

Testing garbage bags would require they be used in the household's normal receptacle, carry the type of garbage the household usually produces, sit in the house for as long as garbage usually does and get carried to the curb for pick up in the usual way.

Often a consumer is sent multiple products to try – with instructions to try one for a week, to evaluate it, then to try another for a second week, evaluate it and finally to declare a preference and provide comparative measures.

In-home testing has both advantages and disadvantages:

Advantages
- Product used as it normally would be, in the consumer's normal environment
- Prepared and presented as it would be if bought, not the way the manufacturer thinks is best
- Measures the reaction of the *whole* household, not just the respondent
- Provides an opportunity for repeated usage
- Longer trial (e.g., one week) versus a single taste test in a central location
- The reaction is based on cumulative experience

Disadvantages
- More expensive and more time-consuming
- Researcher loses control over how the product is used

We sometimes see different outcomes when a product is tested in-home versus in a central location. Some commonly acknowledged differences are:

- More startling flavours tend to win in malls, while blander flavours tend to win in-home
- Respondents' senses tend to tire after repeated usage in the mall because they are tasting several products in a very short window of time
- Any physical limitations of a product become more apparent during in-home testing because the respondent can spend more time interacting with it.

Many sensory tests, both central location and in-home, are **blind tests** - with no packaging, branding, or other identity. The intention is to get the response to the product itself without the influence of marketing factors. As a result, there is usually no need for finished packaging for the test.

Blind tests are not completely without information. The package may be plain, but the respondent needs to know the category (e.g., chicken soup), and there is a legal requirement that ingredients of edible products be listed on the label to avoid dietary issues or allergic reactions.

When multiple products are to be tested, they must be identified in some way, even in a blind test. The identification is likely to be "try first" and "try second," or "week one" and "week two," or sometimes non-hierarchical identification codes such as 7Q2 and 3N6 are placed on the packages. It's important not to imply any natural order (Product A and Product B) if the product usage is to be rotated.

To eliminate all biases, **double-blind tests** can be conducted. This means that in a central location situation, neither the staff who deal with the respondents nor the respondents who are using the product are aware of the identity of the brands. Instead, a third party is responsible for preparing and labelling the samples and giving them to the facility staff.

Blind testing is particularly important if a dominant or distinctive brand is included in the test. Its image may have more of an impact on reaction to the product than the actual product performance. However, sometimes the product is so distinctive that its identity can't be hidden – for example, a laundry detergent with rainbow speckles or a soft drink with a singularly unique taste. In that case, it may be better to test the product *monadically* - alone rather than paired with another lesser-known product.

Defining Target Respondents

The type of consumers recruited for a sensory product test can vary depending on the marketing decision that is to be made.

The first principle is that the product test is conducted among people who are the **brand's target market**.

> **Example 1.** You would include only
> - parents of infants for a diaper test, or
> - denture wearers for a test of a new denture adhesive, or
> - principal grocery shoppers for a household meal kit

It is important to remember that the target group for any research may not be the same as the **advertising target**.

> **Example 2.** For example, you may be targeting a facial moisturizer at educated women aged 25 to 34 who are fashion conscious, but in reality, many women aspire to fit into this demographic, and a much broader demographic is likely to buy it. It makes more sense to include all women aged 18 to 44 in the product test.

If the test involves a **product that has been "improved,"** and you are going to **tell consumers about the improvements**, it is because you hope to attract new buyers or protect current buyers from a competitive attack. At the same time, you must be careful that you don't lose your current buyers who may have become attached to the current product.

In this case, you would recruit both *current buyers* and *non-buyers* of the brand. For efficiency, you might choose to exclude those who are not buying the category because they would be more difficult to win over by the reformulated product. Special attention might be paid to 'light' users to see if the improvement might increase the frequency of their use.

> **Example**. Sorelaw is a company that manufactures an odour-removing powder for refrigerators. They have added a new ingredient that will not only remove odours but replace them with a series of fresh scents. This should be tested among anyone who uses freshener products in their refrigerators. It might attract those who do not use the product, but it would be a challenge to change their behaviour, and you might not be able to trust their reaction in a product test.

A product test may involve a **change in the formulation** that is not revealed to consumers, for example, when a less expensive ingredient is being substituted to reduce production costs. In this case, the intent of the research will be to see if respondents notice, and if they do, what impact that might have on purchase interest. In this case, it is critical to test among the product's own customers to be assured that they will not be dissatisfied with the change and switch to a different brand.

> **Example**. Borreal, a manufacturer of premium chocolates, has found that the price of Brazilian cocoa, a key ingredient, has been driven up by a combination of higher demand and tighter land-use regulations. They have sourced less expensive cocoa from another country, but the flavour is less intense, so some artificial enhancers will have to be added to replicate the current taste. Borreal needs to test the current formulation and the new formulation to see if the change would be noticeable to current consumers.

If a product test is a **head-to-head comparison between competitors' products** to establish an understanding of perceived strengths and weaknesses, it makes sense to recruit people who are buying any of the products in the category but pay particular attention to those who are currently buying the brands being tested.

> **Example**. Happy Plastic Wrap is the market leader but is faced with a new entrant that is making superiority claims. Happy needs to see how consumers are reacting to the new product to understand the potential extent of lost business before they embark on some new product development of their own.

If a product is ground-breaking and may **create a new category**, it's important to test the product among the broadest possible definition of the market.

Example. Sloops, a lawn care company, recognizes that homeowners have trouble finding the time to cut the grass and have invented a durable growth-limited ground cover hybrid that can be scattered by hand that will cover the lawn in a matter of days and then stop growing. This instant lawn carpet will revolutionize home maintenance and should be tested among anyone with a flat, outdoor space that they maintain (including balconies).

Because the sample is expensive in product testing, it is important to be as efficient as possible in the sample design. When testing a new flavour for a product line, it makes sense to test it only among those who have a predisposition to that flavour. For instance, don't ask people who generally dislike orange soft drinks to try a new orange flavoured beverage. It is unlikely they will like it.

Simulated Test Markets

The fondest desire of any brand manager is to predict future sales. This is particularly important with a new product that will require significant investments

- to manufacture and distribute it,
- to convince retailers to put it on the shelves and
- to advertise so consumers know it is available.

If the initial investment is significant, the risk of failure is high. Sales forecasts can reduce the risk of failure. The sooner you can understand how well it will sell, the lower the risk is.

A generation (or two) ago, the new product would be placed in a store in a smaller, more isolated community, local advertising might replicate the planned national rollout, and the marketer and retailer would sit back to see how consumers reacted by measuring real-life purchases.

Of course, everyone knew where these 'test markets' were located, and competitors could easily observe the results. In the interim, fragmentation and globalization have weakened the impact of *local* media.

In the late 1960s and early 1970s, marketing researchers began to develop **Simulated Test Markets (STMs)** - mathematical models that use consumer reaction to an initial exposure (like advertising), collect reaction to in-home usage, add in the manufacturer's marketing plan, and project trial and repeat purchasing.

When the model analyzes the respondent data, those inputs become volumetric sales projections that can inform companies' financial managers (who know the internal costs) to see if the profit projected would offset the investment required – essentially whether or not they would earn a profit.

The model can also be used to determine how much would have to be spent on marketing to achieve the desired level of sales and profits.

Regardless of which model is considered, several key principles are shared among STMs:
1. **Initial exposure.** The individual respondents are shown a concept of the new product idea, simulating the initial exposure they would have when they first see the product advertised or on the shelf. There are variations on how the concept is shown:
    a. as part of a clutter reel – an ad mixed in with other advertisements.
    b. in isolation – like an informative magazine ad that one might stumble across

c. as a simple pack shot with the only the information that appears on the pack – to replicate initial exposure at shelf when no advertising is planned
2. **Competitive context**. During the initial exposure, simulated test markets generally try to replicate the competitive context of the store.
   a. Some models ask respondents to evaluate the product they purchase most often to gain a benchmark for each individual respondent.
   b. Some display the new product on a shelf with its current or eventual competitors
   c. In some cases, a simple brand and price list sets the scene.
3. **Purchase decision**. Respondents evaluate the concept and decide whether or not they are likely to buy it. The purchase decision may be as simple as a 'purchase intent,' but in some of the more sophisticated models, it is an actual shopping exercise – either at an actual shelf or more likely from a virtual shelf embedded in an online questionnaire. The shelf can be quite sophisticated, with the ability to pick up the pack, turn it around to read the side or back panels and place it in a shopping cart.
4. **Product trial**. The actual product is placed in subjects' homes, either sent home with them from a central facility or mall intercept interview or couriered to them after completing an online survey. The respondents are asked to use it as they normally would use a similar product. Over a few days, they develop their own opinion of how well it meets their households' needs.
5. **Repurchase decision**. After a usage period, they are sent a second questionnaire and asked to declare their interest in buying the product a second time. This 'repeat purchase' is an important part of any product's continued success.
6. **Cannibalization.** Sales obtained at the expense of other brands from the same manufacturer. A company would be interested in the "net" impact of the new launch on their sales and profits. If the new launch does well but draws most of its sales from other products the company sells, it may not be beneficial in the long run. 'Replacement' questions, such as, "What would you buy this instead of?" can be asked.
7. **Product Improvement**. The second part of the study also focuses on respondents' evaluations of the product's performance. Does it live up to the expectations set by the initial exposure (positioning/advertising)? Does it compare favourably enough to what consumers are currently using to justify its replacement? Are there characteristics that can be emphasized that manufacturers should feature more prominently to gain more of a competitive advantage? Are there flaws that the manufacturer can improve upon before the product is launched to improve its chances for success?

Several simulated test market models have been developed over the decades –Assessor, Sprinter, ESP, Designor, BASES. The field approach may be similar, but there are some key differences:

- Some require only current category users participate in the test, while others include a broader sampling of consumers.
- Some use a simple declaration of purchase interest to model sales potential. In contrast, others use a series of key indicator questions that they feel are better indicators of future intent – relevance, believability, uniqueness, expensiveness, for example.

The prediction models make use of several different approaches:

- **Preference model**. This model employs a constant-sum paired comparison to measure consumer preference. Often referred to as a "chip game," respondents are repeatedly asked to indicate their preferences among pairs of brands in their consideration set by dividing 11 imaginary poker chips between the two brands in each pair. The preference information is then converted into purchase probabilities using the logit model of consumer choice. The share for the test brand is then used to estimate its actual in-market purchases.
- **Trial and Repeat model**. 'Trial' occurs when a consumer decides to buy a product for the first time. A **repeat** occurs when a consumer uses the product and decides to buy it a second time and thereafter.
- **Benchmarking**. A new product generally must either displace at least some of the sales of a product consumers are currently buying or create new sales. The scores that a new product receives from a survey respondent should compare favourably to how they score their 'most often' used product on the same measures if it is to make it into their shopping cart.

Some models integrate the impact of 'key influencers' – interviewing doctors or pharmacists to see if they would prescribe/recommend it or interviewing young children in front of their parents to see if they would 'nag' their parent into buying it and impact the purchase decision.

Normative Databases

Some companies maintain a large database of past new product launches and rely on the premise that people's responses to any new product will be similar to their responses to previous new products. A big advantage of this procedure is that comparisons can be made to past successes and past failures to estimate the sales and market share of the new product.

There is criticism that some proportion of the products in these databases were not successful when launched so that the comparison is on 'average' performance when, increasingly, a product has to be 'exceptional' to succeed. Some databases present comparisons in 'quintiles' so that manufacturers can target the 'top quintile' as a better measure of success.

Product Test Designs

Pure Monadic Test

The monadic test is used in those situations where the product would be conspicuous if presented in comparison to another. For example, the brand might be the dominant brand and thus easily recognizable, or the brand might have a distinctive form or features that would overshadow any other brand in a comparison test. The **Pure Monadic Test** can often answer the question of acceptability for the brand but is not able to provide any information on comparative grounds. The key characteristics of the pure monadic design are:

- Only one product is tried and evaluated by each respondent.

- The findings are compared to norms or historical test data collected in an identical fashion or to concurrent tests (another cell) on other products.
- The findings are compared to each respondent's perception of how the product they use most often performs on the same measures.
- It can be used when there is no logical comparison.

A monadic test gives us a better sense of how people would use a product in everyday life when they only use one product at a time. However, because it doesn't give us a head-to-head comparison from each respondent, it is not particularly sensitive to small differences between competing products.

Sequential Monadic Test

In a **sequential monadic test,** each respondent sees more than one product. But they evaluate each on its own. So, the interview looks like a series of two or more pure monadic tests, one after the other.

> **Example**. A respondent tastes a breakfast pastry with raisins and apricots and is asked the key performance indicators for this product. Then the same respondent tastes a breakfast pastry with sun-dried tomatoes and slices of sausage and evaluates it. Then the respondent tastes a family dessert pastry that has chocolate with raisins and apricots and evaluates that product.

While we are asking respondents to evaluate each product on its own, we cannot remove the first product from their minds when we give them the second product, etc. The first product may taint perceptions of products that follow. The questions they answer when evaluating the first product also sensitize them about what to look for when they try the second product.

You can see how a 'superstar' product might diminish the scores of less spectacular ideas, even if, on their own, they are strong.

The major benefit of this approach is that it is more cost-effective, and the impacts can be mitigated somewhat by randomizing the order in which the products are tried.

Paired Comparison

The **paired comparison** method makes use of the impact one product has on the other. It is used to evaluate new formulations, product _re_formulations, and testing the client's product versus the competitive product.

The design for a paired comparison has the respondent try one product without evaluating it, then try a second product, and finally, comparatively evaluate the two products at the same time.

> **Example**. A respondent is asked to taste a small glass of beer, then taste a small glass of another beer, and finally is asked to rate which they prefer on a list of attributes, including colour, aroma, amount of bubbles, initial taste, after taste, refreshing, filling, etc.

This approach is best suited for comparisons of easily consumed products. It might not be well suited, for example, to a facial moisturizer because the product would have to be used for several days to judge its impact. By the time the second product has been used, respondents might forget how the first felt on their skin.

Paired comparisons are a sensitive procedure that emphasizes differences between two products and is particularly useful when evaluating a single dimension (e.g., level of sweetness).

However, given the comparative nature of the design, we would not use it for *absolute* measures. We couldn't compare a product's scores to those of a product in another test if the comparative products are different.

Proto-monadic Paired Comparisons

The **proto-monadic paired comparisons method** is one of the most widely used designs in product testing. Proto-monadic, paired comparisons occur when respondents try one product and evaluate it, then try a second product and evaluate it, and then comparatively evaluate the pair of products.

From one respondent to the next, the order of usage is reversed, so that each product is impacted by the test of the other product half of the time. We generally look at the results of "first exposure" to get a clean, monadic read. Still, we can also get comparative and preference information that we need to make decisions.

Here is a typical, step-by-step procedure for a proto-monadic paired comparison:

1. **Screen**: The respondents are initially contacted, screened on the sample requirements (e.g., brand decision-makers, age, category usage) and asked if they would like to participate in the study. Once they qualify and consent, they are sent the product. If a mall-intercept screening method is used, they can take the product home with them (particularly useful if the product needs to remain refrigerated or frozen). If an online survey is used to screen, the product is mailed or shipped by courier.
2. **Try First**: The respondent is given the product and usage instructions, along with a means for recording their reaction – such as a paper or digital questionnaire. The respondent records product usage details, the overall rating of the brand, and reasons for rating the product either positively or negatively.
3. **Try Second**: One week later, the respondent records and submits their reaction to the first product (e.g., by filling out an online questionnaire) and turns to the second product. It some cases it may have been delivered at the same time as the first (with Try Second clearly indicated on the label), but in cases where there is a concern that a consumer will try the two products simultaneously or in the wrong order, it may be sent as a separate delivery along with instructions and another means to record their reaction.
4. **Comparative Evaluation**: At the end of the second week, the household is asked to record their reaction to the second product, and then continue on to answer questions on the comparison between the two products.

The analysis begins by comparing the responses for the two products *when each was tried first*. This monadic analysis of 'first exposure' opinions eliminates any source of bias from one product on the other. This approach provides absolute estimates of the value of each product when experienced by themselves.

The next phase of the analysis is to look at the comparative scores after the second product is tried. In these questions, the wording is looking for a comparative measure (e.g., "Which of the two products did you prefer for 'level of sweetness'").

Comparative evaluations are much more discriminating than monadic scores, accentuating even smaller differences that may exist between products. This makes it appropriate in categories where advances are made in small steps. However, it can also be more removed from real-life situations because preference or difference judgements might be made on inconsequential differences – things that don't really matter to people in real life.

Triangle Test

The **Triangle Test** is used *only* to discern if there is a difference between two products. The triangle test occurs when the respondent is presented with two units of one product and one unit of a second product, tries all three products and is asked to comparatively evaluate the "three" products. The respondent is then asked to select the "different" product after all have been tried.

The expectation is that "false differences" are identified, and if two of the products are identical, the degree of 'false differences' can be established, and the true differentiation measured.

Researchers often mistrust the triangle test. There are documented instances in which respondents could not distinguish products that were clearly different. Some feel that the task is too complex, too threatening, or the product interaction is too strong to be reliable.

How are Product Testing Results Used?

The main uses of product testing can be summarized as:
- Understanding how consumers react and if they would change behaviour having tried the product (buy a new product, turn away from a reformulated product, etc.)
- Projecting future sales to decide whether to launch it or not
- Understanding product issues that might require reformulation, repackaging or re-positioning
- Understanding perceptual benefits that can be highlighted in marketing
- Understanding perceptual flaws that can be counteracted in marketing

Many manufacturers now take it for granted that new products *must* be tested rigorously before they are introduced. Sophisticated simulated test market modelling has become a key tool for innovative companies and volumetric forecasts are a regular part of brand management.

Marketing Communications Research

Promotion is one of the traditional four Ps of marketing. The American Marketing Association website includes this definition of promotion: "According to the Association of National Advertisers (ANA), promotion marketing includes tactics that encourage short-term purchase, influence trial and quantity of purchase, and are very measurable in volume, share and profit." The Common Language Marketing Dictionary defines a promotional campaign as, "An **advertising** or **marketing campaign** is a set of coordinated, specific activities that are based on a common theme and are designed to promote a product, service or business through different advertising media." The message in an advertisement can be product-related, service-specific, or focused on an organization.

The immediate objective of any advertisement is to shift or reinforce consumers' perceptions, preferences or behaviours in favour of the advertiser. Of course, it is unrealistic to expect every single advertisement to accomplish all these goals. Sometimes, the purpose of an advertisement can simply be to inform the consumers about the availability of a product or service, or it can be to create a favourable impression of the advertiser. In fact, every advertising campaign has a two-fold effect on the consumer: the short-term and the long-term effect.

The **long-range objective** of an advertisement is to persuade many consumers to buy a product or service. Most advertising research tends to deal with how well advertising is accomplishing that task.

> When I write an advertisement, I don't want you to tell me that you find it 'creative.' I want you to find it so interesting that you buy the product. When Aeschines spoke, they said, 'How well he speaks.' But when Demosthenes spoke, they said, 'Let us march against Philip.' (David Ogilvy)

The **short-term effects** of an advertising campaign would include:
- increasing product awareness;
- creating greater recognition of what the product has to offer;
- creating a positive image of the product such that it increases the probability of purchase;
- persuading the consumer actually to buy the product;
- persuading the consumer to buy the product again; and
- reinforcing purchase satisfaction.

The long-term effects of advertising relate to creating and reinforcing a consistent and viable brand image among a solid community of repeat brand buyers. Brand image refers to the general perception of a brand as, for example, being expensive or inexpensive, being of low or high quality, being widely or not widely available, etc. Such a brand image implies a consistent and viable user image.

> Image means personality. Products, like people, have personalities, and they can make or break them in the marketplace. The personality of a product is an amalgam of many things—its name, its packaging, its price, the style of its advertising, and, above all, the nature of the product. (David Ogilvy)

How Does Advertising Work?

There is no satisfactory explanation about how advertising works. In fact, some people maintain that the effects of advertisements are very different from what is usually supposed. All we have is a series of models that are simple formalizations of individual points of view as to how advertising is *supposed* to work.

These models are neither correct nor incorrect. They are simply alternative hypotheses with little or no conclusive proof. But they do provide a framework for testing advertising on certain criteria.

Several **hierarchy-of-effects models** have been developed over the past few decades to help explain the processes through which advertising works. **Hierarchy-of-effects models** are usually descriptions of the stages that a consumer is hypothesized to pass through during the purchasing cycle. These stages include being unaware of the product through to purchase and then through to post-purchase feedback.

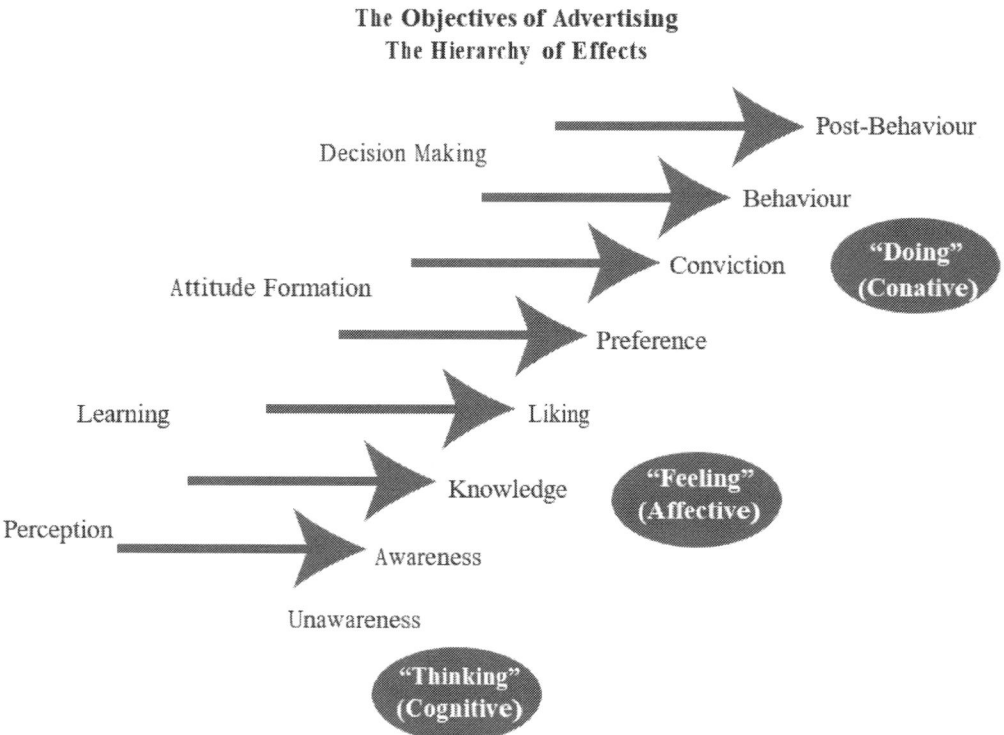

These models include AIDA (Awareness, Interest, Desire, Action) and DAGMAR (Defining Advertising Goals for Measured Advertising Results), which is the work of Elridge and others. One generalized approach offers **cognition** as the stage of attitude formation in which a person recognizes an object and learns about it while **affect** as the stage of attitude formation in which feelings and emotional responses toward an object or action are developed. **Conation** is the stage of attitude formation in which motivations for action are developed.

Experience has shown that none of these hierarchy-of-effects models is *always* correct regarding the sequence of steps on the road to converting a person into a consumer of a product. The sequence can change dramatically depending on the product category and the nature of the consumers. Also, this should not be looked at as a linear path. Rather, advertising is a complex phenomenon with several different beginnings, potential for substantial feedback during the process, and possibly simultaneous activities happening but with the persistent long-run objective of causing the behaviour to benefit the advertiser. The main benefit of these models seems to be that they focus attention on the important triad of **COGNITION-AFFECT-CONATION** (i.e., learning-feeling-doing that occurs during the purchasing process).

Advertising Decisions

Advertising decisions cover the following areas:
1. What to say in an advertisement (Strategy)
2. Who to say it to (Target Audience)
3. How to say it (Creative Strategy)
4. How often to say it (Minimizing Wear-out)
5. Where to say it (Media Strategy)
6. How much to spend on it (Optimizing the Budget)

Although all the above are legitimate areas of investigation, most advertising research relates to refining and evaluating (1) and (3). Secondary information, segmentation research, large-scale media usage studies, and prior knowledge often cover the remaining areas.

The advertisements that are evaluated can pertain to any media: digital, radio, TV, newspapers, magazines, point-of-purchase, outdoor, or direct mail. Each medium has its own strengths and weaknesses, and testing procedures will vary depending on the medium.

Communications Research

Ideally, every advertisement or "communication" should have some stated objectives, such as "to increase brand awareness among the target audience" or "to persuade consumers to use more of the brand advertised." Communication research is the systematic evaluation of how well these objectives have been accomplished through the advertisement. Communication research can test any aspect of communication such as intrusiveness, appeal, the transmission of information, influence on attitudes, memorability and persuasiveness. (Keep in mind that measurement of audience size is not communication research.) The methods used can be qualitative, quantitative or both.

Several dimensions may be measured in communication research. Some of the more common measures are brand recall, message recall, change in attitudes, brand or user image, purchase intent and diagnostic measures such as strengths and weaknesses. Questions that pertain to these measures do not necessarily have a standardized form. They may be open-ended or closed-ended, structured or unstructured, aided or unaided, scaled or non-scaled.

The usefulness of these measures is very dependent on the purpose for which they are collected. For example, how useful is the brand recall measure? If you believe in the hierarchy-of-effects models mentioned earlier, you might want to collect the brand recall information because, according to this model, awareness is a critical variable. On the other hand, if you go by proven ideas, you may not care much for brand recall information since it has not been conclusively shown to be related to product purchase. In practice, the measures included in a communication research study depend on several factors such as past studies, standard practice in a given industry or agency at any given time, and the researcher's notion of how advertising works.

Research Techniques

Some research techniques are common to all media, including focus groups, mall-intercept interviews, online and telephone tracking. Although these techniques have already been discussed, we will see here how some of them relate to advertising research.

Mall-intercept Interviews can be used to evaluate measures such as brand and message recall, purchase intent, brand image, and diagnostic information. Respondents can be asked to view an advertisement along with other ads and then be tested for recall. Or the researcher may want to solicit comments on a given set of ads. This method also provides for splitting the sample into two groups (test and control) and for follow-up interviews if necessary.

Telephone Tracking Studies can be used to measure the effect of a given campaign by interviewing people before and after the campaign. Brand awareness, brand image, purchase interest, and awareness of the advertisement are some of the aspects that can be measured. Its main advantage is that the test takes place in a natural setting rather than a shopping mall.

Some disadvantages of this method are the possible confusion related to which ad the research is referring to, uncontrolled exposure to ads, and no control of extraneous factors related to campaign effectiveness. Also, this procedure cannot be used effectively for diagnostic purposes. Most other tests are related to a specific medium.

Online Research provides the ability to show respondents "print" or video ads and ask them to compare and react in other ways to the ads. This can be done without interviewers being present and without the threat of the respondents viewing ads out of sequence.

The various methodologies that can be used are implemented and combined in ways that are suitable to the particular technique used at the time. The following procedures give a general view of the types of studies that are used in advertising research.

Perception Analyzer is a method of measuring the creative value of a commercial, second-by-second, as the responder views the commercial.

Respondents are invited to a central location where they are asked to watch or listen to the test material and record their responses by turning a dial on a specially designed, hand-held response meter. Their movements are transmitted directly to a computer and analyzed immediately so researchers and the client can see it in real-time. The responses are superimposed over the test material and can be viewed carefully at a later point to see exactly where consumers react positively and negatively.

The respondents' answers are completely anonymous, enhancing feedback from those who might have difficulty expressing how an ad makes them feel.

Here is what a typical group session might look like:

- **Participant Profile:** Attitudinal, behavioural, and demographic information are obtained and can be used to analyze the commercial testing information by shopper segment.
- **Baseline Profile:** Categorical questions are used to elicit brand preference and intention-to-purchase information. A videotape of a typical walk down the aisle in a supermarket, for example, is shown to respondents. They are asked to indicate on their hand-held dials which sections of the display are most interesting and likely to attract their attention.

- **Reaction Profile:** The respondents view the target commercial and competitive commercials interspersed with a 20-minute clutter tape. Respondents' reaction to the test material, according to the criteria specified by the moderator, is registered through the hand-held dials. The evaluative criteria may be appeal, persuasiveness, believability, likability, and so on.
- **Post-test Profile:** After responding to the clutter reel of commercials, respondents record their recall of the advertising and the perceived message in writing. Then, they use their dials to enter those messages. The walk-down-the aisle videotape is shown a second time, and respondents once again indicate which displays attract their attention. Each commercial is viewed two or three times and evaluated relative to the several different criteria. A battery of semantic scales stimulates the comprehensive evaluative profile.
- **Refocus:** Each commercial is shown a fourth time. The moderator then leads a discussion with the respondents, examining those issues of interest to the viewing client.

Clients can view the information instantly and also receive reports after the data have been analyzed using appropriate statistical procedures. Although the Perception Analyzer is used most frequently to test television commercials, it is also used to test radio commercials, new products, animatic productions (roughed-out executions or animated drawings, which are developed prior to incurring the expense of a full production of the commercial), broadcast talent, logos, movies, and music. Some providers of Perception Analyzer, or dials-based research are moving their methods more towards online implementation.

While many research approaches are designed to optimize advertising material before it is released (**Copy Testing**), research is also needed to track how effective the advertising is once it has been launched (**Ad Tracking**). Is it reaching the intended target with the intended message? Is it convincing people to react, is it making the appropriate brand linkage and at what point is it beginning to wear out?

Day-After-Recall (DAR) research is a tracking methodology that identifies whether or not the advertising is effective. The term *effective* can be misleading since the objective of the advertising can vary from creating awareness through to convincing a purchaser that she or he made the right decision.

The name is descriptive of the procedure. The day after a commercial is aired on television, respondents are called and asked if they watched the program within which the commercial appeared the preceding day. If they did, they are asked to name the commercials that they remember appearing during that program. This is 'unaided recall.' If they do not name the test commercial, they are asked whether they saw the "Whiskas commercial," for example. This is 'aided recall.' Those who did are asked to describe what they remember of the commercial they saw. The percentage of viewers who correctly name the commercial and remember parts of it is 'validated recall,' and this number is compared to historical normative percentages that have been measured for commercials advertising products in the same product category.

Two important measures are used in advertising tracking:
- **Brand linkage** – Consumers may remember the ad, but not which brand it was advertising. If the brand linkage doesn't register, even the best ad of all time will have little benefit for the brand.

- **Wear out** – Over time, even a great ad can fade into background noise and lose its effectiveness. At worst, it can become annoying and begin to have a deleterious effect on the brand. Ad tracking has measures to gauge when that line is crossed, and a researcher will advise the client that it is time to develop new creative.

Go-To-Market Tactics

Marketing mix decisions that are part of any brand's launch and market success include:
- **Pricing**. What is the optimal price in the competitive context of the shelf,
- **Packaging**. Which packaging design will best represent the product's advantages,
- **Shelf optimization**. How many line extensions and flavours is optimal – maximizing interest while minimizing manufacturing, distributing and listing costs.

Pricing Research

Many pricing decisions are made on a **cost-plus** basis, adding the *desired profit* onto the estimated costs of *producing, distributing and marketing the brand*. However, it is generally the market, including consumers, that ultimately guarantees the survival of the product and the attendant profits.

The price of a product—when not controlled by regulatory agencies—is simply the value that the manufacturer or marketer has placed on the item. The effectiveness of that price is driven by **supply and demand** – if people want the product to fulfill their needs (*demand*), and if there are no other products that will do so at a price people are willing to pay (*supply*), then they are likely to buy the product.

A company must gauge supply and demand to be able to set a price that will attract consumers while at the same time covering costs and returning a profit. Pricing research provides the consumer feedback they need to reduce the risk of making the wrong decision.

The wrong price can kill a product that could have been a potential winner. One common mistake relates to **price elasticity**: the belief that if prices were much lower, people would buy much more. Such economic truths are not universal and need to be tested in different contexts.

A marketing strategy based on **price discounting** can lead a company and its copycat competitors to financial disaster. On the other hand, a company that develops a marketing strategy that attempts to **associate high prices with quality and value** must be very certain that people perceive the quality and value the luxury connotation and that there are sufficient respondents in some elite segment that will buy the product.

If *moral* pricing is an extraneous consideration, there is no *fair* price for a product. Pricing should then be viewed within the context of three marketing environment variables: the product, the consumer and the competition. All three variables are potentially measurable through research.

The Role of Marketing Research

Some pricing methods are **product-oriented**, some **market-oriented**, and others **competition-oriented**. Marketing research is seldom relevant to *product-oriented* pricing techniques and highly relevant to *market, consumer* and *competition-oriented* pricing techniques.

We need to ask some **fundamental questions** about the competition and consumers to make sense of the market's reaction to prices. Here are a few suggested questions:

About the competition
- Are substitute products available?
- What are their regular and feature prices?
- How is the competition likely to react to this price?
- Have competitors' pricing strategies affected your sales in the past?
- Have competitors' sales been responsive to price changes?

About the consumer
- Does your product fill a basic need?
- How large is your market?
- How much will people pay?
- How much would they buy?
- Is the product price-sensitive?
- How is the product bought?
- What are the motives for buying this product?
- What savings can be passed on to the buyer?
- What new benefits can be provided?
- Is the product in the "shop around" category?
- Is there a general price awareness among consumers for this product?

Some of these questions can be answered by secondary research and general knowledge, some by third-party subscription data, and yet others require ad hoc research. Some questions may require more than one approach.

Let us assume that we have overcome all these hurdles and avoided all the pitfalls. Let's also assume that the marketer has considered alternative pricing strategies and has chosen the appropriate ones. Still, the marketer and the researcher must answer several questions before settling on an appropriate research technique.

1. **Is ad hoc research needed at all?** There are some instances in which research is not critical for pricing decisions. Products that are known to have high brand loyalty and low price elasticity, monopolistic brands with no major negative perception, brands that have inflexible cost-plus consideration and mature brands considering price increases in line with general market trends fall into this category. Research can provide additional information but is generally used to confirm what the marketer already knows.

2. **Can we use econometric models instead?** These models, which use economic variables to forecast the effect of price changes, may be adequate in some situations. For instance, when a product is known to respond to changes in consumer disposable income, inflation rate, or competitive price environment, these factors can be built into a model, and decisions can be based on the outcome as predicted by the model.

3. **Can secondary research be used instead?** Data sources readily available to the marketer may offer adequate indications of the possible impacts of price changes. Secondary data can also be incorporated into econometric models. Some of the more common sources of secondary data are:

- competitive price-lists
- competitive advertising expenditure
- competitive advertising and promotional literature
- customer feedback
- salesforce feedback
- published literature on the product category
- professional and trade associations
- financial and annual reports of competitors
- government statistics
- census data
- industry trend data (published sources/internal sources)
- product pricing trends (published sources/internal sources)

Not all of these sources are available for every product; however, at least a few sources should be available for any given product.

Pricing Research Techniques

At some point, it is necessary to conduct specific pricing research work. The following pricing research techniques are commonly used.

Monadic Price Testing

"Monadic" means testing one price with each respondent, asking them to consider whether they would buy a product for that specific price. Pricing is one of those areas where the direction of interest is always known. For example, if a respondent is asked, "Would you buy this car for $26,300?" and the respondent says 'no,' they understand there's a chance the price will go down, and they will be asked again. Everyone knows that bargaining on car prices is routine.

In any research, it is important to avoid situations where respondents understand that the focus is the price. They understand that marketing research gives them opportunities to influence product design (we often tell them so in the introduction to a survey), so, many respondents will answer obvious pricing questions in ways that they think will reduce future prices of the product. In other words, simply asking price questions opens the way for potential bias.

The essence of monadic price testing is with the use of a **test-and-control experimental design** where each respondent sees only one price. The design calls for at least two separate groups, or cells, of respondents. Each *additional* price point requires an *additional* sample cell of respondents who see only that price. If the potential range of prices for the product is fairly broad, this might result in a large number of cells. This is shown in the table below.

To minimize sampling error, it is important to have fairly **large samples** in each cell so that variations in reaction are statistically readable and to **match the respondents** across the cells so that variations truly reflect the impact of only the price variation and not sample differences. The better way to match the cells is through quotas imposed at the recruiting phase, although the weighting of the sample during the analysis process is acceptable.

In some designs, a competitive context is added – with two or more competing products and their prices shown along with the test product. Respondents might be asked which of the products they are most likely to buy or how likely they would be to buy each (on a 5-point scale) or how they would share their next ten purchases across the range of products.

Experimental Allocation of Monthly Internet Fees to Sample Cells

Sample Cell	Sample Size and Requirements	Stimulus (Monthly Recurring Charge)	Response (Measurement)
Cell 1	$n_1 = 600$ (R, M)	$X_1 = \$24.95$ monthly	$O_1 =$ Purchase Intention
Cell 2	$n_2 = 600$ (R, M)	$X_2 = \$34.95$ monthly	$O_2 =$ Purchase Intention
Cell 3	$n_3 = 600$ (R, M)	$X_3 = \$44.95$ monthly	$O_3 =$ Purchase Intention
Cell 4	$n_4 = 600$ (R, M)	$X_4 = \$54.95$ monthly	$O_4 =$ Purchase Intention

Gabor Granger

Gabor Granger is a fairly commonly used and direct technique that can be embedded in another piece of research (e.g., a concept test) to **find the price that optimizes revenue**. Responses can be predictable (lower prices dominate), but it does give us a sense of pricing elasticity.

It generally starts with a range of **3 or 5 expected price points** for a product. Respondents are asked if they would buy a product at a specific price. The next question depends on how they respond. If "no," they are asked again at a lower price. But, if they answer "yes," they are asked again at a higher price. The process can be repeated one more time. But the risk is always that respondents anticipate that the price will go down if they say no.

The starting point is generally the price that had been shown earlier in the research (e.g., on the concept) and often the mid-point in the scale. A more scientific design may randomize the start point on the scale, so different respondents are initially shown different price points first.

The results show the proportion that would be likely to buy at each price point, and when this proportion is multiplied by the price point it represents, the result is a revenue number. Of course, it is not an actual sales forecast, so it is generally shown as an index where 100 is the highest revenue generated.

The key learning here may be that even though potential buyers are lost when the price rises, the increased price may still bring in more revenue.

> Example. Swish laundry detergent is launching a smaller 'condo size' bottle of concentrated soap. They conduct a concept test to measure potential sales volumetrics using the price that they are most likely to be selling it at - $11.95 for 20 loads (1 litre). At the end of the questionnaire, they embed a Gabor Granger – asking again for purchase interest at $11.95.
>
> Those who say they would not buy it at that price are then shown $9.95 while those who had said they would buy it at $11.95 are shown $14.95. Both are asked about their purchase intent.
>
> Among that first group, those who would buy it at $9.95 move on to the next area of questioning. Those who still say they would not buy it at $9.95 are given one last chance to say yes to $8.95.
>
> Among the **second** group, those who are not willing to pay $14.95 move on to the next area of questioning. Those who are still interested in buying at $14.95 are pushed higher and asked if they would buy it at $15.95.

The Van Westendorp Price Sensitivity Meter

Another fairly common technique is based on the Van Westendorp (VW) economic theories of pricing elasticity. It is an 'open-ended' approach that requires a 'clean read,' often a **separate cell** on a concept test, in which no prices are given.

In one variation of the technique, respondents are shown a concept for a product, with no prices attached, and are asked the following six questions (The questions in bold are the only ones in the van Westendorp model.)

- **At what price is this product too expensive for you to consider buying?**
- **At what price is it expensive but you would consider buying it?**
- How likely would you be to buy it at this price point?
- **At what price is it a real bargain?**
- How likely would you be to buy it at this price point?
- **At what price is it so cheap that you would not consider it worth buying**

The four price points from each respondent and their purchase intentions for the two prices at which they would be willing to buy are compiled, and the results provide:

The range of acceptable price points

The optimal price point for penetration (number of people who would buy)

The optimal price point for revenue (people x price)

Example (contd.) Swish wants to get a completely 'clean' read on the pricing sensitivity for their 'condo size' concentrated laundry detergent and are willing to spend a little more for a Van Westendorp cell in addition to the concept test. A completely separate group of respondents matched demographically to the main concept test cell are shown the same concept but with no price and are asked the six VW questions. The results show that while $9.95 is the price at which the largest proportion of respondents are willing to buy the product, the revenue is higher when the price is set at $11.95. Fewer people are willing to buy the detergent at $11.95, but the higher price more than off-sets the loss of buyers.

While the van Westendorp Price Sensitivity Meter can provide some useful findings, it is not founded on sound economic theory. There have been some alterations to the PSM, such as the two purchase intent questions, that help to provide somewhat more solid insights into pricing.

Conjoint Analysis

The pricing techniques, such as Gabor-Granger and PSM, are not sophisticated enough to provide robust answers to pricing questions. The most robust alternative technique is conjoint analysis, also called discrete choice experiments (which is described in Unit 9).

Packaging Research

As a product nears launch date, other go-to-market decisions arise. One of the most important is the packaging design.

If we are dealing with a **line extension**, the pack design decision may focus on colour variations, an illustration of a flavour, placement of the flavour name, the font used, or any flashes to draw attention to the new offer.

However, if we are about to launch a **brand-new product**, then the packaging design plays an extremely important role at shelf. Every aspect of it can be tested.

Sometimes the **package is the innovation** itself. Upside down ketchup bottles, resealable snack bags, tetra packs that can be punctured with a sharp straw are all relatively recent packaging innovations.

Packaging must perform several functions:
- Attract attention at the shelf (stand-out)
- Create a desire to buy (persuasion)
- Transmit the information that the manufacturer wants (communications)
- And create the necessary brand linkage.

Several approaches can be taken for package testing. One of the key determining points is accurately identifying exactly what needs to be tested.
- If it is **just the graphics** on the front of the pack when we are dealing with a colour variation for a new flavour, then on-line research where a digital image is shown is perfectly acceptable.
- However, if there is a **functional element** that needs to be tested, perhaps a difference in size or shape or hand fit, or an 'easy-open' or 'resealable' function, then it may be important to put the product into respondents' hands.

If we need a **hands-on** test, we will treat this like the product tests described above – with product placement through a central location or a mall intercept or by sending the product out to respondents to use in their homes. Of course, this requires significant investment in creating prototypes that can be tested in these 'touch-and-feel' scenarios.

Developments in digital research, particularly **interactive virtual shelves**, mean that most packaging research can now be done at an earlier stage using virtual packaging mock-ups rather than physical prototypes.

Digital shelves allow respondents to 'shop' for a product on a realistic-looking shelf that would represent their usual store. Each variation in the product's packaging design can be placed on the shelf amongst its competition to see what impact it has on consumers' decisions.

The design might be **monadic**, where each respondent is shown a single shelf (with one of the pack variations) and makes a purchase decision. The impact of the different pack designs is measured across multiple cells where different respondents see different designs.

New developments in technology now allow us to **measure response times** - how long it takes for a respondent to make a choice and respond. We might test **'findability'** by asking respondents to look for the new design on the shelf and see how long it takes. With different respondents looking for different designs, we can measure which version makes it easier to find.

Brand linkage might be tested by showing a version of the new pack design, with the brand name obscured and asking them to select the brand that produces the product.

Eye Tracking

Eye-tracking is a method that follows where a respondent is looking when they are exposed to a shelf or a package – what do they see first and what path do their eyes follow. This is an excellent way to determine if a new pack will stand out on the shelf if design elements are attracting the attention that they need if something 'disappears' into the design, and if the new communications pieces are even registering.

Eye-tracking is done at a central location with specialized equipment that can track eye movement. A respondent sits down in front of a large monitor with a sensor that is calibrated so the computer can record what the respondent is looking at.

When an **image of the shelf** is put up on the screen, the respondent looks over it as they would a shelf in the store. With different respondents looking at the same shelf in which different alternative pack designs have been inserted, we can understand which design is more likely to **attract** the eye. We can also measure '**dwell** times' – how long a respondent stops to look at a particular pack.

Once the 'stand out' on the shelf is tested, eye tracking can also measure how respondents look at the **pack itself**. Instead of an image of the shelf, the respondent is shown an image of the new pack design and the equipment tracks where the eye moves. What attracts attention first? Where does the eye go next? Where does it spend more time? Does the eye even pass over the new piece of information that has been inserted?

With separate, matched samples, the research can identify the package design that attracts attention faster and the composition that helps consumers see the most important communication elements of the package.

If the study is designed to 'upgrade' the packaging, it is important to test the **current pack** as well. An 'improved' pack may not work better than the tried and true original design.

Line Optimization

At some point, there may be too many products in a line, and new additions are not bringing in incremental sales. Because manufacturers pay retailers "listing fees" for each product they put on the shelf, it is important to have 'just enough' items and no more.

The most common type of line optimization research is a "**TURF**" analysis, which stands for Total Unduplicated Reach and Frequency. Respondents are asked how likely they would be to buy each item in a proposed line and how often they would buy each. The analytical modelling will indicate, at which point new buyers are not being brought in and which combination will maximize sales volume (people x frequency).

> **Example**. Lemongina has a line of 5 fruit flavoured sodas on the market and is considering the launch of several new ones from among the eight additional flavours they have developed. But they would only do so if the new flavours will bring in incremental sales. They would be willing to drop some of the flavours from their current line if the new ones are stronger. They also recognize that some of the new flavours may be 'infrequent switch-ins' – bought only seasonally or for special occasions. They initiate a research project that identifies current and potential brand buyers,

shows them the full line of flavours and introduces the new ones, asking purchase intent, frequency expectation and 'occasion associations' for each. The line optimization analysis reveals that the optimal line has nine flavours in it and that the best combination includes 4 of the five current products and 5 of the new ones.

Research for Specialized Fields

Business-to-business Marketing Research

Business-to-business (B to B) marketing research refers to research conducted to understand better the nature and potential of the exchanges **between businesses**. The key determining feature is that the respondents are **answering on behalf of their organization** rather than as individual consumers or voters or citizens.

> **Example 1**. Border Buddy Inc. is a customs brokerage firm that works with importers and exporters to move their products across borders from where they are manufactured to where they are sold. They advise on customs duties, assist in the completion of import/export paperwork, provide warehouses and agents at the border crossing to manage the physical movement and approval processes. They have been operating for 75 years, but new management realizes that the digital marketplace is opening up new opportunities, and the company has to stay at the forefront if it is to succeed and flourish. They commission research to understand better how their customers – largely small and mid-sized manufacturing companies -- perceive Border Buddy and its key competitors and what drives them to choose between them.
>
> **Example 2**. Legaleeze is a software development company that serves the legal community. They own several case citator packages (for different legal jurisdictions), accounting software specifically designed for law firm billing, etc. They are in the process of designing a new tool to sync lawyers' schedules with court schedules to minimize conflicts when cases are delayed. There are several features that they could build into this new software and are looking for marketing research that will optimize the package in the eyes of those who make software acquisition decisions for law firms.
>
> **Example 3**. Appleseed Brothers is a growing, eco-friendly, grounds maintenance firm that has contracts to cut grass, maintain lawns and gardens and remove snow for large suburban corporate complexes in their home city. They are on the threshold of an ambitious expansion into new markets. They want to ensure they price their offer right, particularly given that competition, largely smaller, family-owned companies, is very different city to city. They are looking for a pricing optimization study that would ensure each of their offers is competitively priced before they put together their pitches.

Business-to-business (B-to-B) research makes extensive use of secondary data (see Chapter 3 for more details). Even when primary research is used to answer the information needs of a B-to-B study, it can be supplemented by reliable secondary data that are readily available. This might include government census data on market sizes and composition, industry association statistics on sales, the Annual Reports of major players in a sector, etc.

There are more similarities than differences between the way marketing research is conducted with consumers (B-to-C) and the way it is conducted with business representatives as respondents (B-to-B).

It is key to remember that the respondents are still people who may have faulty memories, short patience, and differing degrees of engagement in the questionnaire. Also, business respondents may have concerns about protecting their organization's intellectual property and competitive advantages.

Here are some of the key differences between B2B and B2C research.

Sample Definition and Generation

One of the first steps in designing any business-to-business study is deciding **who** is likely to provide the **responses you need**.

- It might be *purchasing agents* or *procurement officers* if the targets are larger organizations and your client wants to sell them office or cleaning supplies, packaging materials, or plant equipment, or
- It might be the *research and development team* if your client is selling alternative product ingredients, or
- It might be the Director of *human resources, information technology, accounting* or *legal counsel* if your client is selling software packages for people or information management, accounting or legal management, or
- It might be the *CEO* if your client is an industry association or government body intent on compiling confidence measures for the economy, or
- It might be the *owner/President* if your intended target is small businesses.

The target may be those who 'influence' consumers:

- It might be doctors, pharmacists or other health care professionals if measuring the potential to recommend over-the-counter health care products like cough and cold products
- It might be salesmen (appliance, cars, etc.) to understand what support material they feel is most useful when consumers ask questions about various offers on the floor, etc. (the potential list is endless.)

In B-to-B research, a **sample source** for a given target audience may not always be readily available. There are specialized online panels that focus on, for example, health care professionals. Industry associations and commercial sources (such as Dunn and Bradstreet) may have lists of members, and perhaps even those within the organization with specific responsibilities. But even when they are available, individuals change jobs, and it is difficult to maintain an accurate list.

More often than not, the process to find business respondents involves:

- Deciding on the business sectors that are to be targeted (e.g., retail, food, oil and gas, insurance and banking, customs brokerage, etc.)

- Collect a list of companies operating in the target sector(s), perhaps tiered by size (large multinationals, major national competitors, small to mid-sized local competitors) with whatever contact information is available.
- Call the organization to get the name of the person in the role you need to interview (procurement, CFO, R&D etc.) and contact information – a phone number or e-mail
- Call to make an appointment for an interview/e-mail questionnaire invitation

It is relatively difficult to get employee contact information from an organization on a cold call. They have become increasingly protective of their employees' time and privacy. An alternative is to use personal connections and introductions to find out who is in what role at target organizations, or to use the social media equivalents such as 'LinkedIn' to find specific people in the industry.

The research team may still have to do additional screening before locating the appropriate respondent to find not only the person who has the correct responsibilities, but who is also willing to participate in the survey.

Sample Size

In consumer marketing research, the target population is generally very large (e.g., all women aged 18 to 44 years), so the sample usually includes only a small fraction of the total population. In B-to-B marketing research, the target population can be very small (e.g., those who make software decisions in legal firms). Hence, it is not unusual to interview a large proportion of the population, sometimes even everyone in the population.

Some business sectors might have fewer than 100 or even 50 firms that comprise the relevant population. In cases like this, we can have confidence in the results of a very small sample.

> Example
> You are a manufacturer of sonography equipment for the oil industry and need the feedback from Vice Presidents of exploration in your prime markets of Alberta and Texas. There are only 50 people who hold this title, so you will be very happy to be able to get the reaction of 15 of them. Because of the group's relative homogeneity (similar education, experience, business pressure and work environments), even this small sample reflects the full population.

Questionnaires and Interviewers

The respondents in B-to-B studies are usually managers with extensive knowledge in their area of practice. The questions must be accurately and intelligently worded to ensure they get the answers that are needed but also to ensure respondents feel their time is well-spent.

If interviewers are involved, they must be able to ask the questions correctly and understand and record the answers accurately. They should be knowledgeable about the product in question, so the ideal interviewer may be professionals who have actually worked in that business sector.

> **Example.** Research on prescription medicines often involves highly technical jargon for the medical conditions and symptoms that are being explored and complicated names for the competitive set of medications that doctors are using. Specialized organizations working in this field would hire

researchers and interviewers who have pharmaceutical or health care training (e.g., pharma sales or nursing).

Costs

B-to-B marketing research generally involves interviewing a specific person in an organization. This could mean taking the time and making multiple calls/inquiries to identify the right person and make an appointment for an interview or gain agreement to participate in an online survey. This is an extensive time investment before the interview even takes place.

Interviewers are likely to be more senior, better trained and more knowledgeable than the average interviewer used in consumer research.

It is common to give these specialized respondents an incentive or 'honorarium' to gain their participation. Incentives are generally fairly hefty in business-to-business research because the respondent is acting in a professional capacity and will think of their time commitment in terms of what they are paid, or how they bill their time out to clients (think lawyers, doctors, accountants, etc.). Occasionally, when the subject is a 'good cause,' a donation to a charity is an acceptable incentive rather than a monetary payment.

When higher-level managers need to be interviewed in-depth, interviews are often scheduled at their offices. If a representative national sample is needed, you may need to send well-trained professional interviewers across the country. All of this results in a much higher cost-per-interview than would be seen in consumer research.

Availability of Background Information

In consumer marketing research, when a respondent is approached, we collect extensive demographic information in addition to information on the topic of interest. In B-to-B research, we are not interested in the respondent's personal demographics (other than, perhaps, experience on the job). What we do want to understand are characteristics (or firmographics) of the company. This might include the number of employees, major clients, annual revenue, markets covered and advertising expenditure.

If the company is publicly owned, these characteristics are often available from other sources, such as Annual Reports or publicly released information. A company's website is often the first stop to see what information can be gleaned and therefore needn't be asked in an interview.

Type of Products

What approach we take may depend on the nature of the product or service that is being researched.
- Does the **product** involve significant investment from the client? A new piece of equipment for a plant might require interviewing at a different level in an organization and using a more complex set of criteria than researching a new type of cleaning supplies.
- Is the **potential customer base** extensive or restricted? If there are very few potential buyers in a business-to-business environment, they may be 'turned off' by frequent requests to participate in research, particularly if some of the topics are more important to

the client organization than they are to the respondent's organization. It may, in these circumstances, be important to restrict research to only the most crucial decisions or to combine all information needs into one single annual study.

- How much **product-specific expertise** does the target respondent have? Is the respondent a qualified professional engineer who carefully evaluates products, or is he more of a clerical type who routinely issues purchase orders and buys based on the lowest price only? The more skilled the respondent, the more careful the research must be about product knowledge.

- Is the product **distributed** through **wholesale** channels, or sold **directly**? Does the client organization's sales staff have a direct relationship with the potential respondent? This may facilitate the creation of the sample list, or sample frame. However, it may also have a significant impact on the relationship between the organization's sales staff and their customers. In situations where a personal relationship exists, the sales team should be involved in designing the survey and introducing the interviewer or questionnaire link. Although highly unusual, you may consider using the sales team as interviewers – but there may be significant biases introduced because of conflicting agendas.

- Is it a **standard product or service,** or does it involve **custom engineering**? Products that require custom engineering, such as defense equipment, need a different research approach from standard products. For custom products, the critical factor is the expertise that is required to match the customer need. For standard products, on the other hand, the critical factor is the quality of the product already produced. Long-term relationships are more common for custom products than for standard products. A wide range of products falls between these two categories, i.e., standard components customized to suit customer needs. Standard products are sometimes called commodities when the same basic product can be obtained from several suppliers. The prices for commodities tend to be consistently low for all suppliers. However, some suppliers of commodities have been able to enhance the equity of their products by adding customer service that results in customers paying somewhat more for those brands.

Who Carries out Business-to-business Research?

Most business-to-business research studies are structurally similar to consumer marketing research studies and can be easily designed, managed and analyzed by most marketing research firms.

When special factors significantly alter procedures, perhaps because specialized knowledge of the subject matter is required, or unusual sampling procedures must be employed, marketing research firms can bring in 'subject matter experts', consultants with the specialized knowledge required, to collaborate. Increasingly, 'virtual firms' are bringing together experts in a variety of fields to work on specific projects.

> **Example.** The Greater City Airport Authority is embarking on a new master plan to improve services for the companies who run concessions in and around the two airports under its jurisdiction. These include food service companies that feed travelers, retail chains that keep them occupied, airport

taxi and limousine services that get them to and from the airports, hotel chains that house them in the vicinity of the airport, and of course, the airlines. They are looking for a research firm to create a consultation and feedback program with these partner organizations. A marketing research firm can improve its chances for success by adding consultants to its team of marketing research experts who understand airport planning and operations and the requirements of hospitality and transportation companies. It might, for example, team up with an operations manager who retired from the airport recently and a consultant well known in the hospitality sector.

In areas where there is a consistent flow of work, for example, legal and pharmaceutical research, there are specialized firms (or specialized divisions within firms) that focus on the sectors' specific needs.

Pharmaceutical Research

Marketing research for the pharmaceutical industry can be divided into two groups:
- Research for **'over-the-counter'** consumer products, like pain relievers, cough and cold products, laxatives, yeast infection kits, etc., where the consumers can make purchase decisions on their own, and buy without a prescription, and
- Research on ethical or **prescription** products, where the health care professional (generally a physician) must know about and understand the product and recommend or write a prescription for a patient to buy it.

'Over-the-counter' research among consumers, or patients, for the pharmaceutical industry is conducted like any other type of consumer research. The biggest challenge is in ensuring the language used in the questionnaire is 'consumer friendly.'

On the other hand, pharmaceutical marketing research carried out with physicians (including specialists), pharmacists, nurse practitioners, and other health care professionals differ from consumer market research in the following ways:

Sample Source

- Several Internet research agencies provide panels comprised of health care professionals who are willing to take part in research studies. Those surveys are fielded just like any web-based, self-completion panel study would be fielded.
- In many cases, personal interviews may be required, and, for these, appointments are nearly always arranged over the telephone before the actual interviews are conducted.
- Healthcare professional samples do not regularly use probability selection procedures due to the difficulty of identifying and contacting qualified respondents. In cases with very specialized professions, 'snowball' or 'referral' sampling is required where one recruited respondent is asked to recommend other colleagues who might participate. However, when possible, probability samples should be sought.

Sample Size

- **The Challenge**. For instance, there may be 41,500 general and family physicians in Canada in 2017, but only a few thousand obstetricians and gynecologists, and perhaps 1,000 gastroenterologists.). As a result, creating a sample for a specific specialization is challenging and returning to them regularly for ongoing research programs is extremely difficult.
- It is not unusual for a sample of 30 doctors to be considered robust enough for this branch of marketing research. This can be justified because participants are relatively homogeneous in their education, professional development and work environments.

Questionnaires and Interview

Researchers who work in this branch of marketing research must be conversant in the **highly specialized language** of the medical and pharmaceutical professions.

- They must know the conditions of the subject of the research, and they must be able to identify (and pronounce) the drugs and treatments that are used to treat these conditions and understand the benefits that each is meant to deliver.
- This is required both when writing comprehensible questionnaires, and when analyzing the results and looking for strategic insights.
- As a result, many pharmaceutical market researchers have an education or background in pharmacology.
- Interviewers should be experienced and confident, be comfortable with the language used in the questionnaires and be able to understand and accurately record the answers.

Incentives and Costs

- In most cases, respondents are offered incentives to participate in interviews. The incentive is related both to the time required to complete the questionnaire and to the target respondents' degree of specialization. A 15-minute interview with a general practitioner may require an incentive of a few hundred dollars, while a similar interview with a specialist might require double that amount.
- The specialized knowledge required of researchers and interviewers means that the costs of conducting this type of research are relatively high.

Even with the small samples, homogeneity of the respondents allows us to use multivariate analytic techniques such as perceptual maps, conjoint, factor, and regression analyses in this branch of research. However, some samples of physicians can be quite diverse, and analysts must carefully explore the data before treating the sample as a homogeneous whole. And, some samples might be so small that they support only univariate or bivariate analyses. The client must be fully aware of the hazards of small non-random samples before embarking on such a study.

Legal Research

The legal profession uses marketing research techniques for some very specific purposes. Here are a few examples:

- **Claims Support**. The most common legal application of marketing research is to prove a claim that the product is superior to its competitor. According to truth-in-advertising regulations, commonly heard tag lines such as "nine out of ten doctors recommend," "the fastest internet speed in Canada" or "the taste preferred by today's teens," etc., must be backed up by empirical evidence, particularly when challenged by a competitor.
- **Copyright Infringement**. When an organization feels that its intellectual property has been compromised or copied by another organization, it may choose to sue to ensure that practice is stopped. This may involve proving to a court that consumers are likely to be confused or that the opponent is attempting to "pass-off" its product as being that of the plaintiff. A marketing research study can be created that would measure the degree of confusion.
- **Libel, Defamation etc**. If a claim is made that a particular action has harmed someone's reputation, marketing research might be conducted among a relevant population to prove that they think less of the person/organization since the action happened.
- **Test Jury Trials**. When a large or important case is tried before a jury, a team of lawyers may decide to test their arguments before a 'test jury' before it is presented to the actual jury. This test jury is recruited much as a focus group would be, but to the same demographic specifications as the actual jury. Arguments are presented, and the test jury provides feedback and insights that would help the lawyers fine-tune the arguments they eventually use.

Working in this sector requires a solid understanding of jurisprudence, of what would hold up in court, of what could be attacked by the lawyers on the other side, and when too much information might undermine an argument. For example, if five questions are asked in a survey, and three of them back up the argument, the court could demand to see the two that were not shown, and they may undermine the argument. In a case like this, the study might be repeated, and only the three questions that support the argument included.

In some of these situations, the researcher may be required in court as an '**expert witness**' to defend the study methodology and results. The researcher who takes on this role must be very experienced, have solid credentials, and the strength to stand up to cross-examination. It is not unusual that the expert witness is required in court over several days waiting to be called to provide their testimony. It's best to build this into any cost estimates (perhaps as an hourly rate).

It is primarily because of the need to provide expert testimony – taking a senior researcher out of circulation for a couple of days – that legal research is left to specialized firms.

Polling

Polling is the branch of the marketing research field that focuses on respondents as 'voters' or 'citizens' rather than as consumers. It tracks the rising and falling fortunes of politicians and parties, of governments and public institutions. It measures where the public stands on specific issues and the impact that might have on how they vote.

- **Governments** use polling to help them make decisions that the public supports.

- **Advocacy groups** use polling to try to influence public policy decisions by showing, for example, that the majority of the public is on their side.
- Polling also helps **companies** keep track of their own corporate reputation and how their actions might impact the way the public perceives them.
- The **media** uses polling to attract readers and eyeballs. The political horse race is exciting. Public interest polls are entertaining.

Polling and *marketing research* tend to be separate in the minds of the public. The media, in particular, tend to separate a small number of high-profile firms who work for political parties or release polls to the media.

In reality, many major research houses do some form of polling – more as a way to raise their profile than as a profit-making line of business. These firms claim that polling forms anywhere from 5 percent to 20 percent of their work, the rest being standard marketing research.

Polling results can play an important role in determining public policy. Those studies are also often highly visible and potentially divisive when published in the media. A good pollster knows that the story should be about the results, not about the methodology. It is extremely important that polling is carried out using acceptable research procedures, including the appropriate relevant population, a defensible sampling frame, carefully worded questions and appropriate weighting.

This is particularly true when **political polling** is done in the lead-up to an election; the voting results are the 'ultimate poll.' If the "Polls" are shown to have missed the mark on election day – for example, predicting one party will win and in the end does not, or missing the lead that one party has over another – then the entire marketing research industry is questioned about its accuracy.

Polling does not pose any major methodological problems to a competent researcher who is comfortable with sampling frames and weighting procedures. Because polling results are time-sensitive, the interviews have traditionally been conducted by phone. However, in recent years, fine-tuning online methodologies has led to a shift towards that methodology. Large samples of pre-recruited respondents might be asked in advance to complete a survey after a major debate, with results compiled overnight and released the next morning.

The bigger challenge is in creating a sample that matches the most relevant population. For *political* polling, being a voter is not enough to qualify. It is more important that the respondents represent those voters who are **most likely to cast a vote** on election day.

Predicting voting patterns is challenging with a relatively disengaged population, particularly given the lack of party loyalty that leads many voters to wait until the last moment, even until they are standing in the voting booth, to make up their minds.

One of the issues that have been debated for some time in the media is whether political polling influences the way people vote, and if it does, whether political polling during elections should be banned altogether. Current evidence shows that political polling exerts only limited influence in affecting the final outcome of elections. Another argument is that if the media and political parties can see polling results right up until the last minute on election day, why shouldn't the public have access to the same information.

Pollsters will also conduct **'exit polls'** on voting day – interviewing a cross-section of voters across the country as they leave the polling stations to ask how they had voted. These help predict the outcome, but more importantly, provide demographic information that is very helpful for understanding how different sub-groups of the population voted – younger versus older, men versus women and different ethnic groups.

The word 'poll' has been misused as well. Non-representative **voting tools on websites** are effectively 'man-on-the-street' interviews. With no attention given to proper sampling techniques, they provide a channel for those who have strong opinions to express and can very easily be manipulated. Website polls and similar voting tools do not belong in a textbook on marketing research.

Concluding Comments

In this unit, we have discussed a wide range of ways in which marketing research creates value by helping organizations minimize risk and maximize benefits. It does this by providing the insights and information needed to make more informed decisions.

The broad view covered some of the more common marketing issues that can be addressed, including:
- consumer understanding,
- market landscaping and brand equity,
- innovation development,
- marketing communications,
- go-to-market tactics (e.g., pricing, packaging and promotions research), and
- specialized fields including business to business (B2B), political, legal and pharmaceutical marketing research.

At this point, the reader should have a stronger understanding of which approach is most appropriate for each issue that needs to be addressed.

UNIT 12

What are the Responsibilities of Marketing Researchers?

Ethics and responsibilities are about how we treat each other -- our role as responsible professional citizens in our society. Professional marketing research associations around the globe have prepared guidelines to help us establish a common understanding that can guide our behaviour and improve the likelihood of harmonious business and personal relations.

Let's begin with the relationships that marketing researchers should be concerned about, in no particular order:

- Researcher as **colleague**: The responsibility we have to the firm that employs us, to our colleagues, employees and business partners;

- Researcher as **client**: The responsibilities we have to our suppliers, and service providers, whether we are on the client-side of marketing research or a research supplier with several service providers of his or her own;
- Researcher as **supplier**: The responsibility we have when providing a service to our clients, including our internal client-side clients.

It is perhaps unique to marketing research that we also have a set of ethics and responsibilities that guide our relationship with the *public* as respondents. Without the willing participation of respondents, marketing research would not function. Our ethical concern for the privacy, security and dignity of those who provide us with their attitudes and personal information is the foundation of our business and must always be of paramount consideration.

The rapid development of artificial intelligence and the role that it is beginning to play in marketing research opens new ethical considerations that we have only begun to examine.

Researcher as Colleague

As in any profession, we have a responsibility to act ethically towards those in our work environment. These are covered in many countries by **labour laws** and **employment standards** that set out minimum wages, working conditions, appropriate hours, overtime and vacation expectations.

In many countries, workplace relationships are also governed by **human rights codes** that ensure a safe workplace free from discrimination and harassment. While certainly not universal, these codes can cover age, sex, race, colour, ancestry, ethnic origin, creed (religion), place of origin, physical ability, sexual orientation, gender identity, marital status, family status or any other distinguishing characteristics.

Marketing researchers have responsibilities to their organizations to act ethically towards others. The law will often hold the employer liable for the unethical, discriminatory or harassing behaviours of its employees.

The fair and respectful treatment of colleagues has important implications for the employer. Marketing research is a relatively mobile profession and it is not unusual for a supplier-side researcher to move to the client-side. So, the **junior staffer** on your team today may **become your client** a few years down the road.

If, during their time with you, they saw that the company respects its clients, acts ethically, strives for excellence on every project, seeks to be creative and forward-thinking, etc., they are likely to be interested in hiring you for work if they move to the client-side.

We have a responsibility to our colleagues to be **financially responsible**. For researchers on the client-side, this may mean:
- questioning whether a new piece of research is essential, and whether or not the information needs can be met by publicly available data or past research in the archive;
- carefully thinking through the project objectives and fully scoping out the research brief accurately so the suppliers can fairly cost out the project;
- asking for competitive bids on all RFPs over a minimum size to ensure that the company is getting the best value for their money;

- ensuring the appropriate contracts or statements of work are in place so that everyone has a clear understanding of what is expected of them;
- negotiating master services agreements and volume discounts or rebates if your business with one regular supplier is substantial;
- being wary of "scope creep" from internal clients and ensuring the objectives are respected through the design process to avoid additional charges from the suppliers and ensuring that your requests as the client do not put an unnecessary burden on suppliers, making sure invoices arrive and are paid on time to avoid penalties and to respect suppliers, some of whom may be tiny firms or managing tight cash flows.

For researchers in supplier-side firms, being financially responsible means:
- charging fairly for time and effort (low-balling to win a project undervalues staff time, minimizes the company's profitability and sets a precedent that is hard to sustain);
- ensuring proposals fully describe what will be delivered and spell out limits, with specific up-charges if those limits are breached;
- building contingencies into proposals (e.g. +/- 10%) to ensure minor cost over-runs can be covered without unduly putting pressure on a client's budget and not charging the full fee when projects are executed more efficiently;
- ensuring all contracts or statements-of-work fully reflect what you have contracted to do and spell out timelines to ensure your team is not surprised by unreasonable or shifting expectations;
- resisting "scope creep" to ensure questionnaire length, overly frequent corrections, etc., do not drive up costs;
- tracking all expenses throughout the project to ensure flags are raised when there is the risk of a cost over-run, for example, when the incidence of the intended target is lower than expected, the survey is longer than anticipated, or an unanticipated number of hours are being spent on analysis (early warning of potential cost over-runs will allow those involved to make informed decisions about allocating more budget or cutting back on scope);
- making sure invoices are issued promptly with specified payment expectations and diligently following up with the client if invoices are not paid on time.

Researchers have a **responsibility to the next generation** of our fellow researchers to instill in them the love and fascination we feel for marketing research and ensuring they become the best researchers they can be through professional development and mentoring.

Many educational institutions run 'research analyst' programs that include **internships**. More experienced researchers should consider taking on interns to give them solid, on-the-job training. These interns should, of course, be paid a living wage so they do not suffer undue hardships in the pursuit of experience.

Mentorships are an important part of the learning process and can only improve the skills of marketing research practitioners. One of the appealing aspects of marketing research is the team structure that pairs up experienced researchers with more junior analysts on projects. All parties should treat these as on-going learning opportunities.

Reverse mentorships present opportunities that may not be fully recognized. Younger members of our profession have grown up in a different time, maybe more plugged into current trends, are likely to be more adept at emerging technologies and are closer to the pulse of younger consumers. An experienced team leader should take full advantage of this complimentary experience and ask for input and advice from younger colleagues.

Education doesn't end on graduation day. **Professional development** is essential to reinforce what we've learned and up-grade our skills, particularly in a world of fast-paced change. Both client- and supplier-side firms should have budgets available to permit all staff to take courses that relate not just to their current positions, but to their aspirations. Consider courses that reinforce time-honoured basics (e.g., sampling, statistical and analytical techniques) as well as emerging technologies.

Researcher as Client

All researchers can be clients on some level.

- Client-side researchers hire research firms (or independent researchers) to conduct studies;
- research firms rent focus group facilities, buy samples, and engage field houses or providers of statistical analysis;
- focus group facilities engage with independent recruiters to find respondents or caterers to provide refreshments; and
- field houses hire interviewers often on an 'as needed' contract basis.

Marketing research clients span the full range of business sectors, including the following examples:

- **governments** (including all levels, federal, provincial and municipal) hire researchers to provide feedback from their constituents;
- **political parties** test new policy ideas and track their progress;
- **media** use polls to create headlines, but also to test out new initiatives and track the performance of existing ones;
- **not-for-profit and charitable organizations** use research to understand which pitches or programs may be most likely to attract donations and volunteers;
- **resource companies** commission studies on how to deal with environmental concerns;
- **manufacturers** use research to help them fine-tune new product development, optimize positioning, test their advertising and track wear out;
- **retailers** use a wide variety of research: to position a new product, to find optimal mixes and optimal product arrangement on the shelves (planograms) to ensure consumers find what they are looking for and to ensure that all products sell as quickly as possible (turnover) to maximize profit;
- **industry associations** collect information on consumer reaction to government policy to advocate for changes; and

- **law firms** use to test in-court arguments or build evidence about consumer confusion.

A large client, such as PepsiCo or Coke, Nestle or P&G, Ford or Toyota, Citibank or HSBC bank, phone companies, airlines and technology firms can have extensive ranges of needs that could require almost every conceivable type of marketing research service over the course of a year: focus groups, in-depth personal interviews, combined qualitative/quantitative studies, very large surveys, the highest levels of quantitative analysis and others. At the other end of the scale are small or local clients. They may invest a significant proportion of their annual marketing budget in single market understanding studies that may rarely, if ever, be repeated.

Regardless of the size of the client, a professional researcher will treat them all with respect and invest the time required to do exceptional work within the statement-of-work and study scope.

On the **client-side**, the researcher must respect both the professionalism and business obligations of their providers. The best client-provider relationship is a partnership, which is manifest in a number of the following ways.

Being Informed

Marketing research is an evolving practice. New methodologies emerge to meet the demands of changing business practices; new technologies enter the field and change how we work, attitudes can shift at blinding speed – driven by our constant connectivity. When the COVID-19 pandemic hit in 2020, the marketing research industry was already well-positioned to conduct socially distanced research online and through video connections. As artificial intelligence begins to make inroads, we are quickly becoming masters of its benefits and wary of its threats.

Client-side researchers must stay up-to-date on the offerings of the research providers in their market. The best way to do this is to invite them in for capabilities presentations regularly. Regularly scheduled 'show-and-tell' opportunities have become the norm in some client organizations to ensure their insights team is aware of the latest developments.

The benefit of this is that when a new business need arises within the client organization, the client researcher knows what tools are available and whom to call.

Sharing Information

The more a provider knows about your business, the better equipped they are to help meet your research needs. Keep your providers up-to-date on developments in your company; let them know what other research you are conducting and what you are learning. In this way, new projects are more likely to complement rather than replicate what you already know.

When asking for bids for new work, it may be a good idea to inform suppliers about the available budget. This will let your providers show what can be done within your budget, avoiding the frustration of a 'Cadillac' bid for a 'Chevy' budget and vice versa.

Being Responsive

There are many time pressures and demands in today's workplace. It is easy to put aside a response until you have 'more time.' Unfortunately, doing so when the answer is critical to the continuity of a research project may have serious implications. A brief needs to go out to providers early enough to give them time to prepare a proper bid. A provider-selection decision needs to be made quickly so the project timeline isn't compressed with a fixed delivery date. A questionnaire would need to be approved promptly so fieldwork can start on time.

It is all too common for a 'slow-to-respond' client to create delays at the start of a project, leading to compressed analysis timelines because the report/presentation deadline is unmovable. This client is actually harming their organization by reducing the 'reflection' time that adds depth to the analysis. Also, time delays can cost suppliers money.

Avoiding Unnecessary Proposals

A client may be curious about how a research study would be tackled and might be tempted to ask for bids, simply to get a sense of scope. There is nothing wrong with this and research providers are happy to help a client or potential client understand their capabilities.

However, keep in mind the fact that preparing proposals requires an investment of time and resources for the research provider. Avoid making frivolous requests for proposals if there is no prospect of a project going ahead. Similarly, minimize the number of firms you ask for bids. Three is generally an accepted number. Also, it is respectful and ethical to inform suppliers when proposals are solicited from more than one supplier.

The best approach is to develop professional relationships with several suppliers so that you can learn what they do and rely on them to build your own understanding of approaches and capabilities.

Respecting Intellectual Property

Providers' proposals and reports often include methodologies and techniques that are part of that firm's intellectual property. It is unethical to share one research firm's approach with its competitors without permission.

Avoiding Scope Creep

Scope creep should be a particular concern to both client-side and supplier-side researchers. "While we are at it …" is a problematic phrase if it means adding another target group to the survey sample, or an additional series of questions to the questionnaire.

> **Example.** Elizabeth is an insight manager for a significant confections manufacturer and has commissioned a "children's candy" usage and attitude study from her trusted supplier Josee. The objective of the study is to understand trick-or-treat behaviour at Halloween – involving school-aged children aged 5 to 17 years.
>
> In the iterative questionnaire design process, Elizabeth's internal client, a brand manager on one of the company's lines, begins to wonder how Halloween differs from 'everyday' occasions and whether parents behave differently when buying candy for their children versus trick-or-treat candy for other children. These new questions are logical extensions of the project objectives and could provide invaluable insight into the marketplace. However, they would involve exploring additional 'occasions' with each respondent – increasing the length of the questionnaire.

Elizabeth wants her brand manager to get maximum value from the study and Josee might be tempted to take on the additional requirements without objections given her close business relationship with Elizabeth. However, neither are doing their companies any favours. The longer questionnaire will put more burden on respondents and result in more 'incomplete' surveys, lower data quality and ultimately, higher field costs. The additional questions will require more analysis time and potential delays in delivering the report. In the end, everyone will suffer some disappointment.

From the business perspective, the most responsible action would be for both Elizabeth and Josee to push back on the additional requirements and explain that more budget and time would be required to add in the new requests.

On-Time Payments

Cash flow is always a concern in the consulting business, and marketing research is no different. Professional salaries, office overhead, respondent incentives, field and data processing staff all must be paid on time and the clients' payments are the only source of revenue.

Most research providers will invoice a client for 'out of pocket' and design expenses at the beginning of the project and the remainder when the report is delivered. Longer projects or ongoing tracking programs will require interim invoicing. As turn-around times become shorter and shorter for marketing research, it is now often the norm to invoice for 100 percent of the project work at once.

Any proposal or statement-of-work should spell out payment terms and conditions. Large client organizations and their regular suppliers will often have a Master Services Agreement (MSA) that has been negotiated to cover all aspects of the relationship including intellectual property rights, confidentiality, exclusivity agreements, cancellation terms and billing terms. With an MSA in place, there is no need to negotiate a new contract for every project.

In some MSAs, there may be a built-in penalty for late payment of invoices. In others, there may be rebates offered for a big book of business – for example, if the client commissions $1,000,000 worth of business, they may get a discount of 3 percent; on the *next* $500,000 they may get a rebate of 4 percent. These rebates could be contingent on "on-time" payment. If the invoice for a project is not paid on time, the project doesn't count towards the discount.

Contingencies

Both the client and the research provider should be aware that they cannot always foresee all outcomes on a research project. Cost overruns can happen. Clients generally work with fixed budgets and cannot always go back to the well for more money once the contract is signed.

It is a good idea for both the research client and provider to build a contingency into any project budget – an amount of money that can be accessed if costs increase, but that will remain with the client if everything runs as predicted. It is relatively common for projects to build this in as a "plus or minus 10%" provision in a bid. That contingency range may expand for highly innovative work or very exploratory research studies.

Challenging the Easy Answers

Marketing research is fast-paced, and we often find ourselves charging through the analysis to meet deadlines. The thoughtful reflection that can lead to real insights requires time.

One of the responsibilities of a client-side researcher is to ensure the timelines provide this time for reflection. At the same time, the client has the responsibility to think through the conclusions in the context of their understanding and knowledge and challenge conclusions that may be too facile.

The best client-provider relationship is one in which both parties work through the conclusions *together* to provide the client organization with insightful direction and the suppliers with viable business opportunities.

Researcher as Partner

There are different models of client-provider relationships, but at heart, it is a mutually beneficial partnership. The provider gains business, earns a salary and perhaps a profit and can grow professionally through fresh experiences. The client benefits from the support of a provider who can combine technical expertise, broader multi-client experience and an understanding of the business needs of the client's organization. Ultimately, a stable relationship with a trusted provider makes the client look good.

A partnership encompasses all the responsibilities mentioned above, but the critical element is mutual support and respect. Pressures and stresses can beset both the client and the provider within their organizations – clients have their own demanding decision deadlines, skeptical internal clients and budget pressures. In contrast, providers deal with often unpredictable field conditions, occasional errors and quality concerns and their own budget pressures. These stresses can create strains in the relationship and can lead to abusive language, hair-trigger escalations and unreasonable demands. Both clients and providers must understand that they both succeed when each of them can succeed.

Research providers have their own providers – field houses, independent moderators, sample suppliers, analytics teams, scripting and web-survey hosting companies, etc. Many of these principles apply as well. A research firm should appreciate a field house that recommends improvements to a screener, or a web-survey hosting team that identifies a potential error in questionnaire logic and all benefit from working together.

Researcher as Provider

Supplier-side researchers work:
- as *employees* of large *global* companies such as Ipsos, Nielson, Kantar, QuintilesIMS or GfK
- as *employees* of mid-sized and larger *national* firms
- as part of a smaller boutique *partnership*

- as *independent researchers* – a practice that is relatively common in more specialized parts of the business such as qualitative moderating or advanced analytics

Supplier side researchers may be *broad generalists or* may have found a narrow *niche* in the industry where their expertise provides considerable value.

Researchers on the **client-side** are *also* providers. A large marketing firm like Kraft-Heinz, PepsiCo or Proctor and Gamble have insights departments staffed by professional marketing researchers. Their clients are brand managers, marketing managers, sales departments and the C-suite (e.g. Chief Executive Officer, Chief Operating Officer, Chief Financial Officer, Chief Marketing Officer). These internal research staff serve as internal consultants and treat the colleagues they serve as clients.

Provider/Client Relationships

The relationship between research providers and their clients can take many forms.
- The **auto-updater** may be tasked with providing regular updates on ongoing programs, perhaps working with a template that is populated with new results every quarter, providing little analysis and no insight. This may be a requirement of the job, but it is often a missed opportunity to add value based on education or experience. This role can increasingly be replaced with automation – a scripting program that pulls data out of a dataset and into a dashboard.
- The **order taker** takes instructions from a client without questioning, challenging or suggesting. The client may be experienced and know precisely is what is wanted or may be locked in routine tasks. In either situation, the client is missing an opportunity to learn from a different perspective.
- The **supplier** responds to RFPs with thoughtful proposals and dutifully executes studies as promised. They may ask questions and challenge the assumptions or requested approaches. Their reports may be replete with in-depth analysis and value-added insight. But once the project is complete, the report delivered, and the presentation done, the supplier retires into the background and waits for the next RFP.
- The **partner** has an ongoing relationship with the client, is kept informed on organizational strategy, consults on longer-term planning, provides perspectives on industry developments that may or may not be related to specific projects, recommends and plans research programs and projects and is involved in the decisions that stem from any research.

The less involved roles may be assigned by the client organization, who may want nothing more than an updating service, or they may be roles that an unambitious researcher fulfills. There is a clear continuum in which a provider can add more value, have more impact, and become more critical to the organization.

Mutual respect between all parties is vital to the success of marketing research projects. Most just want to be treated fairly, honestly, and with respect. At the same time, there is an element of self-interest in any research project. The client, understandably, wants to further her career and will do so if seen by influential managers as an effective contributor. A provider who helps the client achieve this will create a long-term relationship of respect, mutual benefit, and the production of valuable information for the organization.

The research provider becomes a true partner by following several **key principles**:

Client and Provider Needs

Client Needs   ### Provider Needs

Client Needs	Provider Needs
Knowledge of marketing research	Knowledge of marketing research
Experience in marketing research	Experience in marketing research
Genuine desire to satisfy expectations for marketing information	Works to resolve internal project conflicts before directing the provider
Delivers what was promised	Provides information/sample as promised
Delivers on time	Maintains internal timeline
Honesty in all matters	Honesty in all matters
Goes beyond the call-of-duty when needed	Responsive client
Is a team player	Is a team player
Provides high quality in all deliverables	Manages internal expectations/interactions
Acts professionally in all matters	Acts professionally in all matters
Maintains regular communication of progress	Knowledge of and experience in the business sector and category
Maintains strict confidentiality	Protects intellectual property

Stay Informed

The research provider who understands the client's business is more likely to be considered a trusted adviser.

The starting point is to understand how the client's organization measures success. How does a private sector client organization make money? A media client, for example, provides consumers with content but earns money by selling advertising.

Providers can stay informed by watching consumer trends in that client's sector, looking for new opportunities for them to innovate. This may involve scanning trade publications and websites or watching news feeds for public domain information that may help them in their daily work. It clearly requires keeping up with developments at the client's own organization – changes in management, new product launches, mergers and acquisitions, etc.

It also means staying on top of the impact of past research-based decisions. If a provider has recommended the launch of a new product, where is it gaining it greatest success? How are consumers reacting to it? Does there appear to be any competitive reaction? Where are the ads showing up? How is it being shelved in stores?

This can mean simply paying attention when online, when shopping, when moving through the city and when reading news articles. More importantly, it means staying in touch with the client even when there are no new projects in the offing – the occasional catch-up call or lunch together.

Develop Strong Communications and Listening skills

Strong provider-client relationships are built over time by working together on projects together. But there is always a starting point, that first approach, that first pitch, proposal and project. It is crucial to start on the right foot by developing open two-way communications.

Good communication requires strong listening skills. The research provider should strive to develop a comfortable rapport with each client and this is best achieved in an environment that puts 'listening' first. E-mails and texts may be the norm to *exchange information* today, but they do not lend themselves to *listening*.

The best way to develop rapport is through face-to-face meetings. The more informal the setting, the easier it will be to get to know each other. Small talk, body language, facial expressions are all part of getting to know the person who is your client or your provider.

In a world that may require social-distancing, or when clients live in different cities, video meetings (e.g., via Zoom or MS Teams) may be an excellent alternative.

This need to create rapport through listening extends beyond the immediate contact person in the client organization to other parties. The goal is to understand the organization's decision needs and you might miss important information that is filtered out if you have only one point of contact.

Broader communications benefits the immediate client contact as well. She must often convince others in the organization that the research provider is the best person to do a particular project. When this project is successful, the reputation of the immediate client is enhanced. A provider who knows and understands the end client is more likely to deliver the decision information needed and make everyone look good.

It is important to meet with the immediate client and *other stakeholders* at the beginning of a project to ensure all are in alignment with the objectives, that expectations are set realistically for the outcome and that timelines are agreed upon. Identifying any expectations that are out of line at this point will save a lot of grief later.

Strong communication skills are needed throughout the project:

- Objectives set for a project may be a 'laundry list' of wishes for the future that could never be covered by a single project. It is important to listen to the players and help them separate out the 'need to know' from the 'nice to know.'
- Developing a good questionnaire may require balancing the information needs of several stakeholders in the project. Greater need is not always aligned with higher authority, so diplomacy may be required to navigate these treacherous waters.
- Clients sometimes seem oblivious to timelines, expecting research providers to make up time lost when client inputs and approvals are delayed. It is important to keep clients informed continuously if schedules are slipping.
- It is rare, and less than optimal, to deliver a final report without some back-and-forth discussions to ensure:
    o you appreciate the client's interpretation of the findings and how the recommendations fit with the corporate perspective;
    o the client understands and is comfortable with the findings and the recommendations; and
    o the client can help you position the recommendations when communicating them to the rest of the client organization to ensure they are sensitive to different agendas.

When presenting to those who will use the information, you might encounter individuals who are skeptical of the findings. Some people routinely challenge any new information; others may feel their perspective is threatened by ideas introduced from outside; still others simply need to be convinced of the value of the findings.

If you don't already know the other players, you should always ask the client to prepare you for the diverse personalities in the audience and their agendas so the presentation can be fashioned to respond to their needs. Excellent communication skills will help build rapport quickly at the beginning of the presentation and handle challenges in professional and respectful ways that take the presentation to a successful conclusion.

Bid Responsibly

At the beginning of each project, the research provider should strive to write a proposal that accurately reflects the effort involved in responding to the client's objectives.

The prospective research provider must include **realistic costs** in the proposal. Low-balling might occur if a provider expects bidding to be very tight and has a strong desire to win the project – perhaps to break into a new client and push out an incumbent. This may be unethical but is also just bad business practice. A low bid might win the project, but in the end, it could result in low-quality work or mid-project requests to increase the budget, and longer-term, sets an unsustainable precedent. Research clients will have trouble explaining to internal managers how the first project with a new supplier was so affordable, but subsequent projects are more expensive.

Project bids for quantitative surveys must **specify realistic response and incidence rates**. It would be unethical to suggest unattainable incidence rates just so field costs would appear lower. Invariably, this would trigger requests for a higher budget or reduction in deliverables mid-project once the true incidence and response rates are revealed. If these rates are truly unknown, the provider must point this out to the client and make them aware that costs will increase if these rates are lower than quoted. Alternatively, the proposal can contain two or three levels of incidence and response rates with the corresponding costs included. These are legitimate and transparent practices.

In today's fast-paced business environment, no schedule is fast-enough. It is tempting to describe *shorter-than-realistic* **timelines** in proposals and then make excuses when projects actually take longer. This, however, puts the client in a difficult situation where they have promised a recommendation to internal clients by a specific date. Product or advertising development schedules, major meetings or pitches may be established based on those unrealistically short timelines. If the research supplier does not deliver the final report at the promised date to the direct client, internal deadlines will be missed with the client taking the blame. That will usually brand the research provider as too big a risk to ever use again.

Be careful when offering a schedule that meets the client deadline but requires quick turnaround on their feedback, approvals and sign-offs, particularly if you know their approval process can't move that quickly.

Keep the Paperwork Up to Date

Expectations can change during the project and, if they do, the key players should be **informed in writing**. Any disagreements or misunderstandings can then be resolved immediately, and the solution documented by the end of the project.

Some clients have so many projects going on simultaneously that they may, from time to time, lose track of details or confuse projects. It is important that proposals or 'statements of work' be kept up to date to minimize future misunderstandings. Frequent, transparent and honest communications are the essence of proper project management.

Most providers have deep commitments to clients and the success of their projects. This devotion might drive them to **exceed the client's expectations**. This is good as long as the client understands that the extra work is 'over-delivering' at a cost to the provider. Setting precedents that are unsustainable for future projects can damage both the provider and the client on future projects.

Put Quality Control First

In a business where accuracy is so important, a research provider's credibility and respect hinge on getting it right. The embarrassment caused by errors and the delays that result in the need to fix them will stay in a client's memory far longer than a well-executed project.

Quality problems can cost the research company not only their reputation but also their profit margin when they try to correct errors that have occurred.

Budgets and timelines in proposals must include provisions for **quality checks** at every stage of project execution. Discussions about cutting costs and shortening timelines should always point out the implications for quality control.

Quality management means paying close attention to the details at all stages of the marketing research project.

- Double and triple check all costings that go into a proposal. Watch for misplaced decimals, double-check any currency conversions, run the timelines by all departments to make sure they can deliver their parts within the time allotted, recheck the research objectives to make sure you haven't missed anything.
- Get a second set of eyes to double-check questionnaire logic and wording. Have several people test links for online surveys and make sure you go through every single logic pathway at least once to make sure you end up in the right place.
- Check translations side-by-side with the original questionnaire to ensure errors have not been made, response categories have not shifted positions and phrases are not missing.
- Create systematic logic checks on tabular data. Make sure all of the banner headings are accurately set up by checking them against the questions they are created from (e.g., check the region banner against the question that asks respondents what region they live in), make sure the skip patterns specified in the questionnaire are accurately reflected in the tables and double-check that the sample bases for each table are what they should be.
- Double-check all data pulled into reports, have a second set of eyes, perhaps those of a more senior person, review the logic and do spot checks back to tables.

- Don't rely only on 'spell-check.' Have an editor proofread all reports for accuracy and brevity and correct all spelling and grammar errors.

Manage Time Efficiently

Adhering to strict timelines is a critically important skill for both client-side and supplier-side researchers. Decisions must be made, products developed, ad campaigns ready to go by concrete deadlines and research needs to deliver the decision inputs at precisely the right time. When the window passes, the opportunity may be lost forever and the value of the marketing research information can drop to zero.

Almost every stage of the marketing research project can cause delays. Identifying the steps that might take longer than expected can be explicitly identified using processes such as the Project Evaluation and Review Technique (PERT), the Critical Path Method (CPM) and Gantt charts. Specialized scheduling software can record the details of each stage and diagram the information to estimate the total time for project completion accurately.

As each project stage is completed, the information in these software programs update the remaining project components and report any expected issues that might cause missed deadlines.

Avoid Surprises

No one wants to hear that a timeline has lengthened or a project has gone over budget, or that an error in the data has been discovered. However, the sooner the client knows this, the sooner contingency plans can be developed. It is easier to reschedule a final presentation several weeks before than a few days earlier.

What makes this approach easier is regular updates. Prepare a project progress report that can be updated and sent to the client every week. Communicate the positive progress but use this to give early warnings of potential issues that may arise.

The client will learn that if there is an issue, they will be kept in the loop, and this can build confidence and set up a solid partnership.

Regular updates will help the client appear 'on top of things' on her end as well. Others will ask how the project is going and your client will always have an answer.

Make It Right

Each researcher has the responsibility to protect not only their reputation but that of the firm and the industry. If you discover an error or roadblock, you owe it to the client to let her know as soon as possible, with one or more solutions ready.

These solutions may involve re-fielding a questionnaire, conducting more interviews, re-running tables, re-pulling a report, etc. There may be both hard, direct costs and soft costs, like your own time. Such costs should be allocated to the individual or department that made the error. Knowing that this is your corporate policy is an added incentive to all employees to double and triple-check their work at each phase of a project and avoid costly and embarrassing errors.

Analyze Thoughtfully

An expert research provider will *avoid* "auto-analysis" (creating a bar graph for every question, writing headlines that put the chart into words). Thoughtful reports start with the clients' challenge – the business decision they must make once they receive the results of the study - and keep this at the forefront as the data is analyzed. The purpose is to help make better marketing decisions not to generate as much report material as possible.

The analysis and reporting should be organized to tell the story that answers the clients' questions. Some researchers go so far as to "write the script" at the proposal phase. *This is what we will be telling you once the study is done.*

The report and the presentation should focus only on the telling of that story. Any extraneous findings, any numbers that don't drive towards that conclusion, should be left in the tables, or at most, charted in the appendix.

Protect data

Some clients require that data be stored in the country in which it is collected to ensure that all relevant privacy laws are understood and respected.

An added issue is the use of data in 'training' artificial intelligence. An AI application will keep and use the data on which it has been used to further develop its algorithms. This may be counter to intellectual property requirements, the data security requirements of your clients and the privacy of your participants. If your data is used to 'train' AI, it is the legal equivalent of keeping it in a database indefinitely. All personal information should be scrubbed from the database before being used with an AI application. If dealing with European participant data, request and verify General Data Protection Regulation compliance certificates from your providers. [5]

Keep a Close Eye on Costs

The research supplier owes it to the client to keep close tabs on project costs. Client budgets are often tightly constrained and a significant series of approvals have probably been sought and received to fund the project. The provider may have been chosen over other bidders to conduct the project. So, going back to the well for more money will put the client in an awkward position.

Smaller markets tend to be more price-sensitive.

For example, a particular type of study may cost the same in Canada and the United States, but the research impacts a market that is ten times larger in the U.S.

It follows that clients in smaller markets have smaller budgets, conduct less research overall and are likely to be more concerned about getting value for their money.

Cost increases over the course of a project often involve **fieldwork issues**. When preparing costs for proposals, response rates and incidence rates must be estimated. This can be done relatively accurately. Past research provides a reasonable basis for future cost expectations. But if there is any uncertainty with costing, those concerns must be spelled out carefully in the proposal.

---

[5] Sidi Lemine, Jade Kite's AI Insider, May 3, 2023

It is always a good idea to build **contingencies** into a project budget, for example, +/- 10 percent on the price, in case actual response and incidence rates differ from those assumed in the costing. These contingencies protect the research supplier if costing estimates are slightly off, but they also protect the client from having to go back through the approvals process for small increments to project costs.

Other potential threats to sound financial management include:

- **Hours for questionnaire design**. Preparing a questionnaire for a one-off, the custom-designed study requires more hours than preparing a standardized or repeating study for field. Dealing with a single client for feedback and approvals can be more efficient than dealing with several people, each with different interests. It is important to estimate hours carefully, knowing who you will be dealing with.
- **Custom analyses expectations**. These require more complex questionnaire designs and lengthen the questionnaire design process. For example, setting up a conjoint study requires negotiation on which attributes to include and how many levels for each. For the actual analysis, you will need to brief and supervise the analytics team, review and approve their outputs at each phase and be familiar enough with the final deliverables that you can answer technical questions. These all require more professional hours than would a standard study. Custom analysis can be so robust that clients often **request more** information once they see the promised outputs, for example, run on sub-groups, or digging more in-depth on specific facets. The initial proposal should be clear about what is included and what will require additional funding.
- **Client inputs**. When clients are involved in providing inputs to the study design (e.g., brand lists and images, respondent sample) or the analysis (e.g., marketing plans, sales data etc.), professional time will be required to interact with the client or others in their organization, to review what is provided and perhaps to clarify or ask for further information. Sufficient professional time should be included in the project costs to cover this.

The provision of **sample lists** by the client can expedite a project or substantially stall the timeline. The client may believe the lists are easy to assemble and send, but the lists may be out-of-date with a high proportion of unusable records. They may need to be reformatted for research purposes. As a result, they may require more time than expected to develop and provide. Sufficient hours must also be forecast to review, clean and format any lists that are provided so they can be used in the research provider's sample list. It would be an excellent idea to evaluate the client list before finalizing the project costs, but this is rarely possible.

The research provider may have more control over field costs if the operations team is **in-house** than if the fielding has been sub-contracted to another firm.

Prompt invoicing is another key component of sound financial management. It helps clients keep track of their budgets and supports the research provider's cash flow. The proposal should spell out payment protocols to ensure there is no misunderstanding.

There might be an invoice when the project is launched to cover out-of-pocket and design costs and a final invoice when the project is done. There may be milestone payments for longer-term projects and tracking programs. There might be an invoice at the beginning to cover the full project cost because the whole project is turned around in a week or less.

In any of these cases, payment terms – how long the provider should expect to wait for the cheque to arrive – should be agreed to in advance. Larger clients and their principal suppliers often have Master Services Agreements that spell this out so that it does not have to be negotiated for each project.

Manage the Project Team Efficiently

When a research provider pitches a new project to a client, they are offering knowledge that will support better marketing decisions. The **people assigned to the project** are an important part of the package that the client is asked to buy.

It makes sense that the pitch specifies who will be working on the project and the role each will play. Clients may be very upset to have other people substituted after the proposal is accepted.

Careful thought should be given when creating a project team not only to provide the knowledge, experience and talents that the project requires, but also to try to **match personalities** between the team and the client.

> **Example.** Joshua is a very methodical and detail-oriented researcher. He tells a good story but takes his time to build towards his conclusions. Sheila is a confident and decisive client who trusts her suppliers and just needs to know the bottom line. She is impatient and irritable whenever she has to sit through one of Joshua's step-by-step presentations. On the other hand, Brad is a skeptical client who wants to see all of the proof before accepting the conclusions. It makes so much more sense to assign Joshua to Brad's projects than to Sheila's.

A research provider who is aware of and carefully thinks through each of these roles and responsibilities will build strong and mutually supportive relationships with his or her clients.

Responsibilities to the Public

The most compelling responsibility of marketing researchers is to the public, those who are called upon to respond to marketing research surveys or participate in qualitative research. Without the goodwill of respondents, there would be no marketing research as it is now practiced.

At the core of our responsibilities is the concept of **respect**. We must respect the integrity and safety of the person, protect their identity and personal information and respect their time and intelligence.

Many of our responsibilities towards the public have been encapsulated over the years in legislation and codes of conduct.

This is increasingly important as public confidence is undermined by the online compilation of big databases and growing impetus to mining them for corporate or political advantage. Recent events have brought these concerns into the headlines with security breaches from firms like Yahoo!, Target, Equifax, and, more recently, Facebook, which in 2018 was alleged to have enabled Cambridge Analytica to use its data to influence politics. These news stories will only make the public more cynical about the motives of those who collect personal data. This is a serious concern for the marketing research industry.

If it is to build and maintain the public's confidence, the industry must adhere to a solid set of principles. As an example, let's consider The Canadian Research and Insights Council (CRIC) in Canada. (Similar organizations exist in other countries as well.) CRIC is an association of marketing research companies in Canada. CRIC's website states that: "The objectives of the CRIC Public Opinion Research Standards and Disclosure Requirements as applied to research released into the public domain are:

- "To support sound and ethical practices in the disclosure of research;
- To ensure research is unbiased and supports decision-making in public, private and not-for-profit sectors;
- To enhance public trust and improve the public's understanding of the use of research;
- To ensure the appropriate transparency and disclosure of research results and methods of studies."

(See https://www.canadianresearchinsightscouncil.ca/wp-content/uploads/2019/09/CRIC-Public-Opinion-Research-Standards-and-Disclosure-Requirements-1.pdf)

CRIC sets out principles that are universally relevant in marketing and survey research and establish a solid foundation for understanding the key relationships in the marketing research profession. Those principles encompass the ESOMAR (world association of opinion and marketing research professionals) Code of Marketing and Social Research, comply with international standards (See https://www.esomar.org/uploads/public/knowledge-and-standards/codes-and-guidelines/ICCESOMAR_Code_English_.pdf) and include:

I. Principles of Professional Responsibility in Our Dealings with People;

II. Principles of Professional Practice in the Conduct of Our Work; and

III. Standard of Disclosure

Codes of conduct are more effective when there are mechanisms for **complaint**, **evaluation**, **judgement** and **consequences**. Some associations have standards committees that receive and adjudicate complaints. Some publish the results of those judgements. Some professional organizations can withdraw an individual organization's membership if a violation of the code of conduct is deemed to have occurred. With legislation in place, the consequences become even more severe and may lead to fines or jail time.

Most educational institutions have ethics committees that must approve any academic or institutional research conducted using human subjects within their communities. These regulations can be substantially more restrictive than the codes of conduct and ethics of the professional marketing research associations and any government legislation.

Right to Privacy

The top-of-mind concern for many is the **right to privacy**.

The right to privacy has been recognized explicitly in legislation throughout the developed world, spurred primarily by the increasing volume of telemarketing, targeted marketing, scams, identity theft, spam and malware.

Canada's Federal Government introduced legislation in 2004 (and revised it in 2019), includes *The Privacy Act* and the *Personal Information Protection and Electronic Documents Act*, or PIPEDA (www.priv.gc.ca/en/privacy-topics/privacy-laws-in-canada). The purpose of this legislation has been to force compliance to a comprehensive set of privacy rules for businesses that involve electronic means. The section about the marketing research sector was based on input from the Canadian marketing research industry associations and reflects their codes of conduct.

Canada's legislation covers all personal information that is collected, used, or transmitted and revealed to others by private sector organizations during their commercial operations. The main provisions of the Act are:

- Organizations are required to seek the consent of individuals before collecting, using, or disclosing their personal information;
- Organizations must protect personal information with security safeguards appropriate to the sensitivity of the information; and
- Individuals may access personal information about themselves held by an organization and have it corrected, if necessary.

Regarding privacy, CRIC states explicitly, "We recognize the importance of preventing unintended disclosure of personally identifiable information. We will act following all applicable best practices, laws, regulations, and data owner rules governing the handling and storage of such information." (See https://www.canadianresearchinsightscouncil.ca/wp-content/uploads/2019/09/CRIC-Public-Opinion-Research-Standards-and-Disclosure-Requirements-1.pdf)

The ten core principles of PIPEDA that businesses must follow are:
1. Accountability
2. Identifying purposes
3. Consent
4. Limiting collection
5. Limiting use, disclosure, and retention
6. Accuracy
7. Safeguards
8. Openness
9. Individual access
10. Challenging compliance

The **principle of consent** is core to both the legislation and the industry's codes of conduct. The requirement is that the information only is used for the purposes for which **consent** was obtained. This creates the need to inform respondents about the nature of the project and to get their explicit, rather than implicit, agreement to participate in the study. The respondent must consent to participate and embedded within that is the right to withdraw their participation at any time – to quit the interview when they want.

This becomes particularly important when the researcher passes respondent information to the client after the survey is completed, perhaps for additional analysis, data mining, re-contact, database merging etc. Consent obligations mean that this can only be done with the respondent's prior and explicit permission.

There is a key difference between 'implied' and 'explicit' consent. **Implied consent** requires that respondents take the initiative to tell the interviewer/researcher that they no longer wanted to participate. The most obvious confirmation of the lack of consent is termination of the interview by the respondent. **Explicit consent** explicitly asks the respondent if the information can be used for specific purposes and requires an affirmative answer.

Privacy legislation can prevent the use of a client contact list for a research project if those on the list have not explicitly agreed to be contacted for that purpose. Privacy statements provided by companies to their customers, stating how their personal information might be used is a way to abide by this type of privacy legislation.

Informed participation goes beyond just agreeing to participate. Some regulations require that the respondents be informed about the length and subject of the interview, about the sponsor and the potential use of the findings.

In Europe, the **General Data Protection Regulation** (GDPR) went into effect in May 2018 and has a significant impact on research and marketing activities around the world. It is a new set of privacy regulations with the intent to modernize the way personal information is handled. The GDPR is 88 pages of additional rules and spells out severe fines for non-compliance. The penalties are based on the revenue of the offending firm, so everyone has a big incentive to comply.

Practical Applications of both Privacy and Consent regulations also mean audio or video recording, or video streaming of any interaction is not allowed unless the respondent signs an informed release agreement. This applies, of course, to all focus groups, which routinely audio-video-record and/or live stream the session. But it also has implications for passive capture of information through recording devices. Cameras used to track traffic patterns through stores, wearable devices that record what a shopper might be looking at (e.g., cameras embedded in eyeglasses) are problematic if they capture the images of those who have not agreed to participate in the study.

Concluding Comments

Professionalism, ethics, responsibility and establishing and maintaining good relationships are core to being successful in the marketing research industry. That applies to both those who produce marketing insights and those who use them.

Members of the public who provide their opinions and information to marketing research professionals are the foundation of this commercial sector. Without respondents, the marketing research industry would not function. Everything we do must focus on respecting and protecting them and their personal information.

Correspondingly, marketing research provides value to consumers by ensuring products and services meet their needs better than if their feedback had not been heard. We must continually keep this duty in mind.

At the end of the day, all those who play a role in market research provide significant value back to society, but only if we work very hard to establish and maintain the industry's ethical integrity.

UNIT 13

How to Carry Out Global Marketing Research

Global marketing research – multi-country research that takes place in at least one region outside the country from which it was commissioned – is a rapidly growing field. The move to a more globalized economy, the emergence of new economies and the search for new markets as established markets mature, all contribute to this phenomenon.

Consolidation within the marketing research industry as large multi-nationals buy up local firms has also contributed to globalization. Centres of excellence in one or two countries may be involved in projects around the globe.

Global marketing research can be challenging, but it is an opportunity for marketing researchers to practice the art and science of their craft truly. All the technical principles that are discussed elsewhere in this book are just as critical in global research as they are in domestic research but, in global research, many more variables come into play. Culture, politics, technological development in the countries of interest and in the research firm's local operating divisions are just some of the factors that need to be considered and accounted for as research is being designed, implemented, analyzed, and presented.

Global research can be very high-profile within the client organization and subject to a higher degree of scrutiny than domestic research. In many cases, a global research project can represent one of the client company's larger research expenditures, and multi-region studies typically mean more senior stakeholders are in the mix.

Global marketing research can be complex, but it can also be fascinating and an excellent learning opportunity if undertaken with some core learning and the guidance of someone with global experience.

How is Global Research Different from Local Research?

The basic principles of marketing research apply in global marketing research, but additional factors are layered on the research process, both in the markets where the research will occur and across the client and research supplier organizations involved in the study.

Local Markets

When a research project is being undertaken in multiple countries, several factors can have implications for how the study is designed.

- There will likely be multiple languages involved – so translation and transcreation (explained later in this unit) become a critical part of the survey design process and one that adds time and cost to the project.
- Differences between the cultures of the local countries, or even between regions within one country, need to be considered. Factors like gender roles, social norms around talking to strangers, and social hierarchy, among others, will all need to be considered as sampling and data collection decisions are being made.
- Methodological decisions will need to consider the level of technological advancement in each region. Is access to the Internet comparable across countries, what is the level of mobile phone penetration?
- Political stability can play a part, too. Are regions of the country inaccessible? Does a government control TV or social media? Does the political situation hamper the expression of opinions?
- Every nation has its own public holidays. A research plan should include an understanding of key holidays and closures. It would be important to know, for example, when planning research in the spring in Japan, that Golden Week falls in April or May and is a week-long

holiday. Similarly, the Christian Holy Week closes down much of Latin America around the same time.

Clients and Suppliers

Just as there are important nuances for research markets and respondents, there are some differences for those commissioning and conducting global research.

- With more markets comes more stakeholders. Effectively managing or conducting a global study means the core project team will have more members (across country and function within the sponsoring company and the research company). The extended team will be even larger – once translators, local moderators and interviewers, etc., are added to the mix. Superior project management skills and a diplomat's touch become part of the global researcher's essential toolkit. It is important that the core team meet at regular intervals to align on key aspects of study approach and design, and that it is understood who key decision-makers are.
- Language is also a factor when working across an organization. When working across countries, it is highly likely that some of the stakeholders and decision-makers on a global team will be functioning in a language that is not their primary one. It is even more important in global research to speak and write clearly, avoid jargon and idiomatic expressions and to follow up phone calls with written minutes of key decisions. Sending out pre-reads with clear directions on what decisions need to be made or have been made is a best practice in global research.
- With multiple regions comes multiple time zones. A study that has Asian, North American, and European client and supplier stakeholders can have differences of 12 or more hours. Efficient and advanced meeting scheduling becomes important – as does rotating meetings, so the same teams are not always getting the "night shift" or the early morning wake-up calls.

Smaller country clients do not typically have the same resources that a major market client does. While a U.S. or UK office might have a full team of marketing researchers, divided by brand or research type, a market like Canada or a smaller European country might have a *marketer* who is doing "double-duty," taking on responsibilities for research in addition to their marketing or brand management responsibilities. As such, they may not be able to react as quickly to requests for time or input as can their counterparts in larger markets. They may also not be classically trained researchers and less familiar with the process and some of the decisions that need to be made and their implications. In these situations, the research supplier would do well to act as a consultant to help the client through the process.

What Factors Affect Global Research

In this section, we will cover some of the key factors that have implications for marketing research and explore the potential impact these can have on various stages of the global marketing research process.

External factors are environmental factors in the local market that need to be considered and accounted for, should they be found to have a bearing on the specific study. Naresh Malhotra identified seven environmental factors that can impact the design and implementation of a global study – Government, Legal, Economic, Structural, Informational/Technological, Socio-cultural, and Marketing (Malhotra p. 18).

Researchers must do an "external factor audit" in global studies to ensure they are thinking through potential implications and not making assumptions about a market based on their own perspectives. The following are some examples of each external factor that can have an impact on global research.

Government

The local government can affect marketing research in a variety of ways, including but not limited to:

- In countries where citizens may have fears about expressing opinions, particularly to strangers, there may be a reluctance to respond freely to surveys, even those not seemingly sensitive in nature.
- Secondary data from some government sources can be unavailable or inaccurate.
- Some sectors that are private in some countries may be publicly controlled in others (e.g., healthcare, media), leading to very different consumer dynamics.

Legal

The advent of the Internet and social media has resulted in a heightened interest in individual privacy and the development of laws to protect it.

Privacy laws may be significantly different from one jurisdiction to the next. In some countries, a consumer can only be contacted if they have given prior permission or if the organization that is reaching out has an existing relationship with them. As a result, client-supplied sample may be unavailable if customers on lists have not agreed before-hand to be interviewed. Or the questionnaire link may need to be sent out by the client to their own list, rather than by the research house, requiring extensive coordination and even additional training for the client's employees.

One such law that has significant implications for the practice of marketing research is the General Data Protection Regulation (GDPR) in Europe. In place since 2018, this regulation has instituted new requirements for research conducted in Europe. Some practical examples of what this means include:

- All data (qualitative and quantitative) must be anonymized;
- Very explicit, clear opt-in requirements for videotaping;
- Limitations on remote viewing of qualitative research by those outside of the research market.

Research in Europe must be GDPR-compliant. For more information, the European Research Federation and ESOMAR have published the General Data Protection Regulation (GDPR) Guidance Note for the Research Sector. Appropriate use of different legal bases under the GDPR on this subject can be found at (https://www.esomar.org/uploads/public/government-affairs/position-papers/EFAMRO-ESOMAR_GDPR-Guidance-Note_Legal-Choice.pdf)

Economic

It is important to understand the economic situation in each country both strategically and for practical purposes.
- What is the standard of living for the average person in your target group? Can they realistically provide feedback on the goods or services you are researching? Or is it out of their consideration set?
- Will the honorarium offered for qualitative research in one market need to be different from others due to the economics of the region?
- Are the income categories, education levels and "social class" categories used in the questionnaire appropriate for each market? How should they be adjusted to reflect the true social structure of the local market?
- Does social class create barriers for research? For example, are there some neighbourhoods that cannot be accessed, either because they are within gated, secure communities or because the neighbourhoods are too dangerous?

Structural

What is the structure of the local market? Are citizens largely urban-based, or are they rurally dispersed? How are goods and services moved throughout the country? These questions can play a role in global marketing research when you are creating test markets and/or need to get products into the hands of respondents for the research to occur.

Informational/Technological

Although online research is the fastest-growing method of data collection globally, it cannot be assumed that all respondents in each country will have equal access to the Internet. Some key questions to be asked to avoid non-response bias or misrepresentative data:
- Do more people access the internet via mobile than desktop in a region? If so, is my survey optimized for mobile?
- Does the average person in the target demographic have private access to the Internet? Or will completing a survey on a sensitive subject be visible and therefore risky?
- Will the elements of your questionnaire (images, video links, 'gamification') require more bandwidth than is readily available to key target groups in a local market? Can you accomplish the same with a 'light,' easy-to-download, questionnaire?

Socio-cultural

Language is perhaps the most obvious accommodation that must be considered when conducting global marketing research. High-quality translation or transcreation of survey instruments is critical. "Transcreation" refers to creating versions of the questionnaire that are as relevant and understandable and that carry the same meaning in the local languages as the original version.

There are often cultural differences that need to be accounted for that are less easy to spot, particularly in face-to-face research.

- In some countries, it may not be appropriate to conduct mixed focus groups – by gender, by age, by social status.
- In others, the interviewer-respondent dynamic is very important, and someone of similar age or social standing would be required as the interviewer or moderator.
- Socio-cultural factors can also influence methodology; in Japan, physicians still prefer to have a professional interviewer interview them in person, preferably in their own office, rather than a phone interview.
- In some cultures, it is important to 'get to the point' and keep the questionnaire as short as possible. In others, pleasantries must be exchanged first to establish a connection and show respect.

Knowing the cultural norms of each region is important throughout the research process. Local researchers and clients can help fill in some of this information, in conjunction with secondary sources.

It is crucial to understand that these socio-cultural factors are just as important when dealing with colleagues and collaborators in other markets as they are in dealing with respondents.

Marketing

Different markets within a sampling frame may have different levels of marketing sophistication. While respondents in more mature markets may be very familiar with the concept of rating scales and questionnaires, this might not be the case in all markets, and guidance should be taken from local researchers on what is the norm.

What You Should Consider in Global Research Processes

While it may be more complex and nuanced and involve more stakeholders, global marketing research follows the same process as all other research – from problem definition to design to data collection to analysis to reporting of findings. Here are some things to consider that have unique or heightened importance at each step of the global marketing research process.

Problem Definition

It is important in global marketing research to look at your overall project problem definition in the context of each country. Does the same problem exist in that market, or is there a region-specific difference? As stated earlier in this chapter, secondary research or consultation with local experts (within the client or research organizations) can help researchers understand the local situation and dynamics.

Design

Study design (along with data collection) is one of two key stages that may require the most exploration and accommodation in a global research project to ensure internal or external bias is not being built into the study. In the design stage of a global marketing research project, the three aspects that require close examination are selection of a survey method, sampling, and questionnaire design, especially scaling.

Methodology

Because all research methods may not be equally viable in all the markets being researched, the decision about which methodology to use is critical. For example, in a case where the decision has been made to do a *quantitative* study, it will be necessary to evaluate the feasibility of specific quantitative approaches in each region. Factors like internet penetration (for online research), telephone penetration (for telephone studies), and access to the target group (for face-to-face studies) all need to be considered.

If a preferred method works in most but not all markets, there are a few options:
- Continue with the preferred method and weight the data to overcome the disparity;
- Move to a method that works in all markets;
- Move to a multi-modal (i.e., multi-methodology) approach, accept potential differences due to data collection, and attempt to mitigate them in analysis or report outlier markets separately.

If the decision is to conduct *qualitative* research, the choice of the **moderator** is extremely important. For the most part, the moderator should be a local researcher who speaks like the local consumers and will understand the full context of what they are saying. Local moderators should be consulted, if not involved, in the creation of the recruitment and discussion guides.

Sampling

Identifying and gaining access to the correct sample can pose some unique challenges in marketing research. It cannot be assumed that purchase dynamics are consistent across markets. Factors like gender roles, economic power, and market structure can affect who is making purchasing decisions and who is purchasing.

Developing a sample frame can also have its challenges.
- Target information may not be available or, if provided from government sources, may be dated and/or unreliable
- Access to participants may be difficult due to gender or social status
- Houses may not be numbered
- Unstable political situations that cause undocumented movement of people

Questionnaire Design

In the quest for global consistency, questionnaire design is presented with several additional challenges:

- Even countries that speak the same language and seem to be culturally very similar to each other have **unique words or phrases**. Some expressions may mean different things in different cultures. For example:
    - An elevator, truck and trunk in North America are a lift, a lorry and a boot in the UK.
    - The store where over-the-counter medications can be bought might be called a pharmacy in one country, a drug store in another and a chemist in a third. In some counties, peddlers can supply these medications out of baskets or carts.
    - A single-family home may, in one country, mean any dwelling in which a family can live, while another more specifically uses the term to describe a detached house surrounded by property.
- What may be considered a straightforward question in one culture could be considered **offensive or inappropriate** in another. For example, household income may not be an appropriate question in every country.
- Race may be a commonly-asked classifier in the United States but might lead to discomfort and anger elsewhere.
- Gender questions that go beyond male/female classifications are increasingly required in many markets but would be considered offensive in more traditional societies.
- Questions on marital status and household composition can include a more extensive list of options in more liberal societies.
- Social roles might be handled differently. In some cultures, "Are you the head of your household?" might be considered inappropriate because it suggests that one person is in charge of others when in fact, two spouses share equal responsibility for a household.

Some concepts simply **don't exist** in every culture. For example:

- Socio-economic classes might be easily defined in Europe, but in North America, income might be the only appropriate measure.
- Professional or occupational categories might be very different from country to country, including the status that they imply.
- Second homes might be common in some parts of the world, and might be called cottages, cabins, camps, dachas or vacation, country or weekend houses. Elsewhere the concept might be unimaginable. This is important when we are asking people to describe their living conditions.
- Brand **lists**, retailers, channels are all appreciably different from country to country.

Even within one country, regional variations present a challenge to effective question-wording. This is particularly true in countries that have regions or populations that speak a different language or belong to a different ethnic group.

It is important to understand that these challenges exist and to be open to adapting our methodologies to local market realities. Any team that manages a multi-country study from a central location should get someone with an in-depth knowledge of the language and culture of *each* target country or region to proof-read the questionnaire before it is fielded in that country.

Measurement and Scaling

How closed-ended questions are asked matters. The more complex questions (e.g., interval or ratio scales) may yield more precise results but these scales may be difficult to use for respondents who are less familiar with them or are less educated. If the sample includes those with less experience with binary numbers and scales, choice or pick-any questions should be explored.

Because some cultures are less comfortable providing negative feedback, scale endpoints and verbal descriptors need to be carefully considered to ensure bias is not introduced. (See Analysis section that follows for ways to mitigate this bias.)

One way that potential bias introduced by numerical scales and labelled scalar points can be mitigated is using MaxDiff analysis. In MaxDiff analysis, participants are not asked to rate the importance of a single attribute but, rather, are given a set of attributes and asked to choose which of these is the most important and which is least important. Other dimensions can be substituted for importance, e.g., liking. For this reason, MaxDiff is frequently used in studies that require cross-cultural comparisons. The analysis of these simple "most," "least," answers provides ratio-scaled measurements.

Translation / Transcreation

It is generally necessary to translate a questionnaire into other languages when working internationally, or in countries with more than one common language.

Translating the questionnaire *accurately* is just as crucial as getting the wording right in the first place. An accurate translation will not only carry the same meaning as the original version but the same tone. Using the term "transcreation" reminds us that we have to create a culturally and linguistically appropriate research instrument for each market.

Ideally, the researcher who wrote the original version speaks the other languages and can ensure all versions reflect the same meaning and intention. However, that is generally not the case, and a third party is required to do the translation and check accuracy. Here are some essential tips to increase the chances of success.

- Use an *experienced translator* who specializes in questionnaires and has the appropriate questionnaire design training.
- Have a *research colleague* who understands the second language review the translation. Sometimes this is best done side-by-side where the author reads the original version out loud, and the colleague follows along with the translation, stopping to ask clarifications on intention.
- Pay particular attention to *subsidiary phrases* in the questionnaire wording that are important and often lost in a translation. Some key examples are: 'if any,' 'or not,' 'or another member of your household,' 'in the past 12 months', 'on this one occasion,' etc.

The question still makes sense if these are missing, but some fundamental meaning and permission may be lost.
- Simple tests like comparing the *number of response options* in each version will reveal if something has been inadvertently missed.
- Pay special attention to *respondent instructions* like 'please choose all that apply' or 'select one only.' If something has been block copied as a starting point for translation, these instructions are often overlooked.

In a case where no-one in the organization can check the translated version of the questionnaire, you may have to ask for a **'back translation'** in which *another* translator re-translates the questionnaire back into its original language. The idea is that if the first translation was well done, the back translation would recreate the original questionnaire. Unfortunately, language is so complex, and there are so many ways to say what we want to in each language, that a back translation rarely returns to exactly the same starting point. We then have to judge which attempt created the gap. We would be well advised to have a discussion with both translators after the exercise to work through anything that makes you uncomfortable in the back translation.

One thing is certain, NEVER use automated translation programs like Google Translate for something as important as questionnaire wording. They are not yet at a point where they can understand and recreate meaning and tone.

Data Collection

At this stage in the process, a design and analysis plan will be in place, and then the study is ready to implement. The success of the project will be in the hands of scores of research professionals in several countries. Here are some critical factors to increase the likelihood of a successful outcome.
- Provide detailed written supervisor, interviewer, or moderator instructions in the local language.
- If possible, conduct live, country-level briefings.
- For qualitative research, employ a moderator who lives in or understands the local culture and have country-level moderators view other country research, where local laws allow.
- Accept that how respondents are recruited for qualitative research may vary from market to market and include intercepting potential respondents, cold calling, or friend and family referrals.

Analysis

Scaled data. As we saw in our units on questionnaire design and measurement, choosing a suitable scale is not a straightforward decision. When we get to global research, the problems get even more complicated. Evidence shows that people from different cultures use the same scale differently. For example, in some cultures, consumers tend to gravitate towards the higher (favourable) end of the scale and avoid the lower end. So, a rating of 8 on a 10-point scale may not mean the same thing in Japan as it does in Canada and the U.S. It is difficult to interpret the data if a rating of 8 means 'very good' in one country and 'above average' in another. One possible solution would be to label each scale point but that can become messy and tedious.

Differences arising out of culturally specific scale usage may often be statistically significant, but whether they are commercially relevant is another matter. Unfortunately, it is not possible to offer a uniform measure or definition of commercial significance as it is for statistical significance. To address this, some researchers standardize data from global studies for the purposes of comparison. The most frequently used data transformation is that which is applied to scales. It should be noted that there is debate in the research community about the advisability of normalizing scalar data across countries.

The problems of scaling are often handled using 'data translation' techniques such as

1. **Developing norms** for different countries and interpreting each country's ratings according to these norms.
2. **Standardizing the data** for all countries, so they become comparable (See standard scores explained in Unit 9.) The first step in data transformation is to calculate the mean and standard deviation for each data set that will be compared. The mean is then subtracted from each data point, and the resulting data points divided by the standard deviation. The resulting transformed scale data sets will all have a common mean of 'zero' and a standard deviation of 'one.' Similar transformations may be applied to other scales.
3. **Using a multiple regression** model in which explanatory variables could include countries.
4. **Employing the MaxDiff technique** in which the scale values are indirectly derived. In the MaxDiff technique, the respondent is not asked to use a rating scale. Rather they are given a choice of 4 or 5 alternatives and asked to indicate what they like/prefer the most and what like/prefer the least. The scale's values are then indirectly derived. Conjoint analysis, aka, discrete choice experiments, can attain similar benefits.

Scaling problems can also happen within countries that have more than one distinct culture. For example, in Canada, one-third of the population lives in the province of Quebec. Quebec has a distinct culture and its residents have different beliefs, values, and behaviour compared to those living in the rest of Canada. French Canadians also tend to use scales differently. Any research that included Canada would need to ensure that participants from Québec were weighted appropriately and that this data was viewed separately and as part of the whole Canadian dataset to see what special analysis might be required.

Reporting and Presentation

The reporting and presentation of research data is a critical finishing step in the process and one that will have implications for its credibility, adoption and perception of success. So, how results are going to be reported and used should be discussed and agreed to in the design stage of the global research process. Often reports are required at the aggregate global level as well as at the individual local market level. Knowing upfront how results are going to be used will help the researchers design reports that will be valued.

It is always a good idea to have someone familiar with each of the local countries vet the report to ensure interpretations and context are relevant and sensitive. For qualitative reports, the local moderators who were involved in the research should be allowed to vet the report to ensure any references to their work are accurately described.

Because a multi-market study can take longer than a smaller scope study, some markets may want a topline (or interim) report. This should also be agreed to in the design phase as layering this on later adds inefficiency and, potentially, cost to the system.

If a presentation is part of the plan, it will likely have remote participants. Because of time zones, researchers may consider a series of presentations to accommodate clients in different parts of the world and give the results a regional emphasis. Where possible, local relevance is added if a local moderator or analyst can provide market-specific commentary.

Whether results are presented in one large meeting or several smaller ones, global best practices should be observed: clear, concise communication without idiomatic expressions, preferably with results sent ahead as a pre-read.

What are some Practical Considerations?

Procurement

The move towards procurement-driven supplier selection is not unique to global research but, because of the higher level of investment, it is more wide-spread. Procurement departments have been instituted in large corporations to ensure the quality and cost-effectiveness of goods and services by sourcing multiple proposals and negotiating value. Most procurement processes will require at least three proposals from different firms, describing the full approach, the scope of work and pricing.

In global marketing research, one of the deciding factors can be the global footprint of the bidding company – does it have wholly-owned offices in each of the target regions, or will it have to subcontract work in certain areas. Several research companies with a global presence or network relationships are prominent in global marketing research, like Ipsos, IQVia, Kantar and GfK, for example.

Resources for Global Market Research

There are some valuable resources for researchers exploring global marketing research.

Secondary Research

Secondary sources allow researchers to gain insight into markets before (or instead of) conducting primary research and provide information to help make decisions about sampling, data collection, and other important parts of the research process. They can also be used to help frame or refine questions for primary research.

There are two broad categories of secondary data. *Internal* data is generated by and belongs to the client company and can include things like sales reports, call center data, social listening reports and data housed in customer relationship management (CRM) databases. *External* data is generated by organizations outside the company sponsoring the research.

National or government sources of secondary data, like Statistics Canada, for example, are good starting points, especially when looking for demographic information or incidence data. Most governments have this data, compiled via census or ad hoc surveys. They are made readily available to promote the country to investors.

Several global resources can be useful in understanding global markets, like the United Nations, The World Trade Association, The World Health Organization and The World Bank.

Internal secondary data can also have a role in global marketing research, especially to answer the question, "has this question been answered before?" Some of the foundational insights being sought may exist in company databases and/or custom surveys.

As with domestic research, artificial intelligence is increasingly a starting point for global secondary research. Concerns about the source of the information assembled may be heightened by a lack of awareness about other countries and an inability to cross-check sources.

Market Research Associations

There are many local or regional marketing research associations, some with reciprocal agreements, that can be a source of insight into local practices and regulations surrounding marketing research. ESOMAR (Europe and international), CRIC (Canada), Insights Association (U.S.), AAPOR (U.S.), QRCA (U.S.), Market Research Society (UK), are some examples of these types of not-for-profit organizations.

Concluding Comments

Global marketing research is an excellent opportunity for marketing researchers to combine solid technical and project management skills with the softer skills of a diplomat and motivator. Several external factors can have implications throughout the research process but can be avoided or mitigated with preparation, collaboration, and skill.

Manufactured by Amazon.ca
Bolton, ON